EMERGING

CONTEMPORARY READINGS FOR WRITERS

EMERGING

CONTEMPORARY READINGS FOR WRITERS

FOURTH EDITION

BARCLAY BARRIOS
Florida Atlantic University

Boston | New York

For Bedford/St. Martin's

Vice President, Editorial, Macmillan Learning Humanities: Edwin Hill
Executive Program Director for English: Leasa Burton
Senior Program Manager: John E. Sullivan III
Executive Marketing Manager: Joy Fisher Williams
Director of Content Development: Jane Knetzger
Executive Developmental Editor: Christina Gerogiannis
Associate Content Project Manager: Matt Glazer
Workflow Project Manager: Lisa McDowell
Production Supervisor: Robert Cherry
Photo Researcher: Kerri Wilson, Lumina Datamatics, Inc.
Media Product Manager: Rand Thomas
Manager of Publishing Services: Andrea Cava
Editorial Assistant: Cari Goldfine
Project Management: Lumina Datamatics, Inc.
Composition: Lumina Datamatics, Inc.
Text Permissions Researcher: Elaine Kosta, Lumina Datamatics, Inc.
Photo Permissions Editor: Angela Boehler
Permissions Manager: Kalina Ingham
Design Director, Content Management: Diana Blume
Cover Design: William Boardman
Cover Image: Leonard Gertz / Getty Images
Printing and Binding: LSC Communications

Manufactured in the United States of America.

3 4 5 6 23 22 21 20 19

For information, write: Bedford/St. Martin's, 75 Arlington Street, Boston, MA 02116

ISBN 978-1-319-05629-2

Acknowledgments

Text acknowledgments and copyrights appear at the back of the book on pages 483–484, which constitute an extension of the copyright page. Art acknowledgments and copyrights appear on the same page as the art selections they cover.

PREFACE FOR INSTRUCTORS

Emerging/Thinking

One of the fundamental facts of teaching writing is that when students leave our classrooms, they *go*: They go to other classes, go to their jobs after school, go hang out with friends, go into their disciplines, go into their careers, go into the world, in so many ways go back to their increasingly busy lives. The challenge for us as instructors is to help students acquire the skills of critical reading, thinking, and writing that will allow them to succeed in these diverse contexts.

Emerging seeks to address this challenge. It offers sustained readings that present complex ideas in approachable language; it encourages critical thinking and writing skills by prompting students to make connections among readings; it draws from a broad cross section of themes and disciplines in order to present students with numerous points of entry and identification; and it introduces emerging problems—such as cultural polarization (in social, educational, and political dimensions), the impact of technology (from Twitter to brain science), race and social issues (such as privilege, microaggressions, and gender roles), and the dilemmas of ethics (ways to advocate change, for instance, and the relations between art and philanthropy)—that have not yet been solved and settled.

The readings are organized alphabetically to open up possibilities for connections. (Alternative tables of contents highlight disciplinary concerns and thematic clusters.) Because they consist of entire book chapters or complete articles, readings can stand on their own as originally intended. However, the readings in *Emerging* were chosen because they connect to each other in interesting and illuminating ways. The issues under discussion resonate across readings, genres, and disciplines, prompting students to think about each selection in multiple dimensions. These resonant connections are shown through "tags" indicating central concepts treated in the selections. Several tags for each piece are listed in the table of contents, in each headnote, and for each assignment sequence—highlighting concepts such as "community," "globalism," "identity," "culture," "social change" and "adolescence and adulthood." Thus one can see at a glance the possibilities for thematic connections among the readings. Connections with other authors are also highlighted in the table of contents, in each headnote, and through the assignment sequences (included at the back of the book; see p. 463). The assignment sequences suggest a succession of readings that are linked conceptually so that one assignment sequence provides the structure for an entire semester. (Sequences are further explained on the next page.)

Emerging/Reading

Because students ultimately enter diverse disciplines, the readings are drawn from across fields of knowledge located both inside and outside the academy. Political science, sociology, journalism, anthropology, economics, and art are some of the disciplines one might expect to find in such a collection, but *Emerging* also includes readings from photography, public health, psychology, philosophy, epigenetics, technology, and law. The author of each selection addresses his or her concerns to an audience outside the discipline—a useful model for students who eventually will need to communicate beyond the boundaries of their chosen fields. Many of the readings also represent cross-disciplinary work—a photographer thinking about economics, a musician thinking about education—since the walls between departments in academia are becoming increasingly permeable.

Yet despite this disciplinary grounding, the readings, though challenging, are accessible, written as they are with a general audience in mind. The readings thus demonstrate multiple ways in which complex ideas and issues can be presented in formal yet approachable language. The accessible nature of the essays also allows for many readings longer than those typically seen in first-year composition anthologies, because the level of writing makes them comprehensible to students. Yet even the briefer readings are substantive, providing numerous opportunities for nuanced arguments.

Of course, in addition to referencing emerging issues, the title of this collection refers also to the students in first-year composition courses, who themselves are emerging as readers, thinkers, and writers. By providing them with challenging texts along with the tools needed to decode, interpret, and deploy these texts, *Emerging* helps college readers develop the skills they will need as they move into working with the difficult theoretical texts presented in their choice of majors—and ultimately into their twenty-first-century careers.

Emerging/Writing

One of the philosophical tenets supporting *Emerging* is that students need to be prepared to deal with emerging issues in their jobs and lives, and to do so, they not only must acquire information about these issues (since such information will continually change) but also must possess an ability to think critically in relation to them. The editorial apparatus in *Emerging* includes the following features that will help students develop the skills needed to become fluid, reflective, and critically self-aware writers:

- **Part One: Emerging as a Critical Thinker and Academic Writer.** Part One presents the key skills of academic success: the ability to read critically, argue, use evidence, research, and revise.

- **Part Two: Readings.** Each reading in Part Two includes a variety of questions to help students practice the skills of critical thinking, explained in detail on pages 2–3.

- **Part Three: Assignment Sequences.** In order to stress the iterative processes of thinking and writing, eight assignment sequences are included in the back of the book, each of which uses multiple selections to engage students' thinking about a central theme, issue, or problem. Each sequence frames a project extensive enough for an entire semester's work and can be easily adapted for individual classes, and two of the sequences prompt students to conduct outside research.

Additionally, the apparatus accompanying each reading provides substantial help for students while featuring innovative approaches to understanding the essays and their relation to the world outside the classroom:

- **Headnotes.** A headnote preceding each reading selection provides biographical information about the author and describes the context of the larger work from which the reading has been taken.
- **Questions for Critical Reading.** These questions direct students to central concepts, issues, and ideas from the essay in order to prompt a directed rereading of the text while providing a guide for the students' own interpretive moves.
- **Exploring Context.** In order to leverage students' existing literacies with digital technologies, these questions ask students to use the web and other electronic sources to contextualize each reading further, using sites and tools such as Facebook and Twitter.
- **Questions for Connecting.** Because thinking across essays provides particular circumstances for critical thinking, these opportunities for writing ask students to make connections between essays and to apply and synthesize authors' ideas.
- **Language Matters.** The Language Matters questions are a unique feature of this reader. These questions address issues of grammar and writing through the context of the essays, presenting language not as a set of rules to be memorized but as a system of meaning-making that can also be used as a tool for analysis.
- **Assignments for Writing.** Each reading has Assignments for Writing questions that ask students to build on the work they've done in the other questions of the apparatus and create a piece of writing with a sustained argument supported by textual engagement.

What's New

New readings on a wider variety of topics. Fifteen selections are new, broadening the range of topics in *Emerging*. Authors of the readings include public intellectuals, many with familiar names. For instance, novelist Michael Chabon reflects on his son's love of fashion and the universal search for community, a place where you belong. Essayist Leslie Jamison traces the complicated path to obtaining an elusive medical diagnosis in order to consider the limits of our compassion for another's suffering. And journalist Adrien Chen explores the influence of social media on our beliefs—and makes a case for radical empathy.

An overarching theme explores the central question of our time: How can we get along? While the readings in the fourth edition span a variety of topics—and can be read and taught any number of ways—the through-line of this edition is one of the most urgent ethical and practical questions in America today: What do we do about polarization? Divergence of opinion is part of the problem; the larger part is an increasing refusal to even talk to others who are different in terms of their politics, culture, or social position. The lack of conversation stymies any solution and initiates a solipsistic cycle that only exacerbates the problem. In a diverse and connected world, we must find a way to get along. Instructors will find the materials and advice necessary to stage productive conversations across these social and political divides in order to encourage conversation, understanding, and empathy.

New multimodal assignments throughout the book offer instructors new options for students to write and compose in a variety of media.

Four new or substantially revised assignment sequences provide a convenient way to structure selected readings into a coherent course. They ask four challenging questions to spark students' interest and to guide them on a substantive academic project: How Do We Face the Challenge of Race?, What Does Ethical Conflict Look Like in a Globalized World?, How Can We Get Along?, and What Is the Role of Art in the World?

Acknowledgments

This collection itself has been a long time emerging, and I would be remiss not to thank the many people who contributed their time, energy, feedback, and support throughout the course of this project.

I would first like to acknowledge past and current colleagues who have played a role in developing this text. Richard E. Miller and Kurt Spellmeyer, both of Rutgers University, through their mentorship and guidance laid the foundations for my approach to composition as reflected in this reader. My department chairs during my time here at Florida Atlantic University, Andrew Furman and Wenying Xu, provided reassurance and support as I balanced the work of this text and the work of serving as Director of Writing Programs. The members of the Writing Committee for Florida Atlantic University's Department of English—Jeff Galin, Joanne Jasin, Jennifer Low, Julia Mason, Daniel Murtaugh, and Magdalena Ostas—generously allowed me to shape both this reader and the writing program. The dean's office of the Dorothy F. Schmidt College of Arts and Letters of Florida Atlantic University provided a Summer Teaching Development Award, which aided in the creation of the materials that form the core of the Instructor's Manual.

For this fourth edition I'd like to thank as well Wendy Hinshaw, who took my place as Director of Writing Programs at Florida Atlantic University, and Janelle Blount, who serves as Associate Director of Writing Programs, both of whom enriched this project with input, suggestions for readings, and frequent conversations about the shape of this work. Thanks to Kathleen Moorhead, who has always been a committed and engaging colleague and who offered readings and assignments for this edition as well. Valerie Duff-Strautmann's work on the Instructor's Manual was invaluable; I thank her for coming on board with this project.

I continue to be grateful for the many reviewers who offered helpful suggestions for the first three editions of *Emerging*. Their valuable feedback continues to shape the book. I also wish to thank the reviewers who helped me plan the fourth edition: Bridgett Blaque, Truckee Meadows Community College; Carole Center, University of New England; Jonathan Ceniceroz, Mt. San Antonio College; Michael Cripps, University of New England; Joshua Dickinson, Jefferson Community College; Ana Douglass, Truckee Meadows Community College; Donita Grissom, University of Central Florida; Molly Guerriero, Casper College; Laura Headley, Monterey Peninsula College; Lisa Hibl,

University of Southern Maine; Wendy Hinshaw, Florida Atlantic University; Michael Piotrowski, The University of Toledo; Danielle Santos, North Shore Community College; and Carlton Southworth, SUNY Jefferson Community College.

I cannot say enough about the support I have received from Bedford/St. Martin's. The enthusiasm of Edwin Hill, Leasa Burton, and John Sullivan for this project was always appreciated. My editor, Christina Gerogiannis, reassured me often, kept this project moving along, and came through more than once. Cari Goldfine, in her role as editorial assistant, really helped take some of the load off my plate. I am grateful to Kalina Ingham and Elaine Kosta for clearing text permissions and to Angela Boehler and Kerri Wilson for obtaining art permissions. Matt Glazer and Sumathy Kumaran, along with her colleagues at Lumina Datamatics, expertly guided the manuscript through production. I appreciate their help, as well as the work of marketing manager Joy Fisher Williams.

My thanks to Tom Edwards, who was there when this edition started, and to Tom Elliott, Trae Ellison, and Eric Bladon who offered me support as it drew to a close. I offer this edition in loving memory of my dear and dearly missed husband, Joseph Tocio, who passed away as the third edition was going to press.

—BJB

We're all in. As always.

Bedford/St. Martin's is as passionately committed to the discipline of English as ever, working hard to provide support and services that make it easier for you to teach your course your way.

Find **community support** at the Bedford/St. Martin's English Community (community.macmillan.com), where you can follow our *Bits* blog for new teaching ideas, download titles from our professional resource series, and review projects in the pipeline.

Choose **curriculum solutions** that offer flexible custom options, combining our carefully developed print and digital resources, acclaimed works from Macmillan's trade imprints, and your own course or program materials to provide the exact resources your students need. Our approach to customization makes it possible to create a customized project uniquely suited for your students, and based on your enrollment size, return money to your department and raise your institutional profile with a high-impact author visit through the Macmillan Author Program ("MAP").

Rely on **outstanding service** from your Bedford/St. Martin's sales representative and editorial team. Contact us or visit macmillanlearning.com to learn more about any of the options below.

Choose from Alternative Formats of *Emerging*

Bedford/St. Martin's offers a range of formats. Choose what works best for you and your students:

- *Paperback.* To order the paperback edition, use ISBN 978-1-319-05629-2.
- *Popular e-book formats.* For details of our e-book partners, visit macmillanlearning .com/ebooks.

Select Value Packages

Add value to your text by packaging a Bedford/St. Martin's resource, such as Writer's Help 2.0, with *Emerging* at a significant discount. Contact your sales representative for more information.

Writer's Help 2.0 is a powerful online writing resource that helps students find answers, whether they are searching for writing advice on their own or as part of an assignment.

- **Smart search.** Built on research with more than 1,600 student writers, the smart search in Writer's Help provides reliable results even when students use novice terms, such as *flow* and *unstuck*.
- **Trusted content from our best-selling handbooks.** Choose *Writer's Help 2.0, Hacker Version*, or *Writer's Help 2.0, Lunsford Version*, and ensure that students have clear advice and examples for all of their writing questions.
- **Diagnostics that help establish a baseline for instruction.** Assign diagnostics to identify areas of strength and areas for improvement and to help students plan a course of study. Use visual reports to track performance by topic, class, and student as well as improvement over time.
- **Adaptive exercises that engage students.** Writer's Help 2.0 includes LearningCurve, gamelike online quizzing that adapts to what students already know and helps them focus on what they need to learn.

Student access is packaged with *Emerging* at a significant discount. Order ISBN 978-1-319-02578-6 for *Writer's Help 2.0, Hacker Version*, or ISBN 978-1-319-02576-2 for *Writer's Help 2.0, Lunsford Version*, to ensure your students have easy access to online writing support. Students who rent or buy a used book can purchase access and instructors may request free access at **macmillanlearning.com/writershelp2.**

Instructor Resources

You have a lot to do in your course. We want to make it easy for you to find the support you need—and to get it quickly.

Resources for Teaching Emerging is available as a PDF that can be downloaded from macmillanlearning.com. Visit the instructor resources tab for *Emerging*. In addition to chapter overviews and teaching tips, the instructor's manual includes sample syllabi, correlations to the Council of Writing Program Administrators' Outcomes Statement, and classroom activities.

CONTENTS

Part 3
ASSIGNMENT SEQUENCES

We tend to think of technology as a neutral tool for connection, but as the readings in this sequence make clear, technology such as social media influences our growth, development, and the ways in which we connect to others. These assignments examine the impact of technology not only on our world but also, more profoundly, on what it means to be human.

▶ TAGS: *community, conversation, culture, empathy, ethics, identity, media, photography and video, psychology, relationships, science and technology, social media*

Race remains a contentious issue even after decades of work toward civil rights and despite the reality of a diverse and deeply interconnected world. Notwithstanding any progress made in legal and political arenas, race continues to have fractious social and cultural implications. This sequence of assignments considers the factors that cause race to persist in order to foster conversations on why racial categories continue to have such critical relevance to our world.

▶ TAGS: *civil rights, community, culture, diversity, education, empathy, globalism, identity, psychology, race and ethnicity, social change, tradition*

Gender is a fundamental category of identity that can be simultaneously enabling and disabling to our growth as human beings. But although gender works to determine who we are and who we can be, we also have the ability to change the meaning of gender for ourselves and our world. These assignments explore the consequences of our current system of gender and the ways in which we can work to alter the meaning, function, and relevance of gender.

▶ TAGS: *adolescence and adulthood, community, culture, gender, identity, judgment and decision making, psychology, relationships, sexuality, social change, tradition*

Living in a globalized world doesn't mean we all have to get along; it does mean, however, that we must learn how to mediate cultural differences in order to solve the problems we face in common with others. War, conflict, and terrorism are the alternatives. This sequence of assignments examines an array of issues related to peace and conflict. The essays and assignments suggest tools and concepts needed to advocate for ethical solutions to conflict in a globalized world.

▶ TAGS: *censorship, community, culture, empathy, ethics, globalism, law and justice, media, photography and video, politics, trauma and violence, war and conflict*

Few of us are completely happy with the world around us, but each of us can work toward the world we want to see. Advocating for change is a fundamental ability we can choose to exercise. The readings in this sequence offer strategies and tools for creating small- and large-scale social change.

▶ TAGS: *art, civil rights, collaboration, community, conversation, culture, economics, empathy, ethics, identity, judgment and decision making, law and justice, politics, psychology, race and ethnicity, relationships, social change, tradition*

Education is a political act, since the choice of what is taught, studied, and learned encodes a set of values and a particular way of looking at the world. As students, you might have a particular investment in the ends of education and, certainly, you have ideas about the goals for your own education. These assignments explore education as it exists today and as it may take shape in the future.

▶ TAGS: *adolescence and adulthood, art, community, culture, education, empathy, identity, psychology, race and ethnicity, relationships, social change, tradition*

Polarization is an increasing problem. People aren't simply disagreeing with each other; they're refusing to listen as well. This lack of communication often leads to conflict and only exacerbates issues of polarization. The readings in this sequence of assignments explore what happens when we don't get along while offering tools of empathy and understanding that each of us can use to resolve this problem.

▶ TAGS: *adolescence and adulthood, community, conversation, culture, empathy, ethics, genetics, identity, judgment and decision making, psychology, relationships, social change, social media, trauma and violence*

We may think of making art or other creative activities as somehow set apart from the "real world." Aesthetic activities might appear to be about pleasure and recreation. These readings instead ask you to consider the ways in which the arts can change the world and reveal the deep connections between creative activity and politics, culture, and social change.

▶ TAGS: *art, community, culture, economics, ethics, politics, science and technology, social change, tradition, trauma and violence, war and conflict*

ALTERNATIVE CONTENTS BY DISCIPLINE

ARTS

BUSINESS

EDUCATION

ENGINEERING, TECHNOLOGY, AND COMPUTER SCIENCE

HEALTH, MEDICINE, AND NURSING

HUMANITIES

NATURAL SCIENCES

SOCIAL SCIENCES

THEMATIC CONTENTS

AESTHETICS

CATEGORIZING PEOPLE

FEELING AND THINKING

GETTING ALONG

GLOBAL PROBLEMS AND SOLUTIONS

GROWING UP

ME AND WE

MEDIA AND CULTURE

RIGHTS AND WRONGS

EMERGING

CONTEMPORARY READINGS FOR WRITERS

Part One
EMERGING AS A CRITICAL THINKER AND ACADEMIC WRITER

IN SOME CLASSES, such as biology, sociology, economics, or chemistry, what you learn and what you're tested on is *content*—a knowledge of terms and concepts. In contrast, what you need to learn in a composition class is a *process*—an approach to reading and writing that you will practice with the essays in this book, in class discussions, and by responding to essay assignments. This class is not just about the readings in this book but also about what you can do with them. What you will do with them, of course, is write. And yet it's not entirely accurate to say you're here to learn how to write, either. After all, you already did a lot of writing in high school, and if you couldn't write, you wouldn't have gotten into college. But you will learn a particular *kind* of writing in this class, one that may be new to you: *academic writing*—joining a conversation by researching, weighing, and incorporating what others say into your own work in order to make a point of your own. You'll use academic writing throughout your college career, and the skills you learn in this class will also help you throughout your life. That's because academic writing involves *critical thinking*—the ability to evaluate, assess, apply, and generate ideas—an essential skill no matter what career you choose. Thriving in a career—any career—is never about how much you know but about what you can do with the knowledge you have. College will prepare you for your career by providing you with knowledge (your job here is part memorization), but college will also help you learn how to evaluate knowledge, how to apply it, and how to create it. These are the skills of critical thinking.

Whenever we solve problems or make decisions, we use critical thinking because we gather, evaluate, and apply knowledge to the situation at hand.

What's *Emerging*?

The Readings

College is also, of course, a time for change. You're not just moving into your career—you're moving into a new phase of your life. In this sense, you might think of yourself as an emerging thinker and writer, one who builds on existing skills and expands them in an academic context. In some ways, emerging is also very much the theme of the readings. Each was chosen to give you an opportunity to practice critical thinking through academic writing. But each one also concerns an emerging issue in the world today, something you might have already encountered but also something you will have to deal with as you move on in your life.

Take, for example, Kwame Anthony Appiah's selections "Making Conversation" and "The Primacy of Practice" (pp. 35 and 42), taken from his best-selling book *Cosmopolitanism: Ethics in a World of Strangers*. Although Appiah is a noted philosopher, he's also very skilled at writing to everyday readers like you and me. At the same time, his argument—about how to get along with others who are different from us—requires a lot of thinking. Comprehension is not so much the issue. Appiah lays out his argument logically and supports it with many kinds of evidence (as you will learn to do as well). But the ideas he proposes about cosmopolitanism, about the relationship between what we do and what we value, and about how practices change over time, will require you to think about the implications of his argument, and that kind of work is the start of critical thinking. Figuring out what's in the text is challenging, but even more challenging is figuring out what's *not* in the text: the examples that would challenge Appiah's argument, or new areas where his ideas have value, or modifications of his argument based on your experience or on other things you have read. That's critical thinking.

Other essays invite you to do critical thinking to unearth the ideas that drive the essay. For example, Michael Chabon's "My Son, the Prince of Fashion" (p. 62) appears on the surface to be a simple narrative about a father taking his son to Paris Fashion Week. As a narrative it's easy to follow and maybe even enjoyable to read. But it also works with several ideas about masculinity, sexuality, fashion's relation to hip-hop culture, identity, and family. You just need to do a little critical thinking to find them. What follows will help you do that thinking.

The Support

To support you, each of the readings comes with a set of tools to help you develop your skills as a critical reader, thinker, and writer:

- **Tags.** If you look in the table of contents and at the end of each headnote, you'll find that each reading comes with a number of tags. These tags give you a quick sense of the topics—such as gender or technology—covered in the reading.
- **Headnotes.** The headnotes that appear before each reading provide context. In addition to finding out about the author, you'll learn about the larger context of writing from which the reading is taken, so that you can have a sense of the author's overall project or the other issues in conversation at the time of the essay's publication. Headnotes help you prepare for the reading by giving you a quick sense of what you're about to encounter.
- **Questions for Critical Reading.** As you read the headnotes, you may find that you are already developing questions about the selection you're about to read, questions that can serve as the basis of your critical thinking. Your own questions can be supplemented by the Questions for Critical Reading at the end of each selection, which are specifically designed to focus your reading and thinking in ways that will develop your critical thinking skills while helping you produce the writing asked of you in this class.
- **Exploring Context.** The Exploring Context questions use technology to deepen your understanding of the essay and its context in the world. These questions also underscore the fact that the readings have a life outside of this text where their ideas are discussed, developed, refuted, and extended—a life to which you will contribute through your work in this class.

- **Questions for Connecting.** These questions prompt you to apply your critical reading and thinking skills by relating the current reading to other selections in the book. Connecting the ideas of one author to the ideas or examples of another author is a key skill in critical thinking.
- **Language Matters.** The Language Matters questions at the end of each reading will help you practice skills with language and grammar by asking you to look at how meaning is created in these readings. Thinking critically about the language used by these authors will help you think critically about the language you use in your writing as well, so that you can take these insights back to your own writing.
- **Assignments for Writing.** These questions provide opportunities to join the conversation of these essays. Your instructor may assign these to you or you may wish to use them more informally to help you develop a deeper understanding of the text. Occasionally, these assignments might be multimodal, which means you might respond to them using other tools besides just writing.
- **Assignment Sequences.** There are also a series of assignment sequences in this text; your instructor may choose to use or adapt one for your class. They're termed *sequences* because each assignment builds on the one that came before. In this way, you'll get to see how your understanding of a reading changes as you work with it alongside other readings from the text. As you return to previous readings while developing a central theme of thinking through these assignments, you will refine your critical thinking skills by paying close attention not only to each text but also to the relationships among groups of texts.

Fortunately, just as you've entered class with many writing skills, so too do you enter with skills in critical thinking. Critical thinking, after all, involves processing information, and we live in an information-rich world. So chances are that many of the things you do every day involve some kind of critical thinking; this class will hone those skills and translate them into the academic realm.

For now, it might be helpful to focus on six skills you might already use that correspond to aspects of academic writing and that also will enable you to thrive in the world at large: the abilities to read critically, think critically, argue, support, research, and revise.

The Writer

As you develop these skills in this class, you will emerge not only as a stronger thinker and writer but also as an individual ready to enter your chosen discipline and thereafter your career. The writing you will do within your field may look very different from the writing you do in this class, but the moves you make within your writing for this class—your ability to form and support an argument—will remain the same. Moreover, you will come to find that people working within a discipline never write only for members of that discipline; they write for the general public as well. An engineer will write very specific, very complicated documents for other engineers but will also need to communicate with business associates, salespeople, managers, customers, and investors. No matter what you end up studying, you will need to communicate the concerns of your discipline to others.

The readings in *Emerging* offer good examples. Contrast, for example, the way neuroscientist Sharon Moalem writes in "Changing Our Genes: How Trauma, Bullying, and Royal Jelly Alter Our Genetic Destiny" (p. 289), intended for a general audience, with the way he writes in "Hemochromatosis and the Enigma of Misplaced Iron: Implications for Infectious Disease and Survival," which he wrote with Eugene D. Weinberg and Maire E. Percy for the journal *BioMetals*. Notice, first, that he writes with others when publishing within his field; collaboration is very common in the sciences. Notice, too, the difference in the opening of the journal article, which I have included with its MLA citation:

> Hereditary hemochromatosis is a genetic condition whereby too much iron is absorbed through the diet (Jazwinska 1998). In people with hereditary hemochromatosis, iron overload of parenchymal cells may lead to destruction of the liver, heart, and pancreas. Two mutations (C282Y and H63D) in a "non-classical" HLA class-I gene named HFE have been found to be associated with hereditary hemochromatosis (Feder et al. 1996). (135)

Moalem uses a very different, very specialized language that probably only makes sense to others in the discipline (*parenchymal, HLA class-I gene*), and he and his coauthors cite others in their field as they begin to make their argument ("Jazwinska," "Feder et al."). The article also includes tables that summarize their research and has a full works cited page. Moalem does not use any of these features when writing for us as general readers. Yet in both pieces he works to articulate an argument and support it with evidence: What differs is how it is written and how it is supported. In this class, you will learn the basic ways of thinking and writing necessary for academic arguments. Should you become a neuroscientist like Moalem, you will learn the specific elements of writing like a neuroscientist in your discipline.

Writing is a lifelong skill. As you practice academic writing, you will emerge as a stronger thinker, one capable of communicating your own ideas. You will take that ability with you as you move through your college career and then later as you move into your profession.

And it all begins with reading critically.

Reading Critically

We live in a world saturated with information. Mastering the ability to read critically is crucial to managing these demands, since doing so allows us to select just the information we're looking for. So crucial is this skill to our survival today that we don't even think about it anymore. Indeed, you probably read for information on the web or on your phone every day, and you probably find what you need, too.

Yet while it seems intuitive, reading involves a kind of critical thinking. Though reading is a way to find information, you may find it difficult to find the information you need in these readings. They are probably not the kinds of texts you've read previously in your life or educational career, so they might feel very difficult. That's OK. They're supposed to be challenging, because dealing with difficulty is the best way to develop your skills with critical thinking. Critical thinking is like a muscle: You have to work it in order for it to grow. In other words, if you didn't have to think about what you read in this class, you wouldn't be doing any critical thinking at all.

Strategies for Reading Critically

There are a number of steps you can take to help you read these essays critically:

- **Acknowledge that the reading is hard.** The first step is to acknowledge any difficulty you're having—recognizing it forces you to activate consciously your skills with critical thinking. That is, when you admit it's hard then you can work hard on it.
- **Keep reading the essay.** The second step is to just keep reading, even if you feel you don't understand what you're reading. Often, the opening of an essay might be confusing or disorienting, but as you continue to read, you start to see the argument emerge. Similarly, the author might repeat key points throughout the essay, so by the time you complete the reading, what seemed impossible to understand begins to make sense.
- **Write down what you *did* understand.** After you've completed the reading, you might still feel confused. Write down what you *did* understand—no matter how little that might be and no matter how unsure you are of your understanding. Recognizing what you know is the best way to figure out what you need to learn.
- **Identify specific passages that confused you.** Identifying specific passages that you did not understand is an important strategy, too. By locating any points of confusion, you can focus your critical thinking skills on those passages in order to begin to decode them.
- **Make a list of specific questions.** Make a list of specific questions you have, and then bring those questions to class as a way of guiding the class's discussion to enhance your understanding of the reading.
- **Discuss the reading with peers.** The questions accompanying the reading will give you some help, but your peers are another valuable resource. Discussing the reading with them allows you and your classmates to pool your comprehension—the section you didn't understand might be the one your peers did, and vice versa.
- **Reread the essay at least once, or more.** Finally, reread the essay. Reading, like writing, is a recursive process. We read and reread, just as we write and revise, and each time we get a little more out of it.

Annotating

While reading, one of the things you'll want to search for is the author's argument, the point he or she is trying to make in the selection. In addition, you'll want to search for concepts, terms, or ideas that are unique or central to the author's argument. Reading with a pen, highlighter, laptop, tablet, or sticky notes at hand will help you identify this information. In academic terms, you will be *annotating* the text, adding questions, comments, and notes while highlighting material you feel is important in some way; annotation is the start of critical reading because it identifies the most important information in the essay, and that's exactly the information you need to think about.

You might think of annotation as keeping a running guide of your thoughts while reading. That way, when you return to work with the essay, you have the start of your critical thinking. There are a number of things you might want to pay attention to during this process:

- **Look for the author's argument.** What is the overall point the author wants to make? Consider this one of the central tasks of your reading and annotation, both because you will want to engage this argument and because it will model for you how *you* can make your own point about the issue.
- **Mark key terms, concepts, and ideas.** Pay special attention to any words or phrases in italics or quotation marks. Often this indicates that the author is either introducing an idea and will then go on to define it or making an especially important point. Critical thinking often involves ideas, so it's important for you to locate and identify the ideas of the essay and crucial points often relate to the argument.
- **Mark information you will need again.** For example, there may be certain quotations that strike you as important or puzzling. By annotating these, you will be able to find them quickly for class discussion or while you are writing your paper.
- **Mark words you don't understand.** Look them up on the web or on your phone. This process will enhance your comprehension of the essay.
- **Ask questions in response to the text.** Don't assume that the author's words are gospel truth. Your job as a critical thinker is to evaluate everything the author says based on your knowledge and experience. Whenever you locate a mismatch between what the author says and what you think, note it with a question about the essay.
- **Summarize key points in the margin.** Summarizing the key points will help you map the overall flow of the argument. This process will help you comprehend the essay better and, as with locating the argument, will help you see how to structure your own writing as well.

HOW TO ANNOTATE A READING

- **Read with a pen, a highlighter, or sticky notes at hand.**
- **Use your laptop, tablet, or phone to take notes.**
- **Look for the author's argument.**
- **Mark key terms, concepts, and ideas.**
- **Mark information you will need again.**
- **Mark words you don't understand.**
- **Ask questions in reaction to the text.**
- **Summarize key points in the margin.**

Let's look at an example, an annotated excerpt from "Electric Funeral," Chuck Klosterman's essay about fame and infamy in the digital age:

> Necessity used to be the mother of invention, but then we ran out of things that were necessary. The postmodern mother of invention is desire; we don't really "need" anything new, so we only create what we *want*. This changes the nature of technological competition. Because the internet is obsessed with its own version of non-monetary capitalism, it rewards the volume of response much more than the merits of whatever people are originally responding to. (p. 246)

Look this up

But we do need new things like cures for diseases, right?

Could be important concept

This reminds me of Provan and copying — connection?

Let's look at how these annotation strategies work. For example, in this passage you would want to mark any terms you don't understand, such as *postmodern*, as well as terms the author may be using to form ideas, such as *non-monetary capitalism*. Another set of strategies, though, involves questions you have in reaction to the text, each of which can serve as a point for rereading the text, and relations you see between the text and other essays you have read or your own life experience. Each question you ask or comment you make during your initial reading of the text gives you a new direction for reading the text again—both for an answer to your question and for support for any alternative position you want to take.

Returning to the text and reading it again refines your reading, making it more critical. Rereading is not something we usually do if we're just reading for comprehension; generally we understand enough of what we read that we don't have to read it again. But in an academic context rereading is essential, because critical reading goes beyond comprehension to *evaluation*—determining the accuracy and applicability of the information and ideas of the text. And before we can evaluate, we have to know the key points that need evaluation. The Questions for Critical Reading located at the end of each selection will help you in this process by focusing your rereading on a significant point in the essay—a particular term, concept, or idea that will allow you to read and think critically. Rereading Klosterman's essay with these questions in mind might cause you to pay attention to those parts of the selection where he discusses villainy and examines two internet figures, Kim Dotcom and Julian Assange. These discussions might feel like stories when you read the essay for the first time, but returning to the reading through the Questions for Critical Reading might prompt you to look more closely at how Klosterman uses these two figures to discuss the nature of villainy in relation to technology.

Glossing the Text

Each of these texts is taking part in a larger conversation about a particular topic. You might find parts of a reading confusing because you are jumping into the middle of a conversation without knowing its complete history. At times, then, you will want to go beyond annotating the text by using a skill called *glossing*. A gloss is a quick explanation of a term or concept—think of it as a quick summary of the conversation that has come before what you are reading. You probably already know what a glossary is—a list of terms and their definitions. Some words have already been glossed for you. When you provide your own glosses for a text, you're building your own sort of glossary, filling in technical details you need to understand the text as a whole. There are a number of techniques you can use to gloss parts of the text while you read and annotate it:

- **Look at the context.** Often you can determine a quick sense of a term or concept by looking at the surrounding context or the way the author uses it.
- **Use your phone.** Using a smartphone to look up a word or term can help you confirm what you learn from the context.
- **Use Wikipedia.** Wikipedia is a controversial tool in academia because it has no single source of authority. Instead, everyone writes it, everyone edits it, and anyone can change it. In most cases, you won't want to use Wikipedia as a source for your writing. For one thing, your writing is about critical thinking, which is about ideas, and Wikipedia is more centrally concerned with factual information. At the same time, because it contains so much knowledge, it's a useful source for glossing because it can give you a quick sense of not only a technical term's meaning but also its history.
- **Use a search engine.** Wikipedia is not the only source for information on the web. Indeed, each of its entries includes links to other sites used in compiling the information on that page. Thus you can also do a web search to find a quick gloss.

Let's look at an example of how you might gloss a text as you read and annotate it. Here's a short passage from Francis Fukuyama's "Human Dignity":

> In the words of Nietzsche's Zarathustra, "One has one's little pleasure for the day and one's little pleasure for the night: But one has a regard for health. 'We have invented happiness,' say the last men, and they blink." Indeed both the return of hierarchy and the egalitarian demand for health, safety, and relief of suffering might all go hand in hand if the rulers of the future could provide the masses with enough of the "little poisons" they demanded. (pp. 141–42)

Nineteenth-century German philosopher who often challenged traditional values and morality. (web search)

Philosophical novel where Nietzsche discusses his concept of the "Superman." (Wikipedia)

"A system of organization in which people or groups are ranked one above the other according to status or authority." (dictionary definition)

"Of, relating to, or believing in the principle that all people are equal and deserve equal rights and opportunities." (dictionary definition)

The context of this quotation helps, too. Fukuyama is discussing how Nietzsche foresaw the implications of natural science for human dignity—specifically the possibility of a ranking or hierarchy of humans. These glosses can help you understand Fukuyama's larger argument about human dignity.

Reading Visuals

You may notice that many of the texts you read contain visual elements such as images or graphs. These, too, are opportunities for critical reading. After all, *every text is an image and every image is a text.*

Consider the page you are reading now. Though not readily apparent, it has a number of visual elements—the font selected for the text, the color of the print, the amount of empty or white space around the text and in the margins. Normally, we don't pay attention to the visual elements of printed texts. That's because printed texts are designed to minimize their visual elements so that you can focus on the meaning of the words on the page. But imagine how the meaning of these words would change if they were printed in **bold** or if they used a curly, informal font.

Visual texts often invert this relationship, bringing the visual elements into the foreground and letting words sit in the background or letting them work with or against the meaning suggested by the visual elements. The words and the images together make meaning and, as in all the texts you will read, this meaning is open to interpretation and analysis. In this sense, reading a visual text isn't all that different from reading any other kind of text, and you will want to use many of the same skills with critical reading that you would use with other selections in this book:

- **Identify the elements.** To begin reading a visual text, make note of each of its elements—not only any words it might contain but also each visual item included in the overall image. Each object you see is an element. Think of each element as a sentence. Together, these elements express meaning just as the sentences of a paragraph do. When you identify each element, you are using your skills with annotation.

- **Identify the connections.** Once you've located the elements, think about the relationships between them. Do the visual and textual elements reinforce each other or do they work against each other? What meaning is the author trying to convey in each case? Remember, authors don't include visual elements randomly. If it's there it has some sort of connection to the point the author wants to make or to the feeling the author wants the reader to have.

- **Analyze and interpret the whole.** Just as you would with other readings in the book, you will want to analyze and interpret the visual image as a whole. This again involves critical thinking because you will need to think about not only the *explicit meanings*—what the image as a whole says—but also the *implicit meanings*—what the image as a whole implies.

Reading Arguments

Finding an author's argument, as we've already noted, is a basic goal as you approach each reading. But *reading* an author's argument involves a broader set of skills. Identifying the argument—locating and summarizing it—is the first step of that process. After that, there are a number of questions you can ask yourself in order to understand not only the argument but also its context and the ways in which the author has chosen to pursue that argument. Working through these questions will help you understand the essay more fully; it will also make you more aware of these issues in your own writing.

After reading the essay, ask yourself:

- **What is the larger conversation?** Each of the essays you read here is part of a larger discussion about an issue: ethics, race, digital life. Where do you see the author acknowledging, including, and joining that conversation? How do you imagine you will join it as well?
- **What other voices are in this conversation?** Where does the author bring in other voices? How does the author use quotation? How might you use quotations from this author as you write about the essay?
- **What counts as evidence for the author?** Each discipline has a different standard for evidence, and the standards for evidence in academic and public writing differ as well. Does the author rely on anecdotes or statistics? Does the author use other credible sources? What sources should you use in your own writing?
- **How does the author acknowledge counterarguments?** Why might an author make or avoid this move? When should you acknowledge opposing positions?
- **How does the author acknowledge audience?** What sort of contextual information does the author provide? How does the style of writing reflect the needs of a particular audience?

Thinking Critically

Once you've completed a critical reading, you're ready to do some thinking. Imagine the essay is raw material. Critical thinking is the process of *doing something* with this raw material, making something out of it in order to join the conversation of the text. There are a number of methods you can use to help with your critical thinking. Responding to the essay is a good start because it allows you to record your thoughts and reactions. You can follow that by figuring out how the essay connects to other essays you've read or to your own ideas. Seeing connections is a way to begin to identify the relationships between ideas. Synthesizing these ideas then offers you a means to add to the conversation.

Responding

You can start the process of critical thinking by taking some time to respond to the reading and connecting what you read to your own life, to what you know and think and how you feel. Your instructor might ask you to keep a reading journal or a blog where you can record these initial connections.

For example, here's a short response assignment Risa Shiman, one of the instructors in the writing program in which I teach, recently gave students in one of her classes before they started discussing Peter Singer's "Visible Man: Ethics in a World without Secrets" (p. 353):

> Do the benefits of increased access to information provided by technology outweigh the costs? Why or why not?

Notice that the question isn't long or complicated. The goal is just to get you writing in response to the issues raised by the essay. Here's how one student responded:

> I believe that the benefits of increased access to information provided by technology outweigh the costs. The world as a whole is becoming a more dangerous and unstable place, and any efforts our country can make to protect us should be taken. Threats to the United States are becoming more frequent, and with terrorists successfully executing their 9/11 attacks, I believe we need to do whatever we can to prevent future occurrences from happening. Social media has definitely made it easier to monitor the world's views, thoughts, and opinions, and I wish that information were only used to monitor potential threats. But as Singer points out, corporations use what we put out into the world through social media so they can target their ads according to our consumer habits. But if getting Target coupons in the mail for Pampers diapers and Gerber baby food after you announce your pregnancy on Facebook is one of the things we have to deal with to make our country safer, then that is a small thing I am willing to give up. I also think that having organizations such as WikiLeaks provide a sort of checks and balances on our government is a good thing. Clearly Hillary Clinton was so upset over WikiLeaks's airing the government's dirty laundry because the government got caught, and it's embarrassing. I do understand that leaking some government documents can have a negative effect on our country. But it has been known that there are many corrupt dealings happening on Capitol Hill, and if that sort of threat makes politicians and government officials think twice before making a potential shady deal, then it's about time.

This student starts by articulating his or her beliefs about the issues, relating those opinions to Singer's discussion. These opinions can then become the basis for an argument as they are refined into a definite position and then put more closely into relation with Singer's text.

Connecting as Critical Thinking

Once you've considered your own responses, then it's a good idea to look for connections. Each of the essays you will read here is already connected to the conversation taking place around that author's particular topic. When you read, you might be able to guess some of these connections, but as you think critically about these readings, you will make new connections of your own, which is essential to critical thinking.

The strongest way to evaluate the information in an essay is to test it against other information, such as the ideas expressed in another essay. Connecting the readings might mean using a concept from one piece, such as Francis Fukuyama's idea of "Factor X," to explain another essay, such as Sherry Turkle's "The Empathy Diaries." But it might also mean using the ideas from one essay to modify the ideas in another: elaborating Michael Pollan's idea of the "holon" through Daniel Gilbert's concept of "super-replicators," for example.

Connecting is a kind of critical thinking used by the authors of the essays in this book, too. In "AIDS, Inc.," Helen Epstein uses this move in discussing HIV prevention programs in Africa:

> Ugandans are more likely to know their neighbors and to live near members of their extended families. This in turn may have contributed to what sociologists call "social cohesion"—the tendency of people to talk openly with one another and form trusted relationships. Perhaps this may have facilitated more realistic and open discussion of AIDS, more compassionate attitudes toward infected people, and pragmatic behavior change. (p. 129)

Epstein, a molecular biologist and specialist in public health, connects a concept from sociology, "social cohesion," with HIV prevention in Uganda. In making that connection, she uses the idea to support her argument and to create a new idea about what an effective prevention program should look like. It's the connections between ideas that allow authors like Epstein—and *you*—to make an argument.

In working with these readings, you might feel like there simply are no connections between them, that the topic of each essay is unique. But keep in mind that a connection is not something you find; it's something you *make*. If the connections were already sitting there in the essays, there wouldn't be much critical thinking involved, because there wouldn't be much thinking involved at all. The process of making connections between disparate ideas is part of critical thinking. Sociology and public health might not seem to have much in common, but when we make connections between them, we generate a new understanding of how to slow the spread of HIV.

Strategies for Making Connections

When making connections between the readings for this class, you might want to try a few different strategies:

- **Draw the connections.** Start by listing the important terms, concepts, and ideas from each essay on a sheet of paper. Once you've done that, you can literally draw lines between ideas that have some relation.
- **Use clustering.** You might also try a technique called clustering. Put the main concept of each essay in a circle on a sheet of paper. Draw other circles containing related or subsidiary ideas and connect them with lines to the circles containing the main ideas of the readings. When you find ways to connect the branches of these separate groups, you're locating relationships between the essays that you might want to pursue. Through figuring out exactly what these relationships are, you not only utilize critical thinking but also start the process of forming your own ideas, which you will express in your writing for this class.
- **Use the questions with the readings.** The Questions for Connecting at the end of each reading will also help in this process by asking you to think specifically about one essay in terms of another. These questions will direct you to think about

both essays, giving you an opportunity to use each reading to test the concepts and ideas of the other.

- **Compare the tags.** The tags for each essay show key concepts, some of which overlap with the tags for other selections. Use the lists of the essays' tags in the table of contents to help you see some of the connections between the readings.

Synthesizing

Connecting defines relationships. Synthesizing goes one step further by combining different sources of information to generate something new. Synthesis happens a lot in the real world. For example, a doctor might combine test results, a patient's medical history, and his or her own knowledge to reach a diagnosis; and a businessperson might use a marketing report, recent sales figures, a demographic study, and data on the current economic outlook to craft a business strategy. Whenever you combine multiple sources of information to create new information or ideas, you're *synthesizing*. Synthesis always creates something new; because you'll be using it in this class to create new ideas and thus new knowledge, you'll use it to demonstrate your critical thinking.

All of the authors in this text use synthesis, because all of them are working from what's already been said and written about a subject to say and write something new. You'll do the same. After you've read a piece and connected its ideas to other contexts, you will synthesize the ideas into a new idea, your own idea. That idea will form the center of the writing you do in this class.

Strategies for Synthesizing

There are several techniques you can use to synthesize the ideas of these readings:

- **Combine ideas.** You might, for example, use ideas from two authors and combine them into a new concept that you use in your paper.

- **Apply ideas.** You might instead use a concept from one essay to show the limitations of another author's argument. In this case you would apply the first idea to the second, and in doing so, you'd produce something new, which would be the synthesis you create between the two.

- **Invent your own term.** You might even invent a term all your own, defining and deploying it through your analyses of the readings in the papers you will write. You can define the term using ideas that you pull from multiple readings, connecting and synthesizing them into a new understanding represented by your term.

- **Pay attention to similarities *and* differences.** When synthesizing, you want to ask yourself not simply how the two elements you're working with are alike but also how they're different. Paying attention to both similarities and differences allows you to discover how different ideas fit together in different ways.

Making an Argument

Introduction to Argument

All the processes we've discussed so far take place before you actually start formally writing in response to an assignment. You need to read (and reread), respond, connect, and synthesize in order to begin the process of critical thinking that forms the core of academic writing. Once you've done all that, it's time to form an argument. In academic terms, *argument* involves joining a conversation, taking a stand, or making a point. When you write in this class, you'll be doing all of these things.

You may already be familiar with this academic sense of *argument*, though you may have been introduced to it in different terms. In the grading criteria we use at my school, we make the meaning clear:

> When we use the term "argument" . . . we mean the central, problem-solving idea that drives the paper, a concept that many of us learned to think of as a "thesis." We might also think of this as a "position" or as a "project," all of which suggest that there is a central point the student is trying to make in the paper. The argument will usually show up in a thesis statement on the first page of the paper, but this is not the sole defining characteristic of an argument.
>
> The student should have a goal in a paper, something he or she is trying to accomplish, often defined by a specific, argumentative statement. But even when this statement is absent, the goal is often still apparent, whether as a summation in the conclusion or an underlying/recurring theme of the paper.
>
> An ideal argument will be spelled out in a clear thesis statement and will provide both a direction for the paper and a motivation for that direction (a problem to solve, a goal to accomplish, a position to defend, a project to complete, etc.).

Forming an argument can be really challenging, in part because the word itself can mean so many things—an argument between lovers is quite different from an argument in a courtroom, which is also different from a scientific argument. Rather than thinking of your argument as the position you defend, like an army protecting its territory, try thinking of it as the words you send out into the world, like a participant joining a conversation.

Some Models for Argument

It might be useful to consider some models for argument to give you some sense of how you might think about your own argument. Many of these sound very similar, and that's because they are. Approaching argument from slightly different angles might be all it takes for you to get the hang of it:

- **Conversation.** We've already considered argument as a kind of conversation. With this model, you use the ideas and terms and concepts from one essay to discuss or evaluate the ideas from the other. That is, you put the authors in conversation to make a point about the larger issue.

- **Framing.** Think about your argument as using the ideas from one essay to "frame" the ideas from the other. That is, you examine the second essay using terms and concepts from the first, as though examining the second essay through a frame or lens provided by the first. Your goal would be to change how your readers understand the second essay by helping them view it through the frame provided by the first; thus we learn something new about the second essay from what you write as well as something new about how the ideas of the first essay can be applied in new contexts.
- **Theory and case.** Your argument might use a theory about something from one essay and test it using another essay as a particular case. That is, you evaluate how effective the first author's ideas are when applied to a second text. This is similar to framing, but whereas with framing you are teaching your readers something new about the second essay and its ideas, with this model you are teaching them something new about the first essay and its theories.
- **Application.** An argument might also apply the ideas of one essay to the ideas of the other. That is, you take a term or concept and apply it to the new essay, learning something new either about the term or about the new essay. Consider this a middle ground to the two models discussed above, one where your application of ideas could change the way your readers think about either essay.

Strategies for Forming an Argument

As you begin to work out what you want to argue, there are a number of matters to consider that can help you articulate your argument:

- **Think about the larger conversation.** The connections you find between essays are not just specific terms or ideas or concepts or quotations. There's also a connection in terms of the larger issues. Start by identifying the larger issue shared between the essays, and then think about how each of these essays addresses this issue. For example, if the issue is civil rights, then what does each author say about civil rights, in a larger sense? How does what each says about the topic relate to larger public debates? How might you join in?
- **Think about what you're trying to prove.** Locating the points of connection between essays does show critical thinking. But it's not enough just to prove a connection between two authors. Yes, that takes some thinking, but you also want to think about what the connections *mean*.
- **Think about what we're learning from your paper.** What have you discovered by bringing these essays together? Do the ideas of one author extend the ideas of the other author into a whole new area? Are the ideas of one author limited because of what the other author shows? Can you raise new questions based on ideas from both authors? Adding your voice to the conversation means that you are saying something new about these issues and these essays. Think about what that is.

Points to Consider

When discussing argument in the classes I teach, I share with students the kinds of questions I ask about argument when reading students' papers:

- **And so?** An argument has to have a point. It has to first assert a connection between the two essays but then also answer the question "and so?" *Essay A is like (or unlike) Essay B, and so . . .*
- **What are you trying to achieve?** I often use the term *project* in class instead of *argument*. When you write, you should have a project, something you want to achieve. Other instructors might use terms like *controlling purpose* or *motive*. Regardless, anyone who reads your argument should have a good sense of what you want to achieve in the paper.
- **What knowledge are you making?** An argument is a way of making new knowledge. How do you learn something new? You think about what you know, and then you come to a conclusion. That conclusion is a new piece of knowledge that you can express. Your argument might be: If we just read Essay A we learn X, but after reading Essay B we now learn Y about Essay A. Your argument tells your readers something new, something they haven't thought about before.

Practical Help

Finding your argument is not as hard as it sounds, because you've already done a lot of the work necessary by the time you get to thinking about your argument. In forming an argument, you will probably want to draw from:

- **The assignment or prompt.** We'll talk more about these later in this section and offer some tips on how to decode the focus of an assignment, but for now, consider the assignment a foundation on which you can build your argument. It offers a central focus that you can use to organize your critical thinking and join the conversation.
- **Your annotations.** You will want to go back to your annotations of any selections connected to the assignment. Since you noted the important ideas and concepts in each essay and, most crucially, your own questions or concerns, these annotations will give you a preliminary sense of how you want to respond to each text.
- **Another rereading.** You might find it helpful to read the essays again with either the writing prompt or your specific argument in mind. You might find new areas to annotate with this more focused reading, and that in turn might help you make your argument clearer and stronger.
- **Your connections and synthesis.** Many times strong arguments are built out of the connections you make between the texts. You may, for example, build an argument around the application of an idea from one essay to an example from another. In the process, you will offer a new insight into the essays, which represents your synthesis and your addition to the larger conversation of the texts.

Writing an Argument

All of these tips are meant to help you conceive of your argument. As you start the process of drafting it in writing, keep these points in mind:

- **Don't hide it.** Unlike some other forms of writing that build up to a central point, academic writing places the argument right at the beginning, usually in the introduction, so that the reader can follow the pursuit of that argument and the process of your thinking through the paper. Someone reading your paper should be able to point to a sentence and identify it as your argument. You may have learned to call this type of sentence a *thesis statement* for your paper.
- **Be specific.** Avoid broad statements. Instead, make your argument as specific as possible.
- **Use the essays.** One way to make sure you stay specific is to incorporate the terms from the essays or the names of the authors in your statement of argument.
- **Make a map.** A really strong, clear argument serves as a map for the entire paper. Your reader should be able to predict the organization of the paper from reading your argument. Your argument should tell you exactly what you need to do in the paper and should also tell your reader exactly how you will proceed in the paper.

From Argument to Draft

Once you have a good sense of your argument, you're in a good position to start drafting your paper. Let's look at a student's argument from a class I taught recently:

> A new civil rights can be achieved by replacing idle conversations with meaningful discussions that aid the presence of our true selves through websites that offer a safe place for human interaction.

Given this argument, it's clear the first thing the author will need to discuss is the idea of a "new civil rights," a concept from Kenji Yoshino's essay (p. 454). In the next body paragraph, the author will need to discuss how "idle conversations" prevent these new civil rights and then how "meaningful discussions" can help create them. Next the author will need to argue that such discussions support our "true selves" (another concept from Yoshino) before looking at how all of this can take place on websites that "offer a safe place for human interaction." The argument, in essence, contains an outline of the whole paper.

Once you have a good sense of the shape and flow of your paper as suggested by the map of your argument, it's time to think about how you will support that argument.

Organization and Transitions

As you begin to write your draft, you will want to make sure that your paper has a clear, logical organization. In many ways your paper is a step-by-step record of your thinking which led to the conclusion that is your argument. A well-organized paper lets the reader follow that thinking. In doing so, they will likely reach the same conclusion you did, which in turn means that you will have persuaded them of your argument.

Many writers find it useful to create some sort of outline to help them with their organization. You might start by writing your argument at the top of the page and then breaking down each of its components, as we did just above. Each of these components will be a paragraph in the paper. This outline doesn't have to be formal at all. It just needs to provide you a good guide on what you need to write.

As you write, pay particular attention to your transitions between paragraphs. These act as signposts that help guide the reader through your thinking. You might want to start with strong transition words or phrases. Most handbooks will have a list for you to use. But you may also want to work from the outline you made, taking each point and using it to frame the paragraph you are writing.

Some transitions are red flags for a poor organization, which may confuse the reader and obscure your argument. For example, if you find that you are starting each paragraph with "Another," then you may just be making a list of connections you see between the readings without explaining how those connections work together toward a larger point, your argument.

A good way to test the strength of your organization is to take the first sentence of each body paragraph from your completed draft and copy them into a new document, forming a paragraph made from your topic sentences. This paragraph should read more or less *as* a paragraph. It should sound fluid (one point moves to the next) and it should make sense. If it doesn't, then you may need to revise your transitions, rearrange some paragraphs, or work on making your argument clearer.

One tip to make especially strong transitions is to write one sentence about the point made in the previous paragraph and then one sentence about the point you want to make in the paragraph using this transition, and then combine those two into a single sentence that serves as a transition and topic sentence for your paragraph.

Using Support

Working with Quotations

As you lay out your thinking, you'll need proof to *support*, or provide evidence for, your point in each body paragraph, which in academic writing happens through working with quotations from the texts. When you use quotation in your writing, you support your words and ideas through the words and ideas of others. Quotation supports critical thinking in two ways. First, it provides evidence for your argument, thesis, or position, showing the reader how and why you thought that way and reached the conclusions that led to your argument. Second, integrating quotation into your text itself requires some critical thinking. That's the difference between "having" quotations in your paper and "using" them. It's not enough to drop in a quotation every now and then. You need to think about the function of every quotation you use, its purpose in your paper. Is it defining a term? Supporting an assertion? Connecting ideas? To make that function clear, you will want to explain each quotation you use. That doesn't mean you should summarize or reiterate each quotation; it means you should write about what that piece of text does for your overall project. Think of it as connecting that text to your own text. You might also analyze the quotation in this process. *Analyzing* a quotation means explaining what it says and what it means.

Here's a pattern you can use to incorporate quotation into your paragraphs in ways that show your critical thinking through connection. When I share this with my students, I call it "Barclay's Super-Secret Formula" (though I suppose it's not so secret anymore):

$$C_1 \rightarrow I \rightarrow Q_1 \rightarrow E \rightarrow T \rightarrow Q_2 \rightarrow C_e$$

This pattern for a paragraph is a great way to connect and synthesize quotations from two essays in support of your argument. Let's break this formula down:

1. C_1 is your **claim**. Begin your paragraph with a sentence that contains the main idea you want to make or the connection you want to show between two essays. You might have learned to call this a topic sentence. Regardless, the key is to start with a sentence that lets the reader know exactly what the paragraph will be about. Your claim should be related to your argument and should offer the reader a clear sense of how this paragraph proves a part of the argument.

2. **I** is an **introduction**. After you state your claim for the paragraph, introduce the first quotation. Sometimes you will need a sentence to set up the quotation; other times you might just use an introductory phrase like "Das writes" or "According to Yoshino."

3. Q_1 is your first **quotation**. After you introduce the quotation, provide it. You will want to make sure it's completely accurate and, of course, you will want to provide proper citation (we'll discuss this more below).

4. **E** is an **explanation** of the quotation. After you provide the first quotation, add a sentence that explains that quotation. This can be particularly useful if the quotation contains an idea or concept. You may want to take another sentence or two to explain that idea even more so that your reader completely understands it.

5. **T** is a **transition** sentence. Before you move on to the next quotation, offer some sort of short transition sentence. This transition should provide a sense of the kind of connection you're trying to make in the paragraph as a whole. For example, you might have a sentence like "Cohen's analysis is useful for explaining the spread of HIV in Africa."

6. Q_2 is your **second quotation**, most likely from another essay. This second quotation needs only a brief introduction or signal phrase.

7. C_e is your **explanation of the connection**. Finally, add several sentences that explain the connection you see between the quotations and the way in which this connection supports your overall argument. This part of the formula is, in many ways, the most important part of the paragraph. These sentences should

also explain how the relationship between the quotations supports your argument. These sentences record your critical thinking, allowing you to use the connection you've made between these two authors to support your project for the paper.

Here's an example of what this kind of paragraph looks like:

> The political climate of our current moment is one in which people see those of opposing political parties as inhuman beings that don't need to be treated with a certain level of respect, which is dangerous because it forces people to hide their political beliefs in order to be accepted as humans. Francis Fukuyama states, "We accord beings with Factor X not just human rights but, if they are adults, political rights as well—that is, the right to live in democratic political communities where their rights to speech, religion, association, and political participation are respected" (138). Fukuyama explains that every being that we see as human is supposed to be treated with certain basic rights, leveling the playing field and giving all people the opportunity to be themselves without risking the loss of human dignity. While this should be the way people are always treated, in today's politically charged climate, members of opposing parties must cover their identities or risk being treated as inhuman. Kenji Yoshino writes, "Americans have come to a consensus that people should not be penalized for being different along these dimensions. That consensus, however, does not protect individuals against demands that they mute those differences" (453). What Yoshino sees as the demands to "mute those differences" complicates Fukuyama's argument that all beings are accorded certain rights. With the elections right around the corner, Republicans and Democrats are busy calling one another stupid, inhuman, uninformed, moronic, and immoral in attempts to strip the opposition of their Factor X and make it OK to devalue human life based on a political orientation.

This student begins with a claim about the ways in which political partisanship affects our perceptions of humanity. To prove this claim, the student begins with an idea from Francis Fukuyama: that all humans should have fundamental political rights. He or she then connects this idea to one from Kenji Yoshino about the ways in which we pressure people to hide their differences (such as differences in political points of view). Using both of these ideas, this student is able to show how political slandering devalues the humanity of those involved.

About Citation

It is absolutely essential that you acknowledge the words of others when you use them. In the real world, failure to do so can result in expensive lawsuits and ruined careers.

In the academic world, failure to do so is considered plagiarism. Every time you use the words or ideas of another, you must provide a citation.

You'll no doubt notice that some of the authors you read in this collection do not use citation. Why do you have to if they don't? The answer has a lot to do with *audience*. Whenever we write, we are addressing a particular audience—that's why it's useful to think about this process as joining a conversation. The audience you select determines a lot about how you will write—your tone, for example. It also determines the need for citation. *Academic writing always requires citation because it addresses an academic audience*. Addressing an academic audience doesn't mean using complicated sentences or fancy words. A lot of academic writing has a conversational tone, but it also always uses citation.

Ultimately, there are only a few things you need to know about citation. First, know that it exists. By that I mean that you must know that there are systems in place for you to acknowledge other sources. Second, you must know *what* you are citing. For example, when you cite something from this book, you are actually citing a selection from an edited anthology. Knowing that this is an anthology (as opposed to a *monograph*, a book with a single author) is crucial to figuring out how to cite it properly. Finally, you need to know how to find the right format. A good grammar or reference handbook is an excellent source, but you can also consult reputable websites; there are also web and computer programs that can help you with citation.

About Disciplines

Once you enter your major, you'll learn a specific system for providing that citation—every discipline has its own system. In this class, the system you will likely use is MLA citation, developed through the Modern Language Association, the governing body for the discipline of English. You will probably spend time in class learning the intricacies of this system, but for now remember the basics: Every time you use a quotation or paraphrase, include the author's name and the page number in parentheses at the end of the sentence, just before the period. That's true for visual images as well. Publication information for all your sources should be listed at the end of your paper. Visual images require a special format. You will want to consult a grammar handbook, a citation guide, or a reliable web source for specific information on how to cite these sources.

If you're interested in learning more about the citation system for your discipline, you can perform a web search to find out what system it uses and what specific rules that system has for formatting each reference. As with all citation, it is essential that you provide these references whenever you use someone else's words or ideas.

About Research

Academic Research

Research is also an important skill of critical thinking. But *research* is a much trickier term than it used to be. It used to be that research involved looking up specific subjects on little cards or ponderous indexes of journals in the library and then hunting down books in the library stacks or finding articles on microfilm. It required a good deal of training to do well. These days, most libraries don't even have what was called a "card catalog" any more. For most of us today, though, the basic methods of research are nearly instinctive. If you were given a blank search box, you would know what to do—just type in some search terms and start looking at the results until you find what you need. And in fact we often do this kind of research every day: researching what school to attend, or information on your favorite band, or where to get the best tattoo.

But academic research is very different from this kind of research. When you research on the web, you gather and summarize existing information. When academics do research, their goal is to produce *new* information. Indeed, this is what academics do for a living. Yes, teaching is an important part of our jobs, but conducting research is just as important. We are paid, in a sense, to make new knowledge. And we're not the only ones. Many careers today involve both research and its application. For example, if a medical researcher were simply to gather all the existing information on a disease, that would only be so useful. It is the move from that research to new avenues of treatment for a disease that is valuable. Making new knowledge matters.

You may be asked to produce research in this class. Even if you are not given a research assignment, working with the texts of this book is a kind of research since academic writing, like research, asks you to make new knowledge.

Having Sources, Finding Sources

There's an important difference between having sources, such as the ones presented for you here, and finding sources, such as doing research at the library. You might imagine it as the difference between swimming in a pool and swimming in the ocean. When you work with the texts of this book, you're practicing research in a fairly controlled environment, like swimming in a pool. You don't have to worry, for example, about the quality of the texts in this book because we've done that work for you. If you are asked to do your own research in this class, though, it's a bit like swimming in the ocean: The material you have to deal with can be just as vast, and there are extra dangers in the wild. One way to avoid those dangers is to make sure you are using reliable, academic sources—a particular challenge if you are using the web for your research. Before you use any website in an academic setting, you will want to make sure you evaluate it. You begin that process by asking yourself how you want to use the site. Any site on the web can be used as an example of your ideas or the ideas of any essay. But whenever you take ideas or evidence from websites, you need to be careful about which sites you use. Ask yourself questions such as:

- **Who wrote the material?** Is the site authored by an individual, an organization, a governmental agency? If you can't identify the author, you may want to question its reliability.
- **How qualified is the source?** What makes this author an expert on this material? What are this author's qualifications? If the site doesn't contain information about the qualifications of the author, then you may want to reconsider using it.

- **When was the site last updated?** Often this information will be provided on each page of the site, usually at the bottom of the page. If the site doesn't include any update information, then you will want to ask yourself how current the material is.
- **How stable is the address or URL?** Websites come and go. Generally speaking, websites from established groups or organizations are more stable than websites with their own domain name, which in turn are more stable than websites hosted with a free service.
- **How do you want to use the site in your writing?** Any website can be used as an example, but only those websites that establish their authority should be used for ideas or evidence.

Ideally, academic research goes beyond what you can find on the web. If you are asked to complete a research project for this class, your instructor will probably provide you with an orientation to the library and its resources. *How* you search will probably be familiar to you, but *what* you search will be academic books and journals.

A Formula for Academic Research

Central to academic research is the ability to work with ideas. In your prior educational experience, you may have completed research papers that were more like researching a topic on the web. The assignments for these papers would have asked you to gather information on a topic and then present that information in a written summary. For example, you may have been asked earlier in your schooling career to write a research paper on an important historical figure or event. You would research that topic and write a paper with what you found. But there's not much critical thinking involved in that sort of research paper. In college, you will most likely be asked to work with ideas in your research in order to generate new knowledge.

Ideas are useful because they help us to explain, predict, or change reality; that's why we refine, revise, and use theories. For example, the theory of gravity predicts what will happen to you if you step off a cliff. With that prediction, you can wisely choose not to take that step. Similarly, various economic theories predict how changes will affect standards of living. We can use these theories to make changes to elements like the interest rate in an attempt to change reality. When you research, you will want to focus on ideas. This formula might be useful:

$$I_s(S) = K_n$$

Let's break that down:

1. I_s stands for **Ideas about Stuff**. We might also use terms like *theory, hypothesis, lens, frame,* or *secondary material.* All of these terms indicate a set of ideas about something, whether that something is models of history or of a cell's inner workings. When you do your own research, you will want to make sure you have at least one source that provides you with Ideas about Stuff.

2. **S** stands for **Stuff**. We might also use *practice* (as opposed to *theory*), *experiment* (as opposed to *hypothesis*), *case* (as opposed to *lens* or *frame*), or *primary material* (as opposed to *secondary material*). These terms all suggest materials that show what actually happened—material elements of reality. In your research, you will want a set of texts that offers you this material. Stuff is the stuff you want to study. It might be one person's story, or an account of a historical incident, or the progress of a disease. Anything can be Stuff, even ideas. That is, you might apply one theory of economic change to another in order to synthesize a new theory.

3. K_n stands for **New Knowledge**. When you apply Ideas about Stuff to Stuff, you end up with New Knowledge, whether that is a new and refined theory or a new explanation for how things happen.

In order to work with this formula, you start with a topic that interests you. Ideally, you really care about the material, because that interest will sustain you through the difficult work of performing research to create new knowledge. Once you have a topic in mind, you will want to use some of the critical thinking skills we've already discussed:

- **Start thinking.** Begin by using the methods we discussed to think critically about your topic. Try responding to the topic—writing out your feelings, thoughts, and ideas about the topic—in order to develop some avenues to start your research. You might also use clustering or other brainstorming techniques to begin to narrow your focus.
- **Be specific.** As with an argument, you will want to be very specific about your topic. If you remain broad or vague, you can become overwhelmed by the amount of information you will find.
- **Formulate a question.** Before you start finding sources that offer you Ideas about Stuff and Stuff, you will want to develop a research question. This question is a lot like an argument for your paper. It's specific and focused. It's clear. And it offers you a map for conducting your research. The argument you end up making from your research should answer this question in a meaningful way.

Once you've found sources, you will want to treat them as you would the essays in this book, reading them critically, annotating and glossing them, and identifying key passages you want to work with. By connecting and synthesizing your sources, you begin to create an argument, one that answers the question you started with and that also creates new knowledge through the work you do in the research paper.

Research and Disciplines

As you enter your chosen discipline, you will learn specific methods of research that will probably involve different actions. You might, for example, design a survey for research in sociology or design an experiment for research in chemistry. Nevertheless, the essential elements of research in all disciplines are the same: using ideas in relation to reality in order to add to the conversation of the discipline.

You will also find that not only do the methods of research vary by discipline but the kinds of acceptable evidence vary as well. In the so-called hard sciences, for example, evidence is often statistical, coming from experimental research. In the humanities, including English, evidence is often textual and supported by analysis.

Thus disciplines can approach the same topic very differently, because the knowledge that matters to the discipline (and the ways of finding it) are very different. As you read the essays in *Emerging*, you might find examples of how different disciplines treat specific topics, though it's useful to keep in mind that when these authors write for other members of their discipline, their ideas and evidence (and citation) look even more different.

Revising, Editing, and Proofreading

So far, we've discussed all the stages of critical thinking you'll need to exercise in order to produce a draft of your paper. Each stage relates to a skill you might already use, and each, too, will have value in your future career. Once you've written a draft, making an argument that contributes to the larger conversation and supporting it by working with quotation, there is still more work to be done, because every good piece of writing goes through at least one revision. This is the thirteenth draft of Part One of this book, for example (though to be fair it's also the fourth edition).

Often students think of revision as "fixing" their papers—just correcting all the errors. But that's only part of the process. Revision involves making changes and should produce something new. Again, when we produce something new in the realm of ideas, we're doing critical thinking; revision, then, is also a form of critical thinking. Instead of thinking about the readings of the class, though, revision asks you to think critically about—to evaluate, test, and assess—your own writing.

When we discussed connecting, we said that it's easier to evaluate ideas against something else. The same is true with revision. Often when we write, our initial draft looks fine to us; it seems like our best thinking. This is where connecting with others—in this case, through the process of peer revision—is again useful. As part of my job coordinating the writing classes at my university, I read the class evaluations for all the writing courses, and one thing students say over and over again is that they don't value peer review, because they believe that only the instructor has "the" answer and so only the instructor's comments count. On the contrary, I believe that *peer review is one of the most practical things you'll learn in this class*. In the rest of your life, you won't be asked to write papers, but you will be asked to work with others on committees or teams again and again. Learning to work well with others—to recognize valuable feedback and to give it in turn—is essential.

Peer review gives you practice in testing your ideas with actual readers. As noted above, every piece of writing has an audience, and your peers form part of that audience when it comes to the writing you will do for this class. Since the goal of each paper is to contribute to the conversation started in the texts, and since your classmates have also read and written about the texts, they are the other participants of your written conversation.

That process works in reverse, too. When you read your peers' writing, you will want to bring all your critical thinking skills to bear. You might be tempted to just write

"Good job!" no matter what you think about the writing, for fear of being critical or mean, but that shows no critical thinking. *Critical thinking is not the same as being critical.* When you offer valuable feedback, you're helping your classmates, no matter how negative that feedback might feel to you. Start by reading your peer's paper, using the same skills of critical reading that you used when you read the texts for this class. Annotate it just as you would one of the readings, marking what you think is important and asking questions in the margin when you are lost or confused. Then think critically about what your classmate is saying, using your connection skills—connect what he or she says about the text to what you know about the text, as well as to what you think and have written about the text. Finally, form your response as a way of joining the conversation.

Sample Student Paper

It might be useful for you to see how this all comes together in an actual student paper. Let's start with the assignment, taken from a recent class taught by Kathleen Moorhead, one of the instructors in the writing program in which I teach:

> The essays we've read this semester have discussed how culture influences us, how TV reinforces stereotypes, and a call for a new paradigm to look at all these issues. Peter Singer, in his essay "Visible Man: Ethics in a World without Secrets," asks, "New technology has made greater openness possible, but has this openness made us better off?" (354). When we discussed this in class, most of you answered yes to this question.
>
> The paradox is that even while people espouse the benefits of openness and honesty, the online images and personalities people present are carefully curated. If culture deeply affects how we think, and the daily barrage of media influences how we regard gender and ethnicity, what do our online creations say about us?
>
> **For this paper, using Singer, plus one other author we've read this semester, analyze how society, stereotypes, perceptions—whatever—play roles in how and why we construct online identities that are different from our real-world identities.**
>
> Questions for Exploration:
>
> How do our virtual identities differ from our real-world identities? An online identity is much more than a photograph we post—is our online identity an example of covering? Do cultural influences play a part in constructing online identities? Do gender and/or ethnic stereotypes come into play? Does the fact that we are potentially "seen" online by more people than in our physical reality make a difference? How do virtual realities intersect with our desire for privacy? Our desire to be known?
>
> You do *not* have to answer these questions. They are only to help you get started thinking in case you're stuck. The best questions will be the ones you develop.

You can apply the same critical thinking skills to the text of this assignment as you would to one of the readings in this book. For starters, critically reading the assignment will help you locate key information in writing your response, and you should annotate it as you would a reading. Notice, for example, that one section is in bold, highlighting the main task of the assignment: "For this paper, using Singer, plus one other author we've read this semester, analyze how society, stereotypes, perceptions—whatever—play roles in how and why we construct online identities that are different from our real-world identities." In annotating the assignment, you'd probably want to highlight this sentence so that you know where to focus your own critical thinking and response.

The questions that follow the assignment are not that different from the kinds of questions you might ask yourself when reading Singer and the essay you might choose. Both offer a jumping-off point for your own critical thinking, which can then lead to an argument you might use for your paper.

Here is one student's response to the assignment:

Eye of the Camera

For many people today, it is hard to remember a time when there has not been a security camera watching people's every move. It seems that individuals in newer generations are predisposed to acting a particular way because they are always being watched by these cameras. However, it is not until behind closed doors that people feel safe enough to expose their unique, and possibly imperfect, real-world identities. Because folks refer to some real-world identities as strange, people take action and develop a new kind of identity. This gives individuals an opportunity to cover their real-world identity and form a new virtual identity with no imperfections. In "The New Civil Rights," Kenji Yoshino writes, "In practice, I expect the liberty paradigm to protect the authentic self better than the equality paradigm" (458). In society, individuals have overlooked the importance of a person's worth and authenticity and instead have focused on a set of rules that apply to the behavior and identity of many types of people, and use that paradigm to determine if they will be treated equally. Unfortunately, because people are so judgmental, many individuals use virtual identities to escape from reality and improve their standing in the eyes of others. In this paper I will argue that because technology has shown people a way to cover their real-world identities, it has become harder to reinforce the importance of originality and diversity leading more people to conform to the camera's eye, creating their own desired virtual identity.

Having a virtual identity has let individuals create a world with no imperfections. This is a form of covering. Yoshino defines covering as "to tone down a disfavored identity to fit into the mainstream" (452). For example, if a person's physical identity contains a scar on the left side of their face, that person may use different angles or certain modifications to cover the scar and show a virtual identity without what they view as an imperfection. Covering in this fashion allows individuals to keep what might be seen as a flaw private. After all, in "Visible Man: Ethics in a World without Secrets," Peter Singer notes, "Over the course of Western history, we've developed a desire for more privacy" (355). Covering flaws allows us to keep them private. However, this type of covering means that the real-world identity has been stripped and turned into an identity that can only be viewed virtually.

In some cases, people's virtual identity have shown that they are operating with greater authority than they have in the real world, modifying their characteristics in order to show others what they view as their "perfect" self. This creates a mindset in people that they have the power to manipulate the way the world works. For example, if someone who has been insecure about the size of their lips chooses from one of the many facial construction apps to make their lips look bigger, then they have taken a physical characteristic and have changed it for their virtual identity to receive the type of attention their real-world self would not get. This use of technology to alter identity runs counter to Singer's claim that "New technology has made greater openness possible" (354), as such modifications conceal real-world identities, rather than reveal them. Media and individuals have promoted the idea that people should post pictures of themselves with no imperfections. This leads people to develop unrealistic expectations and to believe they can change whatever they want about themselves.

The mindset that people are able to act as Mother Nature and change whatever they want about themselves is a false sense of reality. People forget the importance of originality and authenticity. Yoshino notes that "Americans have come to a consensus that people should not be penalized for being different . . . That consensus, however, does not protect individuals against demands that they mute those differences" (453). As a result, people go through the lengths they do to make themselves looks different because they have been told that the looks they possess are not good enough and can be better. No doubt we all can be better in the way we look, but some changes are beyond our power and capability. Virtual identities cause people to hold unrealistic expectations of themselves. Not only are people holding others to high standards for their virtual identities, but now also people are holding standards for themselves to try and obtain the best looking profile from their virtual identity. It is not only the expectations of how a person should live their life, but also the expectation for people to look perfect and plastic. Society has set a paradigm promoting people to change their originality to something society sees as acceptable and beautiful, instead of focusing on people's authenticity and the beauty of their real-world identity.

Virtual identities have let people communicate differently from their real-world identities. Not only are people able to change the way they look, but they are able to manipulate perception of less physical real-world identities, such as socioeconomic class. For example, if a boy wants to convince his followers that he has a lot of money and posts a picture with a lot of dollar bills in his hand and captions his picture saying he has cashed his paycheck, many people will see him as a boy who acquires a lot of money and will continue to have money. But when the camera is turned off, it may show that the boy's money is actually birthday money from his grandma — which, if posted, could lead people to think he is rich and spoiled. In choosing how to caption his photo, the boy is hiding his reality behind a virtual self, similar to D. W. Winnicott's theory of True and False Selves, which Yoshino describes as "Like a king castling behind a rook in chess, the more valuable but less powerful piece retreats behind the less valuable but more powerful one" (455). Since this type of language use is basically false, it can undermine Singer's fears of the "breaches of privacy" that result from "connecting with others, sharing information, networking, self-promoting, flirting, and bragging" (355) online. After all, people's language and how they speak is a part of their identity, and to change the vocabulary someone possess online in order to gain more acceptance is deceiving and untrue.

Virtual attention can become addictive to the point that people will go to extreme lengths to obtain the desired attention. It has been proven by researchers that the notifications of "likes" people receive give neurological pleasure in the same way as if someone was giving that person attention. As this addiction develops, people betray who they are and what they believe in order to receive the virtual attention they crave. For example, if a girl decides to post a picture of herself fully clothed, and notices that a picture of her friend in a bikini has received far more "likes" than the fully-clothed girl's, next time she may post a picture showing more skin, even if she does not dress that way in the real world. She will have learned that in order to get the virtual attention and "likes" she craves, she must abandon her real-world identity. If this fully-clothed girl stuck to her real-world identity, she would not go out into public and show lots of skin to receive provocative attention. But because it is viewed as acceptable in her virtual world, she has no problem literally stripping down her identity in order to receive "likes." Singer writes, "With some social standards, the more people do something, the less risky it becomes for each individual" (355). The more people do something, the more others view it as acceptable, even if the behavior is risky—as it is for a young girl to think that showing her body is the key to being liked. This pressure to cover real-world identities is dangerous. Yoshino writes, "If we look closely, we will see that covering is the way many groups are being held back today. The reason racial minorities are pressured to 'act white' is because of white supremacy. The reason women are told to downplay their child-care responsibilities in the workplace is because of patriarchy" (453–54). Instead of sticking to the original self, people act and follow their avatar, seeking attention while continuing dangerous social realities.

Virtual identities are always evolving, causing people to continuously change what they post. Because virtual identities are used to show the world what people view as the perfect person, these posts will constantly change to create and meet new sets of standards that people view as acceptable. What is acceptable today may not be tomorrow. This is where people change and mold their virtual identities to whatever the new acceptable norm is that will get them the virtual attention. This means that a person's virtual identity is constantly evolving and so is how they portray themselves. Peter Singer writes, "The standards of what we want to keep private and what we want to make public are constantly evolving" (355). Singer is right is the sense that something that was once viewed as unacceptable or needing to remain private can evolve into something that no longer needs to be kept private, as social values are evolving. Yoshino discusses this, writing, "When I hesitate before engaging in a public display of same-sex affection, I am not thinking of the state or my employer, but of strangers around me and my own internal censor" (459). Now that same-sex marriage is legal, however, the type of self-censorship that Yoshino describes is less widespread, with many more LGBT individuals posting about their identities and relationships. Over the course of a few years, a group of individuals has been able to shift their true desires and intentions from private to public.

Unfortunately, humans cannot make their real-world identity as malleable as their virtual identity. But, people should have no desire to change and form their real-world identity because it is who they truly are. They are the original copy of themselves, and should be able to express who they are freely, without needing to follow society's demands and cover. However, it is clear that in society today someone's real-world identity is not enough to make an everlasting impression, so instead people must turn to much more foreign and "cool" virtual identities to receive social acceptance. It is sad to see the world evolving more to the camera's eye than to embrace the diversity and originality of the real-world self—which contains value far more permanent than a virtual identity. Many people who are wrapped up in their virtual identity do not realize that soon, very soon, those posts will not be good enough anymore, and the virtual identity they tried so hard to make acceptable is no longer viewed as relevant. Those people are stuck with a virtual identity that requires constant adjustment and change, and a real-world identity that is covered.

Works Cited

Singer, Peter. "Visible Man: Ethics in a World without Secrets." *Emerging: Contemporary Readings for Writers*, 4th ed., edited by Barclay Barrios, Bedford/St. Martin's, 2018, pp. 353–60.

Yoshino, Kenji. "The New Civil Rights." *Emerging: Contemporary Readings for Writers*, 4th ed., edited by Barclay Barrios, Bedford/St. Martin's, 2018, pp. 452–60.

Every paper needs an argument, the main point that the author is posing. The author of this paper makes that argument clear at the end of the introduction: "In this paper I will argue that because technology has shown people a way to cover their real-world identities, it has become harder to reinforce the importance of originality and diversity leading more people to conform to the camera's eye, creating their own desired virtual identity." The argument addresses the prompt by suggesting that the social force of "covering," a concept from Yoshino's essay, plays a role in constructing online identities and further that the result of that force creates virtual identities that are not only different from real-world identities but also less original and diverse. It's also clear that both Yoshino and Singer have a role to play in this argument, since Yoshino discusses covering and Singer discusses cameras and surveillance culture.

Throughout the paper, the author supports this argument by connecting Yoshino and Singer and synthesizing their ideas. Notice the point made in the second paragraph, for example: The author introduces the notion of covering using a quotation from Yoshino and then connects it to the desire for privacy discussed by Singer. By connecting these two essays, the author is able to begin supporting the larger argument that about the gap between online and real-world identities.

As the paper proceeds, each paragraph makes the same moves—connecting the authors to form a synthesis that supports the argument. There are, of course, some stumbles along the way; this author is, after all, still emerging as an academic writer. You might notice, for example, that some paragraphs only draw support from one of the authors, missing the power of synthesizing their ideas. And some of the transitions may feel weak; transitions that place each paragraph in relation to the larger argument tend to be more effective. Similarly, there are some grammatical and language issues that might distract us as readers. And while sometimes the author does a great job of using the texts to create a synthesis, there are certainly places where clearer analysis and connection would be useful.

This is the second, revised draft of this paper, and in many ways it is a success. By the conclusion, the author has managed to provide support and evidence for the argument. That should be your goal when you write in this class, too. Because despite its shortcomings, this paper does demonstrate critical thinking by presenting a clear argument supported with specific examples and quotations from the text. Your work in this class may look very different (in part, because the writing prompts you work with may look very different), but the skills will remain the same. And in the end, these skills are what matter—not just in this class and not just in college, but in your career and your life as well.

Part Two
THE READINGS

KWAME ANTHONY APPIAH

Kwame Anthony Appiah was born in London, grew up in Ghana, and earned a Ph.D. at Cambridge University. He is a professor of philosophy and law at New York University. He has also taught at Princeton, Duke, Harvard, Yale, Cornell, Cambridge, and the University of Ghana. He has published numerous academic books and articles as well as three detective novels. In 2008, Appiah was recognized for his contributions to racial, ethnic, and religious relations when Brandeis University awarded him the first Joseph B. and Toby Gittler Prize.

Appiah's *Cosmopolitanism: Ethics in a World of Strangers* (2006) was one of the first books published in Henry Louis Gates Jr.'s Issues of Our Time series, which aims to tackle the important concerns of the information age. In *Cosmopolitanism*, Appiah examines the imaginary boundaries that have separated people around the world and the ways we can redraw those boundaries. Appiah claims with the book's title that we are all citizens of the world. In the time of al-Qaeda, we can no longer afford to draw significant lines between different groups and regions. Humanity has fundamental commonalities, Appiah suggests, and we should embrace them.

The following selections, "Making Conversation" and "The Primacy of Practice," appear in *Cosmopolitanism* as the introduction and one of the book's chapters. Appiah first defines *cosmopolitanism* and its problems but ultimately determines that practicing a citizenship of the world is not only helpful in a post-9/11 world, but necessary. There is no divide between "us" and "them," he suggests, only a basic moral obligation we have to each other. It is not necessary for people to agree to behave morally for the right reason, or the right god, or the right country or custom. It is only necessary that they agree to behave morally. Conversation, Appiah writes, is the best starting point.

It's tempting to reduce what follows to something as simple as "We should all just get along," but Appiah is also challenging us to think about how we can make that happen. How primal is practice in your own life? Is what you do more important than why you do it?

- TAGS: *collaboration, community, conversation, ethics, globalism, identity, judgment and decision making, politics, social change*
- CONNECTIONS: *Chen, DeGhett, Epstein, Gladwell, Jamison, Lukianoff and Haidt, Southan, Stillman, van Houtryve, Turkle, Watters, Yoshino*

Making Conversation

Our ancestors have been human for a very long time. If a normal baby girl born forty thousand years ago were kidnapped by a time traveler and raised in a normal family in New York, she would be ready for college in eighteen years. She would learn English (along with—who knows?—Spanish or Chinese), understand trigonometry, follow baseball and pop music; she would probably want a pierced tongue and a couple of tattoos. And she would be unrecognizably different from the brothers and sisters she left behind. For most of human history, we were born into small societies of a few score people, bands of hunters and gatherers, and would see, on a typical day, only people we had known most of our lives. Everything our long-ago ancestors ate or wore, every tool they used, every shrine at which they worshipped, was made within that group. Their knowledge came from their ancestors or from their own experiences. That is the world that shaped us, the world in which our nature was formed.

Now, if I walk down New York's Fifth Avenue on an ordinary day, I will have within sight more human beings than most of those prehistoric hunter-gatherers saw in a lifetime. Between then and now some of our forebears settled down and learned agriculture; created villages, towns, and, in the end, cities; discovered the power of writing. But it was a slow process. The population of classical Athens when Socrates* died, at the end of the fifth century BC, could have lived in a few large skyscrapers. Alexander† set off from Macedon to conquer the world three-quarters of a century later with an army of between thirty and forty thousand, which is far fewer people than commute into Des Moines every Monday morning. When, in the first century, the population of Rome reached a million, it was the first city of its size. To keep it fed, the Romans had had to build an empire that brought home grain from Africa. By then, they had already worked out how to live cheek by jowl in societies where most of those who spoke your language and shared your laws and grew the food on your table were people you would never know. It is, I think, little short of miraculous that brains shaped by our long history could have been turned to this new way of life.

Even once we started to build these larger societies, most people knew little about the ways of other tribes, and could affect just a few local lives. Only in the past couple of centuries, as every human community has gradually been drawn into a single web of trade and a global network of information, have we come to a point where each of us can realistically imagine contacting any other of our six billion conspecifics and sending that person something worth having: a radio, an antibiotic, a good idea. Unfortunately, we could also send, through negligence as easily as malice, things that will cause harm: a virus, an airborne pollutant, a bad idea. And the possibilities of good and of ill are multiplied beyond all measure when it comes to policies carried out by governments in our name. Together, we can ruin poor farmers by dumping our subsidized grain into their markets, cripple industries by punitive tariffs, deliver weapons that will kill thousands upon thousands. Together, we can raise standards of living by adopting new policies on trade and aid, prevent or treat diseases with vaccines and pharmaceuticals, take measures against global climate change, encourage resistance to tyranny and a concern for the worth of each human life.

And, of course, the worldwide web of information—radio, television, telephones, the Internet—means not only that we can affect lives everywhere but that we can learn about life anywhere, too. Each person you know about and can affect is someone to whom you have responsibilities: To say this is just to affirm the very idea of morality. The challenge, then, is to take minds and hearts formed over the long millennia of

---

* Socrates: Athenian Greek (469–399 BC); one of the founders of Western philosophy known chiefly through the writings of his students, notably Plato [Ed.].

† Alexander: Alexander the Great (356–323 BC) founded an empire that eventually covered about two million square miles [Ed.].

living in local troops and equip them with ideas and institutions that will allow us to live together as the global tribe we have become.

Under what rubric to proceed? Not "globalization"—a term that once referred to a marketing strategy, and then came to designate a macroeconomic thesis, and now can seem to encompass everything, and nothing. Not "multiculturalism," another shape shifter, which so often designates the disease it purports to cure. With some ambivalence, I have settled on "cosmopolitanism." Its meaning is equally disputed, and celebrations of the "cosmopolitan" can suggest an unpleasant posture of superiority toward the putative provincial. You imagine a Comme des Garçons–clad sophisticate with a platinum frequent-flyer card regarding, with kindly condescension, a ruddy-faced farmer in workman's overalls. And you wince.

5

Maybe, though, the term can be rescued. It has certainly proved a survivor. Cosmopolitanism dates at least to the Cynics* of the fourth century BC, who first coined the expression cosmopolitan, "citizen of the cosmos." The formulation was meant to be paradoxical, and reflected the general Cynic skepticism toward custom and tradition. A citizen—a *politēs*—belonged to a particular *polis,* a city to which he or she owed loyalty. The cosmos referred to the world, not in the sense of the earth, but in the sense of the universe. Talk of cosmopolitanism originally signaled, then, a rejection of the conventional view that every civilized person belonged to a community among communities.

The creed was taken up and elaborated by the Stoics,† beginning in the third century BC, and that fact proved of critical importance in its subsequent intellectual history. For the Stoicism of the Romans—Cicero, Seneca, Epictetus, and the emperor Marcus Aurelius—proved congenial to many Christian intellectuals, once Christianity became the religion of the Roman Empire. It is profoundly ironic that, though Marcus Aurelius sought to suppress the new Christian sect, his extraordinarily personal *Meditations,* a philosophical diary written in the second century AD as he battled to save the Roman Empire from barbarian invaders, has attracted Christian readers for nearly two millennia. Part of its appeal, I think, has always been the way the Stoic emperor's cosmopolitan conviction of the oneness of humanity echoes Saint Paul's insistence that "there is neither Jew nor Greek, there is neither bond nor free, there is neither male nor female: for ye are all one in Christ Jesus."[1]

Cosmopolitanism's later career wasn't without distinction. It underwrote some of the great moral achievements of the Enlightenment, including the 1789 "Declaration of the Rights of Man" and Immanuel Kant's work proposing a "league of nations." In a 1788 essay in his journal *Teutscher Merkur,* Christoph Martin Wieland—once called the German Voltaire—wrote, in a characteristic expression of the ideal, "Cosmopolitans . . . regard all the peoples of the earth as so many branches of a single family, and the universe as a state, of which they, with innumerable other rational beings, are citizens, promoting together under the general laws of nature the perfection of the

*Cynics: Ancient school of Greek philosophy. Cynics advocated a simple life, free from material things, rejecting desires for fame and even health [Ed.].

†Stoics: School of philosophy influenced by the Cynics. Stoics held that destructive emotions should be controlled and that clear thinking would lead to reason [Ed.].

whole, while each in his own fashion is busy about his own well-being."[2] And Voltaire himself—whom nobody, alas, ever called the French Wieland—spoke eloquently of the obligation to understand those with whom we share the planet, linking that need explicitly with our global economic interdependence. "Fed by the products of their soil, dressed in their fabrics, amused by games they invented, instructed even by their ancient moral fables, why would we neglect to understand the mind of these nations, among whom our European traders have traveled ever since they could find a way to get to them?"[3]

So there are two strands that intertwine in the notion of cosmopolitanism. One is the idea that we have obligations to others, obligations that stretch beyond those to whom we are related by the ties of kith and kind, or even the more formal ties of a shared citizenship. The other is that we take seriously the value not just of human life but of particular human lives, which means taking an interest in the practices and beliefs that lend them significance. People are different, the cosmopolitan knows, and there is much to learn from our differences. Because there are so many human possibilities worth exploring, we neither expect nor desire that every person or every society should converge on a single mode of life. Whatever our obligations are to others (or theirs to us) they often have the right to go their own way. As we'll see, there will be times when these two ideals—universal concern and respect for legitimate difference—clash. There's a sense in which cosmopolitanism is the name not of the solution but of the challenge.

Cosmopolitanism is the name not of the solution but of the challenge.

10

A citizen of the world: How far can we take that idea? Are you really supposed to abjure all local allegiances and partialities in the name of this vast abstraction, humanity? Some proponents of cosmopolitanism were pleased to think so; and they often made easy targets of ridicule. "Friend of men, and enemy of almost every man he had to do with," Thomas Carlyle* memorably said of the eighteenth-century physiocrat the Marquis de Mirabeau, who wrote the treatise *L'Ami des hommes* when he wasn't too busy jailing his own son. "A lover of his kind, but a hater of his kindred," Edmund Burke† said of Jean-Jacques Rousseau,‡ who handed each of the five children he fathered to an orphanage.

Yet the impartialist version of the cosmopolitan creed has continued to hold a steely fascination. Virginia Woolf§ once exhorted "freedom from unreal loyalties"—to nation, sex, school, neighborhood, and on and on. Leo Tolstoy,¶ in the same spirit, inveighed against the "stupidity" of patriotism. "To destroy war, destroy patriotism," he wrote in an 1896 essay—a couple of decades before the tsar was swept away by a revolution in the name of the international working class. Some contemporary philosophers have similarly urged that the boundaries of nations are morally irrelevant—accidents of history with no rightful claim on our conscience.

---

*Thomas Carlyle: Scottish essayist and historian (1795–1881) [Ed.].

†Edmund Burke: Anglo-Irish politician and political philosopher (1729–1797) [Ed.].

‡Jean-Jacques Rousseau: French political philosopher (1712–1778) [Ed.].

§Virginia Woolf: English novelist, critic, and essayist (1882–1941) [Ed.].

¶Leo Tolstoy: Russian writer best known for his novels, such as *War and Peace* (1828–1910) [Ed.].

But if there are friends of cosmopolitanism who make me nervous, I am happy to be opposed to cosmopolitanism's noisiest foes. Both Hitler and Stalin—who agreed about little else, save that murder was the first instrument of politics—launched regular invectives against "rootless cosmopolitans"; and while, for both, anti-cosmopolitanism was often just a euphemism for anti-Semitism, they were right to see cosmopolitanism as their enemy. For they both required a kind of loyalty to one portion of humanity—a nation, a class—that ruled out loyalty to all of humanity. And the one thought that cosmopolitans share is that no local loyalty can ever justify forgetting that each human being has responsibilities to every other. Fortunately, we need take sides neither with the nationalist who abandons all foreigners nor with the hard-core cosmopolitan who regards her friends and fellow citizens with icy impartiality. The position worth defending might be called (in both senses) a partial cosmopolitanism.

There's a striking passage, to this point, in George Eliot's *Daniel Deronda*, published in 1876, which was, as it happens, the year when England's first—and, so far, last—Jewish prime minister, Benjamin Disraeli, was elevated to the peerage as Earl of Beaconsfield. Disraeli, though baptized and brought up in the Church of England, always had a proud consciousness of his Jewish ancestry (given the family name, which his father spelled D'Israeli, it would have been hard to ignore). But Deronda, who has been raised in England as a Christian gentleman, discovers his Jewish ancestry only as an adult; and his response is to commit himself to the furtherance of his "hereditary people":

> It was as if he had found an added soul in finding his ancestry—his judgment no longer wandering in the mazes of impartial sympathy, but choosing, with the noble partiality which is man's best strength, the closer fellowship that makes sympathy practical—exchanging that bird's-eye reasonableness which soars to avoid preference and loses all sense of quality, for the generous reasonableness of drawing shoulder to shoulder with men of like inheritance.

Notice that in claiming a Jewish loyalty—an "added soul"—Deronda is not rejecting a human one. As he says to his mother, "I think it would have been right that I should have been brought up with the consciousness that I was a Jew, but it must always have been a good to me to have as wide an instruction and sympathy as possible." This is the same Deronda, after all, who has earlier explained his decision to study abroad in these eminently cosmopolitan terms: "I want to be an Englishman, but I want to understand other points of view. And I want to get rid of a merely English attitude in studies."[4] Loyalties and local allegiances determine more than what we want; they determine who we are. And Eliot's talk of the "closer fellowship that makes sympathy practical" echoes Cicero's claim that "society and human fellowship will be best served if we confer the most kindness on those with whom we are most closely associated."[5] A creed that disdains the partialities of kinfolk and community may have a past, but it has no future.

In the final message my father left for me and my sisters, he wrote, "Remember you are citizens of the world." But as a leader of the independence movement in what was then the Gold Coast, he never saw a conflict between local partialities and a universal morality—between being part of the place you were and a part of a broader human community. Raised with this father and an English mother, who was both deeply connected to our family in England and fully rooted in Ghana, where she has now lived for half a century, I always had a sense of family and tribe that was multiple and overlapping: Nothing could have seemed more commonplace.

Surely nothing *is* more commonplace. In geological terms, it has been a blink of an eye since human beings first left Africa, and there are few spots where we have not found habitation. The urge to migrate is no less "natural" than the urge to settle. At the same time, most of those who have learned the languages and customs of other places haven't done so out of mere curiosity. A few were looking for food for thought; most were looking for food. Thoroughgoing ignorance about the ways of others is largely a privilege of the powerful. The well-traveled polyglot is as likely to be among the worst off as among the best off—as likely to be found in a shantytown as at the Sorbonne. So cosmopolitanism shouldn't be seen as some exalted attainment: it begins with the simple idea that in the human community, as in national communities, we need to develop habits of coexistence: conversation in its older meaning, of living together, association.

And conversation in its modern sense, too. The town of Kumasi, where I grew up, is the capital of Ghana's Asante region, and, when I was a child, its main commercial thoroughfare was called Kingsway Street. In the 1950s, if you wandered down it toward the railway yards at the center of town, you'd first pass by Baboo's Bazaar, which sold imported foods and was run by the eponymous Mr. Baboo—a charming and courteous Indian—with the help of his growing family. Mr. Baboo was active in the Rotary and could always be counted on to make a contribution to the various charitable projects that are among the diversions of Kumasi's middle class, but the truth is that I remember Mr. Baboo mostly because he always had a good stock of candies and because he was always smiling. I can't reconstruct the tour down the rest of the street, for not every store had bonbons to anchor my memories. Still, I remember that we got rice from Irani Brothers; and that we often stopped in on various Lebanese and Syrian families, Muslim and Maronite, and even a philosophical Druze, named Mr. Hanni, who sold imported cloth and who was always ready, as I grew older, for a conversation about the troubles of his native Lebanon. There were other "strangers" among us, too: in the military barracks in the middle of town, you could find many northerners among the "other ranks," privates and NCOs,* their faces etched in distinctive patterns of ethnic scarification. And then there was the occasional European—the Greek architect, the Hungarian artist, the Irish doctor, the Scots engineer, some English barristers and judges, and a wildly international assortment of professors at the university, many of whom, unlike the colonial officials, remained after independence. I never thought to wonder, as a child, why these people traveled so far to live and work in my hometown; still, I was glad they did. Conversations across boundaries can be fraught, all the more so as the world

* NCOs: Noncommissioned officers [Ed.].

grows smaller and the stakes grow larger. It's therefore worth remembering that they can also be a pleasure. What academics sometimes dub "cultural otherness" should prompt neither piety nor consternation.

Cosmopolitanism is an adventure and an ideal: But you can't have any respect for human diversity and expect everyone to become cosmopolitan. The obligations of those who wish to exercise their legitimate freedom to associate with their own kind—to keep the rest of the world away as the Amish do in the United States—are only the same as the basic obligations we all have: to do for others what morality requires. Still, a world in which communities are neatly hived off from one another seems no longer a serious option, if it ever was. And the way of segregation and seclusion has always been anomalous in our perpetually voyaging species. Cosmopolitanism isn't hard work; repudiating it is.

In the wake of 9/11, there has been a lot of fretful discussion about the divide between "us" and "them." What's often taken for granted is a picture of a world in which conflicts arise, ultimately, from conflicts between values. This is what we take to be good; that is what they take to be good. That picture of the world has deep philosophical roots; it is thoughtful, well worked out, plausible. And, I think, wrong.

I should be clear: this book* is not a book about policy, nor is it a contribution to the debates about the true face of globalization. I'm a philosopher by trade, and philosophers rarely write really useful books. All the same, I hope to persuade you that there are interesting conceptual questions that lie beneath the facts of globalization. The cluster of questions I want to take up can seem pretty abstract. How real are values? What do we talk about when we talk about difference? Is any form of relativism right? When do morals and manners clash? Can culture be "owned"? What do we owe strangers by virtue of our shared humanity? But the way these questions play out in our lives isn't so very abstract. By the end, I hope to have made it harder to think of the world as divided between the West and the Rest; between locals and moderns; between a bloodless ethic of profit and a bloody ethic of identity; between "us" and "them." The foreignness of foreigners, the strangeness of strangers: These things are real enough. It's just that we've been encouraged, not least by well-meaning intellectuals, to exaggerate their significance by an order of magnitude.

As I'll be arguing, it is an error—to which we dwellers in a scientific age are peculiarly prone—to resist talk of "objective" values. In the absence of a natural science of right and wrong, someone whose model of knowledge is physics or biology will be inclined to conclude that values are not real; or, at any rate, not real like atoms and nebulae. In the face of this temptation, I want to hold on to at least one important aspect of the objectivity of values: that there are some values that are, and should be, universal, just as there are lots of values that are, and must be, local. We can't hope to reach a final consensus on how to rank and order such values. That's why the model I'll be returning to is that of conversation—and, in particular, conversation between people from different ways of life. The world is 20

*Appiah's *Cosmopolitanism* [BJB].

getting more crowded: In the next half a century the population of our once foraging species will approach nine billion. Depending on the circumstances, conversations across boundaries can be delightful, or just vexing: What they mainly are, though, is inevitable.

The Primacy of Practice

Local Agreements

Among the Asante,* you will be glad to hear, incest between brothers and sisters and parents and children is shunned as *akyiwadee*. You can agree with an Asante that it's wrong, even if you don't accept his explanation of why. If my interest is in discouraging theft, I needn't worry that one person might refrain from theft because she believes in the Golden Rule; another because of her conception of personal integrity; a third because she thinks God frowns on it. I've said that value language helps shape common responses of thought, action, and feeling. But when the issue is what to do, differences in what we think and feel can fall away. We know from our own family lives that conversation doesn't start with agreement on principles. Who but someone in the grip of a terrible theory would want to insist on an agreement on principles before discussing which movie to go to, what to have for dinner, when to go to bed?

Indeed, our political coexistence, as subjects or citizens, depends on being able to agree about practices while disagreeing about their justification. For many long years, in medieval Spain under the Moors and later in the Ottoman Near East, Jews and Christians of various denominations lived under Muslim rule. This modus vivendi† was possible only because the various communities did not have to agree on a set of universal values. In seventeenth-century Holland, starting roughly in the time of Rembrandt, the Sephardic Jewish community began to be increasingly well integrated into Dutch society, and there was a great deal of intellectual as well as social exchange between Christian and Jewish communities. Christian toleration of Jews did not depend on express agreement on fundamental values. Indeed, these historical examples of religious toleration—you might even call them early experiments in multiculturalism—should remind us of the most obvious fact about our own society.

Americans share a willingness to be governed by the system set out in the U.S. Constitution. But that does not require anyone to agree to any particular claims or values. The Bill of Rights tells us, "Congress shall make no law respecting an establishment of religion, or prohibiting the free exercise thereof. . . ." Yet we don't need to agree on what values underlie our acceptance of the First Amendment's treatment of religion. Is it religious toleration as an end in itself? Or is it a Protestant

---

* Asante: A people living primarily in Ghana and the Ivory Coast [Ed.].

† Modus vivendi: Latin phrase meaning mode (or way) of living that accommodates divergent points of view; agreeing to disagree [Ed.].

commitment to the sovereignty of the individual conscience? Is it prudence, which recognizes that trying to force religious conformity on people only leads to civil discord? Or is it skepticism that any religion has it right? Is it to protect the government from religion? Or religion from the government? Or is it some combination of these, or other, aims?

Cass Sunstein, the American legal scholar, has written eloquently that our understanding of Constitutional law is a set of what he calls "incompletely theorized agreements."[6] People mostly agree that it would be wrong for the Congress to pass laws prohibiting the building of mosques, for example, without agreeing exactly as to why. Many of us would, no doubt, mention the First Amendment (even though we don't agree about what values it embodies). But others would ground their judgment not in any particular law but in a conception, say, of democracy or in the equal citizenship of Muslims, neither of which is explicitly mentioned in the Constitution. There is no agreed-upon answer—and the point is there doesn't need to be. We can live together without agreeing on what the values are that make it good to live together; we can agree about what to do in most cases, without agreeing about why it is right.

I don't want to overstate the claim. No doubt there are widely shared values that help Americans live together in amity. But they certainly don't live together successfully because they have a shared theory of value or a shared story as to how to bring "their" values to bear in each case. They each have a pattern of life that they are used to; and neighbors who are, by and large, used to them. So long as this settled pattern is not seriously disrupted, they do not worry over-much about whether their fellow citizens agree with them or their theories about how to live. Americans tend to have, in sum, a broadly liberal reaction when they *do* hear about their fellow citizens' doing something that they would not do themselves: They mostly think it is not their business and not the government's business either. And, as a general rule, their shared Americanness matters to them, although many of their fellow Americans are remarkably unlike themselves. It's just that what they do share can be less substantial than we're inclined to suppose.

Changing Our Minds

It's not surprising, then, that what makes conversation across boundaries worthwhile isn't that we're likely to come to a reasoned agreement about values. I don't say that we can't change minds, but the reasons we exchange in our conversations will seldom do much to persuade others who do not share our fundamental evaluative judgments already. (Remember: the same goes, mutatis mutandis,* for factual judgments.)

When we offer judgments, after all, it's rarely because we have applied well-thought-out principles to a set of facts and deduced an answer. Our efforts to

*Mutatis mutandis: "With the necessary modifications" (Latin) [Ed.].

justify what we have done—or what we plan to do—are typically made up after the event, rationalizations of what we have decided intuitively. And a good deal of what we intuitively take to be right, we take to be right just because it is what we are used to. If you live in a society where children are spanked, you will probably spank your children. You will believe that it is a good way to teach them right from wrong and that, despite the temporary suffering caused by a beating, they will end up better off for it. You will point to the wayward child and say, sotto voce,* that his parents do not know how to discipline him; you will mean that they do not beat him enough. You will also, no doubt, recognize that there are people who beat their children too hard or too often. So you will recognize that beating a child can sometimes be cruel.

Much the same can be said about the practice of female genital cutting. . . . If you've grown up taking it for granted as the normal thing to do, you will probably respond at first with surprise to someone who thinks it is wrong. You will offer reasons for doing it—that unmodified sexual organs are unaesthetic; that the ritual gives young people the opportunity to display courage in their transition to adulthood; that you can see their excitement as they go to their ceremony, their pride when they return. You will say that it is very strange that someone who has not been through it should presume to know whether or not sex is pleasurable for you. And, if someone should try to force you to stop from the outside, you may decide to defend the practice as an expression of your cultural identity. But this is likely to be as much a rationalization as are the arguments of your critics. They say it is mutilation, but is that any more than a reflex response to an unfamiliar practice? They exaggerate the medical risks. They say that female circumcision demeans women, but do not seem to think that male circumcision demeans men.

I am not endorsing these claims, or celebrating the argumentative impasse, or, indeed, the poverty of reason in much discussion within and across cultures. But let's recognize this simple fact: a large part of what we do we do because it *is* just what we do. You get up in the morning at eight-thirty. Why *that* time? You have coffee and cereal. Why not porridge? You send the kids to school. Why not teach them at home? You have to work. Why that job, though? Reasoning—by which I mean the public act of exchanging stated justifications—comes in not when we are going on in the usual way, but when we are thinking about change. And when it comes to change, what moves people is often not an argument from a principle, not a long discussion about values, but just a gradually acquired new way of seeing things.

Reasoning . . . comes in not when we are going on in the usual way, but when we are thinking about change.

My father, for example, came from a society in which neither women nor men were traditionally circumcised. Indeed, circumcision was *akyiwadee*; and since chiefs were supposed to be unblemished, circumcision was a barrier to holding royal office. Nevertheless, as he tells us in his autobiography, he decided as a teenager to have himself circumcised.

* Sotto voce: Italian for "under the breath"; a dramatic lowering of volume for emphasis [Ed.].

> As was the custom in those happy days, the young girls of Adum would gather together in a playing field nearby on moonlight nights to regale themselves by singing traditional songs and dancing from about 7 PM until midnight each day of the week.
>
> . . . On one such night, these girls suddenly started a new song that completely bowled us over: not only were the words profane in the extreme, but they also constituted the most daring challenge to our manhood and courage ever flung at us. More than that, we were being invited to violate an age-old tradition of our ancestors, long respected among our people, namely the taboo on circumcision. Literally translated the words were:
>
> "An uncircumcised penis is detestable, and those who are uncircumcised should come for money from us so that they can get circumcised. We shall never marry the uncircumcised."[7]

To begin with, my father and his friends thought the girls would relent. But they were wrong. And so, after consultation with his mates, my father found himself a *wansam*—a Muslim circumcision specialist—and had the operation performed. (It was, he said, the most painful experience of his life and, if he'd had it to do again, he would have refrained. He did not, of course, have the advantage of the preparation, the companionship of boys of his own age, and the prestige of suffering bravely that would have come if the practice had been an Akan tradition.)

My father offered a reason for this decision: he and his friends conceded that "as our future sweethearts and wives, they were entitled to be heard in their plea in favor of male circumcision, even though they were not prepared to go in for female circumcision, which was also a taboo among our people." This explanation invites a question, however. Why did these young women, in the heart of Asante, decide to urge the young men of Adum to do what was not just untraditional but taboo? One possibility is that circumcision somehow became identified in their minds with being modern. If that was the point, my father would have been sympathetic. He was traditional in some ways; but like many people in Kumasi in the early twentieth century, he was also excited by a modern world that was bringing new music, new technology, new possibilities. To volunteer for circumcision in his society he surely had not just to hear the plea of the young women of Adum but to understand—and agree with—the impulse behind it. And, as I say, it may have been exactly the fact that it was untraditional that made it appealing. Circumcision—especially because it carried with it exclusion from the possibilities of traditional political office—became a way of casting his lot with modernity.

This new fashion among the young people of Adum was analogous to, if more substantial than, the change in taste that has produced a generation of Americans with piercings and tattoos. And that change was not simply the result of argument and debate, either (even though, as anyone who has argued with a teenager about a pierced belly button will attest, people on both sides can come up with a whole slew of arguments). There's some social-psychological truth in the old Flanders & Swann song "The Reluctant Cannibal," about a young "savage" who pushes away from the table and declares, "I won't eat people. Eating people is wrong." His father has all the arguments, such as they are. ("But people have always eaten people, / What else is there to eat? / If the Juju had meant us not to eat people, / He wouldn't have made us of meat!") The son, though, just repeats his newfound conviction: Eating people is wrong. He's just sure of it, he'll say so again and again, and he'll win the day by declamation.

Or take the practice of foot-binding* in China, which persisted for a thousand years—and was largely eradicated within a generation. The anti-foot-binding campaign, in the 1910s and 1920s, did circulate facts about the disadvantages of bound feet, but those couldn't have come as news to most people. Perhaps more effective was the campaign's emphasis that no other country went in for the practice; in the world at large, then, China was "losing face" because of it. Natural-foot societies were formed, with members forswearing the practice and further pledging that their sons would not marry women with bound feet. As the movement took hold, scorn was heaped on older women with bound feet, and they were forced to endure the agonies of unbinding. What had been beautiful became ugly; ornamentation became disfigurement. (The success of the anti-foot-binding campaign was undoubtedly a salutary development, but it was not without its victims. Think of some of the last women whose feet were bound, who had to struggle to find husbands.) The appeal to reason alone can explain neither the custom nor its abolition.

So, too, with other social trends. Just a couple of generations ago, in most of the industrialized world, most people thought that middle-class women would ideally be housewives and mothers. If they had time on their hands, they could engage in charitable work or entertain one another; a few of them might engage in the arts, writing novels, painting, performing in music, theater, and dance. But there was little place for them in the "learned professions"—as lawyers or doctors, priests or rabbis; and if they were to be academics, they would teach young women and probably remain unmarried. They were not likely to make their way in politics, except perhaps at the local level. And they were not made welcome in science. How much of the shift away from these assumptions is the result of arguments? Isn't a significant part of it just the consequence of our getting used to new ways of doing things? The arguments that kept the old pattern in place were not—to put it mildly—terribly good. If the *reasons* for the old sexist way of doing things had been the problem, the women's movement could have been done with in a couple of weeks. There are still people, I know, who think that the ideal life for any woman is making and managing a home. There are more who think that it is an honorable option. Still, the vast majority of Westerners would be appalled at the idea of trying to force women back into these roles. Arguments mattered for the women who made the women's movement and the men who responded to them. This I do not mean to deny. But their greatest achievement has been to change our habits. In the 1950s, if a college-educated woman wanted to go to law or business school, the natural response was "Why?" Now the natural response is "Why not?"

Or consider another example: in much of Europe and North America, in places where a generation ago homosexuals were social outcasts and homosexual acts

*Foot-binding: Ancient Chinese practice of wrapping female feet in order to keep them from growing more than about three inches long, resulting in terrible pain and deformity [Ed.].

were illegal, lesbian and gay couples are increasingly being recognized by their families, by society, and by the law. This is true despite the continued opposition of major religious groups and a significant and persisting undercurrent of social disapproval. Both sides make arguments, some good, most bad, if you apply a philosophical standard of reasoning. But if you ask the social scientists what has produced this change, they will rightly not start with a story about reasons. They will give you a historical account that concludes with a sort of perspectival shift. The increasing presence of "openly gay" people in social life and in the media has changed our habits. Over the last thirty or so years, instead of thinking about the private activity of gay *sex*, many Americans started thinking about the public category of gay *people*. Even those who continue to think of the sex with disgust now find it harder to deny these people their respect and concern (and some of them have learned, as we all did with our own parents, that it's better not to think too much about other people's sex lives anyway).

Now, I don't deny that all the time, at every stage, people were talking, giving each other reasons to do things: accept their children, stop treating homosexuality as a medical disorder, disagree with their churches, come out. Still, the short version of the story is basically this: people got used to lesbians and gay people. I am urging that we should learn about people in other places, take an interest in their civilizations, their arguments, their errors, their achievements, not because that will bring us to agreement, but because it will help us get used to one another. If that is the aim, then the fact that we have all these opportunities for disagreement about values need not put us off. Understanding one another may be hard; it can certainly be interesting. But it doesn't require that we come to agreement.

Fighting for the Good

I've said we can live in harmony without agreeing on underlying values (except, perhaps, the cosmopolitan value of living together). It works the other way, too: We can find ourselves in conflict when we do agree on values. Warring parties are seldom at odds because they have clashing conceptions of "the good." On the contrary, conflict arises most often when two peoples have identified the same thing as good. The fact that both Palestinians and Israelis—in particular, that both observant Muslims and observant Jews—have a special relation to Jerusalem, to the Temple Mount, has been a reliable source of trouble. The problem isn't that they disagree about the importance of Jerusalem: The problem is exactly that they both care for it deeply and, in part, for the same reasons. Muhammad, in the first years of Islam, urged his followers to turn toward Jerusalem in prayer because he had learned the story of Jerusalem from the Jews among whom he lived in Mecca. Nor is it an accident that the West's fiercest adversaries among other societies tend to come from among the most Westernized of the group. *Mon semblable mon frère?** Only if the *frère* you have in mind is Cain.† We all know now

* *Mon semblable mon frère?*: My likeness my brother? A line from French poet Charles Baudelaire's poem "The Reader," which invokes the interconnectedness of reader and author.

† Cain: Biblical son of Adam and Eve who murdered his brother Abel (see Genesis 4:1–8) [Ed.].

that the foot soldiers of al-Qaeda who committed the mass murders at the Twin Towers and the Pentagon were not Bedouins from the desert; not unlettered fellahin.*

Indeed, there's a wider pattern here. Who in Ghana excoriated the British and built the movement for independence? Not the farmers and the peasants. Not the chiefs. It was the Western-educated bourgeoisie. And when in the 1950s Kwame Nkrumah—who went to college in Pennsylvania and lived in London—created a nationalist mass movement, at its core were soldiers who had returned from fighting a war in the British army, urban market women who traded Dutch prints, trade unionists who worked in industries created by colonialism, and the so-called veranda boys, who had been to colonial secondary schools, learned English, studied history and geography in textbooks written in England. Who led the resistance to the British Raj?† An Indian-born South African lawyer, trained in the British courts, whose name was Gandhi; an Indian named Nehru who wore Savile Row suits and sent his daughter to an English boarding school; and Muhammad Ali Jinnah, founder of Pakistan, who joined Lincoln's Inn in London and became a barrister at the age of nineteen.

In Shakespeare's *Tempest,* Caliban, the original inhabitant of an island commandeered by Prospero, roars at his domineering colonizer, "You taught me language and my profit on't / Is, I know how to curse." It is no surprise that Prospero's "abhorred slave" has been a figure of colonial resistance for literary nationalists all around the world. And in borrowing from Caliban, they have also borrowed from Shakespeare. Prospero has told Caliban, 40

> When thou didst not, savage,
> Know thine own meaning, but wouldst gabble like
> A thing most brutish, I endowed thy purposes
> With words that made them known.

Of course, one of the effects of colonialism was not only to give many of the natives a European language, but also to help shape their purposes. The independence movements of the post-1945 world that led to the end of Europe's African and Asian empires were driven by the rhetoric that had guided the Allies' own struggle against Germany and Japan: democracy, freedom, equality. This wasn't a conflict between values. It was a conflict of interests couched in terms of the same values.

The point applies as much within the West as elsewhere. Americans disagree about abortion, many vehemently. They couch this conflict in a language of conflicting values: they are pro-life or pro-choice. But this is a dispute that makes sense only because each side recognizes the very values the other insists upon. The disagreement is about their significance. Both sides respect something like the sanctity of human life. They disagree about such things as why human life is so precious and where it begins. Whatever you want to call those disagreements, it's just a mistake to think that either side doesn't recognize the value at stake here. And the same is true about choice: Americans are not divided about whether it's important to allow people, women and men, to make

---

*Fellahin: Middle Eastern peasant or farmer [Ed.].

†British Raj: Term for British rule in India from 1858 to 1947 [Ed.].

the major medical choices about their own bodies. They are divided about such questions as whether an abortion involves two people—both fetus and mother—or three people, adding in the father, or only one. Furthermore, no sane person on either side thinks that saving human lives or allowing people medical autonomy is the only thing that matters.

Some people will point to disputes about homosexuality and say that there, at least, there really is a conflict between people who do and people who don't regard homosexuality as a perversion. Isn't that a conflict of values? Well, no. Most Americans, on both sides, have the concept of perversion: of sexual acts that are wrong because their objects are inappropriate objects of sexual desire. But not everyone thinks that the fact that an act involves two women or two men makes it perverted. Not everyone who thinks these acts are perverse thinks they should be illegal. Not everyone who thinks they should be illegal thinks that gay and lesbian people should be ostracized. What is at stake, once more, is a battle about the meaning of perversion, about its status as a value, and about how to apply it. It is a reflection of the essentially contestable character of perversion as a term of value. When one turns from the issue of criminalization of gay sex—which is, at least for the moment, unconstitutional in the United States—to the question of gay marriage, all sides of the debate take seriously issues of sexual autonomy, the value of the intimate lives of couples, the meaning of family, and, by way of discussions of perversion, the proper uses of sex.

What makes these conflicts so intense is that they are battles over the meaning of the *same* values, not that they oppose one value, held exclusively by one side, with another, held exclusively by their antagonists. It is, in part, because we have shared horizons of meaning, because these are debates between people who share so many other values and so much else in the way of belief and of habit, that they are as sharp and as painful as they are.

Winners and Losers

45

But the disputes about abortion and gay marriage divide Americans bitterly most of all because they share a society and a government. They are neighbors and fellow citizens. And it is laws governing all of them that are in dispute. What's at stake are their bodies or those of their mothers, their aunts, their sisters, their daughters, their wives, and their friends; those dead fetuses could have been their children or their children's friends.

We should remember this when we think about international human rights treaties. Treaties are law, even when they are weaker than national law. When we seek to embody our concern for strangers in human rights law and when we urge our government to enforce it, we are seeking to change the world of law in every nation on the planet. We have outlawed slavery not just domestically but in international law. And in so doing we have committed ourselves, at a minimum, to the desirability of its eradication everywhere. This is no longer controversial in the capitals of the world. No one defends enslavement. But international treaties define slavery in ways that arguably include debt bondage; and debt bondage is a significant economic institution in parts of South Asia. I hold no brief for debt bondage. Still, we shouldn't be surprised if people whose income and whose style of life depend upon it are angry. Given that we have neighbors—even if only a few—who think that the fact that abortion is permitted in the United States turns the killing of the doctors who perform them into an act of heroism, we should not be surprised that there are strangers—even if only a few—whose anger turns them to violence against us.

I do not fully understand the popularity among Islamist movements in Egypt, Algeria, Iran, and Pakistan of a high-octane anti-Western rhetoric. But I do know one of its roots. It is, to use suitably old-fashioned language, "the woman question." There are Muslims, many of them young men, who feel that forces from outside their society—forces that they might think of as Western or, in a different moment, American—are pressuring them to reshape relations between men and women. Part of that pressure, they feel, comes from our media. Our films and our television programs are crammed with indescribable indecency. Our fashion magazines show women without modesty, women whose presence on many streets in the Muslim world would be a provocation, they think, presenting an almost irresistible temptation to men. Those magazines influence publications in their own countries, pulling them inevitably in the same direction. We permit women to swim almost naked with strange men, which is our business; but it is hard to keep the news of these acts of immodesty from Muslim women and children or to protect Muslim men from the temptations they inevitably create. As the internet spreads, it will get even harder, and their children, especially their girls, will be tempted to ask for these freedoms too. Worse, they say, we are now trying to force our conception of how women and men should behave upon them. We speak of women's rights. We make treaties enshrining these rights. And then we want their governments to enforce them.[8]

Like many people in every nation, I support those treaties, of course; I believe that women, like men, should have the vote, should be entitled to work outside their homes, should be protected from the physical abuse of men, including their fathers, brothers, and husbands. But I also know that the changes that these freedoms would bring will change the balance of power between men and women in everyday life. How do I know this? Because I have lived most of my adult life in the West as it has gone through the latter phases of just such a transition, and I know that the process is not yet complete.

The recent history of America does show that a society can radically change its attitudes—and more importantly, perhaps, its habits—about these issues over a single generation. But it also suggests that some people will stay with the old attitudes, and the whole process will take time. The relations between men and women are not abstractions: They are part of the intimate texture of our everyday lives. We have strong feelings about them, and we have inherited many received ideas. Above all, we have deep *habits* about gender. A man and a woman go out on a date. Our habit is that, even if the woman offers, the man pays. A man and a woman approach an elevator door. The man steps back. A man and a woman kiss in a movie theater. No one takes a second look. Two men walk hand in hand in the high street.* People are embarrassed. They hope their children don't see. They don't know how to explain it to them.

---

*The high street: Term used in the United Kingdom for what Americans call main street [Ed.].

50

Most Americans are against gay marriage, conflicted about abortion, and amazed (and appalled) that a Saudi woman can't get a driver's license. But my guess is that they're not as opposed to gay marriage as they were twenty years ago. Indeed, twenty years ago, most Americans would probably just have thought the whole idea ridiculous. On the other hand, those Americans who are in favor of recognizing gay marriages probably don't have a simple set of reasons why. It just seems right to them, probably, in the way that it just seems wrong to those who disagree. (And probably they're thinking not about couples in the abstract but about Jim and John or Jean and Jane.) The younger they are, the more likely it is that they think that gay marriage is fine. And if they don't, it will often be because they have had religious objections reinforced regularly through life in church, mosque, or temple.

I am a philosopher. I believe in reason. But I have learned in a life of university teaching and research that even the cleverest people are not easily shifted by reason alone—and that can be true even in the most cerebral of realms. One of the great savants of the postwar era, John von Neumann, liked to say, mischievously, that "in mathematics you don't understand things, you just get used to them." In the larger world, outside the academy, people don't always even care whether they *seem* reasonable. Conversation, as I've said, is hardly guaranteed to lead to agreement about what to think and feel. Yet we go wrong if we think the point of conversation is to persuade, and imagine it proceeding as a debate, in which points are scored for the Proposition and the Opposition. Often enough, as Faust said, in the beginning is the deed: practices and not principles are what enable us to live together in peace. Conversations across boundaries of identity—whether national, religious, or something else—begin with the sort of imaginative engagement you get when you read a novel or watch a movie or attend to a work of art that speaks from some place other than your own. So I'm using the word *conversation* not only for literal talk but also as a metaphor for engagement with the experience and the ideas of others. And I stress the role of the imagination here because the encounters, properly conducted, are valuable in themselves. Conversation doesn't have to lead to consensus about anything, especially not values; it's enough that it helps people get used to one another.

NOTES

1. Galatians 3:28. In quoting the Bible, I have used the King James version, except for the Pentateuch, where I have used Robert Alter's powerful modern translation, *The Five Books of Moses* (New York: Norton, 2004).
2. Christoph Martin Wieland, "Das Geheimniß des Kosmopolitenordens," *Teutscher Merkur*, August 1788, p. 107. (Where I give a reference only to a source that is not in English, the translation is mine.)
3. *Essai sur les mœurs et l'esprit des nations*, vol. 16 of *Oeuvres complètes de Voltaire* (Paris: L'Imprimerie de la Société Litteraire-Typographique, 1784), p. 241. Voltaire is speaking specifically here of "the Orient," and especially of China and India, but he would surely not have denied its more general application.
4. George Eliot, *Daniel Deronda* (London: Penguin, 1995), pp. 745, 661–62, 183.
5. Cicero, *De officiis* 1.50.

6. Cass R. Sunstein, "Incompletely Theorized Agreements," *Harvard Law Review* 108 (1995): 1733–72.
7. Joseph Appiah, *Joe Appiah: The Autobiography of an African Patriot* (New York: Praeger, 1990), p. 22.
8. I have put this complaint in the mouth of a Muslim. But the truth is you could hear it from non-Muslims in many places as well. It is less likely to be heard in non-Muslim Africa, because there, by and large (as Amartya Sen has pointed out), women have a less unequal place in public life. See Jean Drèze and Amartya Sen, *Hunger and Public Action* (Oxford: Clarendon Press, 1989).

Questions for Critical Reading

1. As you reread Appiah, use his text to create a definition of what he means by *cosmopolitanism*, working with quotations from Appiah that support your interpretation. Then apply this definition to a current national or world situation. How does it show cosmopolitanism at work, or how might embracing this concept help resolve the situation?

2. According to Appiah, what are some crucial tools needed to enact his vision of cosmopolitanism? Reread his essay to locate quotations in which Appiah discusses these tools. How realistic is his vision? Based on the examples he offers, do you think these tools would be effective? Why or why not?

3. In order to make his argument, Appiah includes some stories from his own life. How does he use these stories? What sort of evidence do they provide? What other forms of evidence does he use? Support your answers by searching for specific examples from the text.

Exploring Context

1. Appiah uses the term *cosmopolitanism* to describe an ability to get along with others in a globalized and deeply connected world, an ability he relates to having conversation. Locate a website that you think represents Appiah's understanding of *cosmopolitan*. What makes it so? What kinds of conversations happen on this site? Locate passages from Appiah's text that support your interpretation of the website as an example of cosmopolitanism. Does the site fit the definition you created in Question 1 of Questions for Critical Reading?

2. Appiah looks at a number of culturally specific practices, including foot-binding in China and circumcision in African nations. Select one of Appiah's examples and use information from the web to prepare a short report on how the practice has changed in its home culture. Are the reasons for these changes consistent with Appiah's arguments?

3. Visit a social networking site such as Twitter or Facebook. If you don't currently have a profile on either site, create one. Explore the site and consider the role it might play in Appiah's vision of cosmopolitanism. Does it promote that ideal? What sorts of conversations does the site allow? Is it the kind of tool you described in Question 2 of Questions for Critical Reading?

Questions for Connecting

1. How do Appiah's insights about conversation confirm Helen Epstein's findings in "AIDS, Inc." (p. 123)? How can AIDS prevention be further promoted in Africa despite differences in values and practices? Synthesize the ideas of these authors to suggest strategies for halting the spread of HIV.

2. One of Appiah's primary concerns is the way in which conversation can create change. Synthesize Appiah's ideas with Malcolm Gladwell's concepts of social change in "Small Change" (p. 191). What role does conversation have in the development of social ties? Does it create more strong ties or weak ties? How does peer pressure act to change practice?

3. Appiah offers examples of how practices have changed as a result of conversations. Extend his work using Adrian Chen's "Unfollow" (p. 73). How does conversation work in these essays to create personal and social change? How does Chen's essay reflect Appiah's notion of cosmopolitanism? Incorporate your work with the definition of *cosmopolitanism* from Question 1 of Questions for Critical Reading.

Language Matters

1. Transition words or phrases help readers move from one idea or unit in an essay to another. In order to practice using transitions, locate a passage in Appiah that you found difficult or confusing. To clarify the thinking of your selected passage, write a short paragraph that could precede your selection, using transitions to ease the difficulty of the passage from Appiah. Think about what Appiah is trying to do in that part of his essay and then clarify that purpose with transition words or phrases. How might the paragraph you write work as a transitional paragraph for Appiah's ideas? How can you more effectively use transitions in your own writing?

2. As an exercise in being concise, summarize Appiah's argument in a haiku, a Japanese form of nonrhyming poetry that has three lines, with five syllables in the first line, seven syllables in the second line, and five in the third. For example:

   Language matters much.
   Working on a haiku can
   Clarify this text.

   Use the haiku to express Appiah's argument in just a few words.

3. If you are not familiar with simple sentences — sentences with just a subject and verb — locate information on them in a grammar handbook or other reference resource. Then choose one of Appiah's key sentences and transform it into a simple sentence or into a series of simple sentences. Does breaking down Appiah's sentence into simple sentences make his ideas easier to understand? When are simple sentences useful? Why didn't Appiah write this whole essay in simple sentences? When should you use these in your own writing? What makes them useful?

Assignments for Writing

1. For Appiah, cosmopolitanism is as much a challenge as a solution to the problems of a globalized world. Using Appiah's sense of the term *cosmopolitanism*, locate the challenges presented by the examples he uses to illustrate his arguments. Then write a paper in which you propose the best strategies for overcoming the challenges presented by cosmopolitanism. In what way does Appiah offer a solution to facing these challenges in an increasingly diverse world? Is the solution Appiah finds in cosmopolitanism adequate in addressing these challenges in a way that respects the diversity of local populations? Use your work in Exploring Context to offer specific examples of successful strategies.
2. Appiah discusses his choice of cosmopolitanism as a rubric for moving forward. At the same time, he discusses the problems of realizing social change. Based on his discussion of the primacy of practice, how can we advocate for change in social practices? Write a paper in which you identify the best tools for achieving social change. In constructing and supporting your argument, you may wish to build on the cultural practice you explored in Question 2 of Exploring Context.
3. Appiah is invested in conversation as an engagement with others, but has this engagement been constructive in the ideological conflicts Appiah discusses? Using one of the examples Appiah describes in the sections "Changing Our Minds" (p. 43) and "Fighting for the Good" (p. 47), write a paper in which you determine whether conversation has helped to resolve the conflict Appiah describes, and if so, how.

NAMIT ARORA

Namit Arora, a graduate of the Indian Institute of Technology, is the creator of Shunya, a website devoted to his writing and photography, which has operated since 2000. His writings have been published in the *Philosopher*, the *Kyoto Journal*, and *Philosophy Now*. Arora is also a prolific photographer whose works have been licensed by over one hundred organizations, including over twenty-five academic institutions. He is a regular contributor to *3 Quarks Daily*, a blog that presents "interesting items from around the web on a daily basis, in the areas of science, design, literature, current affairs, art, and anything else [the editors] deem inherently fascinating," and is the winner of the 3 Quarks Daily 2011 Arts & Literature Prize for his book review of Omprakash Valmiki's *Joothan: A Dalit's Life*.

Arora's "What Do We Deserve?" was published in the *Humanist*, the journal of the American Humanist Association, an organization that advocates a secular, compassionate, and human-based system of ethics. The May/June 2011 issue in which "What Do We Deserve?" was first published also featured articles by Steven Surman, David Niose, and biologist PZ Myers, dealing with morality issues from a distinctly liberal and secular point of view. The articles included in the issue cover topics as diverse as secularism in the military, corporatism, and a critique of "family values" politics, but they are all united through their commitment to a humanist outlook.

In "What Do We Deserve?" Arora examines three forms of economic systems: the libertarian model, the meritocratic model, and the egalitarian model. Arora briefly evaluates each model, ultimately questioning the idea that both the rich and the impoverished "deserve" or have somehow earned their economic positions.

▶ TAGS: *economics, ethics, social justice*

▶ Connections: *Appiah, Chabon, Coates, Fukuyama, Gilbert, Gladwell, Henig, Watters*

What Do We Deserve?

I often think of the good life I have. By most common measures—say, type of work, income, health, leisure, and social status—I'm doing well. Despite the adage, "call no man happy until he is dead," I wonder no less often: How much of my good life do I really deserve? Why me and not so many others?

The dominant narrative has it that I was a bright student, worked harder than most, and competed fairly to gain admission to an Indian Institute of Technology, where my promise was recognized with financial aid from a U.S. university. When I took a chance after graduate school and came to Silicon Valley, I was justly rewarded for my knowledge and labor with a measure of financial security and social status. While many happily accept this narrative, my problem is that I don't buy it. I believe that much of my socioeconomic station in life was not realized by my own doing, but was accidental or due to my being in the right place at the right time.

A pivotal question in market-based societies is "What do we deserve?" In other words, for our learning, natural talents, and labor, what rewards and entitlements are just? How much of what we bring home is fair or unfair, and why? To chase these questions is to be drawn into the thickets of political philosophy and theories of justice. American political philosopher Michael Sandel's 2009 book *Justice: What's the Right Thing to Do?* proves valuable here in synthesizing a few thoughts on the matter, including a review of the three major approaches to distributive economic justice: libertarian, meritocratic, and egalitarian, undermining en route the dominant narrative on my own well-being.

The *libertarian model* of distributive justice favors a free market with well-defined rules that apply to all. "Citizens are assured equal basic liberties, and the distribution of income and wealth is determined by the free market," says Sandel. This model offers a formal equality of opportunity—making it a clear advance over feudal or caste arrangements—so anyone can, in theory, strive to compete and win. But in practice, people don't have real equality of opportunity due to various disadvantages, for example, of family income, social class, gender, race, caste, etc. So while the racetrack may look nice and shiny, the runners don't begin at the same starting point. What does it mean to say that the first to cross the finish line deserves his or her victory? Isn't the contest rigged from the start, based on factors that are arbitrary and derive from accidents of birth?

5

Take my own example. I was born into the upper-caste, riding on eons of unearned privilege over 80 percent of my fellow Indians. I was also a boy raised in a society that lavished far more attention on male students. My parents fell closer to the upper-middle class, had university degrees, and valued education and success—both my grandfathers had risen up to claim senior state government posts. I lived in a kid-friendly neighborhood with parks, playgrounds, and a staff clubhouse. I had role models and access to the right schools and books, the right coaching classes, and peers aspiring for professional careers. My background greatly shaped my ambition and self-confidence and no doubt put me ahead of perhaps 96 percent of other Indians—the odds that I would perform extremely well on standardized academic tests were huge from the start.

The *meritocratic model*, often associated with the United States, recognizes such inequities and tries to correct for socioeconomic disadvantages. At its best, meritocracy takes real equality of opportunity seriously and tries to achieve it through various means: Head Start programs, education and job training, subsidized healthcare and housing, and so forth. Meritocrats admit that market-based distribution of rewards is just only to the extent to which we can reduce endemic socioeconomic disadvantages and bring everyone to comparable starting points. But thereafter, they believe that we are the authors of our own destiny and whoever wins the race is morally deserving of the rewards they obtain from the market—and its flip side, that we morally deserve our failure too, and its consequences. Swiss writer Alain de Botton looked at this phenomenon in the United States in his 2004 documentary film, *Status Anxiety*.

But is this entirely fair? Even if we somehow leveled socioeconomic disparities, the winners of the race would still be the fastest runners, due in part to a natural lottery. People are often born with certain talents and attributes—for instance, oratory, musical acumen, physical beauty and health, athleticism, good memory and cognition, extroversion—that give them unearned advantages. Are their wins not as arbitrary from a moral standpoint as the wins of those born with silver spoons in their mouths?

Further, isn't it dumb luck that our society happens to value certain aptitudes we may have—such as the leap and hand-eye coordination of Michael Jordan, sound-byte witticisms of talk show hosts like Jay Leno, or the algorithmic wizardry of Sergey Brin in the Internet age? A millennium ago, society valued other aptitudes, such as sculpting bronze in Chola India, equine archery on the Mongolian steppes, or reciting epigrammatic verse in Arabia. My own aptitude for science and math served me well in an India looking to industrialize and a United States facing a shortfall of engineers. I might have done less well in an earlier age where the best opportunities were perhaps in mercantile pursuits or the bureaucracy of government.

But how can a system of distributive justice compensate for random natural gifts that happen to be valued in a time and place? We can't level natural gifts across people, can we? The mere thought is bizarre. The American political philosopher John Rawls (1921–2002) had much to say about this in his landmark 1971 book, *A Theory of Justice*, in which he developed his *egalitarian model*. Since we can't undo the inequities of the natural lottery, he writes, we must find a way to address the differences in the rewards that result from them. We should certainly encourage people to hone and exercise their aptitudes, he says, but we should be clear that they do not morally deserve the rewards their aptitudes earn from the market. Since their natural gifts aren't their own doing, and are moreover profitable only in light of the value a community places on them, they must share the rewards with the community.

One might object here: Wait a minute, what about the role of the personal drive and effort we put into cultivating our talents? Don't we deserve the rewards that come from our striving? Not really, says Rawls. Countless factors beyond our choosing influence our ambition and effort, such as our upbringing, our family's work ethic, our childhood experiences, subconscious insecurities, social milieu, career fads, role models, parental and peer pressure, available life paths, lucky breaks, and other contingent factors. It isn't clear how much of it is our own doing, however militantly we may hold the illusion that we create our own life story (an illusion not without psychological and practical payoffs). Even the accident of being firstborn among siblings can be a factor in how hard we strive. Each year, Sandel reports, 75–80 percent of his freshman class at Harvard are firstborns. Besides, effort may be a virtue but even the meritocrats don't think it deserves rewards independent of results or achievement. So, in short, we can't claim to deserve the rewards on the basis of effort either.

Rawls deflates the idea that we morally deserve the rewards of meritocracy. If we [10] accept this, it follows that the house of distributive justice cannot be built on the sands of moral desert (in simple terms, moral desert is a condition by which we are deserving of something, whether good or bad), but must be built on other grounds. Notably, however, Rawls doesn't make a case for equal rewards. Instead, Rawls speaks of the "Difference Principle" in dealing with the inequities of the natural lottery. This principle, says Sandel, "permits income inequalities for the sake of incentives, provided the incentives are needed to improve the lot of the least advantaged." In other words, income inequality is justified only to the extent to which it improves the lot of the most disadvantaged when compared to an equal income arrangement. Only if society is better off as a whole does favoring inequality seem fair. Does this approach diminish the role of human agency and free will when it comes to moral desert? Some say it does, yet the claim seems modest enough, that our achievements have many ingredients, and the contributions from agency or free will are intertwined with the contributions from social and random factors—to the point that it seems unreasonable to give by default all credit to agency or free will, which libertarians try to do in order to justify the rewards of the market. However, some philosophers find an unresolved tension in Rawls's approach to setting up the Difference Principle. (See, for instance, *Egalitarianism, Free Will, and Ultimate Justice* by Saul Smilansky.)

One might ask: Why should we uphold the Difference Principle at all? Is it not an arbitrary construct? No, says Rawls, and invites us to a thought experiment on creating "a hypothetical social contract in an original position of equality." Imagine, he says, that "when we gather to choose the principles [for governing ourselves], we don't know where we will wind up in society. Imagine that we choose behind a 'veil of ignorance' that temporarily prevents us from knowing anything about who we are," including our race, gender, class, talents, intelligence, wealth, and religion (or lack thereof). What principles would we then choose to order our society? Rawls makes a powerful case that, simply out of a desire to minimize our odds of suffering, we will always choose political equality, fair equal opportunity, and the Difference Principle.

Some have argued that the Difference Principle may not get chosen as is, not unless it has a clause to address the unfairness of propping up those who willfully make bad choices or act irresponsibly. Further, is it desirable, or even possible, to choose a social contract from behind the so-called veil of ignorance, as if, in Rawls's words, "from the perspective of eternity," with scant regard for context? Doesn't Rawls implicitly presuppose a people who already value political equality, individualism, and resolving claims through public deliberation? Rawls later downplays its universality but, argues Sandel, even in the United States, Rawls's thought experiment supports an arid secular public space detached from so much that is central to our identities. This includes historical, moral, and religious discourses, which, if squeezed out, often pop up elsewhere in worse forms, such as the religious right. If the point is to enhance the social contract, Sandel adds, political progressives should do so not by asking people to leave their deepest beliefs at home but by engaging them in the public sphere.

In Rawlsian terms, the problem in the United States is not that a minority has grown super rich, but that for decades now, it has done so to the detriment of the lower social classes.

Sandel's basic critique here is that Rawls's concern with the distribution of primary goods—which Rawls defines as "things that every rational man is presumed to want"—is necessary but not sufficient for a social contract. As purposive beings, we should also consider the telos of our choices, such as our common ends as a community, the areas of life worth shielding from the market, the space we should accord to loyalty and patriotism, ties of blood, marriage, tradition, and so on. Still, Rawls's thought experiment retains a powerful moral force and continues to inspire liberals. His theory of justice, writes Sandel, "represents the most compelling case for a more equal society that American political philosophy has yet produced."

Theories of justice may clarify and guide our thoughts, but we still have to figure out how to change the game we want to play and where to draw the lines on the playing field. An open society does this through vigorous public debate. As British philosopher Isaiah Berlin wrote, "people who want to govern themselves must choose how much liberty, equality, and justice they seek and how much they can let go. The price of a free society is that sometimes, perhaps often, we make bad choices." Thereafter, when the rules are in place, "we are entitled to the benefits the rules of the game promise for the exercise of our talents." It is the rules, says Sandel, and not anything outside them, that create "entitlements to legitimate expectations." Entitlements only arise after we have chosen the rules of the competition. Only in this context can we say we deserve something, whether admission to a law school, a certain bonus, or a pension.

In Rawlsian terms, the problem in the United States is not that a minority has grown super rich, but that for decades now, it has done so to the detriment of the lower social classes. The big question is: Why does the majority in a seemingly free society tolerate this, and even happily vote against its own economic interests? A plausible answer is that it is under a self-destructive meritocratic spell that sees social outcomes as moral desert—a spell at least as old as the American frontier but long since repurposed by the corporate control of public institutions and the media: news, film, TV, publishing, and so forth. It parallels a religious spell in more ways than one. Here too, powerful social institutions are invested in clouding our notions of cause and effect. Rather than move towards greater fairness and egalitarianism, they promote a libertarian gospel of the free market with minimal regulation, taxation, and public safety nets. They beguile us into thinking that the lifestyles of the rich and famous are within reach of all, and uphold rags-to-riches stories as exemplary ("If this enterprising slumdog can do it against all odds, so can you!" goes the storyline). All this gets drummed into people's heads to the point that they only blame themselves for their lot and don't think of questioning the rules of the game. 15

What would it take to break *this* spell? For starters, it would require Americans to realize that the distribution of wealth in their society is far less egalitarian than they think it is—a recent survey revealed that Americans think the richest fifth of them own 59 percent of the wealth, while the actual figure is 84 percent. Perhaps living on credit helps create the illusion that the average American has more than he or she does. Americans also believe that their odds of rising to the top are far better than they actually are; social mobility is quite low by international standards. A kid from the poorest fifth of all households has a 1 percent chance of reaching the top 5 percentile income bracket, while a kid from the richest fifth has a 22 percent chance. The task of breaking this spell, then, requires telling new kinds of stories, engaging in vigorous public debate, and employing our best arts of persuasion.

Questions for Critical Reading

1. As you reread, make note of the three different models of economic justice that Arora discusses. Which of these do you feel is the most just? Find quotations from Arora that support your position.

2. What is the "Difference Principle"? Define this term as you reread the essay and consider what role it plays in our current economic system.

3. What roles do media and culture play in our understanding of "what we deserve"? Use Arora's essay to form your response.

Exploring Context

1. Visit We Are the 99 Percent (wearethe99percent.us). How do the images and information you find there support Arora's arguments about economic justice in the United States?
2. Explore the website for the Bureau of Labor Statistics (bls.gov). Apply the information and data you find there to determine the current model of economic justice operating within the United States.
3. Visit the White House's page on Economy and Jobs (https://www.whitehouse.gov/issues/economy-jobs/). How does it imagine economic justice? Which model does it seem to favor?

Questions for Connecting

1. What's the relationship between economic justice and legal justice? Use Andrew Cohen's discussion of the legal dimension of the opioid epidemic in "Race and the Opioid Epidemic" (p. 97) to explore the ways in which economics and law intersect. What roles do race and class play in justice?
2. Daniel Gilbert, in "Reporting Live from Tomorrow" (p. 172), suggests that the relationship between happiness and money is more complicated than we generally think. Synthesize his discussion with Arora's ideas. Which economic model best promote both happiness and justice?
3. In "Preface" and "The New Civil Rights" (p. 452), Kenji Yoshino is concerned not with economic rights but with civil rights. Synthesize his arguments with Arora's to create a more complete model of justice. How might Yoshino's liberty paradigm be applied to economics? What role does the Difference Principle play in civil rights?

Language Matters

1. In some ways, Arora's essay has a very clear but also very rigid organization, reminiscent of the five-paragraph essay. Begin by outlining Arora's argument and then consider how he uses organization to help prove his argument. How do the various sections build to a conclusion? How would the meaning of his essay change if it were rearranged? Apply what you learn to your own writing: How can you use organization to help prove your argument?
2. Arora uses a number of specialized terms such as *libertarian* and *meritocratic*. Note how he defines these terms in his text and then look up their definitions in a dictionary. How well does context function to help a reader define terms? When should you look up a word in the dictionary, and when is it sufficient to determine a word's meaning from the context of its use?

Assignments for Writing

1. Arora discusses three models of economic justice. Write a paper in which you determine which of these models is the most just, using Arora's analysis as well as your own experience. Which model should we pursue? Is there another alternative? Should we combine aspects of each model instead?

2. Arora's essay presupposes that economic justice is an issue worth considering. Evaluate this assumption by writing a paper on the role of justice in economics. Is social justice necessarily linked to economics or wealth? Why should we care about justice? What ramifications (political, social, cultural) do these questions have?

3. In the final line of his essay, Arora suggests that promoting social and economic justice in America requires "telling new kinds of stories, engaging in vigorous public debate, and employing our best arts of persuasion" (p. 59). Write a paper in which you evaluate and extend Arora's suggestions. Are they sufficient to create a more equitable economic structure in America? Are there other strategies necessary as well? Draw on Arora's discussion in making your argument.

MICHAEL CHABON

American novelist and writer **Michael Chabon** holds an M.F.A. in creative writing from the University of California, Irvine. He is a prolific writer, having published numerous novels, short story collections, essay collections, short fiction, children's books, and comic books. His third novel, *The Adventures of Kavalier & Clay* (2000), won the Pulitzer Prize for Fiction in 2001. Chabon has also won or been a finalist for the O. Henry Award, the National Book Critics Circle Award, the Hugo Award, the Nebula Award, and the Fernanda Pivano Award. In 2012, he was inducted into the American Academy of Arts and Letters.

"My Son, the Prince of Fashion" originally appeared in the September 2016 issue of *GQ*. *GQ*, in publication for over fifty years, styles itself as the premier men's magazine, covering men's fashion, style, and culture. Chabon's essay appeared alongside articles on how to use your kitchen to make better cocktails, the visual impact of textured black and white ties, the importance of using luggage tags to spot your bag while traveling, and an article on the "casualer-than-ever" topcoat.

On its surface, Chabon's essay seems to fit seamlessly into this collection of lifestyle-oriented content, as he narrates his journey to Paris Fashion Week with his son and budding fashionista, Abraham. However, as the tale unfolds, Chabon touches on a number of deep and meaningful themes, including bullying, sexuality, parenting, fitting in, and the complex relationship between high fashion and hip-hop culture.

How do you find a community where you belong? How does how you dress express who you are? What challenges did you face in the journey of you becoming you?

- TAGS: *adolescence and adulthood, beauty, community, culture, gender, identity, relationships, sexuality*
- CONNECTIONS: *Appiah, Chen, Fukuyama, Gilbert, Gladwell, Henig, Provan*

My Son, the Prince of Fashion

I took my son to Paris Fashion Week, and all I got was a profound understanding of who he is, what he wants to do with his life, and how it feels to watch a grown man stride down a runway wearing shaggy yellow Muppet pants.

Half an hour late, and just ahead of his minder—he was always a step ahead of his ponderous old minder—Abraham Chabon sauntered into the room where the designer Virgil Abloh was giving a private preview of Off-White's collection for spring-summer 2017 to a small group of reporters, editorial directors, and fashion buyers. Abe's manner was self-conscious, his cheeks flushed, but if his movements were a bit constrained they had an undeniable grace. Saunter was really the only word for it.

"Now, this dude here, that's what I'm talking about," Abloh said, smiling at Abe from the center of the room, the attic of an old photo studio in the Latin Quarter: crisscrossing steel beams, wide pine floorboards, every surface radiant with whitewash except for the gridded slant of windows in the steep-pitched roof. From their folding chairs opposite the atelier windows, the buyers and editors turned to see what Abloh was talking about. So did the four male models lined up and slouching artfully in front of the people in the folding chairs. By the time his minder caught up with him, everyone in the room seemed to have their eyes on Abe. Prompt people never get to make grand entrances.

"Come over here," Abloh said. Abloh was a big man, solidly built, an architect by training who had emerged in the early 2000s from the fizzy intellectual nimbus—one-third hip-hop, one-third hustle, one-third McLarenesque inside joke—surrounding fellow Chicagoan Kanye West. Abloh had made a name for himself in fashion along the avant-garde perimeter of streetwear, screen-printing diagonal crosswalk stripes and cryptic mottoes onto blank Champion tees and dead-stock Rugby Ralph Lauren flannel shirts that he re-sold for dizzying multiples of their original retail price. Abe thought Virgil Abloh was "lit," the highest accolade he could award to anyone or anything. "Come right on over here. Hey, look at you!"

Abe went on over, sleeves rolled, hands thrust into his pockets, tails of his pale gray-green shirt freshly tucked into the waist of his gray twill trousers. In front the shirt lay flat and trim, but it was a little too big, and at the back it bellied out over the top of his skinny black belt. It was Maison Margiela, cleanly tailored, with a narrow collar and covered buttons that gave it a minimalist sleekness. Abe had bought it the day before, on sale, at a shop in Le Marais called Tom Greyhound. He wore a pair of $400 silver Adidas by Raf Simons purchased for $250 on adidasx.com and a pair of Off-White athletic socks. He had pulled the socks up to his knees, where they met the rolled-up cuffs of his trouser legs, vintage-newsboy-style. Money to pay for the "Rafs" had been earned by Abe's raking leaves for neighbors, organizing drawers and closets around the house, running errands, and other odd jobs. His parents had given him the cash he used to buy the Margiela shirt, on the occasion of his bar mitzvah, and the trousers had actually been repurposed from his Appaman bar mitzvah suit. Abe was 13 years and 3 months old, and he did not need to be told, by Virgil Abloh or anyone else, to look at himself. He knew exactly how he looked.

"Hi," Abe said to Abloh, in his husky voice—low-pitched and raspy all his life, heading even lower now and given, at the moment, to random breaking, "I'm Abe."

Some of the people in the room already knew Abe—which tended to get pronounced Ah-*bay*, like the surname of the Japanese prime minister, by the French staffers who put his name on the guest lists for the fourteen shows he attended over the course of Paris Men's Fashion Week. They had met him or seen him around. He was almost always, and by far, the youngest person in the audience, and would likely have stood out for that reason alone, even if he had not dressed himself with such evident consideration and casual art. But it was his clothes and the way he wore them that elicited reporters' attention, and a few had taken enough of an interest to ask him some questions, on the record. The questions tended to run along the same lines: What had he thought of this or that particular collection? What got him interested in clothes? Did he hope to be a fashion designer one day? Why had he come to Fashion Week?

> I'm here with my dad, it's my bar mitzvah present, he's a writer and he's writing about our trip to Fashion Week for *GQ*. I know I want to do something in fashion but I don't know what, maybe design; I do make sketches, mostly streetwear, I like to use fabrics and patterns you kind of wouldn't expect, like,

I don't know, a Japanese textile pattern for a bomber jacket, *or* glen plaid overalls. My older brother got me interested in clothes, it started with sneakers and then it kind of grew, and now I know more about men's fashion than he does. I thought the collection was interesting *or* I thought it was awesome *or* I thought it was a little boring, you know, it didn't really stand out, we've seen a lot of trench coats already this week *or* The quality of the tailoring didn't seem very good *or* I thought it was insane or It was fire or It was totally lit.

Abe's minder noticed that when talking to reporters, Abe almost always found a way to mention the leaf-raking and drawer-organizing, conscious of the atmosphere of privilege and extravagance that permeated the world of fashion. He knew that for a lot of kids his age—good friends of his among them—the price of a pair of "fire" sneakers represented a greater and more important sacrifice than it would for him and his family. But he never directly addressed the ethics of his wearing a shirt that had cost him $225, on sale. He did not offer profound insights into the economics or meaning of style like some pocket-size Roland Barthes bursting with critique and paradox.

Abe was just a kid who loved clothes. He loved talking about them, looking at them, and wearing them, and when it came to men's clothing, in particular the hipper precincts of streetwear, he knew his shit. He could trace the career path of Raf Simons, from Raf to Jil Sander to Dior and now to Calvin Klein. He could identify on sight the designers of countless individual articles of men's clothing—sneakers, shirts, jackets, pants—and when he didn't know for sure, the guesses he made were informed, reasoned, and often correct. He seemed to have memorized a dense tidal chart of recent fashion trends as they ebbed and flooded, witheringly dismissing a runway offering as "fine, for 2014" or "already kind of played out last year." His taste as reflected in the clothes he wore was impeccable, interesting, and, in its way, fearless. 10

It takes a profound love of clothes, and some fairly decent luck, to stumble on somebody who wants to converse about cutting-edge men's fashion at a Rush concert, and yet a year before his trip to Paris, in the aftermath of the Canadian band's last show at Madison Square Garden, Abe had managed to stumble on John Varvatos. Abe had spent that day leading his bemused minder on a pilgrimage through SoHo, from Supreme to Bape to Saint Laurent to Y-3, and now, ears still ringing from the final encore ("Working Man"), Abe reported in detail to Varvatos, with annotations and commentary, on all the looks he had seen downtown. When he was through, Varvatos had turned to Abe's minder—a major Rush fan who was, of course, also Abe's father—and said, "Where'd you *get* this kid?"

"I really have no idea," I said.

Abe had shown up late to his family, too, the fourth of four, graced with a sister on either side of the elder brother. By the time a fourth child comes along, the siblings have usually managed among them to stake out a wide swath of traits, talents, crotchets, flaws, phobias, and strengths. Finding one's difference can often be a fourth child's particular burden and challenge.

For Abe it never seemed to be a challenge at all, and if it was a burden, it was also a gift: From the moment he became himself, what made Abe different—from his siblings, from classmates, from most of the children who have ever lived—was the degree of comfort he felt with being different. Everybody wants to stand out from the crowd, but so few of us have the knack, and fewer still the stomach for bearing up under the crush of conformity. It was always Abe's rare gift not just to stand out, and bear up, but to do those things with panache. And the way in which he expressed his difference most reliably, and with the greatest panache, was through dressing up.

When he was very little—like so many little boys—"dressing up" meant "superhero." At 3 he had been firmly of the opinion that a bright-yellow-and-sky-blue Wolverine costume, or a lop-eared bat cowl, was appropriate attire for any occasion. Later there had been an intense dalliance with a splendid, old-school, singing-cowboy-type western getup—black hat, red shirt embroidered in white, black vest and chaps with chrome conchos, black boots. When he started kindergarten, however, he found that the wearing of costumes to school was not merely discouraged, or permitted only on special days, as in preschool: It was forbidden. It would also, undoubtedly, have incurred an intolerable amount of mockery. Abe's response was to devise, instinctively and privately, what amounted to a kind of secret costume that would fall just within the bounds of "ordinary attire" and school policy. Over the next few years, with increasing frequency, he went to school dressed up as a man—a stylish man.

He had only vague, somewhat cartoonish notions about what constituted adult-male style, centered around certain key articles of clothing, chief among them fedoras, cardigans, button-front shirts, suspenders, and bow ties. He had a little tweed blazer that was a source of deep power for him, as deep as the power of the armor to Marvel's Iron Man. It had a crest embroidered on a patch over the breast pocket and it made him very happy. By the third grade he was wearing his man costume to school almost every day. There had been teasing; one of his two little snap-brims would get snatched off his head now and then, and tossed around the playground. But the teasing had never exceeded Abe's ability or willingness to withstand it, or the joy that he derived from losing himself in clothes. And his stubborn persistence had established a pattern that was thereafter repeated as his taste grew more refined and sophisticated: Little by little, one by one among the other boys in his class, fedoras would crop up, a porkpie here, a trilby there. It was not unusual to spot one of Abe's former tormentors sporting a cardigan or a clip-on tie.

Some nights I used to stand in the doorway of his bedroom, watching him thoughtfully edit the outfit he planned to wear to school the next day. He would lay out its components, making a kind of flat self-portrait on the bedroom floor—oxford shirt tucked inside of cotton sport coat, extra-slim pants (with the adjustable elastic straps inside the waistband stretched to button at the very last hole), argyle socks, the whole thing topped by the ubiquitous hat—and I would try to understand what the kid got out of dressing up every day like a pint-size Ronald Colman out for a tramp across the countryside of Ruritania. Did he like the attention—even if it was negative? Was he trying, by means of the clothes, to differentiate himself from the other boys, or were the clothes merely the readiest expression, to him, of his having been *born* different? Was he trying to set himself apart, or could he simply not help it?

Around the time that Abe was making the transition to middle school, my elder son began to take a strong interest in clothes, particularly streetwear, fed by a burgeoning interest (shared by Abe) in hip-hop. A kind of golden age of streetwear was under way, exemplified by brands such as Supreme, Palace, and A Bathing Ape, manifested through "collabs" between major sneaker manufacturers and the edgier, top-tier designers like Rick Owens and Raf Simons, and represented by hip-hop tastemakers like

It was always Abe's rare gift not just to stand out, and bear up, but to do those things with panache.

A$AP Rocky and the now-disgraced Ian Connor. Abe's elder brother opened the door to this world—Virgil Abloh's world—and Abe had sauntered right in.

Even as he followed his brother into this trend-driven, icon-imitating world, Abe worked to maintain his standard of idiosyncrasy, of standing out, freely incorporating floral patterns, vintage scarves, and the color pink into the outfits he wore into the heteronormative jaws of seventh grade. Small for his age—barely a men's size XS—Abe often had trouble finding anything "fire," in the way of menswear, that would fit him. So he would shop the women's racks, with a sharply editorial eye; a women's XS, he could make work. The Maison Margiela shirt he wore at the Off-White preview was womenswear, and he had chanced upon another favorite shirt, a Tigran Avetisyan, while browsing one of the women's-clothing rooms at Opening Ceremony in L.A.

The sight of him, hanging around the neighborhood with a friend, looking so at ease in the flowing cream-black-and-gray Avetisyan shirt with its bold bands of red at the collar and cuffs and wild graphic pattern, made me realize that I almost literally never saw boys his age wearing anything remotely like it, wearing anything but a T-shirt or an athletic jersey, a hoodie or a flannel. The mantle of uniformity lay vast and heavy across the shoulders of adolescent boys (how vast, how heavy, I remembered well). As before—even worse than before—Abe suffered taunts and teasing for his style of dress and his love of style. But he did not back down; he doubled down. He flew the freak flag of his Tigran Avetisyan shirt high. And though I couldn't fathom the impulse driving my kid to expose himself, every day, to mockery and verbal abuse at school, I admired him for not surrendering, and in time I came to understand the nature of my job as the father of this sartorial wild child: I didn't *need* to fathom Abe or his stylistic impulses; I needed only to let him go where they took him and, for as long as he needed me, to follow along behind. 20

There was only one flaw, as far as Abe was concerned, in the week he spent going to fashion shows: His poky old minder, making him late. His minder was not having anywhere near as great a time. His minder was hot, and bored. Most of all, his minder did not, fundamentally, really give all that much of a fuck about fashion. Clothes, sure. His minder found pleasure in thrift-shopping for vintage western shirts or Hermès neckties, in wearing his favorite Shipley & Halmos suits (gray cashmere, tan corduroy), his Paul Smith shirts and shoulder bag. Less pleasure, perhaps, than he found in books, or records, or cooking, or watching old movies with his wife, but pleasure nonetheless. Clothes were all right with Abe's minder. But they were nothing to build a religion, a hobby, or even a decent obsession around.

Then, one warm June week in Paris, Abe's minder attended his first Men's Fashion Week and discovered that he understood even less. Fashion shows had an unexpected sideshow-freaks-on-parade quality, and when they were not pompous or eccentric, they were just plain goofy. You drove all the way across Paris to get to the venue—a special mapping algorithm seemed to have been employed to ensure that every show was held as far as possible from its predecessor and its successor on the schedule—through the heat of a Paris summer, arrived late yet still waited around outside until your feet hurt, guaranteeing you would be late for the next show, too. Then you sat in a dark, loud, hot, crowded room for another 20 minutes. The lights came on and the music pounded. There would be a wall made out of old car headlights and a sonic wall of EDM, and a bunch of tall, bony, pouting young men with a studied air of opiate addiction would come striding past you, swinging their arms, like little boys pretending to walk like their dads in a game of playing house. This gait was meant to read as "fierce," someone explained to Abe's minder, as was the expression on the models' faces, a universal stony blank, tinged with rouge, onto which it was forbidden to affix a smile.

The looks they modeled ranged in effect from preposterous to functional to arresting, often in the same show. Sometimes the music would not be EDM but Neil Young or Leonard Cohen or the amazing Japanese neo-psychedelic band Kikagaku Moyo. At the Paul Smith show the models just walked—sauntered, really—like the good-looking young dudes they were, and when they saw somebody they knew in the audience, or when they just felt good in the beautiful suits and shirts Paul Smith had dressed them in, they would— heretically—smile. Issey Miyake gave you a first-aid chemical cold pack to break and lay against the sweaty nape of your neck. Once—at the Y-3 show—the pants were inflatable. The whole show would be over in ten minutes yet it would still run overtime, and then you got back into a taxi and rushed algorithmically across town. It was kind of like Disneyland, but instead of a three-minute log flume or roller coaster you got inflatable pants.

Toward the end of one long and particularly trying four-show day for Abe's minder, Abe began to hear about yet another show he was keen to attend. It started at 8 PM and it would be the last of the day. But Abe's minder felt strongly that he had already experienced his last show of the day.

"It's Stéphane Ashpool—he's a really interesting new designer," Abe said. "Everyone says his show last year was amazing. Please, Dad?" 25

But Abe's minder had hardened his heart against Stéphane Ashpool. Fortunately for Abe, certain members of the editorial staff of this publication, who had been telling Abe about last year's Pigalle show and generally testing, to their apparent satisfaction, the breadth and depth of his knowledge of men's clothing, offered to let him come along with them to this year's. There was room in the car. They would see to it that he would be returned to his minder at the rendezvous point, a party at the Musée Picasso.

It turned out that Abe's minder had, possibly, made the wrong decision in choosing not to go to the Pigalle show. A few hours later, Abe showed up at the Picasso vibrating with excitement about the clothes he had seen and, even more, about the remarkable way they had been presented. Instead of the usual solemn palace or dark box pounding with electronica, instead of the usual runway, the Pigalle show had been presented outdoors, at the back of a museum, in a garden. It had taken the form of a faux wedding party, with musicians and a wedding canopy and little round café tables for all the "guests." Food was served. The evening felt cool. Abe had sat with the people from *GQ* and been caught up in the night and the company and the beautiful clothes.

"It was like being at a play," he said. "But also being in it."

"You need to go stand over there," Virgil Abloh told Abe. He pointed at the line of male models, who looked a little taken aback at the turn things had taken but made room for Abe in their ranks.

Abe laughed, and the flush in his cheeks deepened, but he did as he was told, without apparent hesitation or awkwardness. The laughter and the hectic color were not due to embarrassment; Abe was excited and pleased. The presence on his feet of Off-White socks was hardly an accident. Abe was not the kind of boy who would go to a baseball game with his mitt, hoping that a foul ball might come his way and fantasizing 30 that if one did, he might snatch it from the air with such evident skill that he would be offered, on the spot, a contract to play for the home team, but there was definitely an aspect in this moment of the dream come true.

And really, he had nothing to be embarrassed about. Sure, these models were nearly twice his height, and very good-looking, but with all due respect to Virgil Abloh and his stylists, none of the models were dressed any better—or looked more comfortable in what they were wearing—than Abe. Over the past two days of attending shows with his minder, Abe had paid close attention to everything that came down the runways, but he had if anything made an even more careful study of clothes worn by certain young men one saw waiting around outside the venues, standing in line with their elaborate tickets until the people with the clipboards said it was time to go inside. The models on the runways had without question been *fashionably* dressed—from the shaggy yellow Muppet pants and clown-emblazoned transparent breastplates at the Walter Van Beirendonck show to the hyper-flared trousers and fringed jackets *chez* Dries Van Noten to the Mœbius-meets-*Logan's Run,* 1970s post-apocalypse gear on view at the Rick Owens show, his models swaggering gloomily through the subterranean venue like young volunteers to be fed to the robot god, wearing sneakers so enormous that a couple of them tripped over their own toes—but these guys that caught Abe's eye, always two or three or four of them scattered among the waiting crowds, had *style.* The clothes they wore were their own, chosen and tweaked and assembled by them from their own drawers and closets. Often these looks were built around a single, stunning, no doubt exorbitant garment, a dazzling scarlet silk tracksuit, say, paisleyed with light blue and peach paramecia and paired with a yellow bandanna worn as a neckerchief.

The looks Abe made the closest study of, however, were the eclectic ones, the ones that had been assembled out of disparate, perhaps more affordable elements into a surprising whole. One of Abe's favorites had belonged to a handsome black dude he saw outside the Van Beirendonck show. He had a bushy beard and wore an odd felt hat with a broad brim and broad diagonal pleats around its crown, a cross between an Amish number and a Jell-O mold. Over a black mesh undershirt he had on a gold-and-green plaid blazer down the front of which he had stitched groups of black thread in parallel lines like guitar strings. He had stacked tribal bracelets on his wrists and silver tribal earrings curled in his earlobes, and he wore round gold granny glasses. His moon-boot-style sneakers had been precisely distressed, and his black pinstriped trousers, belted with a length of red-and-white jump rope, he wore rolled to the knee. It was a mad jumble of pieces of this and that from here and there, but somehow it all went together. It expressed an idea, and the idea it expressed was not Rick Owens's idea or Juun.J's idea but all the bits and pieces from here and there that made up the mind and history of the guy who had put them on.

Abe had learned a lot from studying this guy's look and the looks of the other dandies—for that was what they were, unpaid, unsponsored, there only to see and be seen and hoist their colors on the humid afternoon air—who showed up for the shows. Every night he had come home and gone through his suitcase, reviewing the elements of the wardrobe he'd brought with him (with a few fresh additions; it was the week of the *soldes*), combining and recombining them, laying out his little self-portrait on the floor. When he woke up in the morning he would have changed his mind about something, or a sudden inspiration would strike. The look he had chosen for the Off-White preview had been tested and revised, in his mind and on his body, and it said whatever it was about himself that he had managed, at this early and still inarticulate moment in the history of his soul, to say. It would bear up to scrutiny. It had been designed to bear up to scrutiny. Indeed it had been designed to *invite* scrutiny, not of the look itself but of the person inside it.

His clothes were not *on* the outside of his body; they *were*—for now—the outside of his body. They were the visible form taken by the way he chose to define himself. None of the gawky young models, standing around flat-footed and hunch-shouldered with their assigned coats and jackets and baggy shorts hanging off them like drop cloths thrown over a dining room set, could say that. Even Virgil Abloh, in his black sweats and black T-shirt, seemed to be wearing Off-White.

Virgil Abloh asked Abe where he was from. Abe said that he was from Oakland. That was not quite true; Abe lived in Berkeley, one block from the Oakland-Berkeley line. Undoubtedly he thought, not without reason, that Oakland sounded, and was, cooler than Berkeley as a place for one to be from. Oakland was the Black Panthers, the impassive cartoon masks thrown up on freeway embankments by graffiti artist GATS, and heroes of hip-hop like Too Short, Mac Dre, Richie Rich, and the Hieroglyphics collective. Berkeley was bearded dudes wearing drug rugs and drawstring pants in the drum circle at the Ashby BART on Saturday mornings.

"This young man understands the idea, here," Virgil Abloh told the reporters, pens poised over their notepads. "This is what I'm trying to do." Abloh invited his assembled guests to consider Abe's look from the ground up. The models were trying to suppress smiles now and not in all cases succeeding.

"First of all," Abloh said, "you got the Adidas—*hold on!*" He went in for a closer look at Abe's shoes. "You wearing *Rafs?*" He offered Abe a congratulatory fist bump. Abe graciously accepted it. "You got the sneakers, and the athletic socks—the *right* athletic socks." He grinned; Abe beamed.

The people in the folding chairs laughed. "So far, everything is coming out of the streetwear context. But then up at the top, the look is something much more tailored. For the young dudes, they're coming out of streetwear labels. Supreme, Bape . . . That's where it starts, right?"

He checked with Abe, who duly, and truthfully, nodded. "But now they're thinking, maybe without getting too expensive, maybe they could take it to a higher level. Good," he said to Abe. "Thank you. Go on, now, go have a seat."

Two days and five shows later Abe arrived, late, for the Off-White show. He had been melancholy all day, and now, as we arrived to find the show halfway over, he sank even further. I felt badly; I had kept us too long at the previous show, Paul Smith.

After the show ended, Abe caught sight of Virgil Abloh backstage, but the designer was surrounded by press and fans. He nodded and smiled at Abe, but they didn't get the chance to speak again. Fashion Week was over. It was time to go home.

"I don't want to go home," Abe said.

"I know," I said. "Paris is fun."

"It's been so exciting for you," I suggested. "You don't want it to end."

"Yeah. No, it's not that."

"What's wrong?" I said. "Tell me, buddy."

But he didn't want to talk about it. We rode in a taxi back to our rented apartment in the 12th Arrondissement. Abe slowly packed up his clothes and laid out the jeans and T-shirt that he planned to wear on the flight home. He grew more silent and sank even deeper into whatever was eating him. He grew tearful. We had an argument. I was tired of fashion and fashion shows. I could only feel that I had had enough and that I wanted to leave and be done. It was hard for me to imagine feeling any other way.

"We had a good time," I said. "You got to do a lot of fun things and meet cool people. You got some nice things to wear. You were in Paris. Now it's time to go home. Come on."

"I don't want to go back," he said.

"We'll come back to Paris. When you grow up, you can live here." 50

"It's not Paris. It's not the clothes."

"The Pigalle show," he said.

"That was your favorite. I wish I'd gone."

He looked at me, a funny expression on his face. I realized that the reason he'd had such a great time that night was because I had *not* been present. I had not been his father, or his friend, this past week. I had only been his minder. I was a drag to have around a fashion show, and because I could not enter fully into the spirit of the occasion, neither could Abe. He was worrying about me, watching me, wondering if I was having a good time or not, if I thought the shaggy Muppet pants, for example, were as stupid as the look on my face seemed to suggest.

"It wasn't the show, really," I suggested as his eyes filled with tears. "Was it? 55

It was the people you were with, the *GQ* guys, the buyers, that dude who owns Wild Style."

"They get it," he said. "They know everything about all the designers, and the house, and that's what they care about. They love to talk about clothes. They love clothes."

You are born into a family and those are your people, and they know you and they love you and if you are lucky they even, on occasion, manage to understand you. And that ought to be enough. But it is never enough. Abe had not been dressing up, styling himself, for all these years because he was trying to prove how different he was from everyone else. He did it in the hope of attracting the attention of somebody else—somewhere, someday—who was the *same.* He was not flying his freak flag; he was sending up a flare, hoping for rescue, for company in the solitude of his passion.

"You were with your people. You found them," I said.

"That's good," I said. "You're early." 60

Questions for Critical Reading

1. While growing up Abe faces some bullying from his peers because of his sense of style. Looking back through the essay, identify passages where Chabon indicates why Abe continued to pursue his unique style despite the teasing he faced. What did fashion offer Abe? Why was it worth so much to him?

2. What is the relationship between fashion and economics? Reread the essay looking for passages where Chabon discusses the link between the two.

3. Write down your thoughts about what it means to be a man. How do *both* Abe and Chabon (in particular through his relationship with his son) complicate your understanding of manhood? Locate quotations where Chabon points to new, revised, or expanded notions of manhood.

Exploring Context

1. Abe's encounter with Virgil Abloh and his Off-White collection play a central role in Chabon's narrative. Explore the website for Off-White at off-white.com. How does the site reflect the relationship between fashion and economics that you identified in Question 2 of Questions for Critical Reading?

2. Although Chabon's essay is centrally concerned with the relationship between father and son, Abe's mother is also an accomplished writer, Ayelet Waldman. Visit her website at ayeletwaldman.com. Based on what you can find of Waldman's writing, thoughts, and beliefs, what role do you imagine she has played in helping Abe become the young man he is? Consider how your answer might relate to your response to Question 3 of Questions for Critical Reading.

3. Visit the website for the Fédération de la Haute Couture et de la Mode, the organization that puts on Parish Fashion Week, at fhcm.paris/en. How does the site present Fashion Week? How does that representation relate to the issues that Chabon discusses in his essay?

Questions for Connecting

1. Robin Marantz Henig maps out some of the complications involved in the relationships between parents and children today as well as the broader challenges of growing up in her essay "What Is It about 20-Somethings?" (p. 201). How do Abe's experiences with his father confirm, extend, or complicate Henig's ideas? Is Abe on the path to emerging adulthood or does his experience suggest there are other paths available to youth today?

2. Kavita Das explores the idea of cool and its relationship to race, ethnicity, and national identity in "(Un)American, (Un)Cool" (p. 102). In what ways does fashion partake of "cool"? How does the relationship between high fashion and black urban hip-hop reflect the ideas that Das writes about?

3. We might consider high fashion a kind of art. According to Rhys Southan in "Is Art a Waste of Time?" (p. 363) Effective Altruism challenges the very notion of art. Use Southan's ideas about art and altruism to examine Chabon's essay. Is fashion a waste of time? What does fashion provide for individuals like Abe? What does that say about effective altruism?

Language Matters

1. Throughout the essay Chabon refers to himself in the third person as Abe's "minder." Using a grammar handbook or other reliable resource, learn the difference between first and third person. Why do you think Chabon chooses this construction? When might it be appropriate to use third person in your own writing?

2. In small groups, select a common grammatical error, such as sentence fragments or subject-verb agreement problems. Select a key quotation from Chabon's text and then change it to represent the error. Share the original and altered quotations in small groups to create a list of error examples and corrections using this essay.

3. Select a section of at least four paragraphs in Chabon's essay. Find the topic sentence of each paragraph and then copy those sentences together to form a new paragraph. Does the paragraph made out of topic sentences make any sense? Does it reflect the flow of Chabon's argument? How can you apply this exercise to your own writing?

Assignments for Writing

1. Issues of identity and community are at the heart of Chabon's narrative. Write a paper in which you use his text to analyze the ways in which self-representation (through clothes or other means) can be used to form an identity and connect to a community. You may find part of your response to Question 1 of Questions for Critical Reading helpful as you make your argument.
2. Write a paper in which you explain the relationship between fashion and economics as suggested by Chabon's essay. In writing your paper, you may want to draw from your responses to Question 2 of Questions for Critical Reading and Question 1 of Exploring Context.
3. In Question 3 of Questions for Critical Reading you explored notions of manhood. Expand on your response by writing a paper determining the ways in which Chabon's essay illustrates changing cultural notions of what it means to be a man.

ADRIAN CHEN

Journalist **Adrian Chen** began his career as a staff writer at Gawker before moving on to the *New Yorker.* His work often centers on internet culture's darker side, including trolls and websites such as 4chan, Reddit, and Silk Road. His writing has also appeared in *Wired,* the *Nation, New York* magazine, and *MIT Technology Review,* and he is the recipient of a Mirror Award from the S. I. Newhouse School of Public Communications at Syracuse University.

The *New Yorker,* where this essay first appeared, offers notable commentary on politics, global affairs, art and popular culture, and science and technology. It also publishes short fiction and poetry and is famous for its cartoons. Along with Chen's essay, the issue of November 23, 2015, included an essay on the role of weather in fiction; a profile of Robert Corrigan, who holds a doctorate in urban rodentology and is known as the Rat Czar; an examination of the website Erowid, which functions as an online encyclopedia of psychoactive drugs and drug experiences; and coverage of the developing presidential race. The cover focused on virtual reality and virtual music.

Chen's essay centers on the story of Megan Phelps-Roper, a prominent member of the Westboro Baptist Church, known for its militant stance against gays and its frequent picketing of funerals. Phelps-Roper was placed in charge of the church's Twitter account and used social media to spread the Westboro doctrine. Along the way, however, she started talking to others on Twitter, conversations that eventually caused her to rethink everything she was taught to believe.

How can social media promote personal or cultural change? Have your experiences using services like Twitter helped you to understand others different from you? How does Chen's essay suggest the power of conversation?

TAGS: *adolescence and adulthood, censorship, community, conversation, empathy, identity, judgment and decision making, media, relationships, religion, social change, social media, tradition, war and conflict*

CONNECTIONS: *Appiah, DeGhett, Gilbert, Gladwell, Klosterman, Konnikova, Turkle, Yoshino*

Unfollow

On December 1, 2009, to commemorate World AIDS Day, Twitter announced a promotion: If users employed the hashtag #red, their tweets would appear highlighted in red. Megan Phelps-Roper, a twenty-three-year-old legal assistant, seized the opportunity. "Thank God for AIDS!" she tweeted that morning. "You won't repent of your rebellion that brought His wrath on you in this incurable scourge, so expect more & worse! #red."

As a member of the Westboro Baptist Church, in Topeka, Kansas, Phelps-Roper believed that AIDS was a curse sent by God. She believed that all manner of other tragedies—war, natural disaster, mass shootings—were warnings from God to a doomed nation, and that it was her duty to spread the news of His righteous judgments.

To protest the increasing acceptance of homosexuality in America, the Westboro Baptist Church picketed the funerals of gay men who died of AIDS and of soldiers killed in Iraq and Afghanistan. Members held signs with slogans like "God Hates Fags" and "Thank God for Dead Soldiers," and the outrage that their efforts attracted had turned the small church, which had fewer than a hundred members, into a global symbol of hatred.

Westboro had long used the Internet to spread its message. In 1994, the church launched a website, www.godhatesfags.com, and early on it had a chat room where visitors could interact with members of Westboro. As a child, Phelps-Roper spent hours there, sparring with strangers. She learned about Twitter in 2008, after reading an article about an American graduate student in Egypt who had used it to notify his friends that he had been arrested while photographing riots. She opened an account but quickly lost interest—at the time, Twitter was still used mostly by early-adopting techies—until someone e-mailed Westboro's website, in the summer of 2009, and asked if the church used the service. Phelps-Roper, who is tall, with voluminous curly hair and pointed features, volunteered to tweet for the congregation. Her posts could be easily monitored, since she worked at Phelps Chartered, the family law firm, beside her mother, Shirley, an attorney. Moreover, Megan was known for her mastery of the Bible and for her ability to spread Westboro's doctrine. "She had a well-sharpened tongue, so to speak," Josh Phelps, one of Megan's cousins and a former member of Westboro, told me.

In August 2009, Phelps-Roper, under the handle @meganphelps, posted a celebratory tweet when Ted Kennedy died ("He defied God at every turn, teaching rebellion against His laws. Ted's in hell!") and a description of a picket that the church held at an American Idol concert in Kansas City ("Totally awesome! Tons going in & taking pics—even tho others tried to block our signs"). On September 1st, her sister Bekah e-mailed church members to explain the utility of Twitter: "Now Megan has 87 followers and more are trickling in all the time. So every time we find something else to picket, or have some new video or picture we want to post (or just something that we see on the news and want to comment about)—87 people get first-hand, gospel commentary from Megan Marie."

A couple of hours after Phelps-Roper posted her tweet on World AIDS Day, she checked her e-mail and discovered numerous automated messages notifying her of new Twitter followers. Her tweet had been discovered by the comedian Michael Ian Black, who had more than a million followers. He was surprised that a member of the Westboro Baptist Church was on Twitter at all. "I sort of thought they would be this fire-and-brimstone sort of Pentecostal anti-technology clan that would be removed from the world," he told me. He tweeted, "Sort of obsessed w/ @meganphelps. Sample tweet: 'AIDS is God's curse on you.' Let her feel your love." The director Kevin Smith and *The Office* star Rainn Wilson mocked her, as did many of their followers. 5

Phelps-Roper was exhilarated by the response. Since elementary school, she had given hundreds of interviews about Westboro, but the reaction on Twitter seemed more real than a quote in a newspaper. "It's not just like 'Yes, all these people are seeing it,'" she told me. "It's proof that people are seeing it and reacting to it." Phelps-Roper spent much of the morning responding to angry tweets, citing Bible passages. "I think your plan is back-firing," she taunted Black. "Your followers are just nasty haters of God! You should do something about that . . . like tell them some truth every once in a while.

Like this: God hates America." That afternoon, as Phelps-Roper picketed a small business in Topeka with other Westboro members, she was still glued to her iPhone. "I did not want to be the one to let it die," she said.

By the end of the day, Phelps-Roper had more than a thousand followers. She took the incident as an encouraging sign that Westboro's message was well suited to social media. She loved that Twitter let her talk to large numbers of people without the filter of a journalist. During the next few months, Phelps-Roper spearheaded Westboro's push into the social-media age, using Twitter to offer a window into life in the church and giving it an air of accessibility.

It was easy for Phelps-Roper to write things on Twitter that made other people cringe. She had been taught the church's vision of God's truth since birth. Her grandfather Fred Phelps established the church in 1955. Megan's mother was the fifth of Phelps's thirteen children. Megan's father, Brent Roper, had joined the church as a teenager. Every Sunday, Megan and her ten siblings sat in Westboro's small wood-panelled church as her grandfather delivered the sermon. Fred Phelps preached a harsh Calvinist doctrine in a resounding Southern drawl. He believed that all people were born depraved, and that only a tiny elect who repented would be saved from Hell. A literalist, Phelps believed that contemporary Christianity, with its emphasis on God's love, preached a perverted version of the Bible. Phelps denounced other Christians so vehemently that when Phelps-Roper was young she thought "Christian" was another word for evil. Phelps believed that God hated unrepentant sinners. God hated the politicians who were allowing the United States to descend into a modern-day Sodom and Gomorrah. He hated the celebrities who glorified fornication.

Phelps also believed that fighting the increasing tolerance of homosexuality was the key moral issue of our time. To illustrate gay sin, he described exotic sex acts in lurid detail. "He would say things like 'These guys are slobbering around on each other and sucking on each other,'" Megan said. In awe of his conviction and deep knowledge of Scripture, she developed a revulsion to homosexuality. "We thought of him as a star in the right hand of God," she said. Westboro had started as an offshoot of Topeka's East Side Baptist Church, but by the time Phelps-Roper was born its congregation was composed mostly of Fred Phelps's adult children and their families.

10

Nevertheless, Phelps-Roper didn't grow up in isolation. Westboro believed that its members could best preach to the wicked by living among them. The children of Westboro attended Topeka public schools, and Phelps-Roper ran track, listened to Sublime CDs, and read Stephen King novels. If you knew the truth in your heart, Westboro believed, even the filthiest products of pop culture couldn't defile you. She was friendly with her classmates and her teachers, but viewed them with extreme suspicion—she knew that they were either intentionally evil or deluded by God. "We would always say, They have nothing to offer us," Phelps-Roper said. She never went to dances. Dating was out of the question. The Westboro students had a reputation for being diligent and polite in class, but at lunch they would picket the school, dodging food hurled at them by incensed classmates.

Phelps-Roper was constantly around family. Nine of Fred Phelps's children were still in the church, and most of them had large families of their own. Many of them worked as lawyers at Phelps Chartered. The church was in a residential neighborhood in southwest Topeka, and its members had bought most of the houses on the block around it. Their backyards were surrounded by a tall fence, creating a huge courtyard that was home to a trampoline, an in-ground pool, a playground, and a running track. They called the Westboro compound the Block, and considered it a sanctuary in a world full of evil. "We did lots of fun normal-kids stuff," Megan said.

The Phelps-Roper home was the biggest on the Block, and a room in the basement acted as a kind of community center for Westboro. An alcove in the kitchen had cubbies for the signs that were used in pickets. On summer afternoons, Shirley led Bible readings for young members. She had a central role in nearly every aspect of Westboro's operations: she was its media coördinator, planned the pickets, and managed Phelps Chartered. A parade of journalists and Westboro members sought meetings with her. Louis Theroux, a British filmmaker who made two documentaries about Westboro, said, "My feeling was that there was a pecking order and there was an unacknowledged hierarchy, and at the top of it was Shirley's family." Starting in middle school, Megan worked side by side with Shirley; among her siblings, she had a uniquely strong bond with her mother. "I felt like I could ask her anything about anything," Megan told me.

Other young Westboro members regarded Shirley with a mixture of fear and respect. "Shirley had a very abrasive personality," Josh Phelps said. But, he added, she could be remarkably tender when dispensing advice or compliments. Megan lacked Shirley's hard edge. "She was just happy in general," her cousin Libby Phelps, one of Megan's close friends, told me.

Shirley, as Westboro's de-facto spokeswoman, granted interviews to almost any outlet, no matter how obscure or adversarial. "She was smart and funny, and would answer impertinent questions and not be offended about it," Megan said. When reporters wanted the perspective of a young person, Shirley let them speak to Megan. In sixth grade, Megan gave her first live interview when she answered a call from a couple of radio d.j.s who wanted to speak to her mother. Megan recalls, "They thought it was hilarious, this eleven-year-old talking about hating Jews."

15 Obedience was one of the most important values that Shirley instilled in Megan. She would sum up the Bible in three words: "Obey. Obey. Obey." The smallest hint of dissent was seen as an intolerable act of rebellion against God. Megan was taught that there would always be a tension between what she felt and thought as a human and what the Bible required of her. But giving place to rebellious thoughts was the first step down the path toward Hell. "The tone of your voice or the look on your face—you could get into so much trouble for these things, because they betray what's in your heart," she said. Her parents took to heart the proverb "He that spareth his rod hateth his son." Her uncle gave them a novelty wooden paddle inscribed with the tongue-in-cheek direction "May be used on any child from 5 to 75," and her father hung it on the wall next to the family photos. The joke hit close to home for Phelps-Roper, who was spanked well into her teens. Sometimes, she told me, "it went too far, for sure." But, she added, "I also always knew that they were just trying to do what God required of them."

As she grew older, she came to find comfort, and even joy, in submitting her will to the word of God. Children in Westboro must make a profession of faith before they are baptized and become full members of the church. One day in June, when she was thirteen, her grandfather baptized her in the shallow end of the Block's pool. "I wanted to do everything right," she said. "I wanted to be good, and I wanted to be obedient, and I wanted to be the object of my parents' pride. I wanted to go to Heaven."

Westboro started picketing in June, 1991, when Phelps-Roper was five years old. Fred Phelps believed that Gage Park, less than a mile from the Block, had become overrun with gay men cruising for sex. Phelps claimed that he was inspired to launch the Great Gage Park Decency Drive, as he called it, after one of his young grandsons was propositioned while biking through the park. The church sought redress from city officials, to no avail, so throughout the summer church members, including Megan, protested every day, walking in a circle while holding signs with messages written in permanent marker such as "Warning! Gays in the Bushes! Watch Your Children!" and "And God Over-Threw Sodom."

The pickets were met with an immediate backlash from the community, but Phelps was not deterred. He had been a committed civil-rights attorney in the nineteen-sixties and seventies, one of the few lawyers to represent black Kansans in discrimination suits, before the state disbarred him, in 1979, for harassing a court reporter who failed to have a transcript ready in time. Now Westboro targeted local churches, politicians, businesses, journalists, and anyone else who criticized Phelps's crusade. Throughout the nineties, Westboro members crisscrossed the country, protesting the funerals of AIDS victims and gay-pride parades. They picketed the funeral of Matthew Shepard, the gay man whose murder, in what was widely believed to be a hate crime, became a rallying cry for gay-rights activists. They picketed high schools, concerts, conferences, and film festivals, no matter how tenuous the connection to homosexuality or other sins. "Eventually, the targets broadened such that everyone was a target," Phelps-Roper said.

Phelps-Roper enjoyed picketing. When the targets were within driving distance, the group packed into a minivan and her grandfather saw them off from his driveway. "At five in the morning, he'd come out and give us all hugs," she said. When they flew, she and Libby recounted "Saturday Night Live" skits. Amazing things happened on the trips. In New Orleans, they ran into Ehud Barak, the former Israeli Prime Minister, and serenaded him with an anti-Semitic parody of Israel's national anthem. Phelps-Roper learned to hold two signs in each hand, a technique that Westboro members called the Butterfly. Her favorite slogans were "God Is Your Enemy," "No Peace for the Wicked," "God Hates Your Idols," and "Mourn for Your Sins." She laughed and sang and smiled in the face of angry crowds. "If you were ever upset or even scared, you do not show it, because this is not the time or the place," she said. Phelps-Roper believed that she was engaged in a profound act of love. Leviticus 19:17 commands, "Thou shalt not hate thy brother in thine heart: thou shalt in any wise rebuke thy neighbor, and not suffer sin upon him." "When you see someone is backing into traffic, you yell at them," Phelps-Roper said. "You don't mope around and say it's such a good idea."

20 One of the most common questions she was asked on the picket line was why she hated gay people so much. She didn't hate gay people, she would reply, God hated gay people. And the rest of the world hated them, too, by cheering them on as they doomed themselves to Hell. "We love these fags more than anyone," she would say.

In the summer of 2005, Westboro began protesting the funerals of soldiers killed in Iraq and Afghanistan, holding signs like "Thank God for IEDs." "They turned the country over to the fags—they're coming home in body bags!" Fred Phelps would say. He believed that 9/11 was God's punishment for America's embrace of homosexuality, but that, instead of repenting, Americans had drowned this warning in a flood of patriotism. Phelps believed that God had killed the soldiers to warn a doomed

America, and that it was the church's job to make this fact explicit for the mourners. The scale of the picketing increased dramatically. One of Phelps-Roper's aunts checked the Department of Defense website every day for notifications of casualties. The outrage sparked by the soldier-funeral protests dwarfed anything that Phelps-Roper had experienced previously. Crowds of rowdy, sometimes violent counterprotesters tried to block their signs with huge American flags. A group of motorcyclists called the Patriot Guard Riders eventually began to follow Westboro members around the country, revving their engines to drown out their singing.

Phelps-Roper picketed her first military funeral in July 2005, in Omaha. She was nineteen years old and a sophomore at Washburn University, a secular public college in Topeka, where many Westboro children went. The Westboro members stood across the street from the church, in a quiet neighborhood in South Omaha, as the mourners filed in. "Everybody's in close quarters, and marines in dress blues are just staring at us with—the word that comes to mind is hateful 'disgust.' Like 'How could you possibly do this?'" Phelps-Roper said. But, before the picket, she asked her mother to walk her through the Bible passages that justified their actions. "I'm, like, O.K., it's there," she said. "This is right." She added, "This was the only hope for mankind, and I was so grateful to be part of this ministry."

In September 2009, when Phelps-Roper began to use Twitter in earnest, Westboro was preparing for the end of the world. Fred Phelps had preached for years that the end was near, but his sermons grew more dire after Barack Obama's election in 2008. Phelps believed that Obama was the Antichrist, and that his Presidency signalled the beginning of the Apocalypse. The sense of looming calamity was heightened by a multimillion-dollar judgment against the church that had been awarded, in 2007, to Albert Snyder, who sued Westboro after it picketed the funeral of his son Matt, a U.S. marine killed in Iraq. Westboro members drew prophecies from the Book of Revelation about how the end might unfold. First, the Supreme Court would overturn the Snyder verdict. The country would be so enraged by Westboro's victory that its members would be forced to flee to Israel. Obama would be crowned king of the world, then lead every nation in war against Israel. Israel would be destroyed, and only a hundred and forty-four thousand Jews who repented for killing Jesus would be spared. (Revelation says that a hundred and forty-four thousand "children of Israel" are "redeemed from among men.") Westboro members would lead these converted Jews through the wilderness until Christ returned and ushered them into Heaven. Phelps-Roper and her family members all got passports, so that they could travel to Israel. One day, she was in the grocery store and picked up a container of yogurt with Oreo pieces. She stared at it, thinking, We won't have modern conveniences like this in the wilderness. Is it better to learn to live without them, or to enjoy them while we can?

Still, she had a hard time believing in aspects of the future foretold by some church members, like the idea that they would soon be living in pink caves in Jordan. "We were making specific predictions about things without having, in my mind, sufficient scriptural support," she said. Many other members shared her bewilderment, she found, and so she turned to Twitter for answers. Most of the prophecies centered on Jews, so she found a list, published by the Jewish Telegraphic Agency, a syndicated news service, of the hundred most influential Jewish Twitter users. She created an account under the pseudonym Marissa Cohen and followed many of the people on the list, hoping to learn if Westboro's prophecies were coming true.

As the prophecies were developed, Westboro expanded the focus of its preaching to include the Jewish community. Members hoped to find the hundred and forty-four thousand repentant Jews. They picketed synagogues and sent anti-Semitic DVDs to Jewish organizations. Westboro called the protests the Fateful Fig Find, after a parable in the Book of Jeremiah that compares Jews who had been captured by the Babylonians to two baskets of figs, one good and one "naughty." Phelps-Roper thought that this initiative was more explicitly supported by the Bible than other parts of the prophecies were, so she threw herself into the effort. She wrote the church's press release: "WBC is looking for the good figs among the Christ-rejecting hypocrites!" She looked at the J.T.A. list of influential Jews and saw that No. 2 was David Abitbol, a Jerusalem-based Web developer and the founder of the Jewish-culture blog Jewlicious. With more than four thousand followers and a habit of engaging with those who tweeted at him, he would be a prime target for Westboro's message of repentance, she figured.

On September 9, 2009, Shirley gave an interview to an Atlanta radio station, and Phelps-Roper shared a quote on Twitter. Phelps-Roper tagged Abitbol in the post so that he would see it. She wrote, "Atlanta: radio guy says 'Finish this sentence: the only good Jew is a . . .' Ma says 'Repentant Jew!' The only answer that suffices @jewlicious." "Thanks Megan!" he responded. "That's handy what with Yom Kippur coming up!" Phelps-Roper posted another tweet, spelling it out more clearly. "Oh & @jewlicious? Your dead rote rituals == true repentance. We know the diff. Rev. 3:9 You keep promoting sin, which belies the ugly truth." "Dead rote rituals?" he responded. "U mean like holding up God Hates Shrimp, err I mean Fag signs up? Your 'ministry' is a joke."

"Anybody's initial response to being confronted with the sort of stuff Westboro Baptist Church says is to tell them to fuck off," Abitbol told me. Abitbol is a large man in his early fifties who often has a shaggy Mohawk, which he typically covers with a Montreal Expos baseball cap. He was familiar with Westboro from its godhatesfags .com website. He had lived in Montreal in the nineties, and had become fascinated with the explosion of hate sites on the early Internet. "Most people, when they first get access to the Internet, the first thing they wanted to see was naked ladies," he told me. "The first thing I wanted to see was something I didn't have access to in Montreal: neo-Nazis and hate groups." There were few widely available search engines at the time, so he spent hours tracking down the websites of Holocaust deniers, anti-Semites, and racists of all types. He and a friend eventually created a directory called Net Hate, which listed the sites along with mocking descriptions. "We didn't want to debate them, we just wanted to make fun of them," he said. As for the Westboro members, "I just thought they were crazy."

Phelps-Roper got into an extended debate with Abitbol on Twitter. "Arguing is fun when you think you have all the answers," she said. But he was harder to get a bead on than other critics she had encountered. He had read the Old Testament in its original Hebrew, and was conversant in the New Testament as well. She was taken aback to see that he signed all his blog posts on Jewlicious with the handle "ck"—for "christ killer"—as if it were a badge of honor. Yet she found him funny and engaging. "I knew he was evil, but he was friendly, so I was especially wary, because you don't want to be seduced away from the truth by a crafty deceiver," Phelps-Roper said.

Abitbol had learned while running Net Hate that relating to hateful people on a human level was the best way to deal with them. He saw that Phelps-Roper had a lot of followers and was an influential person in the church, so he wanted to counter her message. And he wanted to humanize Jews to Westboro. "I wanted to be like really nice so that they would have a hard time hating me," he said. One day, he tweeted about the television show "Gossip Girl," and Phelps-Roper responded jocularly about one of its characters. "You know, for an evil something something, you sure do crack me up," Abitbol responded.

On December 20, 2009, Phelps-Roper was in the basement of her house, for a church function, when she checked Twitter on her phone and saw that Brittany Murphy, the thirty-two-year-old actress, had died. When she read the tweet aloud, other church members reacted with glee, celebrating another righteous judgment from God. "Lots of people were talking about going to picket her funeral," Phelps-Roper said. When Phelps-Roper was younger, news of terrible events had given her a visceral thrill. On 9/11, she was in the crowded hallway of her high school when she overheard someone talking about how an airplane had hit the World Trade Center. "Awesome!" she exclaimed, to the horror of a student next to her. She couldn't wait to picket Ground Zero. (The following March, she and other Westboro members travelled to New York City to protest what they described in a press release as "FDNY fags and terrorists.") But Phelps-Roper had loved Murphy in "Clueless," and she felt an unexpected pang—not quite sadness, but something close—over her death. As she continued scrolling through Twitter, she saw that it was full of people mourning Murphy. The contrast between the grief on Twitter and the buoyant mood in the basement unsettled her. She couldn't bring herself to post a tweet thanking God for Murphy's death. "I felt like I would be such a jackass to go on and post something like that," she said. 30

Her hesitance reflected a growing concern for the feelings of people outside Westboro. Church members disdained human feelings as something that people worshipped instead of the Bible. They even had a sign: "God Hates Your Feelings." They disregarded people's feelings in order to break their idols. Just a few months earlier, the Westboro website had received an e-mail arguing that the church's constant use of the word "fag" was needlessly offensive. "Get a grip, you presumptuous toad," Phelps-Roper had replied. She signed off, "Have a lovely day. You're going to Hell."

But on Twitter Phelps-Roper found that it was better to take a gentler tone. For one thing, Twitter's hundred-and-forty-character limit made it hard to fit both a florid insult and a scriptural point. And if she made things personal the conversation was inevitably derailed by a flood of angry tweets. She still preached God's hate, and still liberally deployed the word "fag," but she also sprinkled her tweets with cheerful exclamations and emoticons. She became adept at deflecting critics with a wry joke. "So, when do you drink the Kool- aid?" one user tweeted at her. "More of a Sunkist lemonade drinker, myself. =)" she replied. Phelps-Roper told me, "We weren't supposed to care about what people thought about us, but I did." As she developed her affable rhetorical style, she justified it with a proverb: "By long forbearing is a prince persuaded, and a soft tongue breaketh the bone."

Other Twitter users were fascinated by the dissonance between Westboro's loathsome reputation and the goofy, pop-culture-obsessed millennial who Phelps-Roper seemed to be on Twitter. "I remember just thinking, How can somebody who appreciates good music believe so many hateful things?" Graham Hughes said. In November 2009, Hughes, then a college student in British Columbia, interviewed Phelps-Roper for a religious-studies class. Afterward, they corresponded frequently on Twitter. When Hughes was hospitalized with a brain infection, Phelps-Roper showed him more concern than many of his real-life friends. "I knew there was a genuine connection between us," he said.

As Phelps-Roper continued to tweet, she developed relationships with more people like Hughes. There was a Jewish marketing consultant in Brooklyn who abhorred Westboro's tactics but supported the church's right to express its views. There was a young Australian guy who tweeted political jokes that she and her younger sister Grace found hilarious. "It was like I was becoming part of a community," Phelps-Roper said. By following her opponents' feeds, she absorbed their thoughts on the world, learned what food they ate, and saw photographs of their babies. "I was beginning to see them as human," she said. When she read about an earthquake that struck off Canada's Pacific coast, she sent a concerned tweet to Graham Hughes: "Isn't this close to you?"

In February 2010, Westboro protested a festival in Long Beach, California, that David Abitbol had organized through Jewlicious. Phelps-Roper's conversations with Abitbol had continued through the winter, and she knew that debating him in person would be more challenging than on Twitter. The church set up its picket a block from the Jewish community center where the festival was taking place. Phelps-Roper held four signs, while an Israeli flag dragged on the ground from her leg. The church members were quickly mobbed by an angry crowd. "Each of us was really surrounded," Phelps-Roper said. "Two really old women came up behind me and started whispering the filthiest stuff I'd ever heard."

She recognized Abitbol from his Twitter avatar. They made some small talk—Abitbol was amused by a sign, held by one of Phelps-Roper's sisters, that said "Your Rabbi Is a Whore"—then began to debate her about Westboro's doctrine. "Our in-person interaction resembled our Twitter interaction," Phelps-Roper said. "Funny, friendly, but definitely on opposite sides and each sticking to our guns." Abitbol asked why Westboro always denounced homosexuality but never mentioned the fact that Leviticus also forbade having sex with a woman who was menstruating. The question embarrassed Phelps-Roper—"I didn't want to talk about it because, ugh"—but it did strike her as an interesting point. As far as she could remember, her grandfather had never addressed that issue from the pulpit. Still, Phelps-Roper enjoyed the exchange with Abitbol. Not long after, she told him that Westboro would be picketing the General Assembly of the Jewish Federations, in New Orleans, that year. Abitbol said that he'd be there, too, and when they met again they exchanged gifts.

Phelps-Roper and Abitbol continued their conversations via e-mail and Twitter's direct-message function. In Phelps-Roper's effort to better understand Westboro's new prophecies, she had bought a copy of "The Complete Idiot's Guide to Understanding Judaism," but she found it more profitable just to ask Abitbol her questions. Here was a real live Orthodox Jew who lived in Israel and was more than happy to enlighten her. During their debates over Scripture, Phelps-Roper sometimes quoted passages from the Old Testament; Abitbol often countered that their meaning differed in the original Hebrew, so Phelps-Roper bought some language-learning software. She figured that, since she would soon be living in Israel awaiting the end of the world, she should learn the language. Abitbol helped her with the vocabulary.

Phelps-Roper still urged Abitbol to repent, but as someone who was concerned about a wayward friend. "I just wish you would obey God and use your considerable platform to warn your audience about the consequences of engaging in conduct that God calls abomination," she e-mailed Abitbol in October 2010.

In response, Abitbol kept pressing Phelps-Roper on Westboro's doctrine. One day, he asked about a Westboro sign that said "Death Penalty for Fags," referring to a commandment from Leviticus. Abitbol pointed out that Jesus had said, "He that is without sin among you, let him first cast a stone." Abitbol knew that at least one member of Westboro had committed a sin that Leviticus also deems a capital crime. Phelps-Roper's oldest brother, Sam, was the product of a relationship that Shirley had had with a man she met while she was in law school, before she married Megan's father.

Shirley's sin of fornication was often thrown in the church members' faces by counterprotesters. Westboro always argued that the difference between Shirley and gay people was that Shirley had repented of her sin, whereas gays marched in pride parades. But Abitbol wrote that if gay people were killed they wouldn't have the opportunity to repent. 40

Phelps-Roper was struck by the double standard, and, as she did whenever she had a question about doctrine, she brought up the issue with her mother. Shirley responded that Romans said gays were "worthy of death," and that if it was good enough for God it was good enough for Westboro. "It was such a settled point that they've been preaching for so long it's almost like it didn't mean anything to her," Phelps-Roper said. Still, she concluded that Westboro was in the wrong. "That was the first time I came to a place where I disagreed, I knew I disagreed, and I didn't accept the answer that they gave," she said. Phelps-Roper knew that to press the issue would create problems for her in the church, so she quietly stopped holding the "Death Penalty for Fags" sign. There were plenty of other signs whose message she still believed in wholeheartedly. She also put an end to the conversations with Abitbol.

Phelps-Roper found it easy to ignore her doubt amid the greater publicity that Westboro was receiving, much of it tied to her Twitter activity. In February 2011, the hacker collective Anonymous declared war against Westboro. On Twitter, Phelps-Roper taunted the group's members as "crybaby hackers." Anonymous retaliated by hacking godhatesfags.com, and blogs seized on the drama. "Thanks, Anonymous! Your efforts to shut up God's word only serve to publish it further," Phelps-Roper tweeted. In March, Westboro members walked out of a screening of the film *Red State*, which spoofed the church. They had been invited by the director, Kevin Smith, with whom Phelps-Roper had kept up a running feud on Twitter since World AIDS Day. Ten days earlier, the Supreme Court had overturned the judgment against Westboro in the Albert Snyder case. Phelps-Roper was inundated with tweets and new followers. That month, she tweeted more than two thousand times; by the end of the month, she had more than seven thousand followers. "That explosion of activity, it was insane," she said.

But as other members of the church joined Twitter they began to question her friendly relations with outsiders. In April 2011, the BBC aired one of Louis Theroux's documentaries about Westboro. In one scene, Phelps-Roper explained how she used Twitter to keep up with a group of four Dutch filmmakers who had visited Westboro in 2010. She showed Theroux a picture of one of the filmmakers, Pepijn Borgwat, a smiling, handsome young man holding a package of chocolate truffles that she and her sister Grace had given to him.

The day after the documentary aired, Sam Phelps-Roper sent an e-mail to church members urging more discretion in their tweets. "I understand the concept of showing the world our brotherly kindness, but we don't have to let it all hang out," he wrote. Megan's father made her block the Dutch journalists from her private Twitter account. "It feels like we are opening ourselves up for entangling ourselves with the affairs or cares of this life," he e-mailed Phelps-Roper and her siblings. Phelps-Roper said, "It made me scared for myself that I wanted that. And so I was, like, 'OK, you gotta step back.'"

Another online relationship proved more threatening. In February 2011, Phelps-Roper began to have conversations on Twitter with a user named @F_K_A. His avatar was Robert Redford in *The Great Gatsby*. He had learned of Westboro after reading an article about the Anonymous hack. "He sent me a tweet, and initially it was like this angry, nasty tweet," Phelps-Roper said. But @F_K_A was disarmed by Phelps-Roper's friendly demeanor. He began to ask her questions about life in Westboro, and, because he was curious instead of condemning, she kept answering them. One day, Phelps-Roper recalled, "I asked him some kind of pointed question about the Bible. He said something like, 'I can't answer that, but I have never been beaten in Words with Friends'"—the popular online Scrabble knockoff. Phelps-Roper replied, "I can't boast the same. =)" She put her Words with Friends username at the end of the tweet.

They began to talk about the church using the in-game chat function, free from Twitter's character limit. @F_K_A told Phelps-Roper to call him C.G. But C.G. remained a mystery. She knew that he was an attorney, but she didn't know where he lived or how old he was. "He was careful not to reveal anything about himself," Phelps-Roper said.

Like David Abitbol, C.G. argued against Westboro's beliefs and practices, but while Abitbol's arguments were doctrinal C.G. was most critical of Westboro's cruelty. "We had the same discussion several times when someone would die," Phelps-Roper said. C.G. urged Phelps-Roper to think of how much hurt it must cause the families of the deceased to see Phelps-Roper and her family rejoicing. Westboro divided people into good and evil, but, Phelps-Roper said, C.G. "always tried to advocate for a third group of people: people who were decent but not religious." She had heard all these arguments before, but they had never affected her as they did when C.G. made them. "I just really liked him," she said. "He seemed to genuinely like people and care about people, and that resonated with me."

He seemed to genuinely like people and care about people, and that resonated with me.

Phelps-Roper increasingly found herself turning to Bible passages where tragedy is not met with joy. The Old Testament prophet Elisha, for example, weeps when he foresees disaster for Israel. One day in July 2011, Phelps-Roper was on Twitter when she came across a link to a series of photographs about a famine in Somalia. The first image was of a tiny malnourished child. She burst into tears at her desk. Her mother asked what was wrong, and Phelps-Roper showed her the gallery. Her mother quickly composed a triumphant blog post about the famine. "Thank God for famine in East Africa!" she wrote. "God is longsuffering and patient, but he repays the wicked TO THEIR FACE!" When Brittany Murphy died, Phelps-Roper had seen the disparity between her reaction and that of the rest of the church as a sign that something was wrong with her. Now the contradiction of her mother's glee and her own sadness made her wonder if something was wrong with the church.

Phelps-Roper's conversations with C.G. often drifted away from morality. C.G. liked indie rock and literary fiction. He introduced Phelps-Roper to bands like the Antlers, Blind Pilot, and Cults—"funnily enough," she said—and to the novels of David Foster Wallace and Marilynne Robinson. "Hipster shit," Phelps-Roper said. He turned her on to the Field Notes brand of notebooks. He poked fun at the inelegant fonts that Westboro used for its press releases. After C.G. complimented her on her grammar, she took pains to make sure that her tweets were free of clunky text-message abbreviations.

As Phelps-Roper developed her relationship with C.G., her sister Grace grew suspicious. "Suddenly, her taste in music started changing," Grace told me. "It annoyed me, because it wasn't coming from Megan. It was coming from him, this question mark of a person that I don't get to know about, but she has some kind of thing with." As young children, Grace and Megan had squabbled constantly, but they had grown close. Grace was seven years younger than Megan, and still in high school at the time. Grace would scroll through Megan's iPhone, asking about the various messages and e-mails. But soon after Megan started talking to C.G. she stopped letting Grace look at her phone. "I remember thinking, What the heck? What are you hiding?" Grace said. 50

For young women in Westboro, having romantic interactions with someone outside the church was forbidden. When Phelps-Roper was growing up, one of her cousins had been pushed out of the church for, among other things, getting entangled with boys; other young women had been harshly punished. Phelps-Roper had long assumed that she would likely never get married, since she was related to almost every male in the church. "I was terrified of even thinking about guys," she said. "It's not just the physical stuff that can get you in trouble." She did her best to displace her feelings for C.G. onto the music and books he recommended, which she fervently consumed. "I was in denial," she said.

Then, on September 30, 2011, she had a dream: It was a beautiful summer day, and she was standing on the driveway of the church. A black car with tinted windows pulled up, and a tall, blond man got out. She couldn't see his face, but she knew it was C.G. She walked up to him, and they embraced. She knew her family could see them on the surveillance cameras that line the Block, but she didn't care. "It was so real, that feeling of wanting to be with him," Phelps-Roper told me. She woke up fighting back tears. "He was not a good person, according to the church," she said. "And the fact that I dreamed about him, and the strong feeling of wanting that relationship, represented huge danger to me." That day, she told C.G. that they couldn't talk anymore. She deleted her Words with Friends account. C.G. deleted his Twitter account.

Phelps-Roper tried to throw herself back into the Westboro community, but the atmosphere had changed while she was distracted by her relationship with C.G. It had started in April 2011. Her mother seemed mysteriously troubled. After Phelps-Roper pressed her parents, they showed her an e-mail they'd received from her oldest brother, Sam, and Steve Drain, another church member. It accused her mother of lacking humility, saying that she was too zealous in correcting other members' behavior and had overreached her authority on a number of occasions, Phelps-Roper told me. Reading the e-mail made her sick with fear. When a Westboro member was singled out for bad behavior, it often triggered a harrowing period of discipline. The smallest transgression could spark another round of punishment, until the member either shaped up or was kicked out of the church.

Shirley's role in the church was reduced dramatically. "My mother was supposed to be primarily a mother and a caretaker," Zach Phelps-Roper, Megan's younger brother, told me. Megan took over picket planning, while Steve Drain became the church's media manager. The Phelps-Roper house was now quiet, as the flow of church members and reporters stopped. "I watched her all my life work so hard and sacrifice so much, and just be so willing to do anything for anybody," Phelps-Roper said. "She had to be put in her place, essentially, and that feeling—it just was really, really wrong to me." (Drain insists that Megan's description of the letter is inaccurate. He said that it was a "disciplinary message," but wouldn't reveal its contents. "We don't air our dirty laundry," he said.)

55

An all-male group of nine elders took control of church affairs. Previously, decisions at Westboro had been hashed out in church meetings, where consensus was required before moving forward. But the elders met separately before bringing their decisions to the rest of the group. The church became more secretive, as members were reluctant to discuss important issues for fear of appearing to go behind the elders' backs.

Women like Shirley and her older sister Margie—an attorney who had argued the Snyder case in front of the Supreme Court—had always been among the most public and influential members of the church. Westboro members drew on stories of powerful women in the Bible, like Deborah, a prophet and judge of Israel. But now the emphasis shifted to passages about women submitting to their husbands. Fred Phelps encouraged church members to read the Evangelical writer John R. Rice's book *Bobbed Hair, Bossy Wives, and Women Preachers*, from 1941, which offered a view of gender roles that was regressive even when it was published. "It suddenly sucked to be a woman," Phelps-Roper said. "It was, like, I would need to get permission from Dad to talk to anybody else."

Westboro women had long been forbidden to cut their hair, and had restrictions on other aspects of their appearance. But now the elders required more severe standards of modesty. Phelps-Roper had to wear high-necked shirts and dresses or shorts that covered her knees. After one shopping trip with her mother and her sisters, Phelps-Roper had to show her clothes to her father and her brother Sam, to make sure that they were appropriate. She was barred from wearing colorful nail polish and her favorite gold sandals to church. Phelps-Roper was upset to learn that some of her cousins lived under more liberal standards. How could God's judgment differ from house to house?

Phelps-Roper's confusion soon turned to outrage. In 2012, she was twenty-six years old, but she was still being treated like a child. Once-minor indignities, like being accompanied by an adult chaperone while eating lunch at a restaurant with other young church members, now seemed unbearable. In April, she was shocked when Westboro expelled a cousin of hers without adhering to the process that the church had always followed, which was derived from the Book of Matthew. Typically, expulsion resulted only after a unanimous decision, but in the cousin's case she was excluded over other members' objections. (Drain recalls no objections, and said, "Everything was done decently and in accordance with Scripture.") "It stopped feeling like this larger-than-life divine institution ordained and led by God, and more like the sniping and sordid activity of men who wanted to be in control," Phelps-Roper said.

She resented the increasing authority wielded by Drain. One of the few Westboro members unrelated to Fred Phelps, Drain had visited Topeka in 2000 to film a skeptical documentary about the church, but he soon became convinced of its message. The next year, he and his family joined the church. He'd long pushed for a larger role in Westboro, and after the elders came to power his influence increased. In February 2012, during the funeral of Whitney Houston in New Jersey, Drain urged Phelps-Roper and other members to tweet poorly Photoshopped images that depicted them haranguing mourners. The media quickly unravelled the hoax. (Drain told me that the fake picket was never meant to be taken literally.)

Phelps-Roper was embarrassed by the debacle. It undermined her own proud claims on Twitter to be spreading God's truth—and lying violated Scripture. In addition, she now had to have all her media appearances approved by Drain. "It seems like he wants to be Pope Steve and for no one else to do anything without his permission," she wrote in her journal. "I hate it so much." 60

Megan's doubt engendered by the "Death Penalty for Fags" sign grew. She started to complain to her mother, saying that the elders were not obeying the Bible. They treated her mother and other members with cruelty when the Bible required brotherly love, she said. The elders acted arrogantly and tolerated no dissent, when God demanded meekness and humility. Phelps-Roper was struck by the similarities between her arguments and what C.G. and David Abitbol had always said about the church. "It was like we were finally doing to ourselves what we had done to everyone else," she said. "Seeing those parallels was really disorienting."

Drain disputed many of Phelps-Roper's characterizations of the changes in the church. He acknowledged that an all-male group of elders assumed preaching duties, but not that this led to a less open atmosphere in the church. "There's definitely more participation than when I first got here, in 2001, when you had one person doing all the sermons," he said, referring to Fred Phelps.

He also denied that women in the church had been significantly marginalized. "Women do a lot at Westboro now, as they always have," he said. Shirley's role was not reduced as a punishment for overstepping her bounds, he said. Instead, after the Snyder decision, other members had volunteered to help her deal with an overwhelming torrent of media. "We lifted her burden," he said. He pointed out that Shirley had recently spoken at a picket protesting Kim Davis, the Kentucky clerk who had refused to issue marriage licenses to gay couples—the church took issue with Davis's remarriages after divorce. (Through Drain, Megan's parents declined to comment.)

Phelps-Roper first considered leaving the church on July 4, 2012. She and Grace were in the basement of another Westboro family's house, painting the walls. The song "Just One," by the indie folk group Blind Pilot—a band that C.G. had recommended—played on the stereo. The lyrics seemed to reflect her dilemma perfectly: "And will I break and will I bow/if I cannot let it go?" Then came the chorus: "I can't believe we get just one." She suddenly thought, What if Westboro had been wrong about everything? What if she was spending her one life hurting people, picking fights with the entire world, for nothing? "It was, like, just the fact that I thought about it, I had to leave right then," she said. "I felt like I was going to jump out of my skin."

The next day, she mentioned the possibility of leaving to Grace. Grace was horrified. "It just sounded ridiculous to even suggest it," Grace told me. "These were the points I brought up: we're never going to see our families again, we're going to go to 65

Hell for eternity, and our life will be meaningless." Megan, still uncertain, agreed. But she plunged into a profound crisis of faith. "It was like flipping a switch," she said. "So many other thoughts came in that I'd never pursued, and that's every doubt that I'd ever had, everything that had ever seemed illogical or off."

When they were together, Megan engaged Grace in interminable theological conversations. When they were apart, Megan detailed her doubts in text messages. One day, she texted Grace, "What if the God of the Bible isn't the God of creation? We don't believe that the Koran has the truth about God. Is it just because we were told forever that this is How Things Are?" She added, "Does it really make you happy when you hear about people dying or starving or being maimed? Do you really want to ask God to hurt people? I ask myself these questions. I think the answer is no. When I'm not scared of the answer, I know the answer is no." Two days later, she texted Grace about Hell: "Why do we think it's real? It's starting to seem made up to scare people into doing what they say." Grace replied, "But what if?"

That day, Grace wrote to Megan, "Our belief in God has always curbed everything. Like, pain & sorrow, I mean. Without that we'd only have our belief in each other. But we are human & humans die. What would we have if we didn't have each other?" For Megan, the answer could be found in other people. "We know what it is to be kind & good to people," she wrote. "We would just have to find somewhere else, other people to love and care about and help, too." Grace wrote back, "I don't want other people." In truth, Megan didn't want other people, either; she desperately wanted things in Westboro to go back to the way they had been. But the idea of living among outsiders was no longer unimaginable.

Phelps-Roper spent the summer and the fall in an existential spiral. She would conclude that everything about Westboro's doctrine was wrong, only to be seized with terror that these thoughts were a test from God, and she was failing. "You literally feel insane," she said. Eventually, her doubts won out. "I just couldn't keep up the charade," she said. "I couldn't bring myself to do the things we were doing and say the things we were saying."

She largely stopped tweeting and tried to avoid journalists on the picket line, for fear that she might say something that revealed her misgivings. At one protest, a journalism student cornered her and asked if she ever got tired of picketing. "I honestly replied no," she wrote in her journal. "It's not about being tired, it's about not believing in it anymore. If I believed it, I could do it forever." In October, Megan finally persuaded Grace to leave. At the end of October, the sisters started secretly moving their possessions to the house of one of their high-school teachers, who agreed to help them. Many of Megan and Grace's young relatives who left the church had slipped away quietly, in order to avoid confronting their families. But the sisters wanted to explain to their parents the reasons behind their decision.

70

As the sisters agonized over whether to leave, they befriended an older man in the church and his wife, eventually becoming allies in discontent. For a while, they all planned to leave together. Then the couple's marriage began to deteriorate, and the husband told Megan and Grace that they were going to divorce. Grace became involved in a brief romantic relationship with the man. After the relationship ended, the wife learned about it, and sent a letter to Megan and Grace's parents revealing both the relationship and the sisters' plan to leave.

On Sunday, November 11th, the family had just returned from church when Megan and Grace were called into their parents' bedroom, where their father began to read the letter out loud. Megan told Grace quietly that they had to leave: "It was like the world was exploding and I didn't want to be around to see it." Their mother tried to calm things down. Their parents wanted to talk things over—they seemed to think that the sisters could be persuaded to stay—but Megan and Grace had made up their minds. As Grace packed, their father came into her room and asked what she wanted the church to do differently. "I want you and everyone else to leave with me," Grace replied. Their parents were stunned, but they didn't try to force the sisters to stay.

As the sisters packed, their younger brother Zach sat at the piano downstairs, crying and playing hymns, which he hoped might change their mind. Other church members stopped by to say goodbye and to warn the sisters of the consequences of their decision. "The fact that I'm coming face to face with the damage that I was doing to them was even worse than anything else that was happening to me," Phelps-Roper said. Her parents told her to say goodbye to her grandfather. She walked over to the residence where her grandparents lived, above the church sanctuary. When Megan told them she was leaving, her grandfather looked at her grandmother and said, "Well, I thought we had a jewel this time."

Megan and Grace's father drove them to a hotel in Topeka, where he had paid for a room, but they were too scared to spend the night alone, so they called the teacher who had agreed to store their boxes. That night, they cried themselves to sleep on couches in his basement. Megan and Grace returned to their house the next day with a U-Haul truck to pick up their remaining possessions. As they walked away for the last time, Shirley called after them, "You know you can always come back."

For the next few months, the sisters drifted. They lived in Lawrence for a month with their cousin Libby, who had also left the church, while Grace finished the first semester of her sophomore year at Washburn. They travelled to Deadwood, South Dakota, because Megan wanted to see the Black Hills. As she drove there, she kept imagining her car careering off the highway—she was so afraid of God's wrath. "We were a mess, crying all the time," she said. Phelps-Roper was tempted to hide in the Black Hills forever, but soon decided that, after spending so many years as the public face of Westboro, she wanted to go public with how she'd left the church, and to start making amends for the hurt she had caused. In February 2013, she wrote a statement on the blogging platform Medium. "Until now, our names have been synonymous with 'God Hates Fags,'" she wrote. "What we can do is try to find a better way to live from here on." She posted a link to the statement on Twitter. It was her first tweet in three months. "Hi," she wrote. Tweets of encouragement and praise poured in. "I expected a lot more people to be unforgiving," she said.

When David Abitbol learned that the sisters had left Westboro, he invited them 75 to speak at the next Jewlicious festival in Long Beach. They agreed, hoping that the experience might help them to find their way, and to finally understand a community that they had vilified for so long. "It was like we were just reaching out and grabbing on to whatever was around," Megan said. Abitbol said, "People, before they met them, were, like, 'So, now they're not batshit-crazy gay haters and we're supposed to love them? Fuck that.'" He added, "And then they heard them speak, and there wasn't a dry eye in the house." The sisters befriended their hosts, an Orthodox rabbi and his family.

They went kosher-grocery shopping together, and Megan and Grace looked after the kids. Grace became especially close with the family, and ended up staying for more than a month. "They were amazing and super-kind," Phelps-Roper said. Abitbol joked about the dramatic role reversal: "'Your Rabbi Is a Whore'? Your rabbi is a *host*."

Megan tried to put herself in situations that challenged the intolerance she had been indoctrinated with. One evening, after speaking at a Jewish festival in Montreal, she and Grace passed a group of drag queens on the sidewalk outside a cabaret. She felt a surge of disgust, but when Grace asked if they could watch the show she agreed. "It felt illicit," she said. "Like, oh, my gosh, I can't believe I'm here." She and Grace ended up dancing onstage during the intermission. Wherever Megan and Grace went, they met people who wanted to help them, despite all the hurt they had caused. The experience solidified Megan's increasing conviction that no person or group could claim a monopoly on moral truth. Slowly, her fears about God's judgment—the first terrifying understanding of her faith as a child, and its most stubborn remnant—faded. "As undeniable as they had seemed before, they seemed just as impossible now," she said.

One Sunday last February, I went with Megan and Grace to visit their old neighborhood. We parked a few blocks from the church and walked down a quiet street lined with ranch-style homes. It was sunny and warm for a winter day in Kansas. Phelps-Roper wore a green polka-dot dress and high leather boots, and her long curly hair—she still hadn't cut it since leaving the church—fell down her back. Now twenty-nine, she lives in a small town in South Dakota, where she works at a title company. Six months after she left the church, she went on a date with C.G. They met in Omaha, in driving distance for both of them, and saw *The Great Gatsby*, the Baz Luhrmann movie. "It's hard to even describe how weird it was," she told me. It was her first date ever, and it was with someone who had become a symbol of the unattainable. "I was quite a bit like a teenager. He put his arm around my waist at one point, and I just stood up so straight." She and C.G. connected as strongly in person as they had online, and they now live together.

When we reached the Block, we walked along the privacy fence. In front of each house where Westboro members live, Megan pointed out colorful numbers on the curb; Grace had helped paint them when she was a teenager. We passed the Phelps-Roper house and came to an intersection. A group of men and boys came toward us. "I can't tell yet, but it sure looks like a group of brothers and cousins," Megan said. First came five of their young cousins, followed by two of their brothers, Sam and Noah. Steve Drain, a large bearded man, trailed behind. They carried tools. Megan later explained that they had probably just come from doing repairs on a Westboro member's house. The group passed us without stopping. Grace called out, "Hi!" Sam nodded and gave a terse smile and a small wave. "Hi, how are you?" he said. Sam and Noah had recently had birthdays, and Megan wished them a belated happy birthday. The sisters said nothing to Drain. The crew quickly disappeared into a house.

We reached the church, an unremarkable white and brown mock-Tudor building on the northeast corner of the Block. A banner advertised a Westboro website, godhatesamerica.com. Two American flags—one of them rainbow colored—flew upside down from a pole. The church sign read "ST. VALENTINE IS A CATHOLIC IDOL AND AN EXCUSE TO FORNICATE! JUDE 7."

Directly across the street stood a house painted in bright, horizontal rainbow stripes. The house had been bought, in 2012, by Planting Peace, a nonprofit group whose mission, according to its website, is "spreading peace in a hurting world." The Equality House, as it's known, is home to a group of young LGBT activists. Planting Peace has worked with former Westboro members to spread its message of tolerance. Megan first visited the house in 2013, after her cousin Libby encouraged her to visit. She sneaked in the back door, for fear of being spotted by her family. 80

Today, Megan and Grace's only connection to Westboro is virtual. Although Phelps-Roper no longer believes that the Bible is the word of God, she still reads it to try to find scriptural arguments that could encourage Westboro to take a more humane approach to the world. Sometimes she'll tweet passages, knowing that church members will see them. After they left the church, Megan and Grace were blocked from Westboro's Twitter accounts, but they created a secret account to follow them. Sometimes, when her mother appears in a video, Megan will loop it over and over, just to hear her voice.

Fred Phelps died in March 2014, at the age of eighty-four. Former members of the church told me that Fred had had a softening of heart at the end of his life and had been excommunicated. (The church denies these claims.) Zach Phelps-Roper, Megan's younger brother, who left the church later that year, said that one of the precipitating events in Fred's exclusion had been expressing kindness toward the Equality House. At a church meeting, Zach recalls, members discussed the episode: "He stepped out the front door of the church and looked at the Rainbow House, the Planting Peace organization, and looked over and said, 'You're good people.'"

Questions for Critical Reading

1. On the surface this essay seems to be a narrative about the life of Megan Phelps-Roper. Assume, though, that Chen is also making an argument. Reread the essay looking for passages that reveal the larger argument that Chen is trying to make. Why might he tell this story in this way to make this argument?
2. Arguments are driven by ideas. As you reread the essay, highlight passages that use ideas. What are the prominent ideas in the piece?
3. What caused Phelps-Roper to change her belief system? Reread the essay and make a list of factors that prompted the change. Which of these seems to have had the biggest role in her transformation? Why do you think that is?

Exploring Context

1. Phelps-Roper continues to tweet. Visit her account at twitter.com/meganphelps. How do her current tweets reflect the transformation Chen documents?
2. Chen also wrote several pieces for *Wired*. Review these essays at wired.com/author/adrian-chen. How does this essay reflect the larger themes of Chen's work?
3. Phelps-Roper has a TED talk about her experience growing up. View it at ted.com. How does this talk reflect the answers you developed for the Questions for Critical Reading?

Questions for Connecting

1. In "The Empathy Diaries" (p. 378) Sherry Turkle suggests that technologies such as Twitter have initiated a flight from meaningful conversation. Use Chen's essay to examine Turkle's ideas. How does Phelps-Roper's experience complicate Turkle's argument? You might want to draw from your work in Questions for Critical Reading as you make your response.

2. Kwame Anthony Appiah's "Making Conversation" and "The Primacy of Practice" (p. 35) focus on the necessity of learning how to get along in a diverse and connected world as well as the complicated relationship between what we do and the values we hold. Apply Appiah's ideas to Chen's essay. How does Chen's text reflect cosmopolitanism? Does the change in Phelps-Roper's values illustrate the mechanisms that Appiah discusses?

3. In "Small Change" (p. 191), Malcolm Gladwell questions the effectiveness of social media in creating change, specifically calling out Twitter. How does Chen's text complicate Gladwell's argument? What factors are necessary for social media to produce change? Were the strong ties that Phelps-Roper ended up forming on Twitter make a critical difference? How can the weak ties of social media be used to generate strong ties?

Language Matters

1. How would you "grade" Chen's essay? In small groups, develop a set of grading criteria and then apply those criteria to Chen's text. What does your group value in writing? What does this class value in writing? How would a different audience, purpose, or context change the criteria and Chen's grade?

2. This article was originally published in a magazine. How does journalistic writing differ from academic writing? Locate one or more sentences from Chen that seem especially to reflect journalism. Rewrite these as academic sentences. What changes? Word choice? Sentence structure? Tone?

3. This essay was published in the *New Yorker* under two titles: "Unfollow" and "Conversion via Twitter." Which is more effective, and why? What role might titles play in your own writing?

Assignments for Writing

1. Write a paper about the power of conversation to create change. Which factors are critical in enabling conversations to change people or the world around them? You may want to use your work from Question 3 of Questions for Critical Reading and Question 3 of Exploring Context.

2. Write a paper in which you develop a strategy we might use to combat the spread of hate on social media. How can we mitigate hate speech while also protecting free speech? Use ideas from Chen's essay about Phelps-Roper's experience to support your argument.

3. In many ways, this essay is about the possibility for redemption. Write a paper in which you examine the factors necessary for redemption and forgiveness. Why were people willing to accept Phelps-Roper after she left Westboro?

TA-NEHISI COATES

American journalist and author **Ta-Nehisi Coates** is a national correspondent for the *Atlantic*, focusing on the intersection of race, culture, and politics. He has served as Martin Luther King, Jr. Visiting Professor for Writing at the Massachusetts Institute of Technology, City University of New York's Journalist-in-Residence, and a Distinguished Writer in Residence at New York University's Arthur L. Carter Journalism Institute. He is the author of several books, including *The Beautiful Struggle: A Father, Two Sons, and an Unlikely Road to Manhood*, a memoir published in 2008, and *Between the World and Me* (2015), from which this selection is taken. *We Were Eight Years in Power*, a collection of essays about the Obama era, was published in 2017. He is the recipient of a "Genius Grant" from the John D. and Catherine T. MacArthur Foundation and his work has won a National Book Award for Nonfiction, the National Magazine Award, the Hillman Prize for Opinion and Analysis Journalism, and the George Polk Award. He is also the writer for the Black Panther series for Marvel Comics.

Between the World and Me, a finalist for the 2016 Pulitzer Prize for General Nonfiction, is written as a letter from Coates to his teenaged son about his experiences being black in the United States, echoing the form of James Baldwin's *The Fire Next Time*. He manages to interlace his autobiographical account of his youth in Baltimore with insights about education and the schools, police and justice, embodiment and disembodiment, and the discipline and danger of the streets.

In the excerpt offered here, Coates considers the complex connections between the streets, the schools, black bodies, prisons, and religion. Though he feels his schooling fostered compliance and resisted his constant curiosity around why things were the way they were, and while religion offers him no solace either, he does find within his grandmother the means to investigate and interrogate the system within which he is embedded: writing.

How does your experience of education differ from Coates's? Where can you identify with his story?

- TAGS: *adolescence and adulthood, civil rights, education, law and justice, race and ethnicity, religion*
- CONNECTIONS: *Appiah, Cohen, Das, Fukuyama, Gilbert, Gladwell, Holmes, Ma, Yang, Yoshino*

From Between the World and Me

If the streets shackled my right leg, the schools shackled my left. Fail to comprehend the streets and you gave up your body now. But fail to comprehend the schools and you gave up your body later. I suffered at the hands of both, but I resent the schools more. There was nothing sanctified about the laws of the streets—the laws were amoral and practical. You rolled with a posse to the party as sure as you wore boots in the snow, or raised an umbrella in the rain. These were rules aimed at something obvious—the great danger that haunted every visit to Shake & Bake, every bus ride downtown. But the laws of the schools were aimed at something distant and vague. What did it mean to, as our elders told us, "grow up and be somebody"? And what precisely did this have to do with an education rendered as rote discipline? To be educated in my Baltimore mostly meant always packing an extra number 2 pencil and working quietly. Educated children walked in single file on the right side of the hallway, raised their hands to use the lavatory, and carried the lavatory pass when en route. Educated children never offered excuses—certainly not childhood itself. The world had no time for the childhoods of black boys and girls. How could the schools? Algebra, Biology, and English were not subjects so much as opportunities to better discipline the body, to practice writing between the lines, copying the directions legibly, memorizing theorems extracted from the world they were created to represent. All of it felt so distant to me. I remember sitting in my seventh-grade French class and not having any idea why I was there. I did not know any French people, and nothing around me suggested I ever would. France was a rock rotating in another galaxy, around another sun, in another sky that I would never cross. Why, precisely, was I sitting in this classroom?

The question was never answered. I was a curious boy, but the schools were not concerned with curiosity. They were concerned with compliance. I loved a few of my teachers. But I cannot say that I truly believed any of them. Some years after I'd left school, after I'd dropped out of college, I heard a few lines from Nas that struck me:

> Ecstasy, coke, you say it's love, it is poison
> Schools where I learn they should be burned, it is poison

That was exactly how I felt back then. I sensed the schools were hiding something, drugging us with false morality so that we would not see, so that we did not ask: Why—for us and only us—is the other side of free will and free spirits an assault upon our bodies? This is not a hyperbolic concern. When our elders presented school to us, they did not present it as a place of high learning but as a means of escape from death and penal warehousing. Fully 60 percent of all young black men who drop out of high school will go to jail. This should disgrace the country. But it does not, and while I couldn't crunch the numbers or plumb the history back then, I sensed that the fear that marked West Baltimore could not be explained by the schools. Schools did not reveal truths, they concealed them. Perhaps they must be burned away so that the heart of this thing might be known.

Fully 60 percent of all young black men who drop out of high school will go to jail. This should disgrace the country.

Unfit for the schools, and in good measure wanting to be unfit for them, and lacking the savvy I needed to master the streets, I felt there could be no escape for me or, honestly, anyone else. The fearless boys and girls who would knuckle up, call on cousins and crews, and, if it came to it, pull guns seemed to have mastered the streets. But their knowledge peaked at seventeen, when they ventured out of their parents' homes and discovered that America had guns and cousins, too. I saw their futures in the tired faces of mothers dragging themselves onto the 28 bus, swatting and cursing at three-year-olds; I saw their futures in the men out on the corner yelling obscenely at some young girl because she would not smile. Some of them stood outside liquor stores waiting on a few dollars for a bottle. We would hand them a twenty and tell them to keep the change. They would dash inside and return with

Red Bull, Mad Dog, or Cisco. Then we would walk to the house of someone whose mother worked nights, play "Fuck tha Police," and drink to our youth. We could not get out. The ground we walked was trip-wired. The air we breathed was toxic. The water stunted our growth. We could not get out.

A year after I watched the boy with the small eyes pull out a gun, my father beat me for letting another boy steal from me. Two years later, he beat me for threatening my ninth-grade teacher. Not being violent enough could cost me my body. Being too violent could cost me my body. We could not get out. I was a capable boy, intelligent, well-liked, but powerfully afraid. And I felt, vaguely, wordlessly, that for a child to be marked off for such a life, to be forced to live in fear was a great injustice. And what was the source of this fear? What was hiding behind the smoke screen of streets and schools? And what did it mean that number 2 pencils, conjugations without context, Pythagorean theorems, handshakes, and head nods were the difference between life and death, were the curtains drawing down between the world and me?

I could not retreat, as did so many, into the church and its mysteries. My parents rejected all dogmas. We spurned the holidays marketed by the people who wanted to be white. We would not stand for their anthems. We would not kneel before their God. And so I had no sense that any just God was on my side. "The meek shall inherit the earth" meant nothing to me. The meek were battered in West Baltimore, stomped out at Walbrook Junction, bashed up on Park Heights, and raped in the showers of the city jail. My understanding of the universe was physical, and its moral arc bent toward chaos then concluded in a box. That was the message of the small-eyed boy, untucking the piece—a child bearing the power to body and banish other children to memory. Fear ruled everything around me, and I knew, as all black people do, that this fear was connected to the Dream out there, to the unworried boys, to pie and pot roast, to the white fences and green lawns nightly beamed into our television sets.

But how? Religion could not tell me. The schools could not tell me. The streets could not help me see beyond the scramble of each day. And I was such a curious boy. I was raised that way. Your grandmother taught me to read when I was only four. She also taught me to write, by which I mean not simply organizing a set of sentences into a series of paragraphs, but organizing them as a means of investigation. When I was in trouble at school (which was quite often) she would make me write about it. The writing had to answer a series of questions: Why did I feel the need to talk at the same time as my teacher? Why did I not believe that my teacher was entitled to respect? How would I want someone to behave while I was talking? What would I do the next time I felt the urge to talk to my friends during a lesson? I have given you these same assignments. I gave them to you not because I thought they would curb your behavior—they certainly did not curb mine—but because these were the earliest acts of interrogation, of drawing myself into consciousness. Your grandmother was not teaching me how to behave in class. She was teaching me how to ruthlessly interrogate the subject that elicited the most sympathy and rationalizing—myself. Here was the lesson: I was not an innocent. My impulses were not filled with unfailing virtue. And feeling that I was as human as anyone, this must be true for other humans. If I was not innocent, then they were not innocent. Could this mix of motivation also affect the stories they tell? The cities they built? The country they claimed as given to them by God?

Questions for Critical Reading

1. What is the relationship between education and success? As you reread Coates's essay, look for places where he talks about the goals of education and the consequences of failing (or even succeeding) in school. How are these inflected by race and class?
2. The whole of Coates's book, from which this is excerpt is taken, is framed as a letter to his son. As you review the essay, consider the impact that form has on content. In what ways does this essay reflect the form of a letter? In what ways is it clear he has a larger audience in mind? How do form and audience interact?
3. What solution was Coates able to find for the problem of education? Consider the role that critical thinking played and locate passages that suggest his definition of critical thinking. In what ways is his solution related to the work you do in this class?

Exploring Context

1. Dena Simmons has a TED talk titled "How Students of Color Confront Imposter Syndrome" that touches on many of the same issues as Coates's essay. View it at ted .com. How does her experience connect to Coates's? How are their paths to success similar? What accounts for their differences? Connect this to your work in Question 1 of Questions for Critical Reading.
2. Explore the website for Baltimore Public Schools at baltimorecityschools.org. How does the site's vision for education relate to Coates's experience of education? Have things changes since Coates went to school? Consider working with your response to Question 3 of Questions for Critical Reading.
3. Visit Coates's website at ta-nehisicoates.com. How does this essay reflect his larger body of work? What consistent themes can you locate in his writing?

Questions for Connecting

1. In "Variety Show" (p. 217), Anna Holmes looks at the challenge of promoting diversity in business and culture. Extend her argument using Coates's experiences. What additional challenges do we face in moving toward a more inclusive culture?
2. Wesley Yang describes a very different educational experience in "Paper Tigers" (p. 435). What makes the education of Asian Americans so different from the experience of Coates? What makes education successful in ethnically and racially diverse environments? What role does socioeconomic class play? Incorporate your work from Questions 1 and 3 of Questions for Critical Reading and Questions 1 and 2 of Exploring Context.
3. Yo-Yo Ma offers a very different vision of education in "Necessary Edges: Arts, Empathy, and Education" (p. 278). Synthesize his goals for education with Coates's lived experience. Does Ma make assumptions about race and class when thinking about education? Does Coates experience through his grandmother the kind of education Ma imagines?

Language Matters

1. Education is closely related to class boundaries. What class boundaries exist in writing? Is slang an issue of class? Can you determine Coates's class from his writing? What class is reflected in academic writing? What role does education play in forming class?
2. Ellipses and brackets are useful punctuation marks when using quotations. Select a long passage from Coates's essay that represents an important part of his essay. How would you use these punctuation marks to incorporate the quotation into your own writing? How might they be instead used, even unintentionally, to misrepresent the meaning of the quotation? How can you be sure you're using these punctuation marks correctly?
3. What is a hyphen? How is it used? Select a passage of this essay and revise it by adding hyphens. When would you use them in your own writing?

Assignments for Writing

1. **Multimodal.** A poster presentation is an academic genre used in many disciplines in which researchers summarize their findings on a poster board, using key data and images. Determine the risks and rewards of education and then make a poster presentation of your findings. Is the goal of education only conformity and discipline? What makes a successful education? You may find your work in Questions 1 and 3 of Questions for Critical Reading, Questions 1 and 2 of Exploring Context, and Questions 2 and 3 of Questions for Connecting a good start in forming your argument.
2. How do we address the problem of race? Write a paper in which you propose strategies for mitigating the impact of race and promoting diversity in the United States. What role does education play in creating diversity? What must we do to overcome racism? You may find your work in Questions 1 and 3 of Questions for Critical Reading, Questions 1 and 2 of Exploring Context, and Questions 1 and 2 of Questions for Connecting a good start in forming your argument.
3. Write a paper about the impact of class on success. Your work in Question 1 of Language Matters and Question 3 of Questions for Connecting might offer a good start. Does class determine education or is education a crucial mechanism for overcoming the limitations of class?

ANDREW COHEN

Andrew Cohen, who holds a JD from Boston University, is a legal analyst for *60 Minutes* and CBS Radio News, a contributing editor for the *Atlantic* on legal affairs, a fellow at the Brennan Center for Justice, and an editor at the Marshall Project. He is the recipient of a Murrow Award, the American Bar Association's Silver Gavel Award (2012), and the Writers' Guild Award for Outstanding Commentary (2012). His work has also appeared in the *Washington Post*, the *Los Angeles Times*, *USA Today*, the *New York Times*, the *Chronicle of Higher Education*, the *National Law Journal*, *US News and World Report*, the *Chicago Tribune*, *Newsweek*, *Time*, and *People*.

"Race and the Opioid Epidemic" was first published in 2015 through the Marshall Project, a nonprofit news organization that reports on the U.S. criminal justice system and named after Thurgood Marshall, the first African American justice of the U.S. Supreme Court. Other stories published around the same time through the Marshall Project concern the death penalty and the use of body cameras on police officers.

In this essay Cohen explores the racial dimensions of the opioid epidemic raging in the United States. Current policies are trending toward treatment and harm reduction for offenders but Cohen contrasts this response to the disproportionate criminal laws of earlier drug epidemics. The victims of those earlier epidemics, centered on crack cocaine and heroin, were seen as primarily black and disenfranchised rather than the white and often affluent users of the current crisis. Sentencing was harsh and Cohen asks us to consider the possibility that race has determined the different reactions to these crises.

How persistent is the racial divide in the United States? Is it possible that the current reaction to opioid addiction is determined by race rather than a more developed medical understanding of the disease of addiction?

- TAGS: *ethics, health and medicine, law and justice, politics, race and ethnicity*
- CONNECTIONS: *Appiah, Coates, Das, Fukuyama, Holmes, Lukianoff and Haidt, Yang, Yoshino*

Race and the Opioid Epidemic

Heroin use and abuse in America has dramatically increased over the past decade. Between 2006 and 2013, federal records reveal, the number of first-time heroin users doubled, from 90,000 to 169,000. Some of those users, no doubt, already are gone. The Centers for Disease Control announced last month that the rate of deadly heroin overdoses nearly quadrupled between 2002 and 2013.

These troubling figures, and a spate of more recent stories and daunting statistics, have prompted officials across the country to implement bold new policies and practices designed to reduce the harm of heroin use. Although there has been some push to enhance criminal sanctions to combat the heroin surge, much of the institutional reaction to the renewed popularity of the drug has sounded in the realm of medicine, not law.

One public official after another, in states both "red" and "blue," has pressed in recent years to treat increased heroin use as a public-safety problem as opposed to a criminal-justice matter best left to police, prosecutors, and judges. This is good news. But it forms a vivid contrast with the harsh reaction a generation ago to the sudden rise in the use of crack cocaine, and from the harsh reaction two generations ago to an earlier heroin epidemic.

What accounts for the differences? Clearly policymakers know more today than they did then about the societal costs of waging a war on drugs, and dispatching low-level, nonviolent drug offenders to prison for decades. The contemporary criminal-justice system places more emphasis on treatment and reform than it did, say, during the Reagan years or when New York's draconian "Rockefeller laws" were passed in the 1970s. But there may be another explanation for the less hysterical reaction, one that few policymakers have been willing to acknowledge: race.

5 Some experts and researchers see in the different responses to these drug epidemics further proof of America's racial divide. Are policymakers going easier today on heroin users (white and often affluent) than their elected predecessors did a generation ago when confronted with crack addicts who were largely black, disenfranchised, and economically bereft? Can we explain the disparate response to the "black" heroin epidemic of the 1960s, in which its use and violent crime were commingled in the public consciousness, and the white heroin "epidemic" today, in which its use is considered a disease to be treated or cured, without using race as part of our explanation?

Marc Mauer, the executive director of the Sentencing Project, a group that targets racial disparities in the criminal-justice system, has been following this issue closely for decades. He agrees there is strong historical precedent for comparing the crises through the prism of race:

> The response to the rise in heroin use follows patterns we've seen over decades of drug scares. When the perception of the user population is primarily people of color, then the response is to demonize and punish. When it's white, then we search for answers. Think of the difference between marijuana attitudes in the "reefer madness" days of the 1930s when the drug was perceived to be used in the "racy" parts of town, and then the 1960s (white) college town explosion in use.

It is now axiomatic that although the crack epidemic of the 1980s devastated communities of color, the legal and political responses to the crisis compounded the tragedy. Crack was an inner-city drug, a street-corner drug, a drug of gangs and guns that white America largely experienced from a distance. Powder cocaine, the more expensive version of the drug, found its way to more affluent users. The federal Anti-Drug Abuse Act, passed in 1986, imposed mandatory-minimum sentences that were far harsher on users of crack cocaine than on those found with the drug in powdered form. The Fair Sentencing Act of 2010 reduced that disparity in sentencing from 100:1 to 18:1, but that remains a striking gap.

The federal Anti-Drug Abuse Act, passed in 1986, imposed mandatory-minimum sentences that were far harsher on users of crack cocaine than on those found with the drug in powdered form.

Indeed, the harsh, punitive reaction to the crack era was the result of mythology about its use, and its users, that later turned out to be false, says Jeffrey Fagan, a Columbia University professor who has long studied the intersection of criminal justice and race. "It was instantly addictive, it created 'superpredators,' you became a sexual deviant, especially if you were a woman, it destroyed maternal instincts," he said. All of that nonsense led to the draconian sentencing laws associated with crack use in the 1980s, Fagan told me.

And that, Fagan says, was the sequel to another criminal-justice crackdown that had taken place decades earlier. A surge in heroin use among blacks in the 1960s was blamed for a rise in violent crime, and provoked a harsh response.

By contrast to those earlier drug crises, the heroin epidemic of the 21st century is largely a white person's scourge. The Centers for Disease Control says the cheap, easily accessible drug is attracting affluent suburbanites and women. Nearly 90 percent of the people who tried heroin for the first time in the past decade are white, according to a study published in JAMA Psychiatry in July 2014, and there is no reason to believe the trend has eased since then. Said the researchers: 10

> Heroin use has changed from an inner-city, minority-centered problem to one that has a more widespread geographical distribution, involving primarily white men and women in their late twenties living outside of large urban areas.

The cause for *this* may be simple. White people addicted to prescription opiates, the sorts of drugs they could conveniently get from a friendly doctor or pharmacist, are finding heroin an obvious (and cheap) substitute now that law-enforcement officials have cracked down on those opiates. The hottest fronts in this war now can be seen in rural states like Vermont and in suburban areas that largely missed the ravages of the crack craze.

And politicians on both sides of the aisle clearly are paying attention to what researchers diplomatically call the "changing face of heroin use." According to the Pew Charitable Trusts, lawmakers in at least twenty-four states and the District of Columbia have enacted laws in the past few years that make naloxone, a prescription drug that helps counter the effect of a heroin overdose, more broadly available. Just three weeks ago, Ohio Governor John Kasich, a Republican presidential candidate, signed emergency legislation to make naxolone available without a prescription.

His neighbor in Kentucky, Senator Rand Paul, another Republican running for the presidency, introduced the Recovery Enhancement for Addiction Treatment Act earlier this year. It would make it easier for doctors to treat heroin users with a drug called buprenorphine. Nearly two dozen states also have passed laws that protect "good Samaritans" who alert doctors or nurses to heroin overdoses.

Such public-health responses were not necessarily unthinkable during the crack-cocaine wave of the 1980s or the heroin epidemic of the 1960s. But the limited public-health measures adopted during those eras were overshadowed by more punitive responses to those crises. Can you imagine the Congress and the White House of 1985 debating a "Recovery Enhancement for Addiction Act" for crack users? Mauer remembers instead the brutal mandatory-sentencing laws of that era sweeping toward passage in Congress in near-record time. What accounts for the difference? "I don't think that's only because we are more thoughtful today," Mauer says.

Questions for Critical Reading

1. What evidence does Cohen provide for his argument? As you reread his essay, take note of passages where he offers support for the idea that there is a racial dimension to the different responses to drug epidemics.

2. What counterarguments might you propose in response to Cohen's essay? Looking back through his text, note places where he anticipates alternative arguments. Does he attempt to account for your counterargument? How persuasive is he in supporting his own argument?

3. What audience do you think Cohen imagined when he was writing this essay? Reread his text and locate passages that indicate this audience. What might he change in his style or use of evidence if he had intended a different audience?

Exploring Context

1. The U.S. Department of Health and Human Services maintains a website about the current opioid epidemic at hhs.gov/opioids. Explore this website with Cohen's argument in mind. Is there any evidence to support a racial component to the epidemic or the government's response to it?

2. Cohen quotes Marc Mauer of the Sentencing Project. Explore the organization's website at sentencingproject.org. What additional evidence for Cohen's argument can you find there?

3. Cohen references a report from the government's Substance Abuse and Mental Health Services Administration. Visit the agency's website at samhsa.gov. What other substance abuse and mental health issues are highlighted by the agency? How does viewing opioid abuse in a larger context shift your understanding of Cohen's argument? Consider using this site to support the counterarguments you proposed in Question 2 of Questions for Critical Reading.

Questions for Connecting

1. **Multimodal.** Ta-Nehisi Coates, in "From *Between the World and Me*" (p. 92), offers his experience of race and its relation to education. Synthesize the arguments of Cohen and Coates in order to determine how pervasive race is in America. Make a poster presentation of your findings. A poster presentation is an academic genre used in many disciplines in which researchers summarize their findings on a poster board, using key data and images. Consider carefully which textual and visual images you will use given the spatial limitations of a poster board. You may also want to use your work from Questions 1 and 2 of Exploring Context.

2. What role should human dignity play in criminal justice? Use Francis Fukuyama's ideas in "Human Dignity" (p. 137) to assess the different legal approaches to addressing drug epidemics. Which is more just when seen through this framework? And if race has played a role, then what does that say about Factor X in relation to race?

3. Kenji Yoshino examines the future of civil rights in "Preface" and "The New Civil Rights" (p. 452). Could his ideas offer a solution to the racialization of drug epidemics? How might we reframe these crimes through Yoshino's model of civil rights?

Language Matters

1. Each discipline has a specific approach to evidence. Use the web to learn how research is done in your intended major or field. How would you pursue Cohen's arguments through that field? How would that discipline make this argument? Would the field demand a particular kind of evidence such as an experiment or a quantitative analysis? Why do different fields have different approaches to research and evidence?
2. In academic writing, it's vital to state a clear, central argument so that the reader can follow that argument as it's proven with evidence in the paper. Find a quotation that you believe is a clear statement of Cohen's argument. Where is it located in the essay? Why does he place it there? Where should you place your argument in your papers for this class?
3. Cohen's essay is relatively short. Outline the essay to trace the argument. How does Cohen manage to make an argument in so little space? What key moves are necessary to make an argument in a short essay? How can you apply these techniques in your own writing?

Assignments for Writing

1. Write a paper in which you propose and support a counterargument to Cohen's suggestion that race is a significant factor in differing approaches to drug epidemics. You may want to start with your work in Question 2 of Questions for Critical Reading as well as any supporting evidence you located in your responses to Exploring Context.
2. What is the best approach to the current opioid epidemic? Write a paper in which you propose a set of governing ideas to inform our policies in response to this epidemic. How might your strategies be reflected in the criminal justice system? You might find support for your argument in the work you did in Exploring Context.
3. Has the impact of race changed in the United States since the much earlier heroin epidemic? Write a paper in which you consider the role of race in this country, with a focus on political and sociocultural issues.

KAVITA DAS

Kavita Das, who holds a B.A. in growth and structure of cities from Bryn Mawr and an M.B.A. from the University of North Carolina, began her career working for the social change sector on issues including homelessness, public health disparity, and racial justice. Many of these same issues are reflected in her writing, which often centers on the intersections of culture, race, feminism, and social justice. Her work has been published in the *Rumpus*, the *Atlantic, VIDA, McSweeney's*, the *Margins, Quartz, Colorlines*, and elsewhere and has been nominated for a Pushcart Prize (2016). Das has been named to the Disquiet Literary Fiction longlist (2016), and was named a finalist for the New Delta Review Ryan R. Gibbs Award for Flash Fiction (2015). She's currently working on a biography about Lakshmi Shankar, a Grammy-nominated Hindustani singer who played a critical role in bringing Indian music to the West.

"(Un)American, (Un)Cool" first appeared in *The Margins*, an online magazine published by the Asian American Writers Workshop, a national not-for-profit arts organization offering several curated platforms for the publication and dissemination of writing by Asian Americans, broadly conceived. Other pieces published around the same time included a roundup of links to web pages about antiblack racism, Asian Americans, and complicity in the wake of the violent Ferguson riots; an interview with spoken poetry duo DarkMatter; and a review of Shyam Selvadurai's novel *The Ghosts They Carried*.

In this essay, Das consider the implications of the absence of Asian Americans in a National Portrait Gallery exhibit focused on the uniquely American concept of "cool." Das looks at the black historical roots of this concept before noting the overwhelmingly white subject matter of the exhibit. Specifically, Asian Americans, Das notes, are severely underrepresented, with only two photographic portraits of the one hundred on display. This absence, she contends, results from a two-pronged issue: Asian Americans are too often seen as neither American nor cool.

- TAGS: *art, community, culture, identity, photography and video, race and ethnicity*
- CONNECTIONS: *Chabon, Coates, Cohen, DeGhett, Fukuyama, Holmes, Lukianoff and Haidt, Provan, Southan, van Houtryve, Watters, Yang, Yoshino*

(Un)American, (Un)Cool

A purplish-blue neon lighted sign that looks more at home in the window of a blues bar than on the walls of the National Portrait Gallery in Washington, D.C., spells out the title of the gallery's current exhibit: *American Cool*. Just beyond the sign, visitors are confronted with one of the exhibit's central questions: "What do we mean when we say someone is cool?"

It's a question that has eluded teenagers and Hollywood producers alike through the years, but according to the exhibit's introductory text, "to be cool means to exude the aura of something new and uncontainable." The curators go further:

> Cool is the opposite of innocence or virtue. Someone cool has a charismatic edge and a dark side. Cool is an earned form of individuality. Each generation

has certain individuals who bring innovation and style to a field of endeavor while projecting a certain charismatic self-possession. They are the figures selected for this exhibition: the successful rebels of American culture.

The origin and concept of *cool*, the exhibit contends, is uniquely American—the term is credited to Lester Young, a 1940s African American jazz saxophonist who coined the term to refer in part to the unflappable attitude he and his fellow African American jazz musicians adopted in the face of Jim Crow-era racism and segregation in the U.S. Young also pioneered the use of the term to express appreciation and enjoyment for the work of other jazz musicians. Over the years, *cool* evolved into a term capturing an intangible quality, one that marries rebelliousness with a laid back self-confidence.

Combining photographic portraiture, history, and biography, the exhibition sets out to both define and document the embodiment of *cool* in the U.S. from the 1940s to present day. Photographic portraits of one hundred individuals selected by curators line the walls of the gallery and are included in an accompanying catalogue bearing the same title. The portraits are stunning and artfully composed; most of them are black-and-white. And as we might expect, many of the featured individuals are instantly recognizable through these iconic images. There's James Dean, Billie Holliday, Marilyn Monroe, Mohammed Ali, Clint Eastwood, Jimi Hendrix, Madonna, Jay Z, Johnny Cash, Bruce Lee, Patti Smith, Andy Warhol, John Travolta, Carlos Santana, and Miles Davis, just to name a few.

5

Some portraits truly capture their subjects at work, especially when it came to musicians. In photographer Roger Marshutz's 1956 portrait of Elvis, the King of Rock and Roll oozes charm while performing live, tilting the mic and reaching for the outstretched hands of his adoring fans. In contrast, Lance Mercer's 1993 portrait of a performing Neil Young depicts him head down, meditatively lost in the riffs of his guitar. Other portraits captured the essence of their very different subjects. Bombshell actress and personality Mae West sits ensconced in furs, cigarette lit, holding court with several men in tuxes whose faces are out of frame, while civil rights and prison abolition activist Angela Davis stands powerfully poised at a mic, likely at a political rally, mouth open and eyes blazing, radiating resistance against oppression.

But beyond the predictable figureheads of this exhibit, the curators provide the following explanation for how they chose all one hundred individuals whose photographic portraits are featured:

> Each cool figure was considered with the following historical rubric in mind and possesses at least three elements of this singular American self-concept:
>
> 1. an original artistic vision carried off with a signature style
> 2. cultural rebellion or transgression for a given generation
> 3. iconic power or instant visual recognition
> 4. a recognized cultural legacy

Alongside easily recognizable figures with iconic power were portraits of individuals I knew little about, such as jazz singer Anita O'Day, drummer Gene Krupa, jazz pianist Willie "The Lion" Smith, surfing pioneer Duke Paoa Kahanamoku, and boxer Jack Johnson. Short biographies accompany each portrait and provide an argument for why each of these cool cats embodies the concept of *American Cool.* It is through these biographies that I got to know new icons and discovered new aspects of familiar figures.

Given that the term *cool* was coined by African American artists and has deep significance to African American history and identity, it is not surprising that thirty African Americans are featured in the exhibit, ranging from Lester Young, who pioneered the term, to Miles Davis and Jay Z. African American writer and activist Rebecca Walker has thought a lot about the historical relationship of coolness to black culture, and the ways in which that relationship has been diminished. In her recently published edited volume of essays, *Black Cool: One Thousand Streams of Blackness*, she and sixteen other writers try to answer the question, "What is Black Cool?" Walker writes: "If blackness is separated from this aesthetic of cool that comes out of our culture . . . we lose the understanding of how much we are actually giving to this world." Similarly, in his *New York* magazine article about the decoupling of cool from blackness, hip-hop artist Questlove writes, "Black is the gold standard for cool, and you don't need to look any further than the coolest thing of the last century, rock and roll, to see the ways in which white culture clearly sensed that the road to cool involved borrowing from black culture."

Sure enough, of the remaining seventy portraits in the *American Cool* exhibit, sixty-five feature White Americans. But what is surprising is that only three portraits of Hispanic Americans and just two portraits of Asian Americans were included. It gets worse. At the end of the exhibit, a wall of text acknowledges that it took considerable discussion and debate for the curators to whittle the exhibit down to just one hundred individuals. Because so many did not make the cut, they offer an *Alt-100* list of the next one hundred whom, although they didn't make it into the exhibit, they believe embody *American Cool.* There is no Asian American included in the *Alt-100* list. Therefore, out of 200 individuals offered up by curators as embodiments of *American Cool*, only two Asian Americans fit the bill.

10 Those two are actor and martial arts icon Bruce Lee and surfing pioneer Duke Paoa Kahanamoku. Lee and Kahanamoku have certainly left an imprint on American culture, but the exclusion of other iconic Asian Americans who embody American Cool is problematic. It is precisely the decades depicted during this exhibit that saw a dramatic rise in the Asian American population, particularly during the past 50 years. And over that half-century, Asian Americans have contributed to the fabric of American cultural life.

Put in the bluntest of terms, are Asian Americans perceived as UnAmerican or UnCool, or both?

So the question remains: How did Asian Americans end up largely excluded from a national exhibit about "American Cool"? Is there something inherent in the concept behind the exhibit or its definition of *American Cool* that left Asian Americans out? Or is the disconnect because of the application of these concepts to Asian Americans? Put in the bluntest of terms, are Asian Americans perceived as UnAmerican or UnCool, or both?

An important place to start is with the exhibit's name and central concept: *American Cool.* We can break the concept down to its two parts (*American* and *cool*) and see how each relates to Asian Americans. While the curators of the exhibition provide their definition of cool and talk about it as a singularly American self-concept, they do not define *American*. American, according to the curators, it seems, is not only self-evident but also universally recognized and accepted.

But we need look no further than last year's Miss America Pageant and this year's National Spelling Bee to see that Asian Americans are not universally accepted as American even when they win quintessentially American competitions. When Nina Davuluri was crowned Miss America in 2014, becoming the first Indian American woman to earn the title, amidst the celebrations on social media were comments such as, "Miss New York is an Indian. With all due respect, this is America." Similarly, just a few months ago when the final four competitors of the Scripps National Spelling Bee ended up being Indian American, Twitter was lit up with comments like, "Okay, an American isn't winning the spelling bee. 4 remaining." Even more recently, Florida Republican congressman Curt Clawson mistook two officials from the Obama administration for representatives from India.

When we revisit the curator's multi-pronged definition of *American Cool*, of particular significance is the definition's last line, which describes individuals who embody *American Cool* as "the successful rebels of American culture." The Merriam-Webster Dictionary defines a rebel as "a person who does not obey rules or normal standards of behavior, dress, etc." Therefore, one can interpret the curator's notion of "successful rebels" as those who not only flouted societal conventions and norms, but managed to make their own innovative vision, if not acceptable to all, then palatable to many. Meanwhile, Asian American communities have both benefited from and been hurt by the "model minority myth" and its very existence suggests that Asian Americans are viewed as predominantly "successful." According to the mythology of this stereotype, Asian Americans have achieved success by playing by the rules, by working hard, and by integrating and assimilating into American culture, not by resisting and pushing the boundaries of those norms.

Not only has the stereotype been used as a weapon against other communities of color, but it also clearly ignores the diversity of Asian American experiences, whether related to differences in social class, language, generation, history, gender, sexual orientation, disability, religion, or immigration status. Historically Asian Americans *have* rebelled against both the traditionally held values of American society and Asian American communities. Among them are Asian American civil rights leaders Yuri Kochiyama and Grace Lee Boggs. The underrepresentation of Asian Americans in the *American Cool* exhibit likely has less to do with the lack of iconic and transgressive Asian Americans who embody *American Cool* and more to do with the fact that the exhibit's definition of *American Cool* is at odds with pervasive stereotypes of Asian Americans. This underscores not only the persistence and impact of racial stereotypes but also the role that unconscious bias can play, even within cultural institutions. 15

Despite the fact that there are 18.2 million Asian Americans in the U.S. (roughly 6 percent of the population) and that Asians now account for the fastest growing immigrant group in the country, they only account for 1 percent of this exhibit. But the question here is less about proportionate representation and much more about the importance of having Asian Americans and Asian American history regarded as American. The National Portrait Gallery plays a key role in creating and documenting a national narrative on American history, contemporary culture, and national identity. To feature Asian Americans in a meaningful way would not only acknowledge the essential role they have played in American history but would also confirm that Asian Americans and Asian American identity are woven into American national identity.

Not far from the National Portrait Gallery's *American Cool* exhibit is the *Beyond Bollywood* exhibit at the Smithsonian Natural History Museum, which examines the history and impact of Indians in America. This landmark exhibition is significant because it is the first on a national scale to focus on Indians in America. But as important as it is to have dedicated exhibitions exploring the specific histories of regional Asian American communities, it is just as important that these communities be substantively included in exhibits about national identity, such as *American Cool*.

Using photographic portraiture, history, and biography, the National Portrait Gallery's *American Cool* exhibition is an attempt to nail down the singular concept of cool in the United States. However, the exhibit inadvertently demonstrates how *cool* can end up a tool of exclusion. Created by African American artists as a transgressive stance against racism and segregation, it has now been widely appropriated and narrowly interpreted by mainstream American culture. The concept can now be used, then, to perpetuate the cultural marginalization of Asian Americans.

The end of the exhibit states,

> American Cool is not the last word on cool but rather the first step toward a new national conversation on this singular American self-concept. Who's on your Cool list? Here are two questions to consider: 1) Did this person bring something entirely new into American culture? 2) Will this person's work or art stand the test of time and history?

So, given this invitation from the curators of American Cool, here are a just a few sorely missed Asian American icons of American Cool:

Ravi Shankar—The late, great sitarist Ravi Shankar is widely regarded as the leader of the movement that brought Indian music to America in the 1960s, and his influence was felt in American music and in world music, spurring George Harrison of the Beatles to dub Shankar "the Godfather of World Music." Although now celebrated as the greatest Indian musician of modern times and as a pioneer, at the time, Shankar faced criticism from some of his fellow Indian musicians for his efforts to collaborate with Western musicians. Most egregious is the fact that the strains of Ravi Shankar's sitar, which were heard at Woodstock and echoed throughout the American Counterculture movement, were left off the companion soundtrack to the *American Cool* exhibit.

George Takei—rose to fame for his role as Hikaru Sulu in the original beloved sci-fi television series *Star Trek*, making him one of the most visible Asian American actors of the twentieth century. But as a child, Takei and his family, along with thousands of other Japanese Americans were forced into internment camps. Takei has long used his platform as an actor to speak out about the treatment of Japanese Americans and Asian Americans and to advocate for LGBTQ rights.

Yuri Kochiyama—was a Japanese American activist and coalition-builder who fought for civil rights alongside African American activists. Kochiyama became a trusted friend of Malcolm X and was by his side when he was assassinated, a haunting moment captured in an iconic photograph. As a Japanese American who experienced internment, she actively advocated for reparations for her fellow Japanese Americans.

Maya Lin—In 1981 at the age of twenty-one, Maya Lin stunned the architecture and design world when her bold, modern design for the Vietnam Veterans Memorial was selected while she was still a Yale undergraduate. Her designs, though once regarded as controversial, have now become iconic of modern American public architecture.

Jhumpa Lahiri—Lahiri's first collection of stories, *Interpreter of Maladies*, won a Pulitzer Prize in 2000. Her subsequent short story collection and novels have garnered numerous awards and prizes making them both critically acclaimed and popular worldwide. Beyond the literary accolades, Lahiri's work serves as an important chronicle of the lives of Indian Americans.

Vera Wang—Wang has established herself as a leading designer of high-end and ready-to-wear fashion. Her elegant wedding dresses have become must-have items for fashionable American brides. But many don't know that well before she entered the realm of design, Wang was a competitive figure skater and her start in fashion was not as a designer but as a fashion editor. After Wang was turned down for the top position at *Vogue* in favor of Anna Wintour, she reinvented herself as a designer.

Margaret Cho—Cho not only broke through the white male barrier of standup comedy in the early 1990s, she even managed to have a mainstream television sitcom focused on a Korean American family, *All American Girl*, which unfortunately was short-lived. She continues to be regarded as a bold and progressive voice in the comedy realm.

Mindy Kaling—Kaling rose to fame because of her role as Kelly Kapoor, on the hit television comedy *The Office*, and parlayed that into her own comedic television series, *The Mindy Project*. But before television, Kaling got her start writing and starring in theatrical comedies, including *Matt and Ben*, which was heralded at the New York Fringe Festival. As the star and producer of her own hit comedy television show, Kaling has not only become one of the most visible Asian Americans but has taken the baton passed by pioneering comedian Margaret Cho in creating a space for Asian American women in American situational comedies.

Vijay Iyer—Iyer is an acclaimed and accomplished jazz musician and composer, winning countless awards, most notably a MacArthur "Genius" Fellowship. In addition to being known for his musical virtuosity in a quintessentially American musical genre, Iyer is also known for his eclectic range, collaborating with musicians of varied backgrounds and genres, expanding the understanding of jazz. Beyond this, Iyer has also used jazz as a platform for dealing with social issues, participating in breakthrough collaborations with veterans of the wars in Iraq and Afghanistan.

Questions for Critical Reading

1. How do stereotypes operate? As you reread Das's text look for passages where she talks about stereotypes and the impact they have. How might we combat stereotypes and why would we want to do so?

2. Das suggests that the National Portrait Gallery exhibit reflects "unconscious bias" (p. 105). Develop a definition of this term from the context of Das's essay. How does this bias operate?

3. What does it mean to be "cool"? Reread Das's text to locate quotations where she defines this concept and its history. Why does she think people have problems seeing Asian Americans as cool?

Exploring Context

1. Using Google or another web search engine, find images of cool. Do these images reflect the definition that Das offers in this essay? Working from your response to Question 3 of Questions for Critical Reading extend or complicate her argument using other images of what is and isn't cool.

2. Visit the website for the National Portrait Gallery's *American Cool* exhibit at npg.si.edu /exhibit/Cool. Does the material on the website further support Das's argument? Consider incorporating your work on unconscious bias from Question 2 of Questions for Critical Reading.

3. At the end of her essay Das offers a list of cool Asian Americans. Using the web, research one of these figures or add one of your own to her list. What additional evidence can you locate for their coolness? Use your work from Question 3 of Questions for Critical Reading.

Questions for Connecting

1. Andrew Cohen looks at the intersection of race and law in "Race and the Opioid Epidemic" (p. 97). In what ways are ideas about race and ethnicity not simply persistent but *pervasive*? Use ideas from both authors to consider the role that race and ethnicity play in different spheres of life. What might it take to generate change?

2. Alexander Provan, in "The Future of Originals" (p. 327), examines the history and future of museums in the digital age. Do the uncertain future of originals and the shifts in modern museums suggest any possibility of future change for exhibits such as the one Das examines? What role does cultural memory play in both essays?

3. Wesley Yang also looks at stereotypes of Asian Americans in "Paper Tigers" (p. 435). Synthesize his discussion with Das's analysis. What challenges do Asian Americans face when it comes to education and cultural acceptance? Does either author offer some hope for a different future?

Language Matters

1. This essay is centered on the power of the image, in this case through photographs. Make your own visuals of the text of this essay. Draw the argument of Das's essay, either by hand or with a graphics program on your computer. How would the inclusion of this drawing affect Das's text? What elements of visual argument do you use to convey Das's meaning?

2. Locate a key passage from Das's text and then revise the quotation you've selected using more informal language or slang. How does this revision change the meaning of the quotation? What audience would be most receptive to your revision? Why did Das choose the tone she used in this essay, and what tone might you choose in your own writing for this class?

3. In a small group, discuss what revision means. If you were going to revise this text, where would you start? What areas need more development?

Assignments for Writing

1. Write a paper in which you explore what it means to be cool. What role does cool have in culture? What is the power of cool? How might we harness this power for social change? You may want to draw from your work in Question 3 of Questions for Critical Reading and Exploring Context as you write your response.

2. What does it mean to be American? Write a paper about the mechanisms used to form national identity. How is it related to race and ethnicity? What role does culture play in creating a national identity? Does unconscious bias shape our understanding? Use your work from Questions for Critical Reading and Exploring Context to help support your argument.

3. How can images shape social change? Write a paper about the power of images using Das's discussion of the National Portrait Gallery exhibit. You may want to start with your work in Questions 1 and 2 of Exploring Context and Question 2 of Questions for Connecting.

TORIE ROSE DEGHETT

Freelance magazine writer **Torie Rose DeGhett** holds an M.A. from Columbia University's Graduate School of Journalism. Her work, focused largely on foreign affairs, has appeared in publications such as the *Atlantic*, the *Guardian*, and *Guernica*. DeGhett also runs *The Political Notebook*, a blog that was recognized as one of *Time*'s "30 Must-See Tumblr Blogs" and that covers diverse topics from national security to hip-hop songs. DeGhett's "The War Photo No One Would Publish" ran in August 2014 as a feature story on *TheAtlantic.com*, a National Magazine Award–winning multimedia publication that covers politics, business, technology, and culture, among other timely topics. On the day that DeGhett's essay was published, *TheAtlantic.com* also featured pieces on America's moral obligations in Iraq, the disproportionate number of women in public relations, and the spread of valley fever, a fungal infection prevalent among poor farmworkers in the American Southwest.

"The War Photo No One Would Publish" centers on the issue of censorship, detailing the account of a graphic Gulf War photo the American press refused to publish. More than twenty years later, through interviews with the photographer and media players of the time, DeGhett examines the circumstances behind taking the haunting photo and the motives behind keeping it out of the headlines. Ultimately, DeGhett argues that incomplete news coverage has the effect of shielding — and even deceiving — the public when it comes to the consequences of war.

How critical is it to expose the unpleasant, and sometimes gory, side of an issue? Should the press protect the public from what some might call unnecessarily explicit images? Or are such images necessary in painting a complete and accurate picture of an event?

- TAGS: *art, censorship, empathy, ethics, judgment and decision making, media, photography and video, politics, science and technology, trauma and violence, war and conflict*
- CONNECTIONS: *Appiah, Chen, Das, Fukuyama, Lukianoff and Haidt, Paumgarten, Provan, Singer, Southan, van Houtryve*

The War Photo No One Would Publish

The Iraqi soldier died attempting to pull himself up over the dashboard of his truck. The flames engulfed his vehicle and incinerated his body, turning him to dusty ash and blackened bone. In a photograph taken soon afterward, the soldier's hand reaches out of the shattered windshield, which frames his face and chest. The colors and textures of his hand and shoulders look like those of the scorched and rusted metal around him. Fire has destroyed most of his features, leaving behind a skeletal face, fixed in a final rictus. He stares without eyes.

On February 28, 1991, Kenneth Jarecke stood in front of the charred man, parked amid the carbonized bodies of his fellow soldiers, and photographed him. At one point, before he died this dramatic mid-retreat death, the soldier had had a name. He'd fought in Saddam Hussein's army and had a rank and an assignment and a unit. He might have been devoted to the dictator who sent him to occupy Kuwait and fight the Americans. Or he might have been an unlucky young man with no prospects, recruited off the streets of Baghdad.

Jarecke took the picture just before a ceasefire officially ended Operation Desert Storm—the U.S.-led military action that drove Saddam Hussein and his troops out of Kuwait, which they had annexed and occupied the previous August. The image and its anonymous subject might have come to symbolize the Gulf War. Instead, it went unpublished in the United States, not because of military obstruction but because of editorial choices. It's hard to calculate the consequences of a photograph's absence. But sanitized images of warfare, the *Atlantic*'s Conor Friedersdorf argues, make it "easier . . . to accept bloodless language" such as 1991 references to "surgical strikes" or modern-day terminology like "kinetic warfare." The Vietnam War, in contrast, was notable for its catalog of chilling and iconic war photography. Some images, like Ron Haeberle's pictures of the My Lai massacre, were initially kept from the public, but other violent images—Nick Ut's scene of child napalm victims and Eddie Adams's photo of a Vietcong man's execution—won Pulitzer Prizes and had a tremendous impact on the outcome of the war.[1]

It's hard to calculate the consequences of a photograph's absence.

Not every gruesome photo reveals an important truth about conflict and combat. Last month, the *New York Times* decided—for valid ethical reasons—to remove images of dead passengers from an online story about Flight MH-17 in Ukraine and replace them with photos of mechanical wreckage.[2] Sometimes though, omitting an image means shielding the public from the messy, imprecise consequences of a war—making the coverage incomplete, and even deceptive.

5 In the case of the charred Iraqi soldier, the hypnotizing and awful photograph ran against the popular myth of the Gulf War as a "video-game war"—a conflict made humane through precision bombing and night-vision equipment. By deciding not to

© Kenneth Jarecke/Contact Press Images

publish it, *Time* magazine and the Associated Press denied the public the opportunity to confront this unknown enemy and consider his excruciating final moments.

The image was not entirely lost. The *Observer* in the United Kingdom and *Libération* in France both published it after the American media refused. Many months later, the photo also appeared in *American Photo*, where it stoked some controversy, but came too late to have a significant impact. All of this surprised the photographer, who had assumed the media would be only too happy to challenge the popular narrative of a clean, uncomplicated war. "When you have an image that disproves that myth," he says today, "then you think it's going to be widely published."

"Let me say up front that I don't like the press," one Air Force officer declared, starting a January 1991 press briefing on a blunt note.[3] The military's bitterness toward the media was in no small part a legacy of the Vietnam coverage decades before. By the time the Gulf War started, the Pentagon had developed access policies that drew on press restrictions used in the U.S. wars in Grenada and Panama in the 1980s. Under this so-called "pool" system, the military grouped print, TV, and radio reporters together with cameramen and photojournalists and sent these small teams on orchestrated press junkets, supervised by Public Affairs Officers (PAOs) who kept a close watch on their charges.

By the time Operation Desert Storm began in mid-January 1991, Kenneth Jarecke had decided he no longer wanted to be a combat photographer—a profession, he says, that "dominates your life." But after Saddam Hussein's invasion of Kuwait in August

"He was fighting to save his life to the very end, till he was completely burned up," Jarecke says of the man he photographed. "He was trying to get out of that truck."

1990, Jarecke developed a low opinion of the photojournalism coming out of Desert Shield, the pre-war operation to build up troops and equipment in the Gulf. "It was one picture after another of a sunset with camels and a tank," he says. War was approaching and Jarecke says he saw a clear need for a different kind of coverage. He felt he could fill that void.

The images were taken at an altitude that erased the human presence on the ground.

After the U.N.'s January 15, 1991, deadline for Iraq's withdrawal from Kuwait came and went, Jarecke, now certain he should go, convinced *Time* magazine to send him to Saudi Arabia. He packed up his cameras and shipped out from Andrews Air Force Base on January 17—the first day of the aerial bombing campaign against Iraq.

Out in the field with the troops, Jarecke recalls, "anybody could challenge you," however absurdly and without reason. He remembers straying 30 feet away from his PAO and having a soldier bark at him, "What are you doing?" Jarecke retorted, "What do you *mean* what am I doing?"

Recounting the scene two decades later, Jarecke still sounds exasperated. "Some first lieutenant telling me, you know, where I'm gonna stand. *In the middle of the desert.*"

As the war picked up in early February, PAOs accompanied Jarecke and several other journalists as they attached to the Army XVIII Airborne Corps and spent two weeks at the Saudi-Iraqi border doing next to nothing. That didn't mean nothing was happening—just that they lacked access to the action.

During the same period, military photojournalist Lee Corkran was embedding with the U.S. Air Force's 614th Tactical Fighter Squadron in Doha, Qatar, and capturing their aerial bombing campaigns. He was there to take pictures for the Pentagon to use as it saw fit—not primarily for media use. In his images, pilots look over their shoulders to check on other planes. Bombs hang off the jets' wings, their sharp-edged darkness contrasting with the soft colors of the clouds and desert below. In the distance, the curvature of the earth is visible. On missions, Corkran's plane would often flip upside down at high speed as the pilots dodged missiles, leaving silvery streaks in the sky. Gravitational forces multiplied the weight of his cameras—so much so that if he had ever needed to eject from the plane, his equipment could have snapped his neck. This was the air war that comprised most of the combat mission in the Gulf that winter.

The scenes Corkran witnessed weren't just off-limits to Jarecke; they were also invisible to viewers in the United States, despite the rise of 24-hour reporting during the conflict. Gulf War television coverage, as Ken Burns wrote at the time, felt cinematic and often sensational, with "distracting theatrics" and "pounding new theme music," as if "the war itself might be a wholly owned subsidiary of television."

Some of the most widely seen images of the air war were shot not by photographers, but rather by unmanned cameras attached to planes and laser-guided bombs. Grainy shots and video footage of the roofs of targeted buildings, moments before impact, became a visual signature of a war that was deeply associated with phrases like "smart bombs" and "surgical strike." The images were taken at an altitude that erased the human presence on the ground. They were black-and-white shots, some with bluish or greenish casts. One from February 1991, published in the photo book *In The Eye of Desert Storm* by the now-defunct Sygma photo agency, showed a bridge that

The burned-out truck, surrounded by corpses, on the "Highway of Death."

was being used as an Iraqi supply route. In another, black plumes of smoke from French bombs blanketed an Iraqi Republican Guard base like ink blots. None of them looked especially violent.

The hardware-focused coverage of the war removed the empathy that Jarecke says is crucial in photography, particularly photography that's meant to document death and violence. "A photographer without empathy," he remarks, "is just taking up space that could be better used."

In late February, during the war's final hours, Jarecke and the rest of his press pool drove across the desert, each of them taking turns behind the wheel. They had been awake for several days straight. "We had no idea where we were. We were in a convoy," Jarecke recalls. He dozed off.

When he woke up, they had parked and the sun was about to rise. It was almost 6 o'clock in the morning. The group received word that a ceasefire was a few hours away, and Jarecke remembers another member of his pool cajoling the press officer into abandoning the convoy and heading toward Kuwait City.

The group figured they were in southern Iraq, somewhere in the desert about 70 miles away from Kuwait City. They began driving toward Kuwait, hitting Highway 8 and stopping to take pictures and record video footage. They came upon a jarring scene: burned-out Iraqi military convoys and incinerated corpses. Jarecke sat in the truck, alone with Patrick Hermanson, a public affairs officer. He moved to get out of the vehicle with his cameras.

Hermanson found the idea of photographing the scene distasteful. When I asked him about the conversation, he recalled asking Jarecke, "What do you need to take a picture of that for?" Implicit in his question was a judgment: There was something dishonorable about photographing the dead.

"I'm not interested in it either," Jarecke recalls replying. He told the officer that he didn't want his mother to see his name next to photographs of corpses. "But if I don't take pictures like these, people like my mom will think war is what they see in movies." As Hermanson remembers, Jarecke added, "It's what I came here to do. It's what I have to do."

"He let me go," Jarecke recounts. "He didn't try to stop me. He could have stopped me because it was technically not allowed under the rules of the pool. But he didn't stop me and I walked over there."

More than two decades later, Hermanson notes that Jarecke's resulting picture was "pretty special." He doesn't need to see the photograph to resurrect the scene in his mind. "It's seared into my memory," he says, "as if it happened yesterday."

The incinerated man stared back at Jarecke through the camera's viewfinder, his blackened arm reaching over the edge of the truck's windshield. Jarecke recalls that he could "see clearly how precious life was to this guy, because he was fighting for it. He was fighting to save his life to the very end, till he was completely burned up. He was trying to get out of that truck."

He wrote later that year in *American Photo* magazine that he "wasn't thinking at all about what was there; if I had thought about how horrific the guy looked I wouldn't have been able to make the picture." Instead, he maintained his emotional remove by attending to the more prosaic and technical elements of photography. He kept himself steady; he concentrated on the focus. The sun shone in through the rear of the destroyed truck and backlit his subject. Another burned body lay directly in front of the vehicle, blocking a close-up shot, so Jarecke used the full 200mm zoom lens on his Canon EOS-1.

In his other shots of the same scene, it is apparent that the soldier could never have survived, even if he had pulled himself up out of the driver's seat and through the window. The desert sand around the truck is scorched. Bodies are piled behind the vehicle, indistinguishable from one another. A lone, burned man lies face down in front of the truck, everything incinerated except the soles of his bare feet. In another photograph, a man lies spread-eagle on the sand, his body burned to the point of disintegration, but his face mostly intact and oddly serene. A dress shoe lies next to his body.

The group continued on across the desert, passing through more stretches of highway littered with the same fire-ravaged bodies and vehicles. Jarecke and his pool were possibly the first members of the Western media to come across these scenes, which appeared along what eventually became known as the Highway of Death, sometimes referred to as the Road to Hell.

The retreating Iraqi soldiers had been trapped. They were frozen in a traffic jam, blocked off by the Americans, by Mutla Ridge, by a minefield. Some fled on foot; the rest were strafed by American planes that swooped overhead, passing again and again to destroy all the vehicles. Milk vans, fire trucks, limousines, and one bulldozer appeared

Iraqi prisoners of war, captured by the U.S. military on their way to Baghdad.
© Kenneth Jarecke/Contact Press Images

in the wreckage alongside armored cars and trucks, and T-55 and T-72 tanks. Most vehicles held fully loaded, but rusting, Kalashnikov variants. According to descriptions from reporters like the *New York Times*'s R. W. Apple and the *Observer*'s Colin Smith, amid the plastic mines, grenades, ammunition, and gas masks, a quadruple-barreled anti-aircraft gun stood crewless and still pointing skyward.[4] Personal items, like a photograph of a child's birthday party and broken crayons, littered the ground beside weapons and body parts. The body count never seems to have been determined, although the BBC puts it in the "thousands."[5]

"In one truck," wrote Colin Smith in a March 3 dispatch for the *Observer*, "the radio had been knocked out of the dashboard but was still wired up and faintly picking up some plaintive Arabic air which sounded so utterly forlorn I thought at first it must be a cry for help."

Following the February 28 ceasefire that ended Desert Storm, Jarecke's film roll with the image of the incinerated soldier reached the Joint Information Bureau in Dhahran, Saudi Arabia, where the military coordinated and corralled the press, and where pool editors received and filed stories and photographs. At that point, with the operation over, the photograph would not have needed to pass through a security screening, says Maryanne Golon, who was the on-site photo editor for *Time* in Saudi Arabia and is now director of photography for the *Washington Post*. Despite the obviously shocking content, she tells me she reacted like an editor in work mode. She selected it, without debate or controversy among the pool editors, to be scanned and transmitted. The image made its way back to the editors' offices in New York City.

Jarecke also made his way from Saudi Arabia to New York. Passing through Heathrow Airport on a layover, he bought a copy of the March 3 edition of the *Observer*. He opened it to find his photograph on page 9, printed at the top across eight columns under the heading, "The real face of war."

That weekend in March, when the *Observer*'s editors made the final decision to print the image, every magazine in North America made the opposite choice. Jarecke's photograph did not even appear on the desks of most U.S. newspaper editors (the exception being the *New York Times*, which had a photo wire service subscription but nonetheless declined to publish the image). The photograph was entirely absent from American media until far past the time when it was relevant to ground reporting from Iraq and Kuwait. Golon says she wasn't surprised by this, even though she'd chosen to transmit it to the American press. "I didn't think there was any chance they'd publish it," she says.

Apart from the *Observer*, the only major news outlet to run the Iraqi soldier's photograph at the time was the Parisian news daily *Libération*, which ran it on March 4. Both newspapers refrained from putting the image on the front page, though they ran it prominently inside. But Aidan Sullivan, the pictures editor for the British *Sunday Times*, told the *British Journal of Photography* on March 14 that he had opted instead for a wide shot of the carnage: a desert highway littered with rubble. He challenged the *Observer*: "We would have thought our readers could work out that a lot of people had died in those vehicles. Do you have to show it to them?"

"We would have thought our readers could work out that a lot of people had died in those vehicles. Do you have to show it to them?"

"There were 1,400 [Iraqi soldiers] in that convoy, and every picture transmitted until that one came, two days after the event, was of debris, bits of equipment," Tony McGrath, the *Observer*'s pictures editor, was quoted as saying in the same article. "No human involvement in it at all; it could have been a scrapyard. That was some dreadful censorship."

The media took it upon themselves to "do what the military censorship did not do," says Robert Pledge, the head of the Contact Press Images photojournalism agency that has represented Jarecke since the 1980s. The night they received the image, Pledge tells me, editors at the Associated Press's New York City offices pulled the photo entirely from the wire service, keeping it off the desks of virtually all of America's newspaper editors. It is unknown precisely how, why, or by whom the AP's decision was handed down.

Vincent Alabiso, who at the time was the executive photo editor for the AP, later distanced himself from the wire service's decision. In 2003, he admitted to *American Journalism Review* that the photograph ought to have gone out on the wire and argued that such a photo would today.[6]

Yet the AP's reaction was repeated at *Time* and *Life*. Both magazines briefly considered the photo, unofficially referred to as "Crispy," for publication. The photo departments even drew up layout plans. *Time*, which had sent Jarecke to the Gulf in the first place, planned for the image to accompany a story about the Highway of Death.

"We fought like crazy to get our editors to let us publish that picture," former photo director Michele Stephenson tells me. As she recalls, Henry Muller, the managing editor, told her, "*Time* is a family magazine." And the image was, when it came down to it, just too disturbing for the outlet to publish. It was, to her recollection, the only instance during the Gulf War where the photo department fought but failed to get an image into print.

James Gaines, the managing editor of *Life*, took responsibility for the ultimate decision not to run Jarecke's image in his own magazine's pages, despite photo director Peter Howe's push to give it a double-page spread. "We thought that this was the stuff of nightmares," Gaines told Ian Buchanan of the *British Journal of Photography* in March 1991. "We have a fairly substantial number of children who read *Life* magazine," he added. Even so, the photograph was published later that month in one of *Life*'s special issues devoted to the Gulf War—not typical reading material for the elementary-school set.

Stella Kramer, who worked as a freelance photo editor for *Life* on four special-edition issues on the Gulf War, tells me that the decision to not publish Jarecke's photo was less about protecting readers than preserving the dominant narrative of the good, clean war. Flipping through 23-year-old issues, Kramer expresses clear distaste at the editorial quality of what she helped to create. The magazines "were very sanitized," she says. "So, that's why these issues are all basically just propaganda." She points out the picture on the cover of the February 25 issue: a young blond boy dwarfed by the American flag he's holding. "As far as Americans were concerned," she remarks, "nobody ever died."

"If pictures tell stories," Lee Corkran tells me, "the story should have a point. So if the point is the utter annihilation of people who were in retreat and all the charred bodies . . . if that's your point, then that's true. And so be it. I mean, war is ugly. It's hideous." To Corkran, who was awarded the Bronze Star for his Gulf War combat photography, pictures like Jarecke's tell important stories about the effects of American and allied airpower. Even Patrick Hermanson, the public affairs officer who originally protested the idea of taking pictures of the scene, now says the media should not have censored the photo.

The U.S. military has now abandoned the pool system it used in 1990 and 1991, and the Internet has changed the way photos reach the public. Even if the AP did refuse to send out a photo, online outlets would certainly run it, and no managing editor would be able to prevent it from being shared across various social platforms, or being the subject of extensive op-ed and blog commentary. If anything, today's controversies often center on the vast abundance of disturbing photographs, and the difficulty of putting them in a meaningful context.[7]

Some have argued that showing bloodshed and trauma repeatedly and sensationally can dull emotional understanding. But never showing these images in the first place guarantees that such an understanding will never develop. "Try to imagine, if only for a moment, what your intellectual, political, and ethical world would be like if you had never seen a photograph," author Susie Linfield asks in *The Cruel Radiance*, her book on photography and political violence. Photos like Jarecke's not only show that bombs drop on real people; they also make the public feel accountable. As David Carr wrote in the *New York Times* in 2003, war photography has "an ability not just to offend the viewer, but to implicate him or her as well."[8]

As an angry 28-year-old Jarecke wrote in *American Photo* in 1991: "If we're big enough to fight a war, we should be big enough to look at it."

NOTES

1. Michael Griffin, "Media Images of War," *Media, War & Conflict* 3, no. 1 (2010): 7–41.
2. Megan Garber, "The Malaysia Air Crash: Should We Publish Pictures of Bodies?" the *Atlantic*, July 17, 2014.
3. Malcolm W. Browne, "Conflicting Censorship Upsets Many Journalists," *New York Times*, January 21, 1991.
4. R. W. Apple Jr., "Death Stalks Desert Despite Cease-Fire," *New York Times*, March 2, 1991.
5. "Flashback: 1991 Gulf War," *BBC News*, March 20, 2003. http://news.bbc.co.uk/2/hi/middle_east/2754103.stm
6. Lori Robertson, "Images of War," *American Journalism Review* (October/November 2004).
7. David Frum, "Photographs as Weapons of War in the Middle East," the *Atlantic*, August 2, 2014.
8. David Carr, "Telling War's Deadly Story at Just Enough Distance," *New York Times*, April 7, 2003.

Questions for Critical Reading

1. Is censorship ever justified? Briefly write down your thoughts on the question. As you reread this essay, add to what you've written by looking for places where DeGhett's essay confirms or challenges your thoughts about censorship.

2. As you reread, take note of the reasons various decision makers used for not publishing the photo. Are these reasons sufficient justification? Support your response with quotations from the text.

3. What gives an image power? Note places in the text that discuss the ability of images to affect viewers.

Exploring Context

1. Explore Kenneth Jarecke's website at kennethjarecke.com. In what ways does his larger body of work reflect the ideas about photography that DeGhett offers? Incorporate your findings into your response from Question 3 of Questions for Critical Reading.

2. View online Nick Ut's image of child napalm victims mentioned by DeGhett. What factors might cause this photo to be published but not Jarecke's? Use quotations from DeGhett to support your answer and then apply your analysis to the rationale for not publishing Jarecke's photograph that you traced in Question 2 of Questions for Critical Reading.

3. **Multimodal.** Use a search engine to look for images of "war photography." How has technology changed the accessibility of images of war? Support your thoughts with quotations from the essay and then make a digital or print collage that reflects your findings about the changes in war photography.

Questions for Connecting

1. Does Jarecke's image meet the standards for art as explained in Rhys Southan's "Is Art a Waste of Time?" (p. 363)? Does the failure of Jarecke to get his image widely published during the war support the idea that art is not as important as Effective Altruism? Are war photographers replaceable? Consider Nick Ut's images from Question 2 of Exploring Context as an additional example in making your argument.
2. In "Visible Man: Ethics in a World without Secrets" (p. 353), Peter Singer suggests that "sousveillance" can be used to hold governments accountable. How does DeGhett's essay complicate Singer's argument? Does sousveillance require free access to publication channels?
3. Kavita Das, in "(Un)American, (Un)Cool," (p. 102) also examines the power of photographs. How does her examination of the exhibit at the National Portrait Gallery reflect similar themes about the ways in which the inclusion or exclusion of images is critical to the production of meaning? You might want to use your work in Question 3 of Questions for Critical Reading.

Language Matters

1. Wordle (wordle.net) is a tool for generating "word clouds" — it transforms text into a visual representation. Use Wordle to create a word cloud for this essay by typing either key quotations or key terms. How does the visual representation enhance or change your understanding of the text?
2. Select a key passage from DeGhett and replace all the verbs with blanks ("________"). Working in small groups, fill in the blanks with verbs and then reflect on which verbs you chose and why. How does the context of each sentence determine which word to use? More important, how significant are verbs to the meaning of a sentence? Could you change DeGhett's entire argument by changing the verbs?
3. Locate the strongest transition in DeGhett's essay. What makes it strong or effective? How can you use this strategy in your own writing?

Assignments for Writing

1. One of DeGhett's central arguments is that photographs such as Jarecke's are powerful tools to examine the consequences of war. Write a paper in which you examine how images can affect conflicts such as war. Do such photographs create empathy or do they numb viewers to violence? Draw from your work on the power of images from Question 3 of Questions for Critical Reading.

2. DeGhett suggests that given the development of technologies such as social media, Jarecke's photograph would have had a very different fate had it been taken today. Write a paper in which you suggest the ways in which technology has changed the power of the media. Use your exploration of war photography from Question 3 of Exploring Context to support your position.

3. In some ways DeGhett's essay is centrally concerned with practices of censorship. Write a paper in which you propose guidelines for an ethics of censorship. In which situations might it be justified? Use your answer from Question 1 for Questions for Critical Reading in making your response.

HELEN EPSTEIN

After earning a Ph.D. in molecular biology from Cambridge University, **Helen Epstein** attended the London School of Hygiene and Tropical Medicine, where she earned an M.Sc. in public health in developing countries. In 1993, while working as a scientist for a biotechnology company in search of an AIDS vaccine, Epstein moved to Uganda, where she witnessed the suffering caused by the virus. Epstein still works in public health care in developing countries. She has published articles in magazines such as the *New York Review of Books* and in 2007 published her book *The Invisible Cure: Africa, the West, and the Fight against AIDS*. Epstein's latest book, *Another Fine Mess: America, Uganda, and the War on Terror*, was published in 2017.

Epstein compiled the information she had gathered in her years as a scientist in Africa, along with her personal observations, to write *The Invisible Cure*. In it she explores the reasons behind the unprecedented AIDS epidemic in Africa and suggests ways to reduce infection rates on that continent. Along the way she corrects the misinformation and misconceptions that Westerners have been using as a guide for aiding Africans who suffer from or are at risk for HIV/AIDS. She points out that programs for prevention might need to be in the hands of Africans themselves in order to account for local cultures. For instance, while campaigns promoting condom usage might be successful in Western countries, this does not mean such campaigns will succeed within other cultures. Instead, listening to and understanding the traditions and customs of individual cultures might lead to more successful approaches to the AIDS epidemic.

In "AIDS, Inc.," a chapter from *The Invisible Cure*, Epstein examines HIV and AIDS prevention programs in Africa. In South Africa, Epstein witnesses a government-run campaign that focuses on creating conversations about sexual activity among the nation's youth in order to help them make informed decisions about sex. However, many of the conversations stop there, leaving out any talk of people who already have AIDS. While the campaign may open up new avenues for youth in terms of sexual responsibility and respect, the lack of conversation surrounding AIDS perpetuates the social stigmas of infected peoples as well as an "out of sight, out of mind" attitude toward the virus. Perhaps, as Epstein points out, campaigns are only as successful as the conversations surrounding them. She points to Uganda — one of the few countries in Africa where the rate of infection has dropped precipitously — as an example of effective conversation. Open conversation among Ugandans about personal experiences with the virus has succeeded in preventing its spread by breaking the cycle of social stigmas surrounding those infected.

What social stigmas concerning HIV and AIDS exist locally and globally? How do these social stigmas interfere with campaigns to prevent the spread of the virus? How might class, race, gender, and religion contribute to the way prevention is approached? While Epstein points out how important conversation is among communities, is it possible to create a global conversation about HIV and AIDS?

- TAGS: *adolescence and adulthood, collaboration, community, conversation, culture, education, globalism, health and medicine, judgment and decision making, media, politics, sexuality, social change*
- CONNECTIONS: *Appiah, Chen, Cohen, Gilbert, Gladwell, Southan, Watters, Yoshino*

AIDS, Inc.

In response to government prevarication over HIV treatment, a vigorous AIDS activist movement emerged in South Africa and a fierce public relations battle ensued. The Treatment Action Campaign, or TAC, along with other activist groups, accused the South African health minister, Manto Tshabalala-Msimang, of "murder" for denying millions of South Africans access to medicine for AIDS. A spokesman from the ANC Youth League then called the activists "paid marketing agents for toxic AIDS drugs from America."[1] An official in the Department of Housing accused journalists who defended the AIDS activists of fanaticism, and quoted Lenin* on how the "press in bourgeois society . . . deceive[s], corrupt[s], and fool[s] the exploited and oppressed mass of the people, the poor."

Meanwhile, across the nation thousands of people were becoming infected daily, from the rural homesteads of the former Bantustans† to the peri-urban townships and squatter camps to the formerly all-white suburbs, now home to a growing black middle class. By 2005, the death rate for young adults had tripled.[2] Surveys showed that nearly everyone in South Africa knew that HIV was sexually transmitted and that it could be prevented with condoms, abstinence, and faithfulness to an uninfected partner. Children were receiving AIDS education in school and condoms were widely available, but these programs made little difference. In the din of the battle between the activists and the government, the deeper message, that HIV was everyone's problem, was lost.

In 1999, a group of public health experts sponsored by the U.S.-based Kaiser Family Foundation stepped into this fray. They were concerned about the worsening AIDS crisis in South Africa and wanted to launch a bold new HIV prevention program for young people. They also knew they had to take account of the South African government's attitudes toward AIDS and AIDS activists. Their program, called loveLife, would soon become South Africa's largest and most ambitious HIV prevention campaign. It aimed both to overcome the limitations of similar campaigns that had failed in the past and, at the same time, to avoid dealing with the issues of AIDS treatment and care that had become so controversial.

Could this work? I wondered. Was it possible to reduce the spread of HIV without involving HIV-positive people and the activists and community groups that supported them? LoveLife had been endorsed at one time or another by the archbishop of Cape Town; Nelson Mandela; the king of the Zulu tribe; Jacob Zuma, South Africa's former deputy president; and even Zanele Mbeki, the wife of the president. In 2003, loveLife's annual $20 million budget was paid for by the South African government, the Kaiser Family Foundation, UNICEF, the Bill and Melinda Gates Foundation, and the Global Fund to Fight AIDS, Tuberculosis, and Malaria. At least South Africa's leaders were beginning to take AIDS seriously, I thought, but what kind of program was this?

---

*Lenin: Vladimir Lenin (1870–1924), a chief figure in the Russian revolution of 1917 (which led to the communist takeover); Lenin was the first head of the USSR [Ed.].

†Bantustans: Areas in South Africa where the black population was kept separate from whites during the policy of apartheid, or racial segregation, in the twentieth century [Ed.].

5 "What we want to do is create a substantive, normative shift in the way young people behave," explained loveLife's director, David Harrison, a white South African doctor, when I met him in his Johannesburg office. The average age at which young South Africans lose their virginity—around seventeen—is not much different from the age at which teenagers in other countries do. What's different, Harrison said, was that many of the young South Africans who were sexually active were very sexually active. They were more likely to start having sex at very young ages, even below the age of fourteen—well below the national average. Those vulnerable young people were more likely to have more than one sexual partner, and they were less likely to use condoms. South African girls were more likely to face sexual coercion or rape, or to exchange sex for money or gifts, all of which placed them at greater risk of HIV infection. For Harrison, the trick was to "get inside the head-space of these young people . . . we have to understand what is driving them into sex—they know what HIV is, but they don't internalize it," he said.

LoveLife's aim was to get young people talking, to each other and to their parents, so they would really understand and act on what they knew. But to reach out to them, you had to use a special language that young people could relate to. According to Harrison, traditional HIV prevention campaigns were too depressing: They tried to scare people into changing their behavior, and this turned kids off. LoveLife's media campaign, on the other hand, was positive and cheerful, and resembled the bright, persuasive modern ad campaigns that many South African kids were very much attracted to.

In the past couple of years, nearly a thousand loveLife billboards had sprouted all along the nation's main roads. They were striking. For example, on one of them, the hands of four women of different races caressed the sculpted back and buttocks of a young black man as though they were appraising an antique newel post. The caption read, "Everyone he's slept with, is sleeping with you." On another, a gorgeous mixed-race couple—the boy looked like Brad Pitt, the girl like an Indian film star—lay in bed, under the caption "No Pressure." Some people told me they found these ads oversexualized and disturbing, but it is hard to see why. On the same roads, there are torsos advertising sexy underwear and half-naked actresses advertising romantic movies. Sex is a potent theme in marketing all sorts of products; loveLife, according to its creators, tries to turn that message around to get young people thinking and talking about sex in more responsible ways and convince them of the virtues of abstinence, fidelity, and the use of condoms.

Harrison calls loveLife "a brand of positive lifestyle." The sexy billboards and similar ads on TV and radio, as well as newspaper inserts that resemble teen gossip magazines, with articles and advice columns about clothes, relationships, and sexual health, were designed, Harrison says, to persuade young people to avoid sex in the same way a sneaker ad tries to seduce them into buying new sneakers, because the players in the ads look so cool. The idea is "to create a brand so strong that young people who want to be hip and cool and the rest of it want to associate with it," Harrison told an interviewer in 2001.[3]

Harrison calls loveLife "a brand of positive lifestyle."

The concept of a "lifestyle brand" originated with the rise of brand advertising in the 1960s, when ads for such products as Pepsi-Cola and Harley-Davidson began to promote not only soft drinks and motorcycles, but also a certain style or aesthetic.

People were urged to "join the Pepsi generation" or ride a Harley-Davidson not just to get around, but to embrace a certain attitude. A Harley wasn't just a bike; it was a macho rebellion, an escape from the workaday world to the open road. In the 1970s, family-planning programs also tried to promote contraceptives in developing countries by tapping into poor people's aspirations for a glamorous Western lifestyle. Campaigns depicted small, well-dressed families surrounded by sleek new commodities, including televisions and cars. Harrison predicted that young South Africans would readily respond to this approach too.

"Kids have changed," Harrison explained. Today's young South Africans weren't like the activists who risked their lives in the anti-apartheid demonstrations at Sharpeville and Soweto. "Seventy-five percent of South African teenagers watch TV every day," Harrison informed me. "Their favorite program is *The Bold and the Beautiful*"—an American soap opera in which glamorous characters struggle with personal crises while wearing and driving some very expensive gear. "They are exposed to the global youth culture of music, fashion, pop icons, and commercial brands. They talk about brands among themselves, even if they can't afford everything they see."

10

The Kaiser Foundation's Michael Sinclair told me that loveLife drew much of its inspiration from the marketing campaign for the soft drink Sprite.[4] In the mid-1990s, sales of Sprite were flagging until the company began an aggressive campaign to embed Sprite in youth culture by sponsoring hip-hop concerts and planting attractive, popular kids in internet chat rooms or college dormitories and paying them to praise or distribute Sprite in an unobtrusive way. Sprite is now one of the most profitable drinks in the world because it managed to exploit what marketing experts call "the cool effect"—meaning the influence that a small number of opinion leaders can have on the norms and behavior of large numbers of their peers. So far, corporate marketers had made the greatest use of the cool effect, but there was speculation that small numbers of trendsetters could change more complex behavior than shopping, such as criminality, suicide, and sexual behavior.[5]

For this reason, loveLife had established a small network of recreation centers for young people, known as Y-Centers, throughout the country. At Y-Centers, young people could learn to play basketball, volleyball, and other sports, as well as learn break dancing, radio broadcasting, and word processing. All Y-Center activities were led by "loveLife GroundBreakers"—older youths, usually in their early twenties, who, like the kids who made Sprite cool, were stylish and cheerful and enthusiastic about their product, in this case, loveLife and its program to encourage safer sexual behavior. If abstinence, monogamy, and condoms all happened to fail, each Y-Center was affiliated with a family-planning clinic that offered contraceptives and treatment for sexually transmitted diseases such as syphilis and gonorrhea. The centers offered no treatment for AIDS symptoms, however, and when I visited, none of them offered HIV testing either.

Any young person could become a Y-Center member, but in order to fully participate in its activities, he or she had to complete a program of seminars about HIV, family planning, and other subjects related to sexuality and growing up. The seminars emphasized the biological aspects of HIV and its prevention, but not the experience of the disease and its effects on people's lives. Members also received training to raise their self-esteem, because, as Harrison told an interviewer in 2001,

> there is a direct correlation between young people's sexual behavior and their sense of confidence in the future. Those young people who feel motivated, who feel that they have something to look forward to—they are the ones who protect themselves, who ensure that they do not get HIV/AIDS. . . . It's all about the social discount rates that young people apply to future benefits.[6]

Dr. Harrison arranged for me to visit a loveLife Y-Center in the archipelago of townships in the flat scrubland south of Johannesburg known as the Vaal Triangle. Millions of people live in these townships, many of them recent migrants from rural South Africa or from neighboring countries. The Vaal, once a patchwork of white-owned farms, is now a residential area for poor blacks. At first, only a few families moved here, because the apartheid government used the notorious pass laws to restrict the tide of impoverished blacks seeking a better life in Johannesburg. But when the apartheid laws were scrapped, people poured in. Today, the roads and other services in the area are insufficient for its huge and growing population, and many people have no electricity and lack easy access to clean water and sanitation. Unemployment exceeds 70 percent and the crime rate is one of the highest in South Africa.[7]

The loveLife Y-Center was a compound of two small lavender buildings surrounded by an iron fence and curling razor wire. Inside the compound, a group of young men in shorts and T-shirts were doing warm-up exercises on the outdoor basketball court, while girls and barefoot children looked on. Inside the main building, another group of boys in fashionably droopy jeans and dreadlocks practiced a hip-hop routine, and two girls in the computer room experimented with Microsoft Word.

Valentine's Day was coming up, and the Y-Center had organized a group discussion for some of its members. About thirty teenagers, most of them in school uniforms, sat around on the floor of a large seminar room and argued about who should pay for what on a Valentine's Day date. A GroundBreaker in a loveLife T-shirt and with a loveLife kerchief tied pirate-style on her head officiated. "I go with my chick and I spend money on her and always we have sex," said a husky boy in a gray school uniform. "And I want to know, what's the difference between my chick and a prostitute?" As we have seen, long-term transactional relationships—in which money or gifts are frequently exchanged—may not be the same as prostitution, but they nevertheless put many township youths at risk of HIV.[8]

"Boys, they are expecting too much from us. They say we are parasites if we don't sleep with them," said a plump girl in the uniform of a local Catholic school.

"The girls, they ask for a lot of things," another boy chimed in.

"Me, I think it is wrong. If most of the boys think Valentine's Day is about buying sex, the boys must stop," a girl said. "We girls must hold our ground."

These young people were certainly talking openly about sexual relationships all right, just as Harrison prescribed. Nevertheless, I felt something was missing. "Do you ever talk about AIDS in those discussion groups?" I asked the GroundBreaker afterward. "We do it indirectly," she replied. "We know that if we just came out and started lecturing them about AIDS, they wouldn't listen. They would just turn off. So we talk about positive things, like making informed choices, sharing responsibility, and positive sexuality."

Was this true? Do young people in South Africa, like their politicians, really want to avoid the subject of AIDS? I wanted to meet young people outside the Y-Center and ask them what they thought about that. A few hundred yards away from the Y-Center stood the headquarters of St. Charles Lwanga, a Catholic organization that carries out a number of activities in the township. Their AIDS program, called Inkanyezi, meaning "star" in Zulu, provides counseling to young people about AIDS and also brings food and other necessities to some four hundred orphans and people living with AIDS in the Vaal.

St. Charles Lwanga was independent of loveLife, and its budget was modest, less than a tenth of what loveLife spent on its billboards alone. The Inkanyezi program was staffed almost entirely by volunteers, whose only compensation was that they were allowed to eat some of the food—usually rice and vegetables—that they prepared for the patients. Lack of funding greatly limited the help that Inkanyezi was able to provide. Although Inkanyezi nurses were able to dispense tuberculosis medicine, antiretroviral drugs were as yet unavailable. Indeed, many of the patients they visited lacked some of the most basic necessities for life and human dignity. Sometimes destitute patients had their water and electricity cut off. But the worst thing was that many of the patients were socially isolated and lived alone in flimsy shacks. The doors were easily broken down and at night neighborhood thugs sometimes came in and stole what little they had. Sometimes the patients were raped.

Justice Showalala, who ran Inkanyezi, organized a meeting for me with a group of about twenty-five young people from Orange Farm. The HIV rate in the area was not known, but several people explained to me how their lives had been changed by the virus. They said they had witnessed extreme prejudice and discrimination against people with AIDS, and they did not know where to turn when they learned that a relative or friend was HIV positive. "People say you shouldn't touch someone with HIV," said one girl. "I have a friend at school who disclosed she has HIV, and the others won't even walk with her." Justice explained how he had offered to introduce some teachers from a local school to some of his HIV-positive clients. "They said, 'If you want me to meet people with AIDS, you better give me a rubber suit.'"

The loveLife Y-Center did little to help young people deal with such confusion, stigma, and shame. "I learned basketball at the Y-Center," one girl told me, "and at meetings we talked about resisting peer pressure, [like when] your friends advise you to break your virginity, to prove you are girl enough. But I was afraid the people there would find out my sister had HIV. We talked about it as though it was someone else's problem."

In general, although sex was openly discussed at the Y-Center, the experience of AIDS was not. The Y-Center offered individual counseling for a small number of young people with HIV, but those who were hungry, homeless, or destitute, or were suffering from the symptoms of AIDS, were told to consult other organizations, including Inkanyezi.

It turns out that talking about the pain, both physical and emotional, that the disease creates is far more difficult than getting over the embarrassment of talking about sex. "I had heard about HIV before," said an Inkanyezi girl, wearing a bright blue T-shirt and matching headband. "But then I found out my mother was HIV positive. I was so shocked, so shocked. I even talked to my teacher about it. She said it can happen to anyone; it must have been from mistakes my mother made, and that I shouldn't make those mistakes in my own life."

"Sometimes, women have no choice," said the older woman sitting next to the girl in blue. She was thin, with intense dark eyes and a deep, wry smile. She was dressed entirely in black, except for a baseball cap with a red ribbon on it—the universal symbol of solidarity with HIV-positive people. "They get infected because of their husbands, and there's nothing they can do.

"It happened like this," the older woman went on. "It was back when we were living in Soweto, before we moved here. One day my daughter and I were washing clothes together," she said, nodding at the girl in blue. "She said she'd had a dream that I was so sick, that I had cancer and I was going to die. I waited until we were done with the washing, and then I told her that I was HIV positive. She said, 'I knew it, you were always sick and always going to support groups.' She was so down, she just cried all day and all night after that. I told her, 'Only God knows why people have this disease. Don't worry, I won't die right away.'

"Once I visited the loveLife Y-Center," the woman continued, "but I just saw children playing. I sat and talked with them, and they were shocked when I said I was HIV positive. I told them about what it was like, and one of them said she would ask the managers whether I could come and talk to a bigger group. But that was about six months ago and they haven't called me. I haven't moved and my number hasn't changed. I don't know why they haven't called."

"I think there should be more counseling and support groups for people who find out their parents are HIV positive," the girl in blue said. "It puts you down, it really gets to you, it haunts you. When you are standing in class and you have to recite a poem or something, I find I can't get anything out of my mouth. I can't concentrate. [The problem] here is ignorance. I didn't care about HIV until I found out about my mother. Then I started to care about these people. I wish many people in our country would also think like that." 30

In 2003, the only African country that had seen a nationwide decline in HIV prevalence was Uganda. Since 1992 the HIV rate had fallen by some two-thirds, a success that saved perhaps a million lives. The programs and policies that led to this success [are discussed elsewhere], but the epidemiologists Rand Stoneburner and Daniel Low-Beer have argued that a powerful role was played by the ordinary, but frank, conversations people had with family, friends, and neighbors—not about sex, but about the frightening, calamitous effects of AIDS itself.[9] Stoneburner and Low-Beer maintain that these painful personal conversations did more than anything else to persuade Ugandans to come to terms with the reality of AIDS, care for the afflicted, and change their behavior. This in turn led to declines in HIV transmission. The researchers found that people in other sub-Saharan African countries were far less likely to have such discussions.

In South Africa, people told Stoneburner and Low-Beer that they had heard about the epidemic from posters, radio, newspapers, and clinics, as well as from occasional mass rallies, schools, and village meetings; but they seldom spoke about it with the people they knew. They were also far less likely to admit knowing someone with AIDS or to be willing to care for an AIDS patient. It may be no coincidence that the HIV rate in South Africa rose higher than it ever did in Uganda, and has taken far longer to fall.

When I was in Uganda during the early 1990s, the HIV rate was already falling, and I vividly recall how the reality of AIDS was alive in people's minds. Kampala taxi drivers talked as passionately about AIDS as taxi drivers elsewhere discuss politics or football. And they talked about it in a way that would seem foreign to many in South Africa because it was so personal: "my sister," "my father," "my neighbor," "my friend."[10]

Ugandans are not unusually compassionate people, and discrimination against people with AIDS persists in some families and institutions. But Ugandans do seem more willing to openly address painful issues in their lives. This courage owes much to the AIDS information campaigns launched by the government of Uganda early on in the epidemic. But it may have other sources as well. Maybe the difference between the ways South Africa and Uganda have dealt with AIDS has historical roots. Both South Africa and Uganda have bitter histories of conflict. But while Uganda was terrorized for decades by a series of brutal leaders, they could not destroy the traditional rhythms of rural family life. Uganda is one of the most fertile countries in Africa; there is enough land for everyone, and most people live as their ancestors did, as peasant farmers and herders. No large settler population displaced huge numbers of people or set up a system to exploit and humiliate them, as happened in South Africa and in many other African countries. This means Ugandans are more likely to know their neighbors and to live near members of their extended families. This in turn may have contributed to what sociologists call "social cohesion"—the tendency of people to talk openly with one another and form trusted relationships. Perhaps this may have facilitated more realistic and open discussion of AIDS, more compassionate attitudes toward infected people, and pragmatic behavior change.

Perhaps many attempts to prevent the spread of HIV fail because those in charge of them don't recognize that the decisions people make about sex are usually a matter of feeling, not calculation. In other words, sexual behavior is determined less by what Dr. Harrison called "discount rates" that young people "apply to future benefits" than by emotional attachments. I thought of the South African girls who said they had lost a sister or a friend to AIDS. If one of them was faced with a persistent, wealthy seducer, what would be more likely to persuade her to decline? The memory of a loveLife billboard, with its flashy, beautiful models? Or the memory of a person she had known who had died?

On the morning before I left South Africa, I attended a loveLife motivational seminar at a school not far from Orange Farm. "These seminars help young people see the future, identify choices, and identify the values that underpin those choices," Harrison had told me. "We help them ask themselves, 'What can you do to chart life's journey and control it as much as possible?'" The seminars were based on Success by Choice, a series devised by Marlon Smith, a California-based African-American motivational speaker. How was Mr. Smith's message of personal empowerment translated to South Africa, I wondered, where children have to contend with poverty, the risk of being robbed or raped, and a grim future of likely unemployment?

About twenty-five children aged ten to fourteen were in the class, and the GroundBreaker asked them to hold their hands out in front of them, pretend they were looking in a mirror, and repeat the following words:

"You are intelligent!"

"You are gifted!"

"There is no one in the world like you!" 40

"I love you!"

The children spoke quietly at first, then louder, as though they were being hypnotized. The GroundBreaker urged them to talk more openly with their parents, to keep themselves clean, and to make positive choices in their lives, especially when it came to sexuality. There was little mention of helping other people, nor was there much advice about how to avoid being raped or harassed by other students as well as teachers, relatives, or strangers, or how to plan a future in a country where unemployment for township blacks was so high.

Then something really odd occurred. One of the GroundBreakers asked the children to stand up because it was time for an "Icebreaker." "This is a little song-and-dance thing we do, to give the children a chance to stretch. It improves their concentration," another GroundBreaker told me. The words of the song were as follows:

Pizza Hut
Pizza Hut
Kentucky Fried Chicken and a Pizza Hut
McDonald's
McDonald's
Kentucky Fried Chicken and a Pizza Hut.

In the dance, the children spread their arms out as though they were rolling out a pizza, or flapped their elbows like chickens.

What kinds of choices was Dr. Harrison really referring to? I wondered. The techniques of marketing attempt to impose scientific principles on human choices. But it seemed a mad experiment to see whether teenagers living through very difficult times could be persuaded to choose a new sexual lifestyle as they might choose a new brand of shampoo, or whether children could be trained to associate safe sex with pizza and self-esteem.

Afterward, I spoke to some of the children who had participated in the seminar. 45 They all knew how to protect themselves from HIV, and they were eager to show off their knowledge about condoms, abstinence, and fidelity within relationships. But they all said they didn't personally know anyone with AIDS; nor did they know of any children who had lost parents to AIDS. They did mention Nkosi Johnson, the brave HIV-positive twelve-year-old boy who became world-famous in 2000 when he stood up at an International Conference on AIDS and challenged the South African president, Thabo Mbeki, to do more for people living with the virus.

In fact, their principal would tell me later, more than twenty children at the school were AIDS orphans, and many more had been forced to drop out because there was no one to pay their expenses after their parents died. The children I spoke to seemed not to know why some of their classmates wore ragged uniforms or had no shoes or stopped showing up at all.

The week before, I had met some teenage girls in Soweto and I had asked them the same question. They answered in the same way: The only person they knew with AIDS was Nkosi Johnson, the famous boy at the AIDS conference. Just as Harrison had warned me, these girls said they were tired of hearing about AIDS. The girls were orphans, although they said their parents had not died of AIDS. I later discovered that, in another part of that same orphanage, there was a nursery where thirty babies and small children, all of them HIV positive, all abandoned by their parents, lay on cots or sat quietly on the floor, struggling for life. No wonder those girls were tired of hearing about HIV. It was right in their midst, within earshot, but the world around them was telling them to look the other way.

A couple of years later, I would meet a group of primary-school students in Kigali, Rwanda. By then, the HIV infection rate in Rwanda had fallen steeply, just as it had in Uganda years earlier. The school was a typical single-story line of classrooms in one of the poorest sections of Kigali. I spoke to the principal first, and he showed me the government-issued manual used for teaching about AIDS, which contained the usual information about abstinence and condoms. The school day had just ended, and he went outside and asked a few students to stay behind and chat with me.[11]

The Rwandan students had no idea in advance what I wanted to talk to them about. But when I asked them the same question I had asked the South African children, "Do you know anyone with AIDS?" their answers floored me. Every one of them had a story about someone they knew who was HIV positive or suffering from AIDS. "I knew a man who had bad lips [sores] and tears all over his skin," said a fourteen-year-old boy. "People stigmatized him and he died because no one was caring for him." Another boy described a woman who was "so thin, she almost died." But then her relatives took her to the hospital, where she was given AIDS treatment. "She got better because people cared for her," he said.

When I asked the Rwandan children whether they had any questions for me, all they wanted to know was what they could do to help people with AIDS. The responses of the South African children were strikingly different. When I asked them if they had questions for me, they quickly changed the subject from AIDS and asked me what America was like and whether I knew any of the pop stars they admired on TV.

The persistent denial of AIDS in South Africa was deeply disturbing. People liked the colorful, frank advertising and the basketball games sponsored by loveLife. But its programs seemed to me to reinforce the denial that posed so many obstacles to preventing HIV in the first place. In 2005, the Global Fund to Fight AIDS, Tuberculosis, and Malaria would come to similar conclusions and terminate its multimillion-dollar grant to loveLife.[12]

The persistent denial of AIDS in South Africa was deeply disturbing.

Epidemiologists are equivocal about whether loveLife had any effect on HIV transmission in South Africa, but during the program's first seven years, HIV infection rates continued to rise steadily.[13]

A more realistic HIV prevention program would have paid less attention to aspirations and dreams unattainable for so many young people, and greater attention to the real circumstances in people's lives that make it hard for them to avoid infection.

It would also have been more frank about the real human consequences of the disease. But that would have meant dealing with some very painful matters that South Africa's policy-makers seemed determined to evade.

It was heartening that Western donors were now spending so much money on AIDS programs in Africa. But the problem with some large foreign-aid programs was that distributing the funds often involved negotiating with governments with a poor record of dealing with AIDS. In addition, the huge sums of money involved were often very difficult to manage, so that small community-based groups that need thousands of dollars, rather than millions—like Inkanyezi in Orange Farm—were often overlooked in favor of overly ambitious megaprojects, whose effectiveness had not been demonstrated and whose premises were open to question. It seemed clear to me that more could be learned from Inkanyezi's attempt to help people deal with the reality of AIDS than from loveLife's attempt to create a new consumerist man and woman for South Africa.

NOTES

1. Helen Schneider, "On the fault-line: The politics of AIDS policy in contemporary South Africa," *Afr Stud* 61:1 (July 1, 2002), 145–67; Samantha Power, "The AIDS Rebel," *New Yorker*, May 19, 2003, pp. 54–67.
2. Rob Dorrington et al., "The Impact of HIV/AIDS on Adult Mortality in South Africa" (Cape Town: Burden of Disease Research Unit, Medical Research Council of South Africa, September 2001); "Mortality and causes of death in South Africa, 2003 and 2004," Statistics South Africa, May 2006.
3. Richard Delate, "The Struggle for Meaning: A Semiotic Analysis of Interpretations of the loveLife His&Hers Billboard Campaign," November 2001, http://www.comminit.com/global/content/struggle-meaning-semiotic-analysis-interpretations-lovelife-hishers-billboard-campaign.
4. Personal communication, February 2003.
5. For more about this, see Malcolm Gladwell, *The Tipping Point* (Boston: Little, Brown, 2000), and Everett Rogers, *Diffusion of Innovations* (New York: Free Press, 1983).
6. Delate, "Struggle for Meaning."
7. See Prishani Naidoo, "Youth Divided: A Review of loveLife's Y-Centre in Orange Farm" (Johannesburg: CADRE Report, 2003).
8. Nancy Luke and Kathleen M. Kurtz, "Cross-Generational and Transactional Sexual Relations in Sub-Saharan Africa: Prevalence of Behavior and Implications for Negotiating Safer Sexual Practices," International Center for Research on Women, 2002, https://www.icrw.org/wp-content/uploads/2016/10/Cross-generational-and-Transactional-Sexual-Relations-in-Sub-Saharan-Africa-Prevalence-of-Behavior-and-Implications-for-Negotiating-Safer-Sexual-Practices.pdf; J. Swart-Kruger and L. M. Richter, "AIDS-related knowledge, attitudes and behaviour among South African street youth: Reflections on power, sexuality and the autonomous self," *Soc Sci Med* 45:6 (1997), 957–66; Editorial, "Reassessing priorities: Identifying the determinants of HIV transmission," *Soc Sci Med 36:5* (1993), iii–viii.
9. Daniel Low-Beer and Rand Stoneburner, "Uganda and the Challenge of AIDS," in *The Political Economy of AIDS in Africa*, eds. Nana Poku and Alan Whiteside (London: Ashgate, 2004).
10. See Helen Epstein, "Fat," *Granta* 49 (1995). Low-Beer and Stoneburner make this observation, too, as do Janice Hogle et al. in *What Happened in Uganda? Declining HIV Prevalence, Behavior Change and the National Response* (USAID, 2002).

11. In 2006, the *Washington Post* reported that the HIV infection rate in Rwanda, once estimated to be 15 percent, was now estimated to be 3 percent. See Craig Timberg, "How AIDS in Africa Was Overstated: Reliance on Data from Urban Prenatal Clinics Skewed Early Projections," *Washington Post*, April 6, 2006, p. A1. Timberg attributed the downward revision to a new U.S. government survey and suggested that the earlier estimate, issued by the UNAIDS program, had been inflated, perhaps to raise money or appease AIDS activists. Although the old UNAIDS statistics were in need of correction, there clearly had been a decline in the true infection rate. A population-based survey carried out in Rwanda in 1986 found that prevalence was 17.8 percent in urban areas and 1.3 percent in rural areas. (Rwandan HIV Seroprevalence Study Group, "Nationwide community-based serological survey of HIV-1 and other human retrovirus infections in a country," *Lancet* 1 (ii) (1989), 941–43.
12. A. E. Pettifor et al., "Young people's sexual health in South Africa: HIV prevalence and sexual behaviors from a nationally representative household survey," *AIDS* 19:14 (September 23, 2005), 1525–34; but see R. Jewkes, "Response to Pettifor et al.," *AIDS* 20:6 (April 4, 2006), 952–53; author reply, 956–58; and W. M. Parker and M. Colvin, "Response to Pettifor et al.," *AIDS* 20:6 (April 4, 2006), 954–55.
13. In 2005, an article in the prestigious medical journal *AIDS* reported that young people who had attended at least one loveLife program were slightly, but significantly, less likely to be HIV positive than those who had not. The author argued that this was consistent with the possibility that loveLife reduced risky sexual behavior. However, there could well be another explanation. From what I saw, loveLife attracted young people who would have been at lower risk of infection in the first place, either because they were wealthier or better educated or less vulnerable to abuse. (While the loveLife study attempted to control for education and wealth, it did not do so rigorously.) Indeed, the tendency to avoid the subject of AIDS would seem to discourage HIV-positive young people from attending loveLife's programs, and this could make it look as though loveLife protected young people when in fact it merely alienated those most at risk. Most loveLife materials were in English, and thus accessible only to young people with higher social status. This would have sent a clear signal to those—often marginalized and vulnerable young people—who could not speak English well that loveLife was not for them. The main author of the article reporting lower HIV rates among young people exposed to loveLife admitted to me in an interview that an anthropologist hired by loveLife itself had come to these same conclusions, but her results remain unpublished. See Pettifor et al., "A community-based study to examine the effect of a youth HIV prevention intervention on young people aged 15–24 in South Africa: results of the baseline survey," *Trop Med Int Health* 10:10 (October 2005), 971–80; but see also Jewkes, "Response to Pettifor et al.," author reply, and Parker and Colvin, "Response to Pettifor." Information re the loveLife anthropologist from Pettifor, personal communication, April 2006.

Questions for Critical Reading

1. What is a *lifestyle brand*? Make note of the definition of the term as you reread Epstein's text. Then find an example of a lifestyle brand from popular culture. How might such an approach be used in health education? How effective might it be? How effective was it in South Africa?

2. Define *social cohesion* using Epstein's text. What role did it play in HIV infection rates in Uganda? How might that role be extended to other countries, including the United States?

3. What do you think would make an effective HIV prevention program for the United States? Compare your vision to Epstein's and her observations on such programs in Africa Would the same strategies be effective in those two different cultural contexts? Supp t your responses with passages from the essay.

Explorir g Context

1. The (RED) campaign (red.org) pairs popular products with fundraising in the fight against AIDS in Africa. Explore the (RED) website. Given Epstein's argument, how successful might this campaign be? How does your work with lifestyle brands from Question 1 of Questions for Critical Reading inform your answer?
2. Use the web to locate information on current HIV infection rates in Africa. Has the situation improved since Epstein wrote her essay, or is it continuing to get worse? What might account for this trend, given Epstein's argument?
3. One of Epstein's central arguments is the usefulness of conversation in combating HIV infection in Africa. How might social networking technologies like Facebook or Twitter help in such a campaign?

Questions for Connecting

1. Kwame Anthony Appiah, in "Making Conversation" and "The Primacy of Practice" (p. 35), examines the mechanisms of cultural change. Apply his ideas to the fight against HIV/AIDS in Africa. How does social cohesion leverage the power of conversation? How might we promote new practices around sex in Africa regardless of the values that people hold? Work with your definition of social cohesion from Question 2 of Questions for Critical Reading as well as your thoughts on effective HIV prevention programs from Question 3 of Questions for Critical Reading.
2. How has imagination failed in the fight against HIV/AIDS in Africa? Use Daniel Gilbert's insights from "Reporting Live from Tomorrow" (p. 172) to expand Epstein's argument. What role do super-replicators play in the spread of the disease? How could they be used to help eradicate it? Are surrogates available? Why aren't they being used, and what effect might they have?
3. Kenji Yoshino, in "Preface" and "The New Civil Rights" (p. 452), suggests that conversation has an important role to play in producing change around civil rights. How does Epstein's argument confirm or complicate Yoshino's ideas? What makes conversation useful in producing social change?

Language Matters

1. Periods are important marks of punctuation, denoting the units of meaning we call sentences. Select a key passage from Epstein's text and type it into a word processor without any capital letters or periods. In class, trade these never-ending sentences and work on replacing the missing punctuation marks. How can you tell when a period is needed in Epstein's text? How can you tell when one is needed in your own text?

2. Outlines can be helpful in creating organization before we start writing, but they can also help us see the organization of any existing piece of writing. Create an outline of Epstein's piece, using a one-sentence summary of each major move of her argument. What sections do you see in her essay? How do they relate to each other? How can you use postdraft outlines of your own papers to check your organization as you revise?

3. Because it is sexually transmitted, HIV/AIDS is a delicate issue for many people. What sort of tone and language does Epstein use to discuss the disease and its transmission? How do her choices reflect both her audience and the delicacy of the subject matter? When would you make similar choices in your own writing?

Assignments for Writing

1. Epstein explores the way children and families address the AIDS crisis in Africa. In a short paper, examine the generational response to HIV/AIDS using Epstein's essay. Here are some questions to help your critical thinking: How do adults handle the discussion of AIDS? Is this separate from the discussion of other sexually transmitted diseases? How do children and young adults handle this topic? How do *you* handle it? You might want to draw on your work on social cohesion from Question 2 of Questions for Critical Reading or your analysis of conversation's potential for combating HIV from Question 3 of Exploring Context.

2. Epstein evaluates a number of approaches to HIV prevention, both formal and informal campaigns. Write a paper in which you assess the role of government in the prevention of diseases like HIV. Consider: What should the role of the government be in addressing the HIV/AIDS crisis? Both loveLife and Inkanyezi are private organizations that address sexually transmitted diseases and HIV/AIDS; should there be a similar government outreach program? What role would that program play? Are ordinary people better at preventing disease? How can a government promote the kind of strategies that were effective in Uganda?

3. **Multimodal.** South Africa's loveLife relies heavily on an advertising campaign. Using your phone or other available technology, make a short video in which you evaluate the role of commercial culture in addressing national crises such as HIV/AIDS. What role should companies and advertisers take upon themselves? How does that differ from what they appear to do? Are they really just out for profit, or do companies have a conscience? Should or can they act on issues that affect national health? You might want to reference your work on (RED) from Question 1 in Exploring Context in making your argument. You will also want to consider the visual factors inherent in video, whether that is your self-presentation, the background, or the interspersing of other video clips; audio also plays an important role, so think about how what you say, how you say it, and background music (if any) shapes your response.

FRANCIS FUKUYAMA

Francis Fukuyama holds a B.A. in classics from Cornell University and a Ph.D. in political science from Harvard University. He is Olivier Nomellini Senior Fellow at the Freeman Spogli Institute for International Studies at Stanford University. As a prominent neoconservative thinker, Fukuyama signed letters to both President Bill Clinton (in 1998) and President George W. Bush (in 2001) advocating the overthrow of Saddam Hussein (at the time, the president of Iraq). However, Fukuyama ultimately disapproved of the 2003 invasion of Iraq, writing publicly that neoconservative ideas had changed and were no longer supportable. Fukuyama is the author of multiple books of political philosophy advocating liberal democracy, including his 2006 publication *America at the Crossroads*, which deals directly with his departure from the neoconservative agenda.

In *Our Posthuman Future: Consequences of the Biotechnology Revolution* (2002), Fukuyama updates an earlier proposal. Fukuyama had, in his book *The End of History and the Last Man* (1992), suggested that the history of humanity is an ideological struggle that is pretty much settled now, with liberal democracy as the eventual and destined end point, an argument he clarified in *America at the Crossroads*, stating that modernization is what wins the ideological struggle and that liberal democracy is merely one of the outcomes of modernization. In *Our Posthuman Future*, he reexamines this argument, taking into account the potential effects of biotechnology on liberal democracy. Now that human behavior can potentially be modified and DNA can be manipulated, Fukuyama asks, how will a political order based on natural equality survive?

In "Human Dignity," a chapter from *Our Posthuman Future*, Fukuyama examines the idea of "Factor X," an "essential human quality . . . that is worthy of a certain minimal level of respect" (p. 138) regardless of our varying individual characteristics, such as skin color, looks, or social class. Modern science, particularly the science of genetic engineering, Fukuyama claims, tends to disagree with the very idea of an essential human quality like Factor X. From this scientific perspective, human beings are the end result of genetic accidents and environmental influences. Fukuyama, however, finds merit in Pope John Paul II's assertion that science can't fully explain how human beings emerge from simple components. If that assertion is correct, Fukuyama speculates, what does this imply about science's ability to understand other complex systems? What does this mean for the future of human consciousness and political systems? In "Human Dignity," Fukuyama asks the reader to consider what happens to the idea of universal human equality when genetic engineering can be used to "improve" human genes.

Given the seemingly inevitable progress of science, which undoubtedly will influence you throughout your life, what does it mean to be human, and how can we preserve the qualities that make us so?

- TAGS: *civil rights, empathy, ethics, genetics, identity, science and technology, social change*
- CONNECTIONS: *Appiah, Coates, Klosterman, Lukianoff and Haidt, Moalem, Singer, Stillman, Turkle, Watters, Yoshino*

Human Dignity

> Is it, then, possible to imagine a new Natural Philosophy, continually conscious that the "natural object" produced by analysis and abstraction is not reality but only a view, and always correcting the abstraction? I hardly know what I am asking for. . . . The regenerate science which I have in mind would not do even to minerals and vegetables what modern science threatens to do to man himself. When it explained it would not explain away. When it spoke of parts it would remember the whole. . . . The analogy between the *Tao* of Man and the instincts of an animal species would mean for it new light cast on the unknown thing, Instinct, by the only known reality of conscience and not a reduction of conscience to the category of Instinct. Its followers would not be free with the words *only* and *merely*. In a word, it would conquer Nature without being at the same time conquered by her and buy knowledge at a lower cost than that of life.
>
> —C. S. LEWIS, *THE ABOLITION OF MAN*[1]

According to the Decree by the Council of Europe on Human Cloning, "The instrumentalisation of human beings through the deliberate creation of genetically identical human beings is contrary to human dignity and thus constitutes a misuse of medicine and biology."[2] Human dignity is one of those concepts that politicians, as well as virtually everyone else in political life, like to throw around, but that almost no one can either define or explain.

Much of politics centers on the question of human dignity and the desire for recognition to which it is related. That is, human beings constantly demand that others recognize their dignity, either as individuals or as members of religious, ethnic, racial, or other kinds of groups. The struggle for recognition is not economic: What we desire is not money but that other human beings respect us in the way we think we deserve. In earlier times, rulers wanted others to recognize their superior worth as king, emperor, or lord. Today, people seek recognition of their equal status as members of formerly disrespected or devalued groups—as women, gays, Ukrainians, the handicapped, Native Americans, and the like.[3]

The demand for an equality of recognition or respect is the dominant passion of modernity, as Tocqueville* noted over 170 years ago in *Democracy in America*.[4] What this means in a liberal democracy is a bit complicated. It is not necessarily that we think we are equal in all important respects, or demand that our lives be the same as everyone else's. Most people accept the fact that a Mozart or an Einstein or a Michael Jordan has talents and abilities that they don't have, and receives recognition and even monetary compensation for what he accomplishes with those talents. We accept, though we don't necessarily like, the fact that resources are distributed unequally based on what James Madison called the "different and unequal faculties of acquiring property." But we also believe that people deserve to keep what they earn and that the faculties for

*Tocqueville: Alexis de Tocqueville (1805–1859); French political thinker and historian best known for his two-volume book *Democracy in America* (1835 and 1840), which examined changing social conditions in American society [Ed.].

working and earning will not be the same for all people. We also accept the fact that we look different, come from different races and ethnicities, are of different sexes, and have different cultures.

Factor X

What the demand for equality of recognition implies is that when we strip all of a person's contingent and accidental characteristics away, there remains some essential human quality underneath that is worthy of a certain minimal level of respect—call it Factor X. Skin color, looks, social class and wealth, gender, cultural background, and even one's natural talents are all accidents of birth relegated to the class of nonessential characteristics. We make decisions on whom to befriend, whom to marry or do business with, or whom to shun at social events on the basis of these secondary characteristics. But in the political realm we are required to respect people equally on the basis of their possession of Factor X. You can cook, eat, torture, enslave, or render the carcass of any creature lacking Factor X, but if you do the same thing to a human being, you are guilty of a "crime against humanity." We accord beings with Factor X not just human rights but, if they are adults, political rights as well—that is, the right to live in democratic political communities where their rights to speech, religion, association, and political participation are respected.

The circle of beings to whom we attribute Factor X has been one of the most contested issues throughout human history. For many societies, including most democratic societies in earlier periods of history, Factor X belonged to a significant subset of the human race, excluding people of certain sexes, economic classes, races, and tribes and people with low intelligence, disabilities, birth defects, and the like. These societies were highly stratified, with different classes possessing more or less of Factor X, and some possessing none at all. Today, for believers in liberal equality, Factor X etches a bright red line around the whole of the human race and requires equality of respect for all of those on the inside, but attributes a lower level of dignity to those outside the boundary. Factor X is the human essence, the most basic meaning of what it is to be human. If all human beings are in fact equal in dignity, then X must be some characteristic universally possessed by them. So what is Factor X, and where does it come from?

For Christians, the answer is fairly easy: It comes from God. Man is created in the image of God, and therefore shares in some of God's sanctity, which entitles human beings to a higher level of respect than the rest of natural creation. In the words of Pope John Paul II, what this means is that "the human individual cannot be subordinated as a pure means or a pure instrument, either to the species or to society; he has value per se. He is a person. With his intellect and his will, he is capable of forming a relationship of communion, solidarity, and self-giving with his peers. . . . It is by virtue of his spiritual soul that the whole person possesses such dignity even in his body."[5]

So what is Factor X, and where does it come from?

Supposing one is not a Christian (or a religious believer of any sort), and doesn't accept the premise that man is created in the image of God. Is there a secular ground for believing that human beings are entitled to a special moral status or dignity?

Perhaps the most famous effort to create a philosophical basis for human dignity was that of Kant,* who argued that Factor X was based on the human capacity for moral choice. That is, human beings could differ in intelligence, wealth, race, and gender, but all were equally able to act according to moral law or not. Human beings had dignity because they alone had free will—not just the subjective illusion of free will but the actual ability to transcend natural determinism and the normal rules of causality. It is the existence of free will that leads to Kant's well-known conclusion that human beings are always to be treated as ends and not as means.

It would be very difficult for any believer in a materialistic account of the universe—which includes the vast majority of natural scientists—to accept the Kantian account of human dignity. The reason is that it forces them to accept a form of dualism—that there is a realm of human freedom parallel to the realm of nature that is not determined by the latter. Most natural scientists would argue that what we believe to be free will is in fact an illusion and that all human decision making can ultimately be traced back to material causes. Human beings decide to do one thing over another because one set of neurons fires rather than another, and those neuronal firings can be traced back to prior material states of the brain. The human decision-making process may be more complex than that of other animals, but there is no sharp dividing line that distinguishes human moral choice from the kinds of choices that are made by other animals. Kant himself does not offer any proof that free will exists; he says that it is simply a necessary postulate of pure practical reason about the nature of morality—hardly an argument that a hard-bitten empirical scientist would accept.

Seize the Power

The problem posed by modern natural science goes even deeper. The very notion that there exists such a thing as a human "essence" has been under relentless attack by modern science for much of the past century and a half. One of the most fundamental assertions of Darwinism† is that species do not have essences.[6] That is, while Aristotle‡ believed in the eternity of the species (i.e., that what we have been labeling "species-typical behavior" is something unchanging), Darwin's theory maintains that this behavior changes in response to the organism's interaction with its environment. What is typical for a species represents a snapshot of the species at one particular moment of evolutionary time; what came before and what comes after will be different. Since Darwinism maintains that there is no cosmic teleology guiding the process of evolution, what seems to be the essence of a species is just an accidental by product of a random evolutionary process.

In this perspective, what we have been calling human nature is merely the species-typical human characteristics and behavior that emerged about 100,000 10

*Kant: Immanuel Kant (1724–1804), German philosopher best known for *Critique of Pure Reason* (1781); he was concerned with questions of how we can know what we know [Ed.].

†Darwinism: Shorthand for naturalist Charles Darwin's idea of evolution by natural selection, the concept that only the species best adapted to their environment survive [Ed.].

‡Aristotle: Greek philosopher and enormously important figure in Western thought. Aristotle (384–322 BC) was a student of Plato and a teacher of Alexander the Great [Ed.].

years ago, during what evolutionary biologists call the "era of evolutionary adaptation"—when the precursors of modern humans were living and breeding on the African savanna. For many, this suggests that human nature has no special status as a guide to morals or values because it is historically contingent. David Hull, for example, argues,

> I do not see why the existence of human universals is all that important. Perhaps all and only people have opposable thumbs, use tools, live in true societies, or what have you. I think that such attributions are either false or vacuous, but even if they were true and significant, the distributions of these particular characters is largely a matter of evolutionary happenstance.[7]

The geneticist Lee Silver, trying to debunk the idea that there is a natural order that could be undermined by genetic engineering, asserts,

> Unfettered evolution is never predetermined [toward some goal], and not necessarily associated with progress—it is simply a response to unpredictable environmental changes. If the asteroid that hit our planet 60 million years ago had flown past instead, there would never have been any human beings at all. And whatever the natural order might be, it is not necessarily good. The smallpox virus was part of the natural order until it was forced into extinction by human intervention.[8]

This inability to define a natural essence doesn't bother either writer. Hull, for example, states that "I, for one, would be extremely uneasy to base something as important as human rights on such temporary contingencies [as human nature] . . . . I fail to see why it matters. I fail to see, for example, why we must all be essentially the same to have rights."[9] Silver, for his part, pooh-poohs fears about genetic engineering on the part of those with religious convictions or those who believe in a natural order. In the future, man will no longer be a slave to his genes, but their master:

> Why not seize this power? Why not control what has been left to chance in the past? Indeed, we control all other aspects of our children's lives and identities through powerful social and environmental influences and, in some cases, with the use of powerful drugs like Ritalin and Prozac. On what basis can we reject positive genetic influences on a person's essence when we accept the rights of parents to benefit their children in every other way?[10]

Why not seize this power, indeed?

Well, let us begin by considering what the consequences of the abandonment of the idea that there is a Factor X, or human essence, that unites all human beings would be for the cherished idea of universal human equality—an idea to which virtually all of the debunkers of the idea of human essences are invariably committed. Hull is right that we don't all need to be the same in order to have rights—but we need to be the same in some one critical respect in order to have *equal* rights. He for one is very concerned that basing human rights on human nature will stigmatize homosexuals, because their sexual orientation differs from the heterosexual norm. But the only basis on which anyone can make an argument in favor of equal rights for gays is to argue that whatever their sexual orientation, *they are people too* in some other respect that is more essential than their sexuality. If you cannot find this common other ground, then there is no reason not to discriminate against them, because in fact they are different creatures from everyone else.

Similarly, Lee Silver, who is so eager to take up the power of genetic engineering to "improve" people, is nonetheless horrified at the possibility that it could be used to create a class of genetically superior people. He paints a scenario in which a class called the GenRich steadily improve the cognitive abilities of their children to the point that they break off from the rest of the human race to form a separate species.

Silver is not horrified by much else that technology may bring us by way of unnatural reproduction—for example, two lesbians producing genetic offspring, or eggs taken from an unborn female fetus to produce a child whose mother had never been born. He dismisses the moral concerns of virtually every religion or traditional moral system with regard to future genetic engineering but draws the line at what he perceives as threats to human equality. He does not seem to understand that, given his premises, there are no possible grounds on which he can object to the GenRich, or the fact that they might assign themselves rights superior to those of the GenPoor. Since there is no stable essence common to all human beings, or rather because that essence is variable and subject to human manipulation, why not create a race born with metaphorical saddles on their backs, and another with boots and spurs to ride them? Why not seize *that* power as well?

The bioethicist Peter Singer, whose appointment to Princeton University caused great controversy because of his advocacy of infanticide and euthanasia under certain circumstances, is simply more consistent than most people on the consequences of abandoning the concept of human dignity. Singer is an unabashed utilitarian: He believes that the single relevant standard for ethics is to minimize suffering in the aggregate for all creatures. Human beings are part of a continuum of life and have no special status in his avowedly Darwinian worldview. This leads him to two perfectly logical conclusions: the need for animal rights, since animals can experience pain and suffering as well as humans, and the downgrading of the rights of infants and elderly people who lack certain key traits, like self-awareness, that would allow them to anticipate pain. The rights of certain animals, in his view, deserve greater respect than those of certain human beings. 15

But Singer is not nearly forthright enough in following these premises through to their logical conclusion, since he remains a committed egalitarian. What he does not explain is why the relief of suffering should remain the only moral good. As usual, the philosopher Friedrich Nietzsche was much more clear-eyed than anyone else in understanding the consequences of modern natural science and the abandonment of the concept of human dignity. Nietzsche had the great insight to see that, on the one hand, once the clear red line around the whole of humanity could no longer be drawn, the way would be paved for a return to a much more hierarchical ordering of society. If there is a continuum of gradations between human and nonhuman, there is a continuum within the type human as well. This would inevitably mean the liberation of the strong from the constraints that a belief in either God or Nature had placed on them. On the other hand, it would lead the rest of mankind to demand health and safety as the only possible goods, since all the higher goals that had once been set for them were now debunked. In the words of Nietzsche's Zarathustra, "One has one's little pleasure for the day and one's little pleasure for the night: But one has a regard for health. 'We have invented happiness,' say the last men, and they blink."[11] Indeed, both the return of hierarchy and the egalitarian demand for health, safety, and relief of suffering might all go hand in hand if the rulers of the future could provide the masses with enough of the "little poisons" they demanded.

It has always struck me that one hundred years after Nietzsche's death, we are much less far down the road to either the superman or the last man than he predicted. Nietzsche once castigated John Stuart Mill as a "flathead" for believing that one could have a semblance of Christian morality in the absence of belief in a Christian God. And yet, in a Europe and an America that have become secularized over the past two generations, we see a lingering belief in the concept of human dignity, which is by now completely cut off from its religious roots. And not just lingering: The idea that one could exclude any group of people on the basis of race, gender, disability, or virtually any other characteristic from the charmed circle of those deserving recognition for human dignity is the one thing that will bring total obloquy on the head of any politician who proposes it. In the words of the philosopher Charles Taylor, "We believe it would be utterly wrong and unfounded to draw the boundaries any narrower than around the whole human race," and should anyone try to do so, "we should immediately ask what distinguished those within from those left out."[12] The idea of the equality of human dignity, deracinated from its Christian or Kantian origins, is held as a matter of religious dogma by the most materialist of natural scientists. The continuing arguments over the moral status of the unborn (about which more later) constitute the only exception to this general rule.

The reasons for the persistence of the idea of the equality of human dignity are complex. Partly it is a matter of the force of habit and what Max Weber once called the "ghost of dead religious beliefs" that continue to haunt us. Partly it is the product of historical accident: The last important political movement to explicitly deny the premise of universal human dignity was Nazism, and the horrifying consequences of the Nazis' racial and eugenic policies were sufficient to inoculate those who experienced them for the next couple of generations.

But another important reason for the persistence of the idea of the universality of human dignity has to do with what we might call the nature of nature itself. Many of the grounds on which certain groups were historically denied their share of human dignity were proven to be simply a matter of prejudice, or else based on cultural and environmental conditions that could be changed. The notions that women were too irrational or emotional to participate in politics, and that immigrants from southern Europe had smaller head sizes and were less intelligent than those from northern Europe, were overturned on the basis of sound, empirical science. That moral order did not completely break down in the West in the wake of the destruction of consensus over traditional religious values should not surprise us either, because moral order comes from within human nature itself and is not something that has to be imposed on human nature by culture.[13]

All of this could change under the impact of future biotechnology. The most clear and present danger is that the large genetic variations between individuals will narrow and become clustered within certain distinct social groups. Today, the "genetic lottery" guarantees that the son or daughter of a rich and successful parent will not

20

necessarily inherit the talents and abilities that created conditions conducive to the parent's success. Of course, there has always been a degree of genetic selection: Assortative mating means that successful people will tend to marry each other and, to the extent that their success is genetically based, will pass on to their children better life opportunities. But in the future, the full weight of modern technology can be put in the service of optimizing the kinds of genes that are passed on to one's offspring. This means that social elites may not just pass on social advantages but embed them genetically as well. This may one day include not only characteristics like intelligence and beauty, but behavioral traits like diligence, competitiveness, and the like.

The genetic lottery is judged as inherently unfair by many because it condemns certain people to lesser intelligence, or bad looks, or disabilities of one sort or another. But in another sense it is profoundly egalitarian, since everyone, regardless of social class, race, or ethnicity, has to play in it. The wealthiest man can and often does have a good-for-nothing son; hence the saying "Shirtsleeves to shirtsleeves in three generations." When the lottery is replaced by choice, we open up a new avenue along which human beings can compete, one that threatens to increase the disparity between the top and bottom of the social hierarchy.

What the emergence of a genetic overclass will do to the idea of universal human dignity is something worth pondering. Today, many bright and successful young people believe that they owe their success to accidents of birth and upbringing but for which their lives might have taken a very different course. They feel themselves, in other words, to be lucky, and they are capable of feeling sympathy for people who are less lucky than they. But to the extent that they become "children of choice" who have been genetically selected by their parents for certain characteristics, they may come to believe increasingly that their success is a matter not just of luck but of good choices and planning on the part of their parents, and hence something deserved. They will look, think, act, and perhaps even feel differently from those who were not similarly chosen, and may come in time to think of themselves as different kinds of creatures. They may, in short, feel themselves to be aristocrats, and unlike aristocrats of old, their claim to better birth will be rooted in nature and not convention.

Aristotle's discussion of slavery in Book I of the *Politics* is instructive on this score. It is often condemned as a justification of Greek slavery, but in fact the discussion is far more sophisticated and is relevant to our thinking about genetic classes. Aristotle makes a distinction between conventional and natural slavery.[14] He argues that slavery would be justified by nature if it were the case that there were people with naturally slavish natures. It is not clear from his discussion that he believes such people exist: Most actual slavery is conventional—that is, it is the result of victory in war or force, or based on the wrong opinion that barbarians as a class should be slaves of Greeks.[15] The noble-born think their nobility comes from nature rather than acquired virtue and that they can pass it on to their children. But, Aristotle notes, nature is "frequently unable to bring this about."[16] So why not, as Lee Silver suggests, "seize this power" to give children genetic advantages and correct the defect of natural equality?

The possibility that biotechnology will permit the emergence of new genetic classes has been frequently noted and condemned by those who have speculated about the future.[17] But the opposite possibility also seems to be entirely plausible—that there will be an impetus toward a much more genetically egalitarian society. For it seems highly unlikely that people in modern democratic societies will sit around complacently if they see elites embedding their advantages genetically in their children.

Indeed, this is one of the few things in a politics of the future that people are likely to rouse themselves to fight over. By this I mean not just fighting metaphorically, in the sense of shouting matches among talking heads on TV and debates in Congress, but actually picking up guns and bombs and using them on other people. There are very few domestic political issues today in our rich, self-satisfied liberal democracies that can cause people to get terribly upset, but the specter of rising genetic inequality may well get people off their couches and into the streets.

If people get upset enough about genetic inequality, there will be two alternative courses of action. The first and most sensible would simply be to forbid the use of biotechnology to enhance human characteristics and decline to compete in this dimension. But the notion of enhancement may become too powerfully attractive to forego, or it may prove difficult to enforce a rule preventing people from enhancing their children, or the courts may declare they have a right to do so. At this point a second possibility opens up, which is to use that same technology to raise up the bottom.[18]

This is the only scenario in which it is plausible that we will see a liberal democracy of the future get back into the business of state-sponsored eugenics. The bad old form of eugenics discriminated against the disabled and less intelligent by forbidding them to have children. In the future, it may be possible to breed children who are more intelligent, more healthy, more "normal." Raising the bottom is something that can only be accomplished through the intervention of the state. Genetic enhancement technology is likely to be expensive and involve some risk, but even if it were relatively cheap and safe, people who are poor and lacking in education would still fail to take advantage of it. So the bright red line of universal human dignity will have to be reinforced by allowing the state to make sure that no one falls outside it.

The politics of breeding future human beings will be very complex. Up to now, the Left has on the whole been opposed to cloning, genetic engineering, and similar biotechnologies for a number of reasons, including traditional humanism, environmental concerns, suspicion of technology and of the corporations that produce it, and fear of eugenics. The Left has historically sought to play down the importance of heredity in favor of social factors in explaining human outcomes. For people on the Left to come around and support genetic engineering for the disadvantaged, they would first have to admit that genes are important in determining intelligence and other types of social outcomes in the first place.

The Left has been more hostile to biotechnology in Europe than in North America. Much of this hostility is driven by the stronger environmental movements there, which have led the campaign, for example, against genetically modified foods. (Whether certain forms of radical environmentalism will translate into hostility to human biotechnology remains to be seen. Some environmentalists see themselves defending nature from human beings, and seem to be more concerned with threats to nonhuman than to human nature.) The Germans in particular remain very sensitive to anything that smacks of eugenics. The philosopher Peter Sloterdijk raised a storm of protest in 1999 when he suggested that it will soon be impossible for people to refuse the power of selection that biotechnology provides them, and that the questions of breeding something "beyond" man that were raised by Nietzsche and Plato could no longer be ignored.[19]

He was condemned by the sociologist Jürgen Habermas, among others, who in other contexts has also come out against human cloning.[20]

On the other hand, there are some on the Left who have begun to make the case for genetic engineering.[21] John Rawls argued in *A Theory of Justice* that the unequal distribution of natural talents was inherently unfair. A Rawlsian should therefore want to make use of biotechnology to equalize life chances by breeding the bottom up, assuming that prudential considerations concerning safety, cost, and the like would be settled. Ronald Dworkin has laid out a case for the right of parents to genetically engineer their children based on a broader concern to protect autonomy,[22] and Laurence Tribe has suggested that a ban on cloning would be wrong because it might create discrimination against children who were cloned in spite of the ban.[23]

It is impossible to know which of these two radically different scenarios—one of growing genetic inequality, the other of growing genetic equality—is more likely to come to pass. But once the technological possibility for biomedical enhancement is realized, it is hard to see how growing genetic inequality would fail to become one of the chief controversies of twenty-first-century politics.

Human Dignity Redux

Denial of the concept of human dignity—that is, of the idea that there is something unique about the human race that entitles every member of the species to a higher moral status than the rest of the natural world—leads us down a very perilous path. We may be compelled ultimately to take this path, but we should do so only with our eyes open. Nietzsche is a much better guide to what lies down that road than the legions of bioethicists and casual academic Darwinians that today are prone to give us moral advice on this subject.

To avoid following that road, we need to take another look at the notion of human dignity, and ask whether there is a way to defend the concept against its detractors that is fully compatible with modern natural science but that also does justice to the full meaning of human specificity. I believe that there is.

In contrast to a number of conservative Protestant denominations that continue to hold a brief for creationism, the Catholic Church by the end of the twentieth century had come to terms with the theory of evolution. In his 1996 message to the Pontifical Academy of Sciences, Pope John Paul II corrected the encyclical *Humani generis* of Pius XII, which maintained that Darwinian evolution was a serious hypothesis but one that remained unproven. The pope stated, "Today, almost half a century after the publication of the Encyclical, new knowledge has led to the recognition of the theory of evolution as more than a hypothesis. It is indeed remarkable that this theory has been progressively accepted by researchers, following a series of discoveries in various fields of knowledge. The convergence, neither sought nor fabricated, of the results of work that was conducted independently is in itself a significant argument in favor of this theory."[24]

But the pope went on to say that while the church can accept the view that man is descended from nonhuman animals, there is an "ontological leap" that occurs somewhere in this evolutionary process.[25] The human soul is something directly created by God: Consequently, "theories of evolution which, in accordance with the philosophies inspiring them, consider the mind as emerging from the forces of living nature, or as a mere epiphenomenon of this matter, are incompatible with the truth about man." The pope continued, "Nor are they able to ground the dignity of the person."

The pope was saying, in other words, that at some point in the 5 million years between man's chimplike forebears and the emergence of modern human beings, a human soul was inserted into us in a way that remains mysterious. Modern natural science can uncover the time line of this process and explicate its material correlates, but it has not fully explained either what the soul is or how it came to be. The church has obviously learned a great deal from modern natural science in the past two centuries and has adjusted its doctrines accordingly. But while many natural scientists would scoff at the idea that they have anything to learn from the church, the pope has pointed to a real weakness in the current state of evolutionary theory, which scientists would do well to ponder. Modern natural science has explained a great deal less about what it means to be human than many scientists think it has.

Parts and Wholes

Many contemporary Darwinians believe that they have demystified the problem of how human beings came to be human through the classical reductionist methods of modern natural science. That is, any higher-order behavior or characteristic, such as language or aggression, can be traced back through the firing of neurons to the biochemical substrate of the brain, which in turn can be understood in terms of the simpler organic compounds of which it is composed. The brain arrived at its present state through a series of incremental evolutionary changes that were driven by random variation, and a process of natural selection by which the requirements of the surrounding environment selected for certain mental characteristics. Every human characteristic can thus be traced back to a prior material cause. If, for example, we today love to listen to Mozart or Beethoven, it is because we have auditory systems that were evolved, in the environment of evolutionary adaptation, to discriminate between certain kinds of sounds that were necessary perhaps to warn us against predators or to help us on a hunt.[26]

The problem with this kind of thinking is not that it is necessarily false but that it is insufficient to explain many of the most salient and unique human traits. The problem lies in the methodology of reductionism itself for understanding complex systems, and particularly biological ones.

Reductionism constitutes, of course, one of the foundations of modern natural science and is responsible for many of its greatest triumphs. You see before you two apparently different substances, the graphite in your pencil lead and the diamond in your engagement ring, and you might be tempted to believe that they were essentially different substances. But reductionist chemistry has taught us that in fact they are both composed of the same simpler substance, carbon, and that the apparent differences are not ones of essence but merely of the way the carbon atoms are bonded. Reductionist physics has been busy over the past century tracing atoms back to subatomic particles and thence back to an even more reduced set of basic forces of nature.

But what is appropriate for domains in physics, like celestial mechanics and fluid dynamics, is not necessarily appropriate for the study of objects at the opposite end of the complexity scale, like most biological systems, because the behavior of complex systems cannot be predicted by simply aggregating or scaling up the behavior of the parts that constitute them.* The distinctive and easily recognizable behavior of a flock of birds or a swarm of bees, for example, is the product of the interaction of individual birds or bees following relatively simple behavioral rules (fly next to a partner, avoid obstacles, and so on), none of which encompasses or defines the behavior of the flock or swarm as a whole. Rather, the group behavior "emerges" as a result of the interaction of the individuals that make it up. In many cases, the relationship between parts and wholes is nonlinear: That is, increasing input A increases output B up to a certain point, whereupon it creates a qualitatively different and unexpected output C. This is true even of relatively simple chemicals like water: H_2O undergoes a phase transition from liquid to solid at 32 degrees Fahrenheit, something that one would not necessarily predict on the basis of knowledge of its chemical composition.

That the behavior of complex wholes cannot be understood as the aggregated behavior of their parts has been understood in the natural sciences for some time now,[27] and has led to the development of the field of so-called nonlinear or "complex adaptive" systems, which try to model the emergence of complexity. This approach is, in a way, the opposite of reductionism: It shows that while wholes can be traced back to their simpler antecedent parts, there is no simple predictive model that allows us to move from the parts to the emergent behaviors of the wholes. Being nonlinear, they may be extremely sensitive to small differences in starting conditions and thus may appear chaotic even when their behavior is completely deterministic.

This means that the behavior of complex systems is much more difficult to understand than the founders of reductionist science once believed. The eighteenth-century astronomer Laplace once said that he could precisely predict the future of the universe on the basis of Newtonian mechanics, if he could know the mass and motion of the universe's constituent parts.[28] No scientist could make this claim today—not just because of the inherent uncertainties introduced by quantum mechanics but also because there exists no reliable methodology for predicting the behavior of complex systems.[29] In the words of Arthur Peacocke, "The concepts and theories . . . that constitute the content of the sciences focusing on the more complex levels are often (not always) logically not reducible to those operative in the sciences that focus on their components."[30] There is a hierarchy of levels of complexity in the sciences, with human beings and human behavior occupying a place at the uppermost level.

Each level can give us some insight into the levels above it, but understanding the lower levels does not allow one to fully understand the higher levels' emergent properties. Researchers in the area of complex adaptive systems have created so-called agent-based models of complex systems, and have applied them in a wide variety of areas, from cell biology to fighting a war to distributing natural gas. It remains to be seen,

*The determinism of classical Newtonian mechanics is based in large measure on the parallelogram rule, which says that the effects of two forces acting on a body can be summed as if each were acting independently of the other. Newton shows that this rule works for celestial bodies like planets and stars, and assumes that it will also work for other natural objects, like animals.

however, whether this approach constitutes a single, coherent methodology applicable to all complex systems.[31] Such models may tell us only that certain systems will remain inherently chaotic and unpredictable, or that prediction rests on a precise knowledge of initial conditions that is unavailable to us. The higher level must thus be understood with a methodology appropriate to its degree of complexity.

We can illustrate the problematic relationship of parts to wholes by reference to one unique domain of human behavior, politics.[32] Aristotle states that man is a political animal by nature. If one were to try to build a case for human dignity based on human specificity, the capability of engaging in politics would certainly constitute one important component of human uniqueness. Yet the idea of our uniqueness in this regard has been challenged. . . . [C]himpanzees and other primates engage in something that looks uncannily like human politics as they struggle and connive to achieve alpha male status. They appear, moreover, to feel the political emotions of pride and shame as they interact with other members of their group. Their political behavior can also apparently be transmitted through nongenetic means, so that political culture would not seem to be the exclusive preserve of human beings.[33] Some observers gleefully cite examples like this to deflate human feelings of self-importance relative to other species.

45

But to confuse human politics with the social behavior of any other species is to mistake parts for wholes. Only human beings can formulate, debate, and modify abstract rules of justice. When Aristotle asserted that man is a political animal by nature, he meant this only in the sense that politics is a potentiality that emerges over time.[34] He notes that human politics did not begin until the first lawgiver established a state and promulgated laws, an event that was of great benefit to mankind but that was contingent on historical developments. This accords with what we know today about the emergence of the state, which took place in parts of the world like Egypt and Babylonia perhaps 10,000 years ago and was most likely related to the development of agriculture. For tens of thousands of years before that, human beings lived in stateless hunter-gatherer societies in which the largest group numbered no more than 50 to 100 individuals, most of them related by kinship.[35] So in a certain sense, while human sociability is obviously natural, it is not clear that humans are political animals by nature.

But Aristotle insists that politics is natural to man despite the fact that it did not exist at all in early periods of human history. He argues that it is human language that allows human beings to formulate laws and abstract principles of justice that are necessary to the creation of a state and of political order. Ethologists have noted that many other species communicate with sounds, and that chimpanzees and other animals can learn human language to a limited extent. But no other species has *human* language—that is, the ability to formulate and communicate abstract principles of action. It is only when these two natural characteristics, human sociability and human language, come together that human politics emerges. Human language obviously evolved to promote sociability, but it is very unlikely that there were evolutionary forces shaping it to become an enabler of politics. It was rather like one of Stephen Jay Gould's spandrels,* something that evolved for one reason but that found another key

* A spandrel is an architectural feature that emerges, unplanned by the architect, from the intersection of a dome and the walls that support it.

purpose when combined in a human whole.[36] Human politics, though natural in an emergent sense, is not reducible to either animal sociability or animal language, which were its precursors.

Consciousness

The area in which the inability of a reductionist materialist science to explain observable phenomena is most glaringly evident is the question of human consciousness. By consciousness I mean subjective mental states: not just the thoughts and images that appear to you as you are thinking or reading this page, but also the sensations, feelings, and emotions that you experience as part of everyday life.

There has been a huge amount of research and theorizing about consciousness over the past two generations, coming in equal measure from the neurosciences and from studies in computer and artificial intelligence (AI). Particularly in the latter field there are many enthusiasts who are convinced that with more powerful computers and new approaches to computing, such as neural networks, we are on the verge of a breakthrough in which mechanical computers will achieve consciousness. There have been conferences and earnest discussions devoted to the question of whether it would be moral to turn off such a machine if and when this breakthrough occurs, and whether we would need to assign rights to conscious machines.

The fact of the matter is that we are nowhere close to a breakthrough; consciousness remains as stubbornly mysterious as it ever was. The problem with the current state of thinking begins with the traditional philosophical problem of the ontological status of consciousness. Subjective mental states, while produced by material biological processes, appear to be of a very different, nonmaterial order from other phenomena. The fear of dualism—that is, the doctrine that there are two essential types of being, material and mental—is so strong among researchers in this field that it has led them to palpably ridiculous conclusions. In the words of the philosopher John Searle,

> Seen from the perspective of the last fifty years, the philosophy of mind, as well as cognitive science and certain branches of psychology, present a very curious spectacle. The most striking feature is how much of mainstream philosophy of mind of the past fifty years seems obviously false . . . . [I]n the philosophy of mind, obvious facts about the mental, such as that we all really do have subjective conscious mental states and that these are not eliminable in favor of anything else, are routinely denied by many, perhaps most, of the advanced thinkers in the subject.[37]

An example of a patently false understanding of consciousness comes from one of the leading experts in the field, Daniel Dennett, whose book *Consciousness Explained* finally comes to the following definition of consciousness: "Human consciousness is *itself* a huge complex of memes (or more exactly, meme-effects in brains) that can best be understood as the operation of a *'von Neumannesque'* virtual machine *implemented* in the *parallel architecture* of a brain that was not designed for any such activities."[38] A naive reader may be excused for thinking that this kind of statement doesn't do much at all to advance our understanding of consciousness. Dennett is saying in effect that human consciousness is simply the by-product of the operations of a certain type of computer, and if we think that there is more to it than that, we have a mistakenly old-fashioned view of what consciousness is. As Searle says of this approach, it works only by denying the existence of what you and I and everyone else understand consciousness to be (that is, subjective feelings).[39]

Similarly, many of the researchers in the field of artificial intelligence sidestep the question of consciousness by in effect changing the subject. They assume that the brain is simply a highly complex type of organic computer that can be identified by its external characteristics. The well-known Turing test asserts that if a machine can perform a cognitive task such as carrying on a conversation in a way that from the outside is indistinguishable from similar activities carried out by a human being, then it is indistinguishable on the inside as well. Why this should be an adequate test of human mentality is a mystery, for the machine will obviously not have any subjective awareness of what it is doing, or feelings about its activities.* This doesn't prevent such authors as Hans Moravec[40] and Ray Kurzweil[41] from predicting that machines, once they reach a requisite level of complexity, will possess human attributes like consciousness as well.[42] If they are right, this will have important consequences for our notions of human dignity, because it will have been conclusively proven that human beings are essentially nothing more than complicated machines that can be made out of silicon and transistors as easily as carbon and neurons.

The likelihood that this will happen seems very remote, however, not so much because machines will never duplicate human intelligence—I suspect they will probably be able to come very close in this regard—but rather because it is impossible to see how they will come to acquire human emotions. It is the stuff of science fiction for an android, robot, or computer to suddenly start experiencing emotions like fear, hope, even sexual desire, but no one has come remotely close to positing how this might come about. The problem is not simply that, like the rest of consciousness, no one understands what emotions are ontologically; no one understands why they came to exist in human biology.

There are of course functional reasons for feelings like pain and pleasure. If we didn't find sex pleasurable we wouldn't reproduce, and if we didn't feel pain from fire we would be burning ourselves constantly. But state-of-the-art thinking in cognitive science maintains that the particular subjective form that the emotions take is not necessary to their function. It is perfectly possible, for example, to design a robot with heat sensors in its fingers connected to an actuator that would pull the robot's hand away from a fire. The robot could keep itself from being burned without having any subjective sense of pain, and it could make decisions on which objectives to fulfill and which activities to avoid on the basis of a mechanical computation of the inputs of different electrical impulses. A Turing test would say it was a human being in its behavior, but it would actually be devoid of the most important quality of a human being, feelings. The actual subjective forms that emotions take are today seen in evolutionary biology and in cognitive science as no more than epiphenomenal to their underlying function;

* Searle's critique of this approach is contained in his "Chinese room" puzzle, which raises the question of whether a computer could be said to understand Chinese any more than a non-Chinese-speaking individual locked in a room who received instructions on how to manipulate a series of symbols in Chinese. See Searle (1997), p. 11.

there are no obvious reasons this form should have been selected for in the course of evolutionary history.[43]

As Robert Wright points out, this leads to the very bizarre outcome that what is most important to us as human beings has no apparent purpose in the material scheme of things by which we became human.[44] For it is the distinctive human gamut of emotions that produces human purposes, goals, objectives, wants, needs, desires, fears, aversions, and the like and hence is the source of human values. While many would list human reason and human moral choice as the most important unique human characteristics that give our species dignity, I would argue that possession of the full human emotional gamut is at least as important, if not more so.

The political theorist Robert McShea demonstrates the importance of human emotions to our commonsense understanding of what it means to be human by asking us to perform the following thought experiment.[45] Suppose you met two creatures on a desert island, both of which had the rational capacity of a human being and hence the ability to carry on a conversation. One had the physical form of a lion but the emotions of a human being, while the other had the physical form of a human being but the emotional characteristics of a lion. Which creature would you feel more comfortable with, which creature would you be more likely to befriend or enter into a moral relationship with? The answer, as countless children's books with sympathetic talking lions suggest, is the lion, because species-typical human emotions are more critical to our sense of our own humanness than either our reason or our physical appearance. The coolly analytical Mr. Spock in the TV series *Star Trek* appears at times more likable than the emotional Mr. Scott only because we suspect that somewhere beneath his rational exterior lurk deeply buried human feelings. Certainly many of the female characters he encountered in the series hoped they could rouse something more than robotic responses from him.

On the other hand, we would regard a Mr. Spock who was truly devoid of any feelings as a psychopath and a monster. If he offered us a benefit, we might accept it but would feel no gratitude because we would know it was the product of rational calculation on his part and not goodwill. If we double-crossed him, we would feel no guilt, because we know that he cannot himself entertain feelings of anger or of having been betrayed. And if circumstances forced us to kill him to save ourselves, or to sacrifice his life in a hostage situation, we would feel no more regret than if we lost any other valuable asset, like a car or a teleporter.[46] Even though we might want to cooperate with this Mr. Spock, we would not regard him as a moral agent entitled to the respect that human beings command. The computer geeks in AI labs who think of themselves as nothing more than complex computer programs and want to download themselves into a computer should worry, since no one would care if they were turned off for good.

We would regard a Mr. Spock who was truly devoid of any feelings as a psychopath and a monster.

So there is a great deal that comes together under the rubric of consciousness that helps define human specificity and hence human dignity, which nonetheless cannot currently be fully explicated by modern natural science. It is not sufficient to argue that some other animals are conscious, or have culture, or have language, for their consciousness does not combine human reason, human language, human moral choice, and human emotions in ways that are capable of producing human politics, human art, or human religion. All of the nonhuman precursors of these human traits that existed in evolutionary history, and all of the material causes and preconditions for their emergence, collectively add up to much less than the human whole. Jared Diamond in his book *The Third Chimpanzee* notes the fact that the chimpanzee and human genomes overlap by more than 98 percent, implying that the differences between the two species are relatively trivial.[47] But for an emergent complex system, small differences can lead to enormous qualitative changes. It is a bit like saying there is no significant difference between ice and liquid water because they differ in temperature by only 1 degree.

Thus one does not have to agree with the pope that God directly inserted a human soul in the course of evolutionary history to acknowledge with him that there was a very important qualitative, if not ontological, leap that occurred at some point in this process. It is this leap from parts to a whole that ultimately has to constitute the basis for human dignity, a concept one can believe in even if one does not begin from the pope's religious premises.

What this whole is and how it came to be remain, in Searle's word, "mysterious." None of the branches of modern natural science that have tried to address this question have done more than scratch the surface, despite the belief of many scientists that they have demystified the entire process. It is common now for many AI researchers to say that consciousness is an "emergent property" of a certain kind of complex computer. But this is no more than an unproven hypothesis based on an analogy with other complex systems. No one has ever seen consciousness emerge under experimental conditions, or even posited a theory as to how this might come about. It would be surprising if the process of "emergence" didn't play an important part in explaining how humans came to be human, but whether that is all there is to the story is something we do not at present know.

This is not to say that the demystification by science will never happen. Searle himself believes that consciousness is a biological property of the brain much like the firing of neurons or the production of neurotransmitters and that biology will someday be able to explain how organic tissue can produce it. He argues that our present problems in understanding consciousness do not require us to adopt a dualistic ontology or abandon the scientific framework of material causation. The problem of how consciousness arose does not require recourse to the direct intervention of God.

It does not, on the other hand, rule it out, either. 60

What to Fight For

If what gives us dignity and a moral status higher than that of other living creatures is related to the fact that we are complex wholes rather than the sum of simple parts, then it is clear that there is no simple answer to the question, What is Factor X? That is, Factor X cannot be reduced to the possession of moral choice, or reason, or language, or sociability, or sentience, or emotions, or consciousness, or any other quality that has been put forth as a ground for human dignity. It is all of these qualities coming together in a human whole that make up Factor X. Every member of the human species possesses a genetic endowment that allows him or her to become a whole human being, an endowment that distinguishes a human in essence from other types of creatures.

A moment's reflection will show that none of the key qualities that contribute to human dignity can exist in the absence of the others. Human reason, for example, is not that of a computer; it is pervaded by emotions, and its functioning is in fact facilitated by the latter.[48] Moral choice cannot exist without reason, needless to say, but it is also grounded in feelings such as pride, anger, shame, and sympathy.[49] Human consciousness is not just individual preferences and instrumental reason, but is shaped intersubjectively by other consciousnesses and their moral evaluations. We are social and political animals not merely because we are capable of game-theoretic reason, but because we are endowed with certain social emotions. Human sentience is not that of a pig or a horse, because it is coupled with human memory and reason.

This protracted discussion of human dignity is intended to answer the following question: What is it that we want to protect from any future advances in biotechnology? The answer is, we want to protect the full range of our complex, evolved natures against attempts at self-modification. We do not want to disrupt either the unity or the continuity of human nature, and thereby the human rights that are based on it.

If Factor X is related to our very complexity and the complex interactions of uniquely human characteristics like moral choice, reason, and a broad emotional gamut, it is reasonable to ask how and why biotechnology would seek to make us less complex. The answer lies in the constant pressure that exists to reduce the ends of biomedicine to utilitarian ones—that is, the attempt to reduce a complex diversity of natural ends and purposes to just a few simple categories like pain and pleasure, or autonomy. There is in particular a constant predisposition to allow the relief of pain and suffering to automatically trump all other human purposes and objectives. For this will be the constant trade-off that biotechnology will pose: We can cure this disease, or prolong this person's life, or make this child more tractable, at the expense of some ineffable human quality like genius, or ambition, or sheer diversity.

That aspect of our complex natures most under threat has to do with our emotional gamut. We will be constantly tempted to think that we understand what "good" and "bad" emotions are, and that we can do nature one better by suppressing the latter, by trying to make people less aggressive, more sociable, more compliant, less depressed. The utilitarian goal of minimizing suffering is itself very problematic. No one can make a brief in favor of pain and suffering, but the fact of the matter is that what we consider to be the highest and most admirable human qualities, both in ourselves and in others, are often related to the way that we react to, confront, overcome, and frequently succumb to pain, suffering, and death. In the absence of these human evils there would be no sympathy, compassion, courage, heroism, solidarity, or strength of character.* A person who has not confronted suffering or death has no depth. Our ability to experience these emotions is what connects us potentially to all other human beings, both living and dead.

Many scientists and researchers would say that we don't need to worry about fencing off human nature, however defined, from biotechnology, because we are a very long way from being able to modify it, and may never achieve the capability. They may

*The Greek root of *sympathy* and the Latin root of *compassion* both refer to the ability to feel another person's pain and suffering.

be right: Human germ-line engineering and the use of recombinant DNA technology on humans are probably much further off than many people assume, though human cloning is not.

But our ability to manipulate human behavior is not dependent on the development of genetic engineering. Virtually everything we can anticipate being able to do through genetic engineering we will most likely be able to do much sooner through neuropharmacology. And we will face large demographic changes in the populations that find new biomedical technologies available to them, not only in terms of age and sex distributions, but in terms of the quality of life of important population groups.

The widespread and rapidly growing use of drugs like Ritalin and Prozac demonstrates just how eager we are to make use of technology to alter ourselves. If one of the key constituents of our nature, something on which we base our notions of dignity, has to do with the gamut of normal emotions shared by human beings, then we are *already* trying to narrow the range for the utilitarian ends of health and convenience.

Psychotropic drugs do not alter the germ line or produce heritable effects in the way that genetic engineering someday might. But they already raise important issues about the meaning of human dignity and are a harbinger of things to come.

When Do We Become Human?

In the near term, the big ethical controversies raised by biotechnology will not be threats to the dignity of normal adult human beings but rather to those who possess something less than the full complement of capabilities that we have defined as characterizing human specificity. The largest group of beings in this category are the unborn, but it could also include infants, the terminally sick, elderly people with debilitating diseases, and the disabled. 70

This issue has already come up with regard to stem cell research and cloning. Embryonic stem cell research requires the deliberate destruction of embryos, while so-called therapeutic cloning requires not just their destruction but their deliberate creation for research purposes prior to destruction. (As bioethicist Leon Kass notes, therapeutic cloning is not therapeutic for the embryo.) Both activities have been strongly condemned by those who believe that life begins at conception and that embryos have full moral status as human beings.

I do not want to rehearse the whole history of the abortion debate and the hotly contested question of when life begins. I personally do not begin with religious convictions on this issue and admit to considerable confusion in trying to think through its rights and wrongs. The question here is, What does the natural-rights approach to human dignity outlined here suggest about the moral status of the unborn, the disabled, and so on? I'm not sure it produces a definitive answer, but it can at least help us frame an answer to the question.

At first blush, a natural-rights doctrine that bases human dignity on the fact that the human species possesses certain unique characteristics would appear to allow a gradation of rights depending on the degree to which any individual member of that species shares in those characteristics. An elderly person with Alzheimer's, for example, has lost the normal adult ability to reason, and therefore that part of his dignity that would permit him to participate in politics by voting or running for office. Reason, moral choice, and possession of the species-typical emotional gamut are things that are shared by virtually all human beings and therefore serve as a basis for universal equality, but individuals possess these traits in greater or lesser amounts: Some are more reasonable, have stronger consciences or more sensitive emotions than others. At one extreme, minute distinctions could be made between individuals based on the degree to which they possess these basic human qualities, with differentiated rights assigned to them on that basis. This has happened before in history; it is called natural aristocracy. The hierarchical system it implies is one of the reasons people have become suspicious of the very concept of natural rights.

There is a strong prudential reason for not being too hierarchical in the assignment of political rights, however. There is, in the first place, no consensus on a precise definition of that list of essential human characteristics that qualify an individual for rights. More important, judgments about the degree to which a given individual possesses one or another of these qualities are very difficult to make, and usually suspect, because the person making the judgment is seldom a disinterested party. Most real-world aristocracies have been conventional rather than natural, with the aristocrats assigning themselves rights that they claimed were natural but that were actually based on force or convention. It is therefore appropriate to approach the question of who qualifies for rights with some liberality.

75

Nonetheless, every contemporary liberal democracy does in fact differentiate rights based on the degree to which individuals or categories of individuals share in certain species-typical characteristics. Children, for example, do not have the rights of adults because their capacities for reason and moral choice are not fully developed; they cannot vote and do not have the freedom of person that their parents do in making choices about where to live, whether to go to school, and so on. Societies strip criminals of basic rights for violating the law, and do so more severely in the case of those regarded as lacking a basic human moral sense. In the United States, they can be deprived even of the right to life for certain kinds of crimes. We do not officially strip Alzheimer's patients of their political rights, but we do restrict their ability to drive and make financial decisions, and in practice they usually cease to exercise their political rights as well.

From a natural-rights perspective, then, one could argue that it is reasonable to assign the unborn different rights from those of either infants or children. A day-old infant may not be capable of reason or moral choice, but it already possesses important elements of the normal human emotional gamut—it can get upset, bond to its mother, expect attention, and the like, in ways that a day-old embryo cannot. It is the violation of the natural and very powerful bonding that takes place between parent and infant, in fact, that makes infanticide such a heinous crime in most societies. That we typically hold funerals after the deaths of infants but not after miscarriages is testimony to the naturalness of this distinction. All of this suggests that it does not make sense to treat embryos as human beings with the same kinds of rights that infants possess.

Against this line of argument, we can pose the following considerations, again not from a religious but from a natural-rights perspective. An embryo may be lacking in some of the basic human characteristics possessed by an infant, but it is also not just another group of cells or tissue, because it has the *potential* to become a full human being. In this respect, it differs from an infant, which also lacks many of the most important characteristics of a normal adult human being, only in the degree to which it has realized its natural potential. This implies that while an embryo can be assigned a lower moral status than an infant, it has a higher moral status than other kinds of cells or tissue that scientists work with. It is therefore reasonable, on nonreligious grounds, to question whether researchers should be free to create, clone, and destroy human embryos at will.

Ontogeny recapitulates phylogeny. We have argued that in the evolutionary process that leads from prehuman ancestor to human beings, there was a qualitative leap that transformed the prehuman precursors of language, reason, and emotion into a human whole that cannot be explained as a simple sum of its parts, and that remains an essentially mysterious process. Something similar happens with the development of every embryo into an infant, child, and adult human being: What starts out as a cluster of organic molecules comes to possess consciousness, reason, the capacity for moral choice, and subjective emotions, in a manner that remains equally mysterious.

Putting these facts together—that an embryo has a moral status somewhere between that of an infant and that of other types of cells and tissue, and that the transformation of the embryo into something with a higher status is a mysterious process—suggests that if we are to do things like harvest stem cells from embryos, we should put a lot of limits and constraints around this activity to make sure that it does not become a precedent for other uses of the unborn that would push the envelope further. To what extent are we willing to create and grow embryos for utilitarian purposes? Supposing some miraculous new cure required cells not from a day-old embryo, but tissue from a month-old fetus? A five-month-old female fetus already has in her ovaries all the eggs she will ever produce as a woman; supposing someone wanted access to them? If we get too used to the idea of cloning embryos for medical purposes, will we know when to stop?

80

If the question of equality in a future biotech world threatens to tear up the Left, the Right will quite literally fall apart over questions related to human dignity. In the United States, the Right (as represented by the Republican Party) is divided between economic libertarians, who like entrepreneurship and technology with minimal regulation, and social conservatives, many of whom are religious, who care about a range of issues including abortion and the family. The coalition between these two groups is usually strong enough to hold up during elections, but it papers over some fundamental differences in outlook. It is not clear that this alliance will survive the emergence of new technologies that, on the one hand, offer enormous health benefits and money-making opportunities for the biotech industry, but, on the other, require violating deeply held ethical norms.

We are thus brought back to the question of politics and political strategies. For if there is a viable concept of human dignity out there, it needs to be defended, not just in philosophical tracts but in the real world of politics, and protected by viable political institutions.

NOTES

1. Clive Staples Lewis, *The Abolition of Man* (New York: Touchstone, 1944), p. 85.
2. Counsel of Europe, Draft Additional Protocol to the Convention on Human Rights and Biomedicine, On the Prohibiting of Cloning Human Beings, Doc. 7884, July 16, 1997.

3. This is the theme of the second part of Francis Fukuyama, *The End of History and the Last Man* (New York: Free Press, 1992).
4. For an interpretation of this passage in Tocqueville, see Francis Fukuyama, "The March of Equality," *Journal of Democracy* 11 (2000): 11–17.
5. John Paul II, "Message to the Pontifical Academy of Sciences," October 22, 1996.
6. Daniel C. Dennett, *Darwin's Dangerous Idea: Evolution and the Meanings of Life* (New York: Simon and Schuster, 1995), pp. 35–39; see also Ernst Mayr, *One Long Argument: Charles Darwin and the Genesis of Modern Evolutionary Thought* (Cambridge, Mass.: Harvard University Press, 1991), pp. 40–42.
7. Michael Ruse and David L. Hull, *The Philosophy of Biology* (New York: Oxford University Press, 1998), p. 385.
8. Lee M. Silver, *Remaking Eden: Cloning and Beyond in a Brave New World* (New York: Avon, 1998), pp. 256–57.
9. Ruse and Hull (1998), p. 385.
10. Silver (1998), p. 277.
11. Friedrich Nietzsche, *Thus Spoke Zarathustra*, First part, section 5, from *The Portable Nietzsche*, ed. Walter Kaufmann (New York: Viking, 1968), p. 130.
12. Charles Taylor, *Sources of the Self: The Making of the Modern Identity* (Cambridge, Mass.: Harvard University Press, 1989), pp. 6–7.
13. For a fuller defense of this proposition, see Francis Fukuyama, *The Great Disruption: Human Nature and the Reconstitution of Social Order*, part II (New York: Free Press, 1999).
14. Aristotle, *Politics* I.2.13, 1254b, 16–24.
15. Ibid., I.2.18, 1255a, 22–38.
16. Ibid., I.2.19, 1255b, 3–5.
17. See, for example, Dan W. Brock, "The Human Genome Project and Human Identity," in *Genes, Humans, and Self-Knowledge*, eds. Robert F. Weir and Susan C. Lawrence et al. (Iowa City: University of Iowa Press, 1994), pp. 18–23.
18. This possibility has already been suggested by Charles Murray. See his "Deeper into the Brain," *National Review* 52 (2000): 46–49.
19. Peter Sloterdijk, "Regeln für den Menschenpark: Ein Antwortschreiben zum Brief über den Humanismus," *Die Zeit*, no. 38, September 16, 1999.
20. Jürgen Habermas, "Nicht die Natur verbietet das Klonen. Wir müssen selbst entscheiden. Eine Replik auf Dieter E. Zimmer," *Die Zeit*, no. 9, February 19, 1998.
21. For a discussion of this issue, see Allen Buchanan and Norman Daniels et al., *From Chance to Choice: Genetics and Justice* (New York and Cambridge: Cambridge University Press, 2000), pp. 17–20. See also Robert H. Blank and Masako N. Darrough, *Biological Differences and Social Equality: Implications for Social Policy* (Westport, Conn.: Greenwood Press, 1983).
22. Ronald M. Dworkin, *Sovereign Virtue: The Theory and Practice of Equality* (Cambridge, Mass.: Harvard University Press, 2000), p. 452.
23. Laurence H. Tribe, "Second Thoughts on Cloning," *New York Times*, December 5, 1997, p. A31.
24. John Paul II (1996).
25. On the meaning of this "ontological leap," see Ernan McMullin, "Biology and the Theology of the Human," in Phillip R. Sloan, ed., *Controlling Our Desires: Historical, Philosophical, Ethical, and Theological Perspectives on the Human Genome Project* (Notre Dame, Ind.: University of Notre Dame Press, 2000), p. 367.
26. It is in fact very difficult to come up with a Darwinian explanation for the human enjoyment of music. See Steven Pinker, *How the Mind Works* (New York: W. W. Norton, 1997), pp. 528–38.

27. See, for example, Arthur Peacocke, "Relating Genetics to Theology on the Map of Scientific Knowledge," in Sloan, ed. (2000), pp. 346–50.
28. Laplace's exact words were: "We ought then to regard the present state of the universe [not just the solar system] as the effect of its anterior state and as the cause of the one which is to follow. Given an intelligence that could comprehend at one instant all the forces by which nature is animated and the respective situation of the beings who compose it—an intelligence sufficiently vast to submit these data [initial conditions] to analysis—it would embrace in the same formula the movements of the greatest bodies in the universe and those of the lightest atom; for it, nothing would be uncertain and the future, as the past, would be present to its eyes. . . . The regularity which astronomy shows us in the movements of the comets doubtless exists also in all phenomena. The curve described by a simple molecule of air or vapor is regulated in a manner just as certain as the planetary orbits; the only difference between them is that which comes from our ignorance." Quoted in *Final Causality in Nature and Human Affairs*, ed. Richard F. Hassing (Washington, D.C.: Catholic University Press, 1997), p. 224.
29. Hassing, ed. (1997), pp. 224–26.
30. Peacocke, in Sloan, ed. (2000), p. 350.
31. McMullin, in Sloan, ed. (2000), p. 374.
32. On this question, see Roger D. Masters, "The Biological Nature of the State," *World Politics* 35 (1983): 161–93.
33. Andrew Goldberg and Christophe Boesch, "The Cultures of Chimpanzees," *Scientific American* 284 (2001): 60–67.
34. Larry Arnhart, *Darwinian Natural Right: The Biological Ethics of Human Nature* (Albany, N.Y.: State University of New York Press, 1998), pp. 61–62.
35. One exception to this appears to be the indigenous peoples of the American Pacific Northwest, a hunter-gatherer society that seems to have developed a state. See Robert Wright, *Nonzero: The Logic of Human Destiny* (New York: Pantheon Books, 2000), pp. 31–38.
36. Stephen Jay Gould and R. C. Lewontin, "The Spandrels of San Marco and the Panglossian Paradigm: A Critique of the Adaptionist Programme," *Proceedings of the Royal Society of London* 205 (1979): 81–98.
37. John R. Searle, *The Mystery of Consciousness* (New York: New York Review Books, 1997).
38. Daniel C. Dennett, *Consciousness Explained* (Boston: Little, Brown, 1991), p. 210.
39. John R. Searle, *The Rediscovery of the Mind* (Cambridge, Mass.: MIT Press, 1992), p. 3.
40. Hans P. Moravec, *Robot: Mere Machine to Transcendent Mind* (New York: Oxford University Press, 1999).
41. Ray Kurzweil, *The Age of Spiritual Machines: When Computers Exceed Human Intelligence* (London: Penguin Books, 2000).
42. For a critique, see Colin McGinn, "Hello HAL," *New York Times Book Review*, January 3, 1999.
43. On this point, see Wright (2000), pp. 306–8.
44. Ibid., pp. 321–22.
45. Robert J. McShea, *Morality and Human Nature: A New Route to Ethical Theory* (Philadelphia: Temple University Press, 1990), p. 77.
46. Daniel Dennett makes the following bizarre statement in *Consciousness Explained:* "But why should it matter, you may want to ask, that a creature's desires are thwarted if they aren't conscious desires? I reply: Why would it matter more if they were conscious—especially if consciousness were a property, as some think, that forever eludes investigation? Why should a 'zombie's' crushed hopes matter less than a conscious person's crushed hopes? There is a trick with mirrors here that should be exposed and

discarded. Consciousness, you say, is what matters, but then you cling to doctrines about consciousness that systematically prevent us from getting any purchase on *why* it matters" (p. 450). Dennett's question begs a more obvious one: What person in the world would care about crushing a zombie's hopes, except to the extent that the zombie was instrumentally useful to that person?

47. Jared Diamond, *The Third Chimpanzee* (New York: HarperCollins, 1992), p. 23.
48. The dualism between reason and emotion—that is, the idea that these are distinct and separable mental qualities—can be traced to Descartes (see *The Passions of the Soul*, Article 47). This dichotomy has been widely accepted since then but is misleading in many ways. The neurophysiologist Antonio Damasio points out that human reasoning invariably involves what he labels somatic markers—emotions that the mind attaches to certain ideas or options in the course of thinking through a problem—that help speed many kinds of calculations. Antonio R. Damasio, *Descartes' Error: Emotion, Reason, and the Human Brain* (New York: Putnam, 1994).
49. That is, the Kantian notion that moral choice is an act of pure reason overriding or suppressing natural emotions is not the way that human beings actually make moral choices. Human beings more typically balance one set of feelings against another and build character by strengthening the pleasurability of good moral choices through habit.

Questions for Critical Reading

1. The idea of a *Factor X* plays a central role in Fukuyama's essay. As you reread this text, locate quotations where Fukuyama defines this term and then provide a definition of the concept in your own words.
2. Do humans have an "essence"? Locate passages from Fukuyama that support your analysis. Does he think there is a human essence? What quotations make his position clear? You will need to reread his text closely and critically to determine his position.
3. As the title of this selection suggests, Fukuyama is centrally concerned with the concept of human dignity in this chapter. Define *human dignity*, using quotations from Fukuyama that support your definition.

Exploring Context

1. Fukuyama opens this chapter by quoting from a decree from the Council of Europe. Visit the council's website at coe.int and search for information on cloning. What else does the council have to say on the issue? How does its position reflect or complicate Fukuyama's argument?
2. Fukuyama turns to complexity theory to recuperate an understanding of the human essence. Conway's Game of Life is a classic mathematical model illustrating how simple rules governing individual parts can combine into very complex wholes. Play the Game of Life at bitstorm.org/gameoflife. Does it reflect the evolution of consciousness? How often does a stable pattern emerge in the game? How does it support or undercut Fukuyama's arguments about Factor X?
3. Fukuyama asks, "What is it that we want to protect from any future advances in biotechnology?" (p. 153). Visit the website of the *American Journal of Bioethics* at

bioethics.net. In browsing through the site, what answers to Fukuyama's question can you find? How can we decide which biotechnologies should be pursued and which would cause us to lose our humanity?

Questions for Connecting

1. Michael Pollan's discussion of "holons" in "The Animals: Practicing Complexity" (p. 313) seems closely related to Fukuyama's use of complexity theory. In what ways are humans and organic farms similar? What insight does Pollan's essay provide on Fukuyama's argument?
2. Kenji Yoshino, in his discussion of civil rights in "Preface" and "The New Civil Rights" (p. 452), is also concerned, to some extent, with what it means to be human. Synthesize Fukuyama's ideas about human dignity and Factor X with Yoshino's model of civil rights. What might a civil rights based on human dignity look like? What challenges might it face?
3. What is the relationship between human dignity and economic justice? Use Namit Arora's discussion in "What Do We Deserve?" (p. 55) to evaluate the ethics of economic systems. Which model best preserves human dignity? What do we deserve just for being human?

Language Matters

1. Select a key paragraph from the essay and then reduce each sentence of the paragraph down to a single subject and verb. What is lost by condensing the sentences in this way? What other grammatical constructions help carry the meaning of a sentence?
2. Select a particularly complex sentence from this essay. Begin by breaking this sentence down into several smaller sentences. Try substituting simpler vocabulary, too. Once you've absorbed the ideas through this process, try stating out loud a summary of what Fukuyama is trying to communicate and then write down what you say. Try these same strategies in your own writing.
3. You're probably familiar with common parts of speech like nouns and verbs. Using Fukuyama's text, create new parts of speech from common combinations of the usual parts of speech. For example, a noun and a verb together might form a "quarplat," an adverb and an adjective might be a "jerbad." Create rules for your parts of speech. When does Fukuyama use the kinds of constructions you've named? When might you?

Assignments for Writing

1. Write a paper in which you explain what it means to be human. In making your argument, you should account for the fact that Fukuyama identifies many different qualities as being necessary to Factor X. Why, then, does he call them collectively *Factor X*? How do you account for the seemingly infinite number of divergent views on what it is to be human? Use your definition of *Factor X* from Question 1 of Questions for Critical Reading.

2. Fukuyama acknowledges the difficulties that a vision of human equality presents when dealing with specific populations, including the elderly, disabled, and terminally ill. Write a paper in which you suggest standards for dealing with these boundary populations in relation to medical advances such as biotechnology. How might you change Fukuyama's working definitions of *Factor X* to be more inclusive? Consider using any specific examples you located from your work with the *American Journal of Bioethics* website in Question 3 of Exploring Context.

3. **Multimodal.** Fukuyama stresses the centrality of human nature in current political and ethical debate. Some environmentalists would consider his discussion anthropocentric. What about natural life beyond human beings? Create a poster presentation in which you extend Fukuyama's discussion of human dignity to account for the natural environment, ecosystems, and other forms of life. A poster presentation is an academic genre used in many disciplines in which researchers summarize their findings on a poster board, using key data and images. You may want to identify those parts of Fukuyama's essay that deal directly with the distinction between the "natural" and "human" worlds as a point of departure for this discussion. You may also want to use the web to learn more about poster presentation and how best to combine text and images in this genre. What happens when we extend the concept of dignity beyond humans? Would it change the way we acquire our food or what we eat? Consider your work with Michael Pollan from Question 1 of Questions for Connecting.

ROXANE GAY

Roxane Gay earned her Ph.D. in rhetoric and technical communication from Michigan Technological University and is currently an associate professor of English at Purdue University. Gay became the talk of the literary world in 2014 with the publication of her novel *An Untamed State* and her essay collection *Bad Feminist*, both of which became *New York Times* best-sellers. Gay, editor of *The Butter* and coeditor of *PANK*, is also the author of *Ayiti* (2011) and *Hunger: A Memoir of (My) Body* (2017). Her work has appeared in *Best American Mystery Stories 2014*, *Best American Short Stories 2012*, *McSweeney's*, *Tin House*, *Virginia Quarterly Review*, and the *New York Times Book Review*, among other publications.

In the essay collection *Bad Feminist*, Gay examines feminism and its inherent complications, often through the lens of pop culture. With honesty and wit, she tackles issues such as race, privilege, and politics with essays on topics such as the token treatment of race in Hollywood, the responsibility of writers when discussing rape culture, and the killing of Trayvon Martin. Throughout it all, she uses irreverence and wit to highlight the complex relations of gender, race, and sexuality.

In this selection, which was originally published in the *Virginia Quarterly Review*, Gay examines her own identity as a feminist in the context of cultural expectation and categorization—or, as she calls it, the "myth" of "essential feminism," which she argues "doesn't allow for the complexities of human experience or individuality" (p. 163). It also, Gay asserts, proves divisive to the movement, in that many reject the feminist label due to stereotypes and negative associations. She ultimately concludes that she is a "bad feminist," but that she "would rather be a bad feminist than no feminist at all" (p. 169).

Do you agree? What are the benefits and detriments of categorization? What are the benefits and detriments that come from rejecting labels?

- TAGS: *community, gender, identity, judgment and decision making, media, race and ethnicity*
- CONNECTIONS: *Appiah, Chabon, Fukuyama, Gilbert, Klosterman, Lukianoff and Haidt, Serano, von Busch*

Bad Feminist

My favorite definition of a feminist is one offered by Su, an Australian woman who, when interviewed for Kathy Bail's 1996 anthology *DIY Feminism*, described them simply as "women who don't want to be treated like shit." This definition is pointed and succinct, but I run into trouble when I try to expand it. I fall short as a feminist. I feel like I am not as committed as I need to be, that I am not living up to feminist ideals because of who and how I choose to be. I feel this tension constantly. As Judith Butler writes in her 1988 essay, "Performative Acts and Gender Constitution": "Performing one's gender wrong initiates a set of punishments both obvious and indirect, and performing it well provides the reassurance that there is an essentialism of gender identity after all." This tension—the idea that there is a right way to be a woman, a right way to be the most essential woman—is ongoing and pervasive.

We see this tension in socially dictated beauty standards—the right way to be a woman is to be thin, to wear make up, to wear the right kind of clothes (not too slutty, not too prude, show a little leg, ladies), and so on. Good women are charming, polite, and unobtrusive. Good women work but are content to earn 77 percent of what men earn. Depending on whom you ask, good women bear children and stay home to raise them without complaint. Good women are modest, chaste, pious, submissive. Women who don't adhere to these standards are the fallen, the undesirable. They are bad women.

Butler's thesis could also apply to feminism. There is an essential feminism, the notion that there are right and wrong ways to be a feminist, and there are consequences for doing feminism wrong.

Essential feminism suggests anger, humorlessness, militancy, unwavering principles, and a prescribed set of rules for how to be a proper feminist woman, or at least a proper white, heterosexual, feminist woman—hate pornography, unilaterally decry the objectification of women, don't cater to the male gaze, hate men, hate sex, focus on career, don't shave. I kid, mostly, with that last one. This is nowhere near an accurate description of feminism, but the movement has been warped by misperception for so long that even people who should know better have bought into this essential image of feminism.

Consider Elizabeth Wurtzel, who, in a June 2012 *Atlantic* article, says, "Real feminists earn a living, have money and means of their own." By Wurtzel's thinking, women who don't "earn a living, have money and means of their own," are fake feminists, undeserving of the label, disappointments to the sisterhood. She takes the idea of essential feminism even further in a September 2012 *Harper's Bazaar* article where she suggests that a good feminist works hard to be beautiful. She says, "Looking great is a matter of feminism. No liberated woman would misrepresent the cause by appearing less than hale and happy." It's too easy to dissect the error of such thinking. She is suggesting that a woman's worth is, in part, determined by her beauty, which is one of the very things feminism works against.

The most significant problem with essential feminism is how it doesn't allow for the complexities of human experience or individuality. There seems to be little room for multiple or discordant points of view. Essential feminism has, for example, led to the rise of the phrase "sex-positive feminism," which creates a clear distinction between feminists who are positive about sex and feminists who aren't—and that in turn creates a self-fulfilling essentialist prophecy.

I sometimes cringe when someone refers to me as a feminist, as if I should be ashamed of my feminism or as if the word *feminist* is an insult. The label is rarely offered in kindness. I am generally called a feminist when I have the nerve to suggest that the misogyny deeply embedded in our culture is a real problem, requiring relentless vigilance. For example, in an essay for *Salon*, I wrote about Daniel Tosh and rape jokes. I try not to read comments because they can get vicious, but I couldn't help but note one commenter who told me I was an "angry blogger woman," which is simply another way of saying "angry feminist." All feminists are angry instead of passionate.

A more direct reprimand came from a man I was dating, during a heated discussion that wasn't quite an argument. He said, "Don't you raise your voice to me," which was strange because I had not raised my voice. I was stunned because no one had ever said such a thing to me. He expounded, at length, about how women should talk to men. When I dismantled his pseudo-theories, he said, "You're some kind of feminist, aren't you?" His tone made it clear that to be a feminist was undesirable. I was not being a good woman. I remained silent, stewing. I thought, "Isn't it obvious I am a feminist, albeit not a very good one?"

I'm not the only outspoken woman who shies away from the feminist label, who fears the consequences of accepting the label.

In an August 2012 interview with *Salon*'s Andrew O'Hehir, actress Melissa Leo, known for playing groundbreaking female roles, said, "Well, I don't think of myself as a feminist at all. As soon as we start labeling and categorizing ourselves and others, that's going to shut down the world. I would never say that. Like, I just did that episode with Louis C.K." 10

Leo is buying into a great many essential feminist myths with her comment. We are categorized and labeled from the moment we come into this world by gender, race, size, hair color, eye color, and so forth. The older we get the more labels and categories we collect. If labeling and categorizing ourselves is going to shut the world down, it has been a long time coming. More disconcerting, though, is the assertion that a feminist wouldn't take a role on Louis C.K.'s sitcom *Louie*, or that a feminist would be unable to find C.K.'s brand of humor amusing. For Leo, there are feminists and then there are women who defy categorization and are willing to embrace career opportunities. In a July 2012 *Guardian* interview, critically acclaimed performance artist Marina Abramović, when asked how she felt about being invited to lead a woman-only lecture, said, "I really had to think about it. I am very clear that I am not a feminist. It puts you into a category and I don't like that. An artist has no gender. All that matters is whether they make good art or bad art. So I thought about it, but then I said yes."

Again, we see this fear of categorization, this fear of being forced into a box that cannot quite accommodate a woman properly. Abramović believes an artist has no gender, but there are many artists who would disagree, whose art is intimately shaped by their gender, such as artist and sculptor Louise Bourgeois, for whom feminism was a significant influence. In a 1982 *Time* article on Bourgeois and her Museum of Modern Art retrospective, Robert Hughes wrote, "The field to which Bourgeois's work constantly returns is female experience, located in the body, sensed from within. 'I try,' she told an interviewer, with regard to one work, 'to give a representation of a woman who is pregnant. She tries to be frightening but she is frightened. She's afraid someone is going to invade her privacy and that she won't be able to defend what she is responsible for.'"

Trailblazing female leaders in the corporate world tend to reject the feminist label, too. Marissa Mayer, who was appointed president and CEO of Yahoo! in July 2012, said in an interview,

> I don't think that I would consider myself a feminist. I think that I certainly believe in equal rights, I believe that women are just as capable, if not more so in a lot of different dimensions, but I don't, I think, have, sort of, the militant drive and the sort of, the chip on the shoulder that sometimes comes with that. And I think it's too bad, but I do think that feminism has become in many ways a more negative word. You know, there are amazing opportunities all over the world for women, and I think that there is more good that comes out of positive energy around that than negative energy.

For Mayer, even though she is a pioneering woman, feminism is associated with militancy. Despite the strides she has made through her career at Google and now Yahoo!, she'd prefer to eschew the label for the sake of so-called positive energy.

15 Audre Lorde once stated, "I am a black feminist. I mean I recognize that my power as well as my primary oppressions come as a result of my blackness as well as my womaness, and therefore my struggles on both of these fronts are inseparable."

As a woman of color, I find that some feminists don't seem terribly concerned with the issues unique to women of color—the ongoing effects of racism and postcolonialism, the status of women in the Third World, working against the trenchant archetypes black women are forced into (angry black woman, mammy, Hottentot, and the like).

White feminists often suggest that by believing there are issues unique to women of color, an unnatural division occurs, impeding solidarity, sisterhood. Other times, white feminists are simply dismissive of these issues. In 2008, prominent blogger Amanda Marcotte was accused of appropriating ideas for her article, "Can a Person Be Illegal?" from the blogger "Brownfemipower," who posted a speech she gave on the same subject a few days prior to the publication of Marcotte's article. The question of where original thought ends and borrowed concepts begin was complicated significantly by the sense that a white person had yet again appropriated the creative work of a person of color.

Around the same time, feminist press Seal Press was taken to task for not devoting enough of their catalogue to women of color, which made senior editor Brooke Warner and other white feminists defensive. Warner went so far as to respond to a comment made by blogger "Blackamazon," on her eponymous blog, saying, "Seal Press here. We WANT more WOC. Not a whole lotta proposals come our way, interestingly. Seems to me it would be more effective to inform us about what you'd like to see rather than hating." In addition to assuming a defensive posture, Warner also placed the burden of her press's diversity on women of color instead of assuming that responsibility as a senior editor. To be fair, Warner was commenting on a blog and perhaps did not think her comment through before posting, but she is neither the first nor will she be the last white feminist to suggest that the responsibility for making feminism and feminist organizations more inclusive lies with women of color.

The feminist blogosphere engaged in an intense debate over these issues, at times so acrimonious that black feminists were labeled "radical black feminists" who were "playing the race card."

20 Such willful ignorance and disinterest in incorporating the issues and concerns of black women into the mainstream feminist project makes me disinclined to own the feminist label until it embraces people like me. Is that my way of essentializing feminism, of suggesting there's a right kind of feminism or a more inclusive feminism? Perhaps. This is all murky for me, but a continued insensitivity toward race is a serious problem in feminist circles.

There's also this: lately, magazines have been telling me there's something wrong with feminism or women trying to achieve a work/life balance or just women in general. *The Atlantic* has led the way in these lamentations. In the aforementioned June 2012 article, Wurtzel, author of *Prozac Nation*, wrote a searing polemic about "1 percent wives," who are hurting feminism and the progress of women by choosing to stay at home rather than enter the workplace. Wurtzel begins the essay provocatively:

> When my mind gets stuck on everything that is wrong with feminism, it brings out the nineteenth century poet in me: Let me count the ways. Most of all, feminism is pretty much a nice girl who really, really wants so badly to be liked by everybody—ladies who lunch, men who hate women, all the morons who demand choice and don't understand responsibility—that it has become the easy lay of social movements.

There are problems with feminism, you see. Wurtzel says so, and she is vigorous in defending her position. Wurtzel goes on to state there is only one kind of equality, economic equality, and until women recognize that and enter the workforce *en masse*, feminists, and wealthy feminists in particular, will continue to fail. They will continue to be bad feminists, falling short of essential ideals of this movement.

The very next issue of *The Atlantic* included Anne-Marie Slaughter writing 12,000 words about the struggles of powerful, successful women to "have it all." She was speaking to a small, elite group of women—wealthy women with very successful careers—while ignoring the millions of women who don't have the privilege of, as Slaughter did, leaving a high-powered position at the State Department to spend more time with her sons. Many women who work do so because they have to. Working has little to do with having it all and much more to do with having food on the table.

Slaughter wrote, "I'd been the woman congratulating herself on her unswerving commitment to the feminist cause, chatting smugly with her dwindling number of college or law-school friends who had reached and maintained their place on the highest rungs of their profession. I'd been the one telling young women at my lectures that you can have it all and do it all, regardless of what field you are in."

The thing is, I am not at all sure that feminism has ever suggested women can have it all. This notion of being able to have it all is always misattributed to feminism when really it's human nature to want it all. 25

Alas, poor feminism. So much responsibility keeps getting piled on the shoulders of a movement whose primary purpose is to achieve equality, in all realms, between men and women. I keep reading these articles and getting angry and tired because these articles tell me that there's no way for women to ever get it right. These articles make it seem like there is, in fact, a right way to be a woman and a wrong way to be a woman. And the standard appears to be ever changing and unachievable.

Which leads me to confess: I am failing as a woman. I am failing as a feminist. To freely accept the feminist label would not be fair to good feminists. If I am, indeed, a feminist, I am a rather bad one.

I want to be independent, but I want to be taken care of and have someone to come home to. I have a job I'm pretty good at. I am in charge of things. I am on committees. People respect me and take my counsel. I want to be strong and professional, but I resent how hard I have to work to be taken seriously, to receive a fraction of the consideration I might otherwise receive. Sometimes I feel an overwhelming need to cry at work so I close my office door and lose it. I want to be in charge and respected and in control, but I want to surrender, completely, in certain aspects of my life.

When I drive to work I listen to thuggish rap at a very loud volume even though the lyrics are degrading to women and offend me to my core. The classic Ying Yang Twins song "Salt Shaker"? It's amazing. "P poppin' til you percolate / First booty on duty no time to wait / Make it work, with your wet T-shirt / Bitch you gotta shake it til your calf muscle hurts."

30 Poetry.

(I am mortified by my music choices.)

I care what people think.

Pink is my favorite color. I used to say my favorite color was black to be cool, but it is pink—all shades of pink. If I have an accessory, it is probably pink. I read *Vogue*, and I'm not doing it ironically though it might seem that way. I once live-tweeted the September issue. I demonstrate little outward evidence of this, but I have a very indulgent fantasy where I have a closet full of pretty shoes and purses and matching outfits. I love dresses. For years I pretended I hated them, but I don't. Maxi-dresses are one of the finest clothing items to become popular in recent memory. I have opinions on Maxi-dresses! I shave my legs! Again, this mortifies me. If I take issue with the unrealistic standards of beauty women are held to, I shouldn't have a secret fondness for fashion and smooth calves, right?

I know nothing about cars. When I take my car to the mechanic, they are speaking a foreign language. A mechanic asks what's wrong with my car, and I lose my mind. I stutter things like, "Well, there's a sound I try to drown out with my radio." The windshield wiper fluid for the rear window of my car no longer sprays the window. It just sprays the air. I don't know how to deal with this. It feels like an expensive problem. I still call my father with questions about cars and am not terribly interested in changing any of my car-related ignorance. I don't want to be good at cars. Good feminists, I assume, are independent enough to address vehicular crises on their own; they are independent enough to care.

35 Despite what people think based on my writing, I very much like men. They're interesting to me, and I mostly wish they would be better about how they treat women so I wouldn't have to call them out so often. And still, I put up with nonsense from unsuitable men even though *I know better* and can do better. I love diamonds and the excess of weddings. I consider certain domestic tasks as gendered, mostly all in my favor as I don't care for chores—lawn care, bug killing, and trash removal, for example, are men's work.

Despite what people think based on my writing, I very much like men.

Sometimes—a lot of the time, honestly—I totally "fake it," because it's easier. I am a fan of orgasms, but they take time, and in many instances I don't want to waste that time. All too often I don't really like the guy enough to explain the calculus of my desire. Then I feel guilty because the sisterhood would not approve. I'm not even sure what the sisterhood is, but the idea of a sisterhood menaces me, quietly reminding me of how bad a feminist I am. Good feminists don't fear the sisterhood because they know they are comporting themselves in sisterhood-approved ways.

I love babies, and I want to have one. I am willing to make certain compromises (not sacrifices) in order to do so—namely maternity leave and slowing down at work to spend more time with my child, writing less so I can be more present in my life. I worry about dying alone, unmarried and childless because I spent so much time pursuing my career and accumulating degrees. This kind of keeps me up at night, but I pretend it doesn't because I am supposed to be evolved. My success, such as it is, is supposed to be enough if I'm a good feminist. It is not enough. It is not even close.

Because I have so many deeply held opinions about gender equality, I feel a lot of pressure to live up to certain ideals. I am supposed to be a good feminist who is having it all, doing it all. Really, though, I'm a woman in her thirties, struggling to accept herself. For so long I told myself I was not this woman—utterly human and flawed. I worked overtime to be anything but this woman, and it was exhausting and unsustainable, and even harder than simply embracing who I am.

And while I may be a bad feminist, I am deeply committed to the issues important to the feminist movement. I have strong opinions about misogyny, institutional sexism that consistently places women at a disadvantage, the inequity in pay, the cult of beauty and thinness, the repeated attacks on reproductive freedom, violence against women, and on and on. I am as committed to fighting fiercely for equality as I am committed to disrupting the notion that there is an essential feminism.

40 I'm the kind of feminist who is appalled by the phrase "legitimate rape" and politicians such as Missouri's Todd Akin, who reaffirmed his commitment to opposing abortion, drawing from pseudo-science and a lax cultural attitude toward rape: "If it's a legitimate rape, the female body has ways to try to shut that whole thing down. But let's assume that maybe that didn't work or something. I think there should be some punishment, but the punishment ought to be on the rapist, and not attacking the child."

Being a feminist, however, even a bad one, has also taught me that the need for feminism and advocacy also applies to seemingly less serious issues.

I'm the kind of feminist who knows it is complete hypocrisy that actress Kristen Stewart is being publicly excoriated for cheating on her boyfriend Robert Pattinson even though, if you believe the tabloid stories, Pattinson cheated on her for years. Being a bad feminist allows me to get riled up when I read that Stewart could be dropped from the *Snow White and the Huntsman* sequel while, say, Chris Brown, a known abuser with anger issues, is still performing at awards shows and selling albums, adored by a legion of ardent fans.

I'm the kind of feminist who looks at the September 2012 issue of *Vogue* with the Edith Wharton photo spread and knows there's a serious problem. Wharton is my favorite writer. I also love *Vogue* or, perhaps, hate to love *Vogue*. This photo spread would normally thrill me. But. Jeffrey Eugenides portrays Henry James, Jonathan Safran Foer portrays architect Ogden Codman Jr., and Junot Díaz portrays diplomat Walter Van Rensselaer Berry. Wharton is portrayed by model Natalia Vodianova; she is gorgeous, and *Vogue* is a fashion magazine, but a great disservice is being done.

The editors of *Vogue* are, apparently, unaware of the famous, talented, contemporary women writers who would be excellent choices for the photo essay. Zadie Smith released a book in September. There's also Karen Russell, Jennifer Egan, Aimee Bender, Nicole Krauss, Julianna Baggott, Alicia Erian, Claire Vaye Watkins, and the list could go on forever.

45 This disservice rises, in part, out of a culture that assumes women writers are less relevant than their male counterparts, that women in general are simply not as important, that their writing is not as critical to arts and letters. This disservice rises

out of a culture where Jonathan Franzen lost the Pulitzer rather than Jennifer Egan winning the award.

All too often, these seemingly smaller issues go unchecked because there are so many more serious issues facing women.

There's more to the problem. Too many women, particularly groundbreaking women and industry leaders, are afraid to be labeled feminists, afraid to stand up and say, "Yes, I am a feminist," for fear of what that label means, for fear of how to live up to it, for fear of feminism as something essential, for fear of the punishments—both obvious and indirect—that come with openly owning feminism or doing feminism wrong.

At some point, I got it into my head that a feminist was a certain kind of woman. I bought into grossly inaccurate myths about who feminists are—militant, perfect in their politics and person, man hating, humorless. I bought into these myths even though, intellectually, I *know* better. I'm not proud of this. I don't want to buy into these myths anymore. I don't want to cavalierly disavow feminism like far too many other women have done.

I also want to be myself. Bad feminism seems like the only way I can both embrace myself as a feminist and be myself.

No matter what issues I have with feminism, I am one. I cannot nor will not deny the importance and absolute necessity of feminism. Like most people, I'm full of contradictions, but I also don't want to be treated like shit for being a woman. 50

I am, therefore, a bad feminist. I would rather be a bad feminist than no feminist at all.

Questions for Critical Reading

1. Develop your own definition of *feminist*. As you reread the essay, pay attention to places where Gay offers her definition of the term. How do your definitions differ? Are you persuaded by Gay's definition?
2. According to Gay, what is "essential feminism"? Note places in the text where Gay discusses essential feminism. What problems are created by this concept?
3. Is Gay a "bad" feminist? Use your own understanding of *feminist* from Question 1 above in formulating your response.

Exploring Context

1. Search the web for "women against feminism" to locate images from a controversial Tumblr campaign. How does Gay's argument respond to the reasons why these women are against feminism?
2. Explore Roxane Gay's website at roxanegay.com. How does her larger body of work reflect the ideas that she presents in this essay? How does your exploration confirm or change your response to Question 3 of Questions for Critical Reading?
3. Use the Meme Generator at memegenerator.net to create your own meme image about feminism. Incorporate your work from Questions 1 and 3 of Questions for Critical Reading.

Questions for Connecting

1. Francis Fukuyama, in "Human Dignity" (p. 137), also discusses the idea of "essence." Use his discussion to reexamine the notion of essential feminism. How does his explanation of the concept further complicate the concept of essential feminism?

2. In some ways Gay's essay is centrally concerned with fitting in, with notions of feminism in this case. Use Michael Chabon's discussion of his son Abe in "My Son, the Prince of Fashion" (p. 62) to form a larger argument about the relative advantages and disadvantages of conforming to an accepted notion of identity, whether in terms of feminism or masculinity.

3. Gay is centrally invested in changing the way women are treated. Apply Kenji Yoshino's ideas about civil rights from "Preface" and "The New Civil Rights" (p. 452) to Gay's concerns about gender. What paradigm of civil rights might produce change? Is Gay forced to "cover" her flavor of feminism? How might conversations about these issues produce change?

Language Matters

1. One common error for writers involves using commas with introductory elements. Review the rules for comma usage in these situations, using a grammar handbook or other reliable reference source. Then find examples from Gay that illustrate these rules. How can you apply these rules to your own writing?

2. Word choice and tone are important in your writing. Select a significant quotation from Gay's text, type it into a blank document in a word processor, and, using a thesaurus (the word processor's, one online, or a printed one), replace every significant word in the sentence with a synonym. Does the sentence still work? How does word choice influence tone and meaning? Why didn't Gay use "fancier" or more "academic" language in this text? Based on what you have discovered, what sort of tone do you think you should use in your writing for this class?

3. Select a key quotation from Gay's text and then translate it into another language using an online tool such as Bing Translator (bing.com/translator) or Google Translate (translate.google.com). You might even choose to translate it several times (from English to French to German to Chinese). Then translate it back into English. The resulting sentence will probably make little sense. Describe what happened to the sentence. Did translation change parts of speech? Verb tense? Sentence structure? What elements of the sentence are key to transmitting Gay's meaning? Do they survive translation? What parts of your own sentences should you thus pay attention to the most?

Assignments for Writing

1. Use Gay's ideas about feminism to write a paper in which you create a definition of *feminism* that avoids notions of "good" or "bad." You will want to make sure the definition you create is open to people of all genders. Draw from your work in Questions for Critical Reading and Question 1 of Exploring Context to help you support your argument.

2. Gay uses several cultural references to support her argument, including popular magazines such as *Vogue*, media figures, and blogs. Write a paper in which you examine the ways in which popular culture supports stereotypes. How might we change or disable these stereotypes in culture? Incorporate your work from Question 3 of Exploring Context.

3. In detailing the ways in which she is a bad feminist, Gay is also detailing the ways in which she is an individual. Thus, in some ways, Gay is using this essay to define herself. Write a paper in which you specify tools an individual can use to negotiate between individual and group identities. You might want to include what you learned about Gay from Question 2 of Exploring Context.

DANIEL GILBERT

Daniel Gilbert is a professor of psychology at Harvard University. He has won a Guggenheim fellowship, as well as the American Psychological Association's Distinguished Scientific Award for an Early Career Contribution to Psychology. In 2002, *Personality and Social Psychology Bulletin* named him one of the fifty most influential social psychologists of the decade. In addition to his book *Stumbling on Happiness* (2006) and his scholarly publications, Gilbert has published works of science fiction as well as contributed to the *New York Times*, the *Los Angeles Times*, *Forbes*, and *Time*. He was elected to the American Academy of Arts and Sciences in 2008.

In *Stumbling on Happiness*, a *New York Times* best-seller, Gilbert applies his expertise to the study of happiness itself. Gilbert argues that people are rarely able to predict with any accuracy how they will feel in the future, and so are often quite wrong about what will make them happy.

In "Reporting Live from Tomorrow," a chapter from *Stumbling on Happiness*, Gilbert suggests that beliefs, just like genes, can be "super-replicators," given to spreading regardless of their usefulness. Thus even beliefs that are based on inaccurate information can provide the means for their own propagation. Gilbert explains why humans, with their unreliable memories and imaginations, are so easily susceptible to such beliefs. Though "the best way to predict our feelings tomorrow is to see how others are feeling today" (p. 182), most of us are unwilling to make use of the experiences of others because we mistakenly believe ourselves to be unique.

The pursuit of happiness is central to our understanding of America — we all want to be happy. But this selection cautions us about predicting our future happiness and in the process provides the tools we need to correct our misapprehensions.

TAGS: *adolescence and adulthood, conversation, culture, empathy, judgment and decision making, psychology*

CONNECTIONS: *Appiah, Chabon, Klosterman, Ma, Moalem, Serano, Stillman, Yang*

Reporting Live from Tomorrow

In Alfred Hitchcock's 1956 remake of *The Man Who Knew Too Much*, Doris Day sang a waltz whose final verse went like this:

> When I was just a child in school,
> I asked my teacher, "What will I try?
> Should I paint pictures, should I sing songs?"
> This was her wise reply:
> "*Que sera, sera.* Whatever will be, will be.
> The future's not ours to see. *Que sera, sera.*"[1]

Now, I don't mean to quibble with the lyricist, and I have nothing but fond memories of Doris Day, but the fact is that this is *not* a particularly wise reply. When a child asks for advice about which of two activities to pursue, a teacher should be able to provide more than a musical cliché. Yes, of *course* the future is hard to see. But we're all heading that way anyhow, and as difficult as it may be to envision, we have to make *some* decisions about which futures to aim for and which to avoid. If we are prone to mistakes when we try to imagine the future, then how *should* we decide what to do?

Even a child knows the answer to that one: We should ask the teacher. One of the benefits of being a social and linguistic animal is that we can capitalize on the experience of others rather than trying to figure everything out for ourselves. For millions of years, human beings have conquered their ignorance by dividing the labor of discovery and then communicating their discoveries to one another, which is why the average newspaper boy in Pittsburgh knows more about the universe than did Galileo, Aristotle, Leonardo,* or any of those other guys who were so smart they only needed one name. We all make ample use of this resource. If you were to write down everything you know and then go back through the list and make a check mark next to the things you know only because somebody told you, you'd develop a repetitive-motion disorder because almost *everything* you know is secondhand. Was Yury Gagarin the first man in space? Is *croissant* a French word? Are there more Chinese than North Dakotans? Does a stitch in time save nine? Most of us know the answers to these questions despite the fact that none of us actually witnessed the launching of *Vostok I*, personally supervised the evolution of language, hand-counted all the people in Beijing and Bismarck, or performed a fully randomized double-blind study of stitching. We know the answers because someone shared them with us. Communication is a kind of "vicarious observation"[2] that allows us to learn about the world without ever leaving the comfort of our Barcaloungers. The six billion interconnected people who cover the surface of our planet constitute a leviathan with twelve billion eyes, and anything that is seen by one pair of eyes can potentially be known to the entire beast in a matter of months, days, or even minutes.

The fact that we can communicate with one another about our experiences should provide a simple solution to the core problem with which this book has been concerned. Yes, our ability to imagine our future emotions is flawed—but that's okay, because we don't have to imagine what it would feel like to marry a lawyer, move to Texas, or eat a snail when there are so many people who have *done* these things and are all too happy to tell us about them. Teachers, neighbors, coworkers, parents, friends, lovers, children, uncles, cousins, coaches, cabdrivers, bartenders, hairstylists, dentists, advertisers—each of these folks has something to say about what it would be like to live in this future rather than that one, and at any point in time we can be fairly sure that one of these folks has actually *had* the experience that we are merely contemplating. Because we are the mammal that shows and tells, each of us has access to information about almost any experience we can possibly imagine—and many that we can't. Guidance counselors tell us about the best careers, critics tell us about the best restaurants, travel agents tell us about the best vacations, and friends tell us about the best travel agents.

---

*Galileo, Aristotle, Leonardo: Three geniuses. Galileo Galilei (1564–1642) was an Italian mathematician and astronomer best known for his extremely controversial belief that the earth revolves around the sun. Aristotle (384–322 BC) was a Greek philosopher and an enormously important figure in Western thought. He was a student of Plato and a teacher of Alexander the Great. Leonardo da Vinci (1452–1519) was an Italian Renaissance painter, sculptor, and scientist best known for the *Mona Lisa* and *The Last Supper* [Ed.].

Every one of us is surrounded by a platoon of Dear Abbys who can recount their own experiences and in so doing tell us which futures are most worth wanting.

Given the overabundance of consultants, role models, gurus, mentors, yentas,* and nosy relatives, we might expect people to do quite well when it comes to making life's most important decisions, such as where to live, where to work, and whom to marry. And yet, the average American moves more than six times,[3] changes jobs more than ten times,[4] and marries more than once,[5] which suggests that most of us are making more than a few poor choices. If humanity is a living library of information about what it feels like to do just about anything that can be done, then why do the people with the library cards make so many bad decisions? There are just two possibilities. The first is that a lot of the advice we receive from others is bad advice that we foolishly accept. The second is that a lot of the advice we receive from others is good advice that we foolishly reject. So which is it? Do we listen too well when others speak, or do we not listen well enough? As we shall see, the answer to that question is *yes*.

Do we listen too well when others speak, or do we not listen well enough? As we shall see, the answer to that question is *yes*.

Super-Replicators

The philosopher Bertrand Russell once claimed that believing is "the most mental thing we do."[6] Perhaps, but it is also the most *social* thing we do. Just as we pass along our genes in an effort to create people whose faces look like ours, so too do we pass along our beliefs in an effort to create people whose minds think like ours. Almost any time we tell anyone anything, we are attempting to change the way their brains operate—attempting to change the way they see the world so that their view of it more closely resembles our own. Just about every assertion—from the sublime ("God has a plan for you") to the mundane ("Turn left at the light, go two miles, and you'll see the Dunkin' Donuts on your right")—is meant to bring the listener's beliefs about the world into harmony with the speaker's. Sometimes these attempts succeed and sometimes they fail. So what determines whether a belief will be successfully transmitted from one mind to another?

The principles that explain why some genes are transmitted more successfully than others also explain why some beliefs are transmitted more successfully than others.[7] Evolutionary biology teaches us that any gene that promotes its own "means of transmission" will be represented in increasing proportions in the population over time. For instance, imagine that a single gene were responsible for the complex development of the neural circuitry that makes orgasms feel so good. For a person having this gene, orgasms would feel . . . well, orgasmic. For a person lacking this gene, orgasms would feel more like sneezes—brief, noisy, physical convulsions that pay rather paltry hedonic dividends. Now, if we took fifty healthy, fertile people who had the gene and fifty healthy, fertile people who didn't, and left them on a hospitable planet for a million years or so, when we returned we would probably find a population of thousands or

*Yenta: A Yiddish slang word meaning a person, especially a woman, who is gossipy and always ready to offer an opinion [Ed.].

millions of people, almost all of whom had the gene. Why? Because a gene that made orgasms feel good would tend to be transmitted from generation to generation simply because people who enjoy orgasms are inclined to do the thing that transmits their genes. The logic is so circular that it is virtually inescapable: Genes tend to be transmitted when they make us do the things that transmit genes. What's more, even *bad* genes—those that make us prone to cancer or heart disease—can become super-replicators if they compensate for these costs by promoting their own means of transmission. For instance, if the gene that made orgasms feel delicious also left us prone to arthritis and tooth decay, that gene might still be represented in increasing proportions because arthritic, toothless people who love orgasms are more likely to have children than are limber, toothy people who do not.

The same logic can explain the transmission of beliefs. If a particular belief has some property that facilitates its own transmission, then that belief tends to be held by an increasing number of minds. As it turns out, there are several such properties that increase a belief's transmissional success, the most obvious of which is accuracy. When someone tells us where to find a parking space downtown or how to bake a cake at high altitude, we adopt that belief and pass it along because it helps us and our friends do the things we want to do, such as parking and baking. As one philosopher noted, "The faculty of communication would not gain ground in evolution unless it was by and large the faculty of transmitting true beliefs."[8] Accurate beliefs give us power, which makes it easy to understand why they are so readily transmitted from one mind to another.

It is a bit more difficult to understand why *inaccurate* beliefs are so readily transmitted from one mind to another—but they are. False beliefs, like bad genes, can and do become super-replicators, and a thought experiment illustrates how this can happen. Imagine a game that is played by two teams, each of which has a thousand players, each of whom is linked to teammates by a telephone. The object of the game is to get one's team to share as many accurate beliefs as possible. When players receive a message that they believe to be accurate, they call a teammate and pass it along. When they receive a message that they believe to be inaccurate, they don't. At the end of the game, the referee blows a whistle and awards each team a point for every accurate belief that the entire team shares and subtracts one point for every inaccurate belief the entire team shares. Now, consider a contest played one sunny day between a team called the Perfects (whose members always transmit accurate beliefs) and a team called the Imperfects (whose members occasionally transmit an inaccurate belief). We should expect the Perfects to win, right?

Not necessarily. In fact, there are some special circumstances under which the Imperfects will beat their pants off. For example, imagine what would happen if one of the Imperfect players sent the false message "Talking on the phone all day and night will ultimately make you very happy," and imagine that other Imperfect players were gullible enough to believe it and pass it on. This message is inaccurate and thus will cost the Imperfects a point in the end. But it may have the compensatory effect of keeping more of the Imperfects on the telephone for more of the time, thus increasing the total number of accurate messages they transmit. Under the right circumstances, the costs of this inaccurate belief would be outweighed by its benefits, namely, that it led players to behave in ways that increased the odds that they would share other accurate beliefs. The lesson to be learned from this game is that inaccurate beliefs can prevail in the belief-transmission game if they somehow facilitate their own "means of transmission." In this case, the means of transmission is not sex but communication, and thus any belief—even a false belief—that increases communication has a good chance of being transmitted over and over again. False beliefs that happen to promote stable societies tend to propagate because people who hold these beliefs tend to live in stable societies, which provide the means by which false beliefs propagate.

Some of our cultural wisdom about happiness looks suspiciously like a super-replicating false belief. Consider money. If you've ever tried to sell anything, then you probably tried to sell it for as much as you possibly could, and other people probably tried to buy it for as little as they possibly could. All the parties involved in the transaction assumed that they would be better off if they ended up with more money rather than less, and this assumption is the bedrock of our economic behavior. Yet, it has far fewer scientific facts to substantiate it than you might expect. Economists and psychologists have spent decades studying the relation between wealth and happiness, and they have generally concluded that wealth increases human happiness when it lifts people out of abject poverty and into the middle class but that it does little to increase happiness thereafter.[9] Americans who earn $50,000 per year are much happier than those who earn $10,000 per year, but Americans who earn $5 million per year are not much happier than those who earn $100,000 per year. People who live in poor nations are much less happy than people who live in moderately wealthy nations, but people who live in moderately wealthy nations are not much less happy than people who live in extremely wealthy nations. Economists explain that wealth has "declining marginal utility," which is a fancy way of saying that it hurts to be hungry, cold, sick, tired, and scared, but once you've bought your way out of these burdens, the rest of your money is an increasingly useless pile of paper.[10]

So once we've earned as much money as we can actually enjoy, we quit working and enjoy it, right? Wrong. People in wealthy countries generally work long and hard to earn more money than they can ever derive pleasure from.[11] This fact puzzles us less than it should. After all, a rat can be motivated to run through a maze that has a cheesy reward at its end, but once the little guy is all topped up, then even the finest Stilton won't get him off his haunches. Once we've eaten our fill of pancakes, more pancakes are not rewarding, hence we stop trying to procure and consume them. But not so, it seems, with money. As Adam Smith, the father of modern economics, wrote in 1776: "The desire for food is limited in every man by the narrow capacity of the human stomach; but the desire of the conveniences and ornaments of building, dress, equipage, and household furniture, seems to have no limit or certain boundary."[12]

If food and money both stop pleasing us once we've had enough of them, then why do we continue to stuff our pockets when we would not continue to stuff our faces? Adam Smith had an answer. He began by acknowledging what most of us suspect anyway, which is that the production of wealth is not necessarily a source of personal happiness.

> In what constitutes the real happiness of human life, [the poor] are in no respect inferior to those who would seem so much above them. In ease of body and peace of mind, all the different ranks of life are nearly upon a level, and the beggar, who suns himself by the side of the highway, possesses that security which kings are fighting for.[13]

That sounds lovely, but if it's true, then we're all in big trouble. If rich kings are no happier than poor beggars, then why should poor beggars stop sunning themselves by the roadside and work to become rich kings? If no one wants to be rich, then we have a significant economic problem, because flourishing economies require that people continually procure and consume one another's goods and services. Market economies require that we all have an insatiable hunger for *stuff*, and if everyone were content with the stuff they had, then the economy would grind to a halt. But if this is a significant *economic* problem, it is not a significant *personal* problem. The chair of the Federal Reserve may wake up every morning with a desire to do what the economy wants, but most of us get up with a desire to do what *we* want, which is to say that the fundamental needs of a vibrant economy and the fundamental needs of a happy individual are not necessarily the same. So what motivates people to work hard every day to do things that will satisfy the economy's needs but not their own? Like so many thinkers, Smith believed that people want just one thing—happiness—hence economies can blossom and grow only if people are deluded into believing that the production of wealth will make them happy.[14] If and only if people hold this false belief will they do enough producing, procuring, and consuming to sustain their economies.

> The pleasures of wealth and greatness . . . strike the imagination as something grand and beautiful and noble, of which the attainment is well worth all the toil and anxiety which we are so apt to bestow upon it. . . . It is this deception which rouses and keeps in continual motion the industry of mankind. It is this which first prompted them to cultivate the ground, to build houses, to found cities and commonwealths, and to invent and improve all the sciences and arts, which ennoble and embellish human life; which have entirely changed the whole face of the globe, have turned the rude forests of nature into agreeable and fertile plains, and made the trackless and barren ocean a new fund of subsistence, and the great high road of communication to the different nations of the earth.[15]

In short, the production of wealth does not necessarily make individuals happy, but it does serve the needs of an economy, which serves the needs of a stable society, which serves as a network for the propagation of delusional beliefs about happiness and wealth. Economies thrive when individuals strive, but because individuals will only strive for their own happiness, it is essential that they mistakenly believe that producing and consuming are routes to personal well-being. Although words such as *delusional* may seem to suggest some sort of shadowy conspiracy orchestrated by a small group of men in dark suits, the belief-transmission game teaches us that the propagation of false beliefs does not require that anyone be *trying* to perpetrate a magnificent fraud on an innocent populace. There is no cabal at the top, no star chamber,* no master manipulator whose clever program of indoctrination and propaganda has duped us all into believing that money can buy us love. Rather, this particular false belief is a super-replicator because holding it causes us to engage in the very activities that perpetuate it.[16]

If parenting is such difficult business, then why do we have such a rosy view of it?

* Star chamber: Secretive and abusive English law court during the fifteenth to seventeenth centuries [Ed.].

The belief-transmission game explains why we believe some things about happiness that simply aren't true. The joy of money is one example. The joy of children is another that for most of us hits a bit closer to home. Every human culture tells its members that having children will make them happy. When people think about their offspring—either imagining future offspring or thinking about their current ones—they tend to conjure up images of cooing babies smiling from their bassinets, adorable toddlers running higgledy-piggledy across the lawn, handsome boys and gorgeous girls playing trumpets and tubas in the school marching band, successful college students going on to have beautiful weddings, satisfying careers, and flawless grandchildren whose affections can be purchased with candy. Prospective parents know that diapers will need changing, that homework will need doing, and that orthodontists will go to Aruba on their life savings, but by and large, they think quite happily about parenthood, which is why most of them eventually leap into it. When parents look back on parenthood, they remember feeling what those who are looking forward to it expect to feel. Few of us are immune to these cheery contemplations. I have a twenty-nine-year-old son, and I am absolutely convinced that he is and always has been one of the greatest sources of joy in my life, having only recently been eclipsed by my two-year-old granddaughter, who is equally adorable but who has not yet asked me to walk behind her and pretend we're unrelated. When people are asked to identify their sources of joy, they do just what I do: They point to their kids.

Yet if we measure the *actual* satisfaction of people who have children, a very different story emerges. . . . couples generally start out quite happy in their marriages and then become progressively less satisfied over the course of their lives together, getting close to their original levels of satisfaction only when their children leave home.[17] Despite what we read in the popular press, the only known symptom of "empty nest syndrome" is increased smiling.[18] Interestingly, this pattern of satisfaction over the life cycle describes women (who are usually the primary caretakers of children) better than men.[19] Careful studies of how women feel as they go about their daily activities show that they are less happy when taking care of their children than when eating, exercising, shopping, napping, or watching television.[20] Indeed, looking after the kids appears to be only slightly more pleasant than doing housework.

None of this should surprise us. Every parent knows that children are a lot of work—a lot of really *hard* work—and although parenting has many rewarding moments, the vast majority of its moments involve dull and selfless service to people who will take decades to become even begrudgingly grateful for what we are doing. If parenting is such difficult business, then why do we have such a rosy view of it? One reason is that we have been talking on the phone all day with society's stockholders—our moms and uncles and personal trainers—who have been transmitting to us an idea that they *believe* to be true but whose accuracy is not the cause of its successful transmission. "Children bring happiness" is a super-replicator. The belief-transmission network of which we are a part cannot operate without a continuously replenished supply of people to do the transmitting, thus the belief that children are a source of happiness becomes a part of our cultural wisdom simply because the opposite belief unravels the fabric of any society that holds it. Indeed, people who believed that children bring misery and despair—and who thus stopped having them—would put their belief-transmission network out of business in around fifty years, hence terminating the belief that terminated them. The Shakers were a utopian farming community that arose in the 1800s and at one time numbered about six thousand. They approved of children, but they did not approve of the natural act that creates them. Over the years, their strict belief in the importance of celibacy caused their network to contract, and today there are just a few elderly Shakers left, transmitting their doomsday belief to no one but themselves.

The belief-transmission game is rigged so that we *must* believe that children and money bring happiness, regardless of whether such beliefs are true. This doesn't mean that we should all now quit our jobs and abandon our families. Rather, it means that while we *believe* we are raising children and earning paychecks to increase our share of happiness, we are actually doing these things for reasons beyond our ken. We are nodes in a social network that arises and falls by a logic of its own, which is why we continue to toil, continue to mate, and continue to be surprised when we do not experience all the joy we so gullibly anticipated.

The Myth of Fingerprints

My friends tell me that I have a tendency to point out problems without offering solutions, but they never tell me what I should do about it. In one chapter after another, I've described the ways in which imagination fails to provide us with accurate previews of our emotional futures. I've claimed that when we imagine our futures we tend to fill in, leave out, and take little account of how differently we will think about the future once we actually get there. I've claimed that neither personal experience nor cultural wisdom compensates for imagination's shortcomings. I've so thoroughly marinated you in the foibles, biases, errors, and mistakes of the human mind that you may wonder how anyone ever manages to make toast without buttering their kneecaps. If so, you will be heartened to learn that there *is* a simple method by which anyone can make strikingly accurate predictions about how they will feel in the future. But you may be disheartened to learn that, by and large, no one wants to use it.

Why do we rely on our imaginations in the first place? Imagination is the poor man's wormhole. We can't do what we'd really *like* to do—namely, travel through time, pay a visit to our future selves, and *see* how happy those selves are—and so we imagine the future instead of actually going there. But if we cannot travel in the dimensions of time, we can travel in the dimensions of space, and the chances are pretty good that somewhere in those other three dimensions there is another human being who is actually *experiencing* the future event that we are merely thinking about. Surely we aren't the first people ever to consider a move to Cincinnati, a career in motel management, another helping of rhubarb pie, or an extramarital affair, and for the most part, those who have already tried these things are more than willing to tell us about them. It is true that when people tell us about their past experiences ("That ice water wasn't really so cold" or "I love taking care of my daughter"), memory's peccadilloes may render their testimony unreliable. But it is also true that when people tell us about their *current* experiences ("How am I feeling right now? I feel like pulling my arm out of this freezing bucket and sticking my teenager's head in it instead!"), they are providing us with the kind of report about their subjective state that is considered the gold standard of happiness measures. If you believe (as I do) that people can generally say how they are feeling at the moment they are asked, then one way to make predictions about our own emotional futures is to find someone who is having the experience we are contemplating and ask them how they feel. Instead of remembering our past experience in order to simulate our future experience, perhaps we should simply ask other people to introspect on their inner states. Perhaps we should give up on remembering and imagining entirely and use other people as *surrogates* for our future selves.

This idea sounds all too simple, and I suspect you have an objection to it that goes something like this: *Yes, other people are probably right now experiencing the very things I am merely contemplating, but I can't use other people's experiences as proxies for my own because those other people are not me. Every human being is as unique as his or her fingerprints, so it won't help me much to learn about how others feel in the situations that I'm facing. Unless these other people are my clones and have had all the same experiences I've had, their reactions and my reactions are bound to differ. I am a walking, talking idiosyncrasy, and thus I am better off basing my predictions on my somewhat fickle imagination than on the reports of people whose preferences, tastes, and emotional proclivities are so radically different from my own.* If that's your objection, then it is a good one—so good that it will take two steps to dismantle it. First let me prove to you that the experience of a single randomly selected individual can sometimes provide a better basis for predicting your future experience than your own imagination can. And then let me show you why you—and I—find this so difficult to believe.

Finding the Solution

Imagination has three shortcomings, and if you didn't know that then you may be reading this book* backward. If you did know that, then you also know that imagination's first shortcoming is its tendency to fill in and leave out without telling us. . . . No one can imagine every feature and consequence of a future event, hence we must consider some and fail to consider others. The problem is that the features and consequences we fail to consider are often quite important. You may recall the study† in which college students were asked to imagine how they would feel a few days after their school's football team played a game against its archrival.[21] The results showed that students overestimated the duration of the game's emotional impact because when they tried to imagine their future experience, they imagined their team winning ("The clock will hit zero, we'll storm the field, everyone will cheer . . .") but failed to imagine what they would be doing afterward ("And then I'll go home and study for my final exams"). Because the students were focused on the game, they failed to imagine how events that happened *after* the game would influence their happiness. So what *should* they have done instead?

They should have abandoned imagination altogether. Consider a study that put people in a similar predicament and then forced them to abandon their imaginations. 25

---

* Gilbert's *Stumbling on Happiness* [BJB]

† Not discussed in this excerpt [BJB]

In this study, a group of volunteers (reporters) first received a delicious prize—a gift certificate from a local ice cream parlor—and then performed a long, boring task in which they counted and recorded geometric shapes that appeared on a computer screen.[22] The reporters then reported how they felt. Next, a new group of volunteers was told that they would also receive a prize and do the same boring task. Some of these new volunteers (simulators) were told what the prize was and were asked to use their imaginations to predict their future feelings. Other volunteers (surrogators) were not told what the prize was but were instead shown the report of a randomly selected reporter. Not knowing what the prize was, they couldn't possibly use their imaginations to predict their future feelings. Instead, they had to rely on the reporter's report. Once all the volunteers had made their predictions, they received the prize, did the long, boring task, and reported how they actually felt. . . . Simulators were not as happy as they thought they would be. Why? Because they failed to imagine how quickly the joy of receiving a gift certificate would fade when it was followed by a long, boring task. This is precisely the same mistake that the college-football fans made. But now look at the results for the surrogators. As you can see, they made extremely accurate predictions of their future happiness. These surrogators didn't know what kind of prize they would receive, but they did know that someone who had received that prize had been less than ecstatic at the conclusion of the boring task. So they shrugged and reasoned that they too would feel less than ecstatic at the conclusion of the boring task—and they were right!

Imagination's second shortcoming is its tendency to project the present onto the future. . . . When imagination paints a picture of the future, many of the details are necessarily missing, and imagination solves this problem by filling in the gaps with details that it borrows from the present. Anyone who has ever shopped on an empty stomach, vowed to quit smoking after stubbing out a cigarette, or proposed marriage while on shore leave* knows that how we feel now can erroneously influence how we *think* we'll feel later. As it turns out, surrogation can remedy this shortcoming too. In one study, volunteers (reporters) ate a few potato chips and reported how much they enjoyed them.[23] Next, a new group of volunteers was fed pretzels, peanut-butter cheese crackers, tortilla chips, bread sticks, and melba toast, which, as you might guess, left them thoroughly stuffed and with little desire for salty snack foods. These stuffed volunteers were then asked to predict how much they would enjoy eating a particular food the next day. Some of these stuffed volunteers (simulators) were told that the food they would eat the next day was potato chips, and they were asked to use their imaginations to predict how they would feel after eating them. Other stuffed volunteers (surrogators) were not told what the next day's food would be but were instead shown the report of one randomly selected reporter. Because surrogators didn't know what the next day's food would be, they couldn't use their imaginations to predict their future enjoyment of it and thus they had to rely on the reporter's report. Once all the volunteers had made their predictions, they went away, returned the next day, ate some potato chips, and reported how much they enjoyed them. . . . Simulators enjoyed eating the potato chips more than they thought they would.

* Shore leave: Time granted to a sailor to spend on land [Ed.].

Why? Because when they made their predictions they had bellies full of pretzels and crackers. But surrogators—who were equally full when they made their predictions—relied on the report of someone without a full belly and hence made much more accurate predictions. It is important to note that the surrogators accurately predicted their future enjoyment of a food despite the fact that they didn't even know what the food was!

Imagination's third shortcoming is its failure to recognize that things will look different once they happen—in particular, that bad things will look a whole lot better. . . . When we imagine losing a job, for instance, we imagine the painful experience ("The boss will march into my office, shut the door behind him . . .") without also imagining how our psychological immune systems will transform its meaning ("I'll come to realize that this was an opportunity to quit retail sales and follow my true calling as a sculptor"). Can surrogation remedy this shortcoming? To find out, researchers arranged for some people to have an unpleasant experience. A group of volunteers (reporters) was told that the experimenter would flip a coin, and if it came up heads, the volunteer would receive a gift certificate to a local pizza parlor. The coin was flipped and—*oh, so sorry*—it came up tails and the reporters received nothing.[24] The reporters then reported how they felt. Next, a new group of volunteers was told about the coin-flipping game and was asked to predict how they would feel if the coin came up tails and they didn't get the pizza gift certificate. Some of these volunteers (simulators) were told the precise monetary value of the gift certificate, and others (surrogators) were instead shown the report of one randomly selected reporter. Once the volunteers had made their predictions, the coin was flipped and—*oh, so sorry*—came up tails. The volunteers then reported how they felt. Simulators felt better than they predicted they'd feel if they lost the coin flip. Why? Because simulators did not realize how quickly and easily they would rationalize the loss ("Pizza is too fattening, and besides, I don't like that restaurant anyway"). But surrogators—who had nothing to go on except the report of another randomly selected individual—assumed that they wouldn't feel too bad after losing the prize and hence made more accurate predictions.

Rejecting the Solution

This trio of studies suggests that when people are deprived of the information that imagination requires and are thus *forced* to use others as surrogates, they make remarkably accurate predictions about their future feelings, which suggests that the best way to predict our feelings tomorrow is to see how others are feeling today.[25] Given the impressive power of this simple technique, we should expect people to go out of their way to use it. But they don't. When an entirely new group of volunteers was told about the three situations I just described—winning a prize, eating a mystery food, or failing to receive a gift certificate—and was then asked whether they would prefer to make predictions about their future feelings based on *(a)* information about the prize, the food, and the certificate; or *(b)* information about how a randomly selected individual felt after winning them, eating them, or losing them, virtually every volunteer chose the former. If you hadn't seen the results of these studies, you'd probably have done the same. If I offered to pay for your dinner at a restaurant if you could accurately predict how much you were going to enjoy it, would you want to see the restaurant's menu or some randomly selected diner's review? If you are like most people, you would prefer to see the menu, and if you are like most people, you would end up buying your own dinner. Why?

Because if you are like most people, then like most people, you don't know you're like most people. Science has given us a lot of facts about the average person, and one of the most reliable of these facts is that the average person doesn't see herself as average. Most students see themselves as more intelligent than the average student,[26] most business managers see themselves as more competent than the average business manager,[27] and most football players see themselves as having better "football sense" than their teammates.[28] Ninety percent of motorists consider themselves to be safer-than-average drivers,[29] and 94 percent of college professors consider themselves to be better-than-average teachers.[30] Ironically, the bias toward seeing ourselves as better than average causes us to see ourselves as less biased than average too.[31] As one research team concluded, "Most of us appear to believe that we are more athletic, intelligent, organized, ethical, logical, interesting, fair-minded, and healthy—not to mention more attractive—than the average person."[32]

If you are like most people, then like most people, you don't know you're like most people.

This tendency to think of ourselves as better than others is not necessarily a manifestation of our unfettered narcissism but may instead be an instance of a more general tendency to think of ourselves as *different* from others—often for better but sometimes for worse. When people are asked about generosity, they claim to perform a greater number of generous acts than others do; but when they are asked about selfishness, they claim to perform a greater number of selfish acts than others do.[33] When people are asked about their ability to perform an easy task, such as driving a car or riding a bike, they rate themselves as better than others; but when they are asked about their ability to perform a difficult task, such as juggling or playing chess, they rate themselves as worse than others.[34] We don't always see ourselves as *superior*, but we almost always see ourselves as *unique*. Even when we do precisely what others do, we tend to think that we're doing it for unique reasons. For instance, we tend to attribute other people's choices to features of the chooser ("Phil picked this class because he's one of those literary types"), but we tend to attribute our own choices to features of the options ("But I picked it because it was easier than economics").[35] We recognize that our decisions are influenced by social norms ("I was too embarrassed to raise my hand in class even though I was terribly confused"), but fail to recognize that others' decisions were similarly influenced ("No one else raised a hand because no one else was as confused as I was").[36] We know that our choices sometimes reflect our aversions ("I voted for Kerry because I couldn't stand Bush"), but we assume that other people's choices reflect their appetites ("If Rebecca voted for Kerry, then she must have liked him").[37] The list of differences is long but the conclusion to be drawn from it is short: The self considers itself to be a very special person.[38]

What makes us think we're so darned special? Three things, at least. First, even if we aren't special, the way we know ourselves is. We are the only people in the world whom we can know from the inside. We *experience* our own thoughts and feelings but must *infer* that other people are experiencing theirs. We all trust that behind those eyes and inside those skulls, our friends and neighbors are having subjective experiences very much like our own, but that trust is an article of faith and not the palpable, self-evident truth that our own subjective experiences constitute. There is a difference between making love and reading about it, and it is the same difference that distinguishes our knowledge of our own mental lives from our knowledge of everyone else's. Because we know ourselves and others by such different means, we gather very different kinds and amounts of information. In every waking moment we monitor the steady stream of thoughts and feelings that runs through our heads, but we only monitor other people's words and deeds, and only when they are in our company. One reason why we seem so special, then, is that we learn about ourselves in such a special way.

The second reason is that we *enjoy* thinking of ourselves as special. Most of us want to fit in well with our peers, but we don't want to fit in too well.[39] We prize our unique identities, and research shows that when people are made to feel too similar to others, their moods quickly sour and they try to distance and distinguish themselves in a variety of ways.[40] If you've ever shown up at a party and found someone else wearing exactly the same dress or necktie that you were wearing, then you know how unsettling it is to share the room with an unwanted twin whose presence temporarily diminishes your sense of individuality. Because we *value* our uniqueness, it isn't surprising that we tend to overestimate it.

The third reason why we tend to overestimate our uniqueness is that we tend to overestimate everyone's uniqueness—that is, we tend to think of people as more different from one another than they actually are. Let's face it: All people are similar in some ways and different in others. The psychologists, biologists, economists, and sociologists who are searching for universal laws of human behavior naturally care about the similarities, but the rest of us care mainly about the differences. Social life involves selecting particular individuals to be our sexual partners, business partners, bowling partners, and more. That task requires that we focus on the things that distinguish one person from another and not on the things that all people share, which is why personal ads are much more likely to mention the advertiser's love of ballet than his love of oxygen. A penchant for respiration explains a great deal about human behavior—for example, why people live on land, become ill at high altitudes, have lungs, resist suffocation, love trees, and so on. It surely explains more than does a person's penchant for ballet. But it does nothing to distinguish one person from another, and thus for ordinary folks who are in the ordinary business of selecting others for commerce, conversation, or copulation, the penchant for air is stunningly irrelevant. Individual similarities are vast, but we don't care much about them because they don't help us do what we are here on earth to do, namely, distinguish Jack from Jill and Jill from Jennifer. As such, these individual similarities are an inconspicuous backdrop against which a small number of relatively minor individual differences stand out in bold relief.

Because we spend so much time searching for, attending to, thinking about, and remembering these differences, we tend to overestimate their magnitude and frequency, and thus end up thinking of people as more varied than they actually are. If you spent all day sorting grapes into different shapes, colors, and kinds, you'd become one of those annoying grapeophiles who talks endlessly about the nuances of flavor and the permutations of texture. You'd come to think of grapes as infinitely varied, and you'd forget that almost all of the really *important* information about a grape can be deduced from the simple fact of its grapehood. Our belief in the variability of others and in the uniqueness of the self is especially powerful when it comes to emotion.[41] Because we can *feel* our own emotions but must *infer* the emotions of others by watching their faces and listening to their voices, we often have the impression that others don't experience the same intensity of emotion that we do, which is why we expect others to recognize our feelings even when we can't recognize theirs.[42] This sense of emotional uniqueness starts early. When kindergarteners are asked how they and others would feel in a variety of situations, they expect to experience unique emotions ("Billy would be sad but I wouldn't") and they provide unique reasons for experiencing them ("I'd tell myself that the hamster was in heaven, but Billy would just cry").[43] When adults make these same kinds of predictions, they do just the same thing.[44]

Our mythical belief in the variability and uniqueness of individuals is the main reason why we refuse to use others as surrogates. After all, surrogation is only useful when we can count on a surrogate to react to an event roughly as we would, and if we believe that people's emotional reactions are more varied than they actually are, then surrogation will seem less useful to us than it actually is. The irony, of course, is that surrogation is a cheap and effective way to predict one's future emotions, but because we don't realize just how similar we all are, we reject this reliable method and rely instead on our imaginations, as flawed and fallible as they may be.

Onward

Despite its watery connotation, the word *hogwash* refers to the feeding—and not to the bathing—of pigs. Hogwash is something that pigs eat, that pigs like, and that pigs need. Farmers provide pigs with hogwash because without it, pigs get grumpy. The word *hogwash* also refers to the falsehoods people tell one another. Like the hogwash that farmers feed their pigs, the hogwash that our friends and teachers and parents feed us is meant to make us happy; but unlike hogwash of the porcine variety, human hogwash does not always achieve its end. As we have seen, ideas can flourish if they preserve the social systems that allow them to be transmitted. Because individuals don't usually feel that it is their personal duty to preserve social systems, these ideas must disguise themselves as prescriptions for individual happiness. We might expect that after spending some time in the world, our experiences would debunk these ideas, but it doesn't always work that way. To learn from our experience we must remember it, and for a variety of reasons, memory is a faithless friend. Practice and coaching get us out of our diapers and into our britches, but they are not enough to get us out of our presents and into our futures. What's so ironic about this predicament is that the information we need to make accurate predictions of our emotional futures is right under our noses, but we don't seem to recognize its aroma. It doesn't always make sense to heed what people tell us when they communicate their beliefs about happiness, but it does make sense to observe how happy they are in different circumstances. Alas, we think of ourselves as unique entities—minds unlike any others—and thus we often reject the lessons that the emotional experience of others has to teach us.

NOTES

1. J. Livingston and R. Evans, "Whatever Will Be, Will Be (Que Sera, Sera)" (1955).
2. W. V. Quine and J. S. Ullian, *The Web of Belief*, 2nd ed. (New York: Random House, 1978), 51.
3. Half of all Americans relocated in the five-year period of 1995–2000, which suggests that the average American relocates about every ten years; B. Berkner and C. S. Faber, *Geographical Mobility, 1995 to 2000* (Washington, D.C.: U.S. Bureau of the Census, 2003).
4. The average baby boomer held roughly ten jobs between the ages of eighteen and thirty-six, which suggests that the average American holds at least this many in a lifetime. Bureau of Labor Statistics, *Number of Jobs Held, Labor Market Activity, and Earnings Growth among Younger Baby Boomers: Results from More Than Two Decades of a Longitudinal Survey*, Bureau of Labor Statistics news release (Washington, D.C.: U.S. Department of Labor, 2002).
5. The U.S. Census Bureau projects that in the coming years, 10 percent of Americans will never marry, 60 percent will marry just once, and 30 percent will marry at least twice. R. M. Kreider and J. M. Fields, *Number, Timing, and Duration of Marriages and Divorces* (Washington, D.C.: U.S. Bureau of the Census, 2002).
6. B. Russell, *The Analysis of Mind* (New York: Macmillan, 1921), 231.
7. The biologist Richard Dawkins refers to these beliefs as *memes*. See R. J. Dawkins, *The Selfish Gene* (Oxford: Oxford University Press, 1976). See also S. Blackmore, *The Meme Machine* (Oxford: Oxford University Press, 2000).
8. D. C. Dennett, *Brainstorms: Philosophical Essays on Mind and Psychology* (Cambridge, Mass.: Bradford/MIT Press, 1981), 18.
9. R. Layard, *Happiness: Lessons from a New Science* (New York: Penguin, 2005); E. Diener and M. E. P. Seligman, "Beyond Money: Toward an Economy of Well-Being," *Psychological Science in the Public Interest* 5: 1–31 (2004); B. S. Frey and A. Stutzer, *Happiness and Economics: How the Economy and Institutions Affect Human Well-Being* (Princeton, N.J.: Princeton University Press, 2002); R. A. Easterlin, "Income and Happiness: Towards a Unified Theory," *Economic Journal* 111: 465–84 (2001); and D. G. Blanchflower and A. J. Oswald, "Well-Being over Time in Britain and the USA," *Journal of Public Economics* 88: 1359–86 (2004).
10. The effect of declining marginal utility is slowed when we spend our money on the things to which we are least likely to adapt. See T. Scitovsky, *The Joyless Economy: The Psychology of Human Satisfaction* (Oxford: Oxford University Press, 1976); L. Van Boven and T. Gilovich, "To Do or to Have? That Is the Question," *Journal of Personality and Social Psychology* 85: 1193–1202 (2003); and R. H. Frank, "How Not to Buy Happiness," *Daedalus: Journal of the American Academy of Arts and Sciences* 133: 69–79 (2004). Not all economists believe in decreasing marginal utility: R. A. Easterlin, "Diminishing Marginal Utility of Income? Caveat Emptor," *Social Indicators Research* 70: 243–326 (2005).
11. J. D. Graaf et al., *Affluenza: The All-Consuming Epidemic* (New York: Berrett-Koehler, 2002); D. Myers, *The American Paradox: Spiritual Hunger in an Age of Plenty* (New Haven: Yale University Press, 2000); R. H. Frank, *Luxury Fever* (Princeton, N.J.: Princeton University Press, 2000); J. B. Schor, *The Overspent American: Why We Want What We Don't Need* (New York: Perennial, 1999); and P. L. Wachtel, *Poverty of Affluence: A Psychological Portrait of the American Way of Life* (New York: Free Press, 1983).
12. Adam Smith, *An Inquiry into the Nature and Causes of the Wealth of Nations* (1776), book 1 (New York: Modern Library, 1994).

13. Adam Smith, *The Theory of Moral Sentiments* (1759; Cambridge: Cambridge University Press, 2002).
14. N. Ashraf, C. Camerer, and G. Loewenstein, "Adam Smith, Behavioral Economist," *Journal of Economic Perspectives* 19: 131–45 (2005).
15. Smith, *The Theory of Moral Sentiments*.
16. Some theorists have argued that societies exhibit a cyclic pattern in which people do come to realize that money doesn't buy happiness but then forget this lesson a generation later. See A. O. Hirschman, *Shifting Involvements: Private Interest and Public Action* (Princeton, N.J.: Princeton University Press, 1982).
17. C. Walker, "Some Variations in Marital Satisfaction," in *Equalities and Inequalities in Family Life*, ed. R. Chester and J. Peel (London: Academic Press, 1977), 127–39.
18. D. Myers, *The Pursuit of Happiness: Discovering the Pathway to Fulfillment, Well-Being, and Enduring Personal Joy* (New York: Avon, 1992), 71.
19. J. A. Feeney, "Attachment Styles, Communication Patterns and Satisfaction across the Life Cycle of Marriage," *Personal Relationships* 1: 333–48 (1994).
20. D. Kahneman et al., "A Survey Method for Characterizing Daily Life Experience: The Day Reconstruction Method," *Science* 306: 1776–80 (2004).
21. T. D. Wilson et al., "Focalism: A Source of Durability Bias in Affective Forecasting," *Journal of Personality and Social Psychology* 78: 821–36 (2000).
22. R. J. Norwick, D. T. Gilbert, and T. D. Wilson, "Surrogation: An Antidote for Errors in Affective Forecasting" (unpublished manuscript, Harvard University, 2005).
23. Ibid.
24. Ibid.
25. This is also the best way to predict our future behavior. For example, people overestimate the likelihood that they will perform a charitable act but correctly estimate the likelihood that others will do the same. This suggests that if we would base predictions of our own behavior on what we see others do, we'd be dead-on. See N. Epley and D. Dunning, "Feeling 'Holier Than Thou': Are Self-Serving Assessments Produced by Errors in Self- or Social-Prediction?" *Journal of Personality and Social Psychology* 79: 861–75 (2000).
26. R. C. Wylie, *The Self-Concept: Theory and Research on Selected Topics*, vol. 2 (Lincoln: University of Nebraska Press, 1979).
27. L. Larwood and W. Whittaker, "Managerial Myopia: Self-Serving Biases in Organizational Planning," *Journal of Applied Psychology* 62: 194–98 (1977).
28. R. B. Felson, "Ambiguity and Bias in the Self-Concept," *Social Psychology Quarterly* 44: 64–69.
29. D. Walton and J. Bathurst, "An Exploration of the Perceptions of the Average Driver's Speed Compared to Perceived Driver Safety and Driving Skill," *Accident Analysis and Prevention* 30: 821–30 (1998).
30. P. Cross, "Not Can But Will College Teachers Be Improved?" *New Directions for Higher Education* 17: 1–15 (1977).
31. E. Pronin, D. Y. Lin, and L. Ross, "The Bias Blind Spot: Perceptions of Bias in Self Versus Others," *Personality and Social Psychology Bulletin* 28: 369–81 (2002).
32. J. Kruger, "Lake Wobegon Be Gone! The 'Below-Average Effect' and the Egocentric Nature of Comparative Ability Judgments," *Journal of Personality and Social Psychology* 77: 221–32 (1999).
33. J. T. Johnson et al., "The 'Barnum Effect' Revisited: Cognitive and Motivational Factors in the Acceptance of Personality Descriptions," *Journal of Personality and Social Psychology* 49: 1378–91 (1985).
34. Kruger, "Lake Wobegon Be Gone!"

35. E. E. Jones and R. E. Nisbett, "The Actor and the Observer: Divergent Perceptions of the Causes of Behavior," in *Attribution: Perceiving the Causes of Behavior*, ed. E. E. Jones et al. (Morristown, N.J.: General Learning Press, 1972); and R. E. Nisbett and E. Borgida, "Attribution and the Psychology of Prediction," *Journal of Personality and Social Psychology* 32: 932–43 (1975).
36. D. T. Miller and C. McFarland, "Pluralistic Ignorance: When Similarity Is Interpreted as Dissimilarity," *Journal of Personality and Social Psychology* 53: 298–305 (1987).
37. D. T. Miller and L. D. Nelson, "Seeing Approach Motivation in the Avoidance Behavior of Others: Implications for an Understanding of Pluralistic Ignorance," *Journal of Personality and Social Psychology* 83: 1066–75 (2002).
38. C. R. Snyder and H. L. Fromkin, "Abnormality as a Positive Characteristic: The Development and Validation of a Scale Measuring Need for Uniqueness," *Journal of Abnormal Psychology* 86: 518–27 (1977).
39. M. B. Brewer, "The Social Self: On Being the Same and Different at the Same Time," *Personality and Social Psychology Bulletin* 17: 475–82 (1991).
40. H. L. Fromkin, "Effects of Experimentally Aroused Feelings of Undistinctiveness upon Valuation of Scarce and Novel Experiences," *Journal of Personality and Social Psychology* 16: 521–29 (1970); and H. L. Fromkin, "Feelings of Interpersonal Undistinctiveness: An Unpleasant Affective State," *Journal of Experimental Research in Personality* 6: 178–85 (1972).
41. R. Karniol, T. Eylon, and S. Rish, "Predicting Your Own and Others' Thoughts and Feelings: More Like a Stranger Than a Friend," *European Journal of Social Psychology* 27: 301–11 (1997); J. T. Johnson, "The Heart on the Sleeve and the Secret Self: Estimations of Hidden Emotion in Self and Acquaintances," *Journal of Personality* 55: 563–82 (1987); and R. Karniol, "Egocentrism Versus Protocentrism: The Status of Self in Social Prediction," *Psychological Review* 110: 564–80 (2003).
42. C. L. Barr and R. E. Kleck, "Self-Other Perception of the Intensity of Facial Expressions of Emotion: Do We Know What We Show?" *Journal of Personality and Social Psychology* 68: 608–18 (1995).
43. R. Karniol and L. Koren, "How Would You Feel? Children's Inferences Regarding Their Own and Others' Affective Reactions," *Cognitive Development* 2: 271–78 (1987).
44. C. McFarland and D. T. Miller, "Judgments of Self-Other Similarity: Just Like Other People, Only More So," *Personality and Social Psychology Bulletin* 16: 475–84 (1990).

Questions for Critical Reading

1. As you reread Gilbert's text, look for the term *super-replicator*. What does this term mean? Develop a definition using Gilbert's text and then offer an example not included in his essay. What function does this concept serve in Gilbert's argument?

2. What does Gilbert mean by *surrogate*? You will notice as you review his essay that Gilbert never explicitly defines the term. Instead, you should read his text critically and construct a definition out of quotations you find that discuss the idea.

3. **Multimodal.** Using Gilbert's text, define *happiness*. As with *surrogate*, you will need to analyze Gilbert's text to construct this definition. What does it mean in the context of this essay, and what does it mean for you? Then, using your phone or another audio recording device, interview others about what happiness means to them to make a podcast. How do these definitions differ and how does this relate to Gilbert's argument?

Exploring Context

1. **Multimodal.** Visit Stripgenerator.com and make a comic strip that represents the argument of Gilbert's essay. Incorporate representations for your definitions of the terms in Questions for Critical Reading.

2. What is "happiness"? Enter "happy," "happiness," and related terms into Google or another search engine. What sort of results do you get? What if you search for images? What does "happiness" look like on the web? Does it match the definition you developed in Question 3 of Questions for Critical Reading?

3. Gilbert suggests that if we want to know how happy we will be in the future, we should ask someone who's already living our goals. Use Yahoo! Answers (answers.yahoo.com) to ask questions about possible plans for your future. Can the web function as a surrogate? Use the definition of *surrogate* that you developed in Question 2 of Questions for Critical Reading in your answer.

Questions for Connecting

1. Gilbert mostly considers surrogates and super-replicators in relation to our future happiness but can these same phenomena promote social change? Apply Gilbert's ideas to Malcolm Gladwell's examination of social change in "Small Change" (p. 191). What kinds of social ties best foster super-replicators? Use your work from Questions 1 and 2 of Questions for Critical Reading.

2. Is there a genetic component to happiness? Consider Sharon Moalem's work on epigenetics and trauma in "Changing Our Genes: How Trauma, Bullying, and Royal Jelly Alter Our Genetic Destiny" (p. 289). Using his analysis, consider whether or not genetic components could complicate our pursuit of happiness, with or without surrogates.

3. In "My Son, the Prince of Fashion" (p. 62), Michael Chabon's son Abe seems to have a good sense of what will make him happy now and in the future. Analyze Chabon's text using Gilbert's ideas. What sort of super-replicators are at work in fashion? Does Abe use surrogates?

Language Matters

1. Locate information on sentence diagrams in a grammar handbook or other reference resource. Then select a key sentence from Gilbert's text and diagram the sentence. What are the different parts of the sentence, and how are they related?

2. Locate a sentence in Gilbert's essay that uses *I* as the subject. When does Gilbert use *I*? When doesn't he? When should you?

3. Take a key sentence from Gilbert. Summarize it and then paraphrase it. What is the difference between a summary, a paraphrase, and a quotation? When would you use each in your writing, and what type of citation does each need?

Assignments for Writing

1. According to Gilbert, surrogates can offer us an accurate sense of our future happiness. Write a paper in which you assess the potential of the kind of surrogates that Gilbert describes. You will want to extend, complicate, or refute Gilbert's argument for surrogates and their reliability in predicting the future. Think about these questions: What role does individuality have in our future happiness? Is Gilbert correct in claiming that we are not as unique as we believe? Can surrogates be used to examine all future events? How can surrogates be used to control social processes? If we are not unique, why do we see ourselves as individuals? Use your definition of *surrogate* from Question 2 of Questions for Critical Reading as well as your work with Yahoo! Answers from Question 3 of Exploring Context.

2. Write a paper in which you evaluate Gilbert's argument about surrogates and their reliability in predicting the future by finding an appropriate surrogate for you and your future happiness. You may wish to use your experience finding a surrogate on the web from Question 3 of Exploring Context in making your argument. Also consider: What role does individuality have in our future happiness? Are surrogate examples more accurate than our imagination? What event in your life did you imagine was going to make you happier than it did?

3. Gilbert defines *super-replicators* as genes or beliefs that are given to transmission regardless of their usefulness. Write a paper in which you extend Gilbert's argument through your own example of a super-replicator that persists in society. How do we communicate our ideas to others? What super-replicators are we passing along to those we come into contact with? Does the validity of a belief correlate to its speed of transmission? What is the role of super-replicators in communicating cultural ideas? Use your definition of the term from Question 1 of Questions for Critical Reading.

MALCOLM GLADWELL

Born in England and raised in Canada before moving to New York City, **Malcolm Gladwell** is a best-selling author and staff writer for the *New Yorker.* He began his career as a reporter for the *Washington Post*, a position he held from 1987 to 1996, before moving on to a staff writing position for the *New Yorker.* He has won a National Magazine Award and was named one of *Time* magazine's 100 most influential people in 2005. Gladwell famously received a $1 million advance for his first book, *The Tipping Point: How Little Things Make a Big Difference* (2000), which became a best-seller. His other books include *Blink: The Power of Thinking without Thinking* (2005), *Outliers: The Story of Success* (2008), and *What the Dog Saw* (2009). His most recent book, 2013's *David and Goliath: Underdogs, Misfits, and the Art of Battling Giants* contains a collection of case studies examining the relationships between disadvantages and success.

The essay presented here, "Small Change," originally appeared in the October 4, 2010, issue of the *New Yorker.* That issue featured the magazine's usual selection of book reviews and short fiction as well as a brief note to the readers that the magazine had finally debuted on the iPad. Given that technological milestone for the publication, it is interesting that Gladwell's contribution to the issue analyzed the role technology played in inciting the "Arab Spring" uprisings of 2010.

In "Small Change," Gladwell discusses the perception that modern social networking technologies such as Facebook and Twitter have been instrumental in organizing mass uprisings in the Middle East in response to the oppressive regimes of the region. While he concedes that traditional social networks led to great successes for American civil rights in the 1960s, Gladwell disagrees with any comparisons made to the power of social networking in the modern age—"The revolution will not be tweeted," as the *New Yorker* put it. "Small Change" looks at the ties that bind us, both "weak ties" and "strong ties." Ultimately, Gladwell suggests that it's the quality of connections that people have (rather than the quantity of them) that leads to success in social change.

▶ TAGS: *civil rights, Facebook, social change, strong tie, technology, Twitter, weak tie*

▶ CONNECTIONS: *Appiah, Chen, Epstein, Konnikova, Turkle, von Busch, Yoshino*

Small Change

At four-thirty in the afternoon on Monday, February 1, 1960, four college students sat down at the lunch counter at the Woolworth's in downtown Greensboro, North Carolina. They were freshmen at North Carolina A&T, a black college a mile or so away.

"I'd like a cup of coffee, please," one of the four, Ezell Blair, said to the waitress.

"We don't serve Negroes here," she replied.

The Woolworth's lunch counter was a long L-shaped bar that could seat sixty-six people, with a standup snack bar at one end. The seats were for whites. The snack bar was for blacks. Another employee, a black woman who worked at the steam table, approached the students and tried to warn them away. "You're acting stupid, ignorant!" she said. They didn't move. Around five-thirty, the front doors to the store were locked. The four still didn't move. Finally, they left by a side door. Outside, a small crowd had gathered, including a photographer from the *Greensboro Record*. "I'll be back tomorrow with A&T College," one of the students said.

5 By next morning, the protest had grown to twenty-seven men and four women, most from the same dormitory as the original four. The men were dressed in suits and ties. The students had brought their schoolwork, and studied as they sat at the counter. On Wednesday, students from Greensboro's "Negro" secondary school, Dudley High, joined in, and the number of protesters swelled to eighty. By Thursday, the protesters numbered three hundred, including three white women, from the Greensboro campus of the University of North Carolina. By Saturday, the sit-in had reached six hundred. People spilled out onto the street. White teenagers waved Confederate flags. Someone threw a firecracker. At noon, the A&T football team arrived. "Here comes the wrecking crew," one of the white students shouted.

By the following Monday, sit-ins had spread to Winston-Salem, twenty-five miles away, and Durham, fifty miles away. The day after that, students at Fayetteville State Teachers College and at Johnson C. Smith College, in Charlotte, joined in, followed on Wednesday by students at St. Augustine's College and Shaw University, in Raleigh. On Thursday and Friday, the protest crossed state lines, surfacing in Hampton and Portsmouth, Virginia, in Rock Hill, South Carolina, and in Chattanooga, Tennessee. By the end of the month, there were sit-ins throughout the South, as far west as Texas. "I asked every student I met what the first day of the sitdowns had been like on his campus," the political theorist Michael Walzer wrote in *Dissent*. "The answer was always the same: 'It was like a fever. Everyone wanted to go.'" Some seventy thousand students eventually took part. Thousands were arrested and untold thousands more radicalized. These events in the early sixties became a civil-rights war that engulfed the South for the rest of the decade—and it happened without email, texting, Facebook, or Twitter.

It happened without e-mail, texting, Facebook, or Twitter.

The world, we are told, is in the midst of a revolution. The new tools of social media have reinvented social activism. With Facebook and Twitter and the like, the traditional relationship between political authority and popular will has been upended, making it easier for the powerless to collaborate, coordinate, and give voice to their concerns. When ten thousand protesters took to the streets in Moldova* in the spring of 2009 to protest against their country's Communist government, the action was dubbed the Twitter Revolution, because of the means by which the demonstrators had been brought together. A few months after that, when student protests rocked Tehran, the State Department took the unusual step of asking Twitter to suspend scheduled maintenance of its website, because the Administration didn't want such a critical organizing tool out of service at the height of the demonstrations. "Without Twitter the people of Iran would not have felt empowered and confident to stand up for freedom and democracy," Mark Pfeifle, a former national-security adviser, later wrote, calling for Twitter to be nominated for the Nobel Peace Prize. Where activists were once defined by their

*Moldova: The Republic of Moldova is located northeast of Romania in Eastern Europe, bordering Ukraine. Formerly a part of the USSR, Moldova elected a communist president in 2001. He resigned in 2009 [Ed.].

causes, they are now defined by their tools. Facebook warriors go online to push for change. "You are the best hope for us all," James K. Glassman, a former senior State Department official, told a crowd of cyber activists at a recent conference sponsored by Facebook, AT&T, Howcast, MTV, and Google. Sites like Facebook, Glassman said, "give the U.S. a significant competitive advantage over terrorists. Some time ago, I said that Al Qaeda was 'eating our lunch on the Internet.' That is no longer the case. Al Qaeda is stuck in Web 1.0. The Internet is now about interactivity and conversation."

These are strong, and puzzling, claims. Why does it matter who is eating whose lunch on the Internet? Are people who log on to their Facebook page really the best hope for us all? As for Moldova's so-called Twitter Revolution, Evgeny Morozov, a scholar at Stanford who has been the most persistent of digital evangelism's critics, points out that Twitter had scant internal significance in Moldova, a country where very few Twitter accounts exist. Nor does it seem to have been a revolution, not least because the protests—as Anne Applebaum suggested in the *Washington Post*—may well have been a bit of stagecraft cooked up by the government. (In a country paranoid about Romanian revanchism,† the protesters flew a Romanian flag over the Parliament building.) In the Iranian case, meanwhile, the people tweeting about the demonstrations were almost all in the West. "It is time to get Twitter's role in the events in Iran right," Golnaz Esfandiari wrote, this past summer, in *Foreign Policy*. "Simply put: There was no Twitter Revolution inside Iran." The cadre of prominent bloggers, like Andrew Sullivan, who championed the role of social media in Iran, Esfandiari continued, misunderstood the situation. "Western journalists who couldn't reach—or didn't bother reaching?—people on the ground in Iran simply scrolled through the English-language tweets posted with tag #iranelection," she wrote. "Through it all, no one seemed to wonder why people trying to coordinate protests in Iran would be writing in any language other than Farsi."

Some of this grandiosity is to be expected. Innovators tend to be solipsists. They often want to cram every stray fact and experience into their new model. As the historian Robert Darnton has written, "The marvels of communication technology in the present have produced a false consciousness about the past—even a sense that communication has no history, or had nothing of importance to consider before the days of television and the Internet." But there is something else at work here, in the outsized enthusiasm for social media. Fifty years after one of the most extraordinary episodes of social upheaval in American history, we seem to have forgotten what activism is.

Greensboro in the early 1960s was the kind of place where racial insubordination was routinely met with violence. The four students who first sat down at the lunch counter were terrified. "I suppose if anyone had come up behind me and yelled 'Boo,' I think I would have fallen off my seat," one of them said later. On the first day, the store manager notified the police chief, who immediately sent two officers to the store. On the third day, a gang of white toughs showed up at the lunch counter and stood ostentatiously behind the protesters, ominously muttering epithets such as "burr-head nigger." A local Ku Klux Klan leader made an appearance. On Saturday, as tensions grew, someone called in a bomb threat, and the entire store had to be evacuated. 10

†Revanchism: French term meaning retaliation or revenge; refers to a policy of attempting to retake lost land or honor [Ed.].

The dangers were even clearer in the Mississippi Freedom Summer Project of 1964, another of the sentinel campaigns of the civil-rights movement. The Student Nonviolent Coordinating Committee recruited hundreds of Northern, largely white unpaid volunteers to run Freedom Schools, register black voters, and raise civil-rights awareness in the Deep South. "No one should go *anywhere* alone, but certainly not in an automobile and certainly not at night," they were instructed. Within days of arriving in Mississippi, three volunteers—Michael Schwerner, James Chaney, and Andrew Goodman—were kidnapped and killed, and, during the rest of the summer, thirty-seven black churches were set on fire and dozens of safe houses were bombed; volunteers were beaten, shot at, arrested, and trailed by pickup trucks full of armed men. A quarter of those in the program dropped out. Activism that challenges the status quo—that attacks deeply rooted problems—is not for the faint of heart.

What makes people capable of this kind of activism? The Stanford sociologist Doug McAdam compared the Freedom Summer dropouts with the participants who stayed, and discovered that the key difference wasn't, as might be expected, ideological fervor. "*All* of the applicants—participants and withdrawals alike—emerge as highly committed, articulate supporters of the goals and values of the summer program," he concluded. What mattered more was an applicant's degree of personal connection to the civil-rights movement. All the volunteers were required to provide a list of personal contacts—the people they wanted kept apprised of their activities—and participants were far more likely than dropouts to have close friends who were also going to Mississippi. High-risk activism, McAdam concluded, is a "strong-tie" phenomenon.

This pattern shows up again and again. One study of the Red Brigades, the Italian terrorist group of the 1970s, found that seventy percent of recruits had at least one good friend already in the organization. The same is true of the men who joined the mujahideen* in Afghanistan. Even revolutionary actions that look spontaneous, like the demonstrations in East Germany that led to the fall of the Berlin Wall,† are, at core, strong-tie phenomena. The opposition movement in East Germany consisted of several hundred groups, each with roughly a dozen members. Each group was in limited contact with the others: at the time, only thirteen percent of East Germans even had a phone. All they knew was that on Monday nights, outside St. Nicholas Church in downtown Leipzig, people gathered to voice their anger at the state. And the primary determinant of who showed up was "critical friends"—the more friends you had who were critical of the regime the more likely you were to join the protest.

So one crucial fact about the four freshmen at the Greensboro lunch counter—David Richmond, Franklin McCain, Ezell Blair, and Joseph McNeil—was their relationship with one another. McNeil was a roommate of Blair's in A&T's Scott Hall dormitory. Richmond roomed with McCain one floor up, and Blair, Richmond, and McCain had all gone to Dudley High School. The four would smuggle beer into the dorm and talk late into the night in Blair and McNeil's room. They would all have remembered the murder of Emmett Till in 1955, the Montgomery bus boycott that same year, and the

---

* Mujahideen: Fighters who resisted the Soviet invasion of Afghanistan in the 1980s [Ed.].

† Berlin Wall: Barrier that divided Berlin, Germany, into communist East and democratic West; it lasted from 1961 to 1989. East Germans discovered while attempting to cross the wall to escape to the West were either captured or killed by East German forces [Ed.].

showdown in Little Rock in 1957. It was McNeil who brought up the idea of a sit-in at Woolworth's. They'd discussed it for nearly a month. Then McNeil came into the dorm room and asked the others if they were ready. There was a pause, and McCain said, in a way that works only with people who talk late into the night with one another, "Are you guys chicken or not?" Ezell Blair worked up the courage the next day to ask for a cup of coffee because he was flanked by his roommate and two good friends from high school.

The kind of activism associated with social media isn't like this at all. The platforms of social media are built around weak ties. Twitter is a way of following (or being followed by) people you may never have met. Facebook is a tool for efficiently managing your acquaintances, for keeping up with the people you would not otherwise be able to stay in touch with. That's why you can have a thousand "friends" on Facebook, as you never could in real life. 15

This is in many ways a wonderful thing. There is strength in weak ties, as the sociologist Mark Granovetter has observed. Our acquaintances—not our friends—are our greatest source of new ideas and information. The Internet lets us exploit the power of these kinds of distant connections with marvelous efficiency. It's terrific at the diffusion of innovation, interdisciplinary collaboration, seamlessly matching up buyers and sellers, and the logistical functions of the dating world. But weak ties seldom lead to high-risk activism.

In a new book called *The Dragonfly Effect: Quick, Effective, and Powerful Ways to Use Social Media to Drive Social Change*, the business consultant Andy Smith and the Stanford Business School professor Jennifer Aaker tell the story of Sameer Bhatia, a young Silicon Valley entrepreneur who came down with acute myelogenous leukemia. It's a perfect illustration of social media's strengths. Bhatia needed a bone-marrow transplant, but he could not find a match among his relatives and friends. The odds were best with a donor of his ethnicity, and there were few South Asians in the national bone-marrow database. So Bhatia's business partner sent out an e-mail explaining Bhatia's plight to more than four hundred of their acquaintances, who forwarded the e-mail to their personal contacts; Facebook pages and YouTube videos were devoted to the Help Sameer campaign. Eventually, nearly twenty-five thousand new people were registered in the bone-marrow database, and Bhatia found a match.

But how did the campaign get so many people to sign up? By not asking too much of them. That's the only way you can get someone you don't really know to do something on your behalf. You can get thousands of people to sign up for a donor registry, because doing so is pretty easy. You have to send in a cheek swab and—in the highly unlikely event that your bone marrow is a good match for someone in need—spend a few hours at the hospital. Donating bone marrow isn't a trivial matter. But it doesn't involve financial or personal risk; it doesn't mean spending a summer being chased by armed men in pickup trucks. It doesn't require that you confront socially entrenched norms and practices. In fact, it's the kind of commitment that will bring only social acknowledgment and praise.

But how did the campaign get so many people to sign up? By not asking too much of them.

The evangelists of social media don't understand this distinction; they seem to believe that a Facebook friend is the same as a real friend and that signing up for a donor registry in Silicon Valley today is activism in the same sense as sitting at a segregated lunch counter in Greensboro in 1960. "Social networks are particularly effective at increasing motivation," Aaker and Smith write. But that's not true. Social networks are effective at increasing *participation*—by lessening the level of motivation that participation requires. The Facebook page of the Save Darfur Coalition has 1,282,339 members, who have donated an average of nine cents apiece. The next biggest Darfur charity on Facebook has 22,073 members, who have donated an average of thirty-five cents. Help Save Darfur has 2,797 members, who have given, on average, fifteen cents. A spokesperson for the Save Darfur Coalition told *Newsweek*, "We wouldn't necessarily gauge someone's value to the advocacy movement based on what they've given. This is a powerful mechanism to engage this critical population. They inform their community, attend events, volunteer. It's not something you can measure by looking at a ledger." In other words, Facebook activism succeeds not by motivating people to make a real sacrifice but by motivating them to do the things that people do when they are not motivated enough to make a real sacrifice. We are a long way from the lunch counters of Greensboro.

The students who joined the sit-ins across the South during the winter of 1960 described the movement as a "fever." But the civil-rights movement was more like a military campaign than like a contagion. In the late 1950s, there had been sixteen sit-ins in various cities throughout the South, fifteen of which were formally organized by civil-rights organizations like the NAACP and CORE. Possible locations for activism were scouted. Plans were drawn up. Movement activists held training sessions and retreats for would-be protesters. The Greensboro Four were a product of this groundwork: all were members of the NAACP Youth Council. They had close ties with the head of the local NAACP chapter. They had been briefed on the earlier wave of sit-ins in Durham, and had been part of a series of movement meetings in activist churches. When the sit-in movement spread from Greensboro throughout the South, it did not spread indiscriminately. It spread to those cities which had preexisting "movement centers"—a core of dedicated and trained activists ready to turn the "fever" into action. 20

The civil-rights movement was high-risk activism. It was also, crucially, strategic activism: a challenge to the establishment mounted with precision and discipline. The NAACP was a centralized organization, run from New York according to highly formalized operating procedures. At the Southern Christian Leadership Conference, Martin Luther King Jr. was the unquestioned authority. At the center of the movement was the black church, which had, as Aldon D. Morris points out in his superb 1984 study, *The Origins of the Civil Rights Movement*, a carefully demarcated division of labor, with various standing committees and disciplined groups. "Each group was task-oriented and coordinated its activities through authority structures," Morris writes. "Individuals were held accountable for their assigned duties, and important conflicts were resolved by the minister, who usually exercised ultimate authority over the congregation."

This is the second crucial distinction between traditional activism and its online variant: social media are not about this kind of hierarchical organization. Facebook and the like are tools for building *networks*, which are the opposite, in structure and character, of hierarchies. Unlike hierarchies, with their rules and procedures, networks aren't controlled by a single central authority. Decisions are made through consensus, and the ties that bind people to the group are loose.

This structure makes networks enormously resilient and adaptable in low-risk situations. Wikipedia is a perfect example. It doesn't have an editor, sitting in New York, who directs and corrects each entry. The effort of putting together each entry is self-organized. If every entry in Wikipedia were to be erased tomorrow, the content would swiftly be restored, because that's what happens when a network of thousands spontaneously devote their time to a task.

There are many things, though, that networks don't do well. Car companies sensibly use a network to organize their hundreds of suppliers, but not to design their cars. No one believes that the articulation of a coherent design philosophy is best handled by a sprawling, leaderless organizational system. Because networks don't have a centralized leadership structure and clear lines of authority, they have real difficulty reaching consensus and setting goals. They can't think strategically; they are chronically prone to conflict and error. How do you make difficult choices about tactics or strategy or philosophical direction when everyone has an equal say?

The Palestine Liberation Organization originated as a network, and the international-relations scholars Mette Eilstrup-Sangiovanni and Calvert Jones argue in a recent essay in *International Security* that this is why it ran into such trouble as it grew: "Structural features typical of networks—the absence of central authority, the unchecked autonomy of rival groups, and the inability to arbitrate quarrels through formal mechanisms—made the PLO excessively vulnerable to outside manipulation and internal strife."

In Germany in the 1970s, they go on, "the far more unified and successful left-wing terrorists tended to organize hierarchically, with professional management and clear divisions of labor. They were concentrated geographically in universities, where they could establish central leadership, trust, and camaraderie through regular, face-to-face meetings." They seldom betrayed their comrades in arms during police interrogations. Their counterparts on the right were organized as decentralized networks, and had no such discipline. These groups were regularly infiltrated, and members, once arrested, easily gave up their comrades. Similarly, al-Qaeda was most dangerous when it was a unified hierarchy. Now that it has dissipated into a network, it has proved far less effective.

The drawbacks of networks scarcely matter if the network isn't interested in systemic change—if it just wants to frighten or humiliate or make a splash—or if it doesn't need to think strategically. But if you're taking on a powerful and organized establishment you have to be a hierarchy. The Montgomery bus boycott required the participation of tens of thousands of people who depended on public transit to get to and from work each day. It lasted a *year*. In order to persuade those people to stay true to the cause, the boycott's organizers tasked each local black church with maintaining morale, and put together a free alternative private carpool service, with forty-eight dispatchers and forty-two pickup stations. Even the White Citizens Council, King later said, conceded that the carpool system moved with "military precision." By the time King came to Birmingham, for the climactic showdown with Police Commissioner Eugene (Bull) Connor, he had a budget of a million dollars, and a hundred full-time staff members on the ground, divided into operational units. The operation itself was divided into steadily escalating phases, mapped out in advance. Support was maintained through consecutive mass meetings rotating from church to church around the city.

Boycotts and sit-ins and nonviolent confrontations—which were the weapons of choice for the civil-rights movement—are high-risk strategies. They leave little room for conflict and error. The moment even one protester deviates from the script and responds to provocation, the moral legitimacy of the entire protest is compromised. Enthusiasts for social media would no doubt have us believe that King's task in Birmingham would have been made infinitely easier had he been able to communicate with his followers through Facebook, and contented himself with tweets from a Birmingham jail. But networks are messy: think of the ceaseless pattern of correction and revision, amendment and debate, that characterizes Wikipedia. If Martin Luther King Jr. had tried to do a wiki-boycott in Montgomery, he would have been steamrollered by the white power structure. And of what use would a digital communication tool be in a town where ninety-eight percent of the black community could be reached every Sunday morning at church? The things that King needed in Birmingham—discipline and strategy—were things that online social media cannot provide.

The bible of the social-media movement is Clay Shirky's *Here Comes Everybody*. Shirky, who teaches at New York University, sets out to demonstrate the organizing power of the Internet, and he begins with the story of Evan, who worked on Wall Street, and his friend Ivanna, after she left her smartphone, an expensive Sidekick, on the back seat of a New York City taxicab. The telephone company transferred the data on Ivanna's lost phone to a new phone, whereupon she and Evan discovered that the Sidekick was now in the hands of a teenager from Queens, who was using it to take photographs of herself and her friends.

When Evan e-mailed the teenager, Sasha, asking for the phone back, she replied that his "white ass" didn't deserve to have it back. Miffed, he set up a web page with her picture and a description of what had happened. He forwarded the link to his friends, and they forwarded it to their friends. Someone found the MySpace page of Sasha's boyfriend, and a link to it found its way onto the site. Someone found her address online and took a video of her home while driving by; Evan posted the video on the site. The story was picked up by the news filter Digg. Evan was now up to ten e-mails a minute. He created a bulletin board for his readers to share their stories, but it crashed under the weight of responses. Evan and Ivanna went to the police, but the police filed the report under "lost," rather than "stolen," which essentially closed the case. "By this point millions of readers were watching," Shirky writes, "and dozens of mainstream news outlets had covered the story." Bowing to the pressure, the NYDP reclassified the item as "stolen." Sasha was arrested, and Evan got his friend's Sidekick back. 30

Shirky's argument is that this is the kind of thing that could never have happened in the pre-Internet age—and he's right. Evan could never have tracked down Sasha. The story of the Sidekick would never have been publicized. An army of people could never have been assembled to wage this fight. The police wouldn't have bowed to the pressure of a lone person who had misplaced something as trivial as a cell phone. The story, to Shirky, illustrates "the ease and speed with which a group can be mobilized for the right kind of cause" in the Internet age.

Shirky considers this model of activism an upgrade. But it is simply a form of organizing which favors the weak-tie connections that give us access to information over the strong-tie connections that help us persevere in the face of danger. It shifts our energies from organizations that promote strategic and disciplined activity and toward those which promote resilience and adaptability. It makes it easier for activists to express themselves, and harder for that expression to have any impact. The instruments of social media are well suited to making the existing social order more efficient. They are not a natural enemy of the status quo. If you are of the opinion that all the world needs is a little buffing around the edges, this should not trouble you. But if you think that there are still lunch counters out there that need integrating it ought to give you pause.

Shirky ends the story of the lost Sidekick by asking, portentously, "What happens next?"—no doubt imagining future waves of digital protesters. But he has already answered the question. What happens next is more of the same. A networked, weak-tie world is good at things like helping Wall Streeters get phones back from teenage girls. *Viva la revolución.**

Questions for Critical Reading

1. Gladwell discusses "strong ties" and "weak ties." As you reread his essay, mark passages where he discusses each term and then define them using Gladwell's text. What role does each play in social change, according to Gladwell?
2. Can social media be used to enact real social change? Consider recent events such as the #MeToo movement. Engage Gladwell's argument using your own perceptions of the power of social media. Does his analysis remain true?
3. According to Gladwell, what are the crucial factors needed to enact social change? As you reread his essay, mark these passages.

Exploring Context

1. Examine your friends list on Facebook or any other social networking site you use regularly. Using Gladwell's distinction between strong and weak ties, categorize your friends. How many do you think you have strong ties with? How many do you have weak ties with? Does your personal experience with social networking confirm or challenge Gladwell's argument?
2. The Occupy Wall Street movement (occupywallst.org) uses many of the social networking tools that Gladwell suggests are insufficient for true social action. Explore the site and use a search engine to locate any more local "occupy" movements. How do these groups use social networking technologies and media? Will they accomplish or have they accomplished social change? Use their experiences to evaluate Gladwell's argument.
3. In 2011, *Time* magazine named the Protestor as the person of the year (time.com/time/person-of-the-year/2011). Explore *Time*'s coverage of protestors. Do protestors use weak or strong ties? What role does social media play in protesting today?

---

* *Viva la revolución:* "Long live the revolution" (Spanish) [Ed.].

Questions for Connecting

1. Civil rights is a central concern of Gladwell's essay. Apply his analysis to Kenji Yoshino's "Preface" and "The New Civil Rights" (p. 452). Yoshino suggests that changes in civil rights should happen outside courtrooms; what mechanisms can Gladwell offer to help achieve Yoshino's vision?
2. Maria Konnikova, in "The Limits of Friendship" (p. 255), also explores the kinds of connections we can make through social media. Synthesize the arguments of these two authors. Are there inherent limits to how we can connect to others online?
3. In "AIDS, Inc." (p. 123) Helen Epstein looks at role that social connections play in preventing the spread of HIV/AIDS in African nations. Use Gladwell to extend her argument. What sorts of ties had the greatest effect in combating HIV/AIDS?

Language Matters

1. Apostrophes indicate possession. Go through Gladwell's text and locate some examples of the apostrophe, which is perhaps one of the most frequently misunderstood marks of punctuation. Given that an apostrophe is a kind of "tie," how might Gladwell's discussion explain the frequent misuse of this punctuation mark? What are the complexities of "possession" in today's world, in writing and in reality?
2. Locate the strongest transition in Gladwell's essay. What makes it strong or effective? How can you use this strategy in your own writing?
3. What are higher- and lower-order concerns in writing? Apply these concepts to Gladwell's writing. What are the higher-order concerns of the essay? Are there any?

Assignments for Writing

1. Gladwell seems to argue that strong-tie connections offer greater possibilities for social change than weak-tie connections. Write a paper in which you confirm, extend, or complicate Gladwell's argument by using your own example of either weak-tie or strong-tie connections and the possibilities they create for change.
2. Are strong-tie connections even possible with social media technologies? Write a paper in which you examine the possibility of strong-tie connections created through social media such as Twitter or Facebook. Use Gladwell's definitions and examples as well as your work from Questions for Critical Reading, Exploring Context, and Questions for Connecting.
3. What makes social change possible? Write a paper in which you synthesize Gladwell's competing concepts of strong-tie connections and weak-tie connections in order to propose ideal strategies for promoting social change. How can the two kinds of ties work together?

ROBIN MARANTZ HENIG

Robin Marantz Henig is a journalist and author whose work focuses on science. Along with daughter Samantha Henig, she wrote the book *Twentysomething: Why Do Young Adults Seem Stuck?*, which was named a best book of the month on Amazon and a must-read on Oprah .com. Henig is also the author of *Pandora's Baby, The Monk in the Garden*, and *A Dancing Matrix*, among other books. Her articles have appeared in *Scientific American, Newsweek, Discover*, and other publications. Henig is the recipient of a Guggenheim fellowship, two National Association of Science Writers Science in Society Awards, and an American Society of Journalists and Authors Career Achievement Award. She holds a master's in journalism from Northwestern University and is a contributing writer for the *New York Times Magazine*.

Henig's ninth and latest book, *Twentysomething*, explores what it means to be in one's twenties today through both neuroscience and psychological research and surveys of more than 120 millennials and baby boomers. The book project came about as a result of this selection, "What Is It about 20-Somethings?," which ran as the cover story for the *New York Times Magazine* in the summer of 2010 alongside stories about elections in Pennsylvania and knock-off tennis shoes from China.

In "What Is It about 20-Somethings?," Henig analyzes the lag in today's 20-somethings' journey to what is traditionally considered adulthood, inquiring whether this period of "emerging adulthood" is a passing, circumstantial trend or a true, psychological life stage that must be accommodated the way other stages, such as adolescence, are. Henig raises this question: Does delaying conventional adult responsibilities allow for "a rich and varied period for self-discovery" or is it simply "self-indulgence" (p. 204)?

What does your experience suggest to you? What do you (or did you) expect from your twenties? What is it like to be 20-something today?

- TAGS: *adolescence and adulthood, economics, identity, psychology, science and technology, social change*
- CONNECTIONS: *Appiah, Chabon, Chen, Gilbert, Klosterman, Konnikova, Lukianoff and Haidt, Paumgarten, Singer, Turkle, Watters*

What Is It about 20-Somethings?

Why are so many people in their 20s taking so long to grow up?

This question pops up everywhere, underlying concerns about "failure to launch" and "boomerang kids." Two new sitcoms feature grown children moving back in with their parents — *$#*! My Dad Says*, starring William Shatner as a divorced curmudgeon whose 20-something son can't make it on his own as a blogger, and *Big Lake*, in which a financial whiz kid loses his Wall Street job and moves back home to rural Pennsylvania. A cover of the *New Yorker* last spring [2010] picked up on the zeitgeist: a young man hangs up his new Ph.D. in his boyhood bedroom, the cardboard box at his feet signaling his plans to move back home now that he's officially overqualified for a job. In the doorway stand his parents, their expressions a mix of resignation, worry, annoyance, and perplexity: how exactly did this happen?

It's happening all over, in all sorts of families, not just young people moving back home but also young people taking longer to reach adulthood overall. It's a development that predates the current economic doldrums, and no one knows yet what the impact will be—on the prospects of the young men and women; on the parents on whom so many of them depend; on society, built on the expectation of an orderly progression in which kids finish school, grow up, start careers, make a family, and eventually retire to live on pensions supported by the next crop of kids who finish school, grow up, start careers, make a family, and on and on. The traditional cycle seems to have gone off course, as young people remain untethered to romantic partners or to permanent homes, going back to school for lack of better options, traveling, avoiding commitments, competing ferociously for unpaid internships or temporary (and often grueling) Teach for America jobs, forestalling the beginning of adult life.

The 20s are a black box, and there is a lot of churning in there. One-third of people in their 20s move to a new residence every year. Forty percent move back home with their parents at least once. They go through an average of seven jobs in their 20s, more job changes than in any other stretch. Two-thirds spend at least some time living with a romantic partner without being married. And marriage occurs later than ever. The median age at first marriage in the early 1970s, when the baby boomers were young, was 21 for women and 23 for men; by 2009 it had climbed to 26 for women and 28 for men, five years in a little more than a generation.

5 We're in the thick of what one sociologist calls "the changing timetable for adulthood." Sociologists traditionally define the "transition to adulthood" as marked by five milestones: completing school, leaving home, becoming financially independent, marrying, and having a child. In 1960, 77 percent of women and 65 percent of men had, by the time they reached 30, passed all five milestones. Among 30-year-olds in 2000, according to data from the United States Census Bureau, fewer than half of the women and one-third of the men had done so. A Canadian study reported that a typical 30-year-old in 2001 had completed the same number of milestones as a 25-year-old in the early '70s.

The whole idea of milestones, of course, is something of an anachronism; it implies a lockstep march toward adulthood that is rare these days. Kids don't shuffle along in unison on the road to maturity. They slouch toward adulthood at an uneven, highly individual pace. Some never achieve all five milestones, including those who are single or childless by choice, or unable to marry even if they wanted to because they're gay. Others reach the milestones completely out of order, advancing professionally before committing to a monogamous relationship, having children young and marrying later, leaving school to go to work and returning to school long after becoming financially secure.

Even if some traditional milestones are never reached, one thing is clear: Getting to what we would generally call adulthood is happening later than ever. But why? That's the subject of lively debate among policy makers and academics. To some, what we're seeing is a transient epiphenomenon, the byproduct of cultural and economic forces. To others, the longer road to adulthood signifies something deep, durable, and maybe better-suited to our neurological hard-wiring. What we're seeing, they insist, is the dawning of a new life stage—a stage that all of us need to adjust to.

Jeffrey Jensen Arnett, a psychology professor at Clark University in Worcester, Mass., is leading the movement to view the 20s as a distinct life stage, which he calls "emerging adulthood." He says what is happening now is analogous to what happened a century ago, when social and economic changes helped create adolescence—a stage we take for granted but one that had to be recognized by psychologists, accepted by society, and accommodated by institutions that served the young. Similar changes at the turn of the 21st century have laid the groundwork for another new stage, Arnett says, between the age of 18 and the late 20s. Among the cultural changes he points to that have led to "emerging adulthood" are the need for more education to survive in an information-based economy; fewer entry-level jobs even after all that schooling; young people feeling less rush to marry because of the general acceptance of premarital sex, cohabitation, and birth control; and young women feeling less rush to have babies given their wide range of career options and their access to assisted reproductive technology if they delay pregnancy beyond their most fertile years.

Just as adolescence has its particular psychological profile, Arnett says, so does emerging adulthood: identity exploration, instability, self-focus, feeling in-between, and a rather poetic characteristic he calls "a sense of possibilities." A few of these, especially identity exploration, are part of adolescence too, but they take on new depth and urgency in the 20s. The stakes are higher when people are approaching the age when options tend to close off and lifelong commitments must be made. Arnett calls it "the age 30 deadline."

10 The issue of whether emerging adulthood is a new stage is being debated most forcefully among scholars, in particular psychologists and sociologists. But its resolution has broader implications. Just look at what happened for teenagers. It took some effort, a century ago, for psychologists to make the case that adolescence was a new developmental stage. Once that happened, social institutions were forced to adapt: education, health care, social services, and the law all changed to address the particular needs of 12- to 18-year-olds. An understanding of the developmental profile of adolescence led, for instance, to the creation of junior high schools in the early 1900s, separating seventh and eighth graders from the younger children in what used to be called primary school. And it led to the recognition that teenagers between 14 and 18, even though they were legally minors, were mature enough to make their own choice of legal guardian in the event of their parents' deaths. If emerging adulthood is an analogous stage, analogous changes are in the wings.

But what would it look like to extend some of the special status of adolescents to young people in their 20s? Our uncertainty about this question is reflected in our scattershot approach to markers of adulthood. People can vote at 18, but in some states they don't age out of foster care until 21. They can join the military at 18, but they can't drink until 21. They can drive at 16, but they can't rent a car until 25 without some hefty surcharges. If they are full-time students, the Internal Revenue Service considers them dependents until 24; those without health insurance will soon be able to stay on their parents' plans even if they're not in school until age 26, or up to 30 in some states. Parents have no access to their child's college records if the child is over 18, but parents' income is taken into account when the child applies for financial aid up to age 24. We seem unable to agree when someone is old enough to take on adult responsibilities. But we're pretty sure it's not simply a matter of age.

If society decides to protect these young people or treat them differently from fully grown adults, how can we do this without becoming all the things that grown children resist—controlling, moralizing, paternalistic? Young people spend their lives lumped into age-related clusters—that's the basis of K–12 schooling—but as they move through their 20s, they diverge. Some 25-year-olds are married homeowners with good jobs and a couple of kids; others are still living with their parents and working at transient jobs, or not working at all. Does that mean we extend some of the protections and special status of adolescence to all people in their 20s? To some of them? Which ones? Decisions like this matter, because failing to protect and support vulnerable young people can lead them down the wrong path at a critical moment, the one that can determine all subsequent paths. But overprotecting and oversupporting them can sometimes make matters worse, turning the "changing timetable of adulthood" into a self-fulfilling prophecy.

The more profound question behind the scholarly intrigue is the one that really captivates parents: whether the prolongation of this unsettled time of life is a good thing or a bad thing. With life spans stretching into the ninth decade, is it better for young people to experiment in their 20s before making choices they'll have to live with for more than half a century? Or is adulthood now so malleable, with marriage and employment options constantly being reassessed, that young people would be better off just getting started on something, or else they'll never catch up, consigned to remain always a few steps behind the early bloomers? Is emerging adulthood a rich and varied period for self-discovery, as Arnett says it is? Or is it just another term for self-indulgence?

The discovery of adolescence is generally dated to 1904, with the publication of the massive study "Adolescence," by G. Stanley Hall, a prominent psychologist and first president of the American Psychological Association. Hall attributed the new stage to social changes at the turn of the 20th century. Child-labor laws kept children under 16 out of the work force, and universal education laws kept them in secondary school, thus prolonging the period of dependence—a dependence that allowed them to address psychological tasks they might have ignored when they took on adult roles straight out of childhood. Hall, the first president of Clark University—the same place, interestingly enough, where Arnett now teaches—described adolescence as a time of "storm and stress," filled with emotional upheaval, sorrow, and rebelliousness. He cited the "curve of despondency" that "starts at 11, rises steadily and rapidly till 15 . . . then falls steadily till 23," and described other characteristics of adolescence, including an increase in sensation seeking, greater susceptibility to media influences (which in 1904 mostly meant "flash literature" and "penny dreadfuls"), and overreliance on peer relationships. Hall's book was flawed, but it marked the beginning of the scientific study of adolescence and helped lead to its eventual acceptance as a distinct stage with its own challenges, behaviors, and biological profile.

15 In the 1990s, Arnett began to suspect that something similar was taking place with young people in their late teens and early 20s. He was teaching human development and family studies at the University of Missouri, studying college-age students, both at the university and in the community around Columbia, Mo. He asked them questions about their lives and their expectations like, "Do you feel you have reached adulthood?"

"I was in my early- to mid-30s myself, and I remember thinking, They're not a thing like me," Arnett told me when we met last spring in Worcester. "I realized that there was something special going on." The young people he spoke to weren't experiencing the upending physical changes that accompany adolescence, but as an age cohort they did seem to have a psychological makeup different from that of people just a little bit younger or a little bit older. This was not how most psychologists were thinking about development at the time, when the eight-stage model of the psychologist Erik Erikson was in vogue. Erikson, one of the first to focus on psychological development past childhood, divided adulthood into three stages—young (roughly ages 20 to 45), middle (about ages 45 to 65), and late (all the rest)—and defined them by the challenges that individuals in a particular stage encounter and must resolve before moving on to the next stage. In young adulthood, according to his model, the primary psychological challenge is "intimacy versus isolation," by which Erikson meant deciding whether to commit to a lifelong intimate relationship and choosing the person to commit to.

But Arnett said "young adulthood" was too broad a term to apply to a 25-year span that included both him and his college students. The 20s are something different from the 30s and 40s, he remembered thinking. And while he agreed that the struggle for intimacy was one task of this period, he said there were other critical tasks as well.

Arnett and I were discussing the evolution of his thinking over lunch at BABA Sushi, a quiet restaurant near his office where he goes so often he knows the sushi chefs by name. He is 53, very tall, and wiry, with clipped steel-gray hair and ice-blue eyes, an intense, serious man. He describes himself as a late bloomer, a onetime emerging adult before anyone had given it a name. After graduating from Michigan State University in 1980, he spent two years playing guitar in bars and restaurants and experimented with girlfriends, drugs, and general recklessness before going for his doctorate in developmental psychology at the University of Virginia. By 1986 he had his first academic job at Oglethorpe University, a small college in Atlanta. There he met his wife, Lene Jensen, the school's smartest psych major, who stunned Arnett when she came to his office one day in 1989, shortly after she graduated, and asked him out on a date. Jensen earned a doctorate in psychology, too, and she also teaches at Clark. She and Arnett have 10-year-old twins, a boy and a girl.

Arnett spent time at Northwestern University and the University of Chicago before moving to the University of Missouri in 1992, beginning his study of young men and women in the college town of Columbia, gradually broadening his sample to include New Orleans, Los Angeles, and San Francisco. He deliberately included working-class young people as well as those who were well off, those who had never gone to college as well as those who were still in school, those who were supporting themselves as well as those whose bills were being paid by their parents. A little more than half of his sample was white, 18 percent African-American, 16 percent Asian-American, and 14 percent Latino.

20

More than 300 interviews and 250 survey responses persuaded Arnett that he was onto something new. This was the era of the Gen X slacker, but Arnett felt that his findings applied beyond one generation. He wrote them up in 2000 in *American Psychologist*, the first time he laid out his theory of "emerging adulthood." According to Google Scholar, which keeps track of such things, the article has been cited in professional books and journals roughly 1,700 times. This makes it, in the world of academia, practically viral. At the very least, the citations indicate that Arnett had come up with a useful term for describing a particular cohort; at best, that he offered a whole new way of thinking about them.

During the period he calls emerging adulthood, Arnett says that young men and women are more self-focused than at any other time of life, less certain about the future, and yet also more optimistic, no matter what their economic background. This is where the "sense of possibilities" comes in, he says; they have not yet tempered their idealistic visions of what awaits. "The dreary, dead-end jobs, the bitter divorces, the disappointing and disrespectful children . . . none of them imagine that this is what the future holds for them," he wrote. Ask them if they agree with the statement "I am very sure that someday I will get to where I want to be in life," and 96 percent of them will say yes. But despite elements that are exciting, even exhilarating, about being this age, there is a downside, too: dread, frustration, uncertainty, a sense of not quite understanding the rules of the game. More than positive or negative feelings, what Arnett heard most often was ambivalence—beginning with his finding that 60 percent of his subjects told him they felt like both grown-ups and not-quite-grown-ups.

Some scientists would argue that this ambivalence reflects what is going on in the brain, which is also both grown-up and not-quite-grown-up. Neuroscientists once thought the brain stops growing shortly after puberty, but now they know it keeps maturing well into the 20s. This new understanding comes largely from a longitudinal study of brain development sponsored by the National Institute of Mental Health, which started following nearly 5,000 children at ages 3 to 16 (the average age at enrollment was about 10). The scientists found the children's brains were not fully mature until at least 25. "In retrospect I wouldn't call it shocking, but it was at the time," Jay Giedd, the director of the study, told me. "The only people who got this right were the car-rental companies."

When the NIMH study began in 1991, Giedd said he and his colleagues expected to stop when the subjects turned 16. "We figured that by 16 their bodies were pretty big physically," he said. But every time the children returned, their brains were found still to be changing. The scientists extended the end date of the study to age 18, then 20, then 22. The subjects' brains were still changing even then. Tellingly, the most significant changes took place in the prefrontal cortex and cerebellum, the regions involved in emotional control and higher-order cognitive function.

As the brain matures, one thing that happens is the pruning of the synapses. Synaptic pruning does not occur willy-nilly; it depends largely on how any one brain pathway is used. By cutting off unused pathways, the brain eventually settles into a structure that's most efficient for the owner of that brain, creating well-worn grooves for the pathways that person uses most. Synaptic pruning intensifies after rapid brain-cell proliferation during childhood and again in the period that encompasses adolescence and the 20s. It is the mechanism of "use it or lose it": the brains we have are shaped largely in response to the demands made of them.

We have come to accept the idea that environmental influences in the first three years of life have long-term consequences for cognition, emotional control, attention, and the like. Is it time to place a similar emphasis, with hopes for a similar outcome, on enriching the cognitive environment of people in their 20s? 25

NIMH scientists also found a time lag between the growth of the limbic system, where emotions originate, and of the prefrontal cortex, which manages those emotions. The limbic system explodes during puberty, but the prefrontal cortex keeps maturing for another 10 years. Giedd said it is logical to suppose—and for now, neuroscientists have to make a lot of logical suppositions—that when the limbic system is fully active but the cortex is still being built, emotions might outweigh rationality. "The prefrontal part is the part that allows you to control your impulses, come up with a long-range strategy, answer the question 'What am I going to do with my life?'" he told me. "That weighing of the future keeps changing into the 20s and 30s."

Among study subjects who enrolled as children, MRI scans have been done so far only to age 25, so scientists have to make another logical supposition about what happens to the brain in the late 20s, the 30s, and beyond. Is it possible that the brain just keeps changing and pruning, for years and years? "Guessing from the shape of the growth curves we have," Giedd's colleague Philip Shaw wrote in an e-mail message, "it does seem that much of the gray matter," where synaptic pruning takes place, "seems to have completed its most dramatic structural change" by age 25. For white matter, where insulation that helps impulses travel faster continues to form, "it does look as if the curves are still going up, suggesting continued growth" after age 25, he wrote, though at a slower rate than before.

None of this is new, of course; the brains of young people have always been works in progress, even when we didn't have sophisticated scanning machinery to chart it precisely. Why, then, is the youthful brain only now arising as an explanation for why people in their 20s are seeming a bit unfinished? Maybe there's an analogy to be found in the hierarchy of needs, a theory put forth in the 1940s by the psychologist Abraham Maslow. According to Maslow, people can pursue more elevated goals only after their basic needs of food, shelter, and sex have been met. What if the brain has its own hierarchy of needs? When people are forced to adopt adult responsibilities early, maybe they just do what they have to do, whether or not their brains are ready. Maybe it's only now, when young people are allowed to forestall adult obligations without fear of public censure, that the rate of societal maturation can finally fall into better sync with the maturation of the brain.

Cultural expectations might also reinforce the delay. The "changing timetable for adulthood" has, in many ways, become internalized by 20-somethings and their parents alike. Today young people don't expect to marry until their late 20s, don't expect to start a family until their 30s, don't expect to be on track for a rewarding career until much later than their parents were. So they make decisions about their futures that reflect this wider time horizon. Many of them would not be ready to take on the trappings of adulthood any earlier even if the opportunity arose; they haven't braced themselves for it.

Nor do parents expect their children to grow up right away—and they might not even want them to. Parents might regret having themselves jumped into marriage or a career and hope for more considered choices for their children. Or they might want to hold on to a reassuring connection with their children as the kids leave home. If they were "helicopter parents"—a term that describes heavily invested parents who hover over their children, swooping down to take charge and solve problems at a moment's notice—they might keep hovering and problem-solving long past the time when their children should be solving problems on their own. This might, in a strange way, be part of what keeps their grown children in the limbo between adolescence and adulthood. It can be hard sometimes to tease out to what extent a child doesn't quite want to grow up and to what extent a parent doesn't quite want to let go.

It is a big deal in developmental psychology to declare the existence of a new stage of life, and Arnett has devoted the past 10 years to making his case. Shortly after his *American Psychologist* article appeared in 2000, he and Jennifer Lynn Tanner, a developmental psychologist at Rutgers University, convened the first conference of what they later called the Society for the Study of Emerging Adulthood. It was held in 2003 at Harvard with an attendance of 75; there have been three more since then, and last year's conference, in Atlanta, had more than 270 attendees. In 2004 Arnett published a book, *Emerging Adulthood: The Winding Road from the Late Teens through the Twenties*, which is still in print and selling well. In 2006 he and Tanner published an edited volume, *Emerging Adults in America: Coming of Age in the 21st Century*, aimed at professionals and academics. Arnett's college textbook, *Adolescence and Emerging Adulthood: A Cultural Approach*, has been in print since 2000 and is now in its fourth edition. Next year he says he hopes to publish another book, this one for the parents of 20-somethings.

If all Arnett's talk about emerging adulthood sounds vaguely familiar . . . well, it should. Forty years ago, an article appeared in the *American Scholar* that declared "a new stage of life" for the period between adolescence and young adulthood. This was 1970, when the oldest members of the baby boom generation—the parents of today's 20-somethings—were 24. Young people of the day "can't seem to 'settle down,'" wrote the Yale psychologist Kenneth Keniston. He called the new stage of life "youth."

Keniston's description of "youth" presages Arnett's description of "emerging adulthood" a generation later. In the late '60s, Keniston wrote that there was "a growing minority of post-adolescents [who] have not settled the questions whose answers once defined adulthood: questions of relationship to the existing society, questions of vocation, questions of social role and lifestyle." Whereas once, such aimlessness was seen only in the "unusually creative or unusually disturbed," he wrote, it was becoming more common and more ordinary in the baby boomers of 1970. Among the salient characteristics of "youth," Keniston wrote, were "pervasive ambivalence toward self and society," "the feeling of absolute freedom, of living in a world of pure possibilities," and "the enormous value placed upon change, transformation and movement"—all characteristics that Arnett now ascribes to "emerging adults."

Arnett readily acknowledges his debt to Keniston; he mentions him in almost everything he has written about emerging adulthood. But he considers the '60s a unique moment, when young people were rebellious and alienated in a way they've never been before or since. And Keniston's views never quite took off, Arnett says, because "youth" wasn't a very good name for it. He has called the label "ambiguous and confusing," not nearly as catchy as his own "emerging adulthood."

For whatever reason Keniston's terminology faded away, it's revealing to read his old article and hear echoes of what's going on with kids today. He was describing the parents of today's young people when they themselves were young—and amazingly, they weren't all that different from their own children now. Keniston's article seems a lovely demonstration of the eternal cycle of life, the perennial conflict between the generations, the gradual resolution of those conflicts. It's reassuring, actually, to think of it as recursive, to imagine that there must always be a cohort of 20-somethings who take their time settling down, just as there must always be a cohort of 50-somethings who worry about it.

Keniston called it youth, Arnett calls it emerging adulthood; whatever it's called, the delayed transition has been observed for years. But it can be in fullest flower only when the young person has some other, nontraditional means of support—which would seem to make the delay something of a luxury item. That's the impression you get reading Arnett's case histories in his books and articles, or the essays in *20 Something Manifesto*, an anthology edited by a Los Angeles writer named Christine Hassler. "It's somewhat terrifying," writes a 25-year-old named Jennifer, "to think about all the things I'm supposed to be doing in order to 'get somewhere' successful: 'Follow your passions, live your dreams, take risks, network with the right people, find mentors, be financially responsible, volunteer, work, think about or go to grad school, fall in love and maintain personal well-being, mental health and nutrition.' When is there time to just be and enjoy?" Adds a 24-year-old from Virginia: "There is pressure to make decisions that will form the foundation for the rest of your life in your 20s. It's almost as if having a range of limited options would be easier."

While the complaints of these young people are heartfelt, they are also the complaints of the privileged. Julie, a 23-year-old New Yorker and contributor to *20 Something Manifesto*, is apparently aware of this. She was coddled her whole life, treated to French horn lessons and summer camp, told she could do anything. "It is a double-edged sword," she writes, "because on the one hand I am so blessed with my experiences and endless options, but on the other hand, I still feel like a child. I feel like my job isn't real because I am not where my parents were at my age. Walking home, in the shoes my father bought me, I still feel I have yet to grow up."

Despite these impressions, Arnett insists that emerging adulthood is not limited to young persons of privilege and that it is not simply a period of self-indulgence. He takes pains in *Emerging Adulthood* to describe some case histories of young men and women from hard-luck backgrounds who use the self-focus and identity exploration of their 20s to transform their lives.

One of these is the case history of Nicole, a 25-year-old African-American who grew up in a housing project in Oakland, Calif. At age 6, Nicole, the eldest, was forced to take control of the household after her mother's mental collapse. By 8, she was sweeping stores and baby-sitting for money to help keep her three siblings fed and housed. "I made a couple bucks and helped my mother out, helped my family out," she told Arnett. She managed to graduate from high school, but with low grades, and got a job as a receptionist at a dermatology clinic. She moved into her own apartment, took night classes at community college, and started to excel. "I needed to experience living out of my mother's home in order to study," she said.

40 In his book, Arnett presents Nicole as a symbol of all the young people from impoverished backgrounds for whom "emerging adulthood represents an opportunity—maybe a last opportunity—to turn one's life around." This is the stage where someone like Nicole can escape an abusive or dysfunctional family and finally pursue her own dreams. Nicole's dreams are powerful—one course away from an associate

degree, she plans to go on for a bachelor's and then a Ph.D. in psychology—but she has not really left her family behind; few people do. She is still supporting her mother and siblings, which is why she works full time even though her progress through school would be quicker if she found a part-time job. Is it only a grim pessimist like me who sees how many roadblocks there will be on the way to achieving those dreams and who wonders what kind of freewheeling emerging adulthood she is supposed to be having?

Of course, Nicole's case is not representative of society as a whole. And many parents—including those who can't really afford it—continue to help their kids financially long past the time they expected to. Two years ago Karen Fingerman, a developmental psychologist at Purdue University, asked parents of grown children whether they provided significant assistance to their sons or daughters. Assistance included giving their children money or help with everyday tasks (practical assistance) as well as advice, companionship, and an attentive ear. Eighty-six percent said they had provided advice in the previous month; less than half had done so in 1988. Two out of three parents had given a son or daughter practical assistance in the previous month; in 1988, only one in three had.

Fingerman took solace in her findings; she said it showed that parents stay connected to their grown children, and she suspects that both parties get something out of it. The survey questions, after all, referred not only to dispensing money but also to offering advice, comfort, and friendship. And another of Fingerman's studies suggests that parents' sense of well-being depends largely on how close they are to their grown children and how their children are faring—objective support for the adage that you're only as happy as your unhappiest child. But the expectation that young men and women won't quite be able to make ends meet on their own, and that parents should be the ones to help bridge the gap, places a terrible burden on parents who might be worrying about their own job security, trying to care for their aging parents, or grieving as their retirement plans become more and more of a pipe dream.

This dependence on Mom and Dad also means that during the 20s the rift between rich and poor becomes entrenched. According to data gathered by the Network on Transitions to Adulthood, a research consortium supported by the John D. and Catherine T. MacArthur Foundation, American parents give an average of 10 percent of their income to their 18- to 21-year-old children. This percentage is basically the same no matter the family's total income, meaning that upper-class kids tend to get more than working-class ones. And wealthier kids have other, less obvious, advantages. When they go to four-year colleges or universities, they get supervised dormitory housing, health care, and alumni networks not available at community colleges. And they often get a leg up on their careers by using parents' contacts to help land an entry-level job—or by using parents as a financial backup when they want to take an interesting internship that doesn't pay.

"You get on a pathway, and pathways have momentum," Jennifer Lynn Tanner of Rutgers told me. "In emerging adulthood, if you spend this time exploring and you get yourself on a pathway that really fits you, then there's going to be this snowball effect of finding the right fit, the right partner, the right job, the right place to live. The less you have at first, the less you're going to get this positive effect compounded over time. You're not going to have the same acceleration."

Even Arnett admits that not every young person goes through a period of "emerging adulthood." It's rare in the developing world, he says, where people have to grow up fast, and it's often skipped in the industrialized world by the people who marry early, by teenage mothers forced to grow up, by young men or women who go straight from high school to whatever job is available without a chance to dabble until they find the perfect fit. Indeed, the majority of humankind would seem to not go through it at all. The fact that emerging adulthood is not universal is one of the strongest arguments against Arnett's claim that it is a new developmental stage. If emerging adulthood is so important, why is it even possible to skip it?

"The core idea of classical stage theory is that all people—underscore 'all'—pass through a series of qualitatively different periods in an invariant and universal sequence in stages that can't be skipped or reordered," Richard Lerner, Bergstrom chairman in applied developmental science at Tufts University, told me. Lerner is a close personal friend of Arnett's; he and his wife, Jacqueline, who is also a psychologist, live 20 miles from Worcester, and they have dinner with Arnett and his wife on a regular basis.

"I think the world of Jeff Arnett," Lerner said. "I think he is a smart, passionate person who is doing great work—not only a smart and productive scholar, but one of the nicest people I ever met in my life."

No matter how much he likes and admires Arnett, however, Lerner says his friend has ignored some of the basic tenets of developmental psychology. According to classical stage theory, he told me, "you must develop what you're supposed to develop when you're supposed to develop it or you'll never adequately develop it."

When I asked Arnett what happens to people who don't have an emerging adulthood, he said it wasn't necessarily a big deal. They might face its developmental tasks—identity exploration, self-focus, experimentation in love, work, and worldview—at a later time, maybe as a midlife crisis, or they might never face them at all, he said. It depends partly on why they missed emerging adulthood in the first place, whether it was by circumstance or by choice.

No, said Lerner, that's not the way it works. To qualify as a developmental stage, emerging adulthood must be both universal and essential. "If you don't develop a skill at the right stage, you'll be working the rest of your life to develop it when you should be moving on," he said. "The rest of your development will be unfavorably altered." The fact that Arnett can be so casual about the heterogeneity of emerging adulthood and its existence in some cultures but not in others—indeed, even in some people but not in their neighbors or friends—is what undermines, for many scholars, his insistence that it's a new life stage.

Why does it matter? Because if the delay in achieving adulthood is just a temporary aberration caused by passing social mores and economic gloom, it's something to struggle through for now, maybe feeling a little sorry for the young people who had the misfortune to come of age in a recession. But if it's a true life stage, we need to start rethinking our definition of normal development and to create systems of education, health care, and social supports that take the new stage into account.

The Network on Transitions to Adulthood has been issuing reports about young people since it was formed in 1999 and often ends up recommending more support for 20-somethings. But more of what, exactly? There aren't institutions set up to serve people in this specific age range; social services from a developmental perspective tend to disappear after adolescence. But it's possible to envision some that might address the restlessness and mobility that Arnett says are typical at this stage and that might make the experimentation of "emerging adulthood" available to more young people. How about expanding programs like City Year, in which 17- to 24-year-olds from diverse backgrounds spend a year mentoring inner-city children in exchange for a stipend, health insurance, child care, cellphone service, and a $5,350 education award? Or a federal program in which a government-sponsored savings account is created for every newborn, to be cashed in at age 21 to support a year's worth of travel, education, or volunteer work—a version of the "baby bonds" program that Hillary Clinton mentioned during her 2008 primary campaign? Maybe we can encourage a kind of socially sanctioned "rumspringa," the temporary moratorium from social responsibilities some Amish offer their young people to allow them to experiment before settling down. It requires only a bit of ingenuity—as well as some societal forbearance and financial commitment—to think of ways to expand some of the programs that now work so well for the elite, like the Fulbright fellowship or the Peace Corps, to make the chance for temporary service and self-examination available to a wider range of young people.

A century ago, it was helpful to start thinking of adolescents as engaged in the work of growing up rather than as merely lazy or rebellious. Only then could society recognize that the educational, medical, mental-health, and social-service needs of this group were unique and that investing in them would have a payoff in the future. Twenty-somethings are engaged in work, too, even if it looks as if they are aimless or failing to pull their weight, Arnett says. But it's a reflection of our collective attitude toward this period that we devote so few resources to keeping them solvent and granting them some measure of security.

The kind of services that might be created if emerging adulthood is accepted as a life stage can be seen during a visit to Yellowbrick, a residential program in Evanston, Ill., that calls itself the only psychiatric treatment facility for emerging adults. "Emerging adults really do have unique developmental tasks to focus on," said Jesse Viner, Yellowbrick's executive medical director. Viner started Yellowbrick in 2005, when he was working in a group psychiatric practice in Chicago and saw the need for a different way to treat this cohort. He is a soft-spoken man who looks like an accountant and sounds like a New Age prophet, peppering his conversation with phrases like "helping to empower their agency."

"Agency" is a tricky concept when parents are paying the full cost of Yellowbrick's comprehensive residential program, which comes to $21,000 a month and is not always covered by insurance. Staff members are aware of the paradox of encouraging a child to separate from Mommy and Daddy when it's on their dime. They address it with a concept they call connected autonomy, which they define as knowing when to stand alone and when to accept help. 55

Patients come to Yellowbrick with a variety of problems: substance abuse, eating disorders, depression, anxiety, or one of the more severe mental illnesses, like schizophrenia or bipolar disorder, that tend to appear in the late teens or early 20s. The demands of imminent independence can worsen mental-health problems or can create new ones for people who have managed up to that point to perform all the expected roles—son or daughter, boyfriend or girlfriend, student, teammate, friend—but get lost when schooling ends and expected roles disappear. That's what happened to one patient who had done well at a top Ivy League college until the last class of the last semester of his last year, when he finished his final paper and could not bring himself to turn it in.

The Yellowbrick philosophy is that young people must meet these challenges without coddling or rescue. Up to 16 patients at a time are housed in the Yellowbrick residence, a four-story apartment building Viner owns. They live in the apartments—which are large, sunny, and lavishly furnished—in groups of three or four, with staff members always on hand to teach the basics of shopping, cooking, cleaning, scheduling, making commitments, and showing up.

Viner let me sit in on daily clinical rounds, scheduled that day for C., a young woman who had been at Yellowbrick for three months. Rounds are like the world's most grueling job interview: the patient sits in front alongside her clinician "advocate," and a dozen or so staff members are arrayed on couches and armchairs around the room, firing questions. C. seemed nervous but pleased with herself, frequently flashing a huge white smile. She is 22, tall, and skinny, and she wore tiny denim shorts and a big T-shirt and vest. She started to fall apart during her junior year at college, plagued by binge drinking and anorexia, and in her first weeks at Yellowbrick her alcohol abuse continued. Most psychiatric facilities would have kicked her out after the first relapse, said Dale Monroe-Cook, Yellowbrick's vice president of clinical operations. "We're doing the opposite: we want the behavior to unfold, and we want to be there in that critical moment, to work with that behavior and help the emerging adult transition to greater independence."

The Yellowbrick staff let C. face her demons and decide how to deal with them. After five relapses, C. asked the staff to take away her ID so she couldn't buy alcohol. Eventually she decided to start going to meetings of Alcoholics Anonymous.

At her rounds in June, C. was able to report that she had been alcohol-free for 30 days. Jesse Viner's wife, Laura Viner, who is a psychologist on staff, started to clap for her, but no one else joined in. "We're on eggshells here," Gary Zurawski, a clinical social worker specializing in substance abuse, confessed to C. "We don't know if we should congratulate you too much." The staff was sensitive about taking away the young woman's motivation to improve her life for her own sake, not for the sake of getting praise from someone else.

60

C. took the discussion about the applause in stride and told the staff she had more good news: in two days she was going to graduate. On time.

The 20s are like the stem cell of human development, the pluripotent moment when any of several outcomes is possible. Decisions and actions during this time have lasting ramifications. The 20s are when most people accumulate almost all of their formal education; when most people meet their future spouses and the friends they will keep; when most people start on the careers that they will stay with for many years. This is when adventures, experiments, travels, relationships are embarked on with an abandon that probably will not happen again.

The 20s are like the stem cell of human development, the pluripotent moment when any of several outcomes is possible.

Does that mean it's a good thing to let 20-somethings meander—or even to encourage them to meander—before they settle down? That's the question that plagues so many of their parents. It's easy to see the advantages to the delay. There is time enough for adulthood and its attendant obligations; maybe if kids take longer to choose their mates and their careers, they'll make fewer mistakes and live happier lives. But it's just as easy to see the drawbacks. As the settling-down sputters along for the "emerging adults," things can get precarious for the rest of us. Parents are helping pay bills they never counted on paying, and social institutions are missing out on young people contributing to productivity and growth. Of course, the recession complicates things, and even if every 20-something were ready to skip the "emerging" moratorium and act like a grown-up, there wouldn't necessarily be jobs for them all. So we're caught in a weird moment, unsure whether to allow young people to keep exploring and questioning or to cut them off and tell them just to find something, anything, to put food on the table and get on with their lives.

Arnett would like to see us choose a middle course. "To be a young American today is to experience both excitement and uncertainty, wide-open possibility and confusion, new freedoms and new fears," he writes in *Emerging Adulthood*. During the timeout they are granted from nonstop, often tedious and dispiriting responsibilities, "emerging adults develop skills for daily living, gain a better understanding of who they are and what they want from life and begin to build a foundation for their adult lives." If it really works that way, if this longer road to adulthood really leads to more insight and better choices, then Arnett's vision of an insightful, sensitive, thoughtful, content, well-honed, self-actualizing crop of grown-ups would indeed be something worth waiting for.

Questions for Critical Reading

1. What is "emerging adulthood"? As you reread, pay attention to the places where Henig defines and develops this term.
2. What are the key milestones that indicate someone has reached adulthood? Use these to develop your own definition of adulthood and then, as you review the essay, note places where Henig discusses both adulthood and emerging adulthood. Revise your response to take Henig's ideas into account.
3. While rereading the essay, consider the economic impact of emerging adulthood. How has economics shaped this life stage, and what would the further economic consequences be if we truly recognized it as a life stage?

Exploring Context

1. Explore Henig's homepage (robinhenig.com). How does this essay fit into her larger interests as an intellectual, journalist, and writer? What connections do you see between this work and some of her other writing?
2. Clark University, where Jeffrey Jensen Arnett (who coined the term *emerging adulthood*) works, has an annual poll of emerging adults. Explore the results of these polls at clarku.edu/clark-poll-emerging-adults/. How does this data complicate Henig's argument?

3. This essay was originally published with a series of portraits of 20-somethings with a distinctive square ratio. Instagram uses that same format. Using Instagram, or looking through its website, select your own series of images to place alongside Henig's text. Do they confirm or complicate her argument?

Questions for Connecting

1. How does emerging adulthood impact education? Consider Henig's argument in light of the points made by Greg Lukianoff and Jonathan Haidt in "The Coddling of the American Mind" (p. 263). Is this new stage of development part of the problem they identify? How does understanding what emerging adulthood is complicate Lukianoff and Haidt's argument?
2. Is Wesley Yang, author of "Paper Tigers" (p. 435), an emerging adult? Read his essay through the lens that Henig provides. How does his additional information about race and stereotypes complicate what Henig wants to say about emerging adults? How might you synthesize the kind of angst he feels with the data you located in Question 2 of Exploring Context?
3. In "Being WEIRD: How Culture Shapes the Mind" (p. 422), Ethan Watters argues that seemingly universal conclusions rendered by social science actually reflect a very specific cultural context. Apply his argument to Henig's text. Is emerging adulthood uniquely Western? How might understanding it as "WEIRD" change our understanding of Henig's text?

Language Matters

1. Sometimes you can get the best feedback from peers by asking them to review a key section of your writing — something you know isn't quite there yet. If you were going to do a targeted peer revision session for Henig, which section of her essay would you choose, and what feedback would you give?
2. What makes a comma unnecessary? Review information on comma usage in a grammar handbook or other reliable source. Then review Henig's essay. Are any of her commas unnecessary? How can you make sure you only use necessary commas in your own writing?
3. Locate materials in a reference book or online on writing a résumé and then make a résumé for this essay. What would be this essay's "career objective"? What would be its "experience"? Whom would it list for references?

Assignments for Writing

1. What's the cost of growing up? Write a paper in which you use Henig's ideas to determine the price of adulthood, in terms not only of economics but also of what is lost and what is gained in the process. Use your work from Question 3 of Questions for Critical Reading and Question 1 of Questions for Connecting.

2. Henig examines the rationale for creating a new life stage called "emerging adulthood." Write a paper in which you evaluate the risks and benefits of confirming emerging adulthood as a recognized life stage. Draw from your work in Questions for Critical Reading and Question 2 of Exploring Context to support your response.

3. One of the elements of emerging adulthood, according to Henig, is a focus on exploring one's passions and life goals. Write a paper in which you balance this self-actualizing purpose with the limitations inherent in emerging adulthood. Is that self-reflection worth it?

ANNA HOLMES

Anna Holmes, who studied journalism at New York University, is a prolific writer and editor and the founder of Jezebel (jezebel.com), the popular blog geared toward women, which she ran until 2010. She is the editor of two books, *Hell Hath No Fury: Women's Letters from the End of the Affair* (2002)—an anthology of break-up letters ranging from Anne Boleyn's letter Henry VIII to Monica Lewinsky's 1997 e-mail to President Bill Clinton—and *The Book of Jezebel: An Illustrated Encyclopedia of Lady Things* (2013), with entries ranging from Abzug to Zits. Her writing has also appeared in the *Washington Post*, the *New Yorker* online, *Salon*, *Glamour*, and the *New York Times*. In 2016 she took a position as senior vice president at First Look Media, where she serves as editor for Topic.com.

"Variety Show" first appeared October 25, 2015, in the online version of the *New York Times Magazine*; it was subsequently published in the print version as well. The *New York Times Magazine* is a supplement to the *New York Times*, featuring longer articles and noted for its photography. Other articles from that date centered on the algorithms that increasingly shape our lives, a profile of a woman who works as a fisherman on Long Island bay, and a review of the memoir of Ben Bernanke, former chairman of the Federal Reserve.

In this essay Holmes considers the ways in which *diversity* has lost all meaning as it has circulated widely in culture. Rather than encouraging truly integrated corporate and cultural environments, the term is implemented through token representatives and lip service to the ideals it represents. Thus any true social change is avoided through an evacuation of meaning from the concept. Diversity becomes an end point, a box to check off, rather than a starting point for a more inclusive world.

How does diversity operate in the environments within which you move? Are they truly diverse? How can we make them so?

▶ TAGS: *civil rights, culture, identity, media, race and ethnicity, social change*

▶ CONNECTIONS: *Appiah, Coates, Cohen, Das, Gay, Gilbert, Lukianoff and Haidt, Watters, Yoshino*

Variety Show

How does a word become so muddled that it loses much of its meaning? How does it go from communicating something idealistic to something cynical and suspect? If that word is *diversity*, the answer is: through a combination of overuse, imprecision, inertia, and self-serving intentions.

Take the recent remarks by the venture capitalist John Doerr at this year's TechCrunch Disrupt conference in September. Doerr, who with his firm, Kleiner Perkins Caufield & Byers, has invested in Google, Facebook, and Amazon, was on hand to discuss diversity in the overwhelmingly white and male Silicon Valley. After explaining that K.P.C.B. had begun putting its employees through training in unconscious bias—the company was the subject of a high-profile 2012 sex-discrimination lawsuit brought by a former executive, Ellen Pao, which Pao lost—the 64-year-old

Harvard Business School graduate professed himself "deeply committed to diversity," adding: "We have two new partners who are so diverse I have a challenge pronouncing their names."

Doerr was quick to issue an apology for what he called "an unfortunate joke," but his conflation of a few additions with substantial changes in corporate hiring and recruitment practices inadvertently revealed what's so irritating about the recent ubiquity of the word *diversity*: It has become both euphemism and cliché, a convenient shorthand that gestures at inclusivity and representation without actually taking them seriously.

Many Silicon Valley firms are scrambling to hire executives to focus on diversity—there's an opening at Airbnb right now for a "Head of Diversity and Belonging." But at the biggest firms, women and minorities still make up an appallingly tiny percentage of the skilled work force. And the few exceptions to this rule are consistently held up as evidence of more widespread change—as if a few individuals could by themselves constitute diversity.

5 When the word is proudly invoked in a corporate context, it acquires a certain sheen. It can give a person or institution moral credibility, a phenomenon that Nancy Leong, a University of Denver law professor, calls "racial capitalism" and defines as "an individual or group deriving value from the racial identity of another person." It's almost as if cheerfully and frequently uttering the word *diversity* is the equivalent of doing the work of actually making it a reality.

This disconnect is not, of course, limited to tech. In this year's annual *Publishers Weekly* survey of book-publishing employees, respondents—89 percent of whom were white—found "no real change" in the racial composition of the work force since last year, despite "increased attention given to diversity." The television and film industries are being investigated by the Equal Employment Opportunity Commission over complaints of sex discrimination. And yet, as is the case in Silicon Valley, small victories are often overenthusiastically celebrated as evidence of larger change. In September, for example, when Viola Davis became the first African American woman to win the Best Actress in a Drama Series Emmy, the moment was cheered in the press as a triumph of racial equity in Hollywood. But just a month before, Stacy L. Smith, a professor of communication at USC who, with other researchers, had just released a damning report that studied gender bias in 700 films made between 2007 and 2014, lamented "the dismal record of diversity, not just for one group, but for females, people of color and the LGBT community."

Why is there such a disparity between the progress that people in power claim they want to enact and what they actually end up doing about it? Part of the problem is that it doesn't seem that anyone has settled on what diversity actually means. Is it a variety of types of people on the stages of awards shows and in the boardrooms of Fortune 500 companies? Is it raw numbers? Is it who is in a position of power to hire and fire and shape external and internal cultures? Is it who isn't in power, but might be someday?

Why is there such a disparity between the progress that people in power claim they want to enact and what they actually end up doing about it?

Adding to the ambiguity is the fact that the definition of *diversity* changes depending on who is doing the talking. The dictionary will tell you that it is "the quality or state of having many different forms, types, ideas," and the word is often used, without controversy, to describe things like the environment and stock-market holdings. But in reality—which is to say, when applied to actual people, not flora, fauna, or financial securities—the notion of diversity feels more fraught, positioning one group (white, male Americans) as the default, and everyone else as the Other. Multiple studies suggest that white Americans understand "diversity" much differently than black Americans. When Reynolds Farley, a demographer at the University of Michigan, researched the attitudes of people in Detroit about the racial composition of residential neighborhoods in 1976, 1992, and 2004, most African Americans considered "integrated" to be a 50/50 mix of white and black, while a majority of whites considered such a ratio much too high for their comfort each time the study was conducted.

Bragging about hiring a few people of color, or women, seems to come from the same interpretive bias, where a small amount is enough. It also puts significant pressure on the few "diverse" folks who are allowed into any given club, where they are expected to be ambassadors of sorts, representing the minority identity while conforming to the majority one. All this can make a person doubt the sincerity of an institution or organization—and question their place within it. When I was starting out in magazines, I was told by a colleague that my hiring was part of the company's diversity push, and that my boss had received a significant bonus as a result of recruiting me. Whether or not it was true, it colored the next few years I spent there, making me wonder whether I was simply some sort of symbol to make the higher-ups feel better about themselves.

10 Diversity "is an empty signifier for me now," says Jeff Chang, the author of 2014's *Who We Be: The Colorization of America*, though "I still strongly believe in the possibility." Chang prefers *equity* to *diversity*, saying that the latter has been "deradicalized" from its roots in the multicultural movements of decades past. He recalls an anecdote about a diversity week at a Texas university where few white students bothered to show up. "Diversity," Chang says, "has become a code word for 'all those other folks.'" The problem with code words is that they're lazy: They're broad rather than specific, and can provide cover for inaction—the "I don't know how to do this or what it means, so can someone else please do the work for me?" maneuver.

Talk is cheap, of course, and sometimes you get the sense that the people talking the most about diversity are the people doing the least effective work on it. In the season premiere of his HBO reality series *Project Greenlight*, Matt Damon explained—to a veteran African American producer, Effie Brown—that focusing on diversity in the casting of a film was more important than promoting diversity among those working behind the camera. It was a striking example not just of mansplaining but also of whitesplaining. His implication—roundly criticized on social media and in industry publications—is that on-screen visibility is everything, when what Hollywood needs just as much, if not more, are black studio executives, writers, directors, and producers: the people who decide what stories are told in the first place.

Maybe it's not surprising that just a month later, the African American director Ava DuVernay made the opposite argument of Damon's at the Elle Women in Hollywood Awards. DuVernay, who made *Selma*, pointed out that of the 100 top-grossing films last year, only two were directed by women. She urged constant vigilance and proactive searching within the industry: "We have to ask our agents about that script by the woman screenwriter. We have to ask, 'Hey, are there any women agents here that I could talk to?' We have to ask our lawyers about women in the office. We have to ask, when we're thinking about directors or D.P.s, 'Will women interview?'" Her words were powerful and refreshingly specific; they were also further evidence that the work of articulating and creating diversity often—usually!—falls to those who are themselves considered "diverse."

It's something I have experienced myself. Over the past few years, numerous editors have reached out to me asking for help in finding writers and editors of color, as if I had special access to the hundreds of talented people writing and thinking on- and off-line. I know they mean well, but I am often appalled by the ease with which they shunt the work of cultivating a bigger variety of voices onto others, and I get the sense that for them, diversity is an end—a box to check off—rather than a starting point from which a more integrated, textured world is brought into being. I'm not the only one to sense that there's a feeling of obligation, rather than excitement, behind the idea. DuVernay herself hinted at this when she, too, admitted that she hates the word. "It feels like medicine," she said in her speech. "*Diversity* is like, 'Ugh, I have to do diversity.' I recognize and celebrate what it is, but that word, to me, is a disconnect. There's an emotional disconnect. *Inclusion* feels closer; *belonging* is even closer."

Questions for Critical Reading

1. What does *diversity* mean? Reread Holmes's essay to formulate a definition that better matches her vision for the word. Locate passages that support this definition.
2. What's the difference between equity and diversity? As you review Holmes's essay, consider the difference that an equity approach might make to the situations she describes.
3. Holmes, quoting Nancy Leong, uses the term *racial capitalism*. Note the definition of this term. How does it operate in relation to her larger argument?

Exploring Context

1. Holmes mentions that the Equal Employment Opportunity Commission (EEOC) was investigating sex discrimination in the film and television industries. Visit the EEOC website at eeoc.gov. Explore the site for information on diversity initiatives. What role does the government play in promoting diversity? How successful is it?
2. Explore the website for the Emmys at emmys.com. Based on what you find there, do you think the issues with diversity in media have changed since Holmes wrote this essay?
3. Using a search engine, locate the website of a major corporation, such as Microsoft or Apple, and look for information on any diversity initiatives the company might have. Connect these to Holmes's analysis. Are some corporations better than others when it comes to truly implementing diversity?

Questions for Connecting

1. In "(Un)American, (Un)Cool" (p. 102), Kavita Das seems to have similar concerns with how diversity operates in the United States. Synthesize her analysis with Holmes's argument. How can you use both essays to propose strategies that would help us move to a more diverse environment? Consider using your responses to Questions for Critical Reading.

2. Might Kenji Yoshino's vision of civil rights in "Preface" and "The New Civil Rights" (p. 452) offer a solution to the problems that Holmes delineates? Apply his analysis to her essay. Which model of civil rights would help us achieve equity? Incorporate your work on diversity and equity from Questions 1 and 2 of Questions for Critical Reading.

3. In "The Coddling of the American Mind" (p. 263), Greg Lukianoff and Jonathan Haidt argue that college campuses suffer from what might be considered an oversensitivity to diversity. How can you reconcile that with Holmes's argument about diversity in the larger culture? Is there something uniquely insular about college? How can their arguments also help explain the tepid response to diversity in the larger world?

Language Matters

1. Considering counterarguments is an important element in academic writing. Propose a series of counterarguments to Holmes's points. How might she respond?

2. Listen to the latest podcast from Grammar Girl at grammar.quickanddirtytips.com. How might you apply what she's talking about in the podcast to this essay? How might you apply it to your writing instead?

3. Holmes uses the relatively new words *mansplaining* and *whitesplaining*. Using a grammar handbook, reference source, or the web, research neologisms. How are new words created? When might you want to create terms in your own writing? What cultural forces enable new or slang words to enter common use?

Assignments for Writing

1. Working from your responses to Questions for Critical Reading, write a paper in which you locate strategies we might use to create a more inclusive world. What would it take to move from diversity to equity? Consider using your responses to Exploring Context and Question 2 of Questions for Connecting to support your argument.

2. Holmes's central contention is that the word *diversity* has lost its meaning. Write a paper in which you describe the processes through which words change or lose meaning, using Holmes's discussion of *diversity* as support. Is it possible for us to change the meaning of *diversity* again? What would need to happen for that to occur?

3. Who is responsible for diversity? Working from Holmes's essay as well as your work in Exploring Context write a paper in which you determine which sectors should take the lead in promoting diversity. The government? Businesses? Cultural institutions? Or does everyone have a role to play? Use your responses to Questions for Critical Reading and Exploring Context to support your answer. You may also find your work in Questions 2 and 3 of Questions for Connecting useful.

LESLIE JAMISON

Leslie Jamison, who holds both an M.F.A. from the Iowa Writers' Workshop and a Ph.D. in English literature from Yale, is an assistant professor and director of the nonfiction writing concentration at Columbia University. She has authored a novel, *The Gin Closet*; a collection of essays, *The Empathy Exams*, from which this selection is taken; and a hybrid work of memoir and journalism called *The Recovering*, which looks at addiction, recovery, and storytelling. Her work has also been published in *Harper's, Oxford American, A Public Space, Boston Review, Virginia Quarterly Review, The Believer,* and the *New York Times*.

New York Times best-seller *The Empathy Exams* is a collection of essays centrally concerned with the experience of pain, both that of the author and that of others. The essays cover a range of topics, including Jamison's experience working as a medical actor, someone paid to mimic a set of symptoms for medical students to diagnose; the troubling voyeurism of *Intervention*, the reality television show focused on addiction; poverty tourism, including a Los Angeles "gang tour" in which former gang members serve as guides while tourists ride in the comfort of an air-conditioned bus through poor neighborhoods; and the West Memphis Three, a trio of teenagers wrongfully imprisoned for the ritualistic murder of three young boys. Throughout these essays, Jamison asks important questions about our ability to understand others and the question of empathy, how we can feel another's pain.

In "Devil's Bait," the selection presented here, Jamison attends a conference of people with Morgellons disease, a condition in which sufferers feel the sensation of something crawling under their skin, often accompanied by strange fibers emerging from the skin—a condition which science has not been able to validate. Jamison questions our ability to feel empathy for others when we aren't sure whether or not the source of their suffering is real.

What are the necessary conditions for us to feel compassion? What does it take for us to feel another's pain?

▶ TAGS: *community, empathy, health and medicine, identity, judgment and decision making, psychology*

▶ CONNECTIONS: *Appiah, Chabon, Epstein, Fukuyama, Gilbert, Stillman, Turkle*

Devil's Bait

Introduction

For Paul, it started with a fishing trip. For Lenny, it was an addict whose knuckles were covered in sores. Dawn found pimples clustered around her swimming goggles. Kendra noticed ingrown hairs. Patricia was attacked by sand flies on a Gulf Coast beach. The sickness can start as blisters, or lesions, or itching, or simply a terrible fog settling over the mind, over the world.

For me, Morgellons disease started as a novelty: people said they had a strange disease, and no one—or hardly anyone—believed them. But there were a lot of them, almost twelve thousand of them, and their numbers were growing. Their illness manifested in lots of ways: sores, itching, fatigue, pain, and something called formication, the sensation of crawling insects. But its defining symptom was always the same: strange fibers emerging from underneath the skin.

In short, people were finding unidentifiable matter coming out of their bodies. Not just fibers but fuzz, specks, and crystals. They didn't know what this matter was, or where it came from, or why it was there, but they knew—and this was what mattered, the important word—that it was *real*.

The diagnosis originated with a woman named Mary Leitao. In 2001, she took her toddler son to the doctor because he had sores on his lip that wouldn't go away. He was complaining of bugs under his skin. The first doctor didn't know what to tell her, and neither did the second, or the third. Eventually, they started telling her something she didn't want to hear: that she might be suffering from Munchausen syndrome by proxy, because they couldn't find anything wrong with her son. Leitao came up with her own diagnosis; Morgellons was born.

Leitao pulled the name from a treatise written by a seventeenth-century doctor named Thomas Browne: 5

> I long ago observed in that Endemial Distemper of little Children in Languedock, called the Morgellons, wherein they critically break out with harsh Hairs on their Backs, which takes off the Unquiet Symptomes of the Disease, and delivers them from Coughs and Convulsions.

Browne's "harsh hairs" were the early ancestors of today's fibers, the threads that form the core of this disease. Magnified photos online show them in red, white, and blue—like the flag—and also black and clear. These fibers are the kind of thing you describe in relation to other kinds of things: jellyfish or wires, animal fur or taffy candy or a fuzz ball off your grandma's sweater. Some are called "goldenheads" because they have a golden-colored bulb. Others look like cobras curling out of the skin, thread-thin but ready to strike. Others simply look sinister, technological, tangled. The magnification in these photos makes it hard to know what you're looking at; if you're even seeing skin.

Patients started bringing these threads and flecks and fuzz to their doctors, storing them in Tupperware or matchboxes, and dermatologists actually developed a phrase for this: "the matchbox sign," a signal that the patient had become so determined to prove his own disease that he could no longer be trusted.

By the mid-2000s, Morgellons had become a controversy in earnest. Self-identified patients started calling themselves "Morgies" and rallying against doctors who diagnosed them with something called delusions of parasitosis (DOP). The CDC launched a full-scale investigation in 2006. Major newspapers published articles: "Is It Disease or Delusion?" (*New York Times*); "CDC Probes Bizarre Morgellons Condition" (*Boston Globe*); "Curious, Controversial Disease Morgellons Confounding Patients, Doctors Alike" (*Los Angeles Times*).

In the meantime, a Morgellons advocacy organization called the Charles E. Holman Foundation started putting together an annual conference in Austin for patients, researchers, and health care providers—basically, anyone who gave a damn. The foundation was named for a man who devoted the last years of his life to investigating the causes of his wife's disease. His widow still runs the gathering. She's still sick.

The conference offers refuge—to her and others—from a world that generally refuses to accept their account of why they suffer. As one presenter wrote to me by e-mail:

> It is bad enough that people are suffering so terribly. But to be the topic of seemingly the biggest joke in the world is way too much for sick people to bear. It is amazing to me that more people with this dreadful illness do not commit suicide. . . . The story is even more bizarre than you may realize. Morgellons is a perfect storm of an illness, complete with heroes, villains, and very complex people trying to do what they think is right.

The CDC finally released the results of its study "Clinical, Epidemiologic, Histopathologic and Molecular Features of an Unexplained Dermopathy" in January 2012. The report is neatly carved into movements—*Introduction, Methods, Results, Discussion, Acknowledgments*—but it offers no easy conclusions. Its authors, the so-called Unexplained Dermopathy Task Force, investigated 115 patients, using skin samples, blood tests, and neurocognitive exams. Their report offers little comfort to Morgies looking for confirmation: "We were not able to conclude based on this study whether this unexplained dermopathy represents a new condition . . . or wider recognition of an existing condition such as delusional infestation." 10

The bottom line? Probably nothing there.

Methods

The Westoak Baptist Church, on Slaughter Lane, is a few miles south of the Austin I'd imagined, a city full of Airstream trailers selling gourmet donuts, vintage shops crammed with animal heads and lace, melancholy guitar riffs floating from ironic cowboy bars. Slaughter Lane isn't vintage lace or cutting-edge donuts or ironic anything; it's Walgreens and Denny's and eventually a parking lot sliced by the spindly shadow of a twenty-foot cross.

The church itself is a low blue building surrounded by temporary trailers. A conference banner reads: *Searching for the Uncommon Thread*. I've arrived at the conference in the aftermath of the CDC report, as the Morgellons community assembles once more—to regroup, to respond, to insist.

A cluster of friendly women stand by the entrance greeting new arrivals. They wear matching shirts printed with the letters DOP slashed by a diagonal red line. Most of the participants at the conference, I will come to realize, give the wholesome, welcoming impression of no-nonsense midwestern housewives. I learn that 70 percent of Morgellons patients are female—and that women are especially vulnerable to the isolating disfigurement and condescension that come attached to the disease.

The greeters direct me past an elaborate buffet of packaged pastries and into the church sanctuary, which is serving as the main conference room. Speakers stand at the makeshift pulpit (a lectern) with their PowerPoint slides projected onto a screen behind them. The stage is cluttered with musical equipment. Each cloth-covered pew holds a single box of Kleenex. There's a special eating area in the back: tables littered with coffee cups, muffin-greased plastic, and the skeletons of grape bunches. The room has one stained-glass window—a dark blue circle holding the milky cataract of a 15 dove—but the colors admit no light. The window is small enough to make the dove look trapped; it's not flying but stuck.

This gathering is something like an AA meeting or a Quaker service: between speakers, people occasionally just walk up to the podium and start sharing. Or else they do it in their chairs, hunched over to get a better look at each other's limbs. They swap cell phone photos. I hear a man tell a woman: "I live in a bare apartment near work; don't have much else." I hear her reply: "But you still work?"

Here's what else I hear: "So you just run the sound waves through your feet . . . you see them coming out as chunks, literally hanging off the skin? . . . you got it from your dad? . . . you gave it to your son? . . . My sons are still young . . . he has fibers in his hair but no lesions on his skin . . . I use a teaspoon of salt and a teaspoon of vitamin C . . . I was drinking Borax for a while but I couldn't keep it up . . . HR told me not to talk about it . . . your arms look better than last year . . . you seem better than last year . . . but you feel better than last year?" I hear someone talking about what her skin is "expressing." I hear someone say, "It's a lonely world." I feel close to the specter of whole years lost.

I discover that the people who can't help whispering during lectures are the ones I want to talk to; that the coffee station is useful because it's a good place to meet people, and because drinking coffee means I'll have to keep going to the bathroom, which is an even better place to meet people. The people I meet don't look disfigured at first glance. But up close, they reveal all kinds of scars and bumps and scabs. They are covered in records—fossils or ruins—of the open, oozing things that once were.

I meet Patricia, wearing a periwinkle pantsuit, who tells me how she got attacked by sand flies one summer and everything changed. I meet Shirley, who thinks her family got sick from camping at a tick-rich place called Rocky Neck. Shirley's daughter has been on antibiotics for so long she has to lie to her doctor about why she needs them.

I meet Dawn, an articulate and graceful nurse from Pittsburgh, whose legs show the white patches I've come to recognize as once-scabbed or lesion-ridden skin. Antibiotics left a pattern of dark patches on her calves that once got her mistaken for an AIDS patient. Since diagnosing herself with Morgellons, Dawn has kept her full-time position as a nurse because she wants to direct her frustration into useful work. 20

"I was so angry at the misdiagnoses for so many years," she says, "being told that it was anxiety, in my head, female stuff. So I tried to spin that anger into something positive. I got my graduate degree; I published an article in a nursing journal,"

I ask her about this phrase: *female stuff.* It's like heart disease, she explains. For a long time women's heart attacks went unnoticed because they were diagnosed as symptoms of anxiety. I realize her disease is part of a complicated history that goes all the way back to nineteenth-century hysteria. Dawn says her coworkers—the nurses, not the doctors—have been remarkably empathetic; and she suggests it's no mere coincidence that most of these nurses are women. Now they come to her whenever they find something strange or unexpected in a wound: fuzz or flakes or threads. She's become an expert in the unexplainable.

I ask Dawn what the hardest part of her disease has been. At first she replies in general terms—"Uncertain future?"—lilting her answer into a question, but soon finds her way to a more specific fear: "Afraid of relationships," she says, "because who's gonna accept me?" She continues, her speaking full of pauses: "I just feel very—what's the word . . . not conspicuous, but very . . . with scars and stuff that I have from this, what guy's gonna like me?"

I tell her I don't see a scarred woman when I look at her; I think she's beautiful. She thanks me for saying so, but I can tell the compliment rang a bit hollow. One comment from a stranger can't reclaim years spent hating the body you live in.

With Dawn I fall into the easy groove of identification—*I've felt that too*—whenever she talks about her body as something that's done her wrong. Her condition seems like a crystallization of what I've always felt about myself—a wrongness in my being that I could never pin or name, so I found things to pin it to: my body, my thighs, my face. This resonance is part of what compels me about Morgellons: it offers a shape for what I've often felt, a container or christening for a certain species of unease. Dis-ease. Though I also feel how every attempt to metaphorize the illness is also an act of violence—an argument against the bodily reality its patients insist upon. 25

My willingness to turn Morgellons into metaphor—as a corporeal manifestation of some abstract human tendency—is dangerous. It obscures the particular and unbidden nature of the suffering in front of me.

It would be too easy to let all these faces dissolve into correlative possibility: Morgies as walking emblems for how hard it is for all of us to live in our own skin. I feel how conveniently these lives could be sculpted to fit the metaphoric structure—or strictures—of the essay itself.

A woman named Rita from Memphis, another nurse, talks to me about doctors—the ones who didn't believe her; the ones who told her she was out of luck, or out of her mind; the one who happened to share her surname but slammed a door in her face anyway. She felt especially wronged by that gesture—the specter of kinship, a shared name, cast aside so forcefully.

Rita tells me she lost her job and husband because of this disease. She tells me she hasn't had health insurance in years. She tells me she can literally see her skin moving. Do I believe her? I nod. I tell myself I can agree with a declaration of pain without being certain I agree with the declaration of its cause.

Rita tells me she handles a Morgellons hotline. People call if they suspect they might have the disease but don't know much about it. I ask her what she tells them. She reassures them, she says. She tells them there are people out there who will believe them. 30

The most important advice she gives? *Don't take specimens in.* That's the number one rule, she says. Otherwise they'll think you're crazy in a heartbeat.

***Don't take specimens in.* That's the number one rule, she says. Otherwise they'll think you're crazy in a heartbeat.**

I once had a specimen of my own. It was a worm in my ankle, a botfly larva I'd brought back from Bolivia. The human botfly lays its egg on a mosquito proboscis, where it is deposited—via mosquito bite—under the skin. In the Amazon, it's no big deal. In New Haven, it's less familiar. I saw mine emerge around midnight: a small pale maggot. That's when I took a cab to the ER. I remember saying: "There's a worm in there," and I remember how everyone looked at me, doctors and nurses: kindly and without belief. Their doubt was like humidity in the air. They asked me if I'd recently taken any mind-altering drugs. The disconnect felt even worse than the worm itself—to live in a world where this thing *was*, while other people lived in a world where it wasn't.

For weeks, down in Bolivia, I'd been living with the suspicion that I had something living under my skin. It was almost a relief to finally see it, bobbing out of my ankle like a tiny white snorkel. I finally knew it was true. It's Othello's Desdemona Problem: fearing the worst is worse than *knowing* the worst. So you eventually start wanting the worst possible thing to happen—finding your wife in bed with another man, or watching the worm finally come into the light. Until the worst happens, it always *might* happen. When it actually does happen? Now, at least, you know.

I remember the shrill intensity of my gratitude when a doctor finally verified the worm. Desdemona really had fucked someone else. It was a relief. Dr. Imaeda pulled it out and gave it to me in a jar. The maggot was the size of a fingernail clipping and the color of dirty snow, covered with tiny black teeth that looked like fuzz. The two gratifications were simultaneous: the worm was gone and I'd been right about it. I had about thirty minutes of peace before I started suspecting there might be another one left behind.

I spent the next few weeks obsessed with the open wound on my ankle, where Imaeda had cut out my maggot, looking for signs of a remaining worm in hiding. I turned from a parasite host—an actual, physical, literal host—into another kind of host: a woman with an idea, a woman who couldn't be convinced otherwise. I made my boyfriend set up "the Vaseline test" with me each night, a technique we'd found online: placing a cap full of Vaseline over the wound so the suffocated worm, this hypothetical second worm, would have no choice but to surface for air once the cap was removed.

No worm emerged, but I didn't give up looking. Maybe the worm was tricky. It had seen what happened to its comrade. I inspected the wound relentlessly for signs of eggs or motion. Anything I found—a stray bit of Band-Aid, a glossy patch of bruised skin or scab—was proof. The idea of the worm—the possibility of the worm—was so much worse than actually having a worm, because I could never get it out. There was no *not-worm* to see, only a worm I never saw.

At the conference, when I hear that Morgellons patients often spend hours with handheld microscopes, inspecting their own skin, I think, *I get that*. I probably spent hours poring over my maggot wound, its ragged edges and possible traces of parasitic life, I found stray bits of hardened skin and weird threads—from bandages or who-knows-what?—and I read them like tea leaves to discern what made me feel so trapped in my own body.

I don't offer my parasite story as decisive fable. Morgellons patients aren't necessarily like the version of me who had a worm or like the version of me who didn't. I honestly don't know what causes the pain they feel: the rustling on their skin, their lesions, the endless threads they find emerging. I only know what I learned from my botfly and its ghost: it was worse when I didn't have the worm than when I did.

It's easy to forget how Sir Thomas Browne insists upon the value of those "harsh hairs" covering the backs of his Languedoc urchins. He suggests that these strange growths take off the "Unquiet Symptoms of the Disease," "delivering" these children from their ailments. Which is to say: physical symptoms can offer some relief. They certainly offer tangible signs that lend themselves to diagnosis; and diagnosis can lend itself to closure.

The Morgellons diagnosis replaces one unquiet, lack of category, with another: lack of cure. Morgellons offers an explanation, a container, and a community. It can be so difficult to admit what satisfactions certain difficulties provide—not satisfaction in the sense of feeling good, or being pleasurable, but in granting some shape or substance to a discontent that might otherwise feel endless. 40

The trouble ends up feeling endless either way, of course—whether it's got a vessel or not. Rita says Morgellons has taken over her whole life; she divides her life into before and after.

Kendra is one of the folks who called Rita's hotline thinking she might be crazy. Now she's here at the conference. She sits on the church steps and smokes a cigarette. She says she probably shouldn't be smoking—gesturing at the church, and then at her scarred face—but she's doing it anyway. Her chin and cheeks show sores covered with pancake makeup. But she's pretty and young, with long dark hair and a purple wide-necked shirt that makes her look like she's headed somewhere else—a day at the pool, maybe—not back into a dim Baptist church to talk about what's living under her skin.

She says the scientific presentations have all gone over her head, but she's looking forward to tomorrow's program: an interactive session with a high-magnification microscope. That's why she came all this way. She's seen things—what she mistook for hairs, and now thinks are fibers—but the microscope will see more. She'll get proof. She can't get it anywhere else. She doesn't have medical insurance and doctors don't believe her anyway. Second opinions run about half-a-month's rent. She's sick of trying to figure this out by herself. "I've messed with a part of my chin," she confesses. "It's almost like trying to pull out a piece of glass." Her chin looks like something raw and reddish has been chalked with beige powder.

Kendra makes a point of telling me she never had acne as a teenager. She wasn't one of the facially marred until she suddenly was. Now she's among others like her. She's glad to be here. It helps, she says, to know she's not the only one. Otherwise she might start thinking she was crazy again.

Folie à deux is the clinical name for shared delusions. Morgellons patients all know the phrase—it's the name of the crime they're charged with. But if *folie à deux* is happening at the conference, it's happening more like *folie à* many, *folie en masse*, an entire Baptist church full of folks having the same nightmare. 45

I ask Kendra if she ever doubts herself. Maybe she's afraid of something that's not actually happening?

"It's a possibility," she nods. "But at the same time, you know, I think I've got a pretty good head on my shoulders. I don't think I've totally lost all my marbles."

She tells me that coming here has made her a little bit afraid: in two years, will she be showing up in some ER with all the skin peeled off her chin? Spitting up bugs in the shower? In twenty years, will she still find her days consumed by this disease—like they already are, only more so?

She says her symptoms seem to be progressing. "Some of these things I'm trying to get out," she pauses, "it's like they move away from me."

I hate the idea that Kendra would find, in this gathering, the inevitable map of some circle of hell she's headed toward. I try to think of people who have told me about getting better, so I can tell Kendra about them. I can't think of anyone. Kendra tells me she feels for the ones who have it worse than she does. 50

Everyone who is born holds dual citizenship," Susan Sontag writes, "in the kingdom of the well and in the kingdom of the sick." Most people live in the former until they are forced to take up residence in the latter. Right now Kendra is living in both. She's not entirely subsumed by sickness yet. She tells me she's meeting a friend for sushi downtown tonight. She can still understand herself outside the context of this disease: someone who does ordinary things, looks forward to the events of an ordinary life.

Only a few minutes ago, Rita was telling me these are the only three days of the year when she doesn't feel totally alone. I wonder if Kendra is following this same path—just lagging a few years behind—toward an era when she'll live full-time in the realm of illness. She says she's been finding it harder and harder to leave her house. She's too embarrassed by her face. I tell her I don't think her face is anything to be embarrassed about. "It's harder when it's your own body," I add awkwardly. "I know that."

And I *do.* I know something about that. It's about your face, but it's also about a thousand other things: an essential feeling of flaw, maybe, or a shame about taking up space, a fear of being seen as ugly or just *seen*—too much, too closely.

Here is the one place Kendra wants to be seen. She wants to be seen up close. She wants magnification. She wants evidence. She wants certainty.

"We can't all be delusional," she says. 55

I nod. Nodding offers me a saving vagueness—I can agree with the emotion without promising anything else. The nod can hold agnosticism and sympathy at once.

"If this weren't happening to me," Kendra continues, "if I was just hearing this from some regular person, I would probably think they were crazy."

Somehow this makes me feel for her as much as anything—that she has the grace to imagine her way into the minds of people who won't imagine hers.

"It's not just happening to you," I say finally. She thinks I mean one thing by that word—*happening*—and I think I mean another: not necessarily fibers under skin but rather some phenomenon of mind or body, maybe both in collusion, expressing god-knows-what into this lonely world.

Before the afternoon session begins, we get a musical interlude. A young man wearing jeans and flannel—somebody's Texan nephew-in-law—performs a rockabilly song about Morgellons: *"We'll guarantee you tears and applause,"* he croons, *"just take on our cause . . ."* He fumbles over the lyrics a few times because it seems like he's only doing this as a favor to his wife's step-aunt, or something like that, but he launches bravely into each song anyway: *"Doctor, doctor won't you tell me what's the matter with me / I got things going wild in my body, can't you see . . ."* The songs are part battle cry, part rain dance, part punchline, part lament. 60

The star of the afternoon session is a physician from Laurieton known casually around the conference as "The Australian." His talk is responding directly to the CDC report, which he calls a "load of hogwash" and a "rocking horse dung pile." He emerges as a kind of swashbuckling Aussie alligator wrestler, pinning this disease to the ground—pulling out his pidgin jujitsu to contrast the good guys (doctors who listen) with the bad guys (doctors who don't). The Australian makes it clear: He listens. He is one of the good.

He shoots to please, to get the crowd fired up, and he succeeds. He offers himself to the room as a fighter. He's talking to the margins and offering these margins the lyrics to an underdog anthem: *Doctor, doctor won't you tell me what's the matter with me . . .* He coins a new piece of jargon: DOD. Which means Delusions of Doctors. This gets applause and a few hoots from the back. The delusion? Of grandeur. The gist? That maybe *delusions of parasitosis* is just a symptom of another delusion: the hubris of thinking you know people's bodies better than they do. The Australian deploys refrain as heckling: the word *delusion* captured and lobbed back at the ones who hurled it first.

The Australian might be an egomaniac or a savior, probably both; but what matters more to me is the collective nerve he hits and the applause he gets, the specter he summons—of countless fruitless visits to countless callous doctors. One senses a hundred identical wounds across this room. Not just pocked legs and skin ribbed with the pale tracks of scars, but also smirks and muttered remarks, hastily scribbled notes, cutting gazes seeing a category, an absurdity, where a person had once been. I'm less moved by the mudslinging and more moved by the once-mud-slung-at, the ones who are clapping, and the sense of liberation underneath their applause. Here at Westoak Baptist, the Morgies get to be people once again.

Results

This isn't an essay about whether or not Morgellons disease is real. That's probably obvious by now. It's an essay about what kinds of reality are considered prerequisites for compassion. It's about this strange sympathetic limbo: Is it wrong to call it empathy when you trust the fact of suffering, but not the source? How do I inhabit someone's pain without inhabiting their particular understanding of that pain? That anxiety is embedded in every layer of this essay; even its language—every verb choice, every qualifier. Do people have parasites or claim to have them? Do they *understand* or *believe* themselves to have them? I wish I could invent a verb tense full of open spaces—a tense that didn't pretend to understand the precise mechanisms of which it spoke; a tense that could admit its own limits. As it is, I can't move an inch, finish a sentence, without running into some crisis of imputation or connotation. Every twist of syntax is an assertion of doubt or reality.

65 Reality means something different to everyone here. Calling Morgellons "real" generally means acknowledging there is actual, inexplicable stuff coming up through human skin whose emergence can't be explained. "Real" means fungus, parasite, bacteria, or virus, some agent causing lesions and sensations, the production of "coffee specks" of dark grain, crystalline fragments, threads, fibers, strings. In an online testimony, one woman calls her arm a sculpture garden. The trouble is that the reality of this garden—in terms of medical diagnosis, at least—depends upon doctors seeing her sculptures as well.

I find that most people at the conference understand the disease as an "us versus them" of some kind—"us" meaning patients, aligned against either the "them" of the disease itself, its parasitic agency, or else the "them" of those doctors who don't believe in it.

The notion that Morgellons patients might be "making it up" is more complicated than it seems. It could mean anything from intentional fabrication to an itch that's gotten out of hand. Itching is powerful: the impulse that tells someone to scratch lights up the same neural pathways as chemical addiction. In a *New Yorker* article titled "The Itch"—like a creature out of sci-fi—Atul Gawande tells the story of a Massachusetts woman with a chronic scalp itch who eventually scratched right into her own brain, and a man who killed himself in the night by scratching into his carotid artery. There was no discernible condition underneath their itches; no way to determine if these itches had begun on their skin or in their minds. It's not clear that itches can even be parsed in these terms. Itching that starts in the mind feels just like itching on the skin—no less real, no more fabricated—and it can begin with something as simple as a thought. It can begin with reading a paragraph like this one. Itching is a feedback loop that testifies to the possibility of symptoms that dwell in a charged and uneasy space between body and mind.

I've come to understand that the distinction made here between "real" and "unreal" doesn't just signify physical versus mental but also implies another binary: the difference between suffering produced by a force outside the self or within it. That's why "self-excoriation" is such a taboo phrase at the conference, and why patients are so deeply offended by any accusation that they've planted fibers on their own skin. These explanations place blame back on the patient and suggest not only that the harm inflicted is less legitimate but also that it's less deserving of compassion or aid. Parasites and bacteria are agents of otherness; easily granted volition as some sinister *they* or *them*, and—in holding this power—they restore the self to a victimized state.

The insistence upon an external agent of damage implies an imagining of the self as a unified entity, a collection of physical, mental, spiritual components all serving the good of some Gestalt whole—the being itself. When really, the self—at least, as I've experienced mine—is much more discordant and self-sabotaging, neither fully integrated nor consistently serving its own good.

During one discussion of possible bacterial causes for Morgellons, a woman raises her hand to make a point that seems incongruous. Maybe there *are* no autoimmune diseases," she says; "they just don't make sense." Her point: why would a body fight itself? Perhaps, she suggests, what seems like an autoimmune disorder is simply the body anticipating a foreign invader that hasn't yet arrived. This makes sense in a way that self-destruction doesn't. Her logic is predicated on the same vision of the self as a united whole. 70

Ironically enough, this insistence upon a unified self seems to testify inadvertently to its inverse, a sense of the self rising up in revolt, The insistence codes as an attempt to dispel a lurking sense of the body's treachery, a sense of sickness as mutiny. The disease must be turned into an *other* so that it can be properly battled.

What does it look like when the self fights itself? When a person is broken into warring factions? Maybe it looks like the cures I see here; scraping or freezing the skin, hitting it with acid or lasers or electricity, scratching the itch or abrading it, taking cocktails of antiparasitic medicines meant for animals three times our size. All these strategies strike me as symptoms of an individual cleaved into conflicting pieces.

The abiding American myth of the self-made man comes attached to another article of faith—an insistence, even—that every self-made man can sustain whatever self he has managed to make. A man divided—thwarting or interrupting his own mechanisms of survival—fails to sustain this myth, disrupts our belief in the absolute efficacy of willpower, and in these failures also forfeits his right to our sympathy. Or so the logic goes. But I wonder why this fractured self shouldn't warrant our compassion just as much as the self besieged? Or maybe even more?

I duck out of the second afternoon session and fall into conversation with two men already involved in a tense exchange near the cookie tray. Paul is a blond Texan wearing a silver-studded belt and stiff jeans. Lenny is from Oklahoma, a well-coiffed man with a curled mustache and a dark tan. Both men wear flannel shirts tucked into their pants.

Paul is a patient, but Lenny's not. Lenny's here because he thinks he may have found the cure. A woman came to him with the disease all over her knuckles and he treated it with a laser. 75

I ask him to rewind: he's a dermatologist?

"Oh no!" he says. "I'm an electrician."

Who knows what kind of lasers he used? *Turned it on that,* he says; the way you'd train a gun on prey. "I turned it on that," he says, "and it killed it."

It killed *it*. The deictics are so vague. Nobody really knows what hurts or what helps. So much uncertainty is sheltered under the broad umbrella of pursuit.

This woman had two years of pain, Lenny says, and nothing helped her until he did. About twenty minutes into the conversation, he also mentions she was a meth addict. He assures us that his laser cleaned her out until there was "no sign left" of any fibers. Lenny mentions something about eggs. "They said you can look underneath where they've been. They'll lay eggs and reappear again." He says there were no eggs when he was done. 80

Paul has a strange look on his face as Lenny describes the cure. It seems he doesn't like the sound of it. "You didn't heal her," he says finally. "It's a virus."

Lenny nods but he's clearly taken aback. He wasn't expecting resistance.

"I've been dealing with this for eight years," Paul continues, "and I would've chopped off my hand, if that would have stopped it from spreading to the rest of my body."

You get the sense—and I don't mean this is a rhetorical or dramatic sense, but a very literal one—that he still might.

If he'd thought a laser would work, Paul continues, he would've used one. "But," he says, "I know it's more than that." 85

Paul looks worse than anyone else I've seen. He's been sick for eight years but only diagnosed himself with Morgellons a year ago. Before that, he had his own name for his illness: the devil's fishing bait. He says he got it on a fishing trip. Sometimes he refers to it as a virus, other times as a parasitic infestation—but the sense of sinister agency remains the same.

Paul's disease is different because you can see it. You can see it a little bit on everyone: an archipelago of scabs on a scalp; caked makeup over sores across a chin; blanched spots on tan calves. But Paul looks damaged in a different way and to a different degree. His right ear is the most obvious. It's a little twisted, a little curled, almost mashed, and it has the smooth, shiny texture of scar tissue all along the juncture between ear and jaw. I realize his mangled ear is probably something Paul did to himself, trying to get something out. *Devil's bait.* He was lured into response, into attack. His face is dotted with red pockmarks; the skin is stained with milky patterns. He's got drop-shaped scars around his eyes like he cried them.

Paul says he came home from that first fateful fishing trip with legs covered in chigger bites. "You could feel the heat coming out of my pants," he says. His whole body was inflamed.

I ask about his symptoms now. He simply shakes his head. "You can never tell what's coming next." Some days, he says, he just lies on the couch and doesn't want to see tomorrow.

I ask whether he gets support from anyone in his life. He does, he says. That's when he tells me about his sister.

At first, she wasn't sympathetic. She assumed he was on drugs when he first told her about his symptoms. But she was the one who eventually discovered Morgellons online and told him about it.

"So she's become a source of support?" I ask.

"Well," he says, "Now she has it too."

They experiment with different cures and compare notes: freezing, insecticides, dewormers for cattle, horses, dogs. A liquid nitrogen compound he injected into his ear. Lately, he says, he's had success with root beer. He pours it over his head, down his face, down his limbs.

He tells me about arriving at the ER one night with blood gushing out of his ear, screaming because he could feel them—*them* again—tearing him up inside. He tells me the doctors told him he was crazy. I tell him nothing. All I want is to look at him a different way than the doctors did that day, to make him feel a different way than they made him feel. One of those ER doctors did a physical examination and noted that his mouth was dry. Paul told them he already knew that. It was hoarse from screaming at them for help.

Paul says he probably spends ten or twelve hours a day just keeping *them* at bay, meaning whatever is inside of him. His voice is full of wariness and fear. *They* lie beyond science or significance, their ceaseless motion.

Paul doesn't seem overly impressed with the conference. Mainly because it hasn't offered a cure, he says, though there's a trace of satisfaction in his disappointment, as if certain suspicions—about futility, impossibility—have been confirmed.

Lenny jumps in again about the laser. Paul's expression verges on annoyance. Perhaps the possibility of an easy fix reduces his own vexed life to a sort of gratuitous Sisyphean labor. A cure doesn't offer hope so much as it discredits the work he's already done—exhausting every possible option, proving each one ineffectual.

Lenny seems oblivious to this. "I'm so sincere," he says, "I'm only saying, this is what we did, and it cured her." He is having a hard time thinking that his news—the news of his laser—could come across as anything but good.

I sit behind Paul through the day's final presentation. I can see he isn't paying attention to the speaker. He's looking at photographs on his computer. They're all of him—his face—mostly in profile, focused on his ear. He shows them to the middle-aged woman sitting beside him. He points to a photo of some metal implement that looks like a pair of tongs: a taser. A few moments later, I hear him whisper, "These were all eggs."

He eventually scoots his chair away from the woman and returns to what he's probably already spent days inspecting: the spectacle of his own body splayed across the screen, parsed into a thousand tiny frames of scarred and bleeding skin. It's a time-lapse arc of disfigurement. Even here, among others who identify with the same malady, he retreats into the terrible privacy of his own broken body. He brings others—strangers, briefly—into this quiet battleground, but it's always just him again, eventually, drawn back into the cloister of his damage, that nearly unfathomable loneliness.

When I leave the church, I find sunlight waiting outside our windowless rooms. The world has been patient. Springtime in Austin is grackles in the trees; a nearly invisible fluttering of bats under the Congress Avenue bridge, a flickering of wings and waft of guano in blue-washed twilight. Austin is beautiful women everywhere, in scarves and sunglasses; BBQ smoke rising into thick sunlight; wind-blown oak leaves skittering across patios where I eat oysters on ice. Austin is throw-a-stone-and-you-hit-a-food-truck, each one gourmet, serving tongue-on-rice, fried avocado tacos, donuts topped with bacon. Dusk holds the clicking metronome of cowboy boots on sidewalks. People with narrative tattoos smoke in the heat. I find a grotto dedicated to the Virgin Mary with an empty beer bottle and a bag of Cheez-Its buried in the gravel.

I walk among the young and healthy and I am more or less one of them. I am trying not to itch. I am trying not to think about whether I'm itching. I am trying not to take my skin for granted. Sometimes my heart beats too fast, or a worm lodges under the skin of my ankle, or I drink too much, or I am too thin, but these are sojourns away from a kingdom I can generally claim—of being *okay*, capable of desire and being desired, full of a sense I belong in the world. But when I leave the Baptist church on Slaughter Lane, I can't quiet the voices of those who no longer feel they belong anywhere. I spend a day in their kingdom and then leave when I please. It feels like a betrayal to come up for air.

Doubting Morgellons hasn't stopped me from being afraid I'll get it. I buffered myself before the conference: "If I come back from Austin thinking I have Morgellons," I told my friends, "you have to tell me I don't have Morgellons." Now that I'm here, I wash my hands a lot. I'm conscious of other people's bodies.

105 Then it starts happening, as I knew it would. After a shower, I notice small blue strands curled like tiny worms across my clavicle. I find what appear to be minuscule spines, little quills, tucked into the crevice of a fortune line on my palm. I've got these fleeting moments of catching sight, catching panic. I'm afraid to submit myself to the public microscope inspection because I'm nervous something will be found and I won't be able to let go of it.

It actually gives me an odd thrill. Maybe some part of me *wants* to find something. I could be my own proof. Or else I could write a first-person story about delusion. I could connect to the disease with filaments of my own, real or imagined, under my skin.

If you look closely enough, of course, skin is always foreign, anyone's—full of strange bumps, botched hairs, hefty freckles, odd patches of flush and rough. The blue fibers are probably just stray threads from a towel, or from my sleeve, the quills not quills at all but just smeared pen ink. But it's in these moments of fear, oddly, that I come closest to experiencing Morgellons the way its patients do: its symptoms physical and sinister, its tactics utterly invasive. Inhabiting their perspective only makes me want to protect myself from what they have. I wonder if these are the only options available to my crippled organs of compassion: I'm either full of disbelief, or else I'm washing my hands in the bathroom.

I'm not the only person at the conference thinking about contagion. One woman stands up to say she needs to know the facts about how Morgellons is really transmitted. She tells the crowd that her family and friends refuse to come to her apartment. She needs proof they can't catch the disease from her couch. It's hard not to speculate. Her family might be afraid of catching her disease, but they might be even more afraid there's nothing to catch; maybe they're keeping their distance from her obsession instead. I hear so much sadness in what she says—*tell me it's not contagious, so everyone will come back*—and so much hope for an answer that might make things better; that might make her less alone.

Kendra tells me she's afraid of getting her friends sick whenever she goes out to dinner with them. I picture her eating sushi downtown—handling her chopsticks so carefully, keeping her wasabi under strict quarantine—so that this *thing* in her—this thing with agency, if not category—won't get into anyone else. Her fear underscores an unspoken tension embedded in the premise of the conference itself: the notion that all these folks with a possibly contagious condition might gather together in the same confined space.

The specter of contagion actually serves a curious double function, On the one hand, as with Kendra, there is the shameful sense of oneself as a potential carrier of infection. But on the other hand the possibility of spreading this disease also suggests that its real—that it could be proven by its manifestation in others. 110

One of the strangest corners of the Morgellons online labyrinth—a complicated network of chat boards, personal testimonies, and high-magnification photographs—is the "Pets with Morgellons" website. I realize quickly that it's neither a joke nor a feel-good photo album. It's not just "pets of [people who have] Morgellons" but "pets [who also have] Morgellons." In a typical entry, a cat named Ika introduces herself and her illness:

> I have been named [for] the Japanese snack of dried cuttlefish . . . Typically I am full of chaotic energy, however lately I have been feeling quite lethargic and VERY itchy. My best friend/mommy thinks that she gave me her skin condition, and she is so very SAD. I think she is even more sad that she passed it on to me than the fact that she has it covering her entire face.

The list continues, a litany of sick animals: a sleek white dog named Jazzy sports itchy paws; two bloodhounds are biting invisible fleas; a Lhasa Apso joins his mother for stretches in an infrared sauna. One entry is an elegy for an Akita named Sinbad:

> It appears that I got the disease at the same time that my beautiful lady owner got it. And after many trips to the vet they had to put me down. I know it was for my own good, but I do miss them a lot. I can still see my master's face, right up close to mine, when the doc put me to sleep . . . I could sniff his breath and feel the pain in his eyes as tears rolled down his face. But, it's ok. I'm alright now. The maddening itching is finally over. I'm finally at peace.

The ending paints resolution over pathos. We read, *I'm finally at peace*, and imagine another who probably isn't: the master who cried when he put his dog to sleep. Who knows what happened to Sinbad? Maybe he really did need to get put down; maybe he was old, or sick with something else. Maybe he wasn't sick at all. But he has become part of an illness narrative—like lesions, or divorces, or the fibers themselves. He is irrefutable proof that suffering has happened, that things have been lost.

The second day of the conference kicks off with a Japanese television documentary about Morgellons. Over there they call it "cotton erupting disease," suggesting a stage prank—a great *poof!*—more than the silent sinister curling of microscopic fibers. The program has been loosely translated. We see a woman standing at her kitchen counter, mixing a livestock antiparasitic called Ivermectin into a glass of water. The Japanese voiceover sounds concerned and the English translator fills in: she knows this antiparasitic isn't for human consumption, but she's using it anyway. She's desperate. We see a map of America with patches of known cases breaking out like lesions over the land, a twisted Manifest Destiny: disease claims community, claims the disordered as kin. Just as fibers attach to an open wound—its wet surface a kind of glue—so does the notion of disease function as an adhesive, gathering anything we can't understand, anything that hurts, anything that will stick. *Transmission by Internet*, some skeptics claim about Morgellons—chat boards as pied pipers, calling all comers. It's true that Morgellons wasn't officially born until 2001. It's grown up alongside the Internet. Its online community has become an authority in its own right. People here don't necessarily agree about the particulars of their shared disease—bacteria, fungus, parasite—but they agree about a feeling of inescapability: wherever you go, the disease follows; whatever you do, it resists.

A woman named Sandra pulls out her cell phone to show me a photo of something she coughed up. It looks like a little albino shrimp. She thinks it's a larva. She photographed it through a jeweler's loupe. She wants a microscope but doesn't have one yet. She put the larva on a book to give a sense of scale. I try to get a good look at the print; I'm curious about what she was reading. My mind seeks the quiet hours—how this woman fills her life beyond the condition of infestation, as that *beyond* keeps getting smaller. 115

Sandra has a theory about the fibers—not that the fibers *are* an organism but that the organisms inside her are gathering these fibers to make their cocoons. This explains why so many of the fibers turn out to be ordinary kinds of thread, dog hairs, or cotton fibers. Their danger is one of purpose, not of kind: creatures making a nest of her body, using the ordinary materials of her life to build a home inside of her.

Once I've squinted long enough at the shrimpish thing, Sandra brings up a video of herself in the bathtub. "These are way beyond fibers," she promises. Only her feet are visible protruding through the surface of the water. The quality is grainy, but it appears the bath is full of wriggling larva. Their forms are hard to feel sure about—everything is dim and a little sludgy—but that's actually what it looks like. She says that a couple years ago there were hundreds coming out of her skin. It's gotten a little better. When she takes a bath, only two or three of those worms come out.

I'm really at a loss. I don't know if what I'm seeing are worms, or where they come from, or what they might be if they're *not* worms, or whether I want them to be worms or not, or what I have to believe about this woman if they aren't worms, or about the world or human bodies or this disease if they *are*. But I do know I see a bunch of little wriggling shadows, and for now I'm glad I'm not a doctor or a scientist or basically anyone who knows anything about anything, because this uncertainty lets me believe Sandra without needing to confirm her. I can dwell with her—for just a moment, at least—in the possibility of those worms, in that horror. She's been alone in it for so long.

I catch sight of Kendra watching Sandra's cell phone. She's wondering if this is what her future holds. I tell her that everyone's disease turns out a little different. But what do I know? Maybe her future looks like this too.

Kendra tells me about sushi last night. It was good. She had fun. She actually ended up buying a painting from the restaurant. She shouldn't have, she says. She doesn't have the money. But she saw it hanging on the wall and couldn't resist. She shows me a cell phone picture: lush braided swirls of oil paint curl from the corners of a parchment-colored square. The braids are jewel toned, deeply saturated, royal purple twined with lavender and turquoise. 120

I think but don't say: *fibers*.

"You know," she says, voice lowered. "It reminds me a little of those things."

I get a sinking feeling. It's that moment in an epidemic movie when the illness spreads beyond its quarantine. Even when Kendra leaves this kingdom of the sick, she finds sickness waiting patiently for her on the other side. She pays three hundred dollars she can't afford just so she can take its portrait home with her. Whatever comfort I took in her sushi outing, it's gone now. Like I said, disease gathers anything that will stick. Even art on restaurant walls starts to look like what's wrong with you, even if you can't see it—can't see, but see everywhere.

During the morning program, the conference organizers pass around a sheet of jokes—"You might be a morgie if"—followed by a list of punchlines: "You scratch more than the dog," "You've been fired by more doctors than bosses," "An acid bath and total body shave sounds like a fun Friday night." Some jokes summon the split between the current self and the self before its disease: "past life regression means remembering any time before Morgellons." Others summon the split between the self and others: "at dinner your family uses oil and vinegar on their salads while you dump them on your hair and body." Some of the jokes I don't even get: "You can't use anything on your computer that requires a USB port because there's NO WAY you're disconnecting your QX-3 Digital Blue."

I look up QX-3 Digital Blue: it's a microscope. The website claims you can use it to "satisfy your basic curiosity of the world around you," which makes me think of Paul's computer—his own body photographed over and over again—how small his world has gotten. 125

I don't see any QX-3s at the conference, but the organizers are holding a lottery to give away some less expensive microscopes: a handful of miniscopes, like small black plums, and their larger cousin the EyeClops, a children's toy. At Amazon, I find the EyeClops advertised in terms of alchemy. "Ordinary to Extraordinary," the description brags, "minuscule salt crystals morph into blocks of ice; hair and carpet turn into giant noodles; and small insects become fearsome creatures." This ad copy transforms the alchemy of Morgellons into a magic trick: examined close-up, our most ordinary parts—even the surface and abrasions of our skin—become wild and terrifying.

My name is automatically entered in the lottery, along with all the other conference attendees, and I end up winning a miniscope. I'm sheepish headed to the stage. What do I need a scope for? I'm here to write about how other people need scopes. I'm given a square box a bit smaller than a Rubik's Cube. I imagine how the scene will play out later tonight: examining my skin in the stale privacy of my hotel room, coming face to face with that razor's edge between skepticism and fear by way of the little widget in my palm.

At the bottom of my sheet of jokes, the title—*You might be a morgie if*—is given one last completing clause: "you laughed out loud and 'got these jokes." I remember that early e-mail—*topic of the biggest joke in the world*—and see why these jokes might matter so much—not simply because they resonate, but because they reclaim the activity of joking itself. Here Morgies are the makers of jokes, not their targets. Every joke recycles the traitorous body into a neatly packaged punchline.

So we get our page of jokes and I get some of them, but not all of them, and Sandra gets an audience for her cell phone slideshow and I get a miniscope I didn't even want and Kendra gets a painting—and, in the end, she also gets the microscope consultation she's been waiting for.

Afterward, I ask her how it went. She tells me it's been confirmed: Rita found threads around her eyes. But she shrugs as she says it—as if the discovery is just an anticlimax; offering none of the resolution or solidity it promised. 130

"I'm fucking myself," Kendra tells me, "the more I try to pick them away."

I agree. I nod.

"The more I try to pick them away," she continues, "the more come . . . like they want to show me I can't get rid of them that easily."

Discussion

In the end, I gave my miniscope away.

I gave it to Sandra, I gave it to her because she was sick of using her jeweler's loupe, because she was sad she hadn't gotten one, and because I felt self-conscious about winning one when I wasn't even looking for fibers in the first place. 135

"That's so generous," she said to me when I gave it to her—and of course I'd been hoping she would say that. I wanted to do nice things for everyone out of a sense of preemptive guilt that I couldn't conceptualize this disease in the same way as those who suffered from it. So I said, *Here, take my miniscope*, in hopes that might make up for everything else.

That's so generous. But maybe it wasn't. Maybe it was just the opposite. Maybe I just took hours of her life away and replaced them with hours spent at the peephole of that microscope, staring at what she wouldn't be able to cure.

A confession: I left the conference early. I actually, embarrassingly, went to *sit by the shitty hotel pool* because I felt emotionally drained and like I deserved it. I baked bare skinned in the Texan sun and watched a woman from the conference come outside and carefully lay her own body, fully clothed, across a reclining chair in the shade.

Acknowledgments

I've left the kingdom of the ill. Dawn and Kendra and Paul and Rita remain. Now I get the sunlight and they don't. They feed themselves horse dewormers and I don't. But I still feel the ache of an uncanny proximity. They have no fear that isn't mine, no dread of self I haven't known. I kept telling them, *I can't imagine*, and every once in a while, softer, *I can.*

When does empathy actually reinforce the pain it wants to console? Does giving people a space to talk about their disease probe it, gaze at it, share it—help them move through it, or simply deepen its hold? Does a gathering like this offer solace or simply confirm the cloister and prerogative of suffering? Maybe it just pushes on the pain until it gets even worse, until it requires more comforting than it did before. The conference seems to confirm, in those who attend, the sense that they will only ever get what they need here. It sharpens the isolation it wants to heal. 140

I can only be myself when I'm here, is something I heard more than once. But every time I left the dim rooms of Westoak Baptist, I found myself wishing its citizens could also be themselves elsewhere, could be themselves anywhere—in the lavish Austin sunshine, for starters, or hunched over artisanal donuts at a picnic table on a warm night. I wanted them to understand themselves as constituted and contoured beyond the margins of illness.

I think of how Paul always does his grocery shopping half an hour before closing time so he won't see anyone he knows; I think of the bald man sitting behind me on the second day, whose name I never learned, who doesn't do much besides shuttle between a bare apartment and an unnamed job; I think of a beautiful woman who wonders how any man could ever love her scarred.

Kendra is terrified by the same assurances that offer her validation. She has proof of fibers in her skin but no hope of getting them out, only a vision of what it might look like to be consumed by this disease entirely: a thousand bloody photographs on her computer, a soup of larvae on her cell phone testifying to the passing days of her life.

What did Kendra say? *Some of these things I'm trying to get out, it's like they move away from me.* Isn't that all of us? Sometimes, we're all trying to purge something. And what we're trying to purge resists our purging. *Devil's bait*—this disease offers a constant feeling of being lured, the promise of resolution dangling just out of reach. These demons belong to all of us: an obsession with our boundaries and visible shapes, a fear of invasion or contamination, an understanding of ourselves as perpetually misunderstood.

But doesn't this search for meaning obfuscate the illness itself? It's another kind of bait, another tied-and-painted fly: the notion that if we understand something well enough, we can make it go away. 145

Everyone I met at the conference was kind. They offered their warmth to me and to each other. I was a visitor to what they knew, but I have been a citizen at times—a citizen subject to that bodily unrest—and I know I'll be one again. I was splitting my time between one Austin and another; I was splitting my time between dim rooms and open skies.

One of the speakers quoted nineteenth-century biologist Thomas Huxley:

> Sit down before fact as a little child, be prepared to give up every preconceived notion, follow humbly wherever and to whatever abyss Nature leads, or you shall learn nothing.

I want to sit down in front of everyone I've heard—listen to their voices in my tape recorder like a child, like an agnostic, like a pluralist. I want to be the compassionate nurse, not the skeptical doctor. I want the abyss, not the verdict. I want to believe everyone, I want everyone to be right. But compassion isn't the same thing as belief. This isn't a lesson I want to learn.

It wasn't until the seventeenth century that the words *pity* and *piety* were fully distinguished. Sympathy was understood as a kind of duty, an obligation to some basic human bond—and what I feel toward this disorder is a kind of piety. I feel an obligation to pay homage or at least accord some reverence to these patients' collective understanding of what makes them hurt. Maybe it's a kind of sympathetic infection in its own right: this need to go-along-with, to nod-along-with, to support; to agree.

Paul said, "I wouldn't tell anyone my crazy-ass symptoms." But he told them to me. He's always been met with disbelief. He called it "typical." Now I'm haunted by that word. For Paul, life has become a pattern and the moral of that pattern is, *you're destined for this*. The disbelief of others is inevitable and so is loneliness; both are just as much a part of this disease as any fiber, any speck or crystal or parasite. 150

I went to Austin because I wanted to be a different kind of listener than the kind these patients had known: doctors winking at their residents, friends biting their lips, skeptics smiling in smug bewilderment. But wanting to be different doesn't make you so. Paul told me his crazy-ass symptoms and I didn't believe him. Or at least, I didn't believe him the way he wanted to be believed. I didn't believe there were parasites laying thousands of eggs under his skin, but I did believe he hurt like there were. Which was typical, I was typical. In writing this essay, how am I doing something he wouldn't understand as betrayal? I want to say, *I heard you*. To say, *I pass no verdicts*. But I can't say these things to him. So instead I say this: I think he can heal. I hope he does.

Questions for Critical Reading

1. Jamison uses a number of subheadings for her essay that are reminiscent of what one might find in a scientific journal article. Review the content in each of these sections to see how it relates to the subheading. What larger argument is Jamison making in using subheadings? How does the content of each section relate to the subheading?
2. Jamison asks, "Is it wrong to call it empathy when you trust the fact of suffering, but not the source?" (p. 230). Develop your own answer to her question. Then, as you reread the essay, look for passages that suggest Jamison's answer to the question.
3. What role does identity play in this essay? As you reread, look for passages where Jamison discusses notions of the self as well as those passages where she talks to "Morgies." How do particular conceptions of self and identity relate to this disease?

Exploring Context

1. Explore the website for the Morgellons Research Foundation (morgellons.org). How does the site reflect the complicated experience of Morgellons that Jamison describes?
2. The Charles E. Holman Morgellons Disease Foundation (thecehf.org) is another organization focused on research and advocacy around Morgellons disease. Explore the site in relation to your response to Exploring Context Question 1. How do the differences between these two sites further evince the complications around this disease?

3. What role does this essay play in Jamison's larger body of writing and thinking? Visit her website at lesliejamison.com. What questions does she tend to explore and how are those questions reflected in this reading?

Questions for Connecting

1. Sarah Stillman represents trauma as a kind of illness in "Hiroshima and the Inheritance of Trauma" (p. 371). Synthesize her discussion with Jamison's exploration of Morgellons to develop a definition of disease that extends beyond the biological to encompass the social aspects of disease. How could using such a definition highlight different issues in health care?

2. Sufferers of Morgellons disease are often disbelieved by medical professionals. Is their human dignity being respected? Use Francis Fukuyama's discussion of the concept in "Human Dignity" (p. 137) to consider how we might approach those with the disease differently.

3. How can Kwame Anthony Appiah's idea of cosmopolitanism in "Making Conversation" and "The Primacy of Practice" (p. 35) change the way we view those with Morgellons disease? How might you apply Appiah's discussion of the relation between practices and values to Jamison's essay?

Language Matters

1. **Multimodal.** Create a series of presentation slides about this essay using PowerPoint or other software. Since such slides are most effective when they contain only a few key points per slide, you will have to locate the most important elements of Jamison's argument; in designing the slides, you should also consider how visual elements like color, font, and alignment can enhance an argument.

2. Systems of citation are a central aspect of academic writing. In this class, you may be asked to use MLA, APA, or some other format for in-text citations. Develop your own system and illustrate it by citing a quotation from Jamison's essay. What kind of information would the citation have to include? What does this then say about how citation systems work—what does every system seem to need? Why are there so many citation systems?

3. What are the differences between editing, proofreading, and revising? What would you do to this essay if you were editing it? Revising it? How can you use these different skills in your own writing?

Assignments for Writing

1. The impacts of disease ripple out from individuals into the larger society. Using Jamison's essay, write a paper in which you examine the social impact of disease. You may want to begin with your work in Questions 2 and 3 of Questions for Critical Reading, Questions 1 and 2 of Exploring Context, and Question 1 of Questions for Connecting.

2. What role do identity and connection play in health? Write a paper using Jamison's essay in which you explore the ways that self and community function in disease and healing. What concepts of self are bound up in Morgellons or other diseases? How do communities like the gathering Jamison attends contribute to healing? Your work in Question 3 of Questions for Critical Reading, Questions 1 and 2 of Exploring Context, and Questions 2 and 3 of Questions for Connecting may be useful in forming your response.

3. How can we promote empathy? Write a paper in which you propose strategies for promoting empathy using Jamison's experience. You may want to start with your work in Question 2 of Questions for Critical Reading.

CHUCK KLOSTERMAN

Cultural critic and best-selling author **Chuck Klosterman** has written eleven books: two novels, five nonfiction narratives, and four essay collections, including *Sex, Drugs, and Cocoa Puffs*; *Killing Yourself to Live*; and *Fargo Rock City*. Known for his oddball style and sharp, witty observations, Klosterman writes primarily about music, pop culture, and sports. He is "The Ethicist" for the *New York Times Magazine*, and his prolific writings have appeared in such publications as *GQ*, *Spin*, and *Esquire*. Klosterman graduated from the University of North Dakota with a degree in journalism in 1994. He served as the Picador Guest Professor for Literature at the University of Leipzig's Institute for American Studies in 2008.

"Electric Funeral" is taken from Klosterman's *New York Times* best-seller, *I Wear the Black Hat: Grappling with Villains (Real and Imagined)*. This 2013 essay collection examines the concept of villainy and the way so-called bad guys are perceived in modern culture, with essays on subjects such as the rock group Eagles, the sitcom *Seinfeld*, Batman, folk hero and hijacker D. B. Cooper, and former president Bill Clinton. Reflecting Klosterman's work as "The Ethicist" for the *New York Times*, *I Wear the Black Hat* grapples with the larger question of good and evil, asking why we call some figures villains and others heroes.

In "Electric Funeral," Klosterman zooms in on technological innovation and the "villains" that champion it, profiling such figures as Perez Hilton, Julian Assange, and even the office IT guy. They have the power and they are the future, Klosterman posits, asserting that this position of power causes resentment, largely because it scares people. He argues that ultimately "the easiest way for any cutthroat person to succeed is to instinctively (and relentlessly) side with the technology of tomorrow, even if that technology is distasteful" (p. 244). From bloggers who matter because of how many followers they have to the founder of the controversial WikiLeaks website, Klosterman looks at the relationship between technological progress and our cultural concepts of villainy.

What do you think makes a villain? What is the nature of good and evil?

▶ TAGS: *culture, ethics, media, politics, science and technology, social change, social media*

▶ CONNECTIONS: *Appiah, Chen, Cohen, Gilbert, Konnikova, Lukianoff and Haidt, Paumgarten, Singer, Turkle, van Houtryve*

Electric Funeral

If you're reading this book* in order, you've just finished a section about Bill Clinton, the forty-second president of the United States. Unless this book† has survived far longer than I anticipate, most readers will picture Clinton as a living, breathing mammal. You remember where you were when he was elected in 1992 and the condition of your life during his two-term tenure. His time as POTUS might feel more recent than

* Klosterman's *I Wear the Black Hat* [BJB]

† Klosterman's *I Wear the Black Hat* [BJB]

it actually is (and perhaps that makes you feel strange). But there's another chunk of readers who had a different experience when they read the essay* (and the size of that chunk will get progressively larger for the rest of eternity). Those in the second camp recall Clinton only vaguely, or not at all. You know he was once the president in the same way you know Woodrow Wilson was once the president. It feels like something that happened long ago. That makes you different from those in the first camp (and for a lot of different reasons). And there's one specific divergence that matters more than most people think: If you're in that first group, your parents worried about how you were affected by the media—and what they worried about was the *content* you were consuming. If you were born in 1960, your parents worried about Black Sabbath; if you were born in 1970, they worried about *Porky's*; if you were born in 1980, they worried about *Beavis and Butt-head*. Their fear was that you'd be changed by the images you saw and the messages you heard, and perhaps they believed that content needed to be regulated. Their concern was tethered to the message. But if you were born after 1990, this is not the case. Instead, your parents were (or are) primarily worried about the *medium* through which all of those things are accessed. The medium is far more problematic than the message. When a father looks at his typically unfocused four-year-old hypnotically immersed with an iPad for three straight hours, he thinks, "Somehow, I know this is bad." It does not matter that the four-year-old might be learning essential skills on that device; what matters is the way such an intense, insular, digital experience will irreparably alter the way he'll experience the non-simulated world. It's normalizing something that was once abnormal, and it's distancing the child from reality. It will transmogrify his brainstem into the opening credit sequence of Gaspar Noé's *Enter the Void*. And the worst part is that there is no other option. If a father stops his son from embracing the online universe, he's stopping him from becoming a competitive adult; it's like refusing to teach him how to drive a car or boil water. You may worry about all the ancillary consequences, but you can't take away the experience. Avoiding the Internet is akin to avoiding everything that matters. This is even true for adults. An author I know once explained why writing became so much more difficult in the twenty-first century: "The biggest problem in my life," he said, "is that my work machine is also my pornography delivery machine."

The future makes the rules.

The future makes the rules, so there's no point in being mad when the future wins. In fact, the easiest way for any cutthroat person to succeed is to instinctively (and relentlessly) side with the technology of tomorrow, even if that technology is distasteful. Time will eventually validate that position. The only downside is that—until that validation occurs—less competitive people will find you annoying and unlikable.

They know they will end up on the right side of history, because the future always wins.

The future will retire undefeated, but it always makes a terrible argument for its own success. The argument is inevitably some version of this: "You might not like where we're going, and tomorrow might be worse than yesterday. But it's still going to happen, whether you like it or not. It's inevitable." And this is what people hate. They hate being *dragged* into the future, and they hate the technocrats who remind them

* "Arrested for Smoking," not included here [BJB]

that this is always, always, always happening. We tend to dislike cultural architects who seem *excited* that the world is changing, particularly when those architects don't seem particularly concerned whether those changes make things worse. They know they will end up on the right side of history, because the future always wins. These are people who have the clearest understanding of what technology can do, but no emotional stake in how its application will change the lives of people who aren't exactly like them. (They know the most and care the least . . . and they kind of think that's funny.) Certainly, this brand of technophobia has always existed. As early as 1899, people like H. G. Wells were expressing apprehension about a future "ruled by an aristocracy of organizers, men who manage railroads and similar vast enterprises." But this is different. This is about the kind of person who will decide what that future is.

Early in the third season of *The Sopranos*, there's a two-episode subplot in which my favorite character (Christopher Moltisanti) sticks up a charity concert at Rutgers University (the musical headliner is Jewel). What's most interesting about this robbery is the person who hands over the money: The role of the terrified box office clerk is portrayed by an unknown actor named Mario Lavandeira. He has only two lines, but the scene—when viewed retroactively—is more culturally significant than everything else that happens in that particular episode. This is because Mario Lavandeira would soon rename himself Perez Hilton and become the first authentically famous blogger, which (of course) made him the most hated blogger of his generation.

[There are no famous bloggers who aren't hated.]

Perez Hilton once claimed that 8.82 million people read his website within a 24-hour period in 2007. The magnitude of this number was disputed by competing gossip sources, but those critics came off like the type of person who wants to argue over the specific number of people killed during the Holocaust: They missed the point entirely. Even if Hilton was tripling his true traffic figures, the audience for what he was doing was massive. And what he was doing was terrible. It was objectively immoral. The crux of his publishing empire was based around defacing copyrighted photos of celebrities (often to imply they were addicted to cocaine). Other central pursuits included the outing of gay celebrities (Perez himself is homosexual) and publishing unauthorized photos of teen celebrities who may or may not be wearing underwear. The apex of his career was when he broke the news of Fidel Castro's death, a report mildly contradicted by Castro's unwillingness to stop living. Hilton was also a judge for the Miss USA Pageant, a referee for a WWE wrestling match, and the star of a VH1 reality show I never actually saw. [I realize Mr. Hilton would likely disagree with my overview of his career and insist that I failed to mention how he's also been involved with numerous sex-positive, pro-youth, anti-bullying initiatives. But I suspect he will totally agree with much of what I'm going to write next, mostly because it makes him look far less culpable than he probably is.]

Whenever you have an audience as large as Hilton's, there's obviously going to be a substantial swath of consumers who adore the person who built it. It would be wrong to say, "Everyone hates Perez Hilton," because that's just not true. But it's pretty hard to find an intelligent person who loves him. (Such individuals exist, but not in great numbers.) It's hard to find a thoughtful person who appreciates the way Hilton's appeal is so hyper-directed at the lowest common denominator. Even his decision to name himself after noted celebutard Paris Hilton perpetuates a desire to produce self-consciously vapid work. So this, it would seem, is why smart people hate him: because of his blog's content. They find his ideas despicable (or so they would argue). Now, Perez would counter that accusation by charging his critics with jealousy. He (and his defenders) would claim that what people truly hate about Perez Hilton is not what he writes; it's the size of his audience and the scale of his reach. That argument is not invalid. For those who live on the Internet, the attention economy matters way more than making money or earning peer respect; there is a slice of the web that would do *anything* to harvest Hilton's readership, even if it meant publishing photos of aborted celebrity fetuses while going bankrupt in the process. In other words, some people hate Perez for his ideas and some people hate Perez because they so desperately want to be like him. And as it turns out, both sides have a point. The reason Perez Hilton became a villain was the intersection of those two qualities: It wasn't just the content, and it wasn't just the success. It was the creeping fear that this type of content would become the *only* way any future person could be successful.

Necessity used to be the mother of invention, but then we ran out of things that were necessary. The postmodern mother of invention is desire; we don't really "need" anything new, so we only create what we *want*. This changes the nature of technological competition. Because the Internet is obsessed with its own version of nonmonetary capitalism, it rewards the volume of response much more than the merits of whatever people are originally responding to. Moreover, there's no downside to creating something that repulses all those who exist outside your audience (in fact, a reasonable degree of outsider hatred usually helps). Intuitively understanding these rules, Hilton only went after the kind of pre-adult who simultaneously loved and loathed celebrity culture to an unhealthy degree; he knew that specific demographic was both expanding and underserved. It was a brilliant business model. It was like he opened a buffet restaurant that served wet garbage in a community where the population of garbage gluttons was much higher (and far more loyal) than anyone had ever realized. And this made all the normal food eaters hate him. Do they hate his product? Sure (although there are many things on the Internet far worse). Do they hate his success? Sure (although he's never been perceived as credible or particularly insightful, so the definition of his success is limited to pure populism). Do they simply think Hilton is a jerk? Yes (and perhaps he is—I have no idea). But none of those individual issues addresses the greater fear. The real reason Perez Hilton is vilified is the combination of a) what he does editorially, b) its level of public import, and c) the undeniable sense that all of this was somehow *inevitable*. Perez Hilton is a villain because he personifies the way desire-based technology drives mass culture toward primitive impulses. Any singular opinion of his work does not matter; the only thing that matters is the collective opinion, which can be dominated by a vocal, splintered minority who knows only that they want what they want. Everyone seems to understand this. And once everyone understands that this is how New Media works, it becomes normative. It becomes the main way we get information about everything (gossip or otherwise). There is no alternative option. By manipulating an audience that is complicit in the manipulation, Perez Hilton can force the rest of us to accept his version of the future.

Hilton is a technocrat, and technocrats inevitably share two unifying beliefs. The first is that they're already winning; the second is that they're going to push things 10 forward, regardless of what that progress entails. Resistance to either principle is futile. Every day we grow closer to a full-on technocratic police state. "I don't care if you like me," Hilton has written. "I just care if you read my website." This is not exactly an original perspective; many writers feel like that, especially when they're young (Hilton was roughly twenty-four when he first experienced success). But the sentiment is disturbing when expressed by Perez. It seems like his entire objective. It's like he vividly sees the relationship between those two adversarial ideas, and everything else is built upon that foundation. And this would be totally fine, assuming we felt as if it was our decision to agree or disagree. But we don't. At this point, we can't walk away from harmful technology. We've ceded control to the machines. The upside is that the machines still have masters. The downside is that we don't usually like who those masters are.

At this point, we can't walk away from harmful technology. We've ceded control to the machines.

When Kim Dotcom was arrested during a 2012 police raid of his home, I had the same series of reactions as everyone else: There's a person literally named "Kim Dotcom"? And this person is a 350-pound, egocentric German multimillionaire who never went to college? And he got famous for being a computer hacker who refers to himself as Dr. Evil? And he lives in a mansion in New Zealand? And he participates in European road races and is the world's best *Modern Warfare 3* player? And he has a beautiful wife of unknown racial origin? And his 24-acre, $30 million estate is populated with life-size statues of giraffes? And he likes to be photographed in his bathtub? Everything about his biography seemed like someone trying to make fun of a Roger Moore–era James Bond movie that was too dumb to exist. I could not believe that *this* was the person the FBI decided to go after in their ongoing dream of controlling the digital future. It seemed as if they were arbitrarily penalizing a cherubic foreigner for being wealthy and ostentatious, and New Zealand eventually deemed the raid illegal.

However, the arrest turned out to be far less arbitrary than I'd thought. Dotcom owned and operated the online service Megaupload. In an interview with Kiwi investigative reporter John Campbell, Dotcom (born Kim Schmitz in 1974) described Megaupload like this: "I basically created a server where I could upload a file and get a unique link, and then I would just email that link to my friend so he would then get the file. And that's how Megaupload was started. It was just a solution to a problem that still exists today." In essence, Dotcom's argument was that he simply made it easier for people to exchange and store digital files that were too large for Gmail or AOL—and when described in this simplified manner, it seems like his motives were utilitarian. But this claim is such a profound distortion of reality that it almost qualifies as a lie, even though (I suppose) it's technically true. Megaupload was a place to steal music. There was no mystery about this; if you knew what Megaupload was, you knew it was a pirating service. There appeared to be dozens of other sites exactly like it. But what I did not realize was the scope of Dotcom's empire: The week after he was arrested, downloading illegal music became almost impossible (not *totally* impossible, but at least ten times more difficult than it had been in 2011). His arrest instantly changed the entire culture of recreational music theft. For most normal adults, ripping music from the Internet went from "a little too easy" to "a little too hard." Megaupload was more central to the process of stealing copyrighted material than every other file sharing source combined. He really *was* the man. Kim Dotcom was not some goofy eccentric being persecuted for the sins of other people. He pretty much ran the Internet (or at least the part of the Internet that people with money actually care about). He denies this, as any wise man would. But even his denials suggest a secret dominance. Here's one exchange from his conversation with Campbell, the first TV interview he gave following his arrest . . .

CAMPBELL: The FBI indictment against you alleges, and I quote, "Copyright infringement on a massive scale, with estimated harm to copyright holders well in excess of five hundred million U.S. dollars."

DOTCOM: Well, that's complete nonsense. If you read the indictment and if you hear what the Prosecution has said in court, those $500 million of damage were just music files from a two-week time period. So they are actually talking about $13 billion U.S. damages within a year, just for music downloads. The entire U.S. music industry is less than $20 billion. So how can one website be responsible for this amount of damage? It's completely mind-boggling and unrealistic.

It *is* mind-boggling. But it isn't unrealistic. While I don't doubt the FBI is using an unusually high estimate, it doesn't seem implausible that $13 billion worth of music was flowing through Megaupload's channels (assuming we pretend a CD is still worth its $14 retail price). Ripping music is not like buying music. It's not a meditative process. When you purchase music, you make a specific choice that (in your mind) justifies the exchange of currency. When you download music illegally, there's nothing to exchange; if you can simply *think* of a record's title and you can type it semi-correctly into a search engine, there's no reason not to drop it into your iTunes. That's pretty much the entire investment—the ability to type a band name into a search field. Megaupload made stealing simple (it was far better than the previous theft iteration, the Napster-like Limewire). The downloading process took (maybe) 45 seconds per album, and—if you elected to never listen to those songs, even once—you lost nothing. People would download albums just because they were bored. Since the advent (and fall) of Napster in 1999, consumers' relationship to music as a commodity completely collapsed. Supply became unlimited, so demand became irrelevant. A better argument from Dotcom would have been that the $13 billion he was accused of "reappropriating" was not actually $13 billion, but merely the projected value of what such exchanges would have been worth in 1998 (and only if the world had become some kind of strange musical utopia where consumers immediately purchased every single album they were remotely intrigued by).

Weirder still is that the charge of music theft isn't even the main reason media conglomerates wanted Dotcom's arrest. Their real concern was the increasing potential for the pirating of feature-length films, which is only feasible through this kind of server (relative to the size of MP3 music clips, film files are massive). The movie industry makes the music industry look like a food co-op (in 2011, global film revenue was $87 billion). Kim Dotcom clearly understood this, which prompted him to make the kind of move usually reserved for the Joker: Despite being under arrest, he wrote an open letter to the *Hollywood Reporter*, mocking the film industry's inability to understand the future of its own vehicle. His twelve-paragraph letter opens like a Tweet: "Dear Hollywood: The Internet frightens you." And he just keeps going . . .

> (paragraph 2): "You get so comfortable with your ways of doing business that any change is perceived as a threat. The problem is, we as a society don't have a choice: The law of human nature is to communicate more efficiently."
>
> (paragraph 4): "My whole life is like a movie. I wouldn't be who I am if it wasn't for the mind-altering glimpse at the future in *Star Wars*. I am at the forefront of creating the cool stuff that will allow creative works to thrive in an Internet age. I have the solutions to your problems. I am not your enemy."
>
> (paragraph 7): "The people of the Internet will unite. They will help me. And they are stronger than you. We will prevail in the war for Internet freedom and innovation that you have launched. We have logic, human nature and the invisible hand on our side."

The document concludes with Dotcom's signature snark: "This open letter is free of copyright. Use it freely." Technically, he's trying to forward his opinion on how copyright law should be applied, based on the principle that the laws governing ownership over intellectual property are outdated and not designed for the machinations of the Internet age. But that's not what interests me. What interests me is his personality and his leverage—and in the case of Dotcom, those qualities are connected. 15

If you've ever worked in an office filled with computers (which, at this point, is the only kind of office that exists), you've undoubtedly had some kind of complicated, one-sided relationship with whoever worked in the IT department. "IT" stands for "information technology." [An easy illustration of the one-sidedness of this relationship can be quickly illustrated by asking random people what the "I" and "T" literally represent in that acronym. You may be surprised by the results.] Now, there are exceptions to every rule, and I don't want to unfairly stereotype anyone. But people fucking hate IT guys. They want to knife them in the throat and pour acid in their ears. They want to see them arrested for the possession of kiddie porn.

There are two reasons why this is.

The first is that workers typically encounter IT people only when something is already wrong with their desktop (there just aren't any situations where you *want* someone to be doing things to your computer that you can't do yourself). But the second reason is the one that matters more. Regardless of their station within the office hierarchy, there's never any debate over how much power the IT department has: It's borderline infinite. They control all, and they have access to everything. They can't fire you, but they could get you fired in 24 hours. You may have a despotic boss who insists he won't take no for an answer, but he'll take it from an IT guy. He'll eat shit from an IT guy, day after day after day.

Specialists in information technology are the new lawyers. Long ago, lawyers realized that they could make themselves culturally essential if they made the vernacular of contracts too complex for anyone to understand except themselves. They made the language of contracts unreadable on purpose. [Easy example: I can write a book, and my editor can edit a book . . . but neither one of us can read and understand the contract that allows those things to happen.] IT workers became similarly unstoppable the moment they realized virtually every machine powering the modern world is too complicated for the average person to fix or calibrate. And they know this. This is what makes an IT guy different from you. He might make less money, he might have less social prestige, and people might look at him in the cafeteria like he's a morlock—*but he can act however he wants*. He can be nice, but only if he feels like it. He can ignore the company dress code. He can lie for no reason whatsoever (because how would anyone understand what he's lying about?). He can smoke weed at lunch, because he'll still understand your iMac better than you. It doesn't matter how he behaves: The IT department dominates technology, and technology dominates the rest of us. And this state of being creates a new kind of personality. It creates someone like Kim Dotcom, a man who's essentially an IT guy for the entire planet.

"I'm an easy target," Mr. Dotcom claims in his defense. "My flamboyance, my history as a hacker. I'm not American, I'm living somewhere in New Zealand, around the world. I have funny number plates on my cars. I'm an easy target." (Kim Dotcom drives around in luxury vehicles with license plates that read GUILTY.) There is, certainly, something endearing about Kim Dotcom's attitude. He acts like a man who finds his own obesity hilarious. His relationship to pop culture gives him a childlike appeal. (He once made himself the main character in a seminal flash-animation film that centered on the cartoonish murder of Bill Gates. He named his animated alter ego Richard Kimball, the wrongly accused hero from *The Fugitive*.) Sometimes it seems like he can't possibly be serious. (After his arrest, he recorded an anti-copyright ABBA-like pop song titled "Mr. President" in which he directly compares himself to Martin Luther King.) In general, Americans enjoy the idea of computer hackers and prefer to imagine them as precocious elves. (Somehow, the touchstone for how hackers behave is still based on Matthew Broderick's performance in the 1983 film *WarGames*.) Dotcom is arrogant, but not unlikable; at the highest possible level, being an IT guy is vaguely cool. Yet his underlying message is troubling. He starts by arguing, "Change is good," which is only a semi-defensible position to begin with. But that evolves into "Change will happen whether you like it or not." He uses phrases like "*The law of human nature is to communicate more efficiently*," which makes it seem like he's proposing something natural and obvious. But all he's really proposing is the business model for his own company (which might not be diabolical, but certainly isn't altruistic). He's trying to initiate an era when content is free and content providers make all the money, but he still wants to frame it like a more grassroots system ("*The people of the Internet will unite*"). Would his espoused structure actually be better? I don't think it's possible to know. But I do know that any argument attacking Dotcom will come from a position of sad technological inferiority. It will seem unsophisticated and antediluvian. It's easier to just embrace Dotcom's viewpoint, even if it's self-serving and unfair; about a year after the initial raid, he launched another sharing service (this time simply called MEGA) that utilizes cloud technology. I suspect it will succeed. He is, in many ways, the most depressing kind of villain: the kind we *must* agree with in order to stay competitive. The only other option is being trampled.

> There is a view that one should never be permitted to be criticized for being—possibly, even in the future—engaged in a contributory act that might be immoral. And that type of arse covering is more important than

saving people's lives. That it is better to let 1000 people die than risk going to save them and possibly running over someone on the way. And that is something I find philosophically repugnant.

These are the words of Julian Assange, the founder of the website WikiLeaks and the most archetypically villainlike villain of the Internet age. His appearance is so Aryan that it seems like he was engineered by the kind of scientist who ends up hiding in Argentina. I assume Assange can laugh, but I have no proof. He's truly a worldwide irritant: Assange has been accused of sexually assaulting two women in Sweden, applied for political asylum in Ecuador, and had a Canadian academic call for his assassination. His brilliance is impolite and self-defined. There is no one else like him; he is truly a New Thing.

If you know what WikiLeaks is, feel free to skip this paragraph. (I'm not going to outline anything you don't already know, nor am I going to take a strong position on its merits or flaws, nor have I seen the film *The Fifth Estate* starring sexy British weirdo Benedict Cumberbatch in the lead role.) If you don't know anything about it, here's a 230-word description: WikiLeaks is a website that publishes classified, present-tense documents from anonymous sources. The site's abiding premise is that the upside of absolute transparency is greater than the potential downside of publicly dumping sensitive information that might theoretically cause damage. The first noteworthy WikiLeaks release was some 2007 footage of a U.S. Apache helicopter killing an Iraqi journalist in Afghanistan (people generally viewed this release positively). The most discussed incident was an avalanche of "diplomatic cables" that went up in 2011; essentially, these were private correspondences American diplomats had exchanged among themselves. Most of these exchanges were more gossipy than meaningful, but it made some high-profile Americans seem crazy and facile. [It also created the impression that WikiLeaks cannot be controlled or regulated, which seemed scarier than the documents themselves.] That same year, WikiLeaks released seventy-five thousand U.S. military documents that came to be known as the Afghan War Diary. The Pentagon wasn't exactly stoked about this. Obviously, the details of all these fiascoes can be found more comprehensively elsewhere. But the takeaway is this: A very confident Australian (Assange) who's fixated on the problematic politics of one country (the United States) has created a way to publish information about that country that would have previously remained hidden (sometimes for valid reasons and sometimes due to corruption). It is journalism that attacks journalism, which is an extremely interesting topic to journalists.

Supporters of WikiLeaks believe it receives the same kind of unjust, reactionary criticism that was once lobbed at the Pentagon Papers (the Pentagon Papers were a classified overview of U.S. military involvement in the Vietnam War, published by the *New York Times* in 1971). Those who are against WikiLeaks counter this argument by noting that the Pentagon Papers were vetted by a news organization and only involved defunct military actions that were at least four years old (the study examined activities only through the year 1967). It's worth noting that the principal whistleblower in the Pentagon Papers (former U.S. military analyst Daniel Ellsberg) has requested a presidential pardon for the principal whistleblower in the WikiLeaks controversy, former U.S. soldier Bradley Manning. I have my own views on this topic, but they're contradictory and unimportant. What intrigues me more is Assange's quote at the top of this section: His statement either confronts (and obliterates) the problem I'm trying to describe, or it simply *is* the problem (described succinctly and expressed with monotone glee).

Assange comes at the media from a bottom-line, non-theoretical, the-ends-justify-the-means perspective that was (perhaps not so coincidentally) first described in Machiavelli's *The Prince*. He's arguing that people are too obsessed with the arcane ethics of print journalism, and he's willing to accept that an action that hurts one person is justified if it helps a hundred or a thousand or ten thousand others. It's an old problem. Perhaps the clearest metaphor for how much this disturbs people is the classic hypothetical of the runaway trolley car: Imagine you are operating a trolley car whose brakes have malfunctioned. You are flying down the tracks at an obscene speed. Up ahead, you see five workers on the track, unaware that this trolley is bearing down on them; if you continue on your current path, the trolley will kill them all. But then you notice an alternate track that will allow you to avoid colliding with the five workers. The only downside is that if you turn onto this alternate route, you will kill a different innocent person (but only one). Do you switch to the alternate track and kill one person in order to save five? [The folks usually credited with the creation and popularization of this dilemma are Philippa Foot and Judith Jarvis Thomson, but I'm roughly paraphrasing how it's described in Michael Sandel's wonderful book *Justice*.]

When you pose this question to any normal reader, they almost always say yes. It seems insane to kill five people instead of one. But that's not the true question; that's just the introduction. The real question is this: Let's say you're *not* operating the runaway trolley. Let's say you're not the conductor. Let's propose that you're just watching this event from a bridge above the track. You realize this runaway trolley is going to kill five people. You notice another person is watching this event alongside you—an extremely obese man. It dawns on you that if you push this man onto the track below, it will derail the trolley. Here again, you are killing one man in order to save five. Do you push the fat man off the bridge?

This second scenario always troubles people more: The most common answer tends to be, "I know these things are basically the same, but I could never push a man to his death." The reason people feel different is due to how the two scenarios position the decision maker. In the first problem, the decision maker is accepting the existing conditions and trying to choose whatever solution hurts the fewest individuals. In the second problem, the decision maker is injecting himself into the situation and taking on the responsibility of the outcome. The first scenario is a reaction. The second is a self-directed choice. What bothers people about WikiLeaks is that it creates a world in which the second scenario is happening constantly, and what bothers people about Assange is the way he makes that choice seem so stupidly self-evident.

Assange's belief is that everyone would be better off if all information was equally (and immediately) available. His critics say, "That's irresponsible. If you just release information—and particularly military information—without considering its sensitivity, someone will get killed." And that's probably true. If WikiLeaks continues in its current iteration, I'm sure it will (eventually) contribute to someone's death. But Assange makes us consider the larger value of that troubling possibility. What if the relentless release of classified information makes every nation less willing to conduct questionable military actions? Will this force all society to become more honest (and wouldn't that future reality be worth the loss of a hundred innocent people in the present)? Or would it actually make things worse? Will the fear of exposure simply prompt political figures to resist creating any paper trail at all? Will *everything* become hidden? I really have no idea. No one does, and that's the discomfort: We don't know if the old way is better (or worse) than the new way. But Assange does not let us choose. He possesses a sweeping technological advantage, and he knows that released information cannot be retracted. He can make us accept his philosophy against our will. Once a document is released, how we feel about the nature of its existence becomes meaningless; it's instantaneously absorbed into the media bloodstream as pure content. This is why Assange can make an argument that openly advocates actions that (in his words) "might be immoral." Those actions are going to happen anyway, so he doesn't have to pretend that they contradict the way we've always viewed morality. He doesn't have to convince us he's right, because our thoughts don't matter. His view of *everything* is like Perez Hilton's view of gossip or Kim Dotcom's view of entertainment: He believes everything longs to be free. And he will make that happen, because he knows how to do it and we don't know how to stop him. He's already beaten everybody. It was never close.

Questions for Critical Reading

1. How would you define *villainy*? What differentiates it from *evil*? Develop your own definition and then, as you reread Klosterman's essay, note places where he supports or challenges your definition. What do you think villainy means to Klosterman?
2. What are the benefits and costs of technology? Locate passages where Klosterman discusses this issue.
3. Klosterman focuses quite a bit on the inevitability of progress. Mark passages where he suggests there is something problematic, if not villainous, about this position.

Exploring Context

1. Kim Dotcom's website is located at kim.com. In what ways does the site suggest that Dotcom has capitalized on his infamy? How does it reflect your work on the inevitability of technological progress from Question 3 of Questions for Critical Reading?
2. Visit Perez Hilton's blog at perezhilton.com. How does the site reinforce or challenge Klosterman's claims about Hilton and villainy?
3. WikiLeaks (wikileaks.org) remains quite an active website. Explore the site. Do you think the information contained there does good or harm?

Questions for Connecting

1. Peter Singer, in "Visible Man: Ethics in a World without Secrets" (p. 353), also examines WikiLeaks. Apply Klosterman's analysis to Singer's essay. Does Singer's discussion confirm or complicate Klosterman's thoughts on the controversial website? Is sousveillance villainous? Use your work from Question 1 of Questions for Critical Reading and Question 3 of Exploring Context in composing your response.

2. Adrian Chen seems to offer a different perspective on technology in "Unfollow" (p. 73). Apply Chen's analysis to Klosterman's argument. How can technology be used as a positive force for social and individual change? How does this complicate notions of "villainy"? Use your work from Questions for Critical Reading in forming your response.

3. Questions of crime and justice surround two of Klosterman's main examples, Kim Dotcom and Julian Assange. How might Andrew Cohen's discussion of the laws around drug epidemics in "Race and the Opioid Epidemic" (p. 97) offer a new context for these issues? Is there a racial dimension to the cases of Dotcom and Assange? How does the additional context of drug sentencing laws help us to rethink the larger concept of villainy?

Language Matters

1. Klosterman offers an analysis of Kim Dotcom's open letter to the *Hollywood Reporter*. Review this passage to see how Klosterman analyzes Dotcom's text. First evaluate Klosterman's analysis and then perform a similar analysis on a passage you feel is important in Klosterman's essay. How might you use these techniques to help you analyze and then improve your own writing?

2. Using Flickr (flickr.com), search for images that illustrate Klosterman's argument. Paste these images into a document to create a visual montage of this essay. What commonalities can you see in the images that weren't immediately apparent in the essay?

3. Drafting and revising are crucial components of the writing process. We often see a published piece of writing as perfect, but imagine earlier drafts of Klosterman's text. How do you think he started this piece? What areas do you think he revised the most? Where do you think you should do the most revision as you draft your own papers?

Assignments for Writing

1. What is villainy? Write a paper in which you develop a definition of *villainy* supported with quotations from Klosterman's text. You may want to draw from your work in Questions for Critical Reading and Exploring Context in developing your argument.

2. Klosterman's analysis of villainy in this essay is closely tied to the sense that the future of technology cannot and should not be stopped. Write a paper in which you examine the costs of technological progress.

3. None of the figures that Klosterman discusses seem particularly evil. Are any of them, then, villains? Select one of the cases that Klosterman uses and then provide your own analysis to determine whether or not that person is in fact a villain. You might find your work from Questions for Critical Reading useful as a starting point, and you may want to use your insights from Exploring Context to support your argument.

MARIA KONNIKOVA

Maria Konnikova was born in Moscow, Russia, and emigrated to the United States as a child. She studied psychology, creative writing, and government at Harvard University before receiving her Ph.D. in psychology from Columbia University. Konnikova's writing has appeared in popular publications such *as The Atlantic*, the *New York Times*, *Slate*, the *New Republic*, the *Wall Street Journal*, *Salon*, and *Scientific American*, and until 2016 she wrote a weekly column for the *New Yorker* online in which she focused on psychology and science. Her *New York Times* best-selling book *Mastermind: How to Think Like Sherlock Holmes* was nominated for the Agatha Award and the Anthony Award for Best Nonfiction.

"The Limits of Friendship" was published October 7, 2014, in the online version of the *New Yorker*. The *New Yorker*, both in print and online, offers notable commentary on politics, global affairs, art and popular culture, and science and technology. It also publishes short fiction and poetry and is famous for its cartoons. The October 7, 2014, online edition also included articles on Ebola, New York's High Line green space, and the role of the website Reddit in Spanish politics.

In this essay, Konnikova explores the Dunbar number, the theoretical number of friends we can really have, and the ways in which social networking is affecting not only this number but also socialization itself. Along with anthropologist and psychologist Robin Dunbar, she questions whether increasingly pervasive virtual interaction will influence the friend groups and social skills of new generations. Asks Konnikova: "So what happens if you're raised from a young age to see virtual interactions as akin to physical ones?" (p. 259).

Are virtual friends replacing actual friends? How many friends do you feel you have?

- TAGS: *community, culture, identity, media, psychology, relationships, science and technology, social change, social media*
- CONNECTIONS: *Appiah, Chen, Epstein, Gilbert, Klosterman, Pollan, Singer, Turkle*

The Limits of Friendship

Robin Dunbar came up with his eponymous number almost by accident. The University of Oxford anthropologist and psychologist (then at University College London) was trying to solve the problem of why primates devote so much time and effort to grooming. In the process of figuring out the solution, he chanced upon a potentially far more intriguing application for his research. At the time, in the nineteen-eighties, the Machiavellian Intelligence Hypothesis (now known as the Social Brain Hypothesis) had just been introduced into anthropological and primatology discourse.[1] It held that primates have large brains because they live in socially complex societies: the larger the group, the larger the brain. Thus, from the size of an animal's neocortex, the frontal lobe in particular, you could theoretically predict the group size for that animal.

Looking at his grooming data, Dunbar made the mental leap to humans. "We also had humans in our data set so it occurred to me to look to see what size group that relationship might predict for humans," he told me recently. Dunbar did the math, using a ratio of neocortical volume to total brain volume and mean group size, and came up with a number.[2] Judging from the size of an average human brain, the number of people the average person could have in her social group was a hundred and fifty. Anything beyond that would be too complicated to handle at optimal processing levels. For the last twenty-two years, Dunbar has been "unpacking and exploring" what that number actually means—and whether our ever-expanding social networks have done anything to change it.

The Dunbar number is actually a series of them. The best known, a hundred and fifty, is the number of people we call casual friends—the people, say, you'd invite to a large party. (In reality, it's a range: a hundred at the low end and two hundred for the more social of us.) From there, through qualitative interviews coupled with analysis of experimental and survey data, Dunbar discovered that the number grows and decreases according to a precise formula, roughly a "rule of three."[3] The next step down, fifty, is the number of people we call close friends—perhaps the people you'd invite to a group dinner. You see them often, but not so much that you consider them to be true intimates. Then there's the circle of fifteen: the friends that you can turn to for sympathy when you need it, the ones you can confide in about most things. The most intimate Dunbar number, five, is your close support group. These are your best friends (and often family members). On the flip side, groups can extend to five hundred, the acquaintance level, and to fifteen hundred, the absolute limit—the people for whom you can put a name to a face. While the group sizes are relatively stable, their composition can be fluid. Your five today may not be your five next week; people drift among layers and sometimes fall out of them altogether.

When Dunbar consulted the anthropological and historical record, he found remarkable consistency in support of his structure. The average group size among modern hunter-gatherer societies (where there was accurate census data) was 148.4 individuals. Company size in professional armies, Dunbar found, was also remarkably close to a hundred and fifty, from the Roman Empire to sixteenth-century Spain to the twentieth-century Soviet Union. Companies, in turn, tended to be broken down into smaller units of around fifty then further divided into sections of between ten and fifteen. At the opposite end, the companies formed battalions that ranged from five hundred and fifty to eight hundred, and even larger regiments.

Dunbar then decided to go beyond the existing evidence and into experimental methods. In one early study, the first empirical demonstration of the Dunbar number in action, he and the Durham University anthropologist Russell Hill examined the destinations of Christmas cards sent from households all over the UK—a socially pervasive practice, Dunbar explained to me, carried out by most typical households.[4] Dunbar and Hill had each household list its Christmas card recipients and rate them on several scales. "When you looked at the pattern, there was a sense that there were distinct subgroups in there," Dunbar said. If you considered the number of people in each sending household and each recipient household, each individual's network was composed of about a hundred and fifty people. And within that network, people fell into circles of relative closeness—family, friends, neighbors, and work colleagues. Those circles conformed to Dunbar's breakdown.

As constant use of social media has become the new normal, however, people have started challenging the continued relevance of Dunbar's number: Isn't it easier to have more friends when we have Facebook, Twitter, and Instagram to help us to cultivate and maintain them? Some, like the University of California, Berkeley, professor Morten Hansen, have pointed out that social media has facilitated more effective collaborations. Our real-world friends tend to know the same people that we do, but, in the online world, we can expand our networks strategically, leading to better business outcomes. Yet, when researchers tried to determine whether virtual networks increase our strong ties as well as our weak ones (the ones that Hansen had focused on), they found that, for now, the essential Dunbar number, a hundred and fifty, has remained constant. When Bruno Gonçalves and his colleagues at Indiana University at Bloomington looked at whether Twitter had changed the number of relationships that users could maintain over a six-month period, they found that, despite the relative ease of Twitter connections as opposed to face-to-face ones, the individuals that they followed could only manage between one and two hundred stable connections. When the Michigan State University researcher Nicole Ellison surveyed a random sample of undergraduates about their Facebook use, she found that while their median number of Facebook friends was three hundred, they only counted an average of seventy-five as actual friends.[5]

There's no question, Dunbar agrees, that networks like Facebook are changing the nature of human interaction. "What Facebook does and why it's been so successful in so many ways is it allows you to keep track of people who would otherwise effectively disappear," he said. But one of the things that keeps face-to-face friendships strong is the nature of shared experience: you laugh together; you dance together; you gape at the hot-dog eaters on Coney Island together.[6] We do have a social-media equivalent—sharing, liking, knowing that all of your friends have looked at the same cat video on YouTube as you did—but it lacks the synchronicity of shared experience. It's like a comedy that you watch by yourself: you won't laugh as loudly or as often, even if you're fully aware that all your friends think it's hysterical. We've seen the same movie, but we can't bond over it in the same way.

With social media, we can easily keep up with the lives and interests of far more than a hundred and fifty people. But without investing the face-to-face time, we lack deeper connections to them, and the time we invest in superficial relationships comes at the expense of more profound ones. We may widen our network to two, three, or four hundred people that we see as friends, not just acquaintances, but keeping up an actual friendship requires resources. "The amount of social capital you have is pretty fixed," Dunbar said. "It involves time investment. If you garner connections with more people, you end up distributing your fixed amount of social capital more thinly so the average capital per person is lower." If we're busy putting in the effort, however minimal, to "like" and comment and interact with an ever-widening network, we have less time and capacity left for our closer groups. Traditionally, it's a sixty-forty split of attention: we spend sixty percent of our time with our core groups of fifty, fifteen, and five, and forty with the larger spheres. Social networks may be growing our base, and, in the process, reversing that balance.

"The amount of social capital you have is pretty fixed."

On an even deeper level, there may be a physiological aspect of friendship that virtual connections can never replace. This wouldn't surprise Dunbar, who discovered his number when he was studying the social bonding that occurs among primates through grooming. Over the past few years, Dunbar and his colleagues have been looking at the importance of touch in sparking the sort of neurological and physiological responses that, in turn, lead to bonding and friendship. "We underestimate how important touch is in the social world," he said. With a light brush on the shoulder, a pat, or a squeeze of the arm or hand, we can communicate a deeper bond than through speaking alone. "Words are easy. But the way someone touches you, even casually, tells you more about what they're thinking of you."

Dunbar already knew that in monkeys grooming activated the endorphin system.[7] Was the same true in humans? In a series of studies, Dunbar and his colleagues demonstrated that very light touch triggers a cascade of endorphins that, in turn, are important for creating personal relationships. Because measuring endorphin release directly is invasive—you either need to perform a spinal tap or a PET scan, and the latter, though considered safe, involves injecting a person with a radioactive tracer—they first looked at endorphin release indirectly. In one study, they examined pain thresholds: how long a person could keep her hand in a bucket of ice water (in a lab), or how long she could maintain a sitting position with no chair present (back against the wall, legs bent at a ninety degree angle) in the field.[8] When your body is flooded with endorphins, you're able to withstand pain for longer than you could before, so pain tolerance is often used as a proxy for endorphin levels. The longer you can stand the pain, the more endorphins have been released into your system. They found that a shared experience of laughter—a synchronous, face-to-face experience—prior to immersion, be it in the lab (watching a neutral or funny movie with others) or in a natural setting (theatre performances at the 2008 Edinburgh Fringe Festival) enabled people to hold their hands in ice or maintain the chair position significantly longer than they'd previously been able to.

Next, in an ongoing study, Dunbar and his colleagues looked at how endorphins were activated in the brain directly, through PET scans, a procedure that lets you look at how different neural receptors uptake endorphins. The researchers saw the same thing that happened with monkeys, and that had earlier been demonstrated with humans that were viewing positive emotional stimuli: when subjects in the scanner were lightly touched, their bodies released endorphins.[9] "We were nervous we wouldn't find anything because the touch was so light," Dunbar said. "Astonishingly, we saw a phenomenal response." In fact, this makes a great deal of sense and answers a lot of longstanding questions about our sensory receptors, he explained. Our skin has a set of neurons, common to all mammals, that respond to light stroking, but not to any other kind of touch. Unlike other touch receptors, which operate on a loop—you touch a hot stove, the nerves fire a signal to the brain, the brain registers pain and fires a signal back for you to withdraw your hand—these receptors are one-way. They talk to the brain, but the brain doesn't communicate back. "We think that's what they exist for, to trigger endorphin responses as a consequence of grooming," Dunbar said. Until social media can replicate that touch, it can't fully replicate social bonding.

But, the truth is, no one really knows how relevant the Dunbar number will remain in a world increasingly dominated by virtual interactions. The brain is incredibly plastic, and, from past research[10] on social interaction, we know that early childhood experience is crucial in developing those parts of the brain that are largely dedicated to social interaction, empathy, and other interpersonal concerns.[11] Deprive a child of interaction and touch early on, and those areas won't develop fully. Envelop her in a huge family or friend group, with plenty of holding and shared experience, and those areas grow bigger. So what happens if you're raised from a young age to see virtual interactions as akin to physical ones? "This is the big imponderable," Dunbar said. "We haven't yet seen an entire generation that's grown up with things like Facebook go through adulthood yet." Dunbar himself doesn't have a firm opinion one way or the other about whether virtual social networks will prove wonderful for friendships or ultimately diminish the number of satisfying interactions one has. "I don't think we have enough evidence to argue either way," he said.

One concern, though, is that some social skills may not develop as effectively when so many interactions exist online. We learn how we are and aren't supposed to act by observing others and then having opportunities to act out our observations ourselves. We aren't born with full social awareness, and Dunbar fears that too much virtual interaction may subvert that education. "In the sandpit of life, when somebody kicks sand in your face, you can't get out of the sandpit. You have to deal with it, learn, compromise," he said. "On the internet, you can pull the plug and walk away. There's no forcing mechanism that makes us have to learn." If you spend most of your time online, you may not get enough in-person group experience to learn how to properly interact on a large scale—a fear that, some early evidence suggests, may be materializing.[12] "It's quite conceivable that we might end up less social in the future, which would be a disaster because we need to be more social—our world has become so large," Dunbar said. The more our virtual friends replace our face-to-face ones, in fact, the more our Dunbar number may shrink.

NOTES

1. *MIT Encyclopedia of Cognitive Science*, s.v. "Machiavellian Intelligence Hypothesis," by Andrew Whiten, http://ai.ato.ms/MITECS/Entry/whiten.html.
2. R. I. M. Dunbar, "Coevolution of Neocortical Size, Group Size and Language in Humans," *Behavioral and Brain Sciences* 16 (1993): 681–735.
3. W.-X. Zhou et al., "Discrete Hierarchical Organization of Social Group Sizes," *Proceedings of the Royal Society* B 272 (2005): 439–44.
4. R. A. Hill and R. I. M. Dunbar, "Social Network Size in Humans," *Human Nature* 14, no. 1 (2003): 53–72.
5. Nicole B. Ellison et al., "Connection Strategies: Social Capital Implications of Facebook-Enabled Communication Practices," *New Media Society* 13 (2011): 873–92.
6. Curtis D. Hardin and Terri D. Conley, "A Relational Approach to Cognition: Shared Experience and Relationship Affirmation in Social Cognition," in *Cognitive Social Psychology: The Princeton Symposium on the Legacy and Future of Social Cognition*, ed. Gordon B. Moskowitz (Mahwah, NJ: Lawrence Erlbaum Associates Publishers, 2001), 3–17.
7. R. I. Dunbar, "The Social Role of Touch in Humans and Primates: Behavioural Function and Neurobiological Mechanisms," *Neuroscience and Biobehavioral Reviews* 34, no. 2 (2010): 260–68.
8. R. I. M. Dunbar et al., "Social Laughter Is Correlated with an Elevated Pain Threshold," *Proceedings of the Royal Society* B 279 (2012): 1161–67.
9. M. J. Koepp et al., "Evidence for Endogenous Opioid Release in the Amygdala during Positive Emotion," *NeuroImage* 44, no. 1 (2009): 252–56.

10. Jack P. Shonkoff and Deborah A. Phillips, eds., *From Neurons to Neighborhoods: The Science of Early Childhood Development* (Washington, DC: National Academy Press, 2000).
11. Charles A. Nelson, "Neural Plasticity and Human Development," *Current Directions in Psychological Science* 8, no. 2 (1999): 42–45.
12. Aimee L. Drolet and Michael W. Morris, "Rapport in Conflict Resolution: Accounting for How Face-to-Face Contact Fosters Mutual Cooperation in Mixed-Motive Conflicts," *Journal of Experimental Social Psychology* 36, no. 1 (2000): 26–50; Mitzi M. Montoya-Weiss et al., "Getting It Together: Temporal Coordination and Conflict Management in Global Virtual Teams," *Academy of Management Journal* 44, no. 6 (2001): 1251–62.

Questions for Critical Reading

1. As you reread, mark passages where Konnikova defines the *Dunbar number* and the *rule of three*. Then explain these terms in your own words, referencing specific passages from Konnikova to support your response.
2. What do you think makes a good friend? List the qualities of close friendship. As you review the essay, consider the effect of social media on friendship.
3. What's the role of biology in social organization? Examine closely those places where Konnikova draws from the research of Robin Dunbar and others. Does biology determine society?

Exploring Context

1. Examine your list of friends on Facebook or another social media or online gaming site. How many of them are "real" friends? Try applying the rule of three to your list of friends. Does your experience confirm or challenge Konnikova's argument?
2. After you've examined your list of friends from Question 1 of Exploring Context, compare that list to the numbers you keep in your phone. Does the number of people you call relate to the Dunbar number? Does your phone reflect closer friendships than your social media presence?
3. Use a web search engine to look for images of the Dunbar number. How do these visual representations help explain the concept?

Questions for Connecting

1. Sherry Turkle, in "The Empathy Diaries" (p. 378), seems to share some of Konnikova's concerns about the impact of social media on our relationships with others. Synthesize her ideas with Konnikova's analysis. How does social media impact our ability to connect? Does Turkle's essay also reflect the relevance of the rule of three? Use your work from Question 1 of Questions for Critical Reading as you make your response.
2. Is there a generational component to the ability to connect in a digital age? How might emerging adults challenge the conventional understanding of the Dunbar number? Use Robin Marantz Henig's work in "What Is It about 20-Somethings?" (p. 201) to complicate Konnikova's argument.

3. Close friendships formed online through social media are deeply impactful for Megan Phelps-Roper in Adrian Chen's "Unfollow" (p. 73). Use Chen's narrative to complicate Konnikova's argument. Does Phelps-Roper reflect the importance of the rule of three? How did her immediate social groups shift and what role did social media play in that shift? You may want to use your work with Konnikova's core concepts from Question 1 of Questions for Critical Reading.

Language Matters

1. Most often Konnikova spells out numbers, though occasionally she uses numerals instead. Using a grammar handbook or other reference resource, review the rules for writing numbers. When should they be spelled out, and when should numerals be used? Apply your findings to Konnikova's text. Does she follow these rules? How can you bring these insights to your own writing?
2. Quotations should always be integrated fluidly. Locate three instances where Konnikova includes quotations. What strategies does she use to integrate quotations into her own sentences? How can you apply these techniques to your own writing?
3. Editors often use correction symbols; your instructor might use them as well. Design symbols to represent some common errors you make. How are design and meaning related? Would your symbols make immediate sense to someone else?

Assignments for Writing

1. Write a paper in which you evaluate virtual friendships. Do they have advantages that Konnikova doesn't consider? You may want to use your work from Question 2 of Questions for Critical Reading and Question 3 of Questions for Connecting.
2. Robin Dunbar's research focuses on the relationship between the social and the biological. Write a paper in which you evaluate the ways in which culture is determined by biology. Are we limited by our biological impulses or can we transcend them? You may find your work from Question 3 of Questions for Critical Reading useful.
3. How does technology influence social and biological evolution? Write a paper in which you use Konnikova's work to consider the ways in which technology is affecting our development. Draw from your work in Question 3 of Questions for Critical Reading in making your response.

GREG LUKIANOFF AND JONATHAN HAIDT

Greg Lukianoff, an attorney who studied at Stanford Law School, is the president of the Foundation for Individual Rights in Education (FIRE), a nonprofit group whose mission focuses on issues of free speech, due process, and civil liberties in academia. He is the author of two books: *Unlearning Liberty: Campus Censorship and the End of American Debate* (2012), which examines the culture of censorship in American colleges and universities, and *Freedom from Speech* (2014), which looks at the rise of speech restrictions around the world. His writing has also appeared in the *Wall Street Journal*, the *Washington Post*, the *New York Times*, and the *Los Angeles Times*, and he has testified before Congress on free speech issues on college campuses. In 2008, he received the Playboy Foundation's first Freedom of Expression Award. **Jonathan Haidt**, who received his Ph.D. from the University of Pennsylvania, is the Thomas Cooley Professor of Ethical Leadership at New York University's Stern School of Business. As a social psychologist, Haidt researches morality and moral emotions. He is the author of *The Happiness Hypothesis: Finding Modern Truth in Ancient Wisdom* (2005), which looks at common philosophical wisdom through a psychological lens, and *The Righteous Mind: Why Good People are Divided by Politics and Religion* (2012), which explores the origins of our currently divided society and offers suggestions for a way to move forward. Together, Lukianoff and Haidt are working on a book called *Misguided Minds.*

"The Coddling of the American Mind" was first published as the cover story for the September 2015 issue of *The Atlantic.* Since 1857, *The Atlantic* has published book reviews and commentary on culture, politics, the economy, and foreign affairs and is known for its politically moderate viewpoint. The September 2015 issue also included pieces on molecular gastronomy, Republican foreign policy, and an essay by Ta-Nehisi Coates, whose work is also included in this textbook.

In this essay, Lukianoff and Haidt examine the rise of speech restrictions on American college campuses, including the demand for trigger warnings in relation to any material that might seem damaging to those who have suffered trauma and the policing of microaggressions, small actions or words that may seem minor or harmless but are thought of as a kind violence. The authors use a range of psychological concepts to argue that such moves harm the atmosphere of education, the promotion of critical thinking, and the very students they are intended to protect.

How does your school police speech? Should it?

- TAGS: *adolescence and adulthood, censorship, civil rights, education, identity, law and justice, psychology, race and ethnicity, social change, trauma and violence*
- CONNECTIONS: *Appiah, Chen, Coates, DeGhett, Fukuyama, Gay, Gilbert, Holmes, Klosterman, Ma, Moalem, Serano, Singer, Stillman, Turkle, von Busch, Yoshino*

The Coddling of the American Mind

Something strange is happening at America's colleges and universities. A movement is arising, undirected and driven largely by students, to scrub campuses clean of words, ideas, and subjects that might cause discomfort or give offense. Last December, Jeannie Suk wrote in an online article for *The New Yorker* about law students asking her fellow professors at Harvard not to teach rape law—or, in one case, even use the word *violate* (as in "that violates the law") lest it cause students distress. In February, Laura Kipnis, a professor at Northwestern University, wrote an essay in *The Chronicle of Higher Education* describing a new campus politics of sexual paranoia—and was then subjected to a long investigation after students who were offended by the article and by a tweet she'd sent filed Title IX complaints against her. In June, a professor protecting himself with a pseudonym wrote an essay for Vox describing how gingerly he now has to teach. "I'm a Liberal Professor, and My Liberal Students Terrify Me," the headline said. A number of popular comedians, including Chris Rock, have stopped performing on college campuses (see Caitlin Flanagan's article in this month's issue). Jerry Seinfeld and Bill Maher have publicly condemned the oversensitivity of college students, saying too many of them can't take a joke.

Two terms have risen quickly from obscurity into common campus parlance. *Microaggressions* are small actions or word choices that seem on their face to have no malicious intent but that are thought of as a kind of violence nonetheless. For example, by some campus guidelines, it is a microaggression to ask an Asian American or Latino American "Where were you born?," because this implies that he or she is not a real American. *Trigger warnings* are alerts that professors are expected to issue if something in a course might cause a strong emotional response. For example, some students have called for warnings that Chinua Achebe's *Things Fall Apart* describes racial violence and that F. Scott Fitzgerald's *The Great Gatsby* portrays misogyny and physical abuse, so that students who have been previously victimized by racism or domestic violence can choose to avoid these works, which they believe might "trigger" a recurrence of past trauma.

Some recent campus actions border on the surreal. In April, at Brandeis University, the Asian American student association sought to raise awareness of microaggressions against Asians through an installation on the steps of an academic hall. The installation gave examples of microaggressions such as "Aren't you supposed to be good at math?" and "I'm colorblind! I don't see race." But a backlash arose among other Asian American students, who felt that the display itself was a microaggression. The association removed the installation, and its president wrote an email to the entire student body apologizing to anyone who was "triggered or hurt by the content of the microaggressions."

This new climate is slowly being institutionalized, and is affecting what can be said in the classroom, even as a basis for discussion. During the 2014–2015 school year, for instance, the deans and department chairs at the 10 University of California system schools were presented by administrators at faculty leader-training sessions with examples of microaggressions. The list of offensive statements included: "America is the land of opportunity" and "I believe the most qualified person should get the job."

5 The press has typically described these developments as a resurgence of political correctness. That's partly right, although there are important differences between what's happening now and what happened in the 1980s and '90s. That movement sought to restrict speech (specifically hate speech aimed at marginalized groups), but it also challenged the literary, philosophical, and historical canon, seeking to widen

it by including more-diverse perspectives. The current movement is largely about emotional well-being. More than the last, it presumes an extraordinary fragility of the collegiate psyche, and therefore elevates the goal of protecting students from psychological harm. The ultimate aim, it seems, is to turn campuses into "safe spaces" where young adults are shielded from words and ideas that make some uncomfortable. And more than the last, this movement seeks to punish anyone who interferes with that aim, even accidentally. You might call this impulse *vindictive protectiveness*. It is creating a culture in which everyone must think twice before speaking up, lest they face charges of insensitivity, aggression, or worse.

It presumes an extraordinary fragility of the collegiate psyche, and therefore elevates the goal of protecting students from psychological harm.

We have been studying this development for a while now, with rising alarm. (Greg Lukianoff is a constitutional lawyer and the president and CEO of the Foundation for Individual Rights in Education, which defends free speech and academic freedom on campus, and has advocated for students and faculty involved in many of the incidents this article describes; Jonathan Haidt is a social psychologist who studies the American culture wars.) The dangers that these trends pose to scholarship and to the quality of American universities are significant; we could write a whole essay detailing them. But in this essay we focus on a different question: What are the effects of this new protectiveness *on the students themselves*? Does it benefit the people it is supposed to help? What exactly are students learning when they spend four years or more in a community that polices unintentional slights, places warning labels on works of classic literature, and in many other ways conveys the sense that words can be forms of violence that require strict control by campus authorities, who are expected to act as both protectors and prosecutors?

There's a saying common in education circles: Don't teach students *what* to think; teach them *how* to think. The idea goes back at least as far as Socrates. Today, what we call the Socratic method is a way of teaching that fosters critical thinking, in part by encouraging students to question their own unexamined beliefs, as well as the received wisdom of those around them. Such questioning sometimes leads to discomfort, and even to anger, on the way to understanding.

But vindictive protectiveness teaches students to think in a very different way. It prepares them poorly for professional life, which often demands intellectual engagement with people and ideas one might find uncongenial or wrong. The harm may be more immediate, too. A campus culture devoted to policing speech and punishing speakers is likely to engender patterns of thought that are surprisingly similar to those long identified by cognitive behavioral therapists as causes of depression and anxiety. The new protectiveness may be teaching students to think pathologically.

How Did We Get Here?

It's difficult to know exactly why vindictive protectiveness has burst forth so powerfully in the past few years. The phenomenon may be related to recent changes in the interpretation of federal anti-discrimination statutes (about which more later). But the answer probably involves generational shifts as well. Childhood itself has changed greatly during the past generation. Many Baby Boomers and Gen Xers can remember riding their bicycles around their hometowns, unchaperoned by adults, by the time they were 8 or 9 years old. In the hours after school, kids were expected to occupy themselves, getting into minor scrapes and learning from their experiences. But "free range" childhood became less common in the 1980s. The surge in crime from the '60s through the early '90s made Baby Boomer parents more protective than their own parents had been. Stories of abducted children appeared more frequently in the news, and in 1984, images of them began showing up on milk cartons. In response, many parents pulled in the reins and worked harder to keep their children safe.

The flight to safety also happened at school. Dangerous play structures were removed from playgrounds; peanut butter was banned from student lunches. After the 1999 Columbine massacre in Colorado, many schools cracked down on bullying, implementing "zero tolerance" policies. In a variety of ways, children born after 1980—the Millennials—got a consistent message from adults: life is dangerous, but adults will do everything in their power to protect you from harm, not just from strangers but from one another as well. 10

These same children grew up in a culture that was (and still is) becoming more politically polarized. Republicans and Democrats have never particularly liked each other, but survey data going back to the 1970s show that on average, their mutual dislike used to be surprisingly mild. Negative feelings have grown steadily stronger, however, particularly since the early 2000s. Political scientists call this process "affective partisan polarization," and it is a very serious problem for any democracy. As each side increasingly demonizes the other, compromise becomes more difficult. A recent study shows that implicit or unconscious biases are now at least as strong across political parties as they are across races.

So it's not hard to imagine why students arriving on campus today might be more desirous of protection and more hostile toward ideological opponents than in generations past. This hostility, and the self-righteousness fueled by strong partisan emotions, can be expected to add force to any moral crusade. A principle of moral psychology is that "morality binds and blinds." Part of what we do when we make moral judgments is express allegiance to a team. But that can interfere with our ability to think critically. Acknowledging that the other side's viewpoint has any merit is risky—your teammates may see you as a traitor.

Social media makes it extraordinarily easy to join crusades, express solidarity and outrage, and shun traitors. Facebook was founded in 2004, and since 2006 it has allowed children as young as 13 to join. This means that the first wave of students who spent all their teen years using Facebook reached college in 2011, and graduated from college only this year.

These first true "social-media natives" may be different from members of previous generations in how they go about sharing their moral judgments and supporting one another in moral campaigns and conflicts. We find much to like about these trends; young people today are engaged with one another, with news stories, and with pro-social endeavors to a greater degree than when the dominant technology was television. But social media has also fundamentally shifted the balance of power in relationships between students and faculty; the latter increasingly fear what students might do to their reputations and careers by stirring up online mobs against them.

15 We do not mean to imply simple causation, but rates of mental illness in young adults have been rising, both on campus and off, in recent decades. Some portion of the increase is surely due to better diagnosis and greater willingness to seek help, but most experts seem to agree that some portion of the trend is real. Nearly all of the campus mental-health directors surveyed in 2013 by the American College Counseling Association reported that the number of students with severe psychological problems was rising at their schools. The rate of emotional distress reported by students themselves is also high, and rising. In a 2014 survey by the American College Health Association, 54 percent of college students surveyed said that they had "felt overwhelming anxiety" in the past 12 months, up from 49 percent in the same survey just five years earlier. Students seem to be reporting more emotional crises; many seem fragile, and this has surely changed the way university faculty and administrators interact with them. The question is whether some of those changes might be doing more harm than good.

The Thinking Cure

For millennia, philosophers have understood that we don't see life as it is; we see a version distorted by our hopes, fears, and other attachments. The Buddha said, "Our life is the creation of our mind." Marcus Aurelius said, "Life itself is but what you deem it." The quest for wisdom in many traditions begins with this insight. Early Buddhists and the Stoics, for example, developed practices for reducing attachments, thinking more clearly, and finding release from the emotional torments of normal mental life.

Cognitive behavioral therapy is a modern embodiment of this ancient wisdom. It is the most extensively studied nonpharmaceutical treatment of mental illness, and is used widely to treat depression, anxiety disorders, eating disorders, and addiction. It can even be of help to schizophrenics. No other form of psychotherapy has been shown to work for a broader range of problems. Studies have generally found that it is as effective as antidepressant drugs (such as Prozac) in the treatment of anxiety and depression. The therapy is relatively quick and easy to learn; after a few months of training, many patients can do it on their own. Unlike drugs, cognitive behavioral therapy keeps working long after treatment is stopped, because it teaches thinking skills that people can continue to use.

The goal is to minimize distorted thinking and see the world more accurately. You start by learning the names of the dozen or so most common cognitive distortions (such as overgeneralizing, discounting positives, and emotional reasoning; see the list at the bottom of this article). Each time you notice yourself falling prey to one of them, you name it, describe the facts of the situation, consider alternative interpretations, and then choose an interpretation of events more in line with those facts. Your emotions follow your new interpretation. In time, this process becomes automatic. When people improve their mental hygiene in this way—when they free themselves from the repetitive irrational thoughts that had previously filled so much of their consciousness—they become less depressed, anxious, and angry.

The parallel to formal education is clear: cognitive behavioral therapy teaches good critical-thinking skills, the sort that educators have striven for so long to impart. By almost any definition, critical thinking requires grounding one's beliefs in evidence rather than in emotion or desire, and learning how to search for and evaluate evidence that might contradict one's initial hypothesis. But does campus life today foster critical thinking? Or does it coax students to think in more-distorted ways?

20 Let's look at recent trends in higher education in light of the distortions that cognitive behavioral therapy identifies. We will draw the names and descriptions of these distortions from David D. Burns's popular book *Feeling Good*, as well as from the second edition of *Treatment Plans and Interventions for Depression and Anxiety Disorders*, by Robert L. Leahy, Stephen J. F. Holland, and Lata K. McGinn.

Higher Education's Embrace of "Emotional Reasoning"

Burns defines *emotional reasoning* as assuming "that your negative emotions necessarily reflect the way things really are: 'I feel it, therefore it must be true.'" Leahy, Holland, and McGinn define it as letting "your feelings guide your interpretation of reality." But, of course, subjective feelings are not always trustworthy guides; unrestrained, they can cause people to lash out at others who have done nothing wrong. Therapy often involves talking yourself down from the idea that each of your emotional responses represents something true or important.

Emotional reasoning dominates many campus debates and discussions. A claim that someone's words are "offensive" is not just an expression of one's own subjective feeling of offendedness. It is, rather, a public charge that the speaker has done something objectively wrong. It is a demand that the speaker apologize or be punished by some authority for committing an offense.

There have always been some people who believe they have a right not to be offended. Yet throughout American history—from the Victorian era to the free-speech activism of the 1960s and '70s—radicals have pushed boundaries and mocked prevailing sensibilities. Sometime in the 1980s, however, college campuses began to focus on preventing offensive speech, especially speech that might be hurtful to women or minority groups. The sentiment underpinning this goal was laudable, but it quickly produced some absurd results.

Among the most famous early examples was the so-called water-buffalo incident at the University of Pennsylvania. In 1993, the university charged an Israeli-born student with racial harassment after he yelled "Shut up, you water buffalo!" to a crowd of black sorority women that was making noise at night outside his dorm-room window. Many scholars and pundits at the time could not see how the term *water buffalo* (a rough translation of a Hebrew insult for a thoughtless or rowdy person) was a racial slur against African Americans, and as a result, the case became international news.

25 Claims of a right not to be offended have continued to arise since then, and universities have continued to privilege them. In a particularly egregious 2008 case, for instance, Indiana University–Purdue University at Indianapolis found a white student guilty of racial harassment for reading a book titled *Notre Dame vs. the Klan*. The book honored student opposition to the Ku Klux Klan when it marched on Notre Dame in 1924. Nonetheless, the picture of a Klan rally on the book's cover offended at least one of the student's co-workers (he was a janitor as well as a student), and that was enough for a guilty finding by the university's Affirmative Action Office.

These examples may seem extreme, but the reasoning behind them has become more commonplace on campus in recent years. Last year, at the University of

St. Thomas, in Minnesota, an event called Hump Day, which would have allowed people to pet a camel, was abruptly canceled. Students had created a Facebook group where they protested the event for animal cruelty, for being a waste of money, and for being insensitive to people from the Middle East. The inspiration for the camel had almost certainly come from a popular TV commercial in which a camel saunters around an office on a Wednesday, celebrating "hump day"; it was devoid of any reference to Middle Eastern peoples. Nevertheless, the group organizing the event announced on its Facebook page that the event would be canceled because the "program [was] dividing people and would make for an uncomfortable and possibly unsafe environment."

Because there is a broad ban in academic circles on "blaming the victim," it is generally considered unacceptable to question the reasonableness (let alone the sincerity) of someone's emotional state, particularly if those emotions are linked to one's group identity. The thin argument "I'm offended" becomes an unbeatable trump card. This leads to what Jonathan Rauch, a contributing editor at this magazine, calls the "offendedness sweepstakes," in which opposing parties use claims of offense as cudgels. In the process, the bar for what we consider unacceptable speech is lowered further and further.

The thin argument "I'm offended" becomes an unbeatable trump card.

Since 2013, new pressure from the federal government has reinforced this trend. Federal anti-discrimination statutes regulate on-campus harassment and unequal treatment based on sex, race, religion, and national origin. Until recently, the Department of Education's Office for Civil Rights acknowledged that speech must be "objectively offensive" before it could be deemed actionable as sexual harassment—it would have to pass the "reasonable person" test. To be prohibited, the office wrote in 2003, allegedly harassing speech would have to go "beyond the mere expression of views, words, symbols or thoughts that some person finds offensive."

But in 2013, the Departments of Justice and Education greatly broadened the definition of sexual harassment to include verbal conduct that is simply "unwelcome." Out of fear of federal investigations, universities are now applying that standard—defining unwelcome speech as harassment—not just to sex, but to race, religion, and veteran status as well. Everyone is supposed to rely upon his or her own subjective feelings to decide whether a comment by a professor or a fellow student is unwelcome, and therefore grounds for a harassment claim. Emotional reasoning is now accepted as evidence.

If our universities are teaching students that their emotions can be used effectively as weapons—or at least as evidence in administrative proceedings—then they are teaching students to nurture a kind of hypersensitivity that will lead them into countless drawn-out conflicts in college and beyond. Schools may be training students in thinking styles that will damage their careers and friendships, along with their mental health. 30

Fortune-Telling and Trigger Warnings

Burns defines *fortune-telling* as "anticipat[ing] that things will turn out badly" and feeling "convinced that your prediction is an already-established fact." Leahy, Holland, and McGinn define it as "predict[ing] the future negatively" or seeing potential danger in an everyday situation. The recent spread of demands for trigger warnings on reading assignments with provocative content is an example of fortune-telling.

The idea that words (or smells or any sensory input) can trigger searing memories of past trauma—and intense fear that it may be repeated—has been around at least since World War I, when psychiatrists began treating soldiers for what is now called post-traumatic stress disorder. But explicit trigger warnings are believed to have originated much more recently, on message boards in the early days of the Internet. Trigger warnings became particularly prevalent in self-help and feminist forums, where they allowed readers who had suffered from traumatic events like sexual assault to avoid graphic content that might trigger flashbacks or panic attacks. Search-engine trends indicate that the phrase broke into mainstream use online around 2011, spiked in 2014, and reached an all-time high in 2015. The use of trigger warnings on campus appears to have followed a similar trajectory; seemingly overnight, students at universities across the country have begun demanding that their professors issue warnings before covering material that might evoke a negative emotional response.

In 2013, a task force composed of administrators, students, recent alumni, and one faculty member at Oberlin College, in Ohio, released an online resource guide for faculty (subsequently retracted in the face of faculty pushback) that included a list of topics warranting trigger warnings. These topics included classism and privilege, among many others. The task force recommended that materials that might trigger negative reactions among students be avoided altogether unless they "contribute directly" to course goals, and suggested that works that were "too important to avoid" be made optional.

It's hard to imagine how novels illustrating classism and privilege could provoke or reactivate the kind of terror that is typically implicated in PTSD. Rather, trigger warnings are sometimes demanded for a long list of ideas and attitudes that some students find politically offensive, in the name of preventing other students from being harmed. This is an example of what psychologists call "motivated reasoning"—we spontaneously generate arguments for conclusions we want to support. Once *you* find something hateful, it is easy to argue that exposure to the hateful thing could traumatize some *other* people. You believe that you know how others will react, and that their reaction could be devastating. Preventing that devastation becomes a moral obligation for the whole community. Books for which students have called publicly for trigger warnings within the past couple of years include Virginia Woolf's *Mrs. Dalloway* (at Rutgers, for "suicidal inclinations") and Ovid's *Metamorphoses* (at Columbia, for sexual assault).

You believe that you know how others will react, and that their reaction could be devastating. Preventing that devastation becomes a moral obligation for the whole community.

35 Jeannie Suk's *New Yorker* essay described the difficulties of teaching rape law in the age of trigger warnings. Some students, she wrote, have pressured their professors to avoid teaching the subject in order to protect themselves and their classmates from potential distress. Suk compares this to trying to teach "a medical student who is training to be a surgeon but who fears that he'll become distressed if he sees or handles blood."

However, there is a deeper problem with trigger warnings. According to the most-basic tenets of psychology, the very idea of helping people with anxiety disorders avoid the things they fear is misguided. A person who is trapped in an elevator during a power outage may panic and think she is going to die. That frightening experience can change neural connections in her amygdala, leading to an elevator phobia. If you want this woman to retain her fear for life, you should help her avoid elevators.

But if you want to help her return to normalcy, you should take your cues from Ivan Pavlov and guide her through a process known as exposure therapy. You might start by asking the woman to merely look at an elevator from a distance—standing in a building lobby, perhaps—until her apprehension begins to subside. If nothing bad happens while she's standing in the lobby—if the fear is not "reinforced"—then she will begin to learn a new association: elevators are not dangerous. (This reduction in fear during exposure is called habituation.) Then, on subsequent days, you might ask her to get closer, and on later days to push the call button, and eventually to step in and go up one floor. This is how the amygdala can get rewired again to associate a previously feared situation with safety or normalcy.

Students who call for trigger warnings may be correct that some of their peers are harboring memories of trauma that could be reactivated by course readings. But they are wrong to try to prevent such reactivations. Students with PTSD should of course get treatment, but they should not try to avoid normal life, with its many opportunities for habituation. Classroom discussions are safe places to be exposed to incidental reminders of trauma (such as the word *violate*). A discussion of violence is unlikely to be followed by actual violence, so it is a good way to help students change the associations that are causing them discomfort. And they'd better get their habituation done in college, because the world beyond college will be far less willing to accommodate requests for trigger warnings and opt-outs.

The expansive use of trigger warnings may also foster unhealthy mental habits in the vastly larger group of students who do not suffer from PTSD or other anxiety disorders. People acquire their fears not just from their own past experiences, but from social learning as well. If everyone around you acts as though something is dangerous—elevators, certain neighborhoods, novels depicting racism—then you are at risk of acquiring that fear too. The psychiatrist Sarah Roff pointed this out last year in an online article for *The Chronicle of Higher Education*. "One of my biggest concerns about trigger warnings," Roff wrote, "is that they will apply not just to those who have experienced trauma, but to all students, creating an atmosphere in which they are encouraged to believe that there is something dangerous or damaging about discussing difficult aspects of our history."

40 In an article published last year by *Inside Higher Ed*, seven humanities professors wrote that the trigger-warning movement was "already having a chilling effect on [their] teaching and pedagogy." They reported their colleagues' receiving "phone calls from deans and other administrators investigating student complaints that they have included 'triggering' material in their courses, with or without warnings." A trigger warning, they wrote, "serves as a guarantee that students will not experience unexpected discomfort and implies that if they do, a contract has been broken." When students come to *expect* trigger warnings for any material that makes them uncomfortable, the easiest way for faculty to stay out of trouble is to avoid material that might upset the most sensitive student in the class.

Magnification, Labeling, and Microaggressions

Burns defines *magnification* as "exaggerat[ing] the importance of things," and Leahy, Holland, and McGinn define *labeling* as "assign[ing] global negative traits to yourself and others." The recent collegiate trend of uncovering allegedly racist, sexist, classist, or otherwise discriminatory microaggressions doesn't *incidentally* teach students to focus on small or accidental slights. Its *purpose* is to get students to focus on them and then relabel the people who have made such remarks as aggressors.

The term *microaggression* originated in the 1970s and referred to subtle, often unconscious racist affronts. The definition has expanded in recent years to include anything that can be perceived as discriminatory on virtually any basis. For example, in 2013, a student group at UCLA staged a sit-in during a class taught by Val Rust, an education professor. The group read a letter aloud expressing their concerns about the campus's hostility toward students of color. Although Rust was not explicitly named, the group quite clearly criticized his teaching as microaggressive. In the course of correcting his students' grammar and spelling, Rust had noted that a student had wrongly capitalized the first letter of the word *indigenous*. Lowercasing the capital *I* was an insult to the student and her ideology, the group claimed.

Even joking about microaggressions can be seen as an aggression, warranting punishment. Last fall, Omar Mahmood, a student at the University of Michigan, wrote a satirical column for a conservative student publication, *The Michigan Review*, poking fun at what he saw as a campus tendency to perceive microaggressions in just about anything. Mahmood was also employed at the campus newspaper, *The Michigan Daily*. *The Daily*'s editors said that the way Mahmood had "satirically mocked the experiences of fellow Daily contributors and minority communities on campus . . . created a conflict of interest." *The Daily* terminated Mahmood after he described the incident to two websites, The College Fix and The Daily Caller. A group of women later vandalized Mahmood's doorway with eggs, hot dogs, gum, and notes with messages such as "Everyone hates you, you violent prick." When speech comes to be seen as a form of violence, vindictive protectiveness can justify a hostile, and perhaps even violent, response.

In March, the student government at Ithaca College, in upstate New York, went so far as to propose the creation of an anonymous microaggression-reporting system. Student sponsors envisioned some form of disciplinary action against "oppressors" engaged in belittling speech. One of the sponsors of the program said that while "not . . . every instance will require trial or some kind of harsh punishment," she wanted the program to be "record-keeping but with impact."

45 Surely people make subtle or thinly veiled racist or sexist remarks on college campuses, and it is right for students to raise questions and initiate discussions about such cases. But the increased focus on microaggressions coupled with the endorsement of emotional reasoning is a formula for a constant state of outrage, even toward well-meaning speakers trying to engage in genuine discussion.

What are we doing to our students if we encourage them to develop extra-thin skin in the years just before they leave the cocoon of adult protection and enter the workforce? Would they not be better prepared to flourish if we taught them to question their own emotional reactions, and to give people the benefit of the doubt?

Teaching Students to Catastrophize and Have Zero Tolerance

Burns defines *catastrophizing* as a kind of magnification that turns "commonplace negative events into nightmarish monsters." Leahy, Holland, and McGinn define it as believing "that what has happened or will happen" is "so awful and unbearable that you won't be able to stand it." Requests for trigger warnings involve catastrophizing, but this way of thinking colors other areas of campus thought as well.

Catastrophizing rhetoric about physical danger is employed by campus administrators more commonly than you might think—sometimes, it seems, with cynical ends in mind. For instance, last year administrators at Bergen Community College, in New Jersey, suspended Francis Schmidt, a professor, after he posted a picture of his daughter on his Google+ account. The photo showed her in a yoga pose, wearing a T-shirt that read "I will take what is mine with fire & blood," a quote from the HBO show *Game of Thrones*. Schmidt had filed a grievance against the school about two months earlier after being passed over for a sabbatical. The quote was interpreted as a threat by a campus administrator, who received a notification after Schmidt posted the picture; it had been sent, automatically, to a whole group of contacts. According to Schmidt, a Bergen security official present at a subsequent meeting between administrators and Schmidt thought the word *fire* could refer to AK-47s.

Then there is the eight-year legal saga at Valdosta State University, in Georgia, where a student was expelled for protesting the construction of a parking garage by posting an allegedly "threatening" collage on Facebook. The collage described the proposed structure as a "memorial" parking garage—a joke referring to a claim by the university president that the garage would be part of his legacy. The president interpreted the collage as a threat against his life.

50

It should be no surprise that students are exhibiting similar sensitivity. At the University of Central Florida in 2013, for example, Hyung-il Jung, an accounting instructor, was suspended after a student reported that Jung had made a threatening comment during a review session. Jung explained to the *Orlando Sentinel* that the material he was reviewing was difficult, and he'd noticed the pained look on students' faces, so he made a joke. "It looks like you guys are being slowly suffocated by these questions," he recalled saying. "Am I on a killing spree or what?"

After the student reported Jung's comment, a group of nearly 20 others emailed the UCF administration explaining that the comment had clearly been made in jest. Nevertheless, UCF suspended Jung from all university duties and demanded that he obtain written certification from a mental-health professional that he was "not a threat to [himself] or to the university community" before he would be allowed to return to campus.

All of these actions teach a common lesson: smart people do, in fact, overreact to innocuous speech, make mountains out of molehills, and seek punishment for anyone whose words make anyone else feel uncomfortable.

Mental Filtering and Disinvitation Season

As Burns defines it, *mental filtering* is "pick[ing] out a negative detail in any situation and dwell[ing] on it exclusively, thus perceiving that the whole situation is negative." Leahy, Holland, and McGinn refer to this as "negative filtering," which they define as "focus[ing] almost exclusively on the negatives and seldom notic[ing] the positives." When applied to campus life, mental filtering allows for simpleminded demonization.

Students and faculty members in large numbers modeled this cognitive distortion during 2014's "disinvitation season." That's the time of year—usually early spring—when commencement speakers are announced and when students and professors demand that some of those speakers be disinvited because of things they have said or done. According to data compiled by the Foundation for Individual Rights in Education, since 2000, at least 240 campaigns have been launched at U.S. universities to prevent public figures from appearing at campus events; most of them have occurred since 2009.

55 Consider two of the most prominent disinvitation targets of 2014: former U.S. Secretary of State Condoleezza Rice and the International Monetary Fund's managing director, Christine Lagarde. Rice was the first black female secretary of state; Lagarde was the first woman to become finance minister of a G8 country and the first female head of the IMF. Both speakers could have been seen as highly successful role models for female students, and Rice for minority students as well. But the critics, in effect, discounted any possibility of something positive coming from those speeches.

Members of an academic community should of course be free to raise questions about Rice's role in the Iraq War or to look skeptically at the IMF's policies. But should dislike of *part* of a person's record disqualify her altogether from sharing her perspectives?

If campus culture conveys the idea that visitors must be pure, with résumés that never offend generally left-leaning campus sensibilities, then higher education will have taken a further step toward intellectual homogeneity and the creation of an environment in which students rarely encounter diverse viewpoints. And universities will have reinforced the belief that it's okay to filter out the positive. If students graduate believing that they can learn nothing from people they dislike or from those with whom they disagree, we will have done them a great intellectual disservice.

What Can We Do Now?

Attempts to shield students from words, ideas, and people that might cause them emotional discomfort are bad for the students. They are bad for the workplace, which will be mired in unending litigation if student expectations of safety are carried forward. And they are bad for American democracy, which is already paralyzed by worsening partisanship. When the ideas, values, and speech of the other side are seen not just as wrong but as willfully aggressive toward innocent victims, it is hard to imagine the kind of mutual respect, negotiation, and compromise that are needed to make politics a positive-sum game.

Rather than trying to protect students from words and ideas that they will inevitably encounter, colleges should do all they can to equip students to thrive in a world full of words and ideas that they cannot control. One of the great truths taught by Buddhism (and Stoicism, Hinduism, and many other traditions) is that you can never achieve happiness by making the world conform to your desires. But you can master your desires and habits of thought. This, of course, is the goal of cognitive behavioral therapy. With this in mind, here are some steps that might help reverse the tide of bad thinking on campus.

60 The biggest single step in the right direction does not involve faculty or university administrators, but rather the federal government, which should release universities from their fear of unreasonable investigation and sanctions by the Department of Education.

Congress should define peer-on-peer harassment according to the Supreme Court's definition in the 1999 case *Davis v. Monroe County Board of Education*. The *Davis* standard holds that a single comment or thoughtless remark by a student does not equal harassment; harassment requires a pattern of objectively offensive behavior by one student that interferes with another student's access to education. Establishing the *Davis* standard would help eliminate universities' impulse to police their students' speech so carefully.

Universities themselves should try to raise consciousness about the need to balance freedom of speech with the need to make all students feel welcome. Talking openly about such conflicting but important values is just the sort of challenging exercise that any diverse but tolerant community must learn to do. Restrictive speech codes should be abandoned.

Universities should also officially and strongly discourage trigger warnings. They should endorse the American Association of University Professors' report on these warnings, which notes, "The presumption that students need to be protected rather than challenged in a classroom is at once infantilizing and anti-intellectual." Professors should be free to use trigger warnings if they choose to do so, but by explicitly discouraging the practice, universities would help fortify the faculty against student requests for such warnings.

Finally, universities should rethink the skills and values they most want to impart to their incoming students. At present, many freshman-orientation programs try to raise student sensitivity to a nearly impossible level. Teaching students to avoid giving unintentional offense is a worthy goal, especially when the students come from many different cultural backgrounds. But students should also be taught how to live in a world full of potential offenses. Why not teach incoming students how to practice cognitive behavioral therapy? Given high and rising rates of mental illness, this simple step would be among the most humane and supportive things a university could do. The cost and time commitment could be kept low: a few group training sessions could be supplemented by websites or apps. But the outcome could pay dividends in many ways. For example, a shared vocabulary about reasoning, common distortions, and the appropriate use of evidence to draw conclusions would facilitate critical thinking and real debate. It would also tone down the perpetual state of outrage that seems to engulf some colleges these days, allowing students' minds to open more widely to new ideas and new people. A greater commitment to formal, public debate on campus—and to the assembly of a more politically diverse faculty—would further serve that goal.

Thomas Jefferson, upon founding the University of Virginia, said:

> This institution will be based on the illimitable freedom of the human mind. For here we are not afraid to follow truth wherever it may lead, nor to tolerate any error so long as reason is left free to combat it.

We believe that this is still—and will always be—the best attitude for American universities. Faculty, administrators, students, and the federal government all have a role to play in restoring universities to their historic mission.

Common Cognitive Distortions

A partial list from Robert L. Leahy, Stephen J. F. Holland, and Lata K. McGinn's *Treatment Plans and Interventions for Depression and Anxiety Disorders* (2012). 65

1. **Mind reading.** You assume that you know what people think without having sufficient evidence of their thoughts. "He thinks I'm a loser."
2. **Fortune-telling.** You predict the future negatively: things will get worse, or there is danger ahead. "I'll fail that exam," or "I won't get the job."
3. **Catastrophizing.** You believe that what has happened or will happen will be so awful and unbearable that you won't be able to stand it. "It would be terrible if I failed."
4. **Labeling.** You assign global negative traits to yourself and others. "I'm undesirable," or "He's a rotten person."
5. **Discounting positives.** You claim that the positive things you or others do are trivial. "That's what wives are supposed to do—so it doesn't count when she's nice to me," or "Those successes were easy, so they don't matter."
6. **Negative filtering.** You focus almost exclusively on the negatives and seldom notice the positives. "Look at all of the people who don't like me."
7. **Overgeneralizing.** You perceive a global pattern of negatives on the basis of a single incident. "This generally happens to me. I seem to fail at a lot of things."
8. **Dichotomous thinking.** You view events or people in all-or-nothing terms. "I get rejected by everyone," or "It was a complete waste of time."
9. **Blaming.** You focus on the other person as the source of your negative feelings, and you refuse to take responsibility for changing yourself. "She's to blame for the way I feel now," or "My parents caused all my problems."
10. **What if?** You keep asking a series of questions about "what if" something happens, and you fail to be satisfied with any of the answers. "Yeah, but what if I get anxious?," or "What if I can't catch my breath?"
11. **Emotional reasoning.** You let your feelings guide your interpretation of reality. "I feel depressed; therefore, my marriage is not working out."
12. **Inability to disconfirm.** You reject any evidence or arguments that might contradict your negative thoughts. For example, when you have the thought *I'm unlovable*, you reject as irrelevant any evidence that people like you. Consequently, your thought cannot be refuted. "That's not the real issue. There are deeper problems. There are other factors."

Questions for Critical Reading

1. Lukianoff and Haidt introduce numerous concepts in support of their argument. As you reread the essay, select the three that you feel are the most important to their argument and locate the passages where these concepts are defined and used. What makes them critical to the argument?
2. What is *critical thinking*? Reread Lukianoff and Haidt's article to look for places where they define and discuss critical thinking. What role does it in play in college? What role does it play beyond college?

3. According to the authors, who is responsible for resolving the issues taking place on college campuses? Reread the essay looking for quotations where they suggest a solution and identify who should implement it.

Exploring Context

1. Lukianoff works for the Foundation for Individual Rights in Education. Visit the foundation's website at thefire.org. How does the material you find there support the authors' argument? Does it suggest a particular bias for either Lukianoff or Haidt? You may also wish to look up your school to see what rating FIRE has given it.
2. Visit Haidt's homepage at people.stern.nyu.edu/jhaidt. How does his work in this essay reflect his larger research interests? You may want to consider viewing some of his TED talks, linked from his page.
3. Which policies govern speech at your school? Search for relevant policies on your school's website. You may want to use your work in Question 1 of Exploring Context to help you. How would Lukianoff and Haidt evaluate your school's policies?

Questions for Connecting

1. How can we balance the goals of a safe, inclusive, and diverse atmosphere for education and a rigorous emphasis on critical thinking and free speech? Where do we draw the line? Work with Anna Holmes's discussion of diversity in "Variety Show" (p. 217) to expand the context of the discussion of race and diversity and to consider how we might synthesize her insights with Lukianoff and Haidt's argument.
2. In "Necessary Edges: Arts, Empathy, and Education" (p. 278), Yo-Yo Ma also offers a vision for education. Synthesize his ideas with the position of Lukianoff and Haidt. Does Ma's emphasis on empathy negate these authors' desire for critical thinking? How might we combine these to create a new model of education? You may want to use your work from Question 2 of Questions for Critical Reading to help you make your response.
3. Julia Serano examines rape culture, which is all too often prevalent on college campuses, in "Why Nice Guys Finish Last" (p. 343). Lukianoff and Haidt chronicle what they argue is an oversensitivity to these issues. Synthesize the arguments of these authors to suggest ways we might effectively address rape culture on college campuses.

Language Matters

1. Locate a key sentence from Lukianoff and Haidt's text and then identify the subject, verb, and object of the sentence. How does the structure of the sentence contribute to their argument? How does it make meaning, and what meaning does it make?
2. Citation is absolutely essential to academic writing, though it plays no role in Lukianoff and Haidt's essay, despite the fact that Haidt is a respected academic. Why don't they use citation? Why is it so important in academic writing? Consider issues of audience and authority as you prepare your answer.

3. Choose a key quotation from the essay. Revise it to make it less effective but still grammatically correct. Would making it a question blunt its force? What about changing it to passive voice? Draw some general conclusions from this experiment. What makes a sentence effective?

Assignments for Writing

1. **Multimodal.** A poster presentation is an academic genre used in many disciplines in which researchers summarize their findings on a poster board, using key data and images. Make a poster presentation in which you modify Lukianoff and Haidt's argument to suggest a balance between what they see as current practice and what they would like to see. You may want to research more about poster presentation on the web to determine how factors like text and images can work cohesively to reflect your work. How can we balance civil liberties like free speech with protection from harms like hate speech on college campuses? You may want to draw from your work in Questions 1 and 3 of Questions for Critical Reading, Questions 1 and 3 of Exploring Context, and Question 2 of Questions for Connecting.
2. Write a paper in which you determine the proper goals of a college education. What role should sensitivity to others play? What about critical thinking? Consider using your responses to Questions 2 and 3 of Questions for Critical Reading and Questions 2 and 3 of Questions for Connecting.
3. Lukianoff and Haidt draw extensively from areas of psychology to support their argument, using a number of specific concepts. Write a paper in which you extend their argument to another social problem by analyzing it using some of their concepts. Your work in Question 1 of Questions for Critical Reading might be a useful place to start.

YO-YO MA

Cellist and songwriter **Yo-Yo Ma** began performing at five years old. In the more than half century since, he has won over seventeen Grammy Awards and has produced more than ninety albums. Ma has received numerous awards, including the World Economic Forum's Crystal Award (2008), the National Medal of Arts (2001), and the Presidential Medal of Freedom (2010); he was recognized as a Kennedy Center Honoree in 2011. He is a graduate of the Juilliard School and Harvard University.

"Necessary Edges: Arts, Empathy, and Education" was originally published on the *World Post*, an online news and blog site created through a partnership between liberal news aggregator the *Huffington Post* and nonpartisan think tank the Berggruen Institute on Governance. The site was launched during the World Economic Forum in Davos, Switzerland, in January 2014, the same month as Ma's essay was published, and features high-profile contributors such as engineer and magnate Elon Musk, founder of electric car company Tesla; Tony Blair, the former prime minister of Great Britain; and Eric Schmidt, the former executive chairman of Google.

In this essay, Ma considers the role of the arts in the world, arguing that the elements of empathy provided by artistic endeavors are essential to the kind of balanced thinking needed today. Ma thus advocates for STEAM education, which incorporates art into the science, technology, engineering, and mathematics curriculum. Together, art and science create an "edge effect" (p. 280) that promotes equilibrium and produces a global culture.

Does art have a role to play in the world? In education?

- TAGS: *art, collaboration, culture, education, empathy, globalism, science and technology*
- CONNECTIONS: *Appiah, DeGhett, Fukuyama, Klosterman, Provan, Southan, Turkle, von Busch, Yang*

Necessary Edges: Arts, Empathy, and Education

In our highly interdependent global civilization, a lot of things are not working.

When I travel around the country and the world to perform, I pick up in my many conversations a growing sense that the first Enlightenment—which posited the rule of reason over emotion and feelings—is getting a little creaky, confining, and even counterproductive.

The neurobiologist Antonio Damasio has written about Descartes's error that, to put it in shorthand, "I think therefore I am." Damasio instead makes the compelling argument, empirically based in neurology, that feeling and emotions as expressed in art and music play a central role in high-level cognitive reasoning.

Advances in neurobiology now make it clear that we humans have dual neural pathways, one for critical thinking and one for empathetic thinking. Only one pathway can be activated at a time, so when one is on, the other is off. Yet we are also aware that wise and balanced judgment results from integrating the critical and empathetic, taking emotions as well as reason into account. While this can't be done in tandem, it does occur, we now know, through a loop-back process of layers of feedback.

These discoveries suggest that a new way of thinking is possible, a new consciousness—perhaps a new Enlightenment—that brings the arts and science back together.

This new consciousness by which we purposely seek to bolster the integrative feedback loops of our dual neural pathways could provide a new energy for creativity in our weary civilization.

This integrative awareness is especially important today as our science-driven, technologically advanced world is breaking down into ever more compartments, specializations, and disciplines—even as the interdependence of globalization is creating more links with other cultures through which empathetic understanding is vital.

To be able to put oneself in another's shoes without prejudgment is an essential skill. Empathy comes when you understand something deeply through arts and literature and can thus make unexpected connections. These parallels bring you closer to things that would otherwise seem far away. Empathy is the ultimate quality that acknowledges our identity as members of one human family.

Visionaries like Elon Musk have spoken of the internet and the planetary reach of the media as a "global thinking circuit." We need to be sure that this connecting circuit is about communication and not just information by fostering both empathetic and critical thinking.

From STEM to STEAM

Because the world economy is so hypercompetitive, much of the focus in education these days from Singapore to Shanghai to American schools is on STEM—science, technology, engineering, and math. As important as that is, it is short-sighted. We need to add the empathetic reasoning of the arts to the mix—STEAM.

The values behind arts integration—collaboration, flexible thinking, and disciplined imagination—lead to the capacity to innovate. A pianist skilled to both read and improvise music is open to listening to what is around him but knows that, to reach excellence, he needs to filter the imagination through the discipline of knowledge. When he performs, you will know instantly if he has achieved that right balance and it works or not.

For me the most proficient way to teach the values of collaboration, flexibility, imagination, and innovation—all skill sets needed in today's world—is through the performing arts. If you have these tools, you can do well in any field from software engineering to the biosciences.

Empathy is the other key tool. Empathy and imagination, the artificial layering of different realities, are linked. Empathy is your capacity to imagine what someone else is going through; what they are thinking, feeling, and perceiving. That will not only give you an outlook on who they are—continually corrected by evidence—but also what your alternative possibilities are.

Empathetic thinking is something that is severely missing in education today that is only STEM oriented. Everyone wants innovation, recovering that inspired and innovative spirit of JFK talking about going to the moon. But you can't skim the top without the rest of it.

The arts teach us that there is something that connects us all and is bigger than each of us. In both places it is a matter of equilibrium, of centering the ego at the right point of balance between the individual and the community. 15

We are all addressing the same issues with different names attached to them.

STEAM will help us get there by resolving the education problem. Kids will then go to school because it is a passion and a privilege, not a requirement.

It's All about Equilibrium

Finding meaning and living—all of what we do as humans in society—occurs in that brain space between life and death. In our industrial societies there is a great deal of controversy these days over what life is and when it begins and how we approach the agony of death which, in industrial society, we try to avoid thinking about. Therefore we spend an unbelievable amount of money on medical care in those last few years before dying.

The arts help us cope with these issues by engaging, not avoiding, the deep emotions of intimate loss involved and retelling over and over again the story of the human condition and its limits. Only then can we can regain our spiritual balance and find meaning in more than trying to technically manage every aspect of our being from womb to tomb.

Necessary Edges

Equilibrium is what all life forms are seeking in order to survive. Evolution is the balance between stability and the changes necessary to cope with new challenges in the environment. 20

On this earth we can only survive within a very narrow bandwidth of conditions—oxygen, hydrogen, light, acidity, temperature.

Within that narrow bandwidth, most of what exists is concentrated in the middle. But, as we see in ecology, there are also "necessary edges." The "edge effect" in ecology occurs at the border where two ecosystems—for example the savannah and forest—meet. At that interface, where there is the least density and the greatest diversity of life forms, each living thing can draw from the core of the two ecosystems. That is where new life forms emerge.

In our advanced species, we also have these "necessary edges." The hard sciences are probing one far end of the bandwidth, searching for the origins of the universe or the secrets of the genome. People in the arts are probing the other far end of the bandwidth. Without the "necessary edges" that interface with a changing environment and find innovative response, the middle will go over the edge like lemmings. Those on the edge are, in effect, the scouts that say "there is a waterfall, there is a ledge, there is danger ahead. Stop. Don't go this way, go that way."

Equilibrium occurs when the information from the edges is available at the core.

Equilibrium occurs when the information from the edges is available at the core. Only when those meridians or pathways that connect the edges to the middle are open will a life form survive, and even prosper. Only when science and the arts, critical and empathetic reasoning, are linked to the mainstream will we find a sustainable balance in society.

What is dangerous is when the center ignores the edges or the edges ignore the center—art for art's sake or science without a humanist and societal perspective. Then we are headed for doomsday without knowing it. 25

Globalization Creates Culture

My musical journeys have reinforced this point of view. What I've found is that the interactions brought about by globalization don't just destroy culture; they can create new culture and invigorate and spread traditions that have existed for ages precisely because of the "edge effect." Sometimes the most interesting things happen at the edge. The intersections there can reveal unexpected connections.

Culture is a fabric composed of gifts from every corner of the world. One way of discovering the world is by digging deeply into its traditions.

I have often used this example: At the core of any cellist's repertoire are the Cello Suites by Bach. At the heart of each suite is a dance movement called the sarabande.

The dance originated with music of the North African Berbers, where it was a slow, sensual dance. It next appeared in Spain, where it was banned because it was considered lewd and lascivious. Spaniards brought it to the Americas, but it also traveled on to France, where it became a courtly dance. In the 1720s, Bach incorporated the sarabande as a movement in his Cello Suites. Today, I play Bach, a Paris-born American musician of Chinese parentage. So who really owns the sarabande? Each culture has adopted the music, investing it with specific meaning, but each culture must share ownership: it belongs to us all.

In 1998, I founded the Silk Road Project to study the flow of ideas among the many cultures between the Mediterranean and the Pacific over several thousand years. When the Silk Road Ensemble performs, we try to bring much of the world together on one stage. Its members are a peer group of virtuosos, masters of living traditions, whether European, Arabic, Azeri, Armenian, Persian, Russian, Central Asian, Indian, Mongolian, Chinese, Korean, or Japanese. They all generously share their knowledge and are curious and eager to learn about other forms of expression. 30

Over the last several years, we have found that every tradition is the result of successful invention. One of the best ways to ensure the survival of traditions is by organic evolution, using all the tools available to us in the present day, from YouTube to the concert hall.

We Are More Than We Can Measure

We live in such a measuring society, people tend to put a person in a box they can put on their mental shelf. People think of me as a cellist because they can see my performances and take my measure as a musician. I think of my life as a musician as only the tip of an iceberg. That is only the audible part of my existence. Underneath the water is the life I'm leading, the thoughts I'm thinking, and the emotions that well up in me.

We all get into trouble if we think the universe only exists of the matter that we can see and measure, and not the anti-matter that is the counterpart that holds it all together.

Michelangelo famously said, "I liberate the statue from the marble." Similarly, my music emerges from the life all around me and the world we all share together. One is the condition of the other.

Questions for Critical Reading

1. What is the role of art? After writing your own thoughts in response to the question, reread Ma's essay, paying attention to his thoughts about the benefits of art. Does his argument confirm or challenge your ideas?
2. Ma draws from neuroscience to make his argument. Note the places in the essay where he discusses empathy. How does empathy function in thinking and decision making?
3. As you reread Ma's essay, look for his definitions of *necessary edges* and *edge effects*. How does he use these ideas to support his argument?

Exploring Context

1. According to Ma, "At the core of any cellist's repertoire are the Cello Suites by Bach" (p. 281). Using a search engine, look for videos of Ma playing Bach. Does his music reflect his argument in this essay? As you watch the entire video, do you observe elements that also support his ideas?
2. Apple is often cited as an example of a company that embodies STEAM education in its mix of technology and design. Explore Apple's website at apple.com, looking for elements that reflect Ma's argument. Does Apple reflect "necessary edges"? Use your work from Question 3 of Questions for Critical Reading in making your response.
3. Ma mentions his Silk Road Project. Explore the website for this endeavor at silkroadproject.org. How does this project reflect Ma's argument about the relationship between art, science, technology, and collaboration?

Questions for Connecting

1. Sherry Turkle's interest in empathy is reflected in the title of her essay, "The Empathy Diaries" (p. 378). However, she seems much more concerned than Ma about our ability to engage with others in a meaningful collaborative way that supports the kind of exchanges Ma thinks we need. Evaluate the arguments of Turkle and Ma to synthesize a position on the presence of empathy today. Are we in a flight from conversation as Turkle suggests or are the kinds of exchanges Ma values more and more likely to occur? Support your response with quotations from both essays; you may also want to draw from your work in Questions for Critical Reading and Questions 2 and 3 of Exploring Context.
2. Does Ma's argument change the answer to Rhys Southan's question "Is Art a Waste of Time?" (p. 363). How does Ma's analysis change the relationship between art and effective altruism? Incorporate your answer from Question 1 of Questions for Critical Reading.

3. In "The Future of Originals" (p. 327), Alexander Provan explores some related issues concerning art and science. Synthesize his argument with Ma's contentions. Is the connection of art and science always beneficial? What conditions are necessary to create the edge effects that Ma describes? Use your work in Questions 1 and 3 of Questions for Critical Reading as well as Questions 2 and 3 of Exploring Context.

Language Matters

1. How do the headings in Ma's essay contribute to your understanding of it? Devise new headings for this essay. Where would you make the divisions?
2. Ma uses a very clear organization to make his argument. Outline his essay and then consider how he uses organization to help prove his argument. How do the various sections build to a conclusion? How would the meaning of his essay change if it were rearranged? Apply what you learn to your own writing: How can you use organization to help prove your argument?
3. Ma uses acronyms in his essay, such as STEM. Review material on acronyms and abbreviations in a grammar handbook or other reliable resource. How well does Ma follow these rules? When should you use acronyms or abbreviations in your own writing? How should they be introduced?

Assignments for Writing

1. What role does empathy play in collaboration? Can collaboration function without it? Working with Ma's ideas about both practices, write a paper in which you examine the relationship between empathy and collaboration. You may want to use your work from Question 2 of Questions for Critical Reading and Question 1 of Questions for Connecting.
2. Consider your goals for your own education and then write a paper using Ma's ideas to argue for the proper aims of education. Should education be focused on career? Do we have an obligation to promote a broader education?
3. Ma draws from ecological concepts in order to support his argument. Extend Ma's argument by writing a paper in which you consider other "edge effects" and "necessary edges." Can we locate these edges *within* the arts or *within* the sciences? Can we locate them *between* art, science, and other areas of human experience? What elements are necessary to reap the benefits of edge effects? What other edges are used in the Silk Road Project? Use your work from Question 3 of Questions for Critical Reading, Questions 1–3 of Exploring Context, and Question 3 of Questions for Connecting to support your argument.

ROBINSON MEYER

Robinson Meyer is a staff writer for *The Atlantic*, where he writes on technology and climate change, particularly as it relates to politics and public policy. His articles have included titles such as "The Zombie Diseases of Climate Change," "The Social Media Star and the Suicide," and "When a Robot Names a New Color of Paint."

The Atlantic, published since 1857, publishes book reviews and commentary on culture, politics, the economy, and foreign affairs and is known for its politically moderate viewpoint. "Is It OK to Enjoy the Warm Winters of Climate Change" was published in the online edition of the magazine on February 23, 2017, alongside essays on the challenges of accessing birth control in the military, polymath David Gelernter's ideas about American life, and the saturation of ordinary objects with technology.

Meyer uses the ethical question of whether or not we should enjoy mild winters resulting from climate change in order to explore the complicated science of climate change, its economic impact, and the ways in which the seriousness of this challenge might enter the consciousness of the general public.

That our climate is changing is increasingly unquestionable. But how can we address this challenge and its consequences?

▶ TAGS: *ethics, globalism, judgment and decision making, science and technology, social change*

▶ CONNECTIONS: *Appiah, Epstein, Gilbert, Gladwell, Pollan*

Is It OK to Enjoy the Warm Winters of Climate Change?

This is not how February is supposed to feel.

From D.C. to Denver, from Charlotte to Chicago, towns and cities across the United States have posted strings of record-breaking summery days in what is normally the final month of winter. Wednesday was only the third time since 1880 that Green Bay, Wisconsin, cracked 60 degrees Fahrenheit in February. Ice on the Great Lakes covers only a quarter of its normal surface area. And parts of Oklahoma and Texas have both already been scorched by 90-degree afternoons.

All in all, the United States has already set more than 2,800 new record high temperatures this month. It has only set 27 record lows.

Most people handle this weather as the gift it is: an opportunity to get outside, run or bike or play catch, and get an early jump on the spring. But for the two-thirds of Americans who are at least fairly worried about global warming, the weather can also prompt anxiety and unease. As one woman told the *Chicago Tribune*: "It's scary, that's my first thing. Because in all my life I've never seen a February this warm." Or as one viral tweet put it:

> Me enjoying this weather but knowing our Earth is danger
>
> — bre (@bre_lliant) 12:05 PM - Feb 19, 2017

If these feelings take the form of a question, it is something like: How much should we really be enjoying weather so unseasonal, so suggestive of the consequences of climate change, when we're doing so little to combat the larger phenomenon? If we think the future consequences of climate change will be very bad, are we allowed to savor them now? 5

There is, of course, no single right answer to this query, and it is an ethical or existential concern as much as a scientific one. But when I posed it to the scientists who encounter climate change's consequences first-hand—in the planet's expanding deserts, deluged coasts, and bleached coral reefs—they said that it was fine to take the good with the bad when it came to upheavals in Earth's long-term climate.

Katherine Hayhoe, an atmospheric scientist at Texas Tech University, told me that people shouldn't hesitate to enjoy unseasonably warm days, whether or not they are caused by climate change.

"It's a good example of how all of the symptoms of a changing climate are not negative. And if there is something good, then enjoying it doesn't make [climate change] any better or worse than it would be otherwise," she said.

Rather, the warm days might prepare people to notice other shifts in how they experience the weather. "As it gets warmer, the negative impacts outweigh the positive impacts," she said. "This will first look like hotter summers, pests moving northward, and our air-conditioning and water bill going up. Having these unusual days that we really notice, it makes us more aware of how other things are changing, too."

For the climate-concerned, this is an encouraging theory of change—and it fits with a body of research that suggests people experiencing unusual warmth are more likely to tell pollsters they believe in global warming. 10

But a study published last year in *Nature* should make advocates pause. It found that, for the vast majority of Americans, the weather became more favorable and pleasant from 1974 to 2013. Over all, winters have gotten generally warmer and more pleasant for "virtually all Americans," while summers have not yet become scorching and oppressively humid.

This change has occurred on a shocking scale: On the "pleasantness index" used by the study, Boston in 2013 was as favorable as New York City was in 1976; and present-day St. Louis is nicer than D.C. or Baltimore four decades hence.

This study stands apart from the rest of the climate literature for several reasons. It examines neither how climate change is shaping the weather—it does not pull out a climate signal from the 40 years of weather change, only looking at weather overall—and it does not treat the entire expanse of the country's land surface area equally. Rather, it wants to know how Americans experience the weather, so its analysis gives more weight to highly populated counties.

The study also omits incidences of extreme weather. Those have increased during the study period, and they will be one of the earliest ways Americans in the Lower 48 experience the consequences of climate change.

"While we're hearing over and over again that climate change is something we should fear, most people are experiencing it in a way that's really quite comfortable," says Megan Mullin, a political scientist at Duke University and one of the authors of the study. "What I take away from this is really a lesson for scientists. My Twitter stream is filled with these maps, over and over again, showing departures from historically average temperatures. In my mind, [that kind of messaging] is not going to motivate the public to treat this as a top priority." 15

And their study also found that that motivation is needed now, because—after the middle of the century—climate change will begin to make summers worse:

> Under a scenario in which greenhouse gas emissions proceed at an unabated rate . . . we estimate that 88 percent of the U.S. public will experience weather at the end of the century that is less preferable than weather in the recent past.

But this switch won't happen "for decades out," said Mullin. And by then it will be too late to adjust policies to meaningfully mitigate climate change.

"Once we're past a certain point, then we can't just flip the switch and say, it's time to address it. What we have to do is start dealing with it now. Partly because of the way our climate system works, but also because of the way our policy system works," she told me.

Many Americans are already feeling the economic consequences of unseasonable warmth.

All this said, many Americans are already feeling the economic consequences of unseasonable warmth. For instance, peach trees require a certain number of chilling hours—that is, exposure to weather below 45 degrees—in order to produce a bountiful crop. Optimally, Georgia's peach-farming regions want to experience about 1,000 chilling hours before the arrival of spring. This year, according to the *Macon Telegraph*, some farms have recorded as few as 470—and they have little hope of seeing temperatures fall again before spring.

This story has been repeated across the country for essentially any plant that requires some amount of wintertime chilling. 20

"Those of us who have office jobs and bike to work may be enjoying these temperatures, there are a large number of stakeholders in the agricultural community who see doom more clearly in them than we do," says Kim Cobb, a climate scientist at Georgia Tech.

"I know without a doubt that should such unseasonably warm temperatures continue into the summer, we will see energy bills spike to astronomical levels, see older residents suffer, and see schoolchildren have to stay inside due to temperatures spiking past human thresholds," she added.

And by the way, are the warm temperatures this month even attributable to the large-scale damage that climate change will wreak? Many climate scientists encouraged some humility. People shouldn't look to any one day's weather for confirmation that climate change exists, they said. Rather, Americans should look at the broader trends: specifically, the century-long, planet-wide warming trend, and the fact that eight of the last 10 years have been among the warmest on record.

"I'm not going to say that this week's warmth is caused by climate change, so I feel free to tell my colleagues to enjoy it," said Cobb. "The staggering and humbling and worrying moment as a scientist comes when we see that 2015 shattered the record for 2014, and 2016 shattered the record for 2015."

Mullin said that people should ultimately try to seek out better and more reliable sources than their personal experience of the weather. 25

"I think of weather as an indicator in the same way that I think about exposure to crime or exposure to unemployment," she told me. "If you know a bunch of people who have lost their jobs, you start to think unemployment is a substantial problem. And then when you start seeing coverage in the newspaper, you might not really know what a baseline level of unemployment is, or should be—but that employment figure jumps out at you, because you know a bunch of people who have lost their jobs."

"It makes sense that people use this information, but we should try really hard not to. Because it's not high-quality information," she said. Rather, we should trust the well-documented trends and studies that point to global warming's existence and urgency.

And Katherine Hayhoe encouraged thinking about any one day's weather through a more nuanced lens. "On the science side, the number-one question often is: Is this global warming or not? I really am convinced that's completely the wrong question to ask," she told me.

It was like, she said, asking if a heart problem is the result of genetics or lifestyle. "For most of us, the answer is both. And saying—'Is this heart attack caused by lifestyle or genetics?'—is pointless, because the answer will be both. We can't change the genetics of our natural weather patterns and variability, but we can change our lifestyle."

30 And right now, our planetary lifestyle involves emitting millions of tons of carbon dioxide into the atmosphere every second and slowly, but surely, warming the globe.

Questions for Critical Reading

1. How does Meyer answer the question of his title? As you reread, note passages where he reveals whether or not we should enjoy milder winters, why, and what else we should keep in mind.

2. What sort of motivation is needed to prompt people to address climate change? Reread Meyer's essay and look for places where he discusses what we might do to help people take action on this problem.

3. As you review Meyer's text, make a list of all the consequences—good and bad—of global climate change. Given its effects, what should we do about this problem?

Exploring Context

1. Explore NASA's site on global climate change (climate.nasa.gov). Extend or complicate Meyer's argument with the information you find there. Based on the site, is it OK to enjoy warm winters? Do the data and predictions that Meyer includes still hold true?

2. At a couple of points in the essay Meyer references conversations around climate change on Twitter (twitter.com). Search the platform for current conversations on the topic. What are people talking about now when it comes to climate change?

3. National Geographic also maintains a site about climate change (nationalgeographic.com/environment/climate-change). How does the information you find there compare to the information at NASA's site? Does it affirm the points Meyer makes in his essay?

Questions for Connecting

1. Knowing climate change is happening and yet also enjoying a mild winter relates to Kwame Anthony Appiah's discussion of the separation between values and practices in "Making Conversation" and "The Primacy of Practice" (p. 35). How can we use his ideas to change our practices around climate even as we value warmer winters?
2. In "Reporting Live from Tomorrow" (p. 172), Daniel Gilbert argues that we are very bad at imagining our futures. Apply Gilbert's insights to Meyer's discussion of climate change. How might our reactions and behaviors around this problem reflect our inability to predict our future? What solutions does Gilbert offer?
3. Helen Epstein discusses approaches to confronting another global crisis in "AIDS, Inc." (p. 123). How might some of the strategies she examines in the fight against HIV/AIDS be used to take action against climate change?

Language Matters

1. Integrating the words of other authors into your writing is an essential skill. In small groups, select a key quotation from Meyer's text and then create three different sentences that integrate that quotation. Have different groups share their results. What general techniques or strategies did people use?
2. Strong organization is self-evident. That is, when a paper is well organized, each paragraph clearly has a place in the whole. Imagine a different order for Meyer's essay. What sections would you place first, and why? What transitions would you need? Why do you think Meyer organized his essay the way he did?
3. Review the rules for verb tense in a grammar handbook or other reference resource. Then select two key quotations from Meyer and change the tenses of the verbs. What difference does tense make to an argument? What are the conventions for verb tense in academic writing?

Assignments for Writing

1. In this essay, Meyer presents climate change as an ethical issue. Using Meyer's essay, write a paper in which you propose a set of ethical standards for determining actions in relation to climate change. Your work in Question 1 of Questions for Critical Reading and Question 1 of Questions for Connecting may be useful as you form your response.
2. What role might social media play in addressing the problem of climate change. Could it be used for advocacy? Does it function to disseminate information and raise awareness? Can it be a tool for social change? Write a paper using Meyer's essay in which you evaluate the role of social media in relation to global climate change. Your work in Question 2 of Exploring Context might be a good starting point for your essay.
3. Write a paper using Meyer's essay in which you offer a set of actions we can take to address the problem of global climate change. Your work in Question 2 of Questions for Critical Reading, Questions 1 and 3 of Exploring Context, and Questions 1 and 3 of Questions for Connecting may be useful.

SHARON MOALEM

Both a medical doctor and a doctor of philosophy, **Sharon Moalem** is a best-selling author whose works include *Survival of the Sickest* and *How Sex Works*. Moalem, whose research deals largely with genetics, is also an inventor and entrepreneur, having cofounded two biotechnology companies. Moalem and his research are often discussed in the mainstream media, from *The Today Show* to the *New York Times*. He earned his Ph.D. in neurogenetics from the University of Toronto and his M.D. at New York's Mount Sinai School of Medicine.

Moalem's most recent book, *Inheritance: How Our Genes Change Our Lives and Our Lives Change Our Genes*, explores the flexibility of genes. Far from being fixed at birth, our genetic inheritance is fluid. Moalem examines the ways in which environmental conditions and lifestyle choices can not only change the expression of our DNA but also alter it in ways that can be passed down for generations. Chapters cover rare genetic disorders, drugs used in athletic doping, and the ways in which insurance companies are using our genetic information.

In "Changing Our Genes: How Trauma, Bullying, and Royal Jelly Alter Our Genetic Destiny," a chapter from *Inheritance*, Moalem explores the science of genetic inheritance not only of physical attributes but also of emotional traits. Based on studies of bees, mice, and humans, Moalem concludes that the effects of trauma, such as bullying, can change our genes and therefore also alter the genes of future generations.

What does this mean when it comes to the way society does, and should, treat post-traumatic stress?

- TAGS: *adolescence and adulthood, food and agriculture, genetics, health and medicine, science and technology, trauma and violence*
- CONNECTIONS: *Appiah, Chabon, Chen, DeGhett, Fukuyama, Lukianoff and Haidt, Pollan, Serano, Stillman, Watters*

Changing Our Genes: How Trauma, Bullying, and Royal Jelly Alter Our Genetic Destiny

Most people know about Mendel's* work with peas. Some have heard of his truncated work with mice. But what most people don't know is that Mendel also worked with honeybees—which he called "my dearest little animals."

Who can blame him for such adulation? Bees are endlessly fascinating and beautiful creatures—and they can tell us a lot about ourselves. For instance, have you ever been witness to the awesome and fearsome sight of an entire colony of bees swarming and on the move? Somewhere in the middle of that ethereal tornado is a queen bee that has left the hive.

*Gregor Mendel: Austrian monk and scientist (1822–1884) whose garden experiments formed the foundation of modern understanding of genetics and heredity.

Who is she to deserve such a grand parade?

Well, just look at her. For starters, just like human fashion models, queens have longer bodies and legs than their sister workers. They're more slender and have smooth, rather than furry, abdomens. Because they often need to protect themselves from entomological coups from younger royal upstarts, queen bees have stingers that can be reused on demand, unlike female worker bees, who die after using their stingers just once. Queen bees can live for years, though some of their workers live only a few weeks. They can also lay thousands of eggs in a day, while all their royal needs are tended to by sterile workers.*

So yeah, she's kind of a big deal.

Given the incredible differences between them, you could easily assume that queens differ genetically from the workers. That would make sense—after all, their physical traits differ considerably from their sister worker bees. But look deeper—DNA deeper—and a very different story emerges. The truth is that, genetically speaking, the queen is nobody special. A queen bee and her female workers can come from the same parents, and they can have completely identical DNA. Yet their behavioral, physiological, and anatomical differences are profound.

Why? Because larval queens eat better.

That's it. That's all. The food they eat changes their genetic expression—in this case through specific genes being turned off or on, a mechanism we call epigenetics. When the colony decides it's time for a new queen, they choose a few lucky larvae and bathe them in royal jelly, a protein- and amino acid–rich secretion produced by glands in the mouths of young worker bees. Initially, all larvae get a taste of royal jelly, but workers are quickly weaned. The little princesses, however, eat and eat and eat until they emerge as a blue-blooded brood of elegant empresses. The one who murders all the rest of her royal sisters first gets to be queen.

Her genes are no different. But her genetic expression? Royal.[1]

Beekeepers have known for centuries—maybe longer—that larvae bathed in royal jelly will produce queens. But until the genome for the western honeybee, *Apis mellifera*, was sequenced in 2006, and the specific details of caste differentiation were worked out in 2011, no one knew exactly why.

Like every other creature on this planet, bees share a lot of genetic sequences with other animals—even us. And researchers quickly noticed that one of these shared codes was for DNA methyltransferase, or Dnmt3, which in mammals can change the expression of certain genes through epigenetic mechanisms.

When researchers used chemicals to shut down the Dnmt3 in hundreds of larvae, they got an entire brood of queens. When they turned it back on in another batch of larvae, they all grew to be workers. So rather than having something more than their workers, as might be expected, queens actually have a little less—the royal jelly the queens eat so much of, it appears, just turns down the volume on the gene that makes honeybees into workers.[2]

---

*Worker honeybees, at times, can lay eggs that will hatch into drones (male bees). But given the complexities of their reproductive genetics, worker bees are incapable of laying eggs that will become other female workers.

Our diet differs from that of bees, of course, but they (and the clever researchers who study them) have given us lots of amazing examples of how our genes express themselves to meet the demands of our lives.[3]

Like humans who fill a series of set roles during their lives—from students to workers to community elders—worker bees also follow a predictable pattern from birth to death. They start as housekeepers and undertakers, keeping the hive clean and, when necessary, disposing of their dead siblings to protect the colony from disease. Most then become nurses, working together to keep tabs on each larval member of the hive more than a thousand times a day. And then, right around the ripe old age of two weeks, they set off to forage for nectar.

A team of scientists from Johns Hopkins University and Arizona State University knew that sometimes, when more nurse bees are needed, foraging bees will go back to do that job. The scientists wanted to know why. So they looked for differences in gene expression, which can be found by searching for chemical "tags" that rest atop certain genes. And indeed, when they compared the nurses with the foragers, those markers were in different places on more than 150 genes.

So they played a little trick. When the foragers were off searching for nectar, the researchers removed the nurses. Not willing to permit their young ones to be neglected, upon their return the forager bees immediately reverted to nurse duties. And just as immediately, their genetic tagging pattern changed.[4]

Genes that weren't being expressed before, now were. Genes that were, now weren't. The foragers weren't just doing another job—they were fulfilling a different genetic destiny.

Now, we might not look like bees. And we might not feel like bees. But we share a striking number of genetic similarities with bees, including Dnmt3.[5]

And just like those bees, our lives can be momentously impacted by genetic expression, for better or for worse.

Take spinach, for instance. Its leaves are rich in a chemical compound called betaine. In nature or on a farm, betaine helps plants deal with environmental stress, such as low water, high salinity, or extreme temperatures. In your body, though, betaine can behave as a methyl donor—part of a chain of chemical events that leaves a mark on your genetic code. And researchers at Oregon State University have found that, in many people who eat spinach, the epigenetic changes can help influence how their cells fight back against genetic mutations caused by a carcinogen in cooked meat. In fact, in tests involving laboratory animals, researchers were able to cut the incidence of colon tumors nearly in half.[6]

In a very small but important way, compounds within spinach can instruct the cells within our bodies to behave differently—just like the royal jelly instructs bees to develop in different ways. So yes, eating spinach seems to be able to change the expression of your genes themselves.

[In an earlier chapter] I told you that Mendel, if Bishop Schaffgotsch had not curtailed his work with mice, might have stumbled upon something even more revolutionary than his theory of inheritance? Well, now I'd like to tell you about how that idea finally came to light.

First of all, it took time. More than 90 years had passed since Mendel's death when, in 1975, geneticists Arthur Riggs and Robin Holliday, working separately in the United

States and Great Britain, respectively, almost simultaneously came upon the idea that, while genes were indeed fixed, they could perhaps be expressed differently in response to an array of stimuli, thus producing a range of traits rather than the fixed characteristics commonly thought to be associated with genetic inheritance.

Suddenly, the idea that the way genes are inherited could only be changed by the epically slow process of mutation was thrown into immediate dispute. But just as Mendel's ideas had been roundly ignored, so too were the theories being offered by Riggs and Holliday. Once again, an idea about genetics that was ahead of its time failed to gain traction.

It would be another quarter century before these ideas—and their profound implications—would gain broader acceptance. And that came as the result of the striking work of a cherub-faced scientist named Randy Jirtle. Like Mendel, Jirtle suspected that there was more to inheritance than met the eye. And, like Mendel, Jirtle suspected the answers could be found in mice.

Experimenting with agouti mice, which carry a gene that renders them plump and bright orange like a Muppet, Jirtle and his associates at Duke University came upon a discovery that, at the time, was simply stunning. By doing nothing more than changing the diet of females by the addition of a few nutrients such as choline, vitamin B12, and folic acid, starting just before conception, their offspring would be smaller, mottled brown, and altogether more mouse-like in appearance. Researchers would later discover that these mice were less susceptible to cancer and diabetes as well.

Same exact DNA. Completely different creature. And the difference was simply a matter of expression. In essence, a change in the mother's diet tagged her offspring's genetic code with a signal to turn off the agouti gene, and that turned-off gene then became inherited and was passed down across generations.

But that's just the beginning. In the fast-paced world of twenty-first-century genetics, Jirtle's Muppets have already been relegated to syndicated reruns. Every day we're learning new ways to alter genetic expression—in the genes of mice and men. The question isn't whether we can intervene; that's now a given. Now we're examining how to do it with new drugs that are already approved for human use, in ways that will hopefully result in longer and healthier lives for ourselves and for our children. What Riggs and Holliday theorized about—and what Jirtle and his colleagues brought into popular acceptance—is now known as epigenetics. Broadly, epigenetics is the study of changes in gene expression that result from life conditions, such as those seen in honeybee larvae that are doused in royal jelly, without changes in the underlying DNA. One of the fastest growing and most exciting areas of epigenetic study is its heritability, the investigation of how these changes can impact the next generation, and every generation down the line.

One common way changes in genetic expression occur is through an epigenetic process called methylation. There are many different ways in which DNA can be modified without the underlying string of nucleotide letters being altered. Methylation works by the use of a chemical compound, in the shape of three-leaf clovers made up of hydrogen and carbon, that is attached to DNA that alters the genetic structure in such a way as to program our cells to be what they're supposed to be and to do what they're supposed to do—or what they've been told to do by previous generations.

Methylation "tags" that turn genes on and off can give us cancer, diabetes, and birth defects. But don't despair—because they can also affect gene expression to give us better health and longevity.

And such epigenetic changes seem to have consequences in some unexpected places. For instance, at a summer weight-loss camp.

Genetic researchers decided to follow a group of 200 Spanish teens who were on a 10-week quest to battle the bulge. What geneticists discovered was that they could actually reverse engineer the campers' summer experience and predict which of the teens would lose the most weight depending on the pattern of methylation—the way their genes were turned off or on—in around five sites in their genome before summer camp even began.[7] Some kids were epigenetically primed to lose the bulge at summer camp while others were going to keep it on, despite diligent adherence to their counselors' dietary protocol.

We're now learning how to apply the knowledge gained from studies such as these to capitalize on our own unique epigenetic makeup. What the teenagers' methylation tags teach us is how critical it is to get to know our own distinctive epigenome in matters of weight loss, and so much else. Learning from these Spanish summer campers, we can start to mine our epigenome to find the information we need for the most optimal weight-loss strategies. For some of us that may mean saving on the exorbitant fees of a summer weight-loss adventure that is destined not to work.

But far from being static, our epigenome, along with the DNA that we've inherited, can also be impacted by what we do to our genes. We're quickly learning that epigenetic modifications, like methylation, are remarkably easy to impact. In recent years geneticists have devised a number of ways to study and even reprogram methylated genes—to turn them on and off, or to crank the volume up or down.

Changing the volume of our genetic expression can mean the difference between a benign growth and a raging malignancy.

These epigenetic changes can be caused by the pills we swallow, the cigarettes we smoke, the drinks we consume, the exercise classes we attend, and the X-rays we undergo.

And we can also do it with stress.

Building on Jirtle's work on agouti mice, scientists in Zurich wanted to see whether early childhood trauma could impact gene expression, so they stole pup mice away from their mothers for three hours, then returned the blind, deaf, and furless little things to their mommies for the rest of the day. The next day, they did it again.

Then, after 14 consecutive days, they stopped. Eventually, as all mice do, the little ones gained sight and hearing, grew some fur, and became adults. But having suffered two weeks of torment, they grew up to become significantly maladjusted little rodents. In particular, they seemed to have trouble evaluating potentially risky places. When put in adverse situations, instead of fighting or figuring it out, they just gave up. And here's the amazing part: They transmitted these behaviors to their own pups—and then to the offspring of their offspring—even if they had no involvement whatsoever in the rearing.[8]

In other words, a trauma in one generation was genetically present two generations down the line. Incredible.

It's definitely worth noting here that the genome for a mouse is about 99 percent similar to ours. And the two genes impacted in the Zurich study—called *Mecp2* and *Crfr2*—are found in mice and people alike.

Of course, we can't be sure that what happens in mice will happen in humans until we do, in fact, see it. That can be challenging to do, because our relatively long lives make it hard to conduct tests that explore generational changes, and when it comes to humans, it's a lot harder to separate nature and nurture.

But that doesn't mean we haven't seen epigenetic changes related to stress in humans. We most certainly have.

Remember when* I asked you to go back to the seventh grade? For some of us going back that far might evoke some rather unpleasant memories, events that, given a choice, we'd rather not recall. The real numbers are hard to come by, but it's thought that at least three quarters of all children have been bullied at some point in their lives, which means there's a good chance you were on the receiving end of such unfortunate experiences yourself while you were growing up. And as some of us have become parents since then, the concern for our children's own experiences and safety both at school and beyond has only grown.

Until very recently, we've been thinking and speaking about the serious and long-term ramifications of bullying in predominantly psychological terms. Everyone agrees that bullying can leave very significant mental scars. The immense psychic pain some children and teens experience can even lead them to consider and act on desires to physically harm themselves.

But what if our experiences of being bullied did a lot more than just saddle us with some serious psychological baggage? Well, to answer that question, a group of researchers from the UK and Canada decided to study sets of monozygotic "identical" twins from the age of five. Besides having identical DNA, each twin pair in the study, up until that point, had never been bullied.

You'll be glad to know that these researchers were not allowed to traumatize their subjects, unlike how the Swiss mice were handled. Instead, they let other children do their scientific dirty work.

After patiently waiting for a few years, the scientists revisited the twins where only one of the pair had been bullied. When they dropped back into their lives, they found the following: present now, at the age of 12, was a striking epigenetic difference that was not there when the children were five years old. The researchers found significant changes only in the twin who was bullied. This means, in no uncertain genetic terms, that bullying isn't just risky in terms of self-harming tendencies for youth and adolescents; it actually changes how our genes work and how they shape our lives, and likely what we pass along to future generations.

What does that change look like genetically? Well, on average, in the bullied twin a gene called *SERT* that codes for a protein that helps move the neurotransmitter serotonin into neurons had significantly more DNA methylation in its promoter region. This change is thought to dial down the amount of protein that can be made from the *SERT* gene—meaning the more it's methylated the more it's "turned off."

The reason these findings are significant is that these epigenetic changes are thought to be able to persist throughout our lives. This means that even if you can't remember the details of being bullied, your genes certainly do.

---

*In the Introduction, not included here [BJB]

But that's not all these researchers found. They also wanted to see if there were any psychological changes between the twins to go along with the genetic ones that they observed. To test that, they subjected the twins to certain types of situational testing, which included public speaking and mental arithmetic—experiences most of us find stressful and would rather avoid. They discovered that one of the twins, the one with a history of being bullied (with a corresponding epigenetic change), had a much lower cortisol response when exposed to those unpleasant situations. Bullying not only turned those children's *SERT* gene to low, it also turned down their levels of cortisol when stressed.

At first this may sound counterintuitive. Cortisol is known as the "stress" hormone and is normally elevated in people under stress. Why, then, would it be blunted in the twin who had a history of being bullied? Wouldn't you think they would be *more* stressed in a heightened situation?

This gets a little complicated, but hang tight: As a response to the persistent bullying trauma, the *SERT* gene of the bullied twin can alter the hypothalamic-pituitary-adrenal (HPA) axis, which normally helps us cope with the stresses and tumbles of daily living. And according to the scientists' findings in the bullied twin, the greater the degree of methylation, the more the *SERT* gene is turned off. The more it's turned off, the more blunted the cortisol response. To understand the sheer depth of this genetic reaction, this type of blunted cortisol response is also often found in people with post-traumatic stress disorder (PTSD).

A spike of cortisol can help us through a tough situation. But having too much cortisol, for too long, can short-circuit our physiology pretty quickly. So, having a blunted cortisol response to stress was the twin's epigenetic reaction to be being bullied day after day. In other words, the twins' epigenome changed in response to protect them from too much sustained cortisol. This compromise is a beneficial epigenetic adaptation in these children that helps them survive persistent bullying. The implications of this are nothing short of staggering.

Many of our genetic responses to our lives work in such a fashion, favoring the short over the long term. Sure, it's easier in the short term to dull our response to persistent stress, but in the long run, epigenetic changes that cause long-term blunted cortisol responses can cause serious psychiatric conditions such as depression and alcoholism. And not to scare you too much, but those epigenetic changes are likely heritable from one generation to the next.

If we're finding such changes in individuals like the bullied twin, then what about traumatic events that affect large swaths of the population?

It all started, tragically, on a crisp and clear Tuesday morning in New York City. More than 2,600 people died in and around New York's World Trade Center on September 11, 2001. Many New Yorkers who were in direct proximity to the attacks were traumatized to the point of suffering from post-traumatic stress disorder in the months and years to come.

And for Rachel Yehuda, a professor of psychiatry and neuroscience at the Traumatic Stress Studies Division at the Mount Sinai Medical Center in New York, the terrible tragedy presented a unique scientific opportunity.

Yehuda had long known that people with PTSD often had lower levels of the stress hormone cortisol in their systems—she'd first seen that effect in combat veterans she studied in the late 1980s. So she knew where to start when she began looking at samples of saliva collected from women who were at or near the Twin Towers on 9/11, and who were pregnant at that time.

Indeed, the women who ultimately developed PTSD had significantly lower levels of cortisol. And so did their babies after birth—especially the ones who were in the third trimester of development when the attacks occurred.

Those babies are older now, and Yehuda and her colleagues are still investigating how they've been impacted by the attacks. And they've already established that the children of the traumatized mothers are likely to become distressed more easily than others.[9]

What does all this mean? Taken together with the animal data we now have, it is safe to conclude that our genes do not forget our experiences, even long after we've sought therapy and feel that we've moved on. Our genes will still register and maintain that trauma.

And so the compelling question remains: Do we or do we not pass on the trauma we experience, be it bullying or 9/11, to the next generation? We previously thought that almost all of these epigenetic marks or annotations that were made on our genetic code, like those made in the margins of a musical score, were wiped clean and removed before conception. As we prepare to leave Mendel behind, we are now learning that this is likely not the case.

Do we or do we not pass on the trauma we experience, be it bullying or 9/11, to the next generation?

It is also becoming apparent that there are actually windows of epigenetic susceptibility in embryonic development. Within these important time frames, environmental stressors such as poor nutrition affect whether certain genes become turned off and on and then affect our epigenome. That's right, our genetic inheritance becomes imprinted during pivotal moments of our fetal lives.

When exactly those moments occur no one yet knows precisely, so to be safe, moms now have a genetic motivation to watch their diets and stress levels consistently throughout gestation. Research is now even showing that factors such as a mother's obesity during pregnancy can cause a metabolic reprogramming in the baby, which puts the baby at risk for conditions such as diabetes.[10] This further buttresses the growing movement within obstetrics and maternal-fetal medicine that discourages pregnant woman from eating for two.

And, as in the example of the traumatized Swiss mice, we've already seen that many of these epigenetic changes can be passed on from one generation to the next. Which makes me think that the likelihood is rather high that in the coming years we'll have overwhelming evidence that humans are not immune from this type of epigenetic traumatic inheritance.

In the meantime, given the tremendous amount we've learned about what inheritance really means and what we can do to impact our genetic legacy—in good ways (spinach, perhaps) and bad (stress, it would appear)—you are far from helpless. While it may not always be possible to break completely free from your genetic inheritance, the more you learn, the more you will come to understand that the choices you make can result in a big difference in this generation, the next one, and possibly everyone else down the line.

Because what we do know is that we are the genetic culmination of our life experiences, as well as every event our parents and ancestors ever lived through and survived—from the most joyous to the most heartrending. By examining our capacity to change our genetic destiny through the choices we make and then pass those changes along through generations, we are now in the midst of fully challenging our cherished Mendelian beliefs regarding inheritance.

NOTES

1. This paper is cited by nearly a hundred others and stands out as a landmark: M. Kamakura (2011). Royalactin induces queen differentiation in honeybees. *Nature*, 473: 478. If you find bees as fascinating as I do, you might like to read this paper as well: A. Chittka and L. Chittka (2010). Epigenetics of royalty. *PLOS Biology*, 8: el000532.
2. F. Lyko et al. (2010). The honeybee epigenomes: Differential methylation of brain DNA in queens and workers. *PLOS Biology*, 8: el000506.
3. R. Kucharski et al. (2008). Nutritional control of reproductive status in honeybees via DNA methylation. *Science*, 319: 1827–1830.
4. B. Herb et al. (2012). Reversible switching between epigenetic states in honeybee behavioral subcastes. *Nature Neuroscience*, 15: 1371–1373.
5. Humans have two different versions, *DNMT3A* and *DNMT3B*, which have shared homology and similarity in the catalytic domain to the Dmnt3 gene found in *Apis mellifera*, the honeybee. If you'd like to read more about this, see the following paper: Y. Wang et al. (2006). Functional CpG methylation system in a social insect. *Science*, 27: 645–647.
6. M. Parasramka et al. (2012). MicroRNA profiling of carcinogen-induced rat colon tumors and the influence of dietary spinach. *Molecular Nutrition & Food Research*, 56: 1259–1269.
7. A. Moleres et al. (2013). Differential DNA methylation patterns between high and low responders to a weight loss intervention in overweight or obese adolescents: The EVASYON study. *FASEB Journal*, 27: 2504–2512.
8. T. Franklin et al. (2010). Epigenetic transmission of the impact of early stress across generations. *Biological Psychiatry*, 68: 408–415.
9. R. Yehuda et al. (2009). Gene expression patterns associated with posttraumatic stress disorder following exposure to the World Trade Center attacks. *Biological Psychiatry*, 66: 708–711; R. Yehuda et al. (2005). Transgenerational effects of posttraumatic stress disorder in babies of mothers exposed to the World Trade Center attacks during pregnancy. *Journal of Clinical Endocrinology & Metabolism*, 90: 4115–4118.
10. S. Sookoian et al. (2013). Fetal metabolic programming and epigenetic modifications: A systems biology approach. *Pediatric Research*, 73: 531–542.

Questions for Critical Reading

1. Moalem covers quite a bit of territory in this piece, moving from bees to the terrorist attacks of September 11, 2001. As you reread this essay, create a quick outline that traces Moalem's moves between these disparate examples, marking significant passages that link the examples together.
2. What factors can change genes? Review the essay and pay close attention to places in the essay where Moalem discusses elements that can change our genetic information. Knowing that our DNA can be affected by what we do, how might we change our behaviors?

3. *Epigenetics* plays a significant role in Moalem's argument. Find passages where Moalem defines the term and then define it in your own words. Try to locate your own example of epigenetics.

Exploring Context

1. Learn more about epigenetics at the Learn Genetics website from the University of Utah at learn.genetics.utah.edu/content/epigenetics. How does this additional information change your understanding of Moalem's argument? Use the information you find to expand your response to Question 3 of Questions for Critical Reading.
2. Moalem was on the Medical and Scientific Advisory Board of Global Genes (globalgenes.org), a site dedicated to rare diseases, many of which are genetic. Visit the site to learn more about this advocacy group. How would a greater understanding of genetic flexibility help with such a project?
3. Sharon Moalem has a Tumblr blog, located at sharonmoalem.tumblr.com. Explore his blog. How do his posts connect to his work in this essay?

Questions for Connecting

1. **Multimodal.** Sarah Stillman makes a very similar argument in "Hiroshima and the Inheritance of Trauma" (p. 371). Synthesize these two essays. What factors, cultural and biological, contribute to the persistence of trauma across generations? Using PowerPoint or other software, prepare a presentation of your findings. As you do so, you will want to consider not only your content but also the design of the slides and the transitions between them and how these factors can impact the effectiveness of your argument. Consider using the web to learn more about effective presentations.
2. Michael Chabon, in "My Son, the Prince of Fashion" (p. 62) discusses the bullying his son Abe endured at school because of his love of fashion. Use Moalem's ideas to analyze this narrative. How does bullying become an even more pressing problem given what Moalem explains? What is it about Abe that allowed him to go on and thrive? How might that complicate Moalem's argument?
3. Moalem suggests that what we eat can have a tremendous epigenetic impact. Synthesize his work with David Foster Wallace's "Consider the Lobster" (p. 406). Given epigenetics, are the moral and ethical decisions involved in eating even more pressing? How so?

Language Matters

1. Use the online mind-mapping tool at bubbl.us to create a map of Moalem's essay. To what extent does his argument function like genes with multiple possible expressions?
2. Moalem uses endnotes to cite his sources. Research the systems of citation for various disciplines. Which ones promote the use of endnotes or footnotes? Given what you learn, can you determine Moalem's discipline? When might you use endnotes or footnotes, given the citation system you're using in this class?

3. Introductions do a lot of important work in your papers: They introduce the authors, the essays, and, most important, your position or argument. How does Moalem introduce this chapter? How effective is his introduction? Why would you want (or not want) to open your paper that way?

Assignments for Writing

1. Moalem examines the scientific relationship between the mind and body in his discussion of epigenetics. Extend his discussion to philosophy by writing a paper about the mind/body relationship. How does epigenetics change our understanding of the relationship between the two?
2. Write a paper about the persistence of trauma. How do traumatic events such as bullying affect victims? Extend Moalem's work on trauma to consider the larger ramifications of practices such as bullying. Use your work from Question 2 of Questions for Connecting.
3. Write a paper in which you use Moalem's ideas to propose an ethics of eating. How might the epigenetic impacts of food change the way we think about eating? Does the fact that the food changes our genetic code imply that there is a moral dimension to our food choices? Use your work in Question 3 of Questions for Connecting.

NICK PAUMGARTEN

Nick Paumgarten is a staff writer for the *New Yorker*, a position he has held since 2005. He still contributes to "The Talk of the Town," a regular feature of the *New Yorker* that he served as deputy editor of from 2000 to 2005. His work at the magazine often focuses on sports, music, and finance.

The *New Yorker*, published nearly weekly since 1925, is known for its highbrow reporting, criticism, cartoons, and literature. Regular contributors include high-profile writers and thinkers such as Malcolm Gladwell and James Surowiecki; Maria Konnikova, also featured in *Emerging*, regularly writes for the magazine as well. The September 22, 2014 issue, from which this essay is taken, featured fiction from Victor Lodato as well as essays on a Wonder Woman museum, the inclusion of plus-size models at recent fashion shows, and Utah's attempt to solve homelessness by giving away homes.

In "We Are a Camera," Paumgarten explores the popularity of GoPro cameras—small, rugged personal video cameras most often mounted on a person and used to document some exciting, extraordinary event. Mountain climbers, bikers, divers, surfers, and others use them to share some of their most daring exploits. As these POV (point of view) videos produced by GoPro cameras become more and more popular, Paumgarten begins to consider the consequences of this technology. Tracing the history of the company and its technology, he examines the ways in which users come to value the footage of an experience more than the experience itself. Moreover, GoPro makes the pervasiveness of cameras feel benign when it may not be so at all.

Have you ever used a GoPro or seen footage? Do videos enhance our memories or replace them?

- TAGS: *art, culture, economics, empathy, media, photography and video, relationships*
- CONNECTIONS: *DeGhett, Klosterman, Ma, Provan, Singer, Southan, Watters*

We Are a Camera

Late one fall afternoon two years ago, Aaron Chase, a professional mountain biker, was riding his bike in the Smoky Mountains, near Sun Valley, Idaho. He'd powered up to a high-altitude ridge and was gazing, less than eagerly, at the trail down toward the backcountry yurt where he and two fellow pro riders were camped for the week. He wasn't feeling well. He was tired, hungry, dehydrated, and a little woozy. In the argot, he was bonking.

He and the others, along with a professional photographer, had spent two days filming video footage of themselves hurtling down steep technical trails and executing tricks off natural features. They had brought along more than a dozen GoPros, the ubiquitous small digital point-of-view cameras.

Chase, who is sponsored by GoPro and is exceptionally adept at using GoPro cameras to make videos, likes to use a camera mount called the 360 Narwhal, after the species of whale with a tusk protruding from its jaw. The mount consists of a lightweight carbon rod affixed to the top of his helmet, like a helicopter rotor, to which he attaches a pair of GoPros, one at each end, a couple of feet from the center, in the manner of two buckets hanging from a carrying pole. The rod can rotate around its center, its movements determined by the cameras' weight and centrifugal momentum. Typically, Chase sets one camera a little farther out from his head than the other and, with subtle tilts of his head, exploits the asymmetry to manipulate the cameras' positions and movements as he rides. He is star athlete, director, and DP. He gives as much thought to getting the shot as he does to nailing the trick.

For two days in the Idaho mountains, Chase's cameras had been rolling virtually nonstop. Now, with his companions lagging behind, he started down the trail, which descended steeply into an alpine meadow. As he accelerated, he noticed, to his left, an elk galloping toward him from the ridge. He glanced at the trail, looked again to his left, and saw a herd, maybe thirty elk, running at full tilt alongside his bike, like a pod of dolphins chasing a boat. After a moment, they rumbled past him and crossed the trail, neither he nor the elk slowing, dust kicking up and glowing in the early-evening sun, amid a thundering of hooves. It was a magical sight. The light was perfect. And, as usual, Chase was wearing two GoPros. Here was his money shot—the stuff of TV ads and real bucks.

Trouble was, neither camera was rolling. What with his headache and the ample footage of the past days, he'd thought to hell with it, and had neglected, just this once, to turn his GoPros on. Now there was no point in riding with the elk. He slowed up and let them pass. "Idiot," he said to himself. "There goes my commercial."

Once the herd was gone, it was as though it'd never been there at all—Sasquatch, E.T., yeti. Pics or it didn't happen. Still, one doesn't often find oneself swept up in a stampede of wild animals. Might as well hope to wingsuit through a triple rainbow. So you'd think that, cameras or not, he'd remember the moment with some fondness. But no. "It was hell," Chase says now.

When the agony of missing the shot trumps the joy of the experience worth shooting, the adventure athlete (climber, surfer, extreme skier) reveals himself to be something else: a filmmaker, a brand, a vessel for the creation of content. He used to just do the thing—plan the killer trip or trick and then complete it, with panache. Maybe a photographer or film crew tagged along, and afterward there'd be a slide show at community centers and high-school gyms, or an article in a magazine. Now the purpose of the trip or trick is the record of it. Life is footage.

Chase's elk came to mind on the morning, in late June, of GoPro's initial public offering. When GoPro goes public, there is no chance of missing the shot. Before the opening bell, legions of GoPro executives, employees, family, and friends gathered on the ground floor of the NASDAQ building, in what is really just a TV studio, facing out onto Times Square. There's no trading floor at NASDAQ, so bell ringings are Potemkin affairs—in this case, not only for the usual phalanx of TV cameras but also for the fifty-odd GoPros the team had brought along, so everyone could chronicle the occasion from a variety of unconventional vantages.

The camera is a relatively simple device. High-tech guts in low-tech disguise—it's "cute and fancy," as the late Sony chairman Akio Morita is supposed to have said of the Walkman. A GoPro Hero 3+, the latest iteration (the tech rumor mill predicts that the Hero 4 will début next month), costs between three hundred and four hundred dollars. Once removed from its waterproof case—to the GoPro what armor was to the knight—it is small and spare. People say "matchbox-size" but it's more like two matchboxes. It has just three buttons and yet, somehow, dozens of settings.

The GoPro is defined as much by its limitations as by its advantages. It has no display, so you can't see what's in the frame. In a way, this doesn't matter, because the wide-angle lens takes in so broad a field (everything in focus, everything lit) that you need only point it in a general direction and you can expect to capture something good. 10

Both the indicator light and the control display are on the front of the camera, so this is where its operator must go to operate it, or to make sure that it is in fact operating. In unedited GoPro shots, the cameraman often appears in closeup in the frame, amid the muffled clatter of finger (or glove) brushing microphone; this routine parenthesis is the GoPro version of a director's slate. (You could cut an hour-long edit of these accidental selfies—a montage of scraped knuckles, double chins, and bloodshot eyes—and call it "Action!") The microphone picks up sound that is very close but misses sound farther away. GoPro shots are often characterized by one-sided conversation, the rattle of straps, or the beatbox fusillade of water and wind. This is one reason a polished GoPro edit is usually set to music. Still, the clarity of the picture, which renders trees, waves, seracs, clouds, and cliffs with a kind of lysergic radiance, flatters the natural world.

On the morning of the IPO, the company's founder, Nick Woodman, who devised a crude version of the camera twelve years ago to get photos of himself surfing, held GoPros, at different times, in his teeth, at arm's length, or on an array of mounts, filming himself and others, who in turn trained their cameras on him and on themselves. Woodman, in jeans and a dark-blue button-down shirt, tan and fit with white teeth and spiky dark hair, led them in impromptu banshee howls, the feral woo-hoos of joyriders everywhere, and chants of "Go Pro! Go Pro! Go Pro!" and with his non-GoPro hand flashed the surfer's hang-loose shaka sign. He pointed a GoPro at himself and howled, "This is really happening!" The camera affirmed it.

Becoming a multibillionaire may not be as rare an occurrence these days as riding a mountain bike through a herd of elk, but it is nonetheless a feat worthy of documentation. GoPro's offering price, of twenty-four dollars a share, valued the company at around three billion dollars. Woodman's father, Dean Woodman, a hale gent of eighty-five who had himself once been a very successful entrepreneur, as a founder of the now defunct San Francisco investment bank Robertson Stephens, and who early on had lent his son two hundred thousand dollars to finance GoPro, came up to him and said, "You look like a rock star."

"I play one on TV," the son said. He is known as the Mad Billionaire, for his hyperactive antics and taste for adventure sports. But when it came time for him to talk, just before the opening, he teared up, presumably at this culmination of so much hard work—years of risks rewarded, doubts dashed, overpromises met, and paternal expectations exceeded. He recovered himself for the cameras. "I'm fired up!" he called out to his employees. "You fired up?"

After the bell, while the GoPro employees milled around and posed for photos, Brad Schmidt, GoPro's creative director, working on a laptop with GoPro editing software, 15 quickly cut the footage into a packet to present to the TV producers who'd be interviewing Woodman and his fellow-executives throughout the day. As Schmidt has said, you don't hunt shots; you "capture" them. (This approach requires lots of work in the cutting room, or what *Surfing* called "a time-warping pain in the edit-ass.") Schmidt scrolled through dozens of vantages, many of them imbued with a kinetic intensity you don't usually see on the set of a stock-market show. "The button shot is amazing," he said; it had captured Woodman reaching down toward the camera to press a lit panel that would initiate the day's trading—the NASDAQ equivalent, perhaps, of getting tubed at Pipeline.

As he worked, half a dozen guests held their GoPros up to the window to film the Jumbotrons in Times Square, which NASDAQ had leased for the occasion in order to display GoPro videos. Among the cavalcade of images was an underwater shot of Woodman's toddler son learning to swim: a private event now magnified into mythology in the hall of mirrors that is our world of cameras and screens.

Woodman had the good fortune to invent a product that was well suited to a world he had not yet imagined. The ripening of the technology in his camera, after a half decade of tinkering, coincided with the fruition of broadband and the emergence of YouTube, Facebook, and other social-media platforms for the wide distribution of video. GoPro rode the wave. What might have been just another camcorder became a leading connector between what goes on in the real world and what goes out in the virtual one—a perfect instrument for the look-at-me age. Its charm lies perhaps in its sublimated conveyance of self, its sneaky tolerable narcissism. GoPro footage is related to the selfie, in its "Here I am" (or "was") ethos, and its wide view and variety of mounts often allow the filmmaker to include himself, or some part of himself, in the shot. But because it primarily points outward it's a record of what an experience looks like, rather than what the person who had the experience looked like when he stopped afterward and arranged his features into his pretested photo face. The result is not as much a selfie as a worldie. It's more like the story you'd tell about an adventure than the photo that would accompany it.

The result is not as much a selfie as a worldie.

Though GoPro is known primarily for its connection to adventure sports, the camera is increasingly used in feature films and on TV, and by professionals of many stripes—musicians, surgeons, chefs. Many BMWs now come with an app to control a GoPro in the dash (in case you want to show the kids your commute). The company has been promoting its use in broadcasting traditional sports. An armada of GoPros greatly enhanced the coverage of last year's America's Cup, in San Francisco Bay, but perhaps they'd shed less light on the mysteries of an NFL line of scrimmage: one imagines indecipherable grunting and rustling, the filmic equivalent of a butt dial. The opposite of this, and the big thing these days, is the footage that comes from mounting GoPros on small quadcopter drones: sublime sweeping shots and heretofore unseen bird's-eye vantages, on the cheap.

As for its broadcast applications, we are still in a relatively primitive stage. A GoPro senior producer described to me the process he came up with last year to get POV footage of Shane Dorian surfing the giant waves at Mavericks, off the coast of Northern

California, to use on a broadcast of a competition there. After Dorian had ridden a wave, a guy on a Jet Ski would zoom over, grab the camera, and then carry it in past the break to a paddleboarder, who'd maneuver through the swirling whitewash to the base of a cliff, over which a member of the broadcast team had lowered a basket. Up went the basket, and an assistant ran the camera over to the broadcast tent.

In going public, GoPro has tried to position itself not just as a camera-maker but as a media company—a producer and distributor of branded content. In this conception, it is hawking not only cameras and accessories (the source, up to now, of pretty much all of GoPro's revenue) but videos, too (a source, up to now, of pretty much no revenue). In the past five years, videos posted by GoPro have attracted half a billion views. On the GoPro channel on YouTube, videos average about half a million viewers each. The company thinks it can capitalize on the fact that thousands of people every day post videos online and, without prompting, tag them as GoPro. 20

Most of them are not the ones that come from their sponsored athletes (or "brand ambassadors"), like Aaron Chase, who are expected to submit footage. They are crowd-sourced—amateur-hour finds that turn pro. For the latter, GoPro pays very little—maybe some accessories or a camera, plus, say, a thousand dollars for the first million views. A cadre of editors at GoPro scours Facebook, YouTube, and Reddit and often reëdits the best and pushes them out on its own channels on YouTube, Pinterest, and other platforms. In the process, the company has nurtured a growing army of amateurs (eager providers of free content) and helped the GoPro name become shorthand not only for all POV cameras, including those made by other manufacturers, but for the genre of short video that has arguably become as much a feature of daily life as the three-minute pop song.

You can probably think of as many viral GoPro videos as you can recent hit singles. Have you seen the one that was shot from the beak of an airborne pelican? The one of the South African mountain biker being robbed by the gunman? The woman giving birth on the sidewalk? The fireman rescuing the kitten? The Lion Whisperer guy? "Toy Robot in Space"? The view from a car wheel or the inside of a fox's mouth or a drone soaring through a Fourth of July fireworks display? Of course you have, and if you haven't I'll send you the link.

The genre is characterized by point of view, by brevity, and by incident. The ones that go viral contain something extraordinary, be it unimaginable risk, uncharted beauty, unlikely encounter, or unexpected twist. The categories bleed. A common critique has been that the presence of the camera prods people to take greater risks as they aspire to virality—Kodak courage, which might now be more properly called GoPro guts. It may not be fair to say that it's the camera that causes people to attempt to brush the ground while flying past an outcrop in a wingsuit, but perhaps seeing it done on film inspires other people to try. Some have attributed this phenomenon to *Jackass*, the MTV program on which a band of pranksters subjected their bodies to clever, horrific abasements, but, really, people have attempted dangerous stunts for attention and money since the invention of the camera. Before there was Johnny Knoxville there was Buster Keaton. GoPro has been sensitive to the contention that their cameras play any role in getting people to do stupid, risky, dangerous, or unlawful things. It offers, with some plausibility, a kind of guns-don't-kill-people argument. Don't blame the camera. A spokesman cited Icarus.

A popular subgenre is the blooper, the so-called GoPro Fail. Sometimes the intention to Be a Hero causes one instead to Be the Schlemiel. There may be violence, but insofar as it ends well, you might call it comic. My favorite GoPro Fail, which first made the rounds in February, 2011, and still circles the Internet in a kind of ongoing viral orbit, was of, and by, a skier named Stefan Ager. The video is a minute and a half long and is shot from Ager's helmet mount. It begins with him and a friend atop a snow-clad peak in Austria, after a three-hour climb. The setting is a sheer ridge, with cliffs seemingly dropping off in all directions. After some giddy panorama shots, he holds his helmet out and turns the camera on himself, revealing a young shaggy dude. He dons the helmet and looks down to put on his skis, which he lays parallel in the snow, along the narrow ridge. He steps into his bindings, the skis drift backward a few inches, and—"Whoa!"—our man goes backward over the precipice. The camera tosses and clicks as Ager—"Aaaah!"—plummets more than a thousand vertical feet down a cliff, bouncing off rocks, before landing—"Oof!"—on the edge of a glacier. He moans a couple of times and then stands up (or so it looks from his shadow, which is topped by a silhouette of the GoPro). He looks around. Somehow, his survival makes the glacier all the more beautiful, even to the viewer. He glances back to where he came from, and then the video ends.

It's the mother of all pratfalls, and I've watched it more than a dozen times. It's had more than three million hits. Last month, when I tracked Ager down, via Facebook, I felt as though I'd found an e-mail address for, say, Lorde. He wrote back, "I am actually not interested in an interview regarding my fall. I am glad that nothing happened and I can keep skiing." 25

Every entrepreneurial success story hardens into legend, and the quickening often occurs around the time of the IPO. GoPro's is as follows: In 1999, during the dot-com boom, Woodman, a recent graduate of the University of California at San Diego and the son of a prominent Bay Area banker, started an online video-game company called Funbug. It failed two years later, amid the dot-com crash, and Woodman, embarrassed over having lost other people's money, decided to take six months off to surf and travel with his girlfriend. While in Indonesia, in 2002, he struck up a friendship with another surfer, named Brad Schmidt. They were both intrigued by the problem of how to get pictures of themselves riding waves. At this point, Woodman's innovation was a wrist wrap fashioned from the ankle end of his surfboard leash, to which, using rubber bands, he affixed a disposable Kodak camera in a waterproof case. He had a sense that the wristband could be marketable, but soon realized, after trying various cameras, that it would get complicated, with regard to licensing and legal permission. So he went to China to have a camera made to his specs.

By 2004, he had a prototype of the GoPro Hero, a clunky 35-mm. box that used film. In the next few years, with Schmidt testing it out on surfing trips and sending back astonishing images, Woodman made refinements, and started making money, too. He travelled around the country in a 1974 VW van he called Biscuit, to surf shops and trade shows (and did a couple of appearances on QVC); to raise extra funds he sold belts made of seashells he'd picked up in Bali. At surfing events, he handed out cameras to pros. One day, he attached a GoPro to the cockpit of a racecar, and everyone at the track became fascinated by both the device and the result. A light bulb: this thing wasn't just for surfers.

Schmidt, fresh out of film school, became the head of GoPro's media division, which distributed as many videos, from an ever-widening circle of sources, as it could—in part, as Schmidt has said, to convince the world that these videos were real. By the end of the decade, the GoPro was commonplace in the world of action sports. Every week seemed to bring a revelatory new vantage on some established exploit or trick. And then people began coming up with new moves and feats, to suit the camera.

The producers at GoPro are often athletes themselves, maybe with some film or photography experience. Woodman has always encouraged his employees to hire their friends. Zak Shelhamer, a photographer and former professional snowboarder, joined the company to help edit and produce snow-sport videos and now runs the adventure-sports division. He told me that he'd recently been talking to a pair of young Frenchmen who were planning to row a boat from Monterey to Hawaii. They'd submitted a proposal for a contest the company ran called How Will You GoPro? They didn't win, but Shelhamer gave them some cameras anyway and promised to take an interest in what they might come back with. In discussing the risks, he mentioned a guy who had tried rowing from Australia to New Zealand. "How'd he do?" one of the Frenchmen asked him.

"He drowned," Shelhamer said.

"How'd they figure that out?"

"They found his camera."

After the IPO, GoPro's stock price almost doubled and began to develop the characteristics of a so-called battleground stock. On one side were the believers, who, implicitly or not, endorsed the company's branded content aspirations. (One Wall Street analyst last week called GoPro a "movement.") On the other side were the skeptics who suspected that the stock's rise had as much to do with a love for the product as for its real long-term prospects—cute and fancy winning out, for now, over hard and cold. They note that bigger companies are now making similar cameras (one can argue which are the best), and so they wonder how long GoPro can stay on top. The cautionary example, cited by doubters and by GoPro itself, is the Flip, the briefly ubiquitous digital camcorder, which got overtaken by smartphones and is now out of business.

The company wants to capitalize on the mass-market home-video urge, the camera's aptitude for capturing what GoPro's president, Tony Bates, calls "life's great moments," and yet retain its reputation as a kind of philosopher's stone, capable of transforming ordinary experience into magical footage. (Two tips: "Slow it down and you look like a pro." "The closer the better.") In some respects, the GoPro is like the Brownie and the Polaroid, devices that democratized photography and revolutionized the way we think about the past and even the way we fashion the present, with an eye to how it will look later, when we linger over photographs of it. But the analogy comes up short, because GoPro videos aspire to go viral. You're sharing the photos of your ski trip not just with your family and a few friends but, if you're any good, with thousands, if not millions, of people. The GoPro, by implication, asks its users to push a little harder, as both subjects and filmmakers. Be a Hero: The premise from the start has been that you, in every way an amateur, can go pro—on both sides of the lens. It's karaoke, but with the full Marshall stack.

The short video synonymous with GoPro is a kind of post-literate diary, a stop on the way to a future in which everything will be filmed from every point of view. Humans have always recorded their experiences, in an array of media and for a variety of reasons. Not until very recently, with the advent of digital photography and video, and unlimited storage and distribution capacity, has it been conceivable to film everything. As we now more than ever communicate through pictures, either still or moving, perhaps our lives come closer to Susan Sontag's imagined "anthology of images." An obvious example is the people who film concerts on their smartphones. Will they ever watch the video? And if they do will it measure up to the concert, which they half missed? Of course not. They film the concert to certify their attendance and convey their good fortune. The frame corroborates.

The computer scientist Gordon Bell, a former Digital Equipment Corporation engineer, an early developer of the Internet, and later a top researcher at Microsoft, spent several years as the main subject of a life-logging experiment called MyLifeBits, inspired by the work of the scientist Vannevar Bush, who, in 1945, wrote, "The camera hound of the future wears on his forehead a lump a little larger than a walnut." (To store all the images, and everything else, Bush envisioned a device called the "memex," short for memory extender.) Bell, in addition to digitizing every document, object, phone conversation, and transaction in his life, wore a Microsoft SenseCam around his neck. It snapped a photo every twenty seconds.

"What you're capturing is one thing," he told me. "The other is when are you going to use it." He'd recently gone to a conference on memory, sponsored by something called the Institute for the Future. Apparently, psychologists and neurologists have discovered that photos or video of an event are more effective than notes or conversation at helping people remember an experience.

Bell is amazed that a surfer in California cornered the market for what he calls go-everywhere cameras. "Where were the Japanese?" he said. "They totally ignored the fact that you could have a camera like this at this price point. But really it's not the camera—it's the Internet."

At any rate, he predicts that eventually GoPros and their ilk, as well as contrivances like Google Glass, will be supplanted by truly wearable cameras, with virtually no volume (a card, or a chip, or, one imagines, an implant in the retina). "Is there a time in the future where people will record everything they see and hear?" Bell asked. "Yes. It's at least a decade away." The difficulty arises in the sorting—a pain in the edit-ass of big-data proportions. "It requires an enormous amount of software."

By now, so much video is being produced that it's hard to imagine a fate for it other than obsolescence. Where does all this video go? If it's in the cloud, will it all come falling back to earth, in an apocalypse of pets, babies, head-cam porn, flight lessons, golf swings, and unicycle tricks?

Earlier this summer, I attended the GoPro Mountain Games, in Vail, Colorado, a competition-cum-festival featuring mountain bikers, rock climbers, and other outdoor athletes. Teeming with GoPros, the village, ersatz Alpine to begin with, felt a little like the set of a ski-town *Brigadoon*. One afternoon, I went whitewater kayaking down Gore Creek with Eric and Dane Jackson, father-and-son professional freestyle kayakers and GoPro ambassadors. The paddling wasn't hard, and yet the Jacksons, who routinely descend steep creeks and giant waterfalls, seemed intent on making my outing into an accomplishment worthy of recording and then foisting onto the world. Now and then, Dane paddled over, spat on his fingers, and rubbed saliva on the lens of the GoPro on the bow of my boat. We drifted past a man who was operating a quadcopter drone with a GoPro attached. It swooped over us and then receded upriver. Above the take-out, in town, a little girl with a GoPro on her forehead passed over us on a zip line. On bridges and banks: GoPros everywhere. We were mayflies, flashing through the frames of strangers.

When we were done, Eric Jackson, using GoPro's editing program, made a thirty-second video of our trip and posted it on his Facebook page. He scrolled down, interested only in how much attention his posts were getting, not in what others had to say. "I don't read any of this," he said. "I don't read Facebook. I don't watch the other videos. I don't want to read everyone else's diaries. I write a diary." He posts a video almost every day, in part to promote himself and his business (he also manufactures kayaks), but also out of some compulsion to leave a record of his exploits—to draw on the walls of the cave.

Two years ago, my son, then ten, won a GoPro in a school raffle. On a ski vacation that spring, he affixed it to the top of his helmet with the standard mount—Tinkywinky, we called him, after the Teletubby with the triangle on its head—and let it roll most of the day, five to fifteen minutes at a stretch. What struck me, while watching some of the footage on a laptop later, was the idiosyncratic ordinariness of it. As he skied, he whistled to himself, made odd sounds, looked around at the mountains, shouted to his brother and his cousin, cried out at the slightest hint of air, and now and then bent forward and filmed upside down through his legs. Even though the camera was turned outward, filled mainly by the sight of the terrain sliding past, it provided, more than anything, a glimpse into the mind of a dreamy and quiet boy—who, to my eyes, during the day, had been just a nose, his features and expressions otherwise hidden by helmet, neck gaiter, and goggles. I didn't need a camera to show me what he looked like to the world, but was delighted to find one that could show me what the world looked like to him. It captured him better than any camera pointed at him could. This was a proxy, of sorts.

This past spring, he again spent a few days skiing with the camera on his head—Tinkywinky at twelve. His best footage came from a powder morning, his first ever in the Rockies; the camera aimed just past the tips of his skis. Every civilian who skis powder with a GoPro on his head gets the same kind of shot, pole tips rhythmically appearing at the edges of the frame, ski tips porpoising in and out of the snow, the occasional whoop of joy. In my son's video, the whistling and whimsical attention of two years before had given way to a devoted concentration and perhaps an earnest attempt to record what he, in the manner of skiers everywhere, deemed a noteworthy experience. Later, he shot footage while following me through gaps in the trees. That night, I watched it—again in the manner of skiers everywhere—for glimpses of myself.

A month later, he had to make a presentation in class, and he decided to do his about the GoPro. Planning to demonstrate his handiwork, he edited the footage, but then, at the last moment, decided it was too commonplace. It wasn't awesome enough—or, anyway, he didn't want his classmates to think that he thought it was

45

awesome. Instead, he featured, in his report, a famous video from the POV of a mountain biker named Kelly McGarry doing a backflip over a canyon gap in Virgin, Utah. My son had become a habitual consumer of GoPro videos. Even as a grommet, he had standards. He no longer thought of it as home video.

At many ski areas nowadays, you can rent a GoPro for the day. The slopes teem with Teletubbies. People have helmet mounts for POV cameras of every make, and even smartphones in waterproof shells. It's not just groms or pros. It's grampas and gapers, too (*gapers* being the shredder's term for hapless wannabes). A ski trip has become a kind of life-logging vacation. People who'd never film a minute of their ordinary lives deem a day riding chairlifts and creeping along groomed trails to be worthy of wall-to-wall coverage. The sense among many serious skiers is that the cameras have contributed to heedless, or at least distracted, behavior in the backcountry. Any attention given to getting the shot, or posing for it, is attention diverted from the task of staying safe. Of course, there is no data to support this, and it could well be mere curmudgeonly grumbling. It's just that there are so many videos of bad stuff happening to backcountry skiers. GoPros have made it possible to see, really for the first time, the way the snowpack jigsaws around you (a skier's version of a land mine's click) when an avalanche kicks off or how it looks and sounds to be buried when the slide comes to a stop.

When it ends badly, the camera can be a kind of black box. A fantasy of the film-everything movement is an end to forensic uncertainty. Wearable POV cameras are also coming into vogue as a tool for soldiers and police. The premise is that reviewability makes for greater accountability—that seeing is knowing. After the Michael Brown shooting, in Ferguson, many commentators, accustomed already to the ubiquity of cameras, were dismayed that there was no footage of the incident. In this instance, we may wish we had some, but a world in which the police film every interaction with the public is not all sweetness and light. You may catch some bad cops, but you'd also hamstring the good ones. By enforcing uninterpretable standards of exchange, a video record has the effect of a mandatory sentence. It deprives the police of discretion, and the public of leniency. There are many things we'd rather not see or have seen.

There are many things we'd rather not see or have seen.

GoPro, like Google Glass, has the insidious effect of making the pervasiveness of cameras seem playful and benign when it may one day be anything but. The *Economist* called the film-everything culture "the people's panopticon"—the suggestion being that with all these nifty devices we might be unwittingly erecting a vast prison of self-administered surveillance.

Andrew Rossig started BASE jumping in 2004, under the tutelage of an Englishman who was a proponent of "bandit jumping"—that is, jumping off things you are not allowed to. He got his first GoPro in 2010. It was much lighter than existing wearable cameras, which typically involved the camera on one side of the helmet and a battery pack on the other, a strain and a threat to the neck. You might say that a BASE jump consists of two main ingredients: the jump itself and the record of it. The GoPro made feasible part two.

Rossig, a carpenter who works in New York City, building movie sets, began nursing an ambition to film himself leaping off all the city's iconic tall structures, but it 50 eventually became clear to him that it wasn't very safe and that the authorities would never permit it. Still, a man could dabble. In 2012, he was arrested, with a fellow BASE jumper named James Brady, while attempting to jump off a thirty-three-story tower in Co-op City, in the Bronx. Not long afterward, they began planning a jump off One World Trade Center, which Brady, an ironworker, had helped to build. They talked about making a movie out of the whole thing or not filming any of it at all. They agreed that it was perhaps unwise and potentially incriminating, at least, to film their conversations and preparations. Still, isn't the point of jumping off an iconic building to create and share a record of the deed? Rossig felt they had to have footage, at least for the benefit one day of children and grandchildren.

One night last September, the two of them, with a third jumper and a lookout man, sneaked through a hole in the security fence at the construction site and walked up the hundred and four flights to the top of the tower. They wore GoPros on their helmets but opted not to turn them on, lest the red indicator lights give them away. Only once they were on top of the tower, at the edge, preparing to leap, did they start shooting.

Each of the three jumpers shot footage. The first jumper pulled his chute immediately and soared way out over the Hudson and then tacked back toward the towers. Brady was the second to go; his video would be the most widely distributed. Rossig went last, did a somersault in the air, and pulled his chute later in the plunge than the others. He actually passed Brady. Altogether, the three original videos have been viewed almost three and a half million times on YouTube. One is struck by the tranquility and silence before the jump, the mixture of reverence and apprehension. Often GoPro undertakings have a frivolous air, but this one's no joke. Their silhouettes are backlit by a vast plain of city lights. One jumper coaxes another, with a gentleness uncommon to GoPro-land. Most striking of all is the vision, once the plummet begins, of the illuminated glass façade of the tower sliding past, the pace accelerating yet oddly slow, almost elegant, with no trace really of violence or terror. In 1878, "Sallie Gardner at a Gallop," in a sense history's first film, depicting a thoroughbred in profile, surprised many viewers who'd previously misconstrued the mechanics of a galloping horse. These days, the drift of One World Trade's lit windows has a similar effect. So this is free fall. The pace shifts abruptly when each jumper pulls his chute. They drift toward the pavement. At the end of each video, the jumper lands in abandoned streets and scurries toward the shadows and a getaway car.

That night, a passerby caught a glimpse of them and called 911. The police checked security footage from the Goldman Sachs building nearby. They noticed a suspicious car, and then, using footage from other cameras in the area, in an ever-widening radius (there are more than four thousand working security cameras and license-plate scanners below Canal Street), they identified the vehicle (apparently, the NYPD keeps a record of every vehicle that crosses into Lower Manhattan) and eventually, in part by subpoenaing cell-phone records, the jumpers themselves, who, in the immediate aftermath of the jump, had dispersed and refrained from calling each other. A month afterward, they got together with thumb drives to watch and share each other's footage of the jump. But once the cops had identified them, five months after the jump, they turned themselves in. It was only then that they posted their jump footage on YouTube, in the hope that the beauty and strangeness of it might persuade the public, if not prosecutors, that they meant no harm.

"The legal advice we got was that we should show we're not bad guys," Rossig said. "If we're going to get in trouble for it, maybe everyone should see how amazing it was. Who else is going to get that camera angle?"

After a week, the videos had attracted more than three million hits. Still, GoPro's media staff did not reach out to them. "They didn't want to be associated with us," Rossig said. 55

He and the others now face numerous charges, including one felony, and as much as seven years in prison. The police have confiscated their cameras.

Questions for Critical Reading

1. As you reread, keep a list of what Paumgarten believes are the problematic consequences of the GoPro camera. Do you feel these problems outweigh the benefits of the camera?
2. What cultural, economic, and technological factors contributed to the success of the GoPro? Review the essay and note passages where Paumgarten discusses the elements that helped this camera thrive.
3. How do you measure the value of an experience? Record your own thoughts and then as you reread the essay consider how Paumgarten feels we should value experiences. How do video cameras affect experience?

Exploring Context

1. Visit GoPro's website at gopro.com. How does the site represent the camera and its abilities? Relate what you find to Paumgarten's argument and to your response from Question 1 of Questions for Critical Reading.
2. Search YouTube for "GoPro" and "GoPro fail." What sorts of experiences do people record with this camera? How do these videos relate to Paumgarten's argument? You may want to incorporate your response from Question 3 of Questions for Critical Reading.
3. Paumgarten ends with the story of the three men who jumped off New York's One World Trade Center. Search YouTube for "NYC base jump" to view the footage of this jump.

Questions for Connecting

1. Peter Singer, in "Visible Man: Ethics in a World without Secrets" (p. 353), also discusses the consequences of a video-saturated culture. Synthesize Singer's and Paumgarten's arguments. What's the relationship between video culture and political power? Incorporate your work from Question 1 of Questions for Critical Reading.
2. Alexander Provan's "The Future of Originals" (p. 327) is similarly concerned with the impact of technology on the value of creative activity. Synthesize his argument with Paumgarten's. How is art changing in the digital age? How can we preserve its cultural value?

3. **Multimodal.** Paumgarten examines the ramifications of this new technology. In "The Empathy Diaries" (p. 378), Sherry Turkle also looks at the consequence of technology. Use both of their texts to propose ethical standards for the development and use of technology. Using PowerPoint or other software prepare a presentation of your response, focusing not only on making sure your slides are concise but also considering the ways in which the design of the slides and the transitions between them can enhance rather than detract from your argument. What factors must we consider as technology continues to develop? Use your work from Questions 2 and 3 of Questions for Critical Reading as you make your response.

Language Matters

1. Use a handbook or other reliable resource to learn how to cite videos. Practice by completing a citation for one of the videos you looked at in Exploring Context.
2. Paumgarten includes personal anecdotes in his essay. What effect do these stories have on the reader? When is it appropriate to use personal anecdotes in academic writing?
3. Consider the relationship between form and content using the videos you looked at in Exploring Context. How do these videos' authors convey information in a video? How do they make arguments in a video? Apply your findings to the form of the academic paper. What kind of content does it allow? What kind of content doesn't "fit," given the space of the form?

Assignments for Writing

1. What has greater value: an experience or the memory of an experience? Write a paper in which you assess the role of memory in our lives. How does memory shape our beliefs and actions? How do we preserve it? Is such preservation more important than experiences themselves? Use your work in Question 3 of Questions for Critical Reading.
2. Paumgarten raises some of the problems surrounding a video-saturated culture. Write a paper in which you propose an ethics of video. In what situations should we promote the use of video? Are there areas where it is not appropriate and should be discouraged?
3. Paumgarten makes it clear that GoPro is as much a cultural phenomenon as a technological one. Write a paper in which you consider the ways in which technology shapes culture. Consider using your work in Exploring Context to support your response.

MICHAEL POLLAN

Michael Pollan is the Knight Professor of Science and Environmental Journalism at the University of California–Berkeley as well as the author of eight books, including *The Omnivore's Dilemma: A Natural History of Four Meals* (2006), *In Defense of Food: An Eater's Manifesto* (2008), *Food Rules: An Eater's Manual* (2009), and *A Natural History of Transformation* (2013). A graduate of Bennington College and Columbia University, Pollan has won multiple journalism awards, and his writing has appeared in *The Norton Book of Nature Writing* (1990), *Best American Essays* (1990 and 2003), and *Best American Science Writing* (2004). Pollan's work can often be seen in the *New York Times*, where he is a contributing writer.

The Omnivore's Dilemma, declared by the *New York Times* to be one of 2006's best nonfiction books, traces three different food chains—the industrial, the pastoral, and the personal—from nature to table. Ultimately, the book is about the politics of eating: what we should eat, why we should eat it, and what impact our eating decisions have.

In "The Animals: Practicing Complexity" from *The Omnivore's Dilemma*, Pollan writes about an alternative to traditional agribusiness and profiles farmer Joel Salatin. With few outside raw materials, Salatin is able to run an incredibly productive farm that mimics a natural ecosystem in which nothing goes to waste. Pollan shows how order arises from the complex system of Salatin's farm, where everything plays a part, from a tree to a cow to the cow's manure, in a system—described as "holon" based—in which each element is simultaneously an individual whole and an active part in a complex system.

For Pollan, the omnivore's dilemma is one we face each day: What to have for dinner? This selection suggests that a healthy and sustainable answer to that question might come not from rejecting agribusiness entirely for an idealized agrarian past but from rethinking the intersection of business, farming, and food.

▶ TAGS: *collaboration, economics, education, food and agriculture*

▶ CONNECTIONS: *Appiah, Fukuyama, Gilbert, Ma, Moalem, Wallace*

The Animals: Practicing Complexity

1. Tuesday Morning

It's not often I wake up at six in the morning to discover I've overslept, but by the time I had hauled my six-foot self out of the five-foot bed in Lucille's microscopic guest room, everyone was already gone and morning chores were nearly done. Shockingly, chores at Polyface commence as soon as the sun comes up (five-ish this time of year) and always before breakfast. Before coffee, that is, not that there was a drop of it to be had on this farm. I couldn't recall the last time I'd even attempted to do anything consequential before breakfast, or before caffeine at the very least.

When I stepped out of the trailer into the warm early morning mist, I could make out two figures—the interns, probably—moving around up on the broad shoulder of hill to the east, where a phalanx of portable chicken pens formed a checkerboard pattern on the grass. Among other things, morning chores consist of feeding and watering the broilers* and moving their pens one length down the hillside. I was supposed to be helping Galen and Peter do this, so I started up the path, somewhat groggily, hoping to get there before they finished.

As I stumbled up the hill, I was struck by how very beautiful the farm looked in the hazy early light. The thick June grass was silvered with dew, the sequence of bright pastures stepping up the hillside dramatically set off by broad expanses of blackish woods. Birdsong stitched the thick blanket of summer air, pierced now and again by the wood clap of chicken pen doors slamming shut. It was hard to believe this hillside had ever been the gullied wreck Joel had described at dinner, and even harder to believe that farming such a damaged landscape so intensively, rather than just letting it be, could restore it to health and yield this beauty. This is not the environmentalist's standard prescription. But Polyface is proof that people can sometimes do more for the health of a place by cultivating it rather than by leaving it alone.

By the time I reached the pasture Galen and Peter had finished moving the pens. Fortunately they were either too kind or too timid to give me a hard time for oversleeping. I grabbed a pair of water buckets, filled them from the big tub in the center of the pasture, and lugged them to the nearest pen. Fifty of these pens were spread out across the damp grass in a serrated formation that had been calibrated to cover every square foot of this meadow in the course of the fifty-six days it takes a broiler to reach slaughter weight; the pens moved ten feet each day, the length of one pen. Each ten-by-twelve, two-foot-tall floorless pen houses seventy birds. A section of the roof is hinged to allow access, and a five-gallon bucket perched atop each unit fed a watering device suspended inside.

5 Directly behind each pen was a perfectly square patch of closely cropped grass resembling a really awful Jackson Pollock painting, thickly spattered with chicken crap in pigments of white, brown, and green. It was amazing what a mess seventy chickens could make in a day. But that was the idea: Give them twenty-four hours to eat the grass and fertilize it with their manure, and then move them onto fresh ground.

Joel developed this novel method for raising broiler chickens in the 1980s and popularized it in his 1993 book, *Pastured Poultry Profit$*, something of a cult classic among grass farmers. (Joel has self-published four other how-to books on farming, and all but one of them has a $ stepping in for an S somewhere in its title.) Left to their own devices, a confined flock of chickens will eventually destroy any patch of land, by pecking the grass down to its roots and poisoning the soil with their extremely "hot," or nitrogenous, manure. This is why the typical free-range chicken yard quickly winds up bereft of plant life and hard as brick. Moving the birds daily keeps both the land and the birds healthy; the broilers escape their pathogens and the varied diet of greens supplies most of their vitamins and minerals. The birds also get a ration of corn, toasted soybeans, and kelp, which we scooped into long troughs in their pens, but Joel claims the fresh grass, along with the worms, grasshoppers, and crickets they peck out of the grass, provides as much as 20 percent of their diet—a significant savings to the farmer and a boon to the birds. Meanwhile, their manure fertilizes the grass, supplying all the nitrogen it needs. The chief reason Polyface Farm is completely self-sufficient in nitrogen is

*Broilers: Chickens raised for their meat rather than for egg production [Ed.].

that a chicken, defecating copiously, pays a visit to virtually every square foot of it at several points during the season. Apart from some greensand (a mineral supplement to replace calcium lost in the meadows), chicken feed is the only important input Joel buys, and the sole off-farm source of fertility. ("The way I look at it, I'm just returning some of the grain that's been extracted from this land over the last 150 years.") The chicken feed not only feeds the broilers but, transformed into chicken crap, feeds the grass that feeds the cows that, as I was about to see, feed the pigs and the laying hens.

After we had finished watering and feeding the broilers, I headed up to the next pasture, where I could hear a tractor idling. Galen had told me Joel was moving the Eggmobile, an operation I'd been eager to watch. The Eggmobile, one of Joel's proudest innovations, is a ramshackle cross between a henhouse and a prairie schooner. Housing four hundred laying hens, this rickety old covered wagon has hinged nesting boxes lined up like saddlebags on either side, allowing someone to retrieve eggs from the outside. I'd first laid eyes on the Eggmobile the night before, parked a couple of paddocks away from the cattle herd. The hens had already climbed the little ramp into the safety of the coop for the night, and before we went down to dinner Joel had latched the trapdoor behind them. Now it was time to move them into a fresh paddock, and Joel was bolting the Eggmobile to the hitch of his tractor. It wasn't quite 7:00 AM yet, but Joel seemed delighted to have someone to talk to, holding forth being one of his greatest pleasures.

"In nature you'll always find birds following herbivores," Joel explained, when I asked him for the theory behind the Eggmobile. "The egret perched on the rhino's nose, the pheasants and turkeys trailing after the bison—that's a symbiotic relationship we're trying to imitate." In each case the birds dine on the insects that would otherwise bother the herbivore; they also pick insect larvae and parasites out of the animal's droppings, breaking the cycle of infestation and disease. "To mimic this symbiosis on a domestic scale, we follow the cattle in their rotation with the Eggmobile. I call these gals our sanitation crew."

Joel climbed onto the tractor, threw it into gear, and slowly towed the rickety contraption fifty yards or so across the meadow to a paddock the cattle had vacated three days earlier. It seems the chickens eschew fresh manure, so he waits three or four days before bringing them in—but not a day longer. That's because the fly larvae in the manure are on a four-day cycle, he explained. "Three days is ideal. That gives the grubs a chance to fatten up nicely, the way the hens like them, but not quite long enough to hatch into flies." The result is prodigious amounts of protein for the hens, the insects supplying as much as a third of their total diet—and making their eggs unusually rich and tasty. By means of this simple little management trick, Joel is able to use his cattle's waste to "grow" large quantities of high-protein chicken feed for free; he says this trims his cost of producing eggs by twenty-five cents per dozen. (Very much his accountant father's son, Joel can tell you the exact economic implication of every synergy on the farm.) The cows further oblige the chickens by shearing the grass; chickens can't navigate in grass more than about six inches tall.

After Joel had maneuvered the Eggmobile into position, he opened the trapdoor, and an eager, gossipy procession of Barred Rocks, Rhode Island Reds, and New Hampshire Whites filed down the little ramp, fanning out across the pasture. The hens picked at the grasses, especially the clover, but mainly they were all over the cowpats, doing this frantic backward-stepping break-dance with their claws to scratch apart 10 the caked manure and expose the meaty morsels within. Unfolding here before us, I realized, was a most impressive form of alchemy: cowpatties in the process of being transformed into exceptionally tasty eggs.

"I'm convinced an Eggmobile would be worth it even if the chickens never laid a single egg. These birds do a more effective job of sanitizing a pasture than anything human, mechanical, or chemical, and the chickens love doing it." Because of the Eggmobile, Joel doesn't have to run his cattle through a headgate to slather Ivomectrin, a systemic parasiticide, on their hides or worm them with toxic chemicals. This is what Joel means when he says the animals do the real work around here. "I'm just the orchestra conductor, making sure everybody's in the right place at the right time."

That day, my second on the farm, as Joel introduced me to each of his intricately layered enterprises, I began to understand just how radically different this sort of farming is from the industrial models I'd observed before, whether in an Iowa cornfield or an organic chicken farm in California. Indeed, it is so different that I found Polyface's system difficult to describe to myself in an orderly way. Industrial processes follow a clear, linear, hierarchical logic that is fairly easy to put into words, probably because words follow a similar logic: First this, then that; put this in here, and then out comes that. But the relationship between cows and chickens on this farm (leaving aside for the moment the other creatures and relationships present here) takes the form of a loop rather than a line, and that makes it hard to know where to start, or how to distinguish between causes and effects, subjects and objects.

I began to understand just how radically different this sort of farming is from the industrial models I'd observed before.

Is what I'm looking at in this pasture a system for producing exceptionally tasty eggs? If so, then the cattle and their manure are a means to an end. Or is it a system for producing grass-fed beef without the use of any chemicals, in which case the chickens, by fertilizing and sanitizing the cow pastures, comprise the means to that end. So does that make their eggs a product or a by-product? And is manure—theirs or the cattle's—a waste product or a raw material? (And what should we call the fly larvae?) Depending on the point of view you take—that of the chicken, cow, or even the grass—the relationship between subject and object, cause and effect, flips.

Joel would say this is precisely the point, and precisely the distinction between a biological and industrial system. "In an ecological system like this everything's connected to everything else, so you can't change one thing without changing ten other things.

"Take the issue of scale. I could sell a whole lot more chickens and eggs than I do. 15 They're my most profitable items, and the market is telling me to produce more of them. Operating under the industrial paradigm,* I could boost production however much I wanted—just buy more chicks and more feed, crank up that machine. But in a biological system you can never do just one thing, and I couldn't add many more chickens without messing up something else.

"Here's an example: This pasture can absorb four hundred units of nitrogen a year. That translates into four visits from the Eggmobile or two passes of a broiler pen. If I ran any more Eggmobiles or broiler pens over it, the chickens would put down more

* Paradigm: Pattern or model [Ed.].

nitrogen than the grass could metabolize. Whatever the grass couldn't absorb would run off, and suddenly I have a pollution problem." Quality would suffer, too. Unless he added more cattle, to produce more grubs for the chickens and to keep the grass short enough for them to eat it, those chickens and eggs would not taste nearly as good as they do.

"It's all connected. This farm is more like an organism than a machine, and like any organism it has its proper scale. A mouse is the size of a mouse for a good reason, and a mouse that was the size of an elephant wouldn't do very well."

Joel likes to quote from an old agricultural textbook he dug out of the stacks at Virginia Tech many years ago. The book, which was published in 1941 by a Cornell Ag professor, offers a stark conclusion that, depending on your point of view, will sound either hopelessly quaint or arresting in its gnomic wisdom: "Farming is not adapted to large-scale operations because of the following reasons: Farming is concerned with plants and animals that live, grow, and die."

"Efficiency" is the term usually invoked to defend large-scale industrial farms, and it usually refers to the economies of scale that can be achieved by the application of technology and standardization. Yet Joel Salatin's farm makes the case for a very different sort of efficiency—the one found in natural systems, with their coevolutionary relationships and reciprocal loops. For example, in nature there is no such thing as a waste problem, since one creature's waste becomes another creature's lunch. What could be more efficient than turning cow pies into eggs? Or running a half-dozen different production systems—cows, broilers, layers, pigs, turkeys—over the same piece of ground every year?

Most of the efficiencies in an industrial system are achieved through simplification: doing lots of the same thing over and over. In agriculture, this usually means a monoculture of a single animal or crop. In fact, the whole history of agriculture is a progressive history of simplification, as humans reduced the biodiversity of their landscapes to a small handful of chosen species. (Wes Jackson calls our species "homo the homogenizer.") With the industrialization of agriculture, the simplifying process reached its logical extreme—in monoculture. This radical specialization permitted standardization and mechanization, leading to the leaps in efficiency claimed by industrial agriculture. Of course, how you choose to measure efficiency makes all the difference, and industrial agriculture measures it, simply, by the yield of one chosen species per acre of land or farmer.

By contrast, the efficiencies of natural systems flow from complexity and interdependence—by definition the very opposite of simplification. To achieve the efficiency represented by turning cow manure into chicken eggs and producing beef without chemicals you need at least two species (cows and chickens), but actually several more as well, including the larvae in the manure and the grasses in the pasture and the bacteria in the cows' rumens. To measure the efficiency of such a complex system you need to count not only all the products it produces (meat, chicken, eggs) but also all the costs it eliminates: antibiotics, wormers, parasiticides, and fertilizers.

Polyface Farm is built on the efficiencies that come from mimicking relationships found in nature, and layering one farm enterprise over another on the same base of land. In effect, Joel is farming in time as well as in space—in four dimensions rather than three. He calls this intricate layering "stacking" and points out that "it is exactly the model God used in building nature." The idea is not to slavishly imitate nature, but to model a natural ecosystem in all its diversity and interdependence, one where all the species "fully express their physiological distinctiveness." He takes advantage of each species' natural proclivities in a way that not only benefits that animal but other species as well. So instead of treating the chicken as a simple egg or protein machine, Polyface honors—and exploits—"the innate distinctive desires of a chicken," which include pecking in the grass and cleaning up after herbivores. The chickens get to do, and eat, what they evolved to do and eat, and in the process the farmer and his cattle both profit. What is the opposite of zero-sum?* I'm not sure, but this is it.

Joel calls each of his stacked farm enterprises a *holon*, a word I'd never encountered before. He told me he picked it up from Allan Nation; when I asked Nation about it, he pointed me to Arthur Koestler, who coined the term in *The Ghost in the Machine*. Koestler felt English lacked a word to express the complex relationship of parts and wholes in a biological or social system. A holon (from the Greek *holos*, or whole, and the suffix *on*, as in proton, suggesting a particle) is an entity that from one perspective appears a self-contained whole, and from another a dependent part. A body organ like the liver is a holon; so is an Eggmobile.

At any given time, Polyface has a dozen or more holons up and running, and on my second day Joel and Daniel introduced me to a handful of them. I visited the Raken House, the former toolshed where Daniel has been raising rabbits for the restaurant trade since he was ten. ("Raken?" "Half rabbit, half chicken," Daniel explained.) When the rabbits aren't out on the pasture in portable hutches, they live in cages suspended over a deep bedding of woodchips, in which I watched several dozen hens avidly pecking away in search of earthworms. Daniel explained that the big problem in raising rabbits indoors is their powerful urine, which produces so much ammonia that it scars their lungs and leaves them vulnerable to infection. To cope with the problem most rabbit farmers add antibiotics to their feed. But the scratching of the hens turns the nitrogenous rabbit pee into the carbonaceous bedding, creating a rich compost teeming with earthworms that feed the hens. Drugs become unnecessary and, considering how many rabbits and chickens lived in it, the air in the Raken was, well, tolerable. "Believe me," Daniel said, "if it weren't for these chickens, you'd be gagging right about now, and your eyes would sting something awful."

Before lunch I helped Galen and Peter move the turkeys, another holon. Moving the turkeys, which happens every three days, means setting up a new "feathernet"—a paddock outlined by portable electric fencing so lightweight I could carry and lay out the entire thing by myself—and then wheeling into it the shademobile, called the Gobbledy-Go. The turkeys rest under the Gobbledy-Go by day and roost on top of it at night. They happily follow the contraption into the fresh pasture to feast on the grass, which they seemed to enjoy even more than the chickens do. A turkey consumes a long blade of grass by neatly folding it over and over again with its beak, as if making origami. Joel likes to run his turkeys in the orchard, where they eat the bugs, mow the grass, and fertilize the trees and vines. (Turkeys will eat much more grass than chickens, and they don't damage crops the way chickens can.) "If you run turkeys in a grape orchard," Joel explained, "you can afford to stock the birds at only seventy percent of normal density, and space the vines at seventy percent of what's standard, because you're getting two crops off the same land. And at seventy percent you get much healthier birds and grapevines than you would at 100 percent. That's the beauty of stacking."

*Zero-sum: Situation or system in which one side gains all and the other loses all [Ed.].

By industry standards, the turkey and grape holon are each less than 100 percent efficient; together, however, they produce more than either enterprise would yield if fully stocked, and they do so without fertilizer, weeding, or pesticide.

I had witnessed one of the most winning examples of stacking in the cattle barn during my first visit to Polyface back in March. The barn is an unfancy open-sided structure where the cattle spend three months during the winter, each day consuming twenty-five pounds of hay and producing fifty pounds of manure. (Water makes up the difference.) But instead of regularly mucking out the barn, Joel leaves the manure in place, every few days covering it with another layer of woodchips or straw. As this layer cake of manure, woodchips, and straw gradually rises beneath the cattle, Joel simply raises the adjustable feed gate from which they get their ration of hay; by winter's end the bedding, and the cattle, can be as much as three feet off the ground. There's one more secret ingredient Joel adds to each layer of this cake: a few bucketfuls of corn. All winter long the layered bedding composts, in the process generating heat to warm the barn (thus reducing the animals' feed requirements), and fermenting the corn. Joel calls it his cattle's electric blanket.

Why the corn? Because there's nothing a pig enjoys more than forty-proof corn, and there's nothing he's better equipped to do than root it out with his powerful snout and exquisite sense of smell. "I call them my pigaerators," Salatin said proudly as he showed me into the barn. As soon as the cows head out to pasture in the spring, several dozen pigs come in, proceeding systematically to turn and aerate the compost in their quest for kernels of alcoholic corn. What had been an anaerobic decomposition suddenly turns aerobic, which dramatically heats and speeds up the process, killing any pathogens. The result, after a few weeks of pigaerating, is a rich, cakey compost ready to use.

"This is the sort of farm machinery I like: never needs its oil changed, appreciates over time, and when you're done with it you eat it." We were sitting on the rail of a wooden paddock, watching the pigs do their thing—a thing, of course, we weren't having to do ourselves. The line about the pigaerators was obviously well-worn. But the cliché that kept banging around in my head was "happy as a pig in shit." Buried clear to their butts in composting manure, a bobbing sea of wriggling hams and corkscrew tails, these were the happiest pigs I'd ever seen.

These were the happiest pigs I'd ever seen.

I couldn't look at their spiraled tails, which cruised above the earthy mass like conning towers on submarines, without thinking about the fate of pigtails in industrial hog production. Simply put, there *are* no pigtails in industrial hog production. Farmers "dock," or snip off, the tails at birth, a practice that makes a certain twisted sense if you follow the logic of industrial efficiency on a hog farm. Piglets in these CAFOs* are weaned from their mothers ten days after birth (compared with thirteen weeks in nature) because they gain weight faster on their drug-fortified feed than on sow's milk. But this premature weaning leaves the pigs with a lifelong craving to suck and chew, a need they gratify in confinement by biting the tail of the animal in front of them. A normal pig would fight off his molester, but a demoralized pig has stopped caring. *Learned helplessness* is the psychological term, and it's not uncommon in CAFOs, where tens of thousands of hogs spend their entire lives ignorant of earth or straw or sunshine, crowded together beneath a metal roof standing on metal slats suspended over a

*CAFOs: Concentrated animal feeding operations [Ed.].

septic tank. It's not surprising that an animal as intelligent as a pig would get depressed under these circumstances, and a depressed pig will allow his tail to be chewed on to the point of infection. Since treating sick pigs is not economically efficient, these underperforming production units are typically clubbed to death on the spot.

Tail docking is the USDA's recommended solution to the porcine "vice" of tail chewing. Using a pair of pliers and no anesthetic, most—but not quite all—of the tail is snipped off. Why leave the little stump? Because the whole point of the exercise is not to remove the object of tail biting so much as to render it even more sensitive. Now a bite to the tail is so painful that even the most demoralized pig will struggle to resist it. Horrible as it is to contemplate, it's not hard to see how the road to such a hog hell is smoothly paved with the logic of industrial efficiency.

A very different concept of efficiency sponsors the hog heaven on display here in Salatin's barn, one predicated on what he calls "the pigness of the pig." These pigs too were being exploited—in this case, tricked into making compost as well as pork. What distinguishes Salatin's system is that it is designed around the natural predilections of the pig rather than around the requirements of a production system to which the pigs are then conformed. Pig happiness is simply the by-product of treating pigs as pigs rather than as "a protein machine with flaws"—flaws such as pig tails and a tendency, when emiserated, to get stressed.

Salatin reached down deep where his pigs were happily rooting and brought a handful of fresh compost right up to my nose. What had been cow manure and woodchips just a few weeks before now smelled as sweet and warm as the forest floor in summertime, a miracle of transubstantiation. As soon as the pigs complete their alchemy, Joel will spread the compost on his pastures. There it will feed the grasses, so the grasses might again feed the cows, the cows the chickens, and so on until the snow falls, in one long, beautiful, and utterly convincing proof that in a world where grass can eat sunlight and food animals can eat grass, there is indeed a free lunch.

2. Tuesday Afternoon

After our own quick lunch (ham salad and deviled eggs), Joel and I drove to town in his pickup to make a delivery and take care of a few errands. It felt sweet to be sitting down for a while, especially after a morning taken up with loading the hay we'd baled the day before into the hayloft. For me this rather harrowing operation involved attempting to catch fifty-pound bales that Galen tossed in my general direction from the top of the hay wagon. The ones that didn't completely knock me over I hoisted onto a conveyor belt that carried them to Daniel and Peter, stationed up in the hayloft. It was an assembly line, more or less, and as soon as I fell behind (or just fell, literally) the hay bales piled up fast at my station; I felt like Lucille Ball at the candy factory. I joked to Joel that, contrary to his claims that the animals did most of the real work on this farm, it seemed to me they'd left plenty of it for us.

On a farm, complexity sounds an awful lot like hard work, Joel's claims to the contrary notwithstanding. As much work as the animals do, that's still us humans out there moving the cattle every evening, dragging the broiler pens across the field before breakfast (something I'd pledged I'd wake up in time for the next day), and towing chicken coops hither and yon according to a schedule tied to the life cycle of fly larvae and the nitrogen load of chicken manure. My guess is that there aren't too many farmers today who are up for either the physical or mental challenge of this sort of farming, not when industrializing promises to simplify the job. Indeed, a large part of the appeal of industrial farming is its panoply of labor- and thought-saving devices: machines of every description to do the physical work, and chemicals to keep crops and animals free from pests with scarcely a thought from the farmer. George Naylor works his fields maybe fifty days out of the year; Joel and Daniel and two interns are out there every day sunrise to sunset for a good chunk of the year.

Yet Joel and Daniel plainly relish their work, partly because it is so varied from day to day and even hour to hour, and partly because they find it endlessly interesting. Wendell Berry has written eloquently about the intellectual work that goes into farming well, especially into solving the novel problems that inevitably crop up in a natural system as complex as a farm. You don't see much of this sort of problem-solving in agriculture today, not when so many solutions come ready-made in plastic bottles. So much of the intelligence and local knowledge in agriculture has been removed from the farm to the laboratory, and then returned to the farm in the form of a chemical or machine. "Whose head is the farmer using?" Berry asks in one of his essays. "Whose head is using the farmer?"

35 "Part of the problem is, you've got a lot of D students left on the farm today," Joel said, as we drove around Staunton* running errands. "The guidance counselors encouraged all the A students to leave home and go to college. There's been a tremendous brain drain in rural America. Of course that suits Wall Street just fine; Wall Street is always trying to extract brainpower and capital from the countryside. First they take the brightest bulbs off the farm and put them to work in Dilbert's cubicle, and then they go after the capital of the dimmer ones who stayed behind, by selling them a bunch of gee-whiz solutions to their problems." This isn't just the farmer's problem, either. "It's a foolish culture that entrusts its food supply to simpletons."

It isn't hard to see why there isn't much institutional support for the sort of low-capital, thought-intensive farming Joel Salatin practices: He buys next to nothing. When a livestock farmer is willing to "practice complexity"—to choreograph the symbiosis of several different animals, each of which has been allowed to behave and eat as they evolved to—he will find he has little need for machinery, fertilizer, and, most strikingly, chemicals. He finds he has no sanitation problem or any of the diseases that result from raising a single animal in a crowded monoculture and then feeding it things it wasn't designed to eat. This is perhaps the greatest efficiency of a farm treated as a biological system: health.

I was struck by the fact that for Joel abjuring agrochemicals and pharmaceuticals is not so much a goal of his farming, as it so often is in organic agriculture, as it is an indication that his farm is functioning well. "In nature health is the default," he pointed out. "Most of the time pests and disease are just nature's way of telling the farmer he's doing something wrong."

At Polyface no one ever told me not to touch the animals, or asked me to put on a biohazard suit before going into the brooder house. The reason I had to wear one

*Staunton: Polyface Farm is located eight miles south of the city of Staunton, Virginia [Ed.].

at Petaluma Poultry is because that system—a monoculture of chickens raised in close confinement—is inherently precarious, and the organic rules' prohibition on antibiotics puts it at a serious disadvantage. Maintaining a single-species animal farm on an industrial scale isn't easy without pharmaceuticals and pesticides. Indeed, that's why these chemicals were invented in the first place, to keep shaky monocultures from collapsing. Sometimes the large-scale organic farmer looks like someone trying to practice industrial agriculture with one hand tied behind his back.

By the same token, a reliance on agrochemicals destroys the information feedback loop on which an attentive farmer depends to improve his farming. "Meds just mask genetic weaknesses," Joel explained one afternoon when we were moving the cattle. "My goal is always to improve the herd, adapt it to the local conditions by careful culling. To do this I need to know: Who has a propensity for pinkeye? For worms? You simply have no clue if you're giving meds all the time.

"So you tell me, who's really *in* this so-called information economy? Those who learn from what they observe on their farm, or those who rely on concoctions from the devil's pantry?" 40

Of course the simplest, most traditional measure of a farm's efficiency is how much food it produces per unit of land; by this yardstick too Polyface is impressively efficient. I asked Joel how much food Polyface produces in a season, and he rattled off the following figures:

30,000 dozen eggs
10,000 broilers
800 stewing hens
50 beeves (representing 25,000 pounds of beef)
250 hogs (25,000 pounds of pork)
1,000 turkeys
500 rabbits

This seemed to me a truly astonishing amount of food from one hundred acres of grass. But when I put it that way to Joel that afternoon—we were riding the ATV up to the very top of the hill to visit the hogs in their summer quarters—he questioned my accounting method. It was far too simple.

"Sure, you can write that we produced all that food from a hundred open acres, but if you really want to be accurate about it, then you've got to count the four hundred and fifty acres of woodlot too." I didn't get that at all. I knew the woodlot was an important source of farm income in the winter—Joel and Daniel operate a small sawmill from which they sell lumber and mill whatever wood they need to build sheds and barns (and Daniel's new house). But what in the world did the forest have to do with producing food?

Joel proceeded to count the ways. Most obviously, the farm's water supply depended on its forests to hold moisture and prevent erosion. Many of the farm's streams and ponds would simply dry up if not for the cover of trees. Nearly all of the farm's 550 acres had been deforested when the Salatins arrived; one of the first things Bill Salatin did was plant trees on all the north-facing slopes.

45 "Feel how cool it is in here." We were passing through a dense stand of oak and hickory. "Those deciduous trees work like an air conditioner. That reduces the stress on the animals in summer."

Suddenly we arrived at a patch of woodland that looked more like a savanna than a forest: The trees had been thinned and all around them grew thick grasses. This was one of the pig paddocks that Joel had carved out of the woods with the help of the pigs themselves. "All we do to make a new pig paddock is fence off a quarter acre of forest, thin out the saplings to let in some light, and then let the pigs do their thing." Their thing includes eating down the brush and rooting around in the stony ground, disturbing the soil in a way that induces the grass seed already present to germinate. Within several weeks, a lush stand of wild rye and foxtail emerges among the trees, and a savanna is born. Shady and cool, this looked like ideal habitat for the sunburn-prone pigs, who were avidly nosing through the tall grass and scratching their backs against the trees. There is something viscerally appealing about a savanna, with its pleasing balance of open grass and trees, and something profoundly heartening about the idea that, together, farmer and pigs could create such beauty here in the middle of a brushy second-growth forest.

But Joel wasn't through counting the benefits of woodland to a farm; idyllic pig habitat was the least of it.

"There's not a spreadsheet in the world that can measure the value of maintaining forest on the northern slopes of a farm. Start with those trees easing the swirling of the air in the pastures. That might not seem like a big deal, but it reduces evaporation in the fields—which means more water for the grass. Plus, a grass plant burns up fifteen percent of its calories just defying gravity, so if you can stop it from being wind whipped, you greatly reduce the energy it uses keeping its photovoltaic array pointed toward the sun. More grass for the cows. That's the efficiency of a hedgerow surrounding a small field, something every farmer used to understand before 'fencerow to fencerow' became USDA mantra."*

Then there is the water-holding capacity of trees, he explained, which on a north slope literally pumps water uphill. Next was all the ways a forest multiplies a farm's biodiversity. More birds on a farm mean fewer insects, but most birds won't venture more than a couple hundred yards from the safety of cover. Like many species, their preferred habitat is the edge between forest and field. The biodiversity of the forest edge also helps control predators. As long as the weasels and coyotes have plenty of chipmunks and voles to eat, they're less likely to venture out and prey on the chickens.

50 There was more. On a steep northern slope trees will produce much more biomass than will grass. "We're growing carbon in the woods for the rest of the farm—not just the firewood to keep us warm in the winter, but also the woodchips that go into making our compost." Making good compost depends on the proper ratio of carbon to nitrogen; the carbon is needed to lock down the more volatile nitrogen. It takes a lot of woodchips to compost chicken or rabbit waste. So the carbon from the woodlots feeds the fields, finding its way into the grass and, from there, into the beef. Which it turns out is not only grass fed but tree fed as well.

These woods represented a whole other order of complexity that I had failed to take into account. I realized that Joel didn't look at this land the same way I did, or

* USDA mantra: Policy of the United States Department of Agriculture [Ed.].

had before this afternoon: as a hundred acres of productive grassland patchworked into four hundred and fifty acres of unproductive forest. It was all of a biological piece, the trees and the grasses and the animals, the wild and the domestic, all part of a single ecological system. By any conventional accounting, the forests here represented a waste of land that could be put to productive use. But if Joel were to cut down the trees to graze more cattle, as any conventional accounting would recommend, the system would no longer be quite as whole or as healthy as it is. *You can't just do one thing.*

For some reason the image that stuck with me from that day was that slender blade of grass in a too big, wind-whipped pasture, burning all those calories just to stand up straight and keep its chloroplasts* aimed at the sun. I'd always thought of the trees and grasses as antagonists—another zero-sum deal in which the gain of the one entails the loss of the other. To a point, this is true: More grass means less forest; more forest less grass. But either-or is a construction more deeply woven into our culture than into nature, where even antagonists depend on one another and the liveliest places are the edges, the in-betweens or both-ands. So it is with the blade of grass and the adjacent forest as, indeed, with all the species sharing this most complicated farm. Relations are what matter most, and the health of the cultivated turns on the health of the wild. Before I came to Polyface I'd read a sentence of Joel's that in its diction had struck me as an awkward hybrid of the economic and the spiritual. I could see now how characteristic that mixing is, and that perhaps the sentence isn't so awkward after all: "One of the greatest assets of a farm is the sheer ecstasy of life."

Questions for Critical Reading

1. What makes Polyface so successful? Locate passages where Pollan describes the key features of this farm, rereading this essay critically to identify the key factors to the farm's success.
2. What is a *holon*? Use Pollan's text to define this term and to offer examples. Then apply the concept to another area by locating your own example of a holon.
3. Pollan subtitles this essay "Practicing Complexity." Use his text to explain what this means, referring to specific quotations or passages that show complexity in practice. You will need to reread critically to determine your answer since Pollan never explains the relationship between this subtitle and his essay.

Exploring Context

1. Learn more about Polyface Farm by visiting its website at polyfacefarms.com. How do you see the ideas that Pollan discusses at work in the farm's website? Use your work on the success of Polyface from Question 1 of Questions for Critical Reading in making your response.
2. Visit the website for the U.S. Department of Agriculture's Organic Regulations at www.ams.usda.gov/rules-regulations/organic. What differences can you locate between

*Chloroplasts: Specialized units in a plant cell responsible for photosynthesis [Ed.].

the philosophy of organic farming at Polyface and that of the U.S. government? Which seems like a better standard for *organic*, and why?

3. Spend some time at Michael Pollan's home page, michaelpollan.com. How does this essay fit into Pollan's other writing? What biases do you think he might have, based on the information you find on his site? Do these biases make a difference in this essay?

Questions for Connecting

1. Sharon Moalem, in "Changing Our Genes: How Trauma, Bullying, and Royal Jelly Alter Our Genetic Destiny" (p. 289), discusses the impact of what we eat on our epigenetic expression. Synthesize his ideas and Pollan's to make an argument for the importance of promoting organic farming.
2. Pollan points out that the kind of farming done at Polyface is thought-intensive and connects that to Salatin's observations about "brain drain," suggesting that it takes a significant education to create a successful system like Polyface. Use Yo-Yo Ma's "Necessary Edges: Arts, Empathy, and Education" (p. 278) to suggest some of the elements such an education might require.
3. David Foster Wallace points to some of the ethical complications of food in "Consider the Lobster" (p. 406). How do the practices of Polyface that Pollan explores complicate Wallace's observation? Is organic farming more "ethical"?

Language Matters

1. Find a passage in Pollan's text that you think is central to his argument. Identify each of the verbs in your selected passage. What are the key verbs? What is the *action* of these sentences? Are there more verbs used in clauses rather than other parts or components of the sentence? What are the implications of each verb's location and the kind of verb used? How can you apply these insights to your own writing?

2. Understanding your audience is a crucial factor in the success of any piece of writing. Looking at Pollan's writing, identify the audience you think he has in mind. How do you know that? What audience should you keep in mind when writing in this class? How can you make sure that your writing reflects that audience?

3. Conjunctions are words that join nouns, phrases, or clauses. Find two quotations that seem to have some relation in Pollan's essay (or choose one from Pollan and one from another essay you've read for this class). Express the relationship between the two quotations using only one conjunction. When might you want to use this same conjunction in your own writing?

Assignments for Writing

1. Pollan reviews farmer Joel Salatin's alternative farming methods, in the process prompting us to question the very nature of farming. By attempting to simplify and sanitize farming, have we moved away from the health and efficiency inherent

in a natural system? Can the benefits of biotechnology outweigh the benefits of symbiosis and nature? As biotechnology pushes science and food toward new frontiers, will we find that the old ways of farming are the better, more healthful ways, or is technologically engineered food simply a measurement of healthy progress, no different than progress in any other arena? Using Pollan's essay, formulate an argument on the relationship between food production methods and health. To support your position, consider the alternatives to Salatin's farming methods, the effect of farming practices on our health, and how the interdependence among the different parts of the farming process affects not only the farmer, the animals, and the farm's products but the consumer as well. Use your work with complexity from Question 3 of Questions for Critical Reading.

2. Using Pollan's essay, write a paper in which you evaluate the efficiency of nature-based farming methods versus the efficiency of biotechnology-based farming methods in food production. What does Pollan mean when he describes Salatin's methods as "holon" based? Why don't we all still farm in the traditional, interdependent manner practiced by Salatin? What are the benefits and disadvantages of "alternative" natural farming? What are the benefits and disadvantages of farming with biotechnology? Are complexity and multiculture more or less efficient than simplicity and monoculture? Use your work with Pollan's essay from Questions for Critical Reading to support your argument.

3. As agribusiness continues to expand in a global economy, will we find that the old ways of farming are the more effective ways, or will we find that current monoculture practices are needed to keep up with the demands of an ever-expanding world population? Using Pollan's essay, write a paper in which you evaluate the advantages of monoculture-based farming methods versus multiculture-based farming methods in food production. What are the benefits and disadvantages of "alternative" natural farming, or what Pollan calls "coevolutionary relationships"? What are the benefits and disadvantages of farming with biotechnology in the form of vaccines, disease-resistant crop varieties, chemical fertilizers, and genetically modified seeds? Are complexity and multiculture necessary to feed the modern world? Are complexity and multiculture more or less efficient than simplicity and monoculture? Draw on your work on complexity from Question 3 of Questions for Critical Reading.

ALEXANDER PROVAN

Artist and author **Alexander Provan** is the editor of Triple Canopy, an online magazine that focuses on digital art and literature and public conversations in an attempt to enrich the public sphere. Provan's work most often focuses on the relationship between technology and social conduct. He is the recipient of a 2015 Creative Capital grant from the Andy Warhol Foundation and has held a fellowship at the Vera List Center for Art and Politics at the New School. His writing has appeared in the *Nation*, the *Believer*, *n+1*, *Bookforum*, *Art in America*, *Artforum*, and *Frieze*, and his art has been exhibited at the 14th Istanbul Biennial, the Whitney Museum of American Art, the New Museum, the Museum Tinguely, and the Museum of Modern Art in New York.

"The Future of Originals" originally appeared in *Art in America* magazine, an illustrated magazine focusing on contemporary art in the United States, artist profiles, exhibition reviews, and other commentary on the production of art today. The October 2016 issue, which featured this essay, was devoted to the "Digitized Museum" and featured analyses of museum website designs, the use and impact of visitors' personal technology on the museum experience, and other articles concerning the ways in which digital technologies are reshaping museums and their visitors.

Provan's piece considers the fate of the original in the era of digital reproduction. Starting with the fact that for many years American museums actively collected casts of statues and busts, Provan notes that transformation that enabled the notion of the original came to be more highly valued. That notion, however, is under attack by increasingly sophisticated means of digital reproduction. This rise in the digital raises the question of data ownership even as it forces us to reexamine the role of art in cultural memory. Some museums, Provan observes, and some artists too, have embraced the digital and used it to advance the creation and curation of art.

What is the role of a museum? Does the "original" have more value than a copy?

- TAGS: *art, culture, ethics, science and technology, tradition*
- CONNECTIONS: *Das, DeGhett, Klosterman, Ma, Paumgarten, Singer, Southan, van Houtryve, von Busch*

The Future of Originals

Museum without Walls

I may enter the Metropolitan Museum of Art, sketchbook and pencil in hand, and walk through the stately hallways until I arrive in gallery 811, where Gustave Courbet's *The Source* (1862) hangs. I may take a seat on the glossy wood bench, place the sketchbook on my lap, train my eyes on the nude woman whose arms thrust into a cascade of spring water, and attempt the most perfect copy. I may not use ballpoint pens, ink, markers, fountain pens, or watercolors, but I may use crayon, pastel, or charcoal if I'm on a supervised tour that grants permission. I may not photograph the painting, even as

The Metropolitan Museum of Art's Great Hall displays marble sculptures.

I witness visitors momentarily pause between me and *The Source*, elevate iPhones, and blithely jab thumbs into screens. I may have to fight the urge to hiss at the offenders, such is my concern for this institution being turned into a classy Instagram backdrop.

If I'm enrolled in the Met's copyist program, which was established in 1872, I may request to copy one work in the permanent collection with oil on canvas or oil-based clay. I may imagine myself as the young painter in inventor Samuel F. B. Morse's monumental painting *Gallery at the Louvre* (1831–33), reproducing the greatest hits of Western art history, making myself more refined with each minute and each brushstroke. After getting clearance from curatorial and security, I may set up my easel and drop cloth four feet from *The Source*, so long as my copy does not exceed thirty-by-thirty inches and differs from the dimensions of the original work by at least 10 percent; or I may sit on the floor and mold my own version of Marble Head of Herakles, a Roman reproduction of a Greek statue attributed to Lysippos, so long as the size doesn't exceed one cubic foot.

In the late 1800s, the Met was very much devoted to procuring and exhibiting copies. "We can never expect to obtain any large collection of original works, but we can obtain casts, which, for students of art and archaeology, and indeed for the general public, are almost their equivalent," reported the Met in 1891.[1] Though originals may have been far-flung, replicas could be configured so as to provide a full impression of the culture of any era or the relationships between styles separated by oceans and centuries. At the time, European institutions were not only accumulating casts but churning out copies of their own artworks to sell to other museums and collectors. The Met's report singled out the Royal Museum in Berlin, which set an example by striving to acquire copies "of all the masterpieces in the different collections of the world, and bring them together under such an arrangement as would best exemplify the progress of the plastic arts at all epochs."[2]

The Met, which lagged behind its compatriots in Boston, Chicago, and Washington, D.C., determined to do the same, and estimated that $100,000 would be required to "follow examples of European nations in developing an artistic perception common to their people, but slightly manifested by Americans." Curator Edward Robinson dispatched agents to Europe to procure and commission replicas of classical statuary. "Doubtless there are many who join us in the wish that every city might have its gallery of reproductions as well as its public library," wrote Robinson in *The Nation* in 1889. He envisioned "a gallery in which children could grow up familiar with the noblest productions of Greece and Italy, in which the laborer could pass some of his holiday hours, and in which the mechanic could find the stimulus to make his own work beautiful as well as good."[3]

By 1902, the Met had amassed 2,607 casts, some of which were displayed to great fanfare in what is now the central hall. Aspiring artists assembled to draft their own impressions of the Parthenon frieze, the Uffizi Wrestlers, Ghiberti's *Gates of Paradise* (1425–52), and Luca della Robbia's *Visitation* (ca. 1445). As Alan Wallach points out in *Exhibiting Contradiction: Essays on the Art Museum in the United States* (1998), the exaltation of replicas is essential not only to American museums but to the cultivation of popular values and tastes in general. The prominence of casts speaks to the importance of all kinds of copying in a country that for so long had very few original works of art and literature. The colonial publishing landscape was crowded with magazines devoted to reprinting, without permission, articles and book excerpts imported from Europe; rampant piracy was understood as the foundation for the fledgling nation's creativity and eventual autonomy.[4]

The colonial publishing landscape was crowded with magazines devoted to reprinting, without permission, articles and book excerpts imported from Europe; rampant piracy was understood as the foundation for the fledgling nation's creativity and eventual autonomy.

Now, the gallery of reproductions is everywhere, much to the benefit of children and laborers and mechanics, so long as they aren't sued by the Recording Industry Association of America or the Motion Picture Association of America or textbook publishers or copyright trolls. Yet museums like the Met, which by the 1940s had warehoused its casts and focused on originals, may still be perceived by most visitors as custodians of unique objects, even as the notion that any object is really unique, or at least formally inimitable, has come to seem dubious. In fact, museums have been turning into manufacturers and managers of images and various other coded representations of artworks, which they circulate to engage and edify audiences as well as to fill coffers. They've resurrected nineteenth-century ideals and wielded twenty-first-century innovations—all while retaining twentieth-century legal teams.

At the gift shop (which in 2015 accounted for 16 percent of the museum's annual revenue), the Met may sell postcards of *The Source* that mark the image as copyrighted, even though the painting is in the public domain. But the Met also makes available online a high-res image of *The Source*, which juxtaposes two age-old symbols of poetic inspiration—the muse and the spring—and refers to Ingres's 1856 nude of the same name. Viewing this image, I can zoom in so close that I can discern the splotches of paint that compose each fleck of water and crease of flesh, and also plaster the image onto pillows and coffee mugs via Zazzle—or perhaps not the same image, but a version in which my signature overlays Courbet's. The online shop of the Rijksmuseum in Amsterdam ("If you ever wanted a Vermeer above your bed, look no further") enables customers to order exquisite reproductions on paper or canvas, complete with the museum's logo on the border, to mark the copy as genuine. The Van Gogh Museum, also in Amsterdam, reproduces paintings like *Sunflowers* (1889) with a 3D-printing process called reliefography and offers the resulting Relievos, which record the contours of both sides of canvases and every indentation and protuberance caused by brushstrokes and the passage of time, for $34,000.

"Anything unique is at risk of vanishing: we make a twin—a notarized copy, a plaster cast, paste diamonds, Thayer's working replicas," writes Hillel Schwartz in his compendious *The Culture of the Copy: Striking Likenesses, Unreasonable Facsimiles* (1996). "An object uncopied is under perpetual siege, valued less for itself than for the struggle to prevent its being copied. The more adept the West has become at the making of copies, the more we have exalted uniqueness. It is within an exuberant world of copies that we arrive at our experience of originality."[5] Museums—in their contradictory treatments of artworks, in their various investments in restricting and freeing information, in their enthusiasm for exploiting intellectual property and ennobling the public—are excellent avatars of our vexed relationship to copying of all kinds. The ways in which we now understand, or fail to understand, the function of museums and art objects (all objects, really) reflect more general confusion about the rights we possess and violations we routinely commit, the kinds of copies that are "good" or "bad," and how reproduction might fortify or degrade the commons.

We revel in the dematerialization of objects and images, and even testify to the erosion of those categories. We herald the everything-on-demand future, to be driven by global migration to the cloud and 3D-printer-powered manufacturing hubs. Yet we remain ensnared by the notion of art and literature as original works that are fixed in a tangible medium of expression. We cling to notions of creativity and property that date to the Industrial Revolution—and even then hardly satisfied anyone—as we handle books, algorithms, databases, YouTube videos, varieties of flora and fauna, geographical indications, trade secrets, and gene sequences.

After Polykleitos

Photographs taken in the early 1900s show gleaming casts of torqued warriors, serene goddesses, and assured statesmen crowded together in museum halls like thoroughbreds assembled for inspection before the race. Only in the following years—as scribes, pantographs, and pointing machines gave way to Electro Copyists, photostats, mimeographs, Speedographs, Ditto machines, Neo-Cyclostyles, and Rotos—did museums in Europe 10 and the United States cement the dichotomy between original and copy. Connoisseurship was professionalized and oligarchs like J. P. Morgan steered the boards of major museums, which began to esteem originals: rare commodities, products of individual genius, artifacts of bygone civilizations, testaments to the collector's discernment and status. Numerous cast collections were secreted into warehouses or destroyed. The Met's casts ended up in a rundown depot in Upper Manhattan, under the West Side Highway. Heads were severed, faces were cracked, limbs were lost, torsos were blackened.

Sensibilities changed as the figures moldered. By the 1980s, casts had come to seem important to the history of art of the nineteenth century. They were useful for the study or conservation of artworks that had been destroyed or degraded by war. They were valuable to teachers who wanted to transport the museum to the classroom. And they jelled with the zeitgeist: Genius and originality were under assault, and there was a vogue for simulacra, pastiche, unending repetition. To copy was to deprive the king of his crown, and also to assert that images were for the taking and recycling, and always had been. Narratives of authorship and authenticity, equally prevalent in art history and copyright law, were undermined (occasionally in both realms at once).[6] As Warhol was deified, the mantle of the avant-garde was claimed by artists like Richard Prince, Jeff Koons, Sarah Charlesworth, and Louise Lawler. Digital technologies were heralded for their potential to grant unfettered access to—i.e., distribute infinite copies of—all the world's information, even all the world's artworks. So after decades in which any art professional who proposed lavishing funds on fragile derivatives of Western classicism might as well have submitted a résumé to the Department of Motor Vehicles, the Met salvaged its collection, embarked on a restoration campaign, and loaned casts to Princeton University, Carnegie Mellon University, and the New York Academy of Art, among dozens of others.

Genius and originality were under assault, and there was a vogue for simulacra, pastiche, unending repetition.

Today, New York's Institute of Classical Architecture and Art (ICAA), where ancient techniques never go out of style, employs 120 casts donated by the Met as teaching aids. A pristine cast of the Diadoumenos, a young athlete fastening a triumphal band to his head, bears the marks of the lost ancient Greek masterpiece, a bronze by Polykleitos, from which it derives. (The cast may also, or may primarily, bear the marks of one of the manifold Roman copies, and, of course, many of those copies were altered and/or made from older replicas.) Posed in an unassuming room with windows overlooking midtown office buildings, the cast is surrounded by plaster busts and friezes placed on boxy plinths, hung from peach walls, rested on the polished wood floor. The Diadoumenos cast strikes me as oddly inert, more like a product of texture mapping and digital extrusion than muses and manual chiseling. It might as well be compressed data inscribed on an imperfect storage medium, one of thousands of copies of copies of mythical originals; each has its own character, a combination of the artist's hand, the mold-making process, and the passage of time.

I'm reminded of the box in my basement packed with booklets of CD-RWs that store albums and movies copied from friends. To me, they now represent the world in which they were burned, however many microprocessor-generations ago, as much as the MP3s and MPEGs imprinted on their surfaces. They might soon be joined by hard drives full of digital models of classical statuary, such as those fabricated by artist Oliver Laric, who has recently devoted himself to making 3D scans of objects from institutional collections and offering them for free online. The resulting caches of STL files—presented with the artists' names, object numbers, materials, and locations, but destined to roam far from the controlled gallery environment—prompt us to ask how and why we encounter originals and reproductions in (and on the websites of) museums, and what is afforded by these various situations and media. For *Lincoln 3D Scans* (2013), commissioned by the Usher Gallery and The Collection in Lincoln, England, Laric scanned scores of sculptures, friezes, chairs, and vessels, which were then published online along with an archive of works by other artists and tinkerers who employ the models. In these scans and subsequent versions of objects, we can see the absorptive quality of chiseled stone being supplanted by manipulable data; the artwork is liberated but also comically compressed as it migrates from marble to the surface of an image.

If plaster casts were expelled from museums because they contradicted elite opinions about authorship and originality, only to be recuperated in an era when museums and collectors competed to acquire artworks that hinged on transgressive copying, they now seem like typical—and typically anachronistic—features of the media landscape. I know, when I look at the ICAA Diadoumenos, that the cast is not the real thing. At the same time, I'm unsure what, if anything, "original" and "copy" mean, given that everything so frequently and promiscuously manifests as objects, images, texts, series of zeros and ones.

Laric, nurtured by this sense of infinite mutability, revives musty bronzes and democratizes collection data, but he evokes the specters as well as the promises of digitization. He joins in the reconfiguration of museums into digital publishers, and the conversion of the objects to which they assign meaning and value into equivalent pieces of content, all in the name of *access* and *engagement*. To me, the *Lincoln 3D Scans* files seem strangely elegiac, as they're marked by deficits of information that are bound to grow as the source becomes more distant, and that speak to a great mass of remaindered data—the ghostly balance of technological progress.

Owning Data

The confusion, enthusiasm, and inventiveness fostered by today's tools for converting between objects, images, and data recall, among other historical episodes, the popularization in the mid-1800s of the electromagnetic telegraph. The telegraph made "one neighborhood of the whole country," according to Morse (who by middle age had given up on painting), and heralded a revolution in communications, but also undercut principles of originality and authorship—as well as the business models based on them.[7] Similarly, the recent dissolution of distance and sudden mobility of media has spooked the acolytes of Sonny Bono and supplicants of Mickey Mouse. From Hollywood film studios, Silicon Valley rec rooms, and Capitol Hill steakhouses, they lust after rights management and insist that copyright continues to stimulate creativity (as gauged by economic output), even as protections are extended for so long that the primary beneficiaries are likely to cash checks on another planet, even as the inextricability of copying and creation gives rise to our best bromides, e.g., remix culture.

Judges are increasingly likely to be asked whether the law might accommodate the prosaic violations of copyright facilitated by digital technologies. Often, rulings issued in disputes between major corporations have reverberating effects. In the 2008 case of *Meshwerks v. Toyota*, Meshwerks, a design studio, was hired by Toyota to produce 3D depictions of cars to be used in a single commercial. Meshwerks sued when Toyota continued to use the wireframes in additional commercials. To make the wireframes, Meshwerks had painstakingly scanned the car from numerous angles, which produced an extremely rough image—a digital maquette, basically. According to Meshwerks, 90 percent of the work was in what followed: the laborious manual "sculpting" of visual data, which took its designers nearly one hundred hours. Toyota asserted that, while a photograph inherently has the mark of originality, simply as a result of a human being's pointing and clicking, a scan is purely mimetic and not eligible for copyright. Siding with Toyota, the Court of Appeals for the Tenth Circuit concluded that any originality in Meshwerks's digital files was an attribute of the cars they depicted.

Charged with making sense of 3D imaging, the court conflated various notions of originality. The Toyota was understood to have the kind of originality associated with artworks (despite the car being a "useful article"), and the wireframe was understood to be a replica (despite being a digital representation, and one that hardly looks like the car). As a precedent, the court cited an earlier case in which Bridgeman Art Library, an English firm that contracted with museums to license photographs of their artworks, sued the American software company Corel, which had produced a CD-ROM that ostensibly duplicated Bridgeman's images of European masterworks. The judge in *Bridgeman* v. *Corel* found that reproductions cannot be copyrighted when they "do nothing more than accurately convey the underlying image," when they are "slavish copies." The decision discounted the creativity and skill of photographers who precisely record existing objects; they might as well be making Xeroxes.[8]

Taken to its logical extreme, this line of legal thinking implies that realism—in photography, drawing, or painting—is akin to making a copy of whatever is depicted. "Put simply, realism is not contrary to originality," writes law professor Edward Lee in "Digital Originality" (2012), which excoriates the *Meshwerks* ruling. "Raw facts are not copyrightable, whereas depictions of the world are."[9] Lee argues that *Meshwerks* is a sign of the legal system's struggle to maintain a coherent definition of authorship as computers take on much of the work associated with creativity. To help courts distinguish between the labor of machine and human, the role of operator and artist, he proposes a "doctrine of digital originality," which requires a consideration of whether or not "the creative powers of the mind" are involved when someone clicks on an iPhone camera or a 3D scanner. But even if such a doctrine were implemented, for how long might we hold on to any notion of where the work of the mind ends and the work of the machine (or algorithm) begins?

According to Marcus Boon's *In Praise of Copying* (2010), our ongoing "cultural crisis" points to the basic "inability of the law to resolve, both intellectually and practically, questions about the identities of objects," which is made conspicuous by the "apparent indifference of the general public to whether the things that they buy are 'real' or 'fake,' 'original' or a 'copy.'"[10] The crisis is only exacerbated by the efforts of markets, galleries, governments, record companies, and fashion brands to regulate the forms and values of goods. Boon suggests we turn away from the legacy of the Platonic distrust of mimesis, which is thought to distort the connection between outward appearance and

20

inner essence, and toward nondualistic and Buddhist philosophy. He proposes that we understand the similarity of original and copied objects as pointing to a common emptiness, a fundamental *lack* of essence shared by all objects, regardless of which came first and which came second.

Of course, the legal system is not about to adopt Mahayana Buddhism, turn away from the illusory realm of appearances, and embrace flux. In the meantime, Boon cheerily suggests we make do with the Internet, which offers "the opportunity to render visible . . . the instability of all the terms and structures which hold together existing intellectual-property regimes, and to point to the madness of modern, capitalist framings of property." If we produce and circulate enough copies, with the aid of BitTorrent and data breaches and 3D scanners and printers, we might drive the courts to admit that certain laws governing intellectual property are not only antiquated but so unenforceable as to seem like fantasy. Then what?

Copyleft adherents, digital utopians, additive-manufacturing entrepreneurs, and trendcasters at magazines from *Wired* to *Harvard Business Review* envision a world in which anyone with a laptop can function as a factory: Grab designs online and print your own home, then decorate it with extruded ancient Greek busts, Alexander Calder mobiles, and Joseph Cornell boxes; maintain your farm by fabricating shovels, chicken feeders, meat grinders, replacement blades, irrigation spigots, and hydroponics systems; mock up one-of-a-kind Lego fortresses with the kids. Artificial scarcity wanes, imports come to seem extraneous, and artisanal producers displace mega-retailers like Walmart. Consumers turn into creative coders and establish decentralized networks that allow them to exchange knowledge and "physibles" and enable them to sate their own appetites for commodities. In the view of Adrian Bowyer, founder of RepRap, an open-source rapid prototyping system that can replicate itself by manufacturing its own parts, 3D printing augurs "Darwinian Marxism": The proletariat takes control of the means of production but "without all that messy and dangerous revolution stuff, and even without all that messy and dangerous industrial stuff."[11]

Cultural Memory

I may be aware of the laws governing intellectual property, but I hardly notice all the violations I engage in (or benefit from) each day: I wake up and grasp for the alarm on my knockoff nightstand, amble into the office, listlessly gaze at the unauthorized reproduction of a recent artwork that occupies my desktop, play an illegally downloaded song, load a pirated version of Adobe Acrobat in order to search a book nabbed from Aaaaarg—and that's all before I've had coffee. In these moments of impulsive breach, I occasionally realize what a chasm exists between the regulation of intellectual property and my daily routine, even my natural instincts.[12]

I've barely changed my behavior, though, except to mask my Internet traffic by paying for a virtual private network. Perhaps the arm of the law is not really so long, or perhaps hardly anyone heeds the occasional examples made by prosecutors and trolls. (It's impossible to say for sure, because so many defendants can't afford decent representation, so they cease and desist rather than make their mark on the legal system.) Nevertheless, to parrot "Areopagitica," John Milton's foundational polemic against licensing, censorship, and the regulation of thought: "I fear yet this iron yoke of outward conformity hath left a slavish print upon our necks; the ghost of a linen decency yet haunts us."[13]

Yet I don't believe we'll reach Shangri-La 2.0 by leveling the distinctions between original and copy, marble statue and CAD model, and insisting on the essential equivalence of all manifestations of all things. To do so is to disavow the meaning that imbues objects as they become vessels for our personal memories and collective histories, as they are marked by our rituals and caresses—which may be trivial when it comes to torrents of Hollywood films and knockoff Louis Vuitton clutches, but paramount when it comes to ancient artifacts and cultural relics (which is how we'll eventually describe torrents and knockoffs). The museum's traditional role as custodian of objects cannot be divorced from the task of registering and manufacturing the value of those objects through research, publication, education, conservation, and exhibition. A sculpture on a pedestal in a museum is always a signifier of meaning to be found elsewhere.

So what, precisely, is copied when one scans and creates 3D-printed versions of an artwork from a museum's collection? The answer depends on the artwork, the museum, and the relationship between the artwork and the museum. Whereas Laric's scans range from Victorian busts of British authors to Bronze Age urns to nineteenth-century Nigerian figurines, German artists Nora Al-Badri and Jan Nikolai Nelles recently captured the iconic bust of Queen Nefertiti that resides at Berlin's Neues Museum. Last October, they walked into the museum—Al-Badri with a customized Microsoft Kinect motion sensor strapped to her chest, concealed by a black leather jacket and vogueish azure scarf—and headed to Room 2.10, which is devoted to the pacific likeness of the Sun Queen. The museum's website indicates that the bust was made with limestone and stucco around 1340 BC by court sculptor Thutmose and used as a model by contemporary portraitists (which is to say the original was designed to be copied). As for provenance, the museum is oddly terse: "She was found in 1912 during the excavations of the German-Orient-Association in the city of Achet-Aton, today known as Amarna."[14] James Simon, a Jewish patron and philanthropist, "funded the excavations in Amarna and acquired ownership of the bust when the finds were divided and bequeathed it to the National Museums in Berlin."

Al-Badri circled the towering vitrine and, whenever the guards seemed distracted, pushed the scarf aside and made a scan.[15] She and Nelles gave the data to designers to assemble a digital model, which was made available for download two months later—as *The Other Nefertiti*—and widely praised for its accuracy, given the circumstances. They then created a 3D-printed version out of polymer resin, which was put on display at the American University at Cairo: an avatar of the bust and a polemic against its appropriation by Germany. Al-Badri and Nelles lament the Neues Museum's failure to even acknowledge that ownership of the bust is highly contested: The Egyptian government claims that fraudulent documents were used to shuttle the statue out of the country, and officials have requested numerous times that it be repatriated; Germany was on the verge of doing so in 1935, but Hitler interceded. ("Nefertiti continually delights me," he wrote, outlining his plan for the bust to be the centerpiece of a new museum devoted to Egyptian antiquities. "I will never relinquish the head of the queen.")

Does the Neues Museum, which has made an extremely precise "museum quality" scan of the bust for the purposes of research and conservation, have the right to stash that data, to treat it as intellectual property rather than a public good? Does the museum have the right to determine who gets to access artworks and cultural heritage? The museum might like to argue that, for those who can afford to visit Berlin, the most enriching and secure environment in which to encounter the bust of Nefertiti is Room 2.10. But why must this preclude schoolchildren and scholars in Cairo and Toronto from scrutinizing Nefertiti's flat-topped headdress and L'Oréal lips? What is lost when high-quality scans begin to circulate alongside thousands of shoddy and illicit iPhone pics? Why should the museum limit digital or physical reproductions so long as they have no effect on the original, especially since the bust of Nefertiti is ostensibly held in the public trust? If the scholarship on markets for designer clothing and knockoffs is any guide, the museum need not be concerned that the half-million people who file through Room 2.10 each year will instead opt to stay at home—or go to Cairo—and satisfy themselves with 3D-printed versions. Perhaps the answer has to do with the potential devaluation of the museum's own copies: 3D-printed and hand-painted replicas, made last year in an edition of one hundred, retail for $10,000.

What is lost when high-quality scans begin to circulate alongside thousands of shoddy and illicit iPhone pics?

Museums around the world may have shut down their plaster cast workshops, but they are increasingly capable of turning digital models into extremely convincing—and therefore marketable—replicas, which will soon only nominally differ from the original artworks. And while Nefertiti may always be on view, the bulk of the Neues Museum's artifacts are warehoused, as tends to be the case with European museums, whose collections keep paying dividends on colonialism. So why not revive the model of the museum devoted to plaster casts, on the basis of reparations for plunder, and repatriate Nefertiti and her ilk?

This proposal heralds the arrival of perfect copies even as it upholds the value of the original—not as an artwork so much as a symbol of the genesis over millennia of Egyptian culture, and its persistence despite the regularity of conquest and desecration by megalomaniacal foreigners. For the symbol to function properly, the object must be possessed. But even if Egypt were to get the bust of Nefertiti returned, the actual sculpture would remain notional to the vast majority of people, whose vacation allowances are nil. And the narrative of the Egyptian nation might just as well be expressed by the proliferation of digital representations of the sculpture as by the gypsum lacquer that has been mottled by the passage of centuries but still enlivens the queen's face. 30

Since the invasion of Iraq, new urgency has been granted to the question of how physical artifacts and their binary manifestations act as stores of cultural memory, especially in light of campaigns to rid territories of the histories of ethnic and religious minorities. Organizations like CyARK, the Million Image Database, Palmyra Photogrammetry, and Learning Sites have been working to create 3D models and virtual reconstructions of damaged and destroyed monuments. (The Institute for Digital Archaeology's 3D-printed marble version of Palmyra's arch, which was assaulted by ISIS last year, was installed in April at London's Trafalgar Square.) Artist Morehshin Allahyari recently reconstituted a statue of King Uthal, ruler of the Roman-era city of Hatra, that was shattered by Islamic State militants at the Mosul Museum last February.[16]

Allahyari made the 3D model of the sculpture available as STL and OBJ files, along with her cache of research, images, maps, and videos; she also stored this data on a flash drive and memory card nestled within a plastic replica. This miniaturized, crystalline figure of a bearded royal seems spectral in contrast to the stone masses being pulverized by smug militants in an ISIS propaganda video—as much an elegy as an act of recovery. Allahyari's 700-megabyte version might be an appropriate container for cultural memory: People can circulate, manipulate, and annotate the files; they can assign their own significance to the work and put it to their own uses; they can claim ownership of the data and limit access, or they can allow the data to degrade and disappear. Which is to say that this transformation also augurs an age of promiscuity for artworks, as they might no longer be bounded by museum walls or tethered to institutions that assume responsibility for taking care of them and shaping their meaning. The alternative is apparent when I gaze through the extruded plastic that makes up King Uthal: I glimpse the outline of data storage devices and nothing of the world in which he ruled.

The Future of Originals

Perhaps the original is most valuable to most people as a source for continual reproduction: Imagine Thutmose's satisfaction at the multiplication of his masterpiece, which might reside, along with all the world's cultural treasures, in a punctiliously regulated, apocalypse-proof underground facility—the art equivalent of the Svalbard Global Seed Vault. Every museum (and every museumgoer) would have access to the same digital store of objects, with copies being instantly materialized and guiltlessly trashed. Blockbuster traveling exhibitions—which cost fortunes, burn through tons of oil, and harm artworks—would be supplanted by shows with low-cost facsimiles and VR versions of legendary performances. Conservation would become as focused on software rot as the decomposition of paints and papers; artworks would become defined as much by parameters for fabricating reproducible objects as certificates and signatures.

We can glimpse something like this future in the farrago of copies made, facilitated, and proscribed by museums like the Met as they uphold their traditional roles while permitting the dematerialization of artworks and diffusion of collections. But the bleeding edge is elsewhere. Consider the Otsuka Museum of Art in Naruto, Japan, founded in 1998 by an industrialist, Masahito Otsuka, who had no art collection but wanted the Japanese people to have access to Western masterpieces, and for his unremarkable hometown to partake of the Bilbao Effect and transform into a cultural hub. Otsuka decided to stock his museum with one thousand reproductions of Western artworks created between the Renaissance and the 1960s, from the Sistine Chapel to Andy Warhol's *Marilyn Diptych* (1962). Whether out of politeness or confusion, Otsuka's son-in-law traveled the world to secure permission to copy works from museums and private collections that, in most cases, hold copyrights only to their own documentary photographs. The museum then created the reproductions with a technique, developed by one of Otsuka's companies, for implanting photographic images in ceramic sheets. The copies preserve the surface textures of the originals and will outlast them by millennia. "Mind blowing museum," reads the TripAdvisor review by MaurTee from Melbourne. "Amazing to have all of the worlds best art work shown in one place. The reproductions are very impressive especially the cave drawings and art work on the walls of chapels located in very remote places in real life."

35 The Spanish company Factum Arte, which specializes in "the production of works that redefine the relationship between two and three dimensions," replicates not only artifacts but entire archaeological sites in order to prevent their degradation. Factum Arte recently worked with Egypt's Supreme Council of Antiquities to create a facsimile of Tutankhamun's tomb by measuring every millimeter of every surface, converting the textures and colors into data with laser scanners, and reconstructing the space via machine-operated blades. The result is "identical to the original at normal viewing distances" and impervious to tourists—those camera-toting, sweat-secreting, humanoid humidifiers. Pilgrims to the prehistoric cave paintings in Lascaux, France, are familiar with this strategy, as the original site was closed in 1963 and visitors were soon directed to a nearby reproduction, Lascaux II. Thanks to stereophotogrammetry, slide projections, 3D photographs, and a unique mortar, a painter named Monique Peytral was able to mimic the hues and textures of the ancient artworks, the effect of seventeen thousand years on earthen pigments.

What might be lost as the greatest hits of human civilization are safely transferred to hard drives? The passage of centuries registered in the fissuring of the supple flesh and glinting pool of Courbet's *The Source*; our sense of ourselves as stewards of objects that testify to our histories and capabilities, given that everything can so simply be stored and retrieved.

Museums offer a concentrated dose of the vexation caused by our stubborn reverence for originality and intensifying devotion to copying, our sensual investment in hallmarks of human achievement and satisfaction with databases of lifeless versions that can be browsed from bed. But they also prompt us to ask how our creations might meaningfully be governed by laws, quotidian behaviors, and collective desires, and how the status of artworks might change as a result. They even use fashionable devices to enable us to see and understand artworks in ways that might previously have been impossible.

Generally, credit is due not to the schemes of digital strategists but to the intervention of artists like Duane Linklater, an Omaskêko Cree artist who lives in Ontario and often describes the mutation of cultural artifacts as they are wrested from their sources and housed in museums. Last year, for an exhibition at the Utah Museum of Fine Arts, Linklater scoured the American Indian collection and made 3D-printed versions of headdresses, clay pots, masks, a totem pole, and a kachina, which were shown alongside prints on linen that reproduce Navajo textiles. The names of the artists of the original works, which were collected between 1875 and 1978 and exhibited in an adjacent gallery, are all unknown to the museum. Linklater's sculptures, made of uncolored plastic resin, are like low-resolution copies, with the detail and workmanship of the originals supplanted by peculiar blurs and abscesses. His prints, derived from photographs of a screen displaying images of the textiles, trade the vivid colors and precise angles of the original patterns for digital effects and distortions.

Linklater's works allegorize the loss of information and, more important, the depletion of cultural significance that occurs when headdresses and masks are given over to pedestals and vitrines, and complex forms of authorship—which may balance individual artistry and collective ownership—are reduced to the conventions of wall labels. Linklater's sculptures suggest that perfect fidelity is always out of reach. But rather than simply register degradation, they testify to the role of the museum, whose unique ability and staggering responsibility is to present objects at once as elements of sacred rites, pedagogical tools, colonialist booty, exquisite artworks, documents of contested histories, and fragments of a highly particular collection. Focused on the relationship between specific objects and specific contexts, Linklater challenges the museum to provide additional explanation rather than circulation, and fix rather than continuously redirect our attention.

While Linklater may be unmoved by the possibility of digital files endlessly trafficking between platforms and users, museums are now all too eager to address us as makers as well as viewers, and indulge our desire for their paralytic—and paralyzing—grip on artworks to be eased. The British Museum organizes "scanathons," which coax visitors to brandish smartphones and make haphazard captures of artworks to be delivered to a crowd-sourced digital archive. The Met's MediaLab invites museumgoers to scan artworks from the collection as part of the occasional "hackathon" or while wandering through the galleries, and posts many of these images and models on platforms for sharing 3D files, such as Sketchfab and Thingiverse. These exercises seem not to be intended to scrutinize the role of the museum in the twenty-first century, much less reform outmoded laws and correct misguided views concerning intellectual property. "We encourage everyone to use our content, which represents the world's cultural heritage, to create their own creative works," reads the Met's Thingiverse profile, a tangle of buzzwords from museum education departments and Silicon Valley. "These are scans for fun, for sharing, and to inspire creativity." In other words, the Met will continue to hoard its "museum-quality models," which would actually be useful to researchers or those wishing to experience an artwork, not a cartoonish distortion, from afar. But at the gift shop you can buy an impeccable marble reproduction of Marble head of a youth, an Ancient Roman copy of a bronze by Polykleitos, for $425 (member price: $382.50).

NOTES

1. The Report of the Committee of the Metropolitan Museum of Art, New York, "Why the Metropolitan Museum New York Should Contain a Full Collection of Casts," 1891, in *U.S. Government Printing Office*, Congressional Serial Set, 1900, pp. 179–82.
2. The International Convention for Promoting Universal Reproductions of Works of Art, instigated by the director of London's Victoria and Albert Museum and signed by fifteen European princes at the Paris International Exhibition of 1867, promoted the exchange and reproduction of plaster casts.
3. Edward Robinson, "The Cost of a Small Museum," *The Nation*, November 21, 1889, p. 405.
4. In *Piracy: The Intellectual Property Wars from Gutenberg to Gates* (2010), Adrian Johns details how unauthorized reprinting undergirded the Enlightenment, and the routine emendation, revision, reordering, and bowdlerization of texts by editors and publishers fostered early American culture. Later, the reproduction of archetypal portraits (with styles and even backgrounds often lifted from likenesses of British aristocrats), newspaper advertisements, and historical scenes via lithographs, engravings, mezzotints, and photogravures led to the development not only of distinctly American art but of an itinerant image of the nation in which citizens recognized themselves. For more on the relationship between visual reproduction and the development of a national culture, see Lucy Ives, "I Would Draw Her Likeness," *Triple Canopy*, no. 20: "Pointing Machines," April 14, 2015.
5. Hillel Schwartz, *The Culture of the Copy: Striking Likenesses, Unreasonable Facsimiles*, New York, Zone Books, 1996, p. 175.

6. "While the avant-garde can be seen as a function of the discourse of originality," wrote Rosalind Krauss in her epochal essay, "The Originality of the Avant-Garde: A Postmodernist Repetition" (1981), "the actual practice of vanguard art tends to reveal that 'originality' is a working assumption that itself emerges from a ground of repetition and recurrence." Krauss questions the authenticity of a cast of Rodin's *The Gates of Hell* made by the French government in 1978. She accepts the legitimacy of the copy, which nevertheless strikes her as inauthentic because it undermines the established relationship between style and historical period, which grants a sense of coherence. She writes: "We do not care if the copyright papers are all in order; for what is at stake are the aesthetic rights of style based on a culture of originals. Sitting in the little theater, watching the newest *Gates* being cast, watching this violation, we want to call out, 'Fraud.'"
7. In *Transporting Visions: The Movement of Images in Early America* (2014), Jennifer L. Roberts describes the telegraph as auguring "a truly cosmic split in the mobility of media." Texts could suddenly be peeled away from pieces of paper and instantaneously transmitted great distances, while paintings and sculptures came to seem remarkably inert, nearly paralyzed. To Roberts, the telegraph, which fundamentally changed the relationship between reproduction and transmission, "names not just a technology but the entire problem of a society struggling with rapidly disintegrating distances and differences." Much the same might now be said of the 3D printer.
8. The judge construed photographs of artworks as "compilations of facts," which cannot be copyrighted, according to *Feist Publications, Inc.* v. *Rural Telephone Service Co.*, the 1991 Supreme Court case that hinged on the unauthorized reproduction of a phone book. In doing so, he set an exceptionally high bar for originality; the implication is that for a work to qualify for copyright, the underlying concept and not just the expression might have to possess originality. This contradicts US law, which protects "original works of authorship fixed in any tangible medium of expression," not ideas. That said, copyright has always been mired in metaphysical conundrums, the thorniest of which may be the distinction between ideas and expressions. "Nobody has ever been able to fix that boundary and nobody ever can," admitted Judge Learned Hand in 1930.
9. Edward Lee, "Digital Originality," *Vanderbilt Journal of Entertainment & Technology Law* 14, no. 4, 2012, p. 929.
10. Marcus Boon, *In Praise of Copying*, Cambridge, Mass., Harvard University Press, 2010, p. 16.
11. Adrian Bowyer, "Wealth Without Money," accessed August 22, 2016, reprap.org.
12. This realization gets more acute when I read about Aaron Swartz being charged with thirteen felonies for downloading 4.8 million articles from JSTOR; random BitTorrent users being sued for trafficking in *Dallas Buyers Club*; Richard Prince struggling to convince judges that his paintings are aesthetically and contextually distinct from photographs employed as source material; and a draft of the Trans-Pacific Partnership trade agreement labeling any unauthorized, temporary reproductions of copyrighted works (which is the most basic operation of computers) as infringements.
13. John Milton, "Areopagitica: A Speech of Mr John Milton for the Liberty of Unlicenc'd Printing, to the Parliament of England," 1644.
14. See: "Room 2.10: Bust of Queen Nefertiti," egyptian-museum-berlin.com.
15. The narrative presented by the artists has been called into question by experts who posit that the quality of the Nefertiti scans is much too high for them to have been produced with the Kinect, especially with the bust enclosed in glass. Some have suggested

that the scans must have been leaked by an employee of the museum or obtained by a hacker. Al-Badri and Nelles have issued ambiguous responses that neither refute nor confirm these claims. "The whole question about originality and authenticity is the same in data as well as in artifacts, and as well in our effort," Al-Badri told Claire Voon of *Hyperallergic*. "Could the Nefertiti Scan Be a Hoax — and Does That Matter?," March 9, 2016, hyperallergic.com.

16. The destroyed sculptures may have themselves been copies. See Justin Huggler, "Statues destroyed by Islamic State in Mosul 'were fakes with originals safely in Baghdad,'" *Telegraph*, March 15, 2015, telegraph.co.uk.

Questions for Critical Reading

1. Provan's essay is centrally concerned with the varying values of copies and originals. Reread his essay and trace his discussion of the relationship between these two. Note passages that reveal the reasons why copies were valued, why originals came to be valued, and what is increasingly valued today.

2. What is the role of a museum? Answer this question for yourself and then review Provan's essay to locate quotations that support your answer. Given his essay, what do you think is the role of a museum for Provan?

3. Who owns data? Reread Provan to look for passages that help you answer that question. How does intellectual property operate today and how, according to Provan, *should* it operate?

Exploring Context

1. Provan opens with a discussion of Gustave Courbet's *The Source*. Using a search engine, look for images of this painting. Relate what you find in terms of quantity and quality of images to Provan's argument. How widely does the digital version of this painting circulate? You may want to pay particular attention to the version on the website for the Metropolitan Museum of Art (metmuseum.org). Consider connecting your response to your response to Question 3 of Questions for Critical Reading.

2. Provan uses *The Other Nefertiti* to illustrate the complex relations between cultural memory, the ownership of art, and digital copying. Visit the site for this project at nefertitihack.alloversky.com. How does the site contribute to Provan's argument?

3. Explore the website for the Otsuka Museum of Art at o-museum.or.jp/english. How does the museum represent itself and its collection? Connect your findings back to Provan's argument.

Questions for Connecting

1. How do issues of digital copying impact the value of making art? Apply Rhys Southan's ideas about art and Effective Altruism in "Is Art a Waste of Time?" (p. 363) to Provan's argument. How does the notion of replaceability resonate in a world of copies? You may want to bring in your analysis of the Otsuka Museum of Art from Question 3 of Exploring Context.

2. **Multimodal.** Otto von Busch, in "Crafting Resistance" (p. 399), suggests that crafting items such as clothing can function as a kind of resistance. Consider the world of digital crafts, such as 3D printing. Using the insights that Provan provides, evaluate whether or not digital crafting can also act as resistance. Then, make a three-dimensional representation of your answer, such as a model, diorama, or 3D-printed object. Working in three dimensions allows you to use space to show the relationships between elements, so use this capacity to your advantage while also considering other elements of design. Your work with *The Other Nefertiti* project in Question 2 of Exploring Context might be useful in making your response.

3. In "Electric Funeral" (p. 243), Chuck Klosterman looks at notions of villainy and the inevitability of a technological future. Use his analysis to evaluate the circulation of digital copies of art. Is it villainous? Is it avoidable? Your work on the ownership of data and the role of museums in Questions 2 and 3 of Questions for Critical Reading might be helpful.

Language Matters

1. Provan is centrally concerned with images. If you were going to include images with this text, which ones would you choose? How would adding images change the meaning of the text? How can visual images support an argument made with words?

2. Indexes help you locate important information quickly. Create a simple index for Provan's essay. What terms or entries would you include? How often do they appear in the text?

3. The most solid transitions come from a statement that directly ties together two paragraphs. Select two paragraphs from Provan's essay. Write a one-sentence summary of the first paragraph and then another one-sentence summary of the second paragraph. Then combine these two sentences into one to form a new transition between the paragraphs. How does your sentence differ from Provan's transition? How can you use this skill in your own writing?

Assignments for Writing

1. What is the value of the original in a world of digital copies? Write a paper in which you examine the relationship between originals and copies, making an argument about how, or if, we should continue to value the idea of an "original." Does it simply offer something to be copied? Does it play a role in cultural memory? Your work in Questions for Critical Reading and Exploring Context might be useful as you support your argument.

2. Museums are traditionally seen as important cultural institutions of preservation. But what is the role of the museum today? Write a paper in which you propose the role of museums in the age of the digital copy. Questions 1 and 2 of Questions for Critical Reading might offer a helpful starting point for your analysis.

3. Write a paper in which you examine the role of intellectual property in the production of art. Who owns art? How is that ownership challenged by digital copying technologies? Your responses to Questions for Critical Reading and Questions for Connecting might offer a good starting point for locating your argument.

JULIA SERANO

Julia Serano, who holds a Ph.D. in biochemistry and molecular biophysics from Columbia University, is a writer, spoken-word performer, and activist. Serano is a frequent speaker on transgender and queer issues and is the author of *Whipping Girl: A Transsexual Woman on Sexism and the Scapegoating of Femininity* (2007) and *Excluded: Making Feminist and Queer Movements More Inclusive* (2013). She has been anthologized in *Trans/Love: Radical Sex, Love & Relationships beyond the Gender Binary* (2011) and *Yes Means Yes!: Visions of Female Sexual Power & a World without Rape* (2008), edited by Jaclyn Friedman and Jessica Valenti.

Yes Means Yes!, where this essay originally appeared, is a feminist anthology that addresses issues of rape and sexuality by arguing that consent requires affirmative declaration—yes means yes. The editors contend that rather than only declaring what they do not want, women should also actively discover what they *do* want. Essays in the collection focus on body image and self-esteem, incest, rape culture, mass media, pornography, and more. Ultimately, *Yes Means Yes!* seeks to deconstruct the rape culture in which we live and foster understanding and respect for female sexual pleasure.

Julia Serano's contribution to the anthology, "Why Nice Guys Finish Last," explores her own somewhat unique perspective on rape culture from her identity as a transgendered woman who transitioned relatively late in life. She notes that rape culture is perpetuated not only by our preconceptions about women (that they are passive "prey") but also by our preconceptions about men (that they are "predators"). Serano attempts to explain why women tend to prefer "assholes" over "nice guys" and how that preference is a symptom of rape culture, and in the process she also illustrates how gendered stereotypes are detrimental to both women and men.

How do you think cultural expectations shape both men and women? How have they shaped you?

▶ TAGS: *culture, empathy, gender, identity, media, race and ethnicity, relationships, sexuality, social change, trauma and violence*

▶ CONNECTIONS: *Appiah, Chabon, Coates, Epstein, Gay, Gilbert, von Busch, Yang, Yoshino*

Why Nice Guys Finish Last

Sexualization and intimidation haunt all of us who move through the world as women. I have had men talk over me, speak down to me, and shout angrily at me when I've tried to deflect their unwanted passes. Strange men have hurled catcalls and sexual innuendos at me, and have graphically described what they'd like to do with me as I pass by them on city streets. I've also survived an attempted date rape. And frankly, I consider myself lucky that nothing more serious than that has happened to me. Needless to say, like all women, I have a great interest in bringing an end to rape culture.

Having said that, being transsexual—having had the experience of navigating my way through the world as male prior to my transition to female—has given me a somewhat different take on rape culture than the view that is often taken for granted among many cisgender (i.e., non-transgender) women. From my perspective, much of the existing rhetoric used to describe and theorize sexual harassment, abuse, and rape is, unfortunately, mired in the concept of "unilateral sexism"—that is, the belief that men are the oppressors and women are the oppressed, end of story.

Some of those who buy into unilateral sexism believe that men are inherently oppressive, dominating, and violent. Others believe that the problem is rooted in patriarchy and male socialization conspiring to condition men to become sexual predators. While there is certainly some truth to the idea that men are socialized to be sexually aggressive, even predatory, this is not the only force at work in their lives. Male children and teenagers are also regularly and explicitly reminded that they should be respectful of girls and women, and are often punished severely for picking on or "playing rough" with, their female peers. Further, the men-are-just-socialized-that-way argument fails to explain the countless men who never sexually abuse or harass women in their lifetime.

The truth is that rape culture is a mindset that affects each and every one of us, shaping how we view and respond to the world, and creating double binds for both women and men. I call this phenomenon the predator/prey mindset, and within it, men can only ever be viewed as sexual aggressors and women as sexual objects.

Rape culture is a mindset that affects each and every one of us.

5 The predator/prey mindset creates many of the double standards that exist in how we view female versus male sexuality. For example, on numerous occasions I've heard heterosexual female friends of mine ogle some man and make comments about how he has a nice ass. While one could certainly make the case that such discussions are "objectifying" or "sexualizing," what strikes me is that they don't *feel* that way. But if I were to overhear a group of men make the exact same comments about a woman, they would *feel* very different. They would *feel* sexualizing.

Similarly, if a male high school teacher were to have sex with one of his female teenage students, we would all be appalled. The incident would clearly *feel* like statutory rape to us. However, when the roles are reversed—when the adult teacher is female and the teenage student is male—it generally *feels* like a completely different thing to us. While it still fits the definition of statutory rape, we often have problems mustering up the *feeling* that the boy has been violated or abused. In fact, after one recent high-profile case, comedian Bill Maher joked that such teenage boys are "lucky," and the audience broke into laughter.

What these anecdotes reveal is that the predator/prey mindset essentially ensures that men cannot be viewed as legitimate sexual objects, nor can women be viewed as legitimate sexual aggressors. This has the effect of rendering invisible instances of man-on-man and woman-on-woman sexual harassment and abuse, and it makes the idea of woman-on-man rape utterly inconceivable. It's also why women cannot simply "turn the tables" and begin sexualizing men. After all, if a woman were to shout catcalls at a man, or were to pinch a guy's ass as he walked by, her actions wouldn't mean the same thing as they would if the roles were reversed. Her actions would likely be seen as suggestive and slutty, rather than intimidating and predatory.

Because of the predator/prey mindset, when a woman does act in a sexually active or aggressive way, she is generally not viewed as a sexual aggressor, but rather as opening herself up to being sexually objectified by others. This is why rape trials have historically dwelled on whether the woman in question was dressed in a revealing or provocative fashion, or whether she met with the man privately, and so on. If she did any of these things, others are likely to view her as inviting her own sexualization, as "asking for it." The underlying assumption is that women should simply know better—they should recognize that they are prey and men are predators, and they should act "appropriately."

What should be becoming increasingly clear is that the predator/prey mindset enables the virgin/whore double bind that feminists have long been rallying against. Women, as prey, are expected to play down their sexuality—to hide or repress it. Good girls, after all, are supposed to be "virgins." Women who do not downplay or repress their sexualities—that is, who do not act like prey—are viewed stereotypically as "whores." As stereotypes, both "virgin" and "whore" are disempowering, because they both frame female sexuality in terms of the predator/prey mindset. This is why reclaiming their sexuality has been such a double-edged sword for women. If a woman embraces her sexuality, it may be personally empowering for her, but she still has to deal with the fact that others will project the "whore" stereotype onto her and assume that she's inviting male sexualization. In other words, a woman may be personally empowered, but she is not seen as being sexually powerful and autonomous in the culture at large. In order for that to happen, we as individuals must begin to challenge our own (as well as other people's) perceptions and interpretations of gender. We must all move beyond viewing the world through the predator/prey mindset.

10

To do that, we must examine an issue that has traditionally received far less attention: the ways in which the predator/prey mindset complicates the lives of men. Trans perspectives (those of trans women, trans men, and other transgender-spectrum people) can be really vital in this regard, as many of us have had the experience of moving through the world as both women and men at different points in our lives, and thus can consider the male position without undermining or dismissing female perspectives (and vice versa). In thinking about these issues, I draw heavily on my own experiences being raised as a boy, and as a young adult who was viewed by others as a heterosexual man (as I am primarily attracted to women). It is not my intention to speak on behalf of all men, both because I never fully identified as male at the time, and also because I had a very specific and privileged male existence (for example, I am white and middle-class). It will take the experiences of other trans folks and cisgender men to fill in the whole picture.

Just as it is difficult for women to navigate their way through the world, given the fact that they are nonconsensually viewed as prey, it is often difficult for men to move through a world in which they are nonconsensually viewed as predators. When I was male-bodied, it was not uncommon for women to cross the street if I was walking behind them at night, or to have female strangers misinterpret innocent things that I said as unsolicited sexual advances. It is telling, I think, that I had to deal with the predator stereotype despite the fact that my appearance was about as unthreatening as it gets: I was a very small and unmasculine/androgynous man. Bigger and more masculine-appearing men have to deal with this stereotype much more than I ever did. Perhaps no issue exacerbates the male predator stereotype more than race.

I have heard several trans men of color say that they feel that the male privilege they have gained since transitioning has been very much offset by the increased visibility and the societal stereotypes of black men as predators that others are constantly projecting onto them.

While the predator stereotype affects men's interactions with women, it probably has an even greater impact on their interactions with children. When I was male-bodied, I found that if I were to interact enthusiastically with children, women would often give me dirty looks. A trans male acquaintance of mine recently told me that the greatest loss he experienced upon transitioning from female to male was his ability to interact freely and enthusiastically with children. He teaches young children and has found that he's had to modify his whole approach—for example, keeping more distance and not being as effusive or affectionate with his students as before—in order to avoid other adults' viewing him as creepy or suspect.

Obviously, men make up the overwhelming majority of sexual predators. But that does not mean that *all* men are necessarily sexual predators. It is important for us to keep in mind that the men-as-predator stereotype is exactly that—a stereotype—and it creates obstacles that all men must navigate, whether they are predators or not. This is especially true for those men who are additionally marginalized with regard to race and class. Given how destructive and injuring sexual abuse and violence are to those who experience them, I wouldn't dare suggest that it is the (potential or actual) victim's fault for propagating these stereotypes. At the same time, the truth is that we cannot begin to have an honest discussion about how to dismantle rape culture unless we are willing to acknowledge the negative impact that this stereotype has on those men who are not predatory.

The predator stereotype also complicates and constrains male sexuality. While many feminists have discussed how the sexual object/prey stereotype creates a double bind for women in which they can only ever be viewed as either "virgins" or "whores," not enough have considered how the sexual aggressor/predator stereotype might create a similar double bind for men. Having experienced this dilemma myself firsthand, I have come to refer to it (for reasons that will be clear in a moment) as the assholes/nice guys double bind. "Assholes" are men who fulfill the men-as-sexual-aggressors stereotype; "nice guys" are the ones who refuse or eschew it.

15 Just as women receive mixed messages in our culture—some encouraging them to be "virgins," others encouraging them to be "whores"—men receive similar mixed messages. As I alluded to earlier, male children often receive lots of explicit encouragement to be respectful of women. Even in adulthood, men who make blatantly sexist comments, or who suggest (in mixed company, at least) that women are "only good for one thing" will often be looked down upon or taken to task for it. So when it comes to their formal socialization, boys/men receive plenty of encouragement to be "nice guys."

The problem is that boys/men receive conflicting messages from society at large. This informal socialization comes mostly from the meanings and expectations that are regularly projected onto women and men, especially in the media and within the context of heterosexual relationships. Just as women are expected to fulfill the stereotype of being sexual objects in order to gain male attention, men are expected to fulfill the sexual aggressor stereotype in order to gain female attention. In other words, they have to act like "assholes." Granted, this isn't true in *all* situations. For example, in the progressive, artsy, and/or queer circles I inhabit nowadays, men who act like "assholes" don't get very far. But in the heterosexual mainstream culture, men who unapologetically act like "assholes" tend to thrive.

This really confused me in my late teens and young adulthood. I had lots of close female friends back then, and it always used to bum me out when they would completely fall for a guy doing the "asshole" routine: acting confident to the point of being cocky, being sexually forward if not downright pushy, and relentlessly teasing girls in a junior high school–esque way with the expectation that they would smile and giggle in response. It always seemed really contrived to me. I suppose I was privy to insider information: I had the experience of interacting regularly with many of those same men *as a man* (not a woman), and in those situations they did not act nearly as cocky or presumptive or dismissive toward me as they did around women they were interested in.

Anyway, time and time again, my female friends would fall for an "asshole" and then be crushed because he never called her the next day, as he'd promised, or because he started bragging to his guy friends about his "sexual conquest," or because he tried to push things along faster and farther sexually than she was willing to go. Sometimes after being hurt by some "asshole," my female friends would come to me for advice or to be consoled. They came to me because I was a "nice guy." In their eyes, I was safe. Respectful. Harmless. Sometimes during these post-"asshole" conversations, my friends would go on a tirade about how all men are jerks and cannot be trusted, or they'd ask, "Why can't I find a guy who will treat me with respect?" Whenever they did this, I would point out that there are lots of guys who are not jerks, who are respectful of women. I'd even name a few. Upon hearing the names I suggested, my friends would invariably say something like "I don't find him attractive" or "I think of him more as a friend."

Just as women who refuse to play the role of sexual object often fail to attract male attention, "nice guys" who refuse to play the role of sexual aggressor typically fail to attract female attention. (Note that I'm not speaking here of the type of man referred to in the feminist blogosphere as a Nice Guy, who is the sort of man who argues that being a "nice guy" entitles him to sex with whomever he wants, thus revealing himself to be merely a closeted "asshole.") In high school and college, I had several male friends who, apparently concerned with the lack of action I was getting, literally told me that women like it when guys act like "assholes." For them, it was just something one did to attract women. And as much as I hate to admit it, it generally seemed to be true. During my college years, I watched a number of "nice guys" transform into "assholes." And when they did, women suddenly became interested in them. The most stunning transformation I witnessed was in this guy who lived in my dorm, whom I'll call Eric. Freshman and sophomore years, he was a super-sweet and respectful guy. Despite the fact that he was fairly good-looking, women were not generally interested in him. Somewhere around junior year, he suddenly began acting like an "asshole" (around women, at least). Instead of engaging women in conversations (as he used to), he would instead relentlessly tease them. The things he would say sounded really dismissive to me, but often the intended recipient would just giggle in response. Suddenly he was

"Nice guys" who refuse to play the role of sexual aggressor typically fail to attract female attention.

picking women up at parties, and I'd occasionally overhear women who never knew Eric back when he was a "nice guy" discussing how cute they thought he was.

The last time I saw Eric was about two years after college. We had both moved to New York City, and a mutual friend came up to visit and suggested that we all go out together. The bar that we went to was really crowded, and at one point, Eric started talking about how in situations like this, he would sometimes fold his arms across his chest and subtly grope women as they walked by. Between the fact that the bar was so crowded and the way he held his arms to obscure his hands, women weren't able to figure out that it was Eric. Upon hearing this, I walked out of the bar, appalled. 20

The reason I tell this story is that it complicates many of the existing presumptions regarding the origins of rape culture. Some have suggested that men are biologically programmed to be sexual predators. The existence of Eric (and others like him) challenges that argument because, after all, he was a "nice guy" for most of his life until about the age of twenty—well after his sex drive kicked in. Eric challenges overly simplistic men-are-socialized-to-be-that-way arguments for the same reason: He made it to early adulthood—well beyond his formative childhood and teenage years—before becoming an "asshole." It would be really hard to make the case that Eric became a sexual predator because he was influenced by media imagery or pornography, or because his male peers egged him on. Like I said, I lived in the same dorm as he did, and I never once saw any guys teasing him for being a "nice guy" or coercing him into being an "asshole." I would argue that the primary reason Eric became sexually aggressive was that he was interested in attracting women. And, as with many men, once Eric began disrespecting women on a regular basis, the lines between flirting and harassment, between sex and violation, between consensual and nonconsensual, became blurred or unimportant to him.

Not to sound corny, but we all want the same things in life: to gain other people's attention, to be adored, to be sexually desired, to be intimate with people we find attractive, and to have great sex. In a culture where women are generally viewed as sexual objects, some women will take on that role in order to gain attention and to feel desirable. By the same token, in a world where men are only ever viewed as sexual aggressors, some men will take on that role in order to gain attention and to feel desirable. So long as the predator/prey mindset predominates and a demand remains for women and men to fulfill those stereotypes, a large percentage of people will continue to gravitate toward them.

This is why single-tact solutions to abolish rape culture will always fail. For instance, many people in both the political/religious Right, as well as many anti-pornography feminists, seem to take what I call the "virgin" approach. Their line of reasoning goes something like this: Because men are predators, we should desexualize women in the culture by, for example, banning pornography and discouraging representations of women (whether media imagery or actual women) that others can interpret as sexually arousing or objectifying. This approach not only is sexually repressive and disempowering for many women, but it also reinforces the idea that men are predators and women are prey. In other words, it reaffirms the very system that it hopes to dismantle.

I also get frustrated by people who think that it's simply up to male allies to call out those men who are sexist or disrespectful of women. While this approach can have some positive effect, I believe that many cisgender women overestimate its potential. First off, it essentially makes the "nice guys" responsible for policing the "assholes." This overlooks the fact that in the heterosexual mainstream, "assholes" are seen as being higher up in the social pecking order than "nice guys," As a result, a "nice guy" calling out an "asshole" about how he needs to be more respectful of women tends to have as much societal clout as if the geeky girl in class were to lecture the cheerleaders about how they shouldn't play dumb and giggle at every joke that the popular boys make. Such comments, when they are made, are often ignored or outright dismissed. Furthermore, I've experienced a number of situations in my life (e.g., high school locker rooms) where I honestly did not feel safe enough to protest the sexist comments that some boys and men make. After all, one of the ways in which the hierarchical status quo is maintained in male circles is through the threat of physical intimidation and violence.

Any attempts to critique men for being sexually aggressive, or to critique women for fulfilling the role of sexual object, will have a very limited effect. These tactics, after all, fail to address the crucial issue of demand. So long as heterosexual women are attracted to men who act like aggressors, and heterosexual men are attracted to women who act like objects, people will continue to fulfill those roles. In contrast, critiques that challenge why individuals desire stereotypical "sex objects" and "sexual aggressors" seem to me to get closer to the root of the problem.

I have heard many feminists critique men who prefer women that fulfill the sexual object stereotype. Many of these critiques (rightfully, I think) suggest that the man in question must be somewhat shallow or insecure if he's willing to settle for someone whom he does not view as his intellectual and emotional equal. What I have seen far less of are critiques of women who are attracted to sexually aggressive men. Perhaps this stems in part from the belief that such comments might be misinterpreted as blaming women for enabling the sexual abuse they receive at the hands of men. While I can understand this reluctance, I nevertheless feel that it is a mistake to ignore this issue, given the fact that many men become sexual aggressors primarily, if not solely, to attract the attention of women. In fact, if heterosexual women suddenly decided en masse that "nice guys" are far sexier than "assholes," it would create a huge shift in the predator/prey dynamic. While I wouldn't suggest that such a change would completely eliminate rape or sexual abuse (because there are clearly other societal forces at work here), I do believe that it would greatly reduce the number of men who harass and disrespect women on a daily basis.

Those feminists who have critiqued the tendency of women to be attracted to sexually aggressive men often refer to the phenomenon as "internalized misogyny." In other words, they presume that because women have been socialized to take shit from men, they have become conditioned to continually seek out men who will treat them like shit. Personally, I find this explanation unsatisfying. I don't think that women are attracted to sexual aggressors because they believe that those men will treat them like shit. Rather, they tend to be attracted to other aspects of sexual aggressors, and only later become disappointed by the way they are treated.

This phenomenon is more accurately viewed as a form of "externalized misogyny." There are a lot of subliminal meanings built into the predator/prey mindset: that men are aggressive and women are passive, that men are strong and women are weak, that men are rebellious and women are harmless, and so on. It is no accident that the meanings associated with women are typically viewed as inferior to, or lamer than, those associated with men. Given this context, I would argue that "nice guys" are generally read as emasculated or effeminized men in our culture. In a world where calling a man "sensitive" is viewed as a pejorative, the very act of showing respect for women often disqualifies a male from being seen as a "real man." I believe that this is a major reason why many heterosexual women are not sexually interested in "nice guys."

I think that women who are attracted to sexual aggressors are primarily drawn to the rebellious, bad-boy image they project—an image that is essentially built into our cultural ideal of maleness. The odd thing is that for many men, fulfilling the aggressor role represents the path of least resistance. How rebellious can it be to fulfill a stereotype? "Nice guys," on the other hand, *are* rebellious, at least in one sense: They buck the system and refuse to reduce themselves to the predator stereotype. It is time that we begin to recognize and celebrate this rebellion.

30 Lots of women I know want to create a world in which women are allowed and encouraged to be sexual without having to be nonconsensually sexualized. This is a laudable goal. But having been on the other side of the gender divide, I would argue that for this to happen, we will also have to work to simultaneously ensure that men can be respectful of women without being *desexualized*. One cannot happen without the other. I think that a lot of men would be eager to work with women to create such a world. A movement that refuses to render invisible and desexualize men who are not predators, and that attempts to debunk both the virgin/whore *and* the asshole/nice guy double binds, would excite and attract many male allies.

Perhaps most important, understanding the predator/prey mindset can help us to recognize that rape culture is reinforced both by people's actions *and* by their perceptions. The system will not be dismantled until all (or at least most) of us learn not to project the predator stereotype onto men and the prey stereotype onto women. Just as we must learn to debunk the many racist, sexist, classist, homophobic, and ageist cultural stereotypes we've absorbed over the course of a lifetime, we must also learn to move beyond predator/prey stereotypes. Honestly, I find this the most personally challenging aspect of this work. Moving through the world as a woman, and having to deal with being harassed by men on a regular basis, makes me wary of letting my guard down in any way. Viewing all men as predators is a convenient self-defense mechanism, but it ignores the countless men who are respectful of women. I am not suggesting that we, as women, ignore the important issue of safety—to do so at this moment in time would be beyond unwise. What I am suggesting is that we won't get to where we want to be until the men-as–predator/sexual aggressor assumption no longer dominates our thinking. It's difficult to imagine getting there from here, but we're going to have to try.

Questions for Critical Reading

1. Serano introduces a number of terms in making her argument. As you reread, take note as she defines *cisgender, unilateral sexism*, the *predator/prey mindset, virgin/whore*, and *internalized/externalized misogyny.*

2. **Multimodal.** *Rape culture* figures prominently in Serano's essay, though she never explicitly defines it. Using what she does say about rape culture, formulate a definition of the term. Then, compose a photo — approved in advance by your instructor and without depicting people — that illustrates rape culture, labeling with a hashtag

provided by your instructor or decided by the class. If posting the photo is part of your class assignment, consider not only the visual composition of the image but also how the use of filters can enhance your meaning.

3. Take a moment to think about the cultural expectations of men. As you review the essay, take note of the ways that Serano claims the socialization of men contributes to rape culture. Do your thoughts confirm her argument?

Exploring Context

1. Visit the blog for *Yes Means Yes!* at yesmeansyesblog.wordpress.com. Read through several entries. How does the blog continue or complement Serano's project?
2. FORCE: Upsetting Rape Culture (upsettingrapeculture.com) is a website dedicated to fighting rape culture. Explore the site to learn more about this concept and the ways in which it can be fought. How does the site change your definition of *rape culture* from Question 2 of Questions for Critical Reading?
3. The "friendzone" is a popular expression to describe the fate of "nice guys." Using the web, do an image search for "friendzone." In what ways does this concept reflect Serano's argument? Relate your findings to your answer about cultural expectations of men from Question 3 of Questions for Critical Reading.

Questions for Connecting

1. Michael Chabon's son Abe in "My Son, the Prince of Fashion" (p. 62) — and Chabon himself — represents a different kind of masculinity and a different way of being a man than that which Serano describes. Synthesize these essays to consider the possibilities and consequences of creating shifts in notions of masculinity. What price does Abe pay? Is gender linked to sexuality? How does rape culture affect them?
2. In "Small Change" (p. 191), Malcolm Gladwell discusses some mechanisms of social change, particularly in relation to the kinds of connections we make in person and through social media. Apply Gladwell's ideas to the problems Serano discusses surrounding masculinity and rape culture. How might strong and weak ties generate change?
3. Serano acknowledges the difficulties in changing our thinking about men and women. Use Kwame Anthony Appiah's ideas from "Making Conversation" and "The Primacy of Practice" (p. 35) to propose strategies to pursue Serano's vision. Can cosmopolitanism help men and women? How does the persistence of rape culture reveal the primacy of practice, and how can we shift that practice?

Language Matters

1. Sentences can be written in either active or passive voice. If you're not sure what these terms mean, look up *active voice* and *passive voice* in a grammar handbook or reference guide. Then select a quotation from Serano's essay that you think is key

to her argument. Identify whether it is written in active or passive voice, noting how you know this to be the case. Then rewrite the sentence in the opposite voice. Is the argument weaker in passive voice or in active voice? Are concepts clearer in one voice or the other? Why or why not? Why might you choose active or passive voice in your own writing?

2. What's the relationship between point of view and authority? Serano suggests that her position as a transgender woman provides a unique perspective on the issues of the essay. Is that a legitimate basis for authority? How do you find your authority to speak when doing academic writing?

3. Serano uses a number of specialized terms. Note how she defines these terms in her text. How well does context function to help a reader define terms? When should you look up a word in the dictionary, and when is it sufficient to determine a word's meaning from the context of its use?

Assignments for Writing

1. Serano works with a number of binaries (virgin/whore, nice guy/asshole). Write a paper in which you propose a solution to the problem of rape culture that avoids binary positions. Is it possible to locate positions for men and women that don't rely on these binaries? What options does Serano suggest that could lead to such a solution? You may want to work with the definitions you developed in Questions 1 and 2 of Questions for Critical Reading as well as your work on cultural expectations of men from Question 3 of Questions for Critical Reading and Question 1 of Questions for Connecting.

2. Serano draws from her experience in order to argue that nice guys finish last. Write a paper in which you synthesize your own experience with Serano's argument, treating your experiences as evidence to be connected to Serano's. Does your experience confirm or complicate Serano's observations?

3. How can we mitigate the power of stereotypes? Using Serano's ideas, write a paper in which you suggest strategies for dismantling stereotypes in culture. You may want to use your work from Question 3 of Questions for Critical Reading and Question 1 of Questions for Connecting.

PETER SINGER

Peter Singer is the Ira W. DeCamp Professor of Bioethics at Princeton University as well as the Laureate Professor at the Centre for Applied Philosophy and Public Ethics at the University of Melbourne. He founded the Centre for Human Bioethics at Monash University, and the Council of Australian Humanist Societies recognized him as Humanist of the Year in 2004. Singer has published dozens of books and essays, but among the best-known books are *Animal Liberation: A New Ethics for Our Treatment of Animals* (1975), *Practical Ethics* (1979), *How Are We to Live? Ethics in an Age of Self-Interest* (1993), and *The Life You Can Save: Acting Now to End World Poverty* (2009). Most recently, he has published *The Most Good You Can Do: How Effective Altruism Is Changing Ideas about Living Ethically* (2015) and *Ethics in the Real World: 82 Brief Essays on Things That Matter* (2016).

Singer's essay "Visible Man: Ethics in a World without Secrets" was published in the August 2011 edition of *Harper's Magazine*. This issue was published as the country neared the tenth anniversary of the 9/11 tragedy, so accompanying articles were on the FBI's attempt to find internal terrorists as well as the limits of remembrance since the terrorist attacks. The issue also included a series of watercolor images by Steve Mumford, produced while embedded with American troops in Afghanistan.

"Visible Man: Ethics in a World without Secrets" focuses on the concepts of transparency and personal privacy. With a focus on the controversial website WikiLeaks (wikileaks.org), Singer discusses the modern-day changes in surveillance technology and how these changes might alter our government as well as our society. While Singer seemingly argues in favor of this transparency, he also makes note of the possibility that information collected by these technologies might be misused. By arguing that surveillance work should both aid and expose government, Singer is encouraging readers to question current views on privacy and examine how new technologies have the ability to affect the future.

TAGS: *censorship, ethics, law and justice, photography and video, politics, science and technology, social change*

CONNECTIONS: *Appiah, Chen, Gilbert, Klosterman, Konnikova, Paumgarten, Turkle, van Houtryve, von Busch, Watters, Yoshino*

Visible Man: Ethics in a World without Secrets

In 1787, the philosopher Jeremy Bentham proposed the construction of a "Panopticon," a circular building with cells along the outer walls and, at the center, a watchtower or "inspector's lodge" from which all the cells could be seen but no one would know, at any given moment, due to a system of blinds and partitions, whether he was actually being observed. Bentham thought this design would be particularly suited to prisons but suggested it could also be applied to factories, hospitals, mental asylums, and schools. Not only would prisoners, workers, the ill, the insane, and students be subject to observation, but also—if the person in charge of the facility visited the inspector's area—the warders, supervisors, caregivers, and teachers. The gradual adoption of this "inspection principle" would, Bentham predicted, create "a new scene of things," transforming the world into a place with "morals reformed, health preserved, industry invigorated, instruction diffused, public burdens lightened."

The modern Panopticon is not a physical building, and it doesn't require the threat of an inspector's presence to be effective. Technological breakthroughs have made it easy to collect, store, and disseminate data on individuals, corporations, and even the government. With surveillance technology like closed-circuit television cameras and digital cameras now linked to the Internet, we have the means to implement Bentham's inspection principle on a much vaster scale. What's more, we have helped construct this new Panopticon, voluntarily giving up troves of personal information. We blog, tweet, and post what we are doing, thinking, and feeling. We allow friends and contacts, and even strangers, to know where we are at any time. We sign away our privacy in exchange for the conveniences of modern living, giving corporations access to information about our financial circumstances and our spending habits, which will then be used to target us for ads or to analyze our consumer habits.

Then there is the information collected without our consent. Since 2001, the number of U.S. government organizations involved in spying on our own citizens, both at home and abroad, has grown rapidly. Every day, the National Security Agency intercepts 1.7 billion emails, phone calls, instant messages, bulletin-board postings, and other communications. This system houses information on thousands of U.S. citizens, many of them not accused of any wrongdoing. Not long ago, when traffic police stopped a driver they had to radio the station and wait while someone checked records. Now, handheld devices instantly call up a person's Social Security number and license status, records of outstanding warrants, and even mug shots. The FBI can also cross-check your fingerprints against its digital archive of 96 million sets.

Yet the guarded have also struck back, in a sense, against their guardians, using organizations like WikiLeaks, which, according to its founder Julian Assange, has released more classified documents than the rest of the world's media combined, to keep tabs on governments and corporations. When Assange gave the *Guardian* 250,000 confidential cables, he did so on a USB drive the size of your little finger. Efforts to close down the WikiLeaks website have proven futile, because the files are mirrored on hundreds of other sites. And in any case, WikiLeaks isn't the only site revealing private information. An array of groups are able to release information anonymously. Governments, corporations, and other organizations interested in protecting privacy will strive to increase security, but they will also have to reckon with the likelihood that such measures are sometimes going to fail.

New technology has made greater openness possible, but has this openness made us better off?

5 New technology has made greater openness possible, but has this openness made us better off? For those who think privacy is an inalienable right, the modern surveillance culture is a means of controlling behavior and stifling dissent. But perhaps the inspection principle, universally applied, could also be the perfection of democracy, the device that allows us to know what our governments are really doing, that keeps tabs

on corporate abuses, and that protects our individual freedoms just as it subjects our personal lives to public scrutiny. In other words, will this technology be a form of tyranny or will it free us from tyranny? Will it upend democracy or strengthen it?

The standards of what we want to keep private and what we want to make public are constantly evolving. Over the course of Western history, we've developed a desire for more privacy, quite possibly as a status symbol, since an impoverished peasant could not afford a house with separate rooms. Today's affluent Americans display their status not only by having a bedroom for each member of the family, plus one for guests, but also by having a bathroom for every bedroom, plus one for visitors so that they do not have to see the family's personal effects. It wasn't always this way. A seventeenth-century Japanese *shunga* depicts a man making love with his wife while their daughter kneels on the floor nearby, practicing calligraphy. The people of Tikopia, a Pacific island inhabited by Polynesians, "find it good to sleep side by side crowding each other, next to their children or their parents or their brothers and sisters, mixing sexes and generations," according to the anthropologist Dorothy Lee. "[A]nd if a widow finds herself alone in her one-room house, she may adopt a child or a brother to allay her intolerable privacy." The Gebusi people in New Guinea live in communal longhouses and are said to "shun privacy," even showing reluctance to look at photos in which they are on their own.

With some social standards, the more people do something, the less risky it becomes for each individual. The first women to wear dresses that did not reach their knees were no doubt looked upon with disapproval, and may have risked unwanted sexual attention; but once many women were revealing more of their legs, the risks dissipated. So too with privacy: when millions of people are prepared to post personal information, doing so becomes less risky for everyone. And those collective, large-scale forfeitures of personal privacy have other benefits as well, as tens of thousands of Egyptians showed when they openly became fans of the Facebook page "We are all Khaled Said," named after a young man who was beaten to death by police in Alexandria. The page became the online hub for the protests that forced the ouster of President Hosni Mubarak.

Whether Facebook and similar sites are reflecting a change in social norms about privacy or are actually driving that change, that half a billion are now on Facebook suggests that people believe the benefits of connecting with others, sharing information, networking, self-promoting, flirting, and bragging outweigh breaches of privacy that accompany such behavior.

More difficult questions arise when the loss of privacy is not in any sense a choice. Bentham's Panopticon has become a symbol of totalitarian intrusion. Michel Foucault* described it as "the perfection of power." We all know that the police can obtain phone records when seeking evidence of involvement in a crime, but most of us would be surprised by the frequency of such requests. Verizon alone receives 90,000 demands for information from law-enforcement agencies annually. Abuses have undoubtedly accompanied the recent increase in government surveillance.

*Michel Foucault: Influential French philosopher and historian (1926–1984), known for his writings on the nature of being, knowledge, and power [Ed.].

One glaring example is the case of Brandon Mayfield, an Oregon attorney and convert to Islam who was jailed on suspicion of involvement in the 2004 Madrid train bombings. After his arrest, Mayfield sued the government and persuaded a federal judge to declare the provision of the Patriot Act that the FBI used in investigating him unconstitutional. But as with most excesses of state power, the cause is not so much the investigative authority of the state as the state's erroneous interpretation of the information it uncovers and the unwarranted detentions that come about as a result. If those same powers were used to foil another 9/11, most Americans would likely applaud.

There is always a danger that the information collected will be misused—whether by regimes seeking to silence opposition or by corporations seeking to profit from more detailed knowledge of their potential customers. The scale and technological sophistication of this data-gathering enterprise allow the government to intercept and store far more information than was possible for secret police of even the most totalitarian states of an earlier era, and the large number of people who have access to sensitive information increases the potential for misuse.* As with any large-scale human activity, if enough people are involved eventually someone will do something corrupt or malicious. That's a drawback to having more data gathered, but one that may well be outweighed by the benefits. We don't really know how many terrorist plots have been foiled because of all this data-gathering.† We have even less idea how many innocent Americans were initially suspected of terrorism but *not* arrested because the enhanced data-gathering permitted under the Patriot Act convinced law-enforcement agents of their innocence. 10

The degree to which a government is repressive does not turn on the methods by which it acquires information about its citizens, or the amount of data it retains. When regimes want to harass their opponents or suppress opposition, they find ways to do it, with or without electronic data. Under President Nixon, the administration used tax audits to harass those on his "enemies list." That was mild compared with how "enemies" were handled during the dirty wars in Argentina, Guatemala, and Chile, and by the Stasi in East Germany. These repressive governments "disappeared" tens of thousands of dissidents, and they targeted their political enemies with what now seem impossibly cumbersome methods of collecting, storing, and sorting data. If such forms of abuse are rare in the United States, it is not because we have prevented the state from gathering electronic data about us. The crucial step in preventing a repressive government from misusing information is to have alert and well-informed citizens with a strong sense of right and wrong who work to keep the government democratic, open, just, and under the rule of law. The technological innovations used by governments and corporations to monitor citizens must be harnessed to monitor those very governments and corporations.

One of the first victories for citizen surveillance came in 1991, when George Holliday videotaped Los Angeles police officers beating Rodney King. Without that video,

*Including those involved in international operations relating to homeland security and intelligence, 854,000 people currently hold top-secret security clearances, according to the *Washington Post*.

†In 2003, FBI director Robert Mueller claimed that the number of thwarted plots was more than one hundred.

yet another LAPD assault on a black man would have passed unnoticed. Instead, racism and violence in police departments became a national issue, two officers went to prison, and King received $3.8 million in civil damages. Since then, videos and photographs, many of them taken on mobile phones, have captured innumerable crimes and injustices. Inverse surveillance—what Steve Mann, professor of computer engineering and proponent of wearing imaging devices, terms "sousveillance"—has become an effective way of informing the world of abuses of power.

We have seen the usefulness of sousveillance again this year in the Middle East, where the disclosure of thousands of diplomatic cables by WikiLeaks helped encourage the Tunisian and Egyptian revolutions, as well as the protest movements that spread to neighboring countries. Yet most government officials vehemently condemned the disclosure of state secrets. Secretary of State Hillary Clinton claimed that WikiLeaks' revelations "tear at the fabric of the proper function of responsible government." In February of this year, at George Washington University, she went further, saying that WikiLeaks had endangered human rights activists who had been in contact with U.S. diplomats, and rejecting the view that governments should conduct their work in full view of their citizens. As a counterexample, she pointed to U.S. efforts to secure nuclear material in the former Soviet states. Here, she claimed, confidentiality was necessary in order to avoid making it easier for terrorists or criminals to find the materials and steal them.

Clinton is right that it is not a good idea to make public the location of insecurely stored nuclear materials, but how much of diplomacy is like that? There may be some justifiable state secrets, but they certainly are few. For nearly all other dealings between nations, openness should be the norm. In any case, Clinton's claim that WikiLeaks releases documents "without regard for the consequences" is, if not deliberately misleading, woefully ignorant. Assange and his colleagues have consistently stated that they are motivated by a belief that a more transparent government will bring better consequences for all, and that leaking information has an inherent tendency toward greater justice, a view Assange laid out on his blog in December 2006, the month in which WikiLeaks published its first document:

> The more secretive or unjust an organization is, the more leaks induce fear and paranoia in its leadership and planning coterie. . . . Since unjust systems, by their nature induce opponents, and in many places barely have the upper hand, leaking leaves them exquisitely vulnerable to those who seek to replace them with more open forms of governance.*

Assange could now claim that WikiLeaks' disclosures have confirmed his theory. 15
For instance, in 2007, months before a national election, WikiLeaks posted a report on corruption commissioned but not released by the Kenyan government. According to Assange, a Kenyan intelligence official found that the leaked report changed the minds of 10 percent of Kenyan voters, enough to shift the outcome of the election.

*Robert Manne, a professor of politics at Australia's La Trobe University and the author of a detailed examination of Assange's writings that appeared recently in *The Monthly*, comments: "There are few original ideas in politics. In the creation of WikiLeaks, Julian Assange was responsible for one."

Two years later, in the aftermath of the global financial crisis, WikiLeaks released documents on dealings by Iceland's Kaupthing Bank, showing that the institution made multibillion-dollar loans, in some cases unsecured, to its major shareholders shortly before it collapsed. Kaupthing's successor, then known as New Kaupthing, obtained an injunction to prevent Iceland's national television network from reporting on the leaked documents but failed to prevent their dissemination. WikiLeaks' revelations stirred an uproar in the Icelandic parliament, which then voted unanimously to strengthen free speech and establish an international prize for freedom of expression. Senior officials of the bank are now facing criminal charges.

And of course, in April 2010, WikiLeaks released thirty-eight minutes of classified cockpit-video footage of two U.S. Army helicopters over a Baghdad suburb. The video showed the helicopter crews engaging in an attack on civilians that killed eighteen people, including two Reuters journalists, and wounded two children. Ever since the attack took place, in 2007, Reuters had unsuccessfully sought a U.S. military inquiry into the deaths of its two employees, as well as access to the cockpit video under the Freedom of Information Act. The United States had claimed that the two journalists were killed during a firefight. Although no action has been taken against the soldiers involved, if the military is ever going to exercise greater restraint when civilian lives are at risk, it will have been compelled to do so through the release of material like this.

Months before the Arab Spring began, Assange was asked whether he would release the trove of secret diplomatic cables that he was rumored to have obtained. Assange said he would, and gave this reason: "These sort of things reveal what the true state of, say, Arab governments are like, the true human rights abuses in those governments." As one young Tunisian wrote to the *Guardian*, his countrymen had known for many years that their leaders were corrupt, but that was not the same as reading the full details of particular incidents, rounded off with statements by American diplomats that corruption was keeping domestic investment low and unemployment high. The success of Tunisia's revolution undoubtedly influenced the rest of the Arab world, putting U.S. diplomats in an uncomfortable predicament. A mere three months after condemning WikiLeaks for releasing stolen documents "without regard to the consequences," Secretary Clinton found herself speaking warmly about one of those outcomes: the movement for reform in the Middle East.

WikiLeaks' revelations have had profound ramifications, but as with any event of this scale, it is not easy to judge whether those consequences are, on the whole, desirable. Assange himself admitted to the *Guardian* that as a result of the leaked corruption report in Kenya, and the violence that swept the country during its elections, 1,300 people were killed and 350,000 displaced; but, he added, 40,000 Kenyan children die every year from malaria, and these and many more are dying because of the role corruption plays in keeping Kenyans poor.* The Kenyan people, Assange believes, had a right to the information in the leaked report because "decision-making that is based upon lies or ignorance can't lead to a good conclusion."

In making that claim, Assange aligned himself with a widely held view in democratic theory, and a standard argument for freedom of speech: elections can express 20

*The United Nations claimed that as many as 600,000 Kenyans were displaced after the election.

the will of the people only if the people are reasonably well informed about the issues on which they base their votes. That does not mean that decision-making based on the truth always leads to better outcomes than decision-making based on ignorance. There is no reason for Assange to be committed to that claim, any more than a supporter of democracy must be committed to the claim that democratic forms of government always reach better decisions than authoritarian regimes. Nor does a belief in the benefits of transparency imply that people must know the truth about everything; but it does suggest that more information is generally better, and so provides grounds for a presumption against withholding the truth.

What of Clinton's claims that the leaks have endangered human rights activists who gave information to American diplomats? When WikiLeaks released 70,000 documents about the war in Afghanistan, in July 2010, Admiral Mike Mullen, chairman of the Joint Chiefs of Staff, said that Assange had blood on his hands, yet no casualties resulting from the leaks have been reported—unless you count the ambassadors forced to step down due to embarrassing revelations. Four months after the documents were released, a senior NATO official told CNN that there had not been a single case of an Afghan needing protection because of the leaks. Of course, that may have been "just pure luck," as Daniel Domscheit-Berg, a WikiLeaks defector, told the *New York Times* in February. Assange himself has admitted that he cannot guarantee that the leaks will not cost lives, but in his view the likelihood that they will save lives justifies the risk.

WikiLeaks has never released the kind of information that Clinton pointed to in defending the need for secrecy. Still, there are other groups out there, such as the Russian anti-corruption site Rospil.info, the European Union site BrusselsLeaks, the Czech PirateLeaks, Anonymous, and so on, that release leaked materials with less scrupulousness. It is entirely possible that there will be leaks that everyone will regret. Yet given that the leaked materials on the wars in Afghanistan and Iraq show tens of thousands of civilian lives lost due to the needless, reckless, and even callous actions of members of the U.S. military, it is impossible to listen to U.S. leaders blame WikiLeaks for endangering innocent lives without hearing the tinkle of shattering glass houses.

In the Panopticon, of course, transparency would not be limited to governments. Animal rights advocates have long said that if slaughterhouses had glass walls, more people would become vegetarian, and seeing the factory farms in which most of the meat, eggs, and milk we consume are produced would be more shocking even than the slaughterhouses. And why should restaurant customers have to rely on occasional visits by health inspectors? Webcams in food-preparation areas could provide additional opportunities for checking on the sanitary conditions of the food we are about to eat.

Bentham may have been right when he suggested that if we all knew that we were, at any time, liable to be observed, our morals would be reformed. Melissa Bateson and her colleagues at England's Newcastle University tested this theory when they put a poster with a pair of eyes above a canteen honesty box. People taking a hot drink put almost three times as much money in the box with the eyes present as they did when the eyes were replaced by a poster of flowers. The mere suggestion that someone was watching encouraged greater honesty. (Assuming that the eyes did not lead people to overpay, the study also implies a disturbing level of routine dishonesty.)

We might also become more altruistic. Dale Miller, a professor of organizational behavior at Stanford University, has pointed out that Americans assume a "norm of self-interest" that makes acting altruistically seem odd or even irrational. Yet Americans perform altruistic acts all the time, and bringing those acts to light might break down the norm that curtails our generosity. Consistent with that hypothesis, researchers at the University of Pennsylvania found that people are likely to give more to listener-sponsored radio stations when they are told that other callers are giving above-average donations. Similarly, when utility companies send customers a comparison of their energy use with the average in their neighborhood, customers with above-average use reduce their consumption. 25

The world before WikiLeaks and Facebook may have seemed a more secure place, but to say whether it was a better world is much more difficult. Will fewer children ultimately die from poverty in Kenya because WikiLeaks released the report on corruption? Will life in the Middle East improve as a result of the revolutions to which WikiLeaks and social media contributed? As the Chinese communist leader Zhou Enlai responded when asked his opinion of the French Revolution of 1789, it is too soon to say. The way we answer the question will depend on whether we share Assange's belief that decision-making leads to better outcomes when based on the truth than when based on lies and ignorance.

Questions for Critical Reading

1. What is *privacy*? Write your own definition of this term. As you reread Singer's essay, mark passages where he explains privacy—especially where he considers how the concept of privacy changes. Can you reconcile your definition with Singer's? What factors cause concepts such as privacy to change meaning?

2. As you reread Singer's text, look for the term *sousveillance*. What does this term mean? Does it support or undermine democracy? Locate quotations from Singer that support your position.

3. How can we balance the rights of the individual with the need for security? Consider this question as you reread Singer's text. What is his position on this question? Mark passages that you feel indicate his answer.

Exploring Context

1. Locate and then review the privacy policy at Facebook or some other site you frequently use. How does the content of that policy relate to Singer's arguments about our willingness to disclose information about ourselves? Given Singer's examples, do you think any privacy policy can protect you? Use your response to Question 1 of Questions for Critical Reading in forming your answer.

2. Explore the website for WikiLeaks (wikileaks.org). Use what you find there to argue whether the site threatens or supports democracy. Incorporate your work from Question 3 of Questions for Critical Reading.

3. Some people have been arrested for recording or taking pictures of police on duty — the kind of "sousveillance" that Singer suggests keeps governments honest. Visit the website Privacy & Technology, maintained by the American Civil Liberties Union (aclu.org/issues/privacy-technology). How does the information you find there change your understanding of Singer's argument? Does it change your response to Question 2 of Questions for Critical Reading?

Questions for Connecting

1. Robinson Meyer explores a different ethical question in "Is It OK to Enjoy the Warm Winters of Climate Change?" (p. 284). Synthesize these two authors to propose best practices for making ethical decisions in our lives. What factors should we consider? How do we balance our needs against larger concerns?
2. Tomas van Houtryve, in "From the Eyes of a Drone" (p. 390), considers the military uses of surveillance drones, expressing his concerns at this "weaponization" of photography. Apply Singer's argument to van Houtryve to consider the ways that drones might be used in sousveillance. Does the public potential of this technology mitigate its military uses? How do van Houtryve's own photographs relate to sousveillance? Use your thoughts on sousveillance from Question 2 of Questions for Critical Reading.
3. In his essays "Preface" and "The New Civil Rights" (p. 452), Kenji Yoshino argues both that we have a tendency to "cover" or downplay parts of our identity and that we need to move to a new model of civil rights, one based on basic rights and freedoms for all individuals. How does the kind of society Singer describes complicate Yoshino's argument? Is it as easy to cover in a society of surveillance with less concern about privacy? Is Yoshino's "liberty paradigm" for civil rights realistic, given social technologies and their impact on privacy?

Language Matters

1. Audience is a primary concern for all writers. Consider the difference between private and public audiences, using Singer's ideas about privacy. How does your writing change based on notions of privacy? What level of privacy, and thus what audience, is reflected in academic writing?
2. Consider how you write for social media — places like Facebook or Twitter. What are the conventions of writing in these arenas, and how do they differ from those of writing in an academic setting? How important is context to writing?
3. The Swedish furniture maker IKEA uses simplistic pictorial instructions to help people assemble furniture. Go to IKEA's website (ikea.com/us/en/), look up a furniture product, and click on the link for "Assembly Instructions" in the Product Information section. Using these instructions as a model, create a pictorial guide to Singer's argument, a set of instructions for understanding his essay.

Assignments for Writing

1. What is the role of privacy in a democracy? Write a paper in which you address this question using ideas from Singer's essay. Should democracies protect privacy? Is transparency necessary for democracy? Use your work from Questions for Critical Reading in making your response.

2. Write a paper in which you determine the ethics of privacy. When, if ever, is it ethical to violate privacy? What ethical standards should we use in determining and protecting privacy? Use Singer's discussion to support your position as well as your work in Questions for Critical Reading. Consider, too, the subtitle of Singer's essay, "Ethics in a World without Secrets."

3. Using Singer's discussion, write a paper in which you trace the evolution and implications of notions of privacy. What forces shape our understanding of privacy? How has privacy changed? What can we do to shape its future?

RHYS SOUTHAN

Rhys Southan is a freelance writer who maintains his own blog, *Let Them Eat Meat*, about veganism from his ex-vegan perspective. His writing has appeared in the *New Inquiry*, the *New York Times*, and *Aeon Magazine*.

Aeon Magazine is an online-only publication founded in 2012 by Paul and Brigid Hains that specializes in publishing original essays almost every day, on topics ranging from science and philosophy to modern society. "Is Art a Waste of Time?" appeared in *Aeon Magazine* on March 20, 2014. In it, Southan explains that an activism movement called "Effective Altruism" has been embraced by a growing group of people who "want to reduce suffering and increase lifespan and happiness" (p. 365) across the world. This seems well and good, but the movement is also caught up in the core concept of replaceability, which suggests that because people who spend their available time creating art are not feeding the homeless, art (and thus all artistic expression) is not worth pursuing.

Does art have a place in our world? What is its function?

- TAGS: *art, community, economics, empathy, ethics, globalism, judgment and decision making, social change*
- CONNECTIONS: *Appiah, Das, DeGhett, Epstein, Klosterman, Ma, Paumgarten, Pollan, Provan, von Busch, Wallace, Watters*

Is Art a Waste of Time?

With less than a week to finish my screenplay for the last round of a big screenwriting competition, I stepped on a train with two members of a growing activism movement called Effective Altruism. Holly Morgan was the managing director for The Life You Can Save, an organization that encourages privileged Westerners to help reduce global poverty. Sam Hilton had organized the London pub meet-up where I'd first heard about the movement (known as "EA" for short; its members are EAs). The pair of them were heading to East Devon with a few others for a cottage retreat, where they were going to relax among sheep and alpacas, visit a ruined abbey, and get some altruism-related writing done. I decided to join them because I liked the idea of finishing my script (a very dark comedy) in the idyllic English countryside, and because I wanted to learn more about the EA goal of doing as much good as you possibly can with your life. We were already halfway there when my second reason for going threatened to undermine my first.

Around Basingstoke, I asked Hilton what EAs thought about using art to improve the world. In the back of my mind I had my own screenplay, and possibly also Steven Soderbergh's 2001 Oscar acceptance speech for best director, which I'd once found inspiring:

> I want to thank anyone who spends a part of their day creating. I don't care if it's a book, a film, a painting, a dance, a piece of theater, a piece of music. Anybody who spends part of their day sharing their experience with us. I think this world would be unlivable without art.

It turns out that this is not a speech that would have resonated with many Effective Altruists. The idea that someone's book, film, painting, or dance could be their way to reduce the world's suffering struck Hilton as bizarre, almost to the point of incoherence. As I watched his furrowing brow struggle to make sense of my question, I started to doubt whether this retreat was an appropriate venue for my screenwriting ambitions after all.

In 1972, the Australian moral philosopher Peter Singer published an essay called "Famine, Affluence, and Morality," which contained the following thought experiment. Suppose you saw a child drowning in a pond: would you jump in and rescue her, even if you hadn't pushed her in? Even if it meant ruining your clothes? It would be highly controversial to say "no"—and yet most of us manage to ignore those dying of poverty and preventable disease all over the world, though we could easily help them. Singer argues that this inconsistency is unjustifiable. The EAs agree, and have dedicated their lives to living out the radical implications of this philosophy. If distance is morally irrelevant, then devastating poverty and preventable disease surround us. Any break we take from working to reduce suffering throughout the world is like having a leisurely nap beside a lake where thousands of children are screaming for our help.

5 The EA movement started coalescing in Oxford in 2009 when the philosophers Toby Ord and William MacAskill came together with around twenty others to work out how to make radical altruism mainstream. MacAskill told me that they went by the jokey moniker "Super Hardcore Do-Gooders," until they came up with "Effective Altruism" in 2011. Along with various other EA-affiliated organizations, Ord and MacAskill co-founded Giving What We Can, which suggests a baseline donation of 10 percent of your income to effective charities.

This is often what EA comes down to: working hard to earn money and then giving as much of it as you can to the needy. Good deeds come in many forms, of course, and there are other ways of making a difference. But the gauntlet that EA throws down is simply this: does your preferred good deed make as much of a difference as simply handing over the money? If not, how good a deed is it really?

Once we'd settled in at the cottage, Hilton and I stepped out for a walk through the bits of forest that hadn't been razed for pasture, and he asked if my script would be one of the best scripts ever written. At the time I thought he was trolling me. I obviously couldn't say "yes," but "no" would somehow feel like an admission of failure. It was only after talking to other EAs that I came to understand what he was getting at. As EAs see it, writing scripts and making movies demands resources that, in the right hands, could have saved lives. If the movie in question is clearly frivolous, this seems impossible to justify ethically. If, on the other hand, you're making the best movie of all time . . . well, it could almost start to be worthwhile. But I told Hilton "no," and felt a lingering sense of futility as we tramped on through the stinging nettles around the cottage.

I did manage to finish the script that weekend, despite Hilton's crushing anti-pep talk. I felt good about it—but something about the movement had captured my interest, and over the following weeks I kept talking to EAs. Like Hilton, most of them seemed doubtful that art had much power to alter the world for the better. And somewhere between submitting my script in September and receiving the regret-to-inform in December, I started to feel like they might have a point.

The central premise of Effective Altruism is alluringly intuitive. Simply put, EAs want to reduce suffering and increase lifespan and happiness. That's it; nothing else matters. As Morgan explained in an email to me:

> I find that most of us seem to ultimately care about something close to the concept of "well-being"—we want everyone to be happy and fulfilled, and we promote anything that leads to humans and animals feeling happy and fulfilled. I rarely meet Effective Altruists who care about, say, beauty, knowledge, life or the environment for their own sake—rather, they tend to find that they care about these things only insofar as they contribute to well-being.

From this point of view, the importance of most individual works of art would have to be negligible compared with, say, deworming 1,000 children. An idea often paraphrased in EA circles is that it doesn't matter who does something—what matters is that it gets done. And though artists often pride themselves on the uniqueness of their individuality, it doesn't follow that they have something uniquely valuable to offer society. On the contrary, says Diego Caleiro, director of the Brazil-based Institute for Ethics, Rationality, and the Future of Humanity, most of them are "counterfactually replaceable": one artist is as pretty much as useful as the next. And of course, the supply is plentiful.

Replaceability is a core concept in EA. The idea is that the only good that counts is what you accomplish over and above what the next person would have done in your place. In equation form, Your Apparent Good Achieved minus the Good Your Counterfactual Replacement Would Have Achieved equals Your Actual Good Achieved. This is a disconcerting calculation, because even if you think you've been doing great work, your final score could be small or negative. While it might seem as though working for a charity makes a major positive impact, you have to remember the other eager applicants who would have worked just as hard if they'd been hired instead. Is the world in which you got the job really better than the world in which the other person did? Maybe not.

It is in the interests of becoming irreplaceable that a lot of EAs promote "earning to give"—getting a well-paid job and donating carefully. If you score a lucrative programming job and then give away half your income, most of your competition probably wouldn't have donated as much money. As far as the great universal calculation of utility is concerned, you have made yourself hard to replace. Artists, meanwhile, paint the beautiful landscape in front of them while the rest of the world burns.

Artists, meanwhile, paint the beautiful landscape in front of them while the rest of the world burns.

Ozzie Gooen, a programmer for the UK-based ethical careers website 80,000 Hours, told me about a satirical superhero he invented to spoof creative people in rich countries who care more about making cool art than helping needy people, yet feel good about themselves because it's better than nothing. "I make the joke of 'Net-Positive Man,'" Gooen said. "He has all the resources and advantages and money, and he goes around the world doing net-positive things. Like he'll see someone drowning in a well, and he's like, 'But don't worry, I'm here. Net positive! Here's a YouTube Video! It's net positive!'"

If, despite all this, you remain committed to a career in the arts, is there any hope for you? In fact, yes: two routes to the praiseworthy life remain open. If you happen to be successful already, you can always earn to give. And if you aren't, perhaps you can use your talent to attract new EA recruits and spread altruistic ideas.

"We're actually very stacked out with people who have good mathematic skills, good philosophy skills," Robert Wiblin, executive director of the Centre for Effective Altruism, told me. "I would really love to have some artists. We really need visual designers. It would be great to have people think about how Effective Altruism could be promoted through art." Aesthetic mavericks who anticipate long wilderness years of rejection and struggle, however, would seem to have little to contribute to the cause. Perhaps they should think about ditching their dreams for what Caleiro calls "an area with higher expected returns."

For an aspiring screenwriter like me, this is a disappointing message. Brian Tomasik, the American writer of the website Essays on Reducing Suffering, told me that artists who abandon their craft to help others should take solace in the theory that all possible artwork already exists somewhere in the quantum multiverse. As he put it: "With reducing suffering, we care about decreasing the quantity that exists, but with artwork, it seems you'd only care about existence or not in a binary fashion. So if all art already exists within some measure, isn't that good enough?"

I actually do find that mildly comforting, if it's true, but I'm not convinced that it will win many supporters to the EA cause. The problem, ironically, might actually be an aesthetic one.

Effective Altruism is part subversive, part conformist: subversive in its radical egalitarianism and its critique of complacent privilege; conformist in that it's another force channeling us towards the traditional success model. The altruistic Übermensch is a hard-working money mover, a clean-cut advocate, or a brilliant innovator of utility-improving devices or ideas. As usual, creative types are ignored if their ideas aren't lucrative or if they don't support a favored ideology. Crass materialism and ethical anti-materialism now seem to share identical means: earning money or rephrasing the ideas of others. But there are plenty of people drawn to the media and the arts who care about making the world better. For them to accept the EA position will often require that they give up what they love to do most. What do EAs say to that? For the most part, they say "tough."

"Effective Altruism would sometimes say that the thing you most enjoy isn't the most moral thing to do."

"What's implied by utilitarianism," explained Michael Bitton, a once-aspiring Canadian filmmaker turned EA, "is that nothing is sacred. Everything that exists is subject to utilitarian calculations. So there's no such thing as, 'Oh, this is art, or, oh, this is my religion, therefore it's exempt from ethical considerations.'" Wiblin has a similar view. "It is true that Effective Altruism would sometimes say that the thing you most enjoy isn't the most moral thing to do," he told me. "And yeah, some people wanted to be writers, but actually instead they should go into development aid or go into activism or something else."

Still, disappointed arts types might be able to console themselves with the thought that not even science is exempt from EA's remorseless logic. "I myself was extremely interested in evolutionary biology," Wiblin said, "and I would have liked to become an academic in that area. But I couldn't really justify it on the effects that it has on helping other people, even though I found it fascinating."

The iron logic of replaceability leaves many dreams dead on the ground, to be sure. But is this a problem with EA as an ideology, or a problem with reality? It would be great if the arts and humanities were hugely beneficial to the world, because they tend to be personally satisfying. Still, if they're not in fact helping much, artists might be operating on some questionable values. Is your self-expression more important than human lives and suffering? Would you rather contribute to the culture of rich societies than work to reduce the suffering of the poor, or of future generations? Is it not arbitrary to fill the world with your own personal spin on things, simply because it's yours?

Here's a simple test to determine if you're creating art for yourself or for the world. If you discovered that someone else had independently come up with a project idea that you'd also had, but they produced and distributed their work first, would you be upset? Or would you be thrilled that this vitally important stuff was out there, altering perspectives and making everything better in a real, quantifiable way—even though it wouldn't increase your social status?

"I think that there's sort of a mass delusion among artists and writers that just because there's almost nothing that confers more privilege and prestige and symbolic capital than art, just because it's high-status, people think it's of a high importance," said the Australian writer Chris Rodley. "And I think that's wrong. Which is probably a weird, contradictory position for someone who wants to do art to take."

Rodley is one of the two EAs I talked to with a media and arts background. The other was Michael Bitton, who is a postgraduate in media production in Toronto. "I wanted to be a filmmaker, and then I thought, 'Well what good does this do?'" he told me. "So I kind of stopped wanting to be a filmmaker."

Despite their reservations, both Rodley and Bitton are investigating the kinds of creative projects with potential to do the most good, on the assumption that it could sometimes make sense for EAs to influence culture through arts and media. For Bitton, this means questioning whether "the traditional criteria of artistic greatness, like the profundity of ideas, or the emotional impact, or originality or timelessness or popularity," automatically translates into good consequences. "The concept of artistic integrity is inherently in opposition to the concept of Effective Altruism," he told me. "I don't think you could go all the way Effective Altruist as an artist without compromising your 'artistic integrity.'" In theory, Bitton suggests, "you could have an artist who's making stuff that he or she has no interest in whatsoever, doesn't like, doesn't find interesting or funny, doesn't know the point of, but that's the optimal work of art according to our magic consequences calculator . . ."

Rodley suggests that EA artists could have something to learn from the medieval period, when social value and impact were the goals of art, before the "art for art's sake mythology" shifted the focus to intrinsic merit. Take the Christian mystery plays: "They were proto-utilitarian art works. A lot of them were trying to save the audience's souls. And what greater utilitarian deed could you accomplish than averting infinite suffering?"

"What greater utilitarian deed could you accomplish than averting infinite suffering?"

Of course, most EAs don't believe in souls, much less eternal damnation, so a return to passion plays and Last Supper paintings isn't what they're suggesting. They're more interested in how we could use art to reduce the suffering of humans, animals, and future beings—including AI computers and emulated minds. I talked to Bitton and Rodley separately, but they converged on some general guidelines for the utilitarian-minded artist.

Firstly, the entertainment value of a project is fleeting, so what really matters is how it influences political or social behavior. That's why narrative, or at least some way of expressing concrete ideas, is essential. "It's hard to see how a vase or something would really impact culture in any one way, because what does it teach you about life?" Bitton said. He suggests that it might be useful to sneak good memes such as "racism is bad" or "sexism is bad" into mainstream fictional works, especially if you can avoid the heavy-handed "very special episode" feel.

Rodley, meanwhile, pointed to experimental sound design as an anti-utilitarian dead end. In general, the avant-garde is suspect because art's impact grows by reaching larger audiences, which gives the advantage to books, films, lyrical songs, video games, and smartphone apps that make altruistic ideas palatable. "Look at Singer's shallow-pond analogy," Rodley said. "In a way, that's sort of an artistic, fictional parable. It's quite striking and has many of the features of a creative work."

Still, if we were to consult our magic utilitarian consequences calculator, how often would it tell us to bother making art at all? Persuasive, progressive art might be better than nothing, but that doesn't make it an optimal use of time and resources. Even if a socially minded piece of media gets enough attention to make a positive impact (rare enough in itself), its noticeable effects are often mixed.

Rodley pointed out that the U.S. TV series *Will & Grace* might have made some Americans more accepting of gay people, but it also arguably imposed "homonormative" expectations on how gay people are supposed to act. Similarly, Harriet Beecher Stowe's novel *Uncle Tom's Cabin* (1852) apparently turned many white Americans against slavery while also perpetuating damaging stereotypes. The U.S. documentary *Searching for Sugar Man* (2012) claims that the music of Sixto Rodriguez helped to inspire anti-apartheid protestors in South Africa, but presents this as an accidental and serendipitous side-effect rather than something Rodriguez could have consciously set out to do. Famous artists have a lot of influence and money to give away to good causes. But, said Rodley: "By definition, most artists are mediocre, and their art doesn't really please many people, if any."

If what you want to do is make the world better, the impact of paying to treat many people with curable diseases might seem a little humdrum compared with the revolution in human consciousness that will surely come when you publish your novel. But if donating to charity feels a bit generic, the lives it saves are not. All of which is to say, when I thought that writing a movie was the best way for me to contribute to the world, I was almost certainly kidding myself. Then again, to some extent, we all do.

"If you accept the shallow-pond analogy, everyone is morally horrific," said Rodley. "Even Peter Singer himself. Everyone can be doing more than they currently are."

For now, that will have to be my justification. I'm not ready to give up writing. I'm not ready to take up some high-paid job that I'd hate in order to reduce the world's suffering. Maybe that will change. For now, call me Net-Positive Man.

Questions for Critical Reading

1. How important do you feel it is to relieve suffering in the world? What are you willing to do to contribute to that goal? As you reread, pay close attention to the definition and practice of *Effective Altruism*. Do you support this philosophy? What do you do that you think is consistent with the practice?
2. According to Effective Altruists, when *is* it OK to make art? Mark the passages where Southan explains justifiable reasons to make art when acting from Effective Altruism.
3. Central to Effective Altruism is the notion of *replaceability*. Note Southan's definition of this term. In what ways does it function within the Effective Altruism movement?

Exploring Context

1. Visit the website for the Centre for Effective Altruism at centreforeffectivealtruism .org. Explore the site to learn more about Effective Altruism. How does the site echo Southan's characterization of this movement?
2. Southan mentions the website 80,000 Hours (80000hours.org). What does the site have to say about your intended career? What techniques does the site use to try to persuade you to make the most of your career in terms of its social impact?
3. The Life You Can Save is another Effective Altruism organization that Southan discusses. Visit its website at thelifeyoucansave.org. Based on the content and design, what audience do you think the site imagines? Does its audience include you?

Questions for Connecting

1. One of the goals of Effective Altruism is to promote the well-being of animals as well as people. Apply Southan's understanding of Effective Altruism to the problem of eating lobsters as detailed by David Foster Wallace in "Consider the Lobster" (p. 406). How might Effective Altruism offer a solution to the challenge of animal suffering? How can we balance well-being with eating? Draw from your work in Question 1 of Questions for Critical Reading as well as your exploration of Effective Altruism in Exploring Context.
2. In "Crafting Resistance" (p. 399), Otto von Busch argues that craft can function as a form of social activism. Synthesize his argument with the philosophy of Effective Altruism that Southan describes. What are the necessary elements for crafting to function as resistance? Does this resistance represent a kind of Effective Altruism?
3. Apply Effective Altruism's standards for art to the war photograph at the center of Torie Rose DeGhett's "The War Photo No One Would Publish" (p. 110). Would Effective Altruism support the publication of this photograph? Is that image "replaceable"?

What good might it have done in the world? Use your work on the value of art and the concept of replaceability from Questions 2 and 3 of Questions for Critical Reading.

Language Matters

1. Southan often uses colons in his writing. Locate several examples of sentences where he uses a colon. Then, using a grammar handbook or other reliable resource, review the rules for colons. Does Southan's usage follow these rules? When might you use colons in your own writing?
2. The television series *Will & Grace* and the novel *Uncle Tom's Cabin* both appear as examples in Southan's essay. Review the rules for using italics for titles using a grammar handbook or other reliable reference source. Would the title of Southan's own essay be italicized?
3. Select a section of the essay and then locate and remove the topic sentence of each paragraph in that section. What strategies did you use to find the topic sentences? How does removing a paragraph's topic sentence affect the meaning of the paragraph?

Assignments for Writing

1. According to Southan, Effective Altruism is "conformist in that it's another force channeling us towards the traditional success model" (p. 366). Write a paper in which you challenge the model of success at the core of Effective Altruism. Does Effective Altruism guide people to high-paying jobs despite their interests? Is money central to success? Use your explorations of Effective Altruism organizations in Exploring Context to support your argument.
2. Which careers are ethical? Using Southan's ideas, write a paper in which you propose standards for working ethically. Is there a way to pursue a career consistent with ethical principles that doesn't involve heavily donating income? Is it more ethical to be true to yourself in your choice of career or to dedicate your work to helping others?
3. The concept of replaceability helps Effective Altruists measure one's contributions to the world. Write a paper in which you analyze the implications of replaceability. What happens if you extend this idea to other areas of life? Does uniqueness exist? Does it hold inherent value? Use your work from Question 3 of Questions for Critical Reading in your response.

SARAH STILLMAN

Sarah Stillman is a staff writer for the *New Yorker* and has served as a visiting scholar at the Arthur L. Carter Journalism Institute at New York University. Her work has also been published in the *Washington Post*, the *Nation*, and the *Atlantic*, and she has received the Hillman Prize, the George Polk Award, and the National Magazine Award.

On August 12, 2014, Stillman's "Hiroshima and the Inheritance of Trauma" was published in the online version of the *New Yorker*, alongside articles documenting the civil unrest in Ferguson, Missouri, and remembering the then recently deceased Robin Williams. Like its print counterpart, the online edition of the *New Yorker* includes thoughtful essays (including those that appear in the print issues), but it also features daily contributions from *New Yorker* writers and artists as well as podcasts, videos, and interactive graphics.

In "Hiroshima and the Inheritance of Trauma," Stillman not only explores the lingering effects of trauma on the person who experiences it (here through the lens of a *hibakusha*, one who survived the atomic bombs in Hiroshima and Nagasaki) but also examines how that trauma becomes "trans-generational" and affects people in the survivor's family and community who have not experienced the trauma directly themselves. Though we often think of trauma as an experience that affects the individual who survives it, Stillman suggests that it is instead a contagious disease, one that can spread across both families and generations. For Shoji, the *hibakusha* at the center of Stillman's essay, part of her recovery from this disease involves telling her story of survival in the aftermath of an atomic bomb.

▶ TAGS: *genetics, health and medicine, psychology, trauma and violence, war and conflict*

▶ CONNECTIONS: *Appiah, Coates, DeGhett, Epstein, Gilbert, Lukianoff and Haidt, Moalem, Paumgarten, Serano, Turkle*

Hiroshima and the Inheritance of Trauma

Sixty-nine years ago last week, a slender woman named Tomiko Shoji was struck and sent aloft by a bright white light. She'd just arrived at her secretarial job, at a tobacco factory, and was standing by the door when the flash occurred; the light's source had a nickname, Little Boy, but it meant nothing to her at the time. She flew backward under the crushing force of the office door, passed out, and awoke with shards of glass in her head and an expanse of bodies around her—some dead, some alive but dazed, and many more, she soon found, floating "like charcoal" in nearby rivers. The nineteen-year-old climbed up and out of the shell of her younger self; she had survived the U.S. atomic bombing of Hiroshima. Nearly seven decades later, Keni Sabath, Shoji's youngest granddaughter, started to wonder: Had the bombing's aftermath reshaped not just the psyche of her *bachan* (grandmother) but also, in ways both culturally and historically particular, her own?

In recent years, a public-health hypothesis has emerged that one of the world's most poorly understood pandemics isn't a conventional virus—like H1N1, say, or some hemorrhagic fever. This hypothesis suggests that untended wartime trauma can move vertically and horizontally through individuals and families, morphing across years, decades, or even centuries. Sabath began considering the prospect as early as high school, after certain overpowering symptoms emerged on a family visit to Hiroshima when she was six. It was Sabath who had arranged for me to visit her *bachan* at her aunt's home in Hilliard, Ohio, where Shoji agreed to share her first full account of the bombing and the family mysteries that followed.

On my way to Hilliard, I carried my copy of John Hersey's *Hiroshima*. (My 1989 edition bears the cover endorsement "Everyone able to read should read it," and I agree.) Its text first appeared as an entire issue of this magazine, on the one-year anniversary of the bombing, and followed the fates of six civilians in the aftermath. Even now, on a more distant anniversary, Hersey's granular rendering gives an urgency to these stories: of a young clerk, Shoji's age, who found herself crushed beneath a pile of books; of a Methodist pastor who charged his way back into the city to help, passing victims whose eyebrows had been singed off and women with the flower patterns of kimonos burned into their skin.

As I entered Shoji's home, on a quiet cul-de-sac, she swept my hand into hers and pressed her cool forehead against mine by way of welcome. Her eldest daughter, Minori, gave me a pair of slippers to wear inside; as the three of us shuffled into the kitchen, where fresh berries and tea cakes awaited, we paused to examine photographs of the Reverend Kiyoshi Tanimoto, the same pastor who weaves his way through Hersey's narrative, and who also, apparently, stood at the center of Shoji's. She first came across him preaching in an open-air bazaar in Hiroshima not long after the bombing; he gave her a piece of paper with information about his church, and she soon converted to Christianity. (He later baptized her grandson, Isao, who served as my translator well into the early evening.) Some of the first words Shoji spoke to me in Japanese were about the Reverend: "He would say, 'Tomiko, why don't we go all over the world together and tell them of our experiences with the bomb?'"

5 Tanimoto made a second career out of his own suggestion; on the fortieth anniversary of the bombing, Hersey wrote a follow-up story for the magazine, "Hiroshima: The Aftermath," in which he described the pastor's extensive U.S. speaking tour to promote peace. But Shoji wasn't ready to speak freely at the time. This past July, the last surviving crew member of the *Enola Gay*, the plane that dropped Little Boy, died in Stone Mountain, Georgia, having given many interviews. By then, Shoji had made up her mind that, in her eighty-eighth year, she would share her own account of what happened on the other side of the bomb. So we began right there, with the flash.

"Radiation! Heat! The wind from the bomb!" When Shoji began to describe her recollections from August 6, 1945, she took on a staccato pattern of speech, gesticulating rapidly. A tiny woman with pixie-gray hair and a sweet, flushed face, she slapped her small hands together and pummeled her head with pinched fingers, as if to imitate flying debris from the blast. At one point, she pretended to fling burned skin across the room like zucchini peels. Then she closed her eyes and went into a deep repose, resurfacing with a sudden phrase: "I'm scared to meet people," she said, speaking in the present tense of her teenage self, who might also be herself at eighty-eight. "Something could just blow up. I've seen it before."

On the morning of the bombing—it was 8:15, the start of the workday—Shoji recalls briefly losing consciousness at the Bureau of Tobacco. "When I got up, I ran down to the first floor, down to the bomb shelter," she said. "All over was smoke; the entire city was covered with smoke. I saw people coming across the bridge just completely black—covered by blood, coming towards us. . . . The whole city was a sea of fire. And then, at night, it rained black rain."

Collecting herself, she began walking with colleagues across the city's many bridges, toward the sea. She caught a train in Hiroshima's west hoping to find her sister, to no avail; en route were whole trolley cars that had been blown off their tracks, filled with singed corpses. After spending the night, she returned home to find a note from the same sister, which read, "You can find me at the school." The two stayed in the school turned shelter for some time thereafter, living in a true dystopia. "There were tens of thousands of flies from the dead bodies," she recalled. "Our greetings to each other became: Are you having diarrhea?"

For all those who perished in the bombing, many more survived, day by day. Only later would some, like Shoji, come to discover that the most devastating aftereffects were like ghosts: coming and going on a whim, wreaking forms of havoc often incomprehensible to outsiders and, sometimes, even to those who suffered it.

The most devastating aftereffects were like ghosts: coming and going on a whim, wreaking forms of havoc often incomprehensible to outsiders.

I'd always assumed, in ignorance, that to survive the atomic bomb—to be a *hibakusha*, or "explosion-affected person"—was to have conferred upon you a certain esteem or deference, not unlike that afforded to the bearer of a Purple Heart. Shoji's family wasted no time correcting me. To be a *hibakusha*, they explained, was not an honorific but a source of shame, a secret to be closely held. Even grandchildren have often feared telling romantic partners of their grandparents' experience, worried that their genetic material would be perceived as spoiled goods. 10

Eventually, Shoji's family planned for her to enter an arranged marriage with a prominent policeman in Taiwan, where she relocated in her early twenties. They kept her *hibakusha* status hushed, and refused to allow the two to talk before the ceremony, so as to better seal the secret. "My hands were shaking, holding my bouquet," Shoji recalled. When her husband learned the news afterward, he spiraled into a rage that never lifted. For the rest of the marriage, Shoji's daughter Minori said, "He felt he'd been cheated."

The next several decades brought a parade of physical ailments that were easily traceable to the bomb: Shoji's eyes and ears gave up early; her insides felt perpetually cold; her teeth fell out, requiring dentures in her forties. But perhaps most debilitating were the psychological symptoms that she didn't think she could attribute to the radiation. "For thirty or forty years, I was so afraid of thunder and lightening," she told me, as one of many examples. "It would just crush me. I just lost control." Raising four daughters was a challenge of another scale. "Nobody understood me; I was like a beggar," she said, recalling that when her children were young she faced almost daily bouts of overwhelming panic. At night, in dreams, she shouted, "The Earth—the Earth is going to fall!" "At the time, I didn't know what was affecting me so badly," Shoji said. "I couldn't talk about it. Even before I opened my mouth, I would collapse with fear."

Minori chimed in, gently stroking her mother's shoulder: "When we would go into her bedroom in the morning, we would see her get so angry—she would throw things. When we were young, I never saw her laugh—she was quiet, and weak." Back then, neither Shoji nor her children spoke openly about this behavior as tied to the bomb. Remarkably, Shoji says that the idea didn't come easily to her. She was unfamiliar with the concept of post-traumatic stress disorder, or shell shock, or its classic presentation (nightmares, flashbacks, hypervigilance); these traits seemed unrelated to her experience. "Every year I have these crazy episodes—my family is so good to me, but I have these outbursts, these moments when I lose control," she said. Years ago, she insists, it all seemed completely inexplicable.

Still, somewhere within her, she began to trace a clear line between her inner state and the events of her nineteenth year. "After I got married, the family would yell at me, and even when I'm beaten, I can't respond, and I don't know why. But deep inside, I remember, oh, that's what it is: the bomb, the aftereffects of the bomb. It's worse than the day of the bomb."

15 Shoji's granddaughter Keni Sabath grew up in Hawaii and Texas, the child of a New Jersey–born Navy JAG officer and a fashionable Taiwan-born language tutor. Like her older sister Zena, Keni often spent her days with her *bachan*, who lived in their home for years before joining Keni's aunt Minori in Ohio. In the summers, the family would travel back to Japan. "I first became aware of my grandmother's experience in a very disturbing way, when I was six years old," Keni Sabath told me after my Ohio visit. "I went to the Peace Park in Hiroshima with my grandmother and my mom. We walked by the river and my mom would translate, 'This river here was turned into a blood river, and people would jump into it and their skin would burn off.'" The family proceeded to the local memorial museum, where life-size wax statues depicted local children fleeing the bombing site, their skin melting and their clothing singed. "The children were my height!" Sabath said. "It was so hard for me to reconcile that hell with the current city. I couldn't understand: How were people over it?"

Sabath's crying became incessant thereafter. She couldn't sleep; each time she saw a plane in the air, she panicked, just as her grandmother continued to do. "My mother ended up taking me to a witch doctor," she told me. "They thought I was haunted by the ghosts of Hiroshima" (called *yurie*, or faint spirits). For years, the *yurie* resurfaced in Sabath each summer, making her anxious, watchful, her eyes skyward.

Each time she saw a plane in the air, she panicked, just as her grandmother continued to do.

In recent years, a growing body of scholarship has sought to better understand accounts like Shoji's and Sabath's through the framework of "trans-generational trauma," which traces experiences of catastrophic loss across the span of a family or a community. A wide range of studies have examined evidence of "secondary trauma" in the children of Holocaust survivors, the wives of Vietnam veterans, and, more informally, in the families of U.S. veterans who've faced PTSD after deployments to Iraq and Afghanistan. In 2007, a study on the wives of fifty-six traumatized war veterans in Croatia found that more than a third of the veterans' wives met the criteria for secondary traumatic stress; often, this meant symptoms "similar to those present in directly traumatized persons: nightmares about the person who was directly traumatized, insomnia, loss of interest, irritability, chronic fatigue, and changes in self-perception, perception of one's own life, and of other people." More recently, speaking to Mac McClelland for an article on trauma in the families of Iraq and Afghanistan war veterans, the clinical psychologist Robert Motta said, "Trauma is really not something that happens to an individual." Instead, he proposed, "Trauma is a contagious disease; it affects everyone that has close contact with a traumatized person."

But even metaphors of trauma as contagion feel inadequate, or even potentially counterproductive; for one thing, they can get mixed up with questions of shame and stigma, seeming to assign blame or stir up anxieties about contamination where the antidote to both is needed. And stigma, too, gets internalized. As a small child, Sabath said, when she began to fear a plane above, "I would think, how could I let the plane know that I was American?" She would beg her father to come along to Japan during the summers, thinking, "My white military dad—a Navy JAG officer—he signaled my identity, my patriotic Americanness." Only in his presence could she feel, as the mixed-race grandchild of a *hibakusha*, that "there is no way you would ever harm us."

When she reached high school, Sabath became a debating champion and made nuclear proliferation her focus. She went on to college at Yale and visited the White House as a student leader for Global Zero, the international nuclear-disarmament group, for which she recently authored a personal essay on her *bachan*'s "scenes of living hell." "I hope you will remember my grandmother's message and act upon it," she wrote.

20 In the late 1950s, the Japanese government began issuing certificates to *hibakusha*, entitling them to certain health benefits, and Shoji became the first survivor living abroad to travel back to Japan to reap the benefits. Over the course of those treatments, Shoji gathered for the first time with other survivors, at healing hot springs. It was in that community that she got her first glimpse of psychological relief, and perhaps began to decipher some of her experiences and speak of them to others. Last fall, she traveled to Yale to say to her granddaughter's classmates, "I want with every breath, with all my strength, to tell people" about the bomb.

In the final pages of Hersey's *Hiroshima*, he observed that many people he met there were often reticent to speak or even think about the ethics of the bomb; instead, they would offer approximations of "*Shikata ga nai*," a Japanese expression that he translated as "It can't be helped. Oh well. Too bad."

At eighty-eight, Shoji seems to have thrown off that cosmic shrug. When we finished in the dining room, her daughter gave me a bundle of pastries and fruit, and we all shuffled to the foyer. The whole family stood in the doorway and waved goodbye. Shoji's cheeks looked pink, and, as I drove off, it was easy to imagine how she might have appeared on her way to work at nineteen, looking up at the August sky.

Questions for Critical Reading

1. Write some notes on your understanding of how a communicable disease like the flu works. As you reread, pay attention to the ways in which Stillman argues that trauma functions like this kind of disease. Does her description of the effects of the Hiroshima bombing match your own understanding of how diseases work? How do they differ? How does your disease model challenge or complicate Stillman?

2. What role does shame play in trauma? As you review the essay, note places where Stillman discusses shame and its effects. What does the role of shame suggest about the link between the body and the mind?

3. **Multimodal.** Does knowing that trauma can be inherited change our moral obligations in relation to war? Consider how our decisions regarding war might change with a different understanding of trauma, supporting your points with passages from Stillman. Then, using your phone or other audio recording software, make a brief podcast in which you interview others about this issue. Are your views common? What might account for the difference between your views and the ones of those you interview?

Exploring Context

1. Hibakusha Stories (hibakushastories.org) is a website dedicated to sharing the stories of *hibakusha* in order to promote disarmament. Explore the site to learn more about other survivors of the nuclear blasts. How do they reflect the kinds of trauma that Stillman examines?

2. Visit the website for the Hiroshima Peace Memorial Museum at hpmmuseum.jp/?lang=eng. Expand your work from Question 1 by looking for additional representations of trauma in relation to Hiroshima. Relate what you find to Stillman's arguments.

3. The National Institute of Mental Health has a site about post-traumatic stress disorder at nimh.nih.gov/health/topics/post-traumatic-stress-disorder-ptsd. Does its representation reflect the idea that trauma can be contagious? How does it represent this disorder? How does it confirm or challenge Stillman's argument? Relate your findings to your work from Question 1 of Questions for Critical Reading.

Questions for Connecting

1. In "Reporting Live from Tomorrow" (p. 172), Daniel Gilbert suggests that we use surrogates to predict our future happiness. Might we use this same method to learn other things? Use Gilbert's ideas to consider the ways in which Shoji serves as a surrogate. In what other ways can surrogates be useful? Use your work from Questions 1 and 2 of Exploring Context to support your response, considering how other survivors act as surrogates.

2. Torie Rose DeGhett also considers the horrors of war in "The War Photo No One Would Publish" (p. 110). Synthesize DeGhett and Stillman to consider the relationship between war and remembrance. How should war shape our memories? If our memories are shaped in this way, how might our decisions about war change? Use your response to expand your answer to Question 3 of Questions for Critical Reading.

3. Shoji's ability to share her experiences helps her to cope with the trauma. Use Sherry Turkle's ideas about meaningful conversation and empathy in "The Empathy Diaries" (p. 378) to help explain why the construction of these sorts of narratives is so useful.

Also consider what's at stake in saving conversation, given Turkle's warnings about technology's impact on conversation.

Language Matters

1. Stillman's essay contains a number of foreign words and phrases, including *hibakusha.* Use a grammar handbook or other reference resource to review the rules for including words from other languages. How well does Stillman conform to these rules? How should you demarcate foreign words in your own writing?

2. At times Stillman uses parentheses to set off information; other times she uses dashes. Review the rules for both of these punctuation marks in a grammar handbook or other reference resource. When should you use one or the other to set of information that is not the main point of your sentence?

3. Stillman uses a translator when she visits Shoji. What special concerns might bilingual speakers have when it comes to academic writing? How does speaking more than one language complicate the process of composition? Consult a grammar handbook or reference source. Does it provide specific resources for writers who speak other languages? What kind of support is included, and why?

Assignments for Writing

1. Stillman suggests that trauma is a contagious disease. Write a paper in which you explore the effects of personal trauma on families. Is trauma a disease? What is the cure? How can families support healing from trauma? Use your work from Questions 1 and 3 from Questions for Connecting in making your argument.

2. Shoji struggles with shame. Using Stillman's ideas, write a paper about the power of shame. Is shame, like trauma, a disease? What does shame cost individuals and families? Use your work from Question 2 of Questions for Critical to make your argument.

3. Embedded in Stillman's argument is the question of ethics in relation to war. Write a paper in which you shape an ethics for war, using Stillman's ideas. Given the nature of trauma, when is war justified? What responsibilities do governments have to those who survive?

SHERRY TURKLE

Sherry Turkle, who holds a joint doctorate in sociology and personality psychology from Harvard, is the Abby Rockefeller Mauzé Professor of the Social Studies of Science and Technology and the director of the Initiative on Technology and Self at Massachusetts Institute of Technology. She is the author of nine books, including *The Second Self: Computers and the Human Spirit* (1984), *Life on the Screen: Identity in the Age of the Internet* (1995), and *Reclaiming Conversation: The Power of Talk in a Digital Age* (2015), from which this excerpt is taken. Her work has also been published in the *New York Times*, *Scientific American*, and *Wired* magazine. She has received a Guggenheim fellowship and a Rockefeller Humanities fellowship, and is a member of the American Academy of Arts and Sciences.

In *Reclaiming Conversation: The Power of Talk in a Digital Age*, Turkle argues that while technology enables communication it also encourages a flight from conversation — we accept mere connection rather than sustained, engaged conversation and the empathy developed by such interactions. Turkle argues for reversing this trend, seeing conversation as a talking cure for the isolation that inevitably results from cold connections via technology, returning us to modes of relating that contribute to personal development and to the health of the public sphere.

Turkle offers an overview of this argument in "The Empathy Diaries," presented here, which serves as the introduction to her book. She explains the impetus for this project, which originated in part with a visit to a middle school in which the faculty were concerned that the students were making only superficial connections with their peers. She turns to nineteenth-century author and philosopher Henry David Thoreau, whose use of three chairs in his isolated cabin on Walden Pond worked as a model for the "virtuous circle" (p. 382) of conversation. Turkle explains that the ubiquity of technology has removed us from this circle and offers suggestions on how we may return to it in order to better connect to ourselves, to others, and to the world around us.

TAGS: *adolescence and adulthood, conversation, empathy, relationships, science and technology, social media*

CONNECTIONS: *Appiah, Chen, Epstein, Gilbert, Jamison, Klosterman, Konnikova, Ma, Paumgarten, Provan, Singer, von Busch, Watters, Yoshino*

The Empathy Diaries

Why a book on conversation? We're talking all the time. We text and post and chat. We may even begin to feel more at home in the world of our screens. Among family and friends, among colleagues and lovers, we turn to our phones instead of each other. We readily admit we would rather send an electronic message or mail than commit to a face-to-face meeting or a telephone call.

This new mediated life has gotten us into trouble. Face-to-face conversation is the most human—and humanizing—thing we do. Fully present to one another, we learn to listen. It's where we develop the capacity for empathy. It's where we experience the joy of being heard, of being understood. And conversation advances self-reflection, the conversations with ourselves that are the cornerstone of early development and continue throughout life.

But these days we find ways around conversation. We hide from each other even as we're constantly connected to each other. For on our screens, we are tempted to present ourselves as we would like to be. Of course, performance is part of any meeting, anywhere, but online and at our leisure, it is easy to compose, edit, and improve as we revise.

We say we turn to our phones when we're "bored." And we often find ourselves bored because we have become accustomed to a constant feed of connection, information, and entertainment. We are forever elsewhere. At class or at church or business meetings, we pay attention to what interests us and then when it doesn't, we look to our devices to find something that does. There is now a word in the dictionary called "phubbing." It means maintaining eye contact while texting. My students tell me they do it all the time and that it's not that hard.

5 We begin to think of ourselves as a tribe of one, loyal to our own party. We check our messages during a quiet moment or when the pull of the online world simply feels irresistible. Even children text each other rather than talk face-to-face with friends—or, for that matter, rather than daydream, where they can take time alone with their thoughts.

We begin to think of ourselves as a tribe of one, loyal to our own party.

It all adds up to a flight from conversation—at least from conversation that is open-ended and spontaneous, conversation in which we play with ideas, in which we allow ourselves to be fully present and vulnerable. Yet these are the conversations where empathy and intimacy flourish and social action gains strength. These are the conversations in which the creative collaborations of education and business thrive.

But these conversations require time and space, and we say we're too busy. Distracted at our dinner tables and living rooms, at our business meetings, and on our streets, we find traces of a new "silent spring"—a term Rachel Carson coined when we were ready to see that with technological change had come an assault on our environment. Now, we have arrived at another moment of recognition. This time, technology is implicated in an assault on empathy. We have learned that even a silent phone inhibits conversations that matter. The very sight of a phone on the landscape leaves us feeling less connected to each other, less invested in each other.

Despite the seriousness of our moment, I write with optimism. Once aware, we can begin to rethink our practices. When we do, conversation is there to reclaim. For the failing connections of our digital world, it is the talking cure.

"They Make Acquaintances, but Their Connections Seem Superficial"

In December 2013, I was contacted by the dean of the Holbrooke School, a middle school in upstate New York. I was asked to consult with its faculty about what they saw as a disturbance in their students' friendship patterns. In her invitation, the dean put it this way: "Students don't seem to be making friendships as before. They make acquaintances, but their connections seem superficial."

The case of the superficial acquaintances in middle school was compelling. It was of a piece with what I was hearing in other schools, about older students. And so it was decided that I would join the Holbrooke teachers on a faculty retreat. I brought along a new notebook; after an hour, I wrote on its cover "The Empathy Diaries." 10

For that's what the Holbrooke teachers are thinking about. Children at Holbrooke are not developing empathy in the way that years of teaching suggested they would. Ava Reade, the dean of the school, says that she rarely intervenes in student social arrangements, but recently she had to. A seventh-grader tried to exclude a classmate from a school social event. Reade called the remiss seventh-grader into her office and asked why it happened. The girl didn't have much to say:

> *[The seventh-grader] was almost robotic in her response. She said, "I don't have feelings about this." She couldn't read the signals that the other student was hurt.*
>
> *These kids aren't cruel. But they are not emotionally developed. Twelve-year-olds play on the playground like eight-year-olds. The way they exclude one another is the way eight-year-olds would play. They don't seem able to put themselves in the place of other children. They say to other students: "You can't play with us."*
>
> *They are not developing that way of relating where they listen and learn how to look at each other and hear each other.*

The Holbrooke teachers are enthusiastic users of educational technology. But on their retreat, they follow what some call the precautionary principle: "Indication of harm, not proof of harm, is our call to action." These teachers believe they see indications of harm. It is a struggle to get children to talk to each other in class, to directly address each other. It is a struggle to get them to meet with faculty. And one teacher observes: "The [students] sit in the dining hall and look at their phones. When they share things together, what they are sharing is what is on their phones." Is this the new conversation? If so, it is not doing the work of the old conversation. As these teachers see it, the old conversation taught empathy. These students seem to understand each other less.

I was invited to Holbrooke because for many decades I have studied children's development in technological culture. I began in the late 1970s, when a few schools were experimenting with personal computers in classrooms or special computer laboratories. I work on this question still, when many children come to school with a tablet or laptop of their own, or one their school has issued.

From the beginning, I found that children used the digital world to play with issues of identity. In the late 1970s and early 1980s, children used simple programming as an expressive medium. A thirteen-year-old who had programmed a graphical world of her own said: "When you program a computer, you put a little piece of your mind into the computer's mind and you come to see yourself differently." Later, when personal computers became portals to online games, children experimented with identity by building avatars. The particulars changed with new games and new computers, but something essential remained constant: Virtual space is a place to explore the self.

15 Also constant was the anxiety of adults around children and machines. From the beginning, teachers and parents worried that computers were *too* compelling. They watched, unhappy, as children became lost in games and forgot about the people around them, preferring, at long stretches, the worlds in the machine.

One sixteen-year-old describes this refuge: "On computers, if things are unpredictable, it's in a predictable way." Programmable worlds can be made exciting, but they also offer new possibilities for a kind of experience that some began to call friction-free. Newton's laws need not apply. Virtual objects can be made to simply glide along. And you, too, can glide along if that's how things are programmed. In virtual worlds, you can face challenging encounters—with scoundrels and wizards and spells—that you know for sure will work out in the end. Or you can die and be reborn. *Real people, with their unpredictable ways, can seem difficult to contend with after one has spent a stretch in simulation.*

From the early days, I saw that computers offer the illusion of companionship without the demands of friendship and then, as the programs got really good, the illusion of friendship without the demands of intimacy. Because, face-to-face, people ask for things that computers never do. With people, things go best if you pay close attention and know how to put yourself in someone else's shoes. Real people demand responses to what they are feeling. And not just any response.

Real people demand responses to what they are feeling. And not just any response.

Time in simulation gets children ready for more time in simulation. Time with people teaches children how to be in a relationship, beginning with the ability to have a conversation. And this brings me back to the anxieties of the Holbrooke teachers. As the Holbrooke middle schoolers began to spend more time texting, they lost practice in face-to-face talk. That means lost practice in the empathic arts—learning to make eye contact, to listen, and to attend to others. Conversation is on the path toward the experience of intimacy, community, and communion. Reclaiming conversation is a step toward reclaiming our most fundamental human values.

Mobile technology is here to stay, along with all the wonders it brings. Yet it is time for us to consider how it may get in the way of other things we hold dear—and how once we recognize this, we can take action: *We can both redesign technology and change how we bring it into our lives.*

A Partisan of Conversation

20 I have spent my professional life as a student of conversation, trained as a sociologist, a teacher, and a clinical psychologist. These vocations have made me a partisan of conversation because they have taught me to appreciate the work that conversation can do—from Socratic classrooms to small talk around water coolers.

My mentor, the sociologist David Riesman, called these vocations "the talking trades." He was right. They rely on conversation and they approach it with high expectations. Each has an answer to the question: What is the work of conversation?

Sociologists and anthropologists use conversation to make sense of the web of relationships at home, at work, and in public life. When things go right, the social scientist's interview becomes an open, easy exchange. This often happens after trust has been established, when the researcher's notebook has been closed, when people who only a few minutes earlier had been "participants" in "your study" realize that there is something in this for them. Your question becomes their question as well. A conversation begins.

In the classroom, conversations carry more than the details of a subject; teachers are there to help students learn how to ask questions and be dissatisfied with easy answers. More than this, conversations with a good teacher communicate that learning isn't all about the answers. It's about what the answers mean. Conversations help students build narratives—whether about gun control or the Civil War—that will allow them to learn and remember in a way that has meaning for them. Without these narratives, you can learn a new fact but not know what to do with it, how to make sense of it. In therapy, conversation explores the meanings of the relationships that animate our lives. It attends to pauses, hesitations, associations, the things that are said through silence. It commits to a kind of conversation that doesn't give "advice" but helps people discover what they have hidden from themselves so they can find their inner compass.

Conversations in these traditions have a lot in common. When they work best, people don't just speak but listen, both to others and to themselves. They allow themselves to be vulnerable. They are fully present and open to where things might go.

You don't need to be in the talking trades to recognize the work conversation can do. I have asked people of all ages and circumstances to tell me about their most important conversations—with children, with friends, with spouses, partners, lovers, and colleagues. It was a question people wanted to answer. They offered the conversation when they fell in love, when they realized that their parents were vulnerable and needed their care, when they understood that their children were no longer children. They offered the conversation when they were confirmed in a career choice because a mentor gave them a chance to run with a quirky idea. 25

With all of this in mind, when I hear lovers say that they prefer to "talk" by editing a text on their smartphones, when I hear families say that they air their differences on email to avoid face-to-face tension, when I hear corporate vice-presidents describe business meetings as "downtime for emptying your inbox," I hear a desire for distraction, comfort, and efficiency. But I also know that these moves won't allow conversation to do the work it can do.

The Virtuous Circle

We are being silenced by our technologies—in a way, "cured of talking." These silences—often in the presence of our children—have led to a crisis of empathy that has diminished us at home, at work, and in public life. I've said that the remedy, most simply, is a talking cure. This book is my case for conversation.

I begin my case by turning to someone many people think of—mistakenly—as a hermit who tried to get away from talk. In 1845, Henry David Thoreau moved to a cabin on Walden Pond in Concord, Massachusetts, to learn to live more "deliberately"— away from the crush of random chatter. But the cabin furniture he chose to secure that ambition suggests no simple "retreat." He said that in his cabin there were "three chairs—one for solitude, two for friendship, and three for society."

These three chairs plot the points on a virtuous circle that links conversation to the capacity for empathy and for self-reflection. In solitude we find ourselves; we prepare ourselves to come to conversation with something to say that is authentic, ours. When we are secure in ourselves we are able to listen to other people and really hear what they have to say. And then in conversation with other people we become better at inner dialogue.

Of course, this virtuous circle is an ideal type, but taking that into account, it works. Solitude reinforces a secure sense of self, and with that, the capacity for empathy. Then, conversation with others provides rich material for self-reflection. Just as alone we prepare to talk together, together we learn how to engage in a more productive solitude.

Technology disrupts this virtuous circle.

The disruptions begin with solitude, Thoreau's first chair. Recent research shows that people are uncomfortable if left alone with their thoughts, even for a few minutes. In one experiment, people were asked to sit quietly—without a phone or a book—for fifteen minutes. At the start of the experiment, they were also asked if they would consider administering electroshocks to themselves if they became bored. They said absolutely not: No matter what, shocking themselves would be out of the question. But after just six minutes alone, a good number of them were doing just that.

These results are stunning, but in a way, not surprising. These days, we see that when people are alone at a stop sign or in the checkout line at the supermarket, they seem almost panicked and they reach for their phones. We are so accustomed to being always connected that being alone seems like a problem technology should solve.

And this is where the virtuous circle breaks down: Afraid of being alone, we struggle to pay attention to ourselves. And what suffers is our ability to pay attention to each other. If we can't find our own center, we lose confidence in what we have to offer others.

Or you can work the circle the other way: We struggle to pay attention to each other, and what suffers is our ability to know ourselves.

We face a flight from conversation that is also a flight from self-reflection, empathy, and mentorship—the virtues of Thoreau's three chairs. *But this flight is not inevitable. When the virtuous circle is broken, conversation cures.*

For there is good news. Despite the pull of our technology, we are resilient. For example, in only five days at a summer camp that bans all electronic devices, children show an increased capacity for empathy as measured by their ability to identify the feelings of others by looking at photographs and videos of people's faces. In my own research at a device-free summer camp, I hear what this resiliency sounds like.

At a nightly cabin chat, a group of fourteen-year-old boys talk about a recent three-day wilderness hike. One can imagine that not that many years ago the most exciting aspect of that hike might have been the idea of "roughing it" or the beauty of unspoiled nature. These days, what makes the biggest impression is time without a phone, what one boy calls "time where you have nothing to do but think quietly and talk to your friends." Another boy uses the cabin chat to reflect on his new taste for silence: "Don't people know that sometimes you can just look out the window of a car and see the world go by and it's wonderful?"

Crossroads

Just as some people will ask, "Why a book about conversation? We're talking all the time," some will say, "Why bring up the negative? You must know about all the wonderful new conversations that happen on the net!" I do know. I've gone to a reunion of my sixth-grade class from PS 216 Brooklyn that could never have happened if not for Facebook. Texts from my daughter, when she was twenty-three, made her seem closer to home even when she took a job on another coast. These from fall 2014: "Hi! I REALLY like *Life After Life*!" "Where do I get challah?" "My roommate and I are going to the party as Elsa and Anna from *Frozen*." All of a sudden, with no warning, on my phone, in my hand, there will be a reference to a book or a food or a Halloween costume that reminds me of our intimacy and infuses my day with her presence. This is pleasurable and to be cherished. The problem comes if these "reminders" of intimacy lead us away from intimacy itself.

Most relationships are a blend of online and off-line interaction. Courtships take place via text. Political debates are sparked and social movements mobilize on websites. Why not focus on the positive—a celebration of these new exchanges? 40

Because these are the stories we tell each other to explain why our technologies are proof of progress. We like to hear these positive stories because they do not discourage us in our pursuit of the new—our new comforts, our new distractions, our new forms of commerce. And we like to hear them because if these are the only stories that matter, then we don't have to attend to other feelings that persist—that we are somehow more lonely than before, that our children are less empathic than they should be for their age, and that it seems nearly impossible to have an uninterrupted conversation at a family dinner.

We catch ourselves not looking into the eyes of our children or taking the time to talk with them just to have a few more hits of our email. Will we summon our attention if, a decade later, fearful of being alone but anxious about attachment, our children show us what it looks like to pay the price? It makes no sense to "match" this disturbing possibility with a happy story about Facebook friendship or Twitter exchanges. This isn't a game in which we can cross our fingers and hope that the good will outweigh the bad. We want to take the good and also make the changes necessary so that we don't pay a price that no technology is worth.

Generations

I remember the generation that first encountered networked personal computers in the 1980s and 1990s. These were machines you "went to" when you wanted to play games, or write, or work with spreadsheets, or send email. Computers offered aids to productivity and many new pleasures—but they did not suggest that text might displace talk.

Only a few years later, there would be cohorts of children who grew up with smartphones, social media, and chatty digital assistants. Today, these children, no longer children, are our teachers, businesspeople, doctors, and parents.

When these new generations consider the idea of a "flight from conversation," they often ask, "Is that really a problem? If you text or iChat, isn't that 'talking'? And 45 besides, you can get your message 'right.' What's wrong with that?" When I talk with them about open-ended conversation, some ask me to specify its "value proposition." Some tell me that conversation seems like "hard work," with many invitations, often treacherous, to imperfection, loss of control, and boredom. Why are these worth fighting for?

Many of the things we all struggle with in love and work can be helped by conversation. Without conversation, studies show that we are less empathic, less connected, less creative and fulfilled. We are diminished, in retreat. But to generations that grew up using their phones to text and message, *these studies may be describing losses they don't feel.* They didn't grow up with a lot of face-to-face talk.

Of course, across the generations, there are those who do not need to be convinced of the value of conversation. But even these partisans of conversation often surprise me. So many of them seem defeated. They say the future has overtaken them. A filmmaker who graduated from college in 2009 tells me that was the year conversation died. I am particularly struck by parents who say they want their children to stop texting at dinner but don't feel they can object when the phones come out. They fear they are too late with their admonishments, that they will be left behind if they don't embrace the new.

I am describing more than a flight from conversation. This is a flight from the responsibilities of mentorship. Technology enchants; it makes us forget what we know about life. The new—any old new—becomes confused with progress. But in our eagerness, we forget our responsibility *to* the new, to the generations that follow us. It is for us to pass on the most precious thing we know how to do: talking to the next generation about our experiences, our history; sharing what we think we did right and wrong.

It is not enough to ask your children to put away their phones. You have to model this behavior and put away *your* phone. If children don't learn how to listen, to stand up for themselves and negotiate with others in classrooms or at family dinner, when will they learn the give-and-take that is necessary for good relationships or, for that matter, for the debate of citizens in a democracy? Reclaiming conversation begins with the acknowledgment that speaking and listening with attention are skills. They can be taught. They take practice and that practice can start now. In your home, in a classroom, at your job.

Stepping Up, Not Stepping Back

There are at least two audiences for this book. One audience needs to be persuaded that a flight from conversation suggests a problem and not an evolution. And it is a problem with a solution: If we make space for conversation, we come back to each other and we come back to ourselves.

And for the audience that feels defeated, whose members mourn an "inevitable" flight from conversation and see themselves as bystanders, I make another case: This is the wrong time to step back. Those who understand how conversation works—no matter what their ages—need to step up and pass on what they know.

We can step up in our families and friendships, but there are also the public conversations of Thoreau's third chair. These conversations, too, need mentors. Here I think of teachers and students: The classroom is a social space where students can see how thinking happens.

College faculty are often shy about asking students to put away their devices in classrooms. Only a few years ago, most professors told me that they didn't want to be their students' "nannies," that this "policing" job was not for them. But we have learned that a student with an open laptop will multitask in class. And we have learned that this will degrade the performance not only of the student with the open machine but of all the students around him or her. These days, faculty are less deferential. Many begin the semester by announcing a device-free classroom policy or specifically set aside class time for "tools down" conversation.

I have met CEOs who now make a point of instructing employees to work out disagreements and apologize to each other *in person*. A new manager, in his mid-thirties, admits that he shies away from face-to-face conversation but is inspired by a weekly "all hands" meeting in his company that is reserved for "just talk." The new manager is insecure about what he can express, but he says of the weekly meeting: "That's a place where I'm learning to have a conversation." In another company, a manager begins her team's meetings by having all laptops and cell phones put into a basket at the door. She's tired of meetings where people do their email.

Beyond school and workplace, there is the public square.

In the media, one often hears a distinctive phrase: "We have to have a national conversation." But the pundits who say it have become accustomed to quick cuts, partisan bickering, and dropping the subject—be it war or weather or racism—when the next news cycle hits. They are also accustomed to talking about news with a "crawl" of unrelated stories scrolling under their images on the screen. That crawl under the news began during the Iran hostage crisis of 1981. No matter what the news, Americans wanted instant updates on the American prisoners in Iran. The hostage crisis ended; the crawl that divides our attention remains. A more satisfying public conversation will require work. But it's important not to confuse the difficult with the impossible. If we commit ourselves, it's work we know how to do. 55

Does the Exception Make the Problem Go Away?

The problem I sum up as a "flight from conversation" doesn't always capture our attention (the technology does!), so it's easy to defer thinking about it. People are still together talking—this looks like conversation—so we may not notice how much our lives have changed. In this way, the flight from conversation is something like climate change: We feel safe in our homes day to day and we usually aren't thinking about "thirty years from now." And in the case of both climate change and conversation, there is the temptation to think that an exception means the problem isn't real or will go away.

Weather patterns may be changing across the planet in alarming ways, but then you are faced with a beautiful sunny day, one of the most beautiful days you have ever seen, and somehow this makes it easier to put the problem out of mind. Similarly, we now rarely give each other our full attention, but every once in a while, we do. We forget how unusual this has become, that many young people are growing up without ever having experienced unbroken conversations either at the dinner table or when they take a walk with parents or friends. For them, phones have always come along.

I often speak to audiences of parents and many describe their difficulties in talking to their children. And then someone will raise a hand and say, "My son loves to talk and he is sixteen years old." As if this means the case is closed.

But the case is not closed. We have not assessed the full human consequences of digital media. We want to focus on its pleasures. Its problems have to do with unintended consequences. To take the measure of these, I follow a path suggested by Thoreau's three chairs: a first for solitude, a second for friendship, and a third for society.

Thoreau said that when conversation became expansive, he brought his guests out into nature. This image leads me to think of a "fourth chair": conversations that Thoreau could not have envisaged. I look at how we have built a "second nature," an artificial nature, and try to enter into dialogue with it. We have built machines that speak, and, in speaking to them, we cannot help but attribute human nature to objects that have none. 60

We have embarked upon a voyage of forgetting. It has several stations. *At a first, we speak through machines* and forget how essential face-to-face conversation is to our relationships, our creativity, and our capacity for empathy. *At a second, we take a further step and speak not just through machines but to machines.* This is a turning point. When we consider conversations with machines about our most human predicaments, we face a moment of reckoning that can bring us to the end of our forgetting. It is an opportunity to reaffirm what makes us most human.

The Moment Is Right to Reclaim Conversation

In 2011, when I published *Alone Together*, a book critical of our inattention to each other in our always-connected lives, I knew I was describing complications that most people did not want to see. As a culture, we were smitten with our technology. Like young lovers, we were afraid that too much talking would spoil the romance. But now, only a few years later, the atmosphere has changed. We are ready to talk. When we have our mobile devices with us, we see that we turn away from our children, romantic partners, and work colleagues. We are ready to reconsider the too-simple enthusiasm of "the more connected we are, the better off we are."

Now, we begin to take the measure of how our communications compel us. We have learned that we get a neurochemical high from connecting. We recognize that we crave a feeling of being "always on" that keeps us from doing our best, being our best. So we allow ourselves a certain disenchantment with what technology has made possible.

We recognize that we need things that social media inhibit. My previous work described an evolving problem; this book is a call to action. It is time to make the course corrections. We have everything we need to begin. We have each other.

Questions for Critical Reading

1. *Conversation* is at the heart of Turkle's essay but what exactly does she mean by that term? Reread the essay to locate passages that define and describe conversation for Turkle. What are the key elements to successful conversation?

2. Review Turkle's essay and identify passages where she explains how technology disrupts connection. Has this been your experience of technology as well? If not, how would you form a counterargument to her text?

3. What, according to Turkle, is the solution to this problem? Review the essay to find quotations that illustrate Turkle's proposed solution.

Exploring Context

1. Visit Turkle's homepage at www.mit.edu/~sturkle. How does this essay fit into her larger research interests? What other materials has she written that might further support or complicate the argument she presents here?

2. Turkle titles this selection "The Empathy Diaries" but what exactly does empathy mean? Using a web search engine, look for images of empathy. Which seem the most fitting for Turkle's use of the term? What other meanings does *empathy* convey?

3. Henry David Thoreau's retreat on Walden Pond is central to Turkle's argument. Visit the website for the Walden Woods Project (walden.org). How does the project relate to Turkle's argument? Does the contemporary status of Walden Pond complicate Turkle's use of Thoreau's work?

Questions for Connecting

1. Kwame Anthony Appiah, in "Making Conversation" and "The Primacy of Practice" (p. 35), argues that conversation is an important component of cosmopolitanism. Use Turkle's argument to complicate Appiah's position. How does technology compound the problems that Appiah sees in an interconnected world? Given Turkle's argument, how can we make Appiah's solutions workable? What role does empathy play in Appiah's text? You may want to use your work from Questions 1 and 3 of Questions for Critical Reading.

2. How can conversation prevent the spread of epidemic diseases? Apply Turkle's insights about conversation and empathy to Helen Epstein's analysis of HIV prevention campaigns in Africa in "AIDS, Inc." (p. 123). Does social cohesion require conversation? Are the problems with the loveLife campaign related to the same problems that Turkle identifies or are there additional challenges in promoting empathy? Your work in Questions for Critical Reading might be useful as you compose your response.

3. Leslie Jamison, in "Devil's Bait" (p. 222), is also concerned with the question of empathy. Apply Turkle's discussion to Jamison's exploration of the challenge of empathy. Does our general disconnection compound the problem faced by those suffering from Morgellons? In what ways does Jamison's engagement with others reflect the solutions that Turkle hopes to see in our world?

Language Matters

1. Section headings can help a reader understand the organization of your writing. Make a list of Turkle's headings. How do they provide insight into the structure of her essay? In what situations might you use headings in your own writing?

2. Meaningful conversation is at the heart of Turkle's project. Working in small groups in class, have a conversation about a common grammatical issue or error, such as the run-on sentence. Should it be considered an error? How important is that error or any one type of error? How does your discussion reflect Turkle's ideas about conversation? Are group members able to engage with empathy?

3. Constellations help us make sense out of the stars — they give the stars meaning by grouping them into meaningful patterns. Examine how sentence structure does the same with words. Select a key quotation from Turkle's essay and then create a map of its different parts. How did you choose to break up the sentence? What relationships can you find among the parts? Are some connections more important than others? That is, if you took out certain parts of the sentence, would it still have the same meaning?

Assignments for Writing

1. Write a paper about the importance of empathy in human relations. What does empathy enable? What must we do to cultivate empathy? Your work in Questions for Critical Reading, Question 2 of Exploring Context, and Question 3 of Questions for Connecting might serve as a good starting point in forming your argument.

2. **Multimodal.** Turkle sees the connections we make via technology as a problem. Use technology (such as a video, podcast, or website) to make a composition in which you propose and defend a counterargument to Turkle's essay. In what ways does technology enable meaningful connection and empathy? Use your work in Questions for Critical Reading to help you shape your argument.

3. Why is conversation important? Write a paper in which you examine the role of conversations in solving national and global problems. Can so simple a practice have profound consequences? What must we do to realize the power of conversation? Your work in Questions for Connecting may be a good place to start.

TOMAS VAN HOUTRYVE

Tomas van Houtryve is a photojournalist and writer, who worked with the Associated Press in Latin America before working freelance on his own artistic and critical projects around the world. His photography has appeared in *Harper's Magazine*, the *Atlantic*, the *New York Times Magazine*, and *National Geographic*.

National Geographic has been published continuously since 1888 and has come to be known for its extensive use of photography in documenting the cultures and natural geography of places all over the world. Van Houtryve's "From the Eyes of a Drone" was published in *Proof*, the online photography journal of *National Geographic*, on August 15, 2014. *Proof* offers a look at the processes of visual storytelling while presenting the work of emerging photographers in order to create conversations about journalism, art, and photography.

In "From the Eyes of a Drone," van Houtryve juxtaposes stunning aerial photography captured by drones with some of the more questionable and nefarious uses of those very same drones. He hopes that we can use the power and mobility of these photography drones for art's sake but wonders about the military uses of photographic drones.

TAGS: *ethics, photography and video, science and technology, war and conflict*

CONNECTIONS: *Das, DeGhett, Klosterman, Paumgarten, Provan, Singer, Southan, Stillman*

From the Eyes of a Drone

For the past fifteen years I've worked as a professional photojournalist, inspired by the camera's ability to connect human beings, document news, and capture beauty. But there is a darker side to how photography is used in our world today. Cameras are increasingly deployed for surveillance, spying, or targeting. I often wonder whether these uses have already eclipsed traditional ones, such as portraiture and fine art. Are we at a point in the evolution of photography where the medium has become weaponized?

Nothing symbolizes this trend better than the rise of drones, robotic aircraft pioneered by the military which rely on their cameras to link remote operators to their targets.

Last year, I started to explore photography's dark side, hoping to engage in the debate about how imaging technology is changing the nature of personal privacy, surveillance, and contemporary warfare.

I started by buying my own consumer drone, and I was surprised by how easy it was to acquire. Hobby shops and online retailers sell small drones equipped with GPS receivers for a few hundred dollars. With a bit of tinkering, I was able to add a high-resolution camera and a system for transmitting live video back to the ground—a greatly simplified version of the system that American pilots use to guide military drones like Reaper and Predator over foreign airspace.

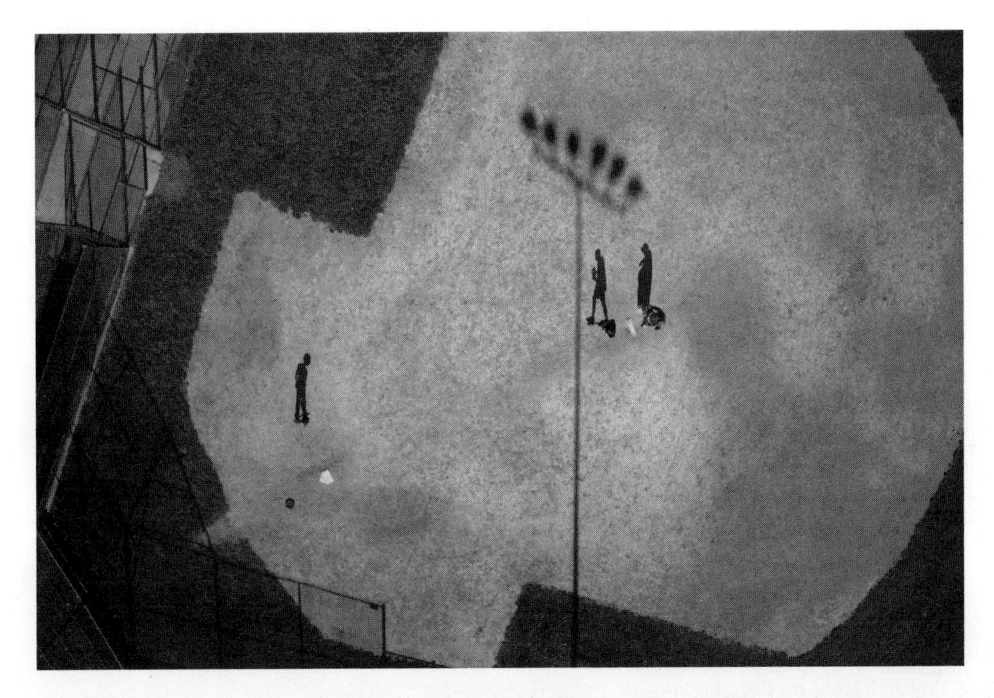

Baseball practice in Montgomery County, Maryland. The FAA issued 1,428 domestic drone permits between 2007 and early 2013. According to records obtained from the agency, the National Institute of Standards and Technology and the U.S. Navy have applied for drone authorization in Montgomery County.

Drones have been used for air strikes over Pakistan for the past decade, marking a significant shift in how America fights wars. Pilots based in Nevada and New Mexico track and record human activity via an infrared video feed. They never leave the ground or cross over hostile territory. Although a huge amount of footage has been collected, the program is classified, and few people have ever seen images of the drone war and its casualties. This seems like a paradox in our thoroughly media-connected age. How can America be involved in a decade-long war where the sky is buzzing with cameras, and yet the public remains totally in the dark? 5

To learn more about the drone war, I looked up reports compiled by investigative journalists and human rights groups. I found the details of many of the strikes startling. A Human Rights Watch report about a drone attack on a wedding in Yemen stated: "The December 12 attack killed 12 men and wounded at least 15 other people, including the bride."[1]

But the testimony of one particular Pakistani boy named Zubair Rehman jarred me the most. In October 2012, Rehman's 67-year-old grandmother was killed by a drone strike while she was picking vegetables outside her home. "I no longer love blue skies," said Rehman. "In fact, I now prefer gray skies. The drones do not fly when the skies are gray."[2]

Residential homes surrounding a circular park are seen from above in Montgomery County, Maryland.
© Tomas van Houtryve/VII Photo Agency

In the past few years, drone use has spread from foreign conflicts to America's domestic airspace. Often, unarmed versions of military aircraft are used, such as the fleet of Predator drones operated by U.S. Customs and Border Protection. Initially, the fleet was meant for border surveillance, but records indicate that drones were lent out hundreds of times to other government entities—including the DEA, the FBI, the Texas Rangers, and local sheriff's departments.[3] The trend of drones used by government security forces is only likely to increase, and some companies such as Amazon are lobbying to put drones to commercial use too.

As drones fill the skies above America, how is the public likely to react? Will the sight of them eventually be as ordinary as seeing an airplane or bird, or will people start wishing for gray skies like the traumatized young Zubair Rehman?

I got a full range of reactions when I flew my own drone in public places earlier this year. Often I would purposely fly my camera over the same type of situations listed in those foreign drone strike reports, such as weddings, funerals, and people entering or leaving religious schools. At other times, I used my drone to look down from the sky over the same areas where the government does aerial surveillance, like along the U.S.-Mexico border. 10

While flying in a park in Maryland, a small girl saw my drone hovering in the sky and asked her mother what it was. I heard the mother answer, "It's a drone, and if you don't do your homework, it's going to go after you!"

A wedding in central Philadelphia. In December 2013, a U.S. drone reportedly struck a wedding in Radda, in central Yemen, killing twelve people and injuring fifteen.

A playground seen from above in Sacramento County, California. The London-based Bureau of Investigative Journalism estimates that over 200 children were killed in drone strikes in Pakistan, Yemen, and Somalia between 2004 and 2013.

"Tent City" jail in Maricopa County, Arizona. Sheriff Joe Arpaio announced in 2013 that he planned to purchase two surveillance drones for the facility, which is already outfitted with perimeter stun fences, four watchtowers, and a facial-recognition system.

On another occasion flying in rural Northern California, a man watched my drone for a long while before approaching me to ask for a look at the control screen. He told me he'd worked as an engineer for a military contractor during the Iraq war, assigned to a team flying the Global Hawk, a large high-altitude surveillance drone. He told me that he worried the technology he had seen as a contractor was moving in a spooky direction, and that the newest weapons systems could decide when to fire or not based on algorithms and lightning-fast calculations, eliminating human will—and judgment—from the battlefield.

And I recently read that graduate students at MIT are experimenting with drones which automatically adapt studio lighting for portraits.[4]

Not everyone I met spoke about the sinister capabilities of drones. Flying near Silicon Valley, a man offered me his business card after I landed in a grassy clearing. He said he was working on a startup company which would manufacture drones to take selfies.

It seems clear that when the next chapter in the evolution of photography is written, drones will have a very prominent role. As more and more cameras take to the skies, my sincere hope is that drones which use photography to celebrate and inspire the best of human values outnumber those designed for darker aims. 15

A U.S. Border Patrol vehicle in San Diego County, California. U.S. Customs and Border Protection has been using Predator drones since 2005. A Freedom of Information Act lawsuit filed in 2012 revealed that the Customs and Border Protection lent its fleet of drones to other government entities — including the DEA, the FBI, the Texas Rangers, and local sheriff's departments — nearly 700 times between 2010 and 2012.

A national war cemetery is seen from above in Philadelphia. In the nearby suburbs, the Horsham Air Guard Base is a drone command center for foreign strikes and surveillance.

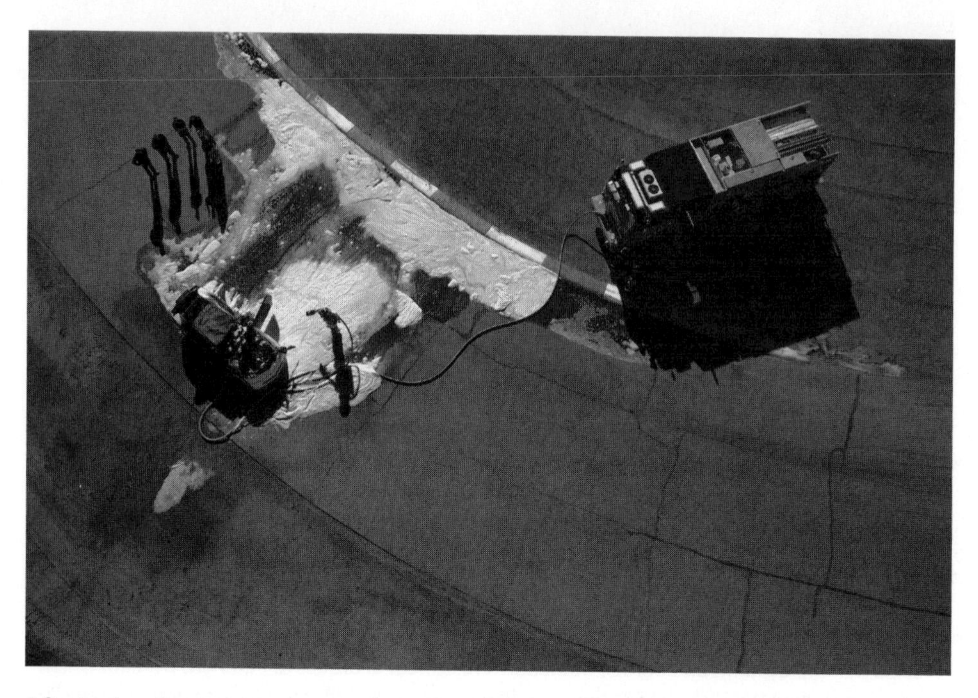

A fire truck and crew respond to a car fire in the Gila River Indian Community in Maricopa County, Arizona. U.S. drone operators are known to engage in "double-tap" strikes, in which consecutive rounds of missiles are fired on the same target, with the second round intended to kill those who respond to the first. The London-based Bureau of Investigative Journalism documented at least five such strikes in Pakistan in 2012.

NOTES

1. Human Rights Watch, "A Wedding That Became a Funeral: US Drone Attack on Marriage Procession in Yemen," *Human Rights Watch*, February 20, 2014.
2. Tomas van Houtryve, "Blue Sky Days," *Harper's*, April 2014, 37.
3. Jennifer Lynch, "Drone Loans: Customs and Border Protection Records 500 Predator Flights for Other Agencies," Electronic Frontier Foundation, September 27, 2013, https://www.eff.org/deeplinks/2013/09/500-cbp-drone-flights-other-agencies.
4. Larry Hardesty, "Drone Lighting: Autonomous Vehicles Could Automatically Assume the Right Positions for Photographic Lighting," *MIT News*, July 11, 2014, http://newsoffice.mit.edu/2014/drone-lighting-0711.

Questions for Critical Reading

1. As you reread, consider closely the relationship between van Houtryve's text and his photographs. How do these images support his argument? In what ways is van Houtryve making a visual argument?

2. What problems does van Houtryve see with the military use of drones? As you review the essay, make a list of these issues. Are van Houtryve's concerns justified?

3. **Multimodal.** Define for yourself the word *weaponized.* What does this term mean for van Houtryve? Mark passages where he discusses the process and its consequences. Then use Instagram to create an image that represents *weaponized.* Tag it with a hashtag provided by your instructor or agreed upon by the class. Be sure to consider carefully the use of filters as well as the subject and composition of the image.

Exploring Context

1. Visit van Houtryve's website at tomasvh.com. How is this essay consistent with van Houtryve's larger body of work?
2. The Predator and Reaper drones that van Houtryve mentions are made by General Atomics Aeronautical (ga-asi.com). Visit this company's website. How does it represent these drones? How does its visual representation of the drones confirm or complicate van Houtryve's argument? Use your findings to expand your answer to Question 2 of Questions for Critical Reading.
3. Parrot (parrot.com/us) manufactures consumer drones like the one van Houtryve uses to capture his photographs. Explore its website, noting the ways Parrot presents and markets its drones. Compare this to the work you did on General Atomics Aeronautical in Question 2.

Questions for Connecting

1. In "Visible Man: Ethics in a World Without Secrets" (p. 353), Peter Singer considers the ramifications of a surveillance culture. Apply his ideas to the use of drones, both military and personal. Does van Houtryve's essay represent a kind of sousveillance? Do drones offer security? At what price?
2. Nick Paumgarten, in "We Are a Camera" (p. 300), looks at another innovation in photographic technology—the GoPro video camera. Synthesize these two essays in order to specify the power of the image today. Do photographs enhance or replace experience? How do new points of view, as conveyed by the GoPro or drones, change our perspective?
3. Rhys Southan, in "Is Art a Waste of Time?" (p. 363), offers a standard for evaluating the usefulness of art through Effective Altruism. Apply the concepts of Effective Altruism to van Houtryve's work as a photographer and to his essay. Is his essay a waste of time? How might we use technology like drones in Effective Altruism?

Language Matters

1. Given the visual nature of this selection, citation is a particular challenge. How should you properly cite van Houtryve's images? Review information on citation in a grammar handbook or other reference resource. Is there a specific format you should use? How would you cite the images, and how would you cite textual quotations from this essay?

2. A complete sentence has a subject and a verb. What is the visual equivalent of a sentence? Consider van Houtryve's photographs as sentences. How can you identify the subject and verb? Consider, for starters, the difference between *subject* in its grammatical sense and the *subject* of a piece of art or writing.

3. Punctuation marks delineate boundaries between words. What is the visual equivalent? Using van Houtryve's photographs, consider what elements act as "punctuation marks." Is the border of a photograph a period? Can the arrangement of elements in an image act as a question mark?

Assignments for Writing

1. Van Houtryve expresses concern about the "weaponization" of drones. Write a paper in which you explore the relationship of technology and war. What role should technology play in combat? Does it save lives or make it easier to take lives? Use your work from Questions 2 and 3 of Questions for Critical Reading and Question 3 of Exploring Context to support your argument.

2. Photographs play an important role in van Houtryve's essay. Write a paper in which you analyze van Houtryve's photographs as a visual argument. What argument does he make with these images? How do the images support that argument? You may want to review the material on analyzing images in Part One (p. 9); also consider using your work from Question 1 of Questions for Critical Reading.

3. Van Houtryve flies his drones through a number of public spaces. Write a paper in which you examine how space determines meaning. How does the setting for van Houtryve's photography influence the meaning of the images? How do people react to the drone based on space? Do different spaces create different meanings for drones and their images?

OTTO VON BUSCH

Otto von Busch, who holds a Ph.D. in design from the School of Design and Craft at the University of Gothenburg in Sweden, is an associate professor of integrated design at the Parsons School of Design at the New School in New York City. His work focuses on "hacktivism" in fashion, where designers engage consumers to transform the relationship between maker and user into a collective experience of empowerment resulting in social activism and engagement.

"Crafting Resistance" was published in *Craftivism: The Art of Craft and Activism* (2014), a collection of essays edited by Betsy Greer. *Craftivism* denotes the use of traditional handmade crafts — including knitting, quilting, and needlepoint — for social activist purposes. Other essays in the collection focused on charity quilting, the social power of upcycling, and the historical politics of the NAMES Project, a collectively created memorial quilt for victims of HIV/AIDS. The essays offer both powerful examples of how crafting can create social change and personal narratives of how these practices create personal change for the crafters as well.

In this selection, von Busch grounds craftivism in the work of nineteenth-century American author and philosopher Henry David Thoreau. Focusing in on do-it-yourself (DIY) clothes and fashion, von Busch notes that even a fairly commercialized site like Etsy can have moments where crafted objects act as a form of resistance. He then moves on to examine the role that crafting had in the movement for India's independence from Great Britain, spearheaded by Mahatma Gandhi. The production of cloth at home (bypassing British textiles) and the production of salt from the ocean (rather than British-taxed salt) were important craft-inflected instances of resistance. He concludes by enumerating some of the necessary factors in using craft as a form of social action and resistance.

▶ TAGS: *art, beauty, civil rights, collaboration, community, culture, economics, globalism, social change, tradition*

▶ CONNECTIONS: *Appiah, Chabon, Ma, Provan, Southan, Turkle, Yoshino*

Crafting Resistance

> "Injustice anywhere is a threat to justice everywhere. We are caught in an inescapable network of mutuality, tied in a single garment of destiny. Whatever affects one directly, affects all indirectly."
>
> —MARTIN LUTHER KING JR.[1]

Since the turn of the century, we have seen a resurgence of both the craft and Do-It-Yourself (DIY) cultures. Many who experienced the waves of activism in the 1970s and '80s make comparisons between the crocheted fashions and dropout cultures of the hippies or punks and their community actions, such as the Greenham Common Women's Peace Camp in the United Kingdom in 1981, and today's craft and activism resurgence, which has much in common with earlier forms of resistance cultures. It can be traced as far back as the nineteenth-century American author Henry David Thoreau's self-built cabin at Walden Pond.

Today, we see a tendency to primarily judge the outcomes of such actions for their aesthetic signature, for their forms and the quality of their craftsmanship. But just as it would be wrong to gauge Thoreau's endeavors based on his skills as a carpenter, it would be wrong to evaluate today's craft only by its merits as objects. Through acts of craft, we still shape forms of resistance. They are examinations of the seams in our social fabric and acts of disobedience.

Thoreau and Resistance

In his essay *Resistance to Civil Government* (1849), Thoreau suggests that it is our fear of punishment that makes us reproduce injustices. Our fear of punishment is our prison, not the prison structure itself. "Under a government which imprisons any unjustly, the true place for a just man is also in prison."[2] Thoreau believed that we must govern ourselves by our conscience and not seek to be ruled, even democratically. "Even voting *for the right* is *doing* nothing for it. It is only expressing to men feebly your desire that it should prevail."[3] To Thoreau, democracy was only a convenient delegation of power and responsibility to a parliament so that we could acquit ourselves from taking necessary action for justice. In other words, by not participating more actively in the fight against injustices, we become complicit in them.

In his epic work *Walden* (1854), Thoreau documents his experiments in what it means to be autonomous. Early in the book, he discusses the role of fashion, pointing out how we are dependent and controlled in this area by the opinions of others. As Thoreau points out, clothes and fashion play an important role in our society, producing a lot of anxiety; they may even act as a cover for conscience: "No man ever stood the lower in my estimation for having a patch in his clothes; yet I am sure that there is greater anxiety, commonly, to have fashionable, or at least clean and unpatched clothes, than to have a sound conscience."[4]

Clothes are not seen as unimportant; they are instead remarkable instruments from which to build independence, and they can reveal our relationship to power if we take them seriously. Thoreau sees our dependence on fashion as reluctance to see that we have power, even though we uncritically adhere to the authority of trends. Not only are our clothes "assimilated to ourselves,"[5] but wearing simple clothing and adopting a critical relation to trends can allow us to have a more independent life.

For Thoreau, our relationship to fashion lies at the core of our independence, as it mirrors our relationship to both government and power. Obeying fashion without conscience is the same as obeying laws we have not set ourselves. By putting our conscience back into the equation, we can remind ourselves of our autonomy. Taking on fashion through craft is more than an issue of expressing identity; it is a way to tackle our relationship to our compliance to being governed. It is a way to be free.

Turning Resistance into Craft

What Thoreau highlights is the struggle for independence inherent in clothing. Fashion may be an identity struggle between belonging and independence, but it is a struggle manifested as part of our social skin, and it is often made from materials open to our intervention. Craft, in the realm of fashion, is a tool that operates directly at the contested front line of identity.

When one sees craft as resistance, it is far too easy to examine it from a perspective of anti-consumerism or an individualistic attempt toward self-sufficiency or homesteading. In such cases, it may seem that craft is yet another counterculture in the spotlight, another subcultural trend that is easily commodified. If we look at craft objects, they are indeed often treated as mere commodities. Even a great arena for craft resurgence such as Etsy is still primarily a venue for the exchange of goods for money, even if other values are also involved.

However, some of the crafts we see at Etsy can also establish other relationships to the world of objects by forming new connections between crafter and buyer. In these, it is possible to disarm some of the fear and social anxiety common throughout consumer culture. As Thoreau saw, the mechanisms of control are internalized in all of us through everyday fear. Peace researcher David Cortright notices that, "We fear the loss of job security or position; we worry how family, friends, and employers will view us. We are so entangled in the comforts of society that we find it difficult to take risks, even for causes we hold dear."[6] The passivity and obedience of the subjects form the basis of how power is executed, as power is founded on obedience. Nobody "holds" power; it is reproduced by the subjects. The prison exists to hold as prisoners people on the outside, through their own fear. In this way, our own latent fear of isolation or even autonomy can be used against us. Therefore resistance is aimed inward as well as outward—to withdraw fear and build inner courage, but also to inspire others, show what is possible, and engage in discussions on what to build together, to form new modes of togetherness beyond fear.

Therefore, resistance is aimed inward as well as outward—to withdraw fear and build inner courage, but also to inspire others, show what is possible, and engage in discussions on what to build together, to form new modes of togetherness beyond fear.

Resistance is thus a struggle against ourselves as much as against external power. Within the current regime of power in consumer society, we may consume sustainably just in order to keep on consuming. Sustainability is, in this sense, a promise to leave things as they were before—so that consumers have no real power except to "vote with our dollars." Consumers are left powerless and in a state of social anxiety if they don't "keep up with the Joneses." In other words, they are not engaged at all, but leave the decisions up to the prison guards. By giving us freedom, craft is training in *not being the prison guard of oneself*. Once we are free, we are then truly able to foment change.

How is resistance and activism enacted through craft? Gandhi's life gives us two well-known examples of craft as resistance against the British Empire. The first is his spinning of *khadi* (homespun cloth) to support the independence movement, thus bypassing the British monopoly on textiles in India. This example takes a frugal position in building autonomy, not unlike Thoreau's self-sufficiency. The other powerful example from Gandhi's life is the Salt March, where justice was manifested through the hands-on craft of independent salt production. Gandhi proposed that instead of buying British salt, which was taxed, Indians march to the sea to make their own salt. Every grain was a manifestation of Indian freedom, made from the abundance of salt in the Indian Ocean. The act itself was very simple, much simpler than spinning cloth, and easily reproduced; it was an action based on accessing abundance rather than signifying thrift. It thus resonates well with our time, a time of abundance, and may inspire us in how to "detoxify" consumerism.

Gandhi's strategy used several components to make it strong:

- The act mobilized participants through simple and palpable means.
- The act accessed a colonized source of abundance and made it public through craft.
- The act bypassed or was a non-reproduction of domination.
- The act exposed oppression by making useful but illegal things.
- The act showed how a tangible result, however small, can emerge from protest.
- The act showed how resistance leads to self-rule (which Gandhi called *swaraj*).

Even though the resistance was violently repressed by the British, the salt campaign was effective in many ways: It was creative and original, easily replicable without the need for extensive training, gave an experience of coherence to everyone involved, and enabled the movement to seize initiative and build momentum toward larger, strategic objectives. It was a craft of being free.

Resistance as the Craft of Two Hands

The resistance proposed by Gandhi can be seen as a form of craft, as it was materialized into action in a constructive manner. It was done by constructing disobedience. Feminist Barbara Deming used a metaphor of the "two hands" to describe this form of resistance, which aims to control and reform the relationship between activist and opponent: "The more the real issues are dramatized, and the struggle raised above the personal, the more control those in nonviolent rebellion begin to gain over the adversary. For they are able at one and the same time to disrupt everything for him, making it impossible for him to operate within the system as usual, and to temper his response to 'this.' [. . .] They have as it were two hands upon him—the one calming him, making him ask questions, as the other makes him move."[7]

This double-handed craft is a refusal to respond violently to the repression of the action and to constrain the escalation of violence or desire for revenge, and to instead focus the action on its moral implications and inform possible dialogue. The action builds the ground for change by incarnating change. One hand stops while the other constructs the alternative; one hand displaces injustice while the other enacts justice. A similar strategy was carried out in mixed-race sit-ins against segregated diners in the American south during the Civil Rights era. At a lunch counter reserved for whites, racism was temporarily displaced when a person of color sat there. In order to oppose the sit-ins, opponents had to stop the constructive act of desegregation, and by doing so, display their racism and reveal the violence of segregation.

Craft resistance in the world of fashion would mean withdrawal of fear from fashion, while not withdrawing from fashion. Instead, resistance is simultaneously crafting alternative forms of togetherness through fashion. This may take the shape of cleverly distributed counterfeit schemes, such as Stephanie Syjuco's *Counterfeit Crochet* project or the Milan-based open-source fashion network Openwear, which runs education, production, and pattern-sharing services for independent designers and users. It is through action that we test our democracy and government, as we touch the seams of society. Craft may, in this sense, act as resistance to obedience. It is a training camp for empowered autonomy. It is fearlessness toward the decrees of consumerism and peer pressure and, in its most expressive form, the violence of fashion. Craft can be a tool for overcoming fear. It is a way to be free. 15

NOTES

1. "Letter from Birmingham Jail," *Martin Luther King Jr. Research and Education Institute*, http://mlk-kpp01.stanford.edu/index.php/resources/article/annotated_letter_from_birmingham/.
2. Thoreau, Henry David. *Walden and Resistance to Civil Government* (New York: W. W. Norton, 1992), p. 235.
3. Thoreau, p. 231.
4. Thoreau, p. 14.
5. Ibid.
6. Cortright, David, *Gandhi and Beyond: Nonviolence for a New Political Age* (Boulder, CO: Paradigm Publishers, 2009), p. 33.
7. Deming, Barbara. *Revolution and Equilibrium* (New York: Grossman Publishers, 1971) p. 207f.

Question for Critical Reading

1. What does von Busch mean by "the craft of two hands" or "double-handed craft"? Review his essay to locate passages that define what he means by this term. Then, offer your own example of this kind of crafting.
2. The relationship between craft and resistance is central to von Busch's argument. Reread his essay and mark passages where he explains how crafting can act as a form of resistance. Are there particular elements necessary in order for it to function in this manner?
3. How does von Busch use historical figures to support his argument? Review his use of Henry David Thoreau and Mahatma Gandhi. Why would he use these figures in his argument? What role do they serve?

Exploring Context

1. Von Busch suggests that even Etsy can have moments when crafted fashions become not simply anti commercial but actively resistant by refiguring the relations between

maker and user. Visit Etsy at etsy.com. Can you find any evidence to support von Busch's argument? Or has Etsy continued to evolve into a commercial venue for craft?

2. **Multimodal.** Von Busch uses Gandhi's Salt March as an example of craft as social resistance. Using a web search engine, do some basic research on the Salt March. What made it successful? Connect what you find to von Busch's argument and then, using PowerPoint or other software, make a presentation about your findings. As you do so, you will want to consider the design elements of the presentation, including the layout of the slides, the choice of font, and the transitions between slides. How do these factors help support your argument? You may want to use the web to learn more about effective presentations.

3. Visit selfpassage (selfpassage.info), a website created and maintained by von Busch. How does this essay fit into his larger projects? What recurrent themes seem to define his work?

Questions for Connecting

1. Sherry Turkle also turns to Thoreau to frame her argument in "The Empathy Diaries" (p. 378). Consider the ways in which Turkle and von Busch are making similar arguments and synthesize their positions to generate a model of social change. What role does conversation play? Can fashion function as a kind of conversation?

2. Clothes and fashion play an important role in Michael Chabon's "My Son, the Prince of Fashion" (p. 62). Complicate von Busch's argument using Chabon's experience with his son Abe. How does fashion operate in ways beyond commercialism? How might someone use fashion not to resist the world but to enable an identity? Does Abe refigure the relationship between designers and consumers?

3. What roles do strong and weak social ties play in von Busch's vision of craftivism and social change? Connect Malcolm Gladwell's analysis in "Small Change" (p. 191) to von Busch. What sort of ties are necessary for "double-handed" activism?

Language Matters

1. Photocopy a couple of pages from von Busch's essay and then cut out each individual paragraph with a pair of scissors. Trade these in small groups. Can everyone put the paragraphs back in the right order? How strong is von Busch's organization? What elements of the paragraphs indicate their order within the piece?

2. Often, a glossary is used to define terms. Create a brief glossary for von Busch's essay. How would you choose which terms to include?

3. Von Busch uses a clear, simple style of writing to discuss a very complex subject. Select a key quotation from his text and break down the parts of each sentence. How does he use language to express difficult concepts clearly? How can you do the same in your writing?

Assignments for Writing

1. Clothing and fashion serve as one of von Busch's primary examples of social change. Extend von Busch's argument by locating another example of a craft or other do-it-yourself activity that can function as a form of resistance and social change. Questions 1 and 2 of Questions for Critical Reading and Question 3 of Questions for Connecting might be useful in supporting your argument.
2. Write a paper in which you identify the necessary factors for enabling successful resistance and social change. How can you abstract from von Busch's argument about craft to extrapolate core factors that are critical for change? Your work in Questions for Critical Reading, Question 2 of Exploring Context, and Questions 1 and 3 of Questions for Connecting may offer useful insights as you shape your argument.
3. Can individuals transform the consumer relationship? Building from von Busch's analysis, write a paper in which you propose strategies for transforming consumerism. Is it possible for individuals to escape consumerism? How can we change the relationship between producer and consumer?

DAVID FOSTER WALLACE

Novelist and essayist **David Foster Wallace** was the Roy E. Disney Professor of Creative Writing at Pomona College until his death in 2008. Highly respected during his lifetime, he was a recipient of the MacArthur fellowship (colloquially known as the "genius grant") from 1997 to 2002, as well as a winner of the Salon Book Award and the Lannan Literary Award for fiction. His significant publications include the novels *The Broom of the System* (1987) and *Infinite Jest* (1996) as well as *Brief Interviews with Hideous Men* (1999), a collection of short stories. Wallace was also a noted essayist, writing for publications such as *Rolling Stone*, *Harper's Magazine*, and the *Atlantic*. Wallace's *The Pale King* (2011), an unfinished novel, was published three years after his death.

In *Consider the Lobster and Other Essays* (2005), the collection from which this selection is taken, Wallace explores a broad range of topics, including the adult film industry's Adult Video News Awards, the criticisms of novelist John Updike, Kafka's wit, the political underbelly of dictionary publications, Senator John McCain, and the seductive and disappointing paradox of sports athlete memoirs. While these topics appear to be unrelated, Wallace's versatility exemplifies his common concern with current concepts of morality. This notion of morality is strikingly clear in the title essay "Consider the Lobster," originally published in *Gourmet* magazine.

Wallace finds it curious that lobster is the one creature that is usually cooked while still alive. Though many people find this practice unproblematic, believing that lobsters cannot feel pain, Wallace observes that lobsters can at least exhibit a preference for not being lowered into a pot of boiling water. This observation leads Wallace to question our justifications for eating lobster, and indeed, our eating of animals altogether. Ultimately, "Consider the Lobster" raises many questions about the practices we engage in as a species, our definitions of pain and suffering, and our understanding of the world around us.

- TAGS: *empathy, ethics, food and agriculture, judgment and decision making*
- CONNECTIONS: *Appiah, Fukuyama, Ma, Moalem, Pollan, Watters*

Consider the Lobster

The enormous, pungent, and extremely well-marketed Maine Lobster Festival is held every late July in the state's midcoast region, meaning the western side of Penobscot Bay, the nerve stem of Maine's lobster industry. What's called the midcoast runs from Owl's Head and Thomaston in the south to Belfast in the north. (Actually, it might extend all the way up to Bucksport, but we were never able to get farther north than Belfast on Route 1, whose summer traffic is, as you can imagine, unimaginable.) The region's two main communities are Camden, with its very old money and yachty harbor and five-star restaurants and phenomenal B&Bs, and Rockland, a serious old fishing town that hosts the festival every summer in historic Harbor Park, right along the water.[1]

[1]There's a comprehensive native apothegm: "Camden by the sea, Rockland by the smell."

Tourism and lobster are the midcoast region's two main industries, and they're both warm-weather enterprises, and the Maine Lobster Festival represents less an intersection of the industries than a deliberate collision, joyful and lucrative and loud. The assigned subject of this *Gourmet* article is the 56th Annual MLF, 30 July–3 August 2003, whose official theme this year was "Lighthouses, Laughter, and Lobster." Total paid attendance was over 100,000, due partly to a national CNN spot in June during which a senior editor of *Food & Wine* magazine hailed the MLF as one of the best food-themed galas in the world. 2003 festival highlights: concerts by Lee Ann Womack and Orleans, annual Maine Sea Goddess beauty pageant, Saturday's big parade, Sunday's William G. Atwood Memorial Crate Race, annual Amateur Cooking Competition, carnival rides and midway attractions and food booths, and the MLF's Main Eating Tent, where something over 25,000 pounds of fresh-caught Maine lobster is consumed after preparation in the World's Largest Lobster Cooker near the grounds' north entrance. Also available are lobster rolls, lobster turnovers, lobster sauté, Down East lobster salad, lobster bisque, lobster ravioli, and deep-fried lobster dumplings. Lobster thermidor is obtainable at a sit-down restaurant called the Black Pearl on Harbor Park's northwest wharf. A large all-pine booth sponsored by the Maine Lobster Promotion Council has free pamphlets with recipes, eating tips, and Lobster Fun Facts. The winner of Friday's Amateur Cooking Competition prepares Saffron Lobster Ramekins, the recipe for which is now available for public downloading at www.mainelobster-festival.com. There are lobster T-shirts and lobster bobblehead dolls and inflatable lobster pool toys and clamp-on lobster hats with big scarlet claws that wobble on springs. Your assigned correspondent saw it all, accompanied by one girlfriend and both his own parents—one of which parents was actually born and raised in Maine, albeit in the extreme northern inland part, which is potato country and a world away from the touristic midcoast.[2]

For practical purposes, everyone knows what a lobster is. As usual, though, there's much more to know than most of us care about—it's all a matter of what your interests are. Taxonomically speaking, a lobster is a marine crustacean of the family Homaridae, characterized by five pairs of jointed legs, the first pair terminating in large pincerish claws used for subduing prey. Like many other species of benthic carnivore, lobsters are both hunters and scavengers. They have stalked eyes, gills on their legs, and antennae. There are a dozen or so different kinds worldwide, of which the relevant species here is the Maine lobster, *Homarus americanus*. The name "lobster" comes from the Old English *loppestre*, which is thought to be a corrupt form of the Latin word for locust combined with the Old English *loppe*, which meant spider.

Moreover, a crustacean is an aquatic arthropod of the class Crustacea, which comprises crabs, shrimp, barnacles, lobsters, and freshwater crayfish. All this is right there in the encyclopedia. And arthropods are members of the phylum Arthropoda, which phylum covers insects, spiders, crustaceans, and centipedes/millipedes, all of whose main commonality, besides the absence of a centralized brain-spine assembly, is a chitinous exoskeleton composed of segments, to which appendages are articulated in pairs.

---

[2]N.B. All personally connected parties have made it clear from the start that they do not want to be talked about in this article.

The point is that lobsters are basically giant sea insects.[3] Like most arthropods, they date from the Jurassic period, biologically so much older than mammalia that they might as well be from another planet. And they are—particularly in their natural brown-green state, brandishing their claws like weapons and with thick antennae awhip—not nice to look at. And it's true that they are garbagemen of the sea, eaters of dead stuff,[4] although they'll also eat some live shellfish, certain kinds of injured fish, and sometimes one another.

The point is that lobsters are basically giant sea insects.

But they are themselves good eating. Or so we think now. Up until sometime in the 1800s, though, lobster was literally low-class food, eaten only by the poor and institutionalized. Even in the harsh penal environment of early America, some colonies had laws against feeding lobsters to inmates more than once a week because it was thought to be cruel and unusual, like making people eat rats. One reason for their low status was how plentiful lobsters were in old New England. "Unbelievable abundance" is how one source describes the situation, including accounts of Plymouth Pilgrims wading out and capturing all they wanted by hand, and of early Boston's seashore being littered with lobsters after hard storms—these latter were treated as a smelly nuisance and ground up for fertilizer. There is also the fact that premodern lobster was cooked dead and then preserved, usually packed in salt or crude hermetic containers. Maine's earliest lobster industry was based around a dozen such seaside canneries in the 1840s, from which lobster was shipped as far away as California, in demand only because it was cheap and high in protein, basically chewable fuel.

Now, of course, lobster is posh, a delicacy, only a step or two down from caviar. The meat is richer and more substantial than most fish, its taste subtle compared to the marine-gaminess of mussels and clams. In the U.S. pop-food imagination, lobster is now the seafood analog to steak, with which it's so often twinned as Surf 'n' Turf on the really expensive part of the chain steakhouse menu.

In fact, one obvious project of the MLF, and of its omnipresently sponsorial Maine Lobster Promotion Council, is to counter the idea that lobster is unusually luxe or unhealthy or expensive, suitable only for effete palates or the occasional blow-the-diet treat. It is emphasized over and over in presentations and pamphlets at the festival that lobster meat has fewer calories, less cholesterol, and less saturated fat than chicken.[5] And in the Main Eating Tent, you can get a "quarter" (industry shorthand for a 1¼-pound lobster), a four-ounce cup of melted butter, a bag of chips, and a soft roll w/butter-pat for around $12.00, which is only slightly more expensive than supper at McDonald's.

Be apprised, though, that the Maine Lobster Festival's democratization of lobster comes with all the massed inconvenience and aesthetic compromise of real democracy. See, for example, the aforementioned Main Eating Tent, for which there is a constant Disneyland-grade queue, and which turns out to be a square quarter mile of

---

[3]Midcoasters' native term for a lobster is, in fact, "bug," as in "Come around on Sunday and we'll cook up some bugs."

[4]Factoid: Lobster traps are usually baited with dead herring.

[5]Of course, the common practice of dipping the lobster meat in melted butter torpedoes all these happy fat-specs, which none of the council's promotional stuff ever mentions, any more than potato industry PR talks about sour cream and bacon bits.

awning-shaded cafeteria lines and rows of long institutional tables at which friend and stranger alike sit cheek by jowl, cracking and chewing and dribbling. It's hot, and the sagged roof traps the steam and the smells, which latter are strong and only partly food-related. It is also loud, and a good percentage of the total noise is masticatory. The suppers come in styrofoam trays, and the soft drinks are iceless and flat, and the coffee is convenience-store coffee in more styrofoam, and the utensils are plastic (there are none of the special long skinny forks for pushing out the tail meat, though a few savvy diners bring their own). Nor do they give you near enough napkins considering how messy lobster is to eat, especially when you're squeezed onto benches alongside children of various ages and vastly different levels of fine-motor development—not to mention the people who've somehow smuggled in their own beer in enormous aisle-blocking coolers, or who all of a sudden produce their own plastic tablecloths and spread them over large portions of tables to try to reserve them (the tables) for their own little groups. And so on. Any one example is no more than a petty inconvenience, of course, but the MLF turns out to be full of irksome little downers like this—see for instance the Main Stage's headliner shows, where it turns out that you have to pay $20 extra for a folding chair if you want to sit down; or the North Tent's mad scramble for the NyQuil-cup-sized samples of finalists' entries handed out after the Cooking Competition; or the much-touted Maine Sea Goddess pageant finals, which turn out to be excruciatingly long and to consist mainly of endless thanks and tributes to local sponsors. Let's not even talk about the grossly inadequate Port-A-San facilities or the fact that there's nowhere to wash your hands before or after eating. What the Maine Lobster Festival really is is a midlevel county fair with a culinary hook, and in this respect it's not unlike Tidewater crab festivals, Midwest corn festivals, Texas chili festivals, etc., and shares with these venues the core paradox of all teeming commercial demotic events: It's not for everyone.[6] Nothing against the euphoric senior editor of

[6]In truth, there's a great deal to be said about the differences between working-class Rockland and the heavily populist flavor of its festival versus comfortable and elitist Camden with its expensive view and shops given entirely over to $200 sweaters and great rows of Victorian homes converted to upscale B&Bs. And about these differences as two sides of the great coin that is U.S. tourism. Very little of which will be said here, except to amplify the above-mentioned paradox and to reveal your assigned correspondent's own preferences. I confess that I have never understood why so many people's idea of a fun vacation is to don flip-flops and sunglasses and crawl through maddening traffic to loud, hot, crowded tourist venues in order to sample a "local flavor" that is by definition ruined by the presence of tourists. This may (as my festival companions keep pointing out) all be a matter of personality and hardwired taste: The fact that I do not like tourist venues means that I'll never understand their appeal and so am probably not the one to talk about it (the supposed appeal). But, since this FN will almost surely not survive magazine-editing anyway, here goes:

As I see it, it probably really is good for the soul to be a tourist, even if it's only once in a while. Not good for the soul in a refreshing or enlivening way, though, but rather in a grim, steely-eyed, let's-look-honestly-at-the-facts-and-find-some-way-to-deal-with-them way. My personal experience has not been that traveling around the country is broadening or relaxing, or that radical changes in place and context have a salutary effect, but rather that intranational tourism is radically constricting, and humbling in the hardest way—hostile to my fantasy of being a true individual, of living somehow outside and above it all. (Coming up is the part that my companions find especially unhappy and repellent, a sure way to spoil the fun of vacation travel.) To be a mass tourist, for me, is to become a pure late-date American: alien, ignorant, greedy for something you cannot ever have, disappointed in a way you can never admit. It is to spoil, by way of sheer ontology, the very unspoiledness you are there to experience. It is to impose yourself on places that in all non-economic ways would be better, realer, without you. It is, in lines and gridlock and transaction after transaction, to confront a dimension of yourself that is as inescapable as it is painful: As a tourist, you become economically significant but existentially loathsome, an insect on a dead thing.

Food & Wine, but I'd be surprised if she'd ever actually been here in Harbor Park, amid crowds of people slapping canal-zone mosquitoes as they eat deep-fried Twinkies and watch Professor Paddywhack on six-foot stilts in a raincoat with plastic lobsters protruding from all directions on springs, terrify their children.

Lobster is essentially a summer food. This is because we now prefer our lobsters fresh, which means they have to be recently caught, which for both tactical and economic reasons takes place at depths less than 25 fathoms. Lobsters tend to be hungriest and most active (i.e., most trappable) at summer water temperatures of 45–50 degrees. In the autumn, most Maine lobsters migrate out into deeper water, either for warmth or to avoid the heavy waves that pound New England's coast all winter. Some burrow into the bottom. They might hibernate; nobody's sure. Summer is also lobsters' molting season—specifically early- to mid-July. Chitinous arthropods grow by molting, rather the way people have to buy bigger clothes as they age and gain weight. Since lobsters can live to be over 100, they can also get to be quite large, as in 30 pounds or more—though truly senior lobsters are rare now because New England's waters are so heavily trapped.[7] Anyway, hence the culinary distinction between hard- and soft-shell lobsters, the latter sometimes a.k.a. shedders. A soft-shell lobster is one that has recently molted. In midcoast restaurants, the summer menu often offers both kinds, with shedders being slightly cheaper even though they're easier to dismantle and the meat is allegedly sweeter. The reason for the discount is that a molting lobster uses a layer of seawater for insulation while its new shell is hardening, so there's slightly less actual meat when you crack open a shedder, plus a redolent gout of water that gets all over everything and can sometimes jet out lemonlike and catch a tablemate right in the eye. If it's winter or you're buying lobster someplace far from New England, on the other hand, you can almost bet that the lobster is a hard-shell, which for obvious reasons travel better.

10

As an à la carte entrée, lobster can be baked, broiled, steamed, grilled, sautéed, stir-fried, or microwaved. The most common method, though, is boiling. If you're someone who enjoys having lobster at home, this is probably the way you do it, since boiling is so easy. You need a large kettle w/cover, which you fill about half full with water (the standard advice is that you want 2.5 quarts of water per lobster). Seawater is optimal, or you can add two tbsp salt per quart from the tap. It also helps to know how much your lobsters weigh. You get the water boiling, put in the lobsters one at a time, cover the kettle, and bring it back up to a boil. Then you bank the heat and let the kettle simmer—ten minutes for the first pound of lobster, then three minutes for each pound after that. (This is assuming you've got hard-shell lobsters, which, again, if you don't live between Boston and Halifax is probably what you've got. For shedders, you're supposed to subtract three minutes from the total.) The reason the kettle's lobsters turn scarlet is that boiling somehow suppresses every pigment in their chitin but one. If you want an easy test of whether the lobsters are done, you try pulling on one of their antennae—if it comes out of the head with minimal effort, you're ready to eat.

---

[7]Datum: In a good year, the U.S. industry produces around 80,000,000 pounds of lobster, and Maine accounts for more than half that total.

A detail so obvious that most recipes don't even bother to mention it is that each lobster is supposed to be alive when you put it in the kettle. This is part of lobster's modern appeal—it's the freshest food there is. There's no decomposition between harvesting and eating. And not only do lobsters require no cleaning or dressing or plucking, they're relatively easy for vendors to keep alive. They come up alive in the traps, are placed in containers of seawater, and can—so long as the water's aerated and the animals' claws are pegged or banded to keep them from tearing one another up under the stresses of captivity[8]—survive right up until they're boiled. Most of us have been in supermarkets or restaurants that feature tanks of live lobsters, from which you can pick out your supper while it watches you point. And part of the overall spectacle of the Maine Lobster Festival is that you can see actual lobstermen's vessels docking at the wharves along the northeast grounds and unloading fresh-caught product, which is transferred by hand or cart 150 yards to the great clear tanks stacked up around the festival's cooker—which is, as mentioned, billed as the World's Largest Lobster Cooker and can process over 100 lobsters at a time for the Main Eating Tent.

So then here is a question that's all but unavoidable at the World's Largest Lobster Cooker, and may arise in kitchens across the U.S.: Is it all right to boil a sentient creature alive just for our gustatory pleasure? A related set of concerns: Is the previous question irksomely PC or sentimental? What does "all right" even mean in this context? Is the whole thing just a matter of personal choice?

As you may or may not know, a certain well-known group called People for the Ethical Treatment of Animals thinks that the morality of lobster-boiling is not just a matter of individual conscience. In fact, one of the very first things we hear about the MLF . . . well, to set the scene: We're coming in by cab from the almost indescribably odd and rustic Knox County Airport[9] very late on the night before the festival opens, sharing the cab with a wealthy political consultant who lives on Vinalhaven Island in the bay half the year (he's headed for the island ferry in Rockland). The consultant and cabdriver are responding to informal journalistic probes about how people who live in the midcoast region actually view the MLF, as in is the festival just a big-dollar tourist thing or is it something local residents look forward to attending, take genuine civic pride in, etc. The cabdriver (who's in his seventies, one of apparently a whole platoon of retirees the cab company puts on to help with the summer rush, and wears a U.S.-flag lapel pin, and drives in what can only be called a very *deliberate* way) assures us that

---

[8]N.B. Similar reasoning underlies the practice of what's termed "debeaking" broiler chickens and brood hens in modern factory farms. Maximum commercial efficiency requires that enormous poultry populations be confined in unnaturally close quarters, under which conditions many birds go crazy and peck one another to death. As a purely observational side-note, be apprised that debeaking is usually an automated process and that the chickens receive no anesthetic. It's not clear to me whether most *Gourmet* readers know about debeaking, or about related practices like dehorning cattle in commercial feed lots, cropping swine's tails in factory hog farms to keep psychotically bored neighbors from chewing them off, and so forth. It so happens that your assigned correspondent knew almost nothing about standard meat-industry operations before starting work on this article.

[9]The terminal used to be somebody's house, for example, and the lost-luggage-reporting room was clearly once a pantry.

locals do endorse and enjoy the MLF, although he himself hasn't gone in years, and now come to think of it no one he and his wife know has, either. However, the demilocal consultant's been to recent festivals a couple times (one gets the impression it was at his wife's behest), of which his most vivid impression was that "you have to line up for an ungodly long time to get your lobsters, and meanwhile there are all these ex–flower children coming up and down along the line handing out pamphlets that say the lobsters die in terrible pain and you shouldn't eat them."

And it turns out that the post-hippies of the consultant's recollection were activists from PETA. There were no PETA people in obvious view at the 2003 MLF,[10] but they've been conspicuous at many of the recent festivals. Since at least the mid-1990s, articles in everything from the *Camden Herald* to the *New York Times* have described PETA urging boycotts of the Maine Lobster Festival, often deploying celebrity spokesmen like Mary Tyler Moore for open letters and ads saying stuff like "Lobsters are extraordinarily sensitive" and "To me, eating a lobster is out of the question." More concrete is the oral testimony of Dick, our florid and extremely gregarious rental-car liaison,[11] to the effect that PETA's been around so much during recent years that a kind of brittlely tolerant homeostasis now obtains between the activists and the festival's locals, e.g.: "We had some incidents a couple years ago. One lady took most of her clothes off and painted herself like a lobster, almost got herself arrested. But for the most part they're let alone. [Rapid series of small ambiguous laughs, which with Dick happens a lot.] They do their thing and we do our thing."

This whole interchange takes place on Route 1, 30 July, during a four-mile, 50-minute ride from the airport[12] to the dealership to sign car-rental papers. Several irreproducible segues down the road from the PETA anecdotes, Dick—whose son-in-law happens to be a professional lobsterman and one of the Main Eating Tent's regular suppliers—explains what he and his family feel is the crucial mitigating factor in the

---

[10]It turned out that one Mr. William R. Rivas-Rivas, a high-ranking PETA official out of the group's Virginia headquarters, was indeed there this year, albeit solo, working the festival's main and side entrances on Saturday, 2 August, handing out pamphlets and adhesive stickers emblazoned with "Being Boiled Hurts," which is the tagline in most of PETA's published material about lobsters. I learned that he'd been there only later, when speaking with Mr. Rivas-Rivas on the phone. I'm not sure how we missed seeing him *in situ* at the festival, and I can't see much to do except apologize for the oversight—although it's also true that Saturday was the day of the big MLF parade through Rockland, which basic journalistic responsibility seemed to require going to (and which, with all due respect, meant that Saturday was maybe not the best day for PETA to work the Harbor Park grounds, especially if it was going to be just one person for one day, since a lot of diehard MLF partisans were off-site watching the parade [which, again with no offense intended, was in truth kind of cheesy and boring, consisting mostly of slow homemade floats and various midcoast people waving at one another, and with an extremely annoying man dressed as Blackbeard ranging up and down the length of the crowd saying, "Arrr" over and over and brandishing a plastic sword at people, etc.; plus it rained]).

[11]By profession, Dick is actually a car salesman; the midcoast region's National Car Rental franchise operates out of a Chevy dealership in Thomaston.

[12]The short version regarding why we were back at the airport after already arriving the previous night involves lost luggage and a miscommunication about where and what the midcoast's National franchise was—Dick came out personally to the airport and got us, out of no evident motive but kindness. (He also talked nonstop the entire way, with a very distinctive speaking style that can be described only as manically laconic; the truth is that I now know more about this man than I do about some members of my own family.)

whole morality-of-boiling-lobsters-alive issue: "There's a part of the brain in people and animals that lets us feel pain, and lobsters' brains don't have this part."

Besides the fact that it's incorrect in about nine different ways, the main reason Dick's statement is interesting is that its thesis is more or less echoed by the festival's own pronouncement on lobsters and pain, which is part of a Test Your Lobster IQ quiz that appears in the 2003 MLF program courtesy of the Maine Lobster Promotion Council:

> The nervous system of a lobster is very simple, and is in fact most similar to the nervous system of the grasshopper. It is decentralized with no brain. There is no cerebral cortex, which in humans is the area of the brain that gives the experience of pain.

Though it sounds more sophisticated, a lot of the neurology in this latter claim is still either false or fuzzy. The human cerebral cortex is the brain-part that deals with higher faculties like reason, metaphysical self-awareness, language, etc. Pain reception is known to be part of a much older and more primitive system of nociceptors and prostaglandins that are managed by the brain stem and thalamus.[13] On the other hand, it is true that the cerebral cortex is involved in what's variously called suffering, distress, or the emotional experience of pain—i.e., experiencing painful stimuli as unpleasant, very unpleasant, unbearable, and so on.

Before we go any further, let's acknowledge that the questions of whether and how different kinds of animals feel pain, and of whether and why it might be justifiable to inflict pain on them in order to eat them, turn out to be extremely complex and difficult. And comparative neuroanatomy is only part of the problem. Since pain is a totally subjective mental experience, we do not have direct access to anyone or anything's pain but our own; and even just the principles by which we can infer that other human beings experience pain and have a legitimate interest in not feeling pain involve hard-core philosophy—metaphysics, epistemology, value theory, ethics. The fact that even the most highly evolved nonhuman mammals can't use language to communicate with us about their subjective mental experience is only the first layer of additional complication in trying to extend our reasoning about pain and morality to animals. And everything gets progressively more abstract and convolved as we move farther and farther out from the higher-type mammals into cattle and swine and dogs and cats and rodents, and then birds and fish, and finally invertebrates like lobsters.

The more important point here, though, is that the whole animal-cruelty-and-eating issue is not just complex, it's also uncomfortable. It is, at any rate, uncomfortable for me, and for just about everyone I know who enjoys a variety of foods and yet does not want to see herself as cruel or unfeeling. As far as I can tell, my own main way of dealing with this conflict has been to avoid thinking about the whole unpleasant

[13]To elaborate by way of example: The common experience of accidentally touching a hot stove and yanking your hand back before you're even aware that anything's going on is explained by the fact that many of the processes by which we detect and avoid painful stimuli do not involve the cortex. In the case of the hand and stove, the brain is bypassed altogether; all the important neurochemical action takes place in the spine.

thing. I should add that it appears to me unlikely that many readers of *Gourmet* wish to think about it, either, or to be queried about the morality of their eating habits in the pages of a culinary monthly. Since, however, the assigned subject of this article is what it was like to attend the 2003 MLF, and thus to spend several days in the midst of a great mass of Americans all eating lobster, and thus to be more or less impelled to think hard about lobster and the experience of buying and eating lobster, it turns out that there is no honest way to avoid certain moral questions.

20 There are several reasons for this. For one thing, it's not just that lobsters get boiled alive, it's that you do it yourself—or at least it's done specifically for you, on-site.[14] As mentioned, the World's Largest Lobster Cooker, which is highlighted as an attraction in the festival's program, is right out there on the MLF's north grounds for everyone to see. Try to imagine a Nebraska Beef Festival[15] at which part of the festivities is watching trucks pull up and the live cattle get driven down the ramp and slaughtered right there on the World's Largest Killing Floor or something—there's no way.

The lobster . . . behaves very much as you or I would behave if we were plunged into boiling water (with the obvious exception of screaming).

The intimacy of the whole thing is maximized at home, which of course is where most lobster gets prepared and eaten (although note already the semiconscious euphemism "prepared," which in the case of lobsters really means killing them right there in our kitchens). The basic scenario is that we come in from the store and make our little preparations like getting the kettle filled and boiling, and then we lift the lobsters out of the bag or whatever retail container they came home in . . . whereupon some uncomfortable things start to happen. However stuporous a lobster is from the trip home, for instance, it tends to come alarmingly to life when placed in boiling water. If you're tilting it from a container into the steaming kettle, the lobster will sometimes try to cling to the container's sides or even to hook its claws over the kettle's rim like a person trying to keep from going over the edge of a roof. And worse is when the lobster's fully immersed. Even if you cover the kettle and turn away, you can usually hear the cover rattling and clanking as the lobster tries to push it off. Or the creature's claws scraping the sides of the kettle as it thrashes around. The lobster, in other

[14]Morality-wise, let's concede that this cuts both ways. Lobster-eating is at least not abetted by the system of corporate factory farms that produces most beef, pork, and chicken. Because, if nothing else, of the way they're marketed and packaged for sale, we eat these latter meats without having to consider that they were once conscious, sentient creatures to whom horrible things were done. (N.B. "Horrible" here meaning really, really horrible. Write off to PETA or peta.org for their free "Meet Your Meat" video, narrated by Mr. Alec Baldwin, if you want to see just about everything meat-related you don't want to see or think about. [N.B.$_2$ Not that PETA's any sort of font of unspun truth. Like many partisans in complex moral disputes, the PETA people are fanatics, and a lot of their rhetoric seems simplistic and self-righteous. But this particular video, replete with actual factory-farm and corporate-slaughterhouse footage, is both credible and traumatizing.])

[15]Is it significant that "lobster," "fish," and "chicken" are our culture's words for both the animal and the meat, whereas most mammals seem to require euphemisms like "beef" and "pork" that help us separate the meat we eat from the living creature the meat once was? Is this evidence that some kind of deep unease about eating higher animals is endemic enough to show up in English usage, but that the unease diminishes as we move out of the mammalian order? (And is "lamb"/"lamb" the counterexample that sinks the whole theory, or are there special, biblico-historical reasons for that equivalence?)

words, behaves very much as you or I would behave if we were plunged into boiling water (with the obvious exception of screaming[16]). A blunter way to say this is that the lobster acts as if it's in terrible pain, causing some cooks to leave the kitchen altogether and to take one of those little lightweight plastic oven-timers with them into another room and wait until the whole process is over.

There happen to be two main criteria that most ethicists agree on for determining whether a living creature has the capacity to suffer and so has genuine interests that it may or may not be our moral duty to consider.[17] One is how much of the neurological hardware required for pain-experience the animal comes equipped with—nociceptors, prostaglandins, neuronal opioid receptors, etc. The other criterion is whether the animal demonstrates behavior associated with pain. And it takes a lot of intellectual gymnastics and behaviorist hairsplitting not to see struggling, thrashing, and lid-clattering as just such pain-behavior. According to marine zoologists, it usually takes lobsters between 35 and 45 seconds to die in boiling water. (No source I could find talks about how long it takes them to die in superheated steam; one rather hopes it's faster.)

There are, of course, other ways to kill your lobster on-site and so achieve maximum freshness. Some cooks' practice is to drive a sharp heavy knife point-first into a spot just above the midpoint between the lobster's eyestalks (more or less where the Third Eye is in human foreheads). This is alleged either to kill the lobster instantly or to render it insensate, and is said at least to eliminate some of the cowardice involved in throwing a creature into boiling water and then fleeing the room. As far as I can tell from talking to proponents of the knife-in-head method, the idea is that it's more violent but ultimately more merciful, plus that a willingness to exert personal agency and accept responsibility for stabbing the lobster's head honors the lobster somehow and entitles one to eat it (there's often a vague sort of Native American spirituality-of-the-hunt flavor to pro-knife arguments). But the problem with the knife method is basic biology: Lobsters' nervous systems operate off not one but several ganglia, a.k.a. nerve bundles, which are sort of wired in series and distributed all along the lobster's underside, from stem to stern. And disabling only the frontal ganglion does not normally result in quick death or unconsciousness.

---

[16]There's a relevant populist myth about the high-pitched whistling sound that sometimes issues from a pot of boiling lobster. The sound is really vented steam from the layer of seawater between the lobster's flesh and its carapace (this is why shedders whistle more than hard-shells), but the pop version has it that the sound is the lobster's rabbit-like death-scream. Lobsters communicate via pheromones in their urine and don't have anything close to the vocal equipment for screaming, but the myth's very persistent—which might, once again, point to a low-level cultural unease about the boiling thing.

[17]"Interests" basically means strong and legitimate preferences, which obviously require some degree of consciousness, responsiveness to stimuli, etc. See, for instance, the utilitarian philosopher Peter Singer, whose 1974 *Animal Liberation* is more or less the bible of the modern animal-rights movement:

> It would be nonsense to say that it was not in the interests of a stone to be kicked along the road by a schoolboy. A stone does not have interests because it cannot suffer. Nothing that we can do to it could possibly make any difference to its welfare. A mouse, on the other hand, does have an interest in not being kicked along the road, because it will suffer if it is.

Another alternative is to put the lobster in cold saltwater and then very slowly bring it up to a full boil. Cooks who advocate this method are going on the analogy to a frog, which can supposedly be kept from jumping out of a boiling pot by heating the water incrementally. In order to save a lot of research-summarizing, I'll simply assure you that the analogy between frogs and lobsters turns out not to hold—plus, if the kettle's water isn't aerated seawater, the immersed lobster suffers from slow suffocation, although usually not decisive enough suffocation to keep it from still thrashing and clattering when the water gets hot enough to kill it. In fact, lobsters boiled incrementally often display a whole bonus set of gruesome, convulsionlike reactions that you don't see in regular boiling.

Ultimately, the only certain virtues of the home-lobotomy and slow-heating methods are comparative, because there are even worse/crueler ways people prepare lobster. Time-thrifty cooks sometimes microwave them alive (usually after poking several vent-holes in the carapace, which is a precaution most shellfish-microwavers learn about the hard way). Live dismemberment, on the other hand, is big in Europe—some chefs cut the lobster in half before cooking; others like to tear off the claws and tail and toss only these parts into the pot. 25

And there's more unhappy news respecting suffering-criterion number one. Lobsters don't have much in the way of eyesight or hearing, but they do have an exquisite tactile sense, one facilitated by hundreds of thousands of tiny hairs that protrude through their carapace. "Thus it is," in the words of T. M. Prudden's industry classic *About Lobster*, "that although encased in what seems a solid, impenetrable armor, the lobster can receive stimuli and impressions from without as readily as if it possessed a soft and delicate skin." And lobsters do have nociceptors,[18] as well as invertebrate versions of the prostaglandins and major neurotransmitters via which our own brains register pain.

Lobsters do not, on the other hand, appear to have the equipment for making or absorbing natural opioids like endorphins and enkephalins, which are what more advanced nervous systems use to try to handle intense pain. From this fact, though, one could conclude either that lobsters are maybe even *more* vulnerable to pain, since they lack mammalian nervous systems' built-in analgesia, or, instead, that the absence of natural opioids implies an absence of the really intense pain-sensations that natural opioids are designed to mitigate. I for one can detect a marked upswing in mood as I contemplate this latter possibility. It could be that their lack of endorphin/enkephalin hardware means that lobsters' raw subjective experience of pain is so radically different from mammals' that it may not even deserve the term "pain." Perhaps lobsters are more like those frontal-lobotomy patients one reads about who report experiencing pain in a totally different way than you and I. These patients evidently do feel physical pain, neurologically speaking, but don't dislike it—though neither do they like it; it's more that they feel it but don't feel anything *about* it—the point being that the pain is not distressing to them or something they want to get

[18]This is the neurological term for special pain-receptors that are "sensitive to potentially damaging extremes of temperature, to mechanical forces, and to chemical substances which are released when body tissues are damaged."

away from. Maybe lobsters, who are also without frontal lobes, are detached from the neurological-registration-of-injury-or-hazard we call pain in just the same way. There is, after all, a difference between (1) pain as a purely neurological event, and (2) actual suffering, which seems crucially to involve an emotional component, an awareness of pain as unpleasant, as something to fear/dislike/want to avoid.

Still, after all the abstract intellection, there remain the facts of the frantically clanking lid, the pathetic clinging to the edge of the pot. Standing at the stove, it is hard to deny in any meaningful way that this is a living creature experiencing pain and wishing to avoid/escape the painful experience. To my lay mind, the lobster's behavior in the kettle appears to be the expression of a *preference*; and it may well be that an ability to form preferences is the decisive criterion for real suffering.[19] The logic of this (preference → suffering) relation may be easiest to see in the negative case. If you cut certain kinds of worms in half, the halves will often keep crawling around and going about their vermiform business as if nothing had happened. When we assert, based on their post-op behavior, that these worms appear not to be suffering, what we're really saying is that there's no sign the worms know anything bad has happened or would *prefer* not to have gotten cut in half.

Lobsters, though, are known to exhibit preferences. Experiments have shown that they can detect changes of only a degree or two in water temperature; one reason for their complex migratory cycles (which can often cover 100-plus miles a year) is to pursue the temperatures they like best.[20] And, as mentioned, they're bottom-dwellers and do not like bright light—if a tank of food-lobsters is out in the sunlight or a store's fluorescence, the lobsters will always congregate in whatever part is darkest. Fairly solitary in the ocean, they also clearly dislike the crowding that's part of their captivity in tanks, since (as also mentioned) one reason why lobsters' claws are banded on capture is to keep them from attacking one another under the stress of close-quarter storage.

---

[19]"Preference" is maybe roughly synonymous with "interests," but it is a better term for our purposes because it's less abstractly philosophical—"preference" seems more personal, and it's the whole idea of a living creature's personal experience that's at issue.

[20]Of course, the most common sort of counterargument here would begin by objecting that "like best" is really just a metaphor, and a misleadingly anthropomorphic one at that. The counterarguer would posit that the lobster seeks to maintain a certain optimal ambient temperature out of nothing but unconscious instinct (with a similar explanation for the low-light affinities upcoming in the main text). The thrust of such a counterargument will be that the lobster's thrashings and clankings in the kettle express not unpreferred pain but involuntary reflexes, like your leg shooting out when the doctor hits your knee. Be advised that there are professional scientists, including many researchers who use animals in experiments, who hold to the view that nonhuman creatures have no real feelings at all, merely "behaviors." Be further advised that this view has a long history that goes all the way back to Descartes, although its modern support comes mostly from behaviorist psychology.

To these what-looks-like-pain-is-really-just-reflexes counterarguments, however, there happen to be all sorts of scientific and pro-animal rights counter-counterarguments. And then further attempted rebuttals and redirects, and so on. Suffice it to say that both the scientific and the philosophical arguments on either side of the animal-suffering issue are involved, abstruse, technical, often informed by self-interest or ideology, and in the end so totally inconclusive that as a practical matter, in the kitchen or restaurant, it all still seems to come down to individual conscience, going with (no pun) your gut.

In any event, at the MLF, standing by the bubbling tanks outside the World's Largest Lobster Cooker, watching the fresh-caught lobsters pile over one another, wave their hobbled claws impotently, huddle in the rear corners, or scrabble frantically back from the glass as you approach, it is difficult not to sense that they're unhappy, or frightened, even if it's some rudimentary version of these feelings . . . and, again, why does rudimentariness even enter into it? Why is a primitive, inarticulate form of suffering less urgent or uncomfortable for the person who's helping to inflict it by paying for the food it results in? I'm not trying to give you a PETA-like screed here—at least I don't think so. I'm trying, rather, to work out and articulate some of the troubling questions that arise amid all the laughter and saltation and community pride of the Maine Lobster Festival. The truth is that if you, the festival attendee, permit yourself to think that lobsters can suffer and would rather not, the MLF begins to take on the aspect of something like a Roman circus or medieval torture-fest.

Does that comparison seem a bit much? If so, exactly why? Or what about this one: Is it possible that future generations will regard our present agribusiness and eating practices in much the same way we now view Nero's entertainments or Mengele's experiments? My own initial reaction is that such a comparison is hysterical, extreme—and yet the reason it seems extreme to me appears to be that I believe animals are less morally important than human beings;[21] and when it comes to defending such a belief, even to myself, I have to acknowledge that (a) I have an obvious selfish interest in this belief, since I like to eat certain kinds of animals and want to be able to keep doing it, and (b) I haven't succeeded in working out any sort of personal ethical system in which the belief is truly defensible instead of just selfishly convenient. 30

Given this article's venue and my own lack of culinary sophistication, I'm curious about whether the reader can identify with any of these reactions and acknowledgments and discomforts. I'm also concerned not to come off as shrill or preachy when what I really am is more like confused. For those *Gourmet* readers who enjoy well-prepared and -presented meals involving beef, veal, lamb, pork, chicken, lobster, etc.: Do you think much about the (possible) moral status and (probable) suffering of the animals involved? If you do, what ethical convictions have you worked out that permit you not just to eat but to savor and enjoy flesh-based viands (since of course refined *enjoyment*, rather than mere ingestion, is the whole point of gastronomy)? If, on the other hand, you'll have no truck with confusions or convictions and regard stuff like the previous paragraph as just so much fatuous navel-gazing, what makes it feel truly okay, inside, to just dismiss the whole thing out of hand? That is, is your refusal to think about any of this the product of actual thought, or is it just that you don't want to think about it? And if the latter, then why not? Do

[21]Meaning *a lot* less important, apparently, since the moral comparison here is not the value of one human's life vs. the value of one animal's life, but rather the value of one animal's life vs. the value of one human's taste for a particular kind of protein. Even the most diehard carniphile will acknowledge that it's possible to live and eat well without consuming animals.

you ever think, even idly, about the possible reasons for your reluctance to think about it? I am not trying to bait anyone here—I'm genuinely curious. After all, isn't being extra aware and attentive and thoughtful about one's food and its overall context part of what distinguishes a real gourmet? Or is all the gourmet's extra attention and sensibility just supposed to be sensuous? Is it really all just a matter of taste and presentation?

These last few queries, though, while sincere, obviously involve much larger and more abstract questions about the connections (if any) between aesthetics and morality—about what the adjective in a phrase like "The Magazine of Good Living" is really supposed to mean—and these questions lead straightaway into such deep and treacherous waters that it's probably best to stop the public discussion right here. There are limits to what even interested persons can ask of each other.

Questions for Critical Reading

1. How does Wallace feel about eating lobsters? As you reread, mark passages that reveal his position on the issue. Does it shift through the essay?
2. Wallace asks, "Is it all right to boil a sentient creature alive just for our gustatory pleasure?" (p. 410). Answer this question for yourself, and then as you review Wallace's essay, locate quotations that support your position.
3. **Multimodal.** Vine was an app that allowed users to make and share six-second looping videos. Recreate this effect using your phone or another video recording device to consider Wallace's discussion of *preference*, which he turns to near the end of his essay. Read this section again closely and then make a six-second video that addresses the following questions: What does Wallace mean by *preference*? What role does it play in his overall argument?

Exploring Context

1. Explore the website for the Maine Lobster Festival (mainelobsterfestival.com). How do both the design and content of the site reflect Wallace's experience attending the festival? Is there anything on the site that addresses the ethical concerns that Wallace raises? Why would the organizers of the festival include or omit such information? Why do you think Wallace raises these concerns?
2. Watch the YouTube video "How to Boil a Live Maine Lobster" by Dan "The Lobster Man" of Lobster Gram. How does Wallace's essay change your reaction to this video? In what ways does the video address Wallace's points about lobsters? Incorporate your response to Question 2 of Questions for Critical Reading.
3. Wallace's essay was originally published in *Gourmet* magazine. Visit Epicurious (epicurious.com), a website with a similar audience. Based on what you find there, how do you think Wallace's original audience reacted to his essay? Why might he have written the essay with this style, focus, and content for such a magazine?

Questions for Connecting

1. Francis Fukuyama, in "Human Dignity" (p. 137), suggests that Factor X plays a role in what we choose to "cook, eat, torture, enslave, or render" (p. 138). Using his ideas about human dignity and Wallace's ideas about lobsters, preference, and pain, formulate ethical guidelines for food. How do we determine which creatures we can ethically eat? Draw from you work on preference in Question 3 of Questions for Critical Reading as well as your responses to the other questions in that section.
2. Sharon Moalem, in "Changing Our Genes: How Trauma, Bullying, and Royal Jelly Alter Our Genetic Destiny" (p. 289), suggests there is evidence that what we eat impacts our genetic expression. Connect his ideas to Wallace's analysis. What other factors should we consider when formulating an ideal diet?
3. Using ideas from Yo-Yo Ma's "Necessary Edges: Arts, Empathy, and Education" (p. 278), discuss the role that empathy plays in decisions about what we eat. What mode of thinking determines our choice of food? Would more empathetic thinking change our approach to eating?

Language Matters

1. Wallace's writing makes frequent use of footnotes. How do they function in his text? When should you use footnotes in your own writing? In considering your response, also review the proper format for footnotes using a grammar handbook or other reliable reference resource.
2. Narrowing one's topic can be a challenge, even for writers like Wallace. Imagine a "research pyramid" for this essay, with the broadest category at the bottom and the most ridiculously specific one at the top point of the pyramid. How many different levels can you find for this essay? Would the essay have been as strong if it were less or more specific? Why did Wallace choose this level of the pyramid for his work?
3. Imagine you could invite Wallace into the discussion in your classroom. What questions would you want to ask him about this essay? Use that experience to think about larger issues. What are the limits of written discourse? How might you anticipate your audience's questions when you write?

Assignments for Writing

1. Wallace asks, "Is it possible that future generations will regard our present agribusiness and eating practices in much the same way we now view Nero's entertainments or Mengele's experiments?" (p. 415). Write a paper in which you address Wallace's query. Rather than answering Wallace's question about an admittedly extreme future with a *yes* or *no*, consider instead the implications of his scenario as you build an argument that articulates how we might define an ethics of creature-based food.

2. Using Wallace for support, take the point of view of either a committed meat eater or a committed vegetarian, arguing your position by drawing on food-related issues such as health, hunger, and treatment of animals. Locate support for your position in Wallace's essay.

3. Wallace suggests an ethics built on "preference" — lobsters, that is, clearly would prefer not to be boiled alive. Evaluate the possibility of a preference-based ethics by locating your own example and connecting it to Wallace's discussion of suffering in animals. Is preference sufficient to make moral and ethical decisions? Can it be expanded to other ethical situations or is it limited to questions of food? You may also want to draw on your work in Questions 1 and 2 of Questions for Connecting.

ETHAN WATTERS

Journalist **Ethan Watters** is the author of *Urban Tribes: A Generation Redefines Friendship, Family, and Commitment* (2003); *Crazy Like Us: The Globalization of the American Psyche* (2010); and, with Richard Ofshe, *Therapy's Delusions: The Myth of the Unconscious and the Exploitation of Today's Walking Worried* (1999). His writing has appeared in such varied magazines as the *New York Times Magazine*, *Wired*, *Details*, *Spin*, and *Pacific Standard*.

Pacific Standard magazine was first published in 2008 under the name *Miller-McCune* for its publisher, the nonprofit Miller-McCune Center for Research, Media, and Public Policy. In keeping with its new name, the magazine seeks to cover stories from a West Coast perspective. Subtitled *The Science of Society*, the magazine covers topics as diverse as politics, health, nature, technology, and culture. On February 25, 2013, the online edition of the magazine published "Being WEIRD: How Culture Shapes the Mind," a featured culture article.

In "Being WEIRD: How Culture Shapes the Mind," Watters looks at the work of anthropologist Joe Henrich, whose work with the "ultimatum game" experiment in isolated small-scale communities around the world revealed that much of what social scientists, economists, and psychologists assumed to be "universal" human behavior was in fact a reflection of a distinctly Western psyche. Henrich and his colleagues use this work and other research to argue that Westerners are *WEIRD*: Western, educated, industrialized, rich, and democratic. Far from serving as examples of the universal, Americans (who form the subjects of many experiments in fields such as psychology) are the "weirdest" of all, with responses indicating that they are the outliers among the outliers. Watters examines the implications of these claims, which threaten the foundation of many disciplines.

Are there universal traits to the human mind? How can we discover them?

- TAGS: *community, culture, economics, education, globalism, psychology*
- CONNECTIONS: *Appiah, Das, Epstein, Fukuyama, Gilbert, Holmes, Konnikova, Lukianoff and Haidt, Ma, Serano, Southan, Turkle, von Busch, Wallace*

Being WEIRD: How Culture Shapes the Mind

In the summer of 1995, a young graduate student in anthropology at UCLA named Joe Henrich traveled to Peru to carry out some fieldwork among the Machiguenga, an indigenous people who live north of Machu Picchu in the Amazon basin. The Machiguenga had traditionally been horticulturalists who lived in single-family, thatch-roofed houses in small hamlets composed of clusters of extended families. For sustenance, they relied on local game and produce from small-scale farming. They shared with their kin but rarely traded with outside groups.

While the setting was fairly typical for an anthropologist, Henrich's research was not. Rather than practice traditional ethnography, he decided to run a behavioral experiment that had been developed by economists. Henrich used a "game"—along the lines of the famous prisoner's dilemma—to see whether isolated cultures shared with the West the same basic instinct for fairness.[1] In doing so, Henrich expected to confirm one of the foundational assumptions underlying such experiments, and indeed underpinning the entire fields of economics and psychology: that humans all share the same cognitive machinery—the same evolved rational and psychological hardwiring.

The test that Henrich introduced to the Machiguenga was called the ultimatum game. The rules are simple: In each game there are two players who remain anonymous to each other. The first player is given an amount of money, say $100, and told that he has to offer some of the cash, in an amount of his choosing, to the other subject. The second player can accept or refuse the split. But there's a hitch: Players know that if the recipient refuses the offer, both leave empty-handed. North Americans, who are the most common subjects for such experiments, usually offer a 50-50 split when on the giving end. When on the receiving end, they show an eagerness to punish the other player for uneven splits at their own expense. In short, Americans show the tendency to be equitable with strangers—and to punish those who are not.

Among the Machiguenga, word quickly spread of the young, square-jawed visitor from America giving away money. The stakes Henrich used in the game with the Machiguenga were not insubstantial—roughly equivalent to the few days' wages they sometimes earned from episodic work with logging or oil companies. So Henrich had no problem finding volunteers. What he had great difficulty with, however, was explaining the rules, as the game struck the Machiguenga as deeply odd.

When he began to run the game it became immediately clear that Machiguengan behavior was dramatically different from that of the average North American. To begin with, the offers from the first player were much lower. In addition, when on the receiving end of the game, the Machiguenga rarely refused even the lowest possible amount. "It just seemed ridiculous to the Machiguenga that you would reject an offer of free money," says Henrich. "They just didn't understand why anyone would sacrifice money to punish someone who had the good luck of getting to play the other role in the game."

The potential implications of the unexpected results were quickly apparent to Henrich. He knew that a vast amount of scholarly literature in the social sciences—particularly in economics and psychology—relied on the ultimatum game and similar experiments. At the heart of most of that research was the implicit assumption that the results revealed evolved psychological traits common to all humans, never mind that the test subjects were nearly always from the industrialized West. Henrich realized that if the Machiguenga results stood up, and if similar differences could be measured across other populations, this assumption of universality would have to be challenged.

What other certainties about "human nature" in social science research would need to be reconsidered when tested across diverse populations?

Henrich had thought he would be adding a small branch to an established tree of knowledge. It turned out he was sawing at the very trunk. He began to wonder: What other certainties about "human nature" in social science research would need to be reconsidered when tested across diverse populations?

Henrich soon landed a grant from the MacArthur Foundation to take his fairness games on the road. With the help of a dozen other colleagues he led a study of fourteen other small-scale societies, in locales from Tanzania to Indonesia. Differences abounded in the behavior of both players in the ultimatum game. In no society did he find people who were purely selfish (that is, who always offered the lowest amount, and never refused a split), but average offers from place to place varied widely and, in some societies—ones where gift-giving is heavily used to curry favor or gain allegiance—the first player would often make overly generous offers in excess of 60 percent, and the second player would often reject them, behaviors almost never observed among Americans.

The research established Henrich as an up-and-coming scholar. In 2004, he was given the U.S. Presidential Early Career Award for young scientists at the White House. But his work also made him a controversial figure. When he presented his research to the anthropology department at the University of British Columbia during a job interview a year later, he recalls a hostile reception. Anthropology is the social science most interested in cultural differences, but the young scholar's methods of using games and statistics to test and compare cultures with the West seemed heavy-handed and invasive to some. "Professors from the anthropology department suggested it was a bad thing that I was doing," Henrich remembers. "The word 'unethical' came up."

10 So instead of toeing the line, he switched teams. A few well-placed people at the University of British Columbia saw great promise in Henrich's work and created a position for him, split between the economics department and the psychology department. It was in the psychology department that he found two kindred spirits in Steven Heine and Ara Norenzayan. Together the three set about writing a paper that they hoped would fundamentally challenge the way social scientists thought about human behavior, cognition, and culture.

A modern liberal arts education gives lots of lip service to the idea of cultural diversity. It's generally agreed that all of us see the world in ways that are sometimes socially and culturally constructed, that pluralism is good, and that ethnocentrism is bad. But beyond that the ideas get muddy. That we should welcome and celebrate people of all backgrounds seems obvious, but the implied corollary—that people from different ethno-cultural origins have particular attributes that add spice to the body politic—becomes more problematic. To avoid stereotyping, it is rarely stated bluntly just exactly what those culturally derived qualities might be. Challenge liberal arts graduates on their appreciation of cultural diversity and you'll often find them retreating to the anodyne notion that under the skin everyone is really alike.

If you take a broad look at the social science curriculum of the last few decades, it becomes a little more clear why modern graduates are so unmoored. The last generation or two of undergraduates have largely been taught by a cohort of social scientists busily doing penance for the racism and Eurocentrism of their predecessors, albeit in different ways. Many anthropologists took to the navel gazing of postmodernism and swore off attempts at rationality and science, which were disparaged as weapons of cultural imperialism.

Economists and psychologists, for their part, did an end run around the issue with the convenient assumption that their job was to study the human mind stripped of culture. The human brain is genetically comparable around the globe, it was agreed, so human hardwiring for much behavior, perception, and cognition should be similarly universal. No need, in that case, to look beyond the convenient population of undergraduates for test subjects. A 2008 survey of the top six psychology journals dramatically shows how common that assumption was: More than 96 percent of the subjects tested in psychological studies from 2003 to 2007 were Westerners—with nearly 70 percent from the United States alone. Put another way: 96 percent of human subjects in these studies came from countries that represent only 12 percent of the world's population.

Henrich's work with the ultimatum game was an example of a small but growing countertrend in the social sciences, one in which researchers look straight at the question of how deeply culture shapes human cognition. His new colleagues in the psychology department, Heine and Norenzayan, were also part of this trend. Heine focused on the different ways people in Western and Eastern cultures perceived the world, reasoned, and understood themselves in relationship to others. Norenzayan's research focused on the ways religious belief influenced bonding and behavior. The three began to compile examples of cross-cultural research that, like Henrich's work with the Machiguenga, challenged long-held assumptions of human psychological universality.

15 Some of that research went back a generation. It was in the 1960s, for instance, that researchers discovered that aspects of visual perception were different from place to place. One of the classics of the literature, the Müller-Lyer illusion, showed that where you grew up would determine to what degree you would fall prey to the illusion that [the] two lines [in the figure on p. 426] are different in length.[2]

Researchers found that Americans perceive the line with the ends feathered outward (B) as being longer than the line with the arrow tips (A). San foragers of the Kalahari, on the other hand, were more likely to see the lines as they are: equal in length. Subjects from more than a dozen cultures were tested, and Americans were at the far end of the distribution—seeing the illusion more dramatically than all others.

More recently psychologists had challenged the universality of research done in the 1950s by pioneering social psychologist Solomon Asch. Asch had discovered that test subjects were often willing to make incorrect judgments on simple perception tests to conform with group pressure. When the test was performed across seventeen societies, however, it turned out that group pressure had a range of influence. Americans were again at the far end of the scale, in this case showing the least tendency to conform to group belief.

As Heine, Norenzayan, and Henrich furthered their search, they began to find research suggesting wide cultural differences almost everywhere they looked: in spatial reasoning, the way we infer the motivations of others, categorization, moral reasoning, the boundaries between the self and others, and other arenas. These differences, they believed, were not genetic. The distinct ways Americans and Machiguengans played the ultimatum game, for instance, wasn't because they had differently evolved brains. Rather, Americans, without fully realizing it, were manifesting a psychological tendency shared with people in other industrialized countries that had been refined and handed down through thousands of generations in ever more complex market economies. When people are constantly doing business with strangers, it helps when they have the desire to go out of their way (with a lawsuit, a call to the Better Business Bureau, or a bad Yelp review) when they feel cheated. Because Machiguengan culture had a different history, their gut feeling about what was fair was distinctly their own. In the small-scale societies with a strong culture of gift-giving, yet another conception of fairness prevailed. There, generous financial offers were turned down because people's minds had been shaped by a cultural norm that taught them that the acceptance of generous gifts brought burdensome obligations. Our economies hadn't been shaped by our sense of fairness; it was the other way around.

The growing body of cross-cultural research that the three researchers were compiling suggested that the mind's capacity to mold itself to cultural and environmental settings was far greater than had been assumed. The most interesting thing about cultures may not be in the observable things they do—the rituals, eating preferences, codes of behavior, and the like—but in the way they mold our most fundamental conscious and unconscious thinking and perception.

For instance, the different ways people perceive the Müller-Lyer illusion likely reflects lifetimes spent in different physical environments. American children, for the most part, grow up in box-shaped rooms of varying dimensions. Surrounded by carpentered corners, visual perception adapts to this strange new environment (strange and new in terms of human history, that is) by learning to perceive converging lines in three dimensions. 20

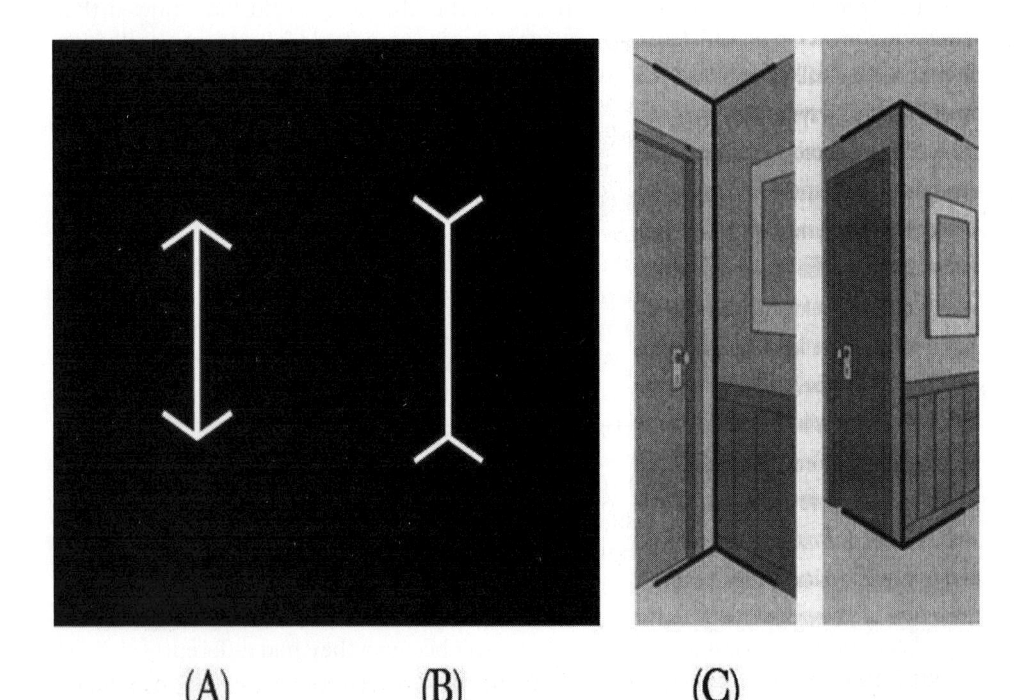

When unconsciously translated in three dimensions, the line with the outward-feathered ends (C) appears farther away and the brain therefore judges it to be longer. The more time one spends in natural environments, where there are no carpentered corners, the less one sees the illusion.

As the three continued their work, they noticed something else that was remarkable: Again and again one group of people appeared to be particularly unusual when compared to other populations—with perceptions, behaviors, and motivations that were almost always sliding down one end of the human bell curve.

In the end they titled their paper "The Weirdest People in the World?"[3] By "weird" they meant both unusual and Western, Educated, Industrialized, Rich, and Democratic. It is not just our Western habits and cultural preferences that are different from the rest of the world, it appears. The very way we think about ourselves and others—and even the way we perceive reality—makes us distinct from other humans on the planet, not to mention from the vast majority of our ancestors. Among Westerners, the data showed that Americans were often the most unusual, leading the researchers to conclude that "American participants are exceptional even within the unusual population of Westerners—outliers among outliers."

Given the data, they concluded that social scientists could not possibly have picked a worse population from which to draw broad generalizations. Researchers had been doing the equivalent of studying penguins while believing that they were learning insights applicable to all birds.

Not long ago I met Henrich, Heine, and Norenzayan for dinner at a small French restaurant in Vancouver, British Columbia, to hear about the reception of their weird paper, which was published in the prestigious journal *Behavioral and Brain Sciences* in 2010. The trio of researchers are young—as professors go—good-humored family men. They recalled that they were nervous as the publication time approached. The paper basically suggested that much of what social scientists thought they knew about fundamental aspects of human cognition was likely only true of one small slice of humanity. They were making such a broadside challenge to whole libraries of research that they steeled themselves to the possibility of becoming outcasts in their own fields.

"We were scared," admitted Henrich. "We were warned that a lot of people were going to be upset."

"We were told we were going to get spit on," interjected Norenzayan.

"Yes," Henrich said. "That we'd go to conferences and no one was going to sit next to us at lunchtime."

Interestingly, they seemed much less concerned that they had used the pejorative acronym WEIRD to describe a significant slice of humanity, although they did admit that they could only have done so to describe their own group. "Really," said Henrich, "the only people we could have called weird are represented right here at this table."

Still, I had to wonder whether describing the Western mind, and the American mind in particular, as weird suggested that our cognition is not just different but somehow malformed or twisted. In their paper the trio pointed out cross-cultural studies that suggest that the "weird" Western mind is the most self-aggrandizing and egotistical on the planet: We are more likely to promote ourselves as individuals versus advancing as a group. WEIRD minds are also more analytic, possessing the tendency to telescope in on an object of interest rather than understanding that object in the context of what is around it.

The WEIRD mind also appears to be unique in terms of how it comes to understand and interact with the natural world. Studies show that Western urban children grow up so closed off in man-made environments that their brains never form a deep or complex connection to the natural world. While studying children from the U.S., researchers have suggested a developmental timeline for what is called "folkbiological reasoning." These studies posit that it is not until children are around seven years old that they stop projecting human qualities onto animals and begin to understand that humans are one animal among many. Compared to Yucatec Maya communities in Mexico, however, Western urban children appear to be developmentally delayed in this regard. Children who grow up constantly interacting with the natural world are much less likely to anthropomorphize other living things into late childhood.

Given that people living in WEIRD societies don't routinely encounter or interact with animals other than humans or pets, it's not surprising that they end up with a rather cartoonish understanding of the natural world. "Indeed," the report concluded, "studying the cognitive development of folkbiology in urban children would seem the equivalent of studying 'normal' physical growth in malnourished children."

During our dinner, I admitted to Heine, Henrich, and Norenzayan that the idea that I can only perceive reality through a distorted cultural lens was unnerving. For me the notion raised all sorts of metaphysical questions: Is my thinking so strange that I have little hope of understanding people from other cultures? Can I mold my own psyche or the psyches of my children to be less WEIRD and more able to think like the rest of the world? If I did, would I be happier?

Henrich reacted with mild concern that I was taking this research so personally. He had not intended, he told me, for his work to be read as postmodern self-help advice. "I think we're really interested in these questions for the questions' sake," he said.

The three insisted that their goal was not to say that one culturally shaped psychology was better or worse than another—only that we'll never truly understand human behavior and cognition until we expand the sample pool beyond its current small slice of humanity. Despite these assurances, however, I found it hard not to read a message between the lines of their research. When they write, for example, that weird children develop their understanding of the natural world in a "culturally and experientially impoverished environment" and that they are in this way the equivalent of "malnourished children," it's difficult to see this as a good thing.

The turn that Henrich, Heine, and Norenzayan are asking social scientists to make is not an easy one: Accounting for the influence of culture on cognition will be a herculean task. Cultures are not monolithic; they can be endlessly parsed. Ethnic backgrounds, religious beliefs, economic status, parenting styles, rural upbringing versus urban or suburban—there are hundreds of cultural differences that individually and in endless combinations influence our

Accounting for the influence of culture on cognition will be a herculean task.

conceptions of fairness, how we categorize things, our method of judging and decision making, and our deeply held beliefs about the nature of the self, among other aspects of our psychological makeup.

We are just at the beginning of learning how these fine-grained cultural differences affect our thinking. Recent research has shown that people in "tight" cultures, those with strong norms and low tolerance for deviant behavior (think India, Malaysia, and Pakistan), develop higher impulse control and more self-monitoring abilities than those from other places. Men raised in the honor culture of the American South have been shown to experience much larger surges of testosterone after insults than do Northerners. Research published late last year suggested psychological differences at the city level too. Compared to San Franciscans, Bostonians' internal sense of self-worth is more dependent on community status and financial and educational achievement. "A cultural difference doesn't have to be big to be important," Norenzayan said. "We're not just talking about comparing New York yuppies to the Dani tribesmen of Papua New Guinea."

As Norenzayan sees it, the last few generations of psychologists have suffered from "physics envy," and they need to get over it. The job, experimental psychologists often assumed, was to push past the content of people's thoughts and see the underlying universal hardware at work. "This is a deeply flawed way of studying human nature," Norenzayan told me, "because the content of our thoughts and their process are intertwined." In other words, if human cognition is shaped by cultural ideas and behavior, it can't be studied without taking into account what those ideas and behaviors are and how they are different from place to place.

This new approach suggests the possibility of reverse-engineering psychological research: Look at cultural content first, cognition and behavior second. Norenzayan's recent work on religious belief is perhaps the best example of the intellectual landscape that is now open for study. When Norenzayan became a student of psychology in 1994, four years after his family had moved from Lebanon to America, he was excited to study the effect of religion on human psychology. "I remember opening textbook after textbook and turning to the index and looking for the word 'religion,'" he told me, "Again and again the very word wouldn't be listed. This was shocking. How could psychology be the science of human behavior and have nothing to say about religion? Where I grew up you'd have to be in a coma not to notice the importance of religion on how people perceive themselves and the world around them."

Norenzayan became interested in how certain religious beliefs, handed down through generations, may have shaped human psychology to make possible the creation of large-scale societies. He has suggested that there may be a connection between the growth of religions that believe in "morally concerned deities"—that is, a god or gods who care if people are good or bad—and the evolution of large cities and nations. To be cooperative in large groups of relative strangers, in other words, might have required the shared belief that an all-powerful being was forever watching over your shoulder. 40

If religion was necessary in the development of large-scale societies, can large-scale societies survive without religion? Norenzayan points to parts of Scandinavia with atheist majorities that seem to be doing just fine. They may have climbed the ladder of religion and effectively kicked it away. Or perhaps, after a thousand years of religious belief, the idea of an unseen entity always watching your behavior remains in our culturally shaped thinking even after the belief in God dissipates or disappears.

Why, I asked Norenzayan, if religion might have been so central to human psychology, have researchers not delved into the topic? "Experimental psychologists are the weirdest of the weird," said Norenzayan. "They are almost the least religious academics, next to biologists. And because academics mostly talk amongst themselves, they could look around and say, 'No one who is important to me is religious, so this must not be very important.'" Indeed, almost every major theorist on human behavior in the last 100 years predicted that it was just a matter of time before religion was a vestige of the past. But the world persists in being a very religious place.

Henrich, Heine, and Norenzayan's fear of being ostracized after the publication of the WEIRD paper turned out to be misplaced. Response to the paper, both published and otherwise, has been nearly universally positive, with more than a few of their colleagues suggesting that the work will spark fundamental changes. "I have no doubt that this paper is going to change the social sciences," said Richard Nisbett, an eminent psychologist at the University of Michigan. "It just puts it all in one place and makes such a bold statement."

More remarkable still, after reading the paper, academics from other disciplines began to come forward with their own mea culpas. Commenting on the paper, two brain researchers from Northwestern University argued that the nascent field of neuroimaging had made the same mistake as psychologists, noting that 90 percent of neuroimaging studies were performed in Western countries.[4] Researchers in motor development similarly suggested that their discipline's body of research ignored how different child-rearing practices around the world can dramatically influence states of development.[5] Two psycholinguistics professors suggested that their colleagues had also made the same mistake: blithely assuming human homogeneity while focusing their research primarily on one rather small slice of humanity.[6]

At its heart, the challenge of the WEIRD paper is not simply to the field of experimental human research (do more cross-cultural studies!); it is a challenge to our Western conception of human nature. For some time now, the most widely accepted answer to the question of why humans, among all animals, have so successfully adapted to environments across the globe is that we have big brains with the ability to learn, improvise, and problem-solve. 45

Henrich has challenged this "cognitive niche" hypothesis with the "cultural niche" hypothesis. He notes that the amount of knowledge in any culture is far greater than the capacity of individuals to learn or figure it all out on their own. He suggests that individuals tap that cultural storehouse of knowledge simply by mimicking (often unconsciously) the behavior and ways of thinking of those around them. We shape a tool in a certain manner, adhere to a food taboo, or think about fairness in a particular way, not because we individually have figured out that behavior's adaptive value, but because we instinctively trust our culture to show us the way. When Henrich asked Fijian women why they avoided certain potentially toxic fish during pregnancy and breastfeeding, he found that many didn't know or had fanciful reasons. Regardless of their personal understanding, by mimicking this culturally adaptive behavior they were protecting their offspring. The unique trick of human psychology, these researchers suggest, might be this: Our big brains are evolved to let local culture lead us in life's dance.

Our big brains are evolved to let local culture lead us in life's dance.

The applications of this new way of looking at the human mind are still in the offing. Henrich suggests that his research about fairness might first be applied to anyone working in international relations or development. People are not "plug and play," as he puts it, and you cannot expect to drop a Western court system or form of government into another culture and expect it to work as it does back home. Those trying to use economic incentives to encourage sustainable land use will similarly need to understand local notions of fairness to have any chance of influencing behavior in predictable ways.

Because of our peculiarly Western way of thinking of ourselves as independent of others, this idea of the culturally shaped mind doesn't go down very easily. Perhaps the richest and most established vein of cultural psychology—that which compares Western and Eastern concepts of the self—goes to the heart of this problem. Heine has spent much of his career following the lead of a seminal paper published in 1991 by Hazel Rose Markus, of Stanford University, and Shinobu Kitayama, who is now at the University of Michigan.[7] Markus and Kitayama suggested that different cultures foster strikingly different views of the self, particularly along one axis: Some cultures regard the self as independent from others; others see the self as interdependent. The interdependent self—which is more the norm in East Asian countries, including Japan and China—connects itself with others in a social group and favors social harmony over self-expression. The independent self—which is most prominent in America—focuses on individual attributes and preferences and thinks of the self as existing apart from the group.

That we in the West develop brains that are wired to see ourselves as separate from others may also be connected to differences in how we reason, Heine argues. Unlike the vast majority of the world, Westerners (and Americans in particular) tend to reason analytically as opposed to holistically. That is, the American mind strives to figure out the world by taking it apart and examining its pieces. Show a Japanese and an American the same cartoon of an aquarium, and the American will remember details mostly about the moving fish while the Japanese observer will likely later be able to describe the seaweed, the bubbles, and other objects in the background. Shown another way, in a different test analytic Americans will do better on something called the "rod and frame" task, where one has to judge whether a line is vertical even though the frame around it is skewed. Americans see the line as apart from the frame, just as they see themselves as apart from the group.

50 Heine and others suggest that such differences may be the echoes of cultural activities and trends going back thousands of years. Whether you think of yourself as interdependent or independent may depend on whether your distant ancestors farmed rice (which required a great deal of shared labor and group cooperation) or herded animals (which rewarded individualism and aggression). Heine points to Nisbett at Michigan, who has argued that the analytic/holistic dichotomy in reasoning styles can be clearly seen, respectively, in Greek and Chinese philosophical writing dating back 2,500 years.[8] These psychological trends and tendencies may echo down generations, hundreds of years after the activity or situation that brought them into existence has disappeared or fundamentally changed.

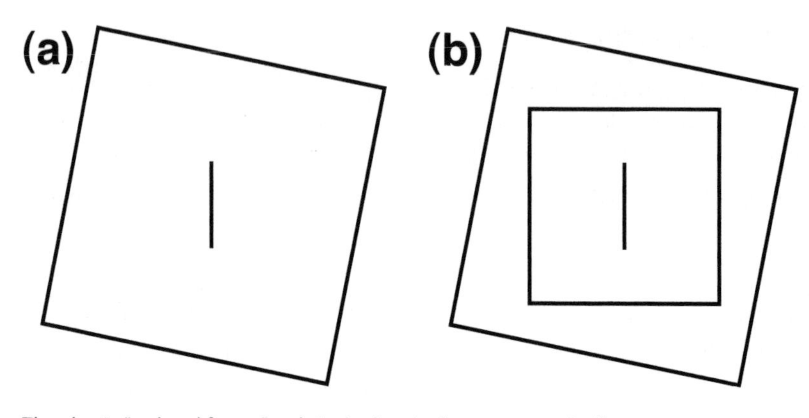

The classic "rod and frame" task: Is the line in the center vertical?

And here is the rub: The culturally shaped analytic/individualistic mind-sets may partly explain why Western researchers have so dramatically failed to take into account the interplay between culture and cognition. In the end, the goal of boiling down human psychology to hardwiring is not surprising given the type of mind that has been designing the studies. Taking an object (in this case the human mind) out of its context is, after all, what distinguishes the analytic reasoning style prevalent in the West. Similarly, we may have underestimated the impact of culture because the very ideas of being subject to the will of larger historical currents and of unconsciously mimicking the cognition of those around us challenges our Western conception of the self as independent and self-determined. The historical missteps of Western researchers, in other words, have been the predictable consequences of the WEIRD mind doing the thinking.

NOTES

1. *Stanford Encyclopedia of Philosophy*, s.v. "Prisoner's Dilemma," revised August 29, 2014, http://plato.stanford.edu/entries/prisoner-dilemma/.
2. "The Muller-Lyer Illusion," Rochester Institute of Technology, http://www.rit.edu/cla/gssp400/muller/muller.html.
3. Joseph Henrich, Steven J. Heine, and Ara Norenzayan, "The Weirdest People in the World?" *Behavioral and Brain Sciences* 33, no. 2–3 (June 2010): 61–83.
4. Joan Y. Chiao and Bobby K. Cheon, "The Weirdest Brains in the World," (Department of Psychology, Northwestern University), http://culturalneuro.psych.northwestern.edu/ChiaoCheon_BBS_inpress.pdf.
5. Lana B. Karasik et al., "WEIRD Walking: Cross-Cultural Research on Motor Development," *Behavioral and Brain Sciences* 33, no. 2–3 (June 2010): 95–96.
6. Asifa Majid and Stephen C. Levinson, "WEIRD Languages Have Misled Us, Too," *Behavioral and Brain Sciences* 33, no. 2–3 (June 2010): 103.
7. Hazel Rose Markus and Shinobu Kitayama, "Culture and the Self: Implications for Cognition, Emotion, and Motivation," *Psychological Review* 98 (1991): 224–253.
8. Richard E. Nisbett et al., "Culture and Systems of Thought: Holistic vs. Analytic Cognition," http://www-personal.umich.edu/~nisbett/images/cultureThought.pdf.

Questions for Critical Reading

1. **Multimodal.** According to Watters, why are Americans "weird"? Locate the definition of *WEIRD* in this context and then note the ways in which Americans are "weird." Make a collage, in print or digitally, using images that represent this definition of *weird*.

2. How does culture shape the human mind? As you reread, note specific examples that show how culture affects cognition.

3. How do Western and Eastern notions of the self differ? Pay attention to Watters's discussion of this distinction. How do these different notions of the self contribute to the problems that Watters traces?

Exploring Context

1. Visit Joe Henrich's website at www2.psych.ubc.ca/~henrich. How has he continued his work on the cultural dependence of seemingly universal traits? Connect the information you find there to Watters's argument.

2. Play the prisoner's dilemma game at serendip.brynmawr.edu/playground/pd.html. Do you feel your choices are shaped by your culture? How might the communities that Henrich studies play the game instead?

3. Using a search engine, find images of "cultural diversity." Do these images confirm Watters's claim that in education notions of cultural diversity rely on the idea that we're all the same underneath the skin?

Questions for Connecting

1. Anna Holmes also critiques "diversity" in her essay "Variety Show" (p. 217). Synthesize both authors' arguments concerning the notion of diversity. What must we do to overcome these challenges and promote a pluralistic culture? Use your work in Question 3 of Exploring Context.

2. In "Human Dignity" (p. 137) Francis Fukuyama claims that humans universally possess "Factor X." Assess his claim using Watters's argument. Does it rely on aspects of the mind that are "weird"? Is it possible to identify universal elements of the human mind?

3. How might Watters's insights be useful in fighting the spread of HIV/AIDS in Africa? Use his ideas about culture and cognition to consider campaigns against the disease as explained by Helen Epstein in "AIDS, Inc." (p. 123). You may want to use your work from Question 3 of Questions for Critical Reading in making your response.

Language Matters

1. How does culture shape language? Consider one aspect of language use in English and make an argument about how it reflects Western notions of the mind and self. How might this aspect of language be different in other cultures?

2. Why doesn't Watters use periods between the letters in the acronym *WEIRD*? Using a grammar handbook or other reliable reference resource, review the rules for acronyms. When should you use periods?

3. The choice of genre often controls the way in which content is presented. Create a summary of Watters's essay as a text message, as a tweet, and as an e-mail. In what ways does form control content?

Assignments for Writing

1. Watters notes that Henrich's findings challenge the notion of diversity as currently practiced in liberal education. Write a paper in which you propose a new model of cultural diversity that takes Henrich's argument into account. What role would Americans play in such a model? How can we promote cultural diversity in ways that aren't "weird"? Use your work from Question 3 of Exploring Context to support your argument.

2. Write a paper in which you examine the ways in which culture shapes thinking. How do cultural practices influence the way we see the world? Use your work from Question 2 of Questions for Critical Reading to help you make your argument.

3. Watters ends with a discussion of Eastern and Western notions of the self. Write a paper in which you synthesize these concepts to create a holistic notion of selfhood. Is the self ultimately independent, interdependent, or a combination of the two? Is it possible to define the self apart from culture? If so, what kind of culture could emerge from blending East and West?

WESLEY YANG

Wesley Yang is a contributing editor at both *Tablet* and *New York* magazines, with more than ten of his essays appearing in both the print and online editions of the latter. His varied articles on race, sexuality, and politics have also been published in noted magazines such as *Salon*, the *New York Observer*, and the *National*.

The May 16, 2011 issue of *New York* magazine, from which this selection was taken, was enveloped in the then-recent killing of Osama bin Laden, which had taken place just over two weeks prior, with blurbs about the event on the cover alongside feature pieces on Lady Gaga. But the cover image, one of Wesley Yang himself in stark closeup fading to white with his own words superimposed over the photo, signified that "Paper Tigers" was indeed the centerpiece of the issue.

In "Paper Tigers," Wesley Yang discusses his own experiences as an Asian American, tying them into the larger picture of Asians functioning in American society. Yang argues that while Asian Americans are indeed the most "successful" ethnic group in the country in terms of education and accumulation of wealth (often trumping the majority demographic—whites), there is a perception in popular culture that Asian Americans are "the products of a timid culture, easily pushed around by more assertive people" (p. 436). Yang asks us to consider the implications of stereotypes—even positive ones—and how they affect not only the viewing of other peoples, but the way those very people being stereotyped integrate into society.

What stereotypes have been applied to you? Is it possible for us to discard stereotypes altogether, especially in the face of continual evidence of their tendency toward misrepresentation?

▶ TAGS: *adolescence and adulthood, civil rights, community, culture, economics, education, identity, race and ethnicity*

▶ CONNECTIONS: *Appiah, Das, Gilbert, Holmes, Ma, Watters, Yoshino*

Paper Tigers

Sometimes I'll glimpse my reflection in a window and feel astonished by what I see. Jet-black hair. Slanted eyes. A pancake-flat surface of yellow-and-green-toned skin. An expression that is nearly reptilian in its impassivity. I've contrived to think of this face as the equal in beauty to any other. But what I feel in these moments is its strangeness to me. It's my face. I can't disclaim it. But what does it have to do with me?

Millions of Americans must feel estranged from their own faces. But every self-estranged individual is estranged in his own way. I, for instance, am the child of Korean immigrants, but I do not speak my parents' native tongue. I have never called my elders by the proper honorific, "big brother" or "big sister." I have never dated a Korean woman. I don't have a Korean friend. Though I am an immigrant, I have never wanted to strive like one.

You could say that I am, in the gently derisive parlance of Asian-Americans, a banana or a Twinkie (yellow on the outside, white on the inside). But while I don't believe our roots necessarily define us, I do believe there are racially inflected assumptions wired into our neural circuitry that we use to sort through the sea of faces we confront. And although I am in most respects devoid of Asian characteristics, I do have an Asian face.

Here is what I sometimes suspect my face signifies to other Americans: an invisible person, barely distinguishable from a mass of faces that resemble it. A conspicuous person standing apart from the crowd and yet devoid of any individuality. An icon of so much that the culture pretends to honor but that it in fact patronizes and exploits. Not just people "who are good at math" and play the violin, but a mass of stifled, repressed, abused, conformist quasi-robots who simply do not matter, socially or culturally.

5 I've always been of two minds about this sequence of stereotypes. On the one hand, it offends me greatly that anyone would think to apply them to me, or to anyone else, simply on the basis of facial characteristics. On the other hand, it also seems to me that there are a lot of Asian people to whom they apply.

Let me summarize my feelings toward Asian values: Fuck filial piety. Fuck grade-grubbing. Fuck Ivy League mania. Fuck deference to authority. Fuck humility and hard work. Fuck harmonious relations. Fuck sacrificing for the future. Fuck earnest, striving middle-class servility.

I understand the reasons Asian parents have raised a generation of children this way. Doctor, lawyer, accountant, engineer: These are good jobs open to whoever works hard enough. What could be wrong with that pursuit? Asians graduate from college at a rate higher than any other ethnic group in America, including whites. They earn a higher median family income than any other ethnic group in America, including whites. This is a stage in a triumphal narrative, and it is a narrative that is much shorter than many remember. Two thirds of the roughly 14 million Asian-Americans are foreign-born. There were less than 39,000 people of Korean descent living in America in 1970, when my elder brother was born. There are around 1 million today.

Asian-American success is typically taken to ratify the American Dream and to prove that minorities can make it in this country without handouts. Still, an undercurrent of racial panic always accompanies the consideration of Asians, and all the more so as China becomes the destination for our industrial base and the banker controlling our burgeoning debt. But if the armies of Chinese factory workers who make our fast fashion and iPads terrify us, and if the collective mass of high-achieving Asian-American students arouse an anxiety about the laxity of American parenting, what of the Asian-American who obeyed everything his parents told him? Does this person really scare anyone?

Earlier this year, the publication of Amy Chua's *Battle Hymn of the Tiger Mother* incited a collective airing out of many varieties of race-based hysteria. But absent from the millions of words written in response to the book was any serious consideration of whether Asian-Americans were in fact taking over this country. If it is true that they are collectively dominating in elite high schools and universities, is it also true that Asian-Americans are dominating in the real world? My strong suspicion was that this was not so, and that the reasons would not be hard to find. If we are a collective juggernaut that inspires such awe and fear, why does it seem that so many Asians are so readily perceived to be, as I myself have felt most of my life, the products of a timid culture, easily pushed around by more assertive people, and thus basically invisible?

A few months ago, I received an email from a young man named Jefferson Mao, who after attending Stuyvesant High School had recently graduated from the University of Chicago. He wanted my advice about "being an Asian writer." This is how he described himself: "I got good grades and I love literature and I want to be a writer and an intellectual; at the same time, I'm the first person in my family to go to college, my parents don't speak English very well, and we don't own the apartment in Flushing that we live in. I mean, I'm proud of my parents and my neighborhood and what I perceive to be my artistic potential or whatever, but sometimes I feel like I'm jumping the gun a generation or two too early." 10

One bright, cold Sunday afternoon, I ride the 7 train to its last stop in Flushing, where the storefront signs are all written in Chinese and the sidewalks are a slow-moving river of impassive faces. Mao is waiting for me at the entrance of the Main Street subway station, and together we walk to a nearby Vietnamese restaurant.

Mao has a round face, with eyes behind rectangular wire-frame glasses. Since graduating, he has been living with his parents, who emigrated from China when Mao was eight years old. His mother is a manicurist; his father is a physical therapist's aide. Lately, Mao has been making the familiar hour-and-a-half ride from Flushing to downtown Manhattan to tutor a white Stuyvesant freshman who lives in Tribeca. And what he feels, sometimes, in the presence of that amiable young man is a pang of regret. Now he understands better what he ought to have done back when he was a Stuyvesant freshman: "Worked half as hard and been twenty times more successful."

Entrance to Stuyvesant, one of the most competitive public high schools in the country, is determined solely by performance on a test: The top 3.7 percent of all New York City students who take the Specialized High Schools Admissions Test hoping to go to Stuyvesant are accepted. There are no set-asides for the underprivileged or, conversely, for alumni or other privileged groups. There is no formula to encourage "diversity" or any nebulous concept of "well-roundedness" or "character." Here we have something like pure meritocracy. This is what it looks like: Asian-Americans, who make up 12.6 percent of New York City, make up 72 percent of the high school.

This year, 569 Asian-Americans scored high enough to earn a slot at Stuyvesant, along with 179 whites, 13 Hispanics, and 12 blacks. Such dramatic overrepresentation, and what it may be read to imply about the intelligence of different groups of New Yorkers, has a way of making people uneasy. But intrinsic intelligence, of course, is precisely what Asians don't believe in. They believe—and have proved—that the constant practice of test-taking will improve the scores of whoever commits to it. All throughout Flushing, as well as in Bayside, one can find "cram schools," or storefront academies, that drill students in test preparation after school, on weekends, and during summer break. "Learning math is not about learning math," an instructor at one called Ivy Prep was quoted in the *New York Times* as saying. "It's about weightlifting. You are pumping the iron of math." Mao puts it more specifically: "You learn quite simply to nail any standardized test you take."

And so there is an additional concern accompanying the rise of the Tiger Children, one focused more on the narrowness of the educational experience a non-Asian child might receive in the company of fanatically preprofessional Asian students. Jenny Tsai, a student who was elected president of her class at the equally competitive New York public school Hunter College High School, remembers frequently hearing that 15 "the school was becoming too Asian, that they would be the downfall of our school." A couple of years ago, she revisited this issue in her senior thesis at Harvard, where she interviewed graduates of elite public schools and found that the white students regarded the Asian students with wariness. (She quotes a music teacher at Stuyvesant describing the dominance of Asians: "They were mediocre kids, but they got in because they were coached.") In 2005, the *Wall Street Journal* reported on "white flight" from a high school in Cupertino, California, that began soon after the children of Asian software engineers had made the place so brutally competitive that a B average could place you in the bottom third of the class.

Colleges have a way of correcting for this imbalance: The Princeton sociologist Thomas Espenshade has calculated that an Asian applicant must, in practice, score 140 points higher on the SAT than a comparable white applicant to have the same chance of admission. This is obviously unfair to the many qualified Asian individuals who are punished for the success of others with similar faces. Upper-middle-class white kids, after all, have their own elite private schools, and their own private tutors, far more expensive than the cram schools, to help them game the education system.

You could frame it, as some aggrieved Asian-Americans do, as a simple issue of equality and press for race-blind quantitative admissions standards. In 2006, a decade after California passed a voter initiative outlawing any racial engineering at the public universities, Asians composed 46 percent of UC–Berkeley's entering class; one could imagine a similar demographic reshuffling in the Ivy League, where Asian-Americans currently make up about 17 percent of undergraduates. But the Ivies, as we all know, have their own private institutional interests at stake in their admissions choices, including some that are arguably defensible. Who can seriously claim that a Harvard University that was 72 percent Asian would deliver the same grooming for elite status its students had gone there to receive?

Somewhere near the middle of his time at Stuyvesant, a vague sense of discontent started to emerge within Mao. He had always felt himself a part of a mob of "nameless, faceless Asian kids," who were "like a part of the décor of the place." He had been content to keep his head down and work toward the goal shared by everyone at Stuyvesant: Harvard. But around the beginning of his senior year, he began to wonder whether this march toward academic success was the only, or best, path.

"You can't help but feel like there must be another way," he explains over a bowl of phô. "It's like, we're being pitted against each other while there are kids out there in the Midwest who can do way less work and be in a garage band or something—and if they're decently intelligent and work decently hard in school . . ."

20 Mao began to study the racially inflected social hierarchies at Stuyvesant, where, in a survey undertaken by the student newspaper this year, slightly more than half of the respondents reported that their friends came from within their own ethnic group. His attention focused on the mostly white (and Manhattan-dwelling) group whose members seemed able to manage the crushing workload while still remaining socially active. "The general gist of most high-school movies is that the pretty cheerleader gets with the big dumb jock, and the nerd is left to bide his time in loneliness. But at some point in the future," he says, "the nerd is going to rule the world, and the dumb jock is going to work in a carwash.

"At Stuy, it's completely different: If you looked at the pinnacle, the girls and the guys are not only good-looking and socially affable, they also get the best grades and star in the school plays and win election to student government. It all converges at the top. It's like training for high society. It was jarring for us Chinese kids. You got the sense that you had to study hard, but it wasn't enough."

Mao was becoming clued in to the fact that there was another hierarchy behind the official one that explained why others were getting what he never had—"a high-school sweetheart" figured prominently on this list—and that this mysterious hierarchy was going to determine what happened to him in life. "You realize there are things you really don't understand about courtship or just acting in a certain way. Things that somehow come naturally to people who go to school in the suburbs and have parents who are culturally assimilated." I pressed him for specifics, and he mentioned that he had visited his white girlfriend's parents' house the past Christmas, where the family had "sat around cooking together and playing Scrabble." This ordinary vision of suburban-American domesticity lingered with Mao: Here, at last, was the setting in which all that implicit knowledge "about social norms and propriety" had been transmitted. There was no cram school that taught these lessons.

Before having heard from Mao, I had considered myself at worst lightly singed by the last embers of Asian alienation. Indeed, given all the incredibly hip Asian artists and fashion designers and so forth you can find in New York, it seemed that this feeling was destined to die out altogether. And yet here it was in a New Yorker more than a dozen years my junior. While it may be true that sections of the Asian-American world are devoid of alienation, there are large swaths where it is as alive as it has ever been.

A few weeks after we meet, Mao puts me in touch with Daniel Chu, his close friend from Stuyvesant. Chu graduated from Williams College last year, having won a creative-writing award for his poetry. He had spent a portion of the $18,000 prize on a trip to China, but now he is back living with his parents in Brooklyn Chinatown.

Chu remembers that during his first semester at Williams, his junior adviser would periodically take him aside. Was he feeling all right? Was something the matter? "I was acclimating myself to the place," he says. "I wasn't totally happy, but I wasn't depressed." But then his new white friends made similar remarks. "They would say, 'Dan, it's kind of hard, sometimes, to tell what you're thinking.'" 25

Chu has a pleasant face, but it would not be wrong to characterize his demeanor as reserved. He speaks in a quiet, unemphatic voice. He doesn't move his features much. He attributes these traits to the atmosphere in his household. "When you grow up in a Chinese home," he says, "you don't talk. You shut up and listen to what your parents tell you to do."

At Stuyvesant, he had hung out in an exclusively Asian world in which friends were determined by which subway lines you traveled. But when he arrived at Williams, Chu slowly became aware of something strange: The white people in the New England wilderness walked around smiling at each other. "When you're in a place like that, everyone is friendly."

He made a point to start smiling more. "It was something that I had to actively practice," he says. "Like, when you have a transaction at a business, you hand over the money—and then you smile." He says that he's made some progress but that there's still plenty of work that remains. "I'm trying to undo eighteen years of a Chinese upbringing. Four years at Williams helps, but only so much." He is conscious of how his father, an IT manager, is treated at work. "He's the best programmer at his office," he says, "but because he doesn't speak English well, he is always passed over."

Though Chu is not merely fluent in English but is officially the most distinguished poet of his class at Williams, he still worries that other aspects of his demeanor might attract the same kind of treatment his father received. "I'm really glad we're having this conversation," he says at one point—it is helpful to be remembering these lessons in self-presentation just as he prepares for job interviews.

30 "I guess what I would like is to become so good at something that my social deficiencies no longer matter," he tells me. Chu is a bright, diligent, impeccably credentialed young man born in the United States. He is optimistic about his ability to earn respect in the world. But he doubts he will ever feel the same comfort in his skin that he glimpsed in the people he met at Williams. That kind of comfort, he says—"I think it's generations away."

While he was still an electrical-engineering student at Berkeley in the nineties, James Hong visited the IBM campus for a series of interviews. An older Asian researcher looked over Hong's résumé and asked him some standard questions. Then he got up without saying a word and closed the door to his office.

"Listen," he told Hong, "I'm going to be honest with you. My generation came to this country because we wanted better for you kids. We did the best we could, leaving our homes and going to graduate school not speaking much English. If you take this job, you are just going to hit the same ceiling we did. They just see me as an Asian Ph.D., never management potential. You are going to get a job offer, but don't take it. Your generation has to go farther than we did, otherwise we did everything for nothing."

The researcher was talking about what some refer to as the "Bamboo Ceiling"—an invisible barrier that maintains a pyramidal racial structure throughout corporate America, with lots of Asians at junior levels, quite a few in middle management, and virtually none in the higher reaches of leadership.

The failure of Asian-Americans to become leaders in the white-collar workplace does not qualify as one of the burning social issues of our time. But it is a part of the bitter undercurrent of Asian-American life that so many Asian graduates of elite universities find that meritocracy as they have understood it comes to an abrupt end after graduation. If between 15 and 20 percent of every Ivy League class is Asian, and if the Ivy Leagues are incubators for the country's leaders, it would stand to reason that Asians would make up some corresponding portion of the leadership class.

It is a part of the bitter undercurrent of Asian-American life that so many Asian graduates of elite universities find that meritocracy as they have understood it comes to an abrupt end after graduation.

35 And yet the numbers tell a different story. According to a recent study, Asian-Americans represent roughly 5 percent of the population but only 0.3 percent of corporate officers, less than 1 percent of corporate board members, and around 2 percent of college presidents. There are nine Asian-American CEOs in the Fortune 500.

In specific fields where Asian-Americans are heavily represented, there is a similar asymmetry. A third of all software engineers in Silicon Valley are Asian, and yet they make up only 6 percent of board members and about 10 percent of corporate officers of the Bay Area's twenty-five largest companies. At the National Institutes of Health, where 21.5 percent of tenure-track scientists are Asians, only 4.7 percent of the lab or branch directors are, according to a study conducted in 2005. One succinct evocation of the situation appeared in the comments section of a website called Yellowworld: "If you're East Asian, you need to attend a top-tier university to land a good high-paying gig. Even if you land that good high-paying gig, the white guy with the pedigree from a mediocre state university will somehow move ahead of you in the ranks simply because he's white."

Jennifer W. Allyn, a managing director for diversity at PricewaterhouseCoopers, works to ensure that "all of the groups feel welcomed and supported and able to thrive and to go as far as their talents will take them." I posed to her the following definition of parity in the corporate workforce: If the current crop of associates is 17 percent Asian, then in fourteen years, when they have all been up for partner review, 17 percent of those who are offered partner will be Asian. Allyn conceded that PricewaterhouseCoopers was not close to reaching that benchmark anytime soon—and that "nobody else is either."

Part of the insidious nature of the Bamboo Ceiling is that it does not seem to be caused by overt racism. A survey of Asian-Pacific-American employees of Fortune 500 companies found that 80 percent reported they were judged not as Asians but as individuals. But only 51 percent reported the existence of Asians in key positions, and only 55 percent agreed that their firms were fully capitalizing on the talents and perspectives of Asians.

More likely, the discrepancy in these numbers is a matter of unconscious bias. Nobody would affirm the proposition that tall men are intrinsically better leaders, for instance. And yet while only 15 percent of the male population is at least six feet tall, 58 percent of all corporate CEOs are. Similarly, nobody would say that Asian people are unfit to be leaders. But subjects in a recently published psychological experiment consistently rated hypothetical employees with Caucasian-sounding names higher in leadership potential than identical ones with Asian names.

Maybe it is simply the case that a traditionally Asian upbringing is the problem. As Allyn points out, in order to be a leader, you must have followers. Associates at PricewaterhouseCoopers are initially judged on how well they do the work they are assigned. "You have to be a doer," as she puts it. They are expected to distinguish themselves with their diligence, at which point they become "super-doers." But being a leader requires different skill sets. "The traits that got you to where you are won't necessarily take you to the next level," says the diversity consultant Jane Hyun, who wrote a book called *Breaking the Bamboo Ceiling*. To become a leader requires taking personal initiative and thinking about how an organization can work differently. It also requires networking, self-promotion, and self-assertion. It's racist to think that any given Asian individual is unlikely to be creative or risk-taking. It's simple cultural observation to say that a group whose education has historically focused on rote memorization and "pumping the iron of math" is, on aggregate, unlikely to yield many people inclined to challenge authority or break with inherited ways of doing things.

Sach Takayasu had been one of the fastest-rising members of her cohort in the marketing department at IBM in New York. But about seven years ago, she felt her progress begin to slow. "I had gotten to the point where I was over delivering, working really long hours, and where doing more of the same wasn't getting me anywhere," she says. It was around this time that she attended a seminar being offered by an organization called Leadership Education for Asian Pacifics. 40

LEAP has parsed the complicated social dynamics responsible for the dearth of Asian-American leaders and has designed training programs that flatter Asian people even as it teaches them to change their behavior to suit white-American expectations. Asians who enter a LEAP program are constantly assured that they will be able to "keep your values, while acquiring new skills," along the way to becoming "culturally competent leaders."

In a presentation to 1,500 Asian-American employees of Microsoft, LEAP president and CEO J. D. Hokoyama laid out his grand synthesis of the Asian predicament in the workplace. "Sometimes people have perceptions about us and our communities which may or may not be true," Hokoyama told the audience. "But they put those perceptions onto us, and then they do something that can be very devastating: They make decisions about us not based on the truth but based on those perceptions." Hokoyama argued that it was not sufficient to rail at these unjust perceptions. In the end, Asian people themselves would have to assume responsibility for unmaking them. This was both a practical matter, he argued, and, in its own way, fair.

Aspiring Asian leaders had to become aware of "the relationship between values, behaviors, and perceptions." He offered the example of Asians who don't speak up at meetings. "So let's say I go to meetings with you and I notice you never say anything. And I ask myself, 'Hmm, I wonder why you're not saying anything. Maybe it's because you don't know what we're talking about. That would be a good reason for not saying anything. Or maybe it's because you're not even interested in the subject matter. Or maybe you think the conversation is beneath you.' So here I'm thinking, because you never say anything at meetings, that you're either dumb, you don't care, or you're arrogant. When maybe it's because you were taught when you were growing up that when the boss is talking, what are you supposed to be doing? Listening."

Takayasu took the weeklong course in 2006. One of the first exercises she encountered involved the group instructor asking for a list of some qualities that they identify with Asians. The students responded: upholding family honor, filial piety, self-restraint. Then the instructor solicited a list of the qualities the members identify with leadership, and invited the students to notice how little overlap there is between the two lists.

At first, Takayasu didn't relate to the others in attendance, who were listing typical Asian values their parents had taught them. "They were all saying things like 'Study hard,' 'Become a doctor or lawyer,' blah, blah, blah. That's not how my parents were. They would worry if they saw me working too hard." Takayasu had spent her childhood shuttling between New York and Tokyo. Her father was an executive at Mitsubishi; her mother was a concert pianist. She was highly assimilated into American culture, fluent in English, poised and confident. "But the more we got into it, as we moved away from the obvious things to the deeper, more fundamental values, I began to see that my upbringing had been very Asian after all. My parents would say, 'Don't create problems. Don't trouble other people.' How Asian is that? It helped to explain 45 why I don't reach out to other people for help." It occurred to Takayasu that she was a little bit "heads down" after all. She was willing to take on difficult assignments without seeking credit for herself. She was reluctant to "toot her own horn."

Takayasu has put her new self-awareness to work at IBM, and she now exhibits a newfound ability for horn tooting. "The things I could write on my résumé as my team's accomplishments: They're really impressive," she says.

The law professor and writer Tim Wu grew up in Canada with a white mother and a Taiwanese father, which allows him an interesting perspective on how whites and Asians perceive each other. After graduating from law school, he took a series of clerkships, and he remembers the subtle ways in which hierarchies were developed among the other young lawyers. "There is this automatic assumption in any legal environment that Asians will have a particular talent for bitter labor," he says, and then goes on to define the word *coolie*, a Chinese term for "bitter labor." "There was this weird self-selection where the Asians would migrate toward the most brutal part of the labor."

By contrast, the white lawyers he encountered had a knack for portraying themselves as above all that. "White people have this instinct that is really important: to give off the impression that they're only going to do the really important work. You're a quarterback. It's a kind of arrogance that Asians are trained not to have. Someone told me not long after I moved to New York that in order to succeed, you have to understand which rules you're supposed to break. If you break the wrong rules, you're finished. And so the easiest thing to do is follow all the rules. But then you consign yourself to a lower status. The real trick is understanding what rules are not meant for you."

This idea of a kind of rule-governed rule-breaking—where the rule book was unwritten but passed along in an innate cultural sense—is perhaps the best explanation I have heard of how the Bamboo Ceiling functions in practice. LEAP appears to be very good at helping Asian workers who are already culturally competent become more self-aware of how their culture and appearance impose barriers to advancement. But I am not sure that a LEAP course is going to be enough to get Jefferson Mao or Daniel Chu the respect and success they crave. The issue is more fundamental, the social dynamics at work more deeply embedded, and the remedial work required may be at a more basic level of comportment.

What if you missed out on the lessons in masculinity taught in the gyms and locker rooms of America's high schools? What if life has failed to make you a socially dominant alpha male who runs the American boardroom and prevails in the American bedroom? What if no one ever taught you how to greet white people and make them comfortable? What if, despite these deficiencies, you no longer possess an immigrant's dutiful forbearance for a secondary position in the American narrative and want to be a player in the scrimmage of American appetite right now, in the present? 50

How do you undo eighteen years of a Chinese upbringing?

This is the implicit question that J. T. Tran has posed to a roomful of Yale undergraduates at a master's tea at Silliman College. His answer is typically Asian: practice. Tran is a pickup artist who goes by the handle Asian Playboy. He travels the globe running "boot camps," mostly for Asian male students, in the art of attraction. Today, he has been invited to Yale by the Asian-American Students Alliance.

"Creepy can be fixed," Tran explains to the standing-room-only crowd. "Many guys just don't realize how to project themselves." These are the people whom Tran spends his days with, a new batch in a new city every week: nice guys, intelligent guys, motivated guys, who never figured out how to be successful with women. Their mothers had kept them at home to study rather than let them date or socialize. Now Tran's company, ABCs of Attraction, offers a remedial education that consists of three four-hour seminars, followed by a supervised night out "in the field," in which J. T., his assistant Gareth Jones, and a tall blonde wing-girl named Sarah force them to approach women. Tuition costs $1,450.

"One of the big things I see with Asian students is what I call the Asian poker face—the lack of range when it comes to facial expressions," Tran says. "How many times has this happened to you?" he asks the crowd. "You'll be out at a party with your white friends, and they will be like—'Dude, are you angry?'" Laughter fills the room. Part of it is psychological, he explains. He recalls one Korean-American student he was teaching. The student was a very dedicated schoolteacher who cared a lot about his students. But none of this was visible. "Sarah was trying to help him, and she was like, 'C'mon, smile, smile,' and he was like . . ." And here Tran mimes the unbearable tension of a face trying to contort itself into a simulacrum of mirth. "He was so completely unpracticed at smiling that he literally could not do it." Eventually, though, the student fought through it, "and when he finally got to smiling he was, like, really cool."

"Sarah was trying to help him, and she was like, 'C'mon, smile, smile,' and he was like . . ." And here Tran mimes the unbearable tension of a face trying to contort itself into a simulacrum of mirth.

55 Tran continues to lay out a story of Asian-American male distress that must be relevant to the lives of at least some of those who have packed Master Krauss's living room. The story he tells is one of Asian-American disadvantage in the sexual marketplace, a disadvantage that he has devoted his life to overturning. Yes, it is about picking up women. Yes, it is about picking up white women. Yes, it is about attracting those women whose hair is the color of the midday sun and eyes are the color of the ocean, and it is about having sex with them. He is not going to apologize for the images of blonde women plastered all over his website. This is what he prefers, what he stands for, and what he is selling: the courage to pursue anyone you want, and the skills to make the person you desire desire you back. White guys do what they want; he is going to do the same.

But it is about much more than this, too. It is about altering the perceptions of Asian men—perceptions that are rooted in the way they behave, which are in turn rooted in the way they were raised—through a course of behavior modification intended to teach them how to be the socially dominant figures that they are not perceived to be. It is a program of, as he puts it to me later, "social change through pickup."

Tran offers his own story as an exemplary Asian underdog. Short, not good-looking, socially inept, sexually null. "If I got a B, I would be whipped," he remembers of his childhood. After college, he worked as an aerospace engineer at Boeing and Raytheon, but internal politics disfavored him. Five years into his career, his entire white cohort had been promoted above him. "I knew I needed to learn about social dynamics, because just working hard wasn't cutting it."

His efforts at dating were likewise "a miserable failure." It was then that he turned to "the seduction community," a group of men on internet message boards like alt.seduction.fast. It began as a "support group for losers" and later turned into a program of self-improvement. Was charisma something you could teach? Could confidence be reduced to a formula? Was it merely something that you either possessed or did not possess, as a function of the experiences you had been through in life, or did it emerge from specific forms of behavior? The members of the group turned their computer-science and engineering brains to the question. They wrote long accounts of their dates and subjected them to collective scrutiny. They searched for patterns in the raw material and filtered these experiences through social-psychological research. They eventually built a model.

This past Valentine's Day, during a weekend boot camp in New York City sponsored by ABCs of Attraction, the model is being played out. Tran and Jones are teaching their students how an alpha male stands (shoulders thrown back, neck fully extended, legs planted slightly wider than the shoulders). "This is going to feel very strange to you if you're used to slouching, but this is actually right," Jones says. They explain how an alpha male walks (no shuffling; pick your feet up entirely off the ground; a slight sway in the shoulders). They identify the proper distance to stand from "targets" (a slightly bent arm's length). They explain the importance of "kino escalation." (You must touch her. You must not be afraid to do this.) They are teaching the importance of sub-communication: what you convey about yourself before a single word has been spoken. They explain the importance of intonation. They explain what intonation is. "Your voice moves up and down in pitch to convey a variety of different emotions."

60 All of this is taught through a series of exercises. "This is going to feel completely artificial," says Jones on the first day of training. "But I need you to do the biggest shit-eating grin you've ever made in your life." Sarah is standing in the corner with her back to the students—three Indian guys, including one in a turban, three Chinese guys, and one Cambodian. The students have to cross the room, walking as an alpha male walks, and then place their hands on her shoulder—firmly but gently—and turn her around. Big smile. Bigger than you've ever smiled before. Raise your glass in a toast. Make eye contact and hold it. Speak loudly and clearly. Take up space without apology. This is what an alpha male does.

Before each student crosses the floor of that bare white cubicle in midtown, Tran asks him a question. "What is good in life?" Tran shouts.

The student then replies, in the loudest, most emphatic voice he can muster: "To crush my enemies, see them driven before me, and to hear the lamentation of their women—in my bed!"

For the intonation exercise, students repeat the phrase "I do what I want" with a variety of different moods.

"Say it like you're happy!" Jones shouts. ("I do what I want.") Say it like you're sad! ("I do what I want." The intonation utterly unchanged.) Like you're sad! ("I . . . do what I want.") Say it like you've just won $5 million! ("I do what I want.")

65 Raj, a 26-year-old Indian virgin, can barely get his voice to alter during intonation exercise. But on Sunday night, on the last evening of the boot camp, I watch him cold-approach a set of women at the Hotel Gansevoort and engage them in conversation for a half-hour. He does not manage to "number close" or "kiss close." But he had done something that not very many people can do.

Of the dozens of Asian-Americans I spoke with for this story, many were successful artists and scientists; or good-looking and socially integrated leaders; or tough, brassy, risk-taking, street-smart entrepreneurs. Of course, there are lots of such people around—do I even have to point that out? They are no more morally worthy than any other kind of Asian person. But they have figured out some useful things.

The lesson about the Bamboo Ceiling that James Hong learned from his interviewer at IBM stuck, and after working for a few years at Hewlett-Packard, he decided to strike off on his own. His first attempts at entrepreneurialism failed, but he finally struck pay dirt with a simple, not terribly refined idea that had a strong primal appeal: hotornot.com. Hong and his co-founder eventually sold the site for roughly $20 million.

Hong ran hotornot.com partly as a kind of incubator to seed in his employees the habits that had served him well. "We used to hire engineers from Berkeley—almost all Asian—who were on the cusp of being entrepreneurial but were instead headed toward jobs at big companies," he says. "We would train them in how to take risk, how to run things themselves. I remember encouraging one employee to read *The Game*—the infamous pickup-artist textbook—"because I figured growing the *cojones* to take risk was applicable to being an entrepreneur."

If the Bamboo Ceiling is ever going to break, it's probably going to have less to do with any form of behavior assimilation than with the emergence of risk-takers whose success obviates the need for Asians to meet someone else's behavioral standard. People like Steve Chen, who was one of the creators of YouTube, or Kai and Charles Huang, who created Guitar Hero. Or Tony Hsieh, the founder of Zappos.com, the online shoe retailer that he sold to Amazon for about a billion dollars in 2009. Hsieh is a short Asian man who speaks tersely and is devoid of obvious charisma. One cannot imagine him being promoted in an American corporation. And yet he has proved that an awkward Asian guy can be a formidable CEO and the unlikeliest of management gurus.

Hsieh didn't have to conform to Western standards of comportment because he adopted early on the Western value of risk-taking. Growing up, he would play recordings of himself in the morning practicing the violin, in lieu of actually practicing. He credits the experience he had running a pizza business at Harvard as more important than anything he learned in class. He had an instinctive sense of what the real world would require of him, and he knew that nothing his parents were teaching him would get him there. 70

You don't, by the way, have to be a Silicon Valley hotshot to break through the Bamboo Ceiling. You can also be a chef like Eddie Huang, whose little restaurant on the Lower East Side, BaoHaus, sells delicious pork buns. Huang grew up in Orlando with a hard-core Tiger Mom and a disciplinarian father. "As a kid, psychologically, my day was all about not getting my ass kicked," he says. He gravitated toward the black kids at school, who also knew something about corporal punishment. He was the smallest member of his football team, but his coach named him MVP in the seventh grade. "I was defensive tackle and right guard because I was just mean. I was nasty. I had this mentality where I was like, 'You're going to accept me or I'm going to fuck you up.'"

Huang had a rough twenties, bumping repeatedly against the Bamboo Ceiling. In college, editors at the Orlando *Sentinel* invited him to write about sports for the paper. But when he visited the offices, "the editor came in and goes, 'Oh, no.' And his exact words: 'You can't write with that face.'" Later, in film class at Columbia, he wrote a script about an Asian-American hot-dog vendor obsessed with his small penis. "The screenwriting teacher was like, 'I love this. You have a lot of Woody Allen in you. But do you think you could change it to Jewish characters?'" Still later, after graduating from Cardozo School of Law, he took a corporate job, where other associates would frequently say, "You have a lot of opinions for an Asian guy."

Finally, Huang decided to open a restaurant. Selling food was precisely the fate his parents wanted their son to avoid, and they didn't talk to him for months after he quit lawyering. But Huang understood instinctively that he couldn't make it work in the professional world his parents wanted him to join. "I've realized that food is one of the only places in America where we are the top dogs," he says. "Guys like David Chang or me—we can hang. There's a younger generation that grew up eating Chinese fast food. They respect our food. They may not respect anything else, but they respect our food."

Rather than strive to make himself acceptable to the world, Huang has chosen to buy his way back in, on his own terms. "What I've learned is that America is about money, and if you can make your culture commodifiable, then you're relevant," he says. "I don't believe anybody agrees with what I say or supports what I do because they truly want to love Asian people. They like my fucking pork buns, and I don't get it twisted."

Sometime during the hundreds of hours he spent among the mostly untouched English-language novels at the Flushing branch of the public library, Jefferson Mao discovered literature's special power of transcendence, a freedom of imagination that can send you beyond the world's hierarchies. He had written to me seeking permission to swerve off the traditional path of professional striving—to devote himself to becoming an artist—but he was unsure of what risks he was willing to take. My answer was highly ambivalent. I recognized in him something of my own youthful ambition. And I knew where that had taken me. 75

Unlike Mao, I was not a poor, first-generation immigrant. I finished school alienated both from Asian culture (which, in my hometown, was barely visible) and the manners and mores of my white peers. But like Mao, I wanted to be an individual. I had refused both cultures as an act of self-assertion. An education spent dutifully acquiring credentials through relentless drilling seemed to me an obscenity. So did adopting the manipulative cheeriness that seemed to secure the popularity of white Americans.

Instead, I set about contriving to live beyond both poles. I wanted what James Baldwin sought as a writer—"a power which outlasts kingdoms." Anything short of that seemed a humiliating compromise. I would become an aristocrat of the spirit, who prides himself on his incompetence in the middling tasks that are the world's business. Who does not seek after material gain. Who is his own law.

This, of course, was madness. A child of Asian immigrants born into the suburbs of New Jersey and educated at Rutgers cannot be a law unto himself. The only way to approximate this is to refuse employment, because you will not be bossed around by people beneath you, and shave your expenses to the bone, because you cannot afford more, and move into a decaying Victorian mansion in Jersey City, so that your sense of eccentric distinction can be preserved in the midst of poverty, and cut yourself free of every form of bourgeois discipline, because these are precisely the habits that will keep you chained to the mediocre fate you consider worse than death.

Throughout my twenties, I proudly turned away from one institution of American life after another (for instance, a steady job), though they had already long since turned away from me. Academe seemed another kind of death—but then again, I had a transcript marred by as many F's as A's. I had come from a culture that was the middle path incarnate. And yet for some people, there can be no middle path, only transcendence or descent into the abyss.

I was descending into the abyss. 80

All this was well deserved. No one had any reason to think I was anything or anyone. And yet I felt entitled to demand this recognition. I knew this was wrong and impermissible; therefore I had to double down on it. The world brings low such people. It brought me low. I haven't had health insurance in ten years. I didn't earn more than $12,000 for eight consecutive years. I went three years in the prime of my adulthood without touching a woman. I did not produce a masterpiece.

I recall one of the strangest conversations I had in the city. A woman came up to me at a party and said she had been moved by a piece of writing I had published. She confessed that prior to reading it, she had never wanted to talk to me, and had always been sure, on the basis of what she could see from across the room that I was nobody worth talking to, that I was in fact someone to avoid.

But she had been wrong about this, she told me: It was now plain to her that I was a person with great reserves of feeling and insight. She did not ask my forgiveness for this brutal misjudgment. Instead, what she wanted to know was—why had I kept that person she had glimpsed in my essay so well hidden? She confessed something of her own hidden sorrow: She had never been beautiful and had decided, early on, that it therefore fell to her to "love the world twice as hard." Why hadn't I done that?

Here was a drunk white lady speaking what so many others over the years must have been insufficiently drunk to tell me. It was the key to many things that had, and had not, happened. I understood this encounter better after learning about LEAP, and visiting Asian Playboy's boot camp. If you are a woman who isn't beautiful, it is a social reality that you will have to work twice as hard to hold anyone's attention. You can either linger on the unfairness of this or you can get with the program. If you are an Asian person who holds himself proudly aloof, nobody will respect that, or find it intriguing, or wonder if that challenging façade hides someone worth getting to know. They will simply write you off as someone not worth the trouble of talking to.

Having glimpsed just how unacceptable the world judges my demeanor, could I too strive to make up for my shortcomings? Practice a shit-eating grin until it becomes natural? Love the world twice as hard? 85

I see the appeal of getting with the program. But this is not my choice. Striving to meet others' expectations may be a necessary cost of assimilation, but I am not going to do it.

Often I think my defiance is just delusional, self-glorifying bullshit that artists have always told themselves to compensate for their poverty and powerlessness. But sometimes I think it's the only thing that has preserved me intact, and that what has been preserved is not just haughty caprice but in fact the meaning of my life. So this is what I told Mao: In lieu of loving the world twice as hard, I care, in the end, about expressing my obdurate singularity at any cost. I love this hard and unyielding part of myself more than any other reward the world has to offer a newly brightened and ingratiating demeanor, and I will bear any costs associated with it.

The first step toward self-reform is to admit your deficiencies. Though my early adulthood has been a protracted education in them, I do not admit mine. I'm fine. It's the rest of you who have a problem. Fuck all y'all.

Amy Chua returned to Yale from a long, exhausting book tour in which one television interviewer had led off by noting that internet commenters were calling her a monster. By that point, she had become practiced at the special kind of self-presentation required of a person under public siege. "I do not think that Chinese parents are superior," she declared at the annual gathering of the Asian-American Students Alliance. "I think there are many ways to be a good parent."

Much of her talk to the students, and indeed much of the conversation surrounding the book, was focused on her own parenting decisions. But just as interesting is how her parents parented her. Chua was plainly the product of a brute-force Chinese education. *Battle Hymn of the Tiger Mother* includes many lessons she was taught by her parents—lessons any LEAP student would recognize. "Be modest, be humble, be simple," her mother told her. "Never complain or make excuses," her father instructed. "If something seems unfair at school, just prove yourself by working twice as hard and being twice as good." 90

In the book, Chua portrays her distaste for corporate law, which she practiced before going into academe. "My entire three years at the firm, I always felt like I was playacting, ridiculous in my suit," she writes. This malaise extended even earlier, to her time as a student. "I didn't care about the rights of criminals the way others did, and I froze whenever a professor called on me. I also wasn't naturally skeptical and questioning; I just wanted to write down everything the professor said and memorize it."

At the AASA gathering at Yale, Chua made the connection between her upbringing and her adult dissatisfaction. "My parents didn't sit around talking about politics and philosophy at the dinner table," she told the students. Even after she had escaped from corporate law and made it onto a law faculty, "I was kind of lost. I just didn't feel the passion." Eventually, she made a name for herself as the author of popular books about foreign policy and became an award-winning teacher. But it's plain that she was no better prepared for legal scholarship than she had been for corporate law. "It took me a long, long time," she said. "And I went through lots and lots of rejection." She recalled her extended search for an academic post, in which she was "just not able to do a good interview, just not able to present myself well."

In other words, *Battle Hymn* provides all the material needed to refute the very cultural polemic for which it was made to stand. Chua's Chinese education had gotten her through an elite schooling, but it left her unprepared for the real world. She does not hide any of this. She had set out, she explained, to write a memoir that was "defiantly self-incriminating"—and the result was a messy jumble of conflicting impulses, part provocation, part self-critique. Western readers rode roughshod over this paradox and made of Chua a kind of Asian minstrel figure. But more than anything else, *Battle Hymn* is a very American project—one no traditional Chinese person would think to undertake. "Even if you hate the book," Chua pointed out, "the one thing it is not is meek."

"The loudest duck gets shot" is a Chinese proverb. "The nail that sticks out gets hammered down" is a Japanese one. Its Western correlative: "The squeaky wheel gets the grease." Chua had told her story and been hammered down. Yet here she was, fresh from her hammering, completely unbowed.

There is something salutary in that proud defiance. And though the debate she sparked about Asian-American life has been of questionable value, we will need more people with the same kind of defiance, willing to push themselves into the spotlight and to make some noise, to beat people up, to seduce women, to make mistakes, to become entrepreneurs, to stop doggedly pursuing official paper emblems attesting to their worthiness, to stop thinking those scraps of paper will secure anyone's happiness, and to dare to be interesting. 95

Questions for Critical Reading

1. We've all heard about the *American Dream*. Before you reread this essay, write a brief definition of what this term means to you. As you review Yang's text, pay attention to how he defines the term. What does it mean to him, and how does he apply it to minorities? Is the "American Dream" the same for all Americans?
2. Look up the meaning of the word *estrangement*. How does Yang define this term? While rereading, take note of places where he discusses estrangement. How does it relate to the argument he wants to make?
3. Yang discusses the "Bamboo Ceiling" (p. 440). Do you agree with his analysis and use of the concept? What other "ceilings" might there be for other classes of people? You might begin your response by looking into the "glass ceiling" faced by women in the workplace.

Exploring Context

1. The popular TV show *Glee* had an episode called "Asian F." Watch a clip of this episode on YouTube and read the comments left in response. How do this clip and viewer reactions reflect the issues that Yang discusses in his essay?
2. In some ways, Yang's essay is a response to Amy Chua's book *Battle Hymn of the Tiger Mother*, in which she discusses a set of culturally inflected parenting techniques that are packed into the term *Tiger Mom*. Visit the Tiger Mom meme (knowyourmeme.com/memes/tiger-mom). How does this meme reflect the themes of Yang's essay?
3. Review the Ivy League college acceptance rates as represented by Bradshaw College Consulting, a company that specializes in helping students get into universities (bradshawcollegeconsulting.com/college_acceptance_rate.html). How do these acceptance rates confirm or complicate Yang's argument? What does the existence of companies such as Bradshaw College Consulting suggest about the claims Yang makes?

Questions for Connecting

1. In "(Un)American, (Un)Cool" (p. 102), Kavita Das also talks about the challenges that Asian Americans face because of stereotypes. Synthesize the ideas in these two essays. Does either author offer a solution to these problems? Do both discuss it in the same terms?

2. Kenji Yoshino, an Asian American himself, talks about the ways we tend to downplay part of our identity — a process he calls "covering" in "Preface" and "The New Civil Rights" (p. 452). What response does Yang offer to Yoshino's concept of covering? Given Yang's argument, what are the possibilities of achieving Yoshino's goals for civil rights?

3. One of the stereotypes that Yang engages centers around Asian American men and their relationship to masculinity. Julia Serano is centrally concerned with masculinity and its relation to rape culture in "Why Nice Guys Finish Last" (p. 343). Are Asian American men the "nice guys" that Serano is talking about. Do programs like the ABCs of Attraction address problems of race and ethnicity at the cost of gender and sexuality? How might Asian American men inhabit masculinity — or redfine in — in ways that fight rape culture rather than feed it?

Language Matters

1. At the start of this selection, Yang uses several sentence fragments (see if you can find them). Why does Yang use these? In what situations might a sentence fragment be acceptable? In what ways does intentional use of sentence fragments rely on an understanding of context and audience? When, if ever, should fragments be used in academic writing?

2. Quotations in academic writing must be of appropriate length. Find a significant passage from the essay and choose the shortest and longest useful quotations from the passage. How short is too short? How long is too long? How might you use quotations of different lengths for different ends?

3. The classic rhetorical triangle is composed of receiver, sender, and message. Using this essay, design a new shape to explain its rhetorical situation: What additional elements should be considered? Would the inclusion of style make a rhetorical square? What elements would be included in a rhetorical hexagon?

Assignments for Writing

1. Yang's essay is centrally concerned with the relationship between stereotypes and the realities behind them. Write a paper on the impact of stereotypes on individuals. In what ways are stereotypes enabling? Can there be positive stereotypes? Is it possible to get rid of stereotypes?

2. How can Asian Americans break through the "Bamboo Ceiling"? Write a paper in which you propose strategies for overcoming this limitation, building on the strategies discussed in Yang's essay and incorporating your work from Question 3 of Questions for Critical Reading.

3. Both education and upbringing play important roles in the lives of the people Yang discusses in his essay. How do these factors interact to shape a person's future? Write a paper in which you discuss the roles of education and parenting in the shaping of an individual. Is it possible to escape these influences? To what end? How does Yang challenge either or both?

KENJI YOSHINO

Kenji Yoshino is the Chief Justice Earl Warren Professor of Constitutional Law at New York University. Previously, Yoshino was a professor of law and the deputy dean of intellectual life at Yale Law School, where he earned a J.D. after graduating from Harvard and Oxford Universities. His articles have appeared in various law journals as well as the *New York Times*, the *Village Voice*, the *Boston Globe*, and the *Nation*. He is the author of *Covering: The Hidden Assault on Our Civil Rights* (2006), *A Thousand Times More Fair: What Shakespeare's Plays Teach Us about Justice* (2011), and *Speak Now: Marriage Equality on Trial* (2015).

Covering offers a unique perspective on the familiar concepts of assimilation and passing, utilizing Yoshino's background experience as both a law scholar and a gay Asian American. Yoshino combines personal narrative and legal argument to lay out a new definition of civil rights. The term *covering*, as Yoshino uses it, means "to tone down a disfavored identity to fit into the mainstream" (p. 452), and Yoshino argues that though Americans value the idea of the melting pot as a model for our culture, that ideal can have unintended negative consequences. Despite our avowed appreciation for multiculturalism, the unstated public expectation is still for people of all genders, sexual orientations, and races to conform to rigid expectations.

The selections here, "Preface" and "The New Civil Rights," form something close to a set of bookends for Yoshino's argument in *Covering*. After defining the concept of covering and the problems caused by it in the "Preface" and investigating the issue of a distinct "True Self" and "False Self" in the second excerpt, Yoshino moves on to propose a new paradigm for civil rights. Questioning the idea of legislating civil rights, Yoshino suggests that the next step may have to occur in bars, restaurants, and internet chat rooms; he also suggests that in order to accommodate an increasingly diverse population, the model of civil rights itself must change. Yoshino points the way by helping us to rethink our model of civil rights and the mechanisms used to bring those rights into existence.

The United States is more diverse than ever. How can we balance the rights of diverse groups with the demands of individuals and the nation?

- TAGS: *civil rights, community, conversation, identity, law and justice, politics, race and ethnicity, social change*
- CONNECTIONS: *Appiah, Chabon, Chen, Coates, Cohen, Das, Epstein, Fukuyama, Holmes, Lukianoff and Haidt, Serano, Southan, Watters, von Busch, Yang*

Preface

Everyone covers. To cover is to tone down a disfavored identity to fit into the mainstream. In our increasingly diverse society, all of us are outside the mainstream in some way. Nonetheless, being deemed mainstream is still often a necessity of social life. For this reason, every reader of this book has covered, whether consciously or not, and sometimes at significant personal cost.

Famous examples of covering abound. Ramón Estévez covered his ethnicity when he changed his name to Martin Sheen, as did Krishna Bhanji when he changed his name to Ben Kingsley. Margaret Thatcher covered her status as a woman when she trained with a voice coach to lower the timbre of her voice. Long after they came out as lesbians, Rosie O'Donnell and Mary Cheney still covered, keeping their same-sex partners out of the public eye. Issur Danielovitch Demsky covered his Judaism when he became Kirk Douglas, as did Joseph Levitch when he became Jerry Lewis. Franklin Delano Roosevelt covered his disability by ensuring his wheelchair was always hidden behind a desk before his Cabinet entered.

I doubt any of these people covered willingly. I suspect they were all bowing to an unjust reality that required them to tone down their stigmatized identities to get along in life. Sheen says he needed to "get a name people could pronounce and connect with" if he "wanted to work commercially." Yet he now regrets having done so, and has exhorted his sons—Emilio and Charlie—to use the family name. One of them has not done so, signaling the enduring force of the covering demand.

In a supposedly enlightened age, the persistence of the covering demand presents a puzzle. Today, race, national origin, sex, religion, and disability are all protected by federal civil rights laws. An increasing number of states and localities include sexual orientation in civil rights laws as well. Albeit with varying degrees of conviction, Americans have come to a consensus that people should not be penalized for being different along these dimensions. That consensus, however, does not protect individuals against demands that they mute those differences. We need an explanation for why the civil rights revolution has stalled on covering.

5 Covering has enjoyed such a robust and stubborn life because it is a form of assimilation. At least since Hector St. John de Crèvecoeur's 1782 *Letters from an American Farmer*, this country has touted assimilation as the way Americans of different backgrounds would be "melted into a new race of men." By the time Israel Zangwill's play of that name was performed in 1908, the "melting pot" had acquired the burnish of an American ideal. Only with the civil rights movement of the 1960s was this ideal challenged in any systematic way, with calls to move "beyond the melting pot" and to "celebrate diversity." And notwithstanding that challenge, assimilation has never lost its hold on the American imagination. Indeed, as our country grows more pluralistic, we have seen a renaissance of the melting pot ideal. Fearful that we are spinning apart into balkanized groups, even liberals like Arthur Schlesinger have called for a recommitment to that ethic. In the United States, as in other industrialized democracies, we are seeing the "return of assimilation."

I recognize the value of assimilation, which is often necessary to fluid social interaction, to peaceful coexistence, and even to the dialogue through which difference is valued. For that reason, this is no simple screed against conformity. What I urge here is that we approach the renaissance of assimilation in this country critically. We must be willing to see the dark side of assimilation, and specifically of covering, which is the most widespread form of assimilation required of us today.

Covering is a hidden assault on our civil rights. We have not been able to see it as such because it has swaddled itself in the benign language of assimilation. But if we look closely, we will see that covering is the way many groups are being held back today. The reason racial minorities are pressured to "act white" is because of white supremacy. The reason women are told to downplay their child-care responsibilities in the workplace is because of patriarchy. And the reason gays are asked not to "flaunt" is because of homophobia. So long as such covering demands persist, American civil rights will not have completed its work.

Unfortunately, the law has yet to perceive covering as a threat. Contemporary civil rights law generally only protects traits that individuals cannot change, like their skin color, chromosomes, or innate sexual orientations. This means that current law will not protect us against most covering demands, because such demands direct themselves at the behavioral aspects of our personhood. This is so despite the fact that covering imposes costs on us all.

The universality of the covering demand, however, is also a potential boon for civil rights advocates. I, too, worry about our current practice of fracturing into groups, each clamoring for state and social solicitude. For this reason, I do not think we can move forward by focusing on old-fashioned group-based identity politics. We must instead build a new civil rights paradigm on what draws us together rather than on what drives us apart. Because covering applies to us all, it provides an issue around which we can make common cause. This is the desire for authenticity, our common human wish to express ourselves without being impeded by unreasoning demands for conformity.

We must instead build a new civil rights paradigm on what draws us together rather than on what drives us apart.

I thought I would make this argument in purely political terms. As a law professor, I have become accustomed to the tones of legal impersonality. But I came to see that I could not compose an argument about the importance of human authenticity without risking such authenticity myself. So I have written this . . . in a more intimate voice, blending memoir with argument. In trying to make the stakes of assimilation vivid, I draw on my attempts to elaborate my identity as a gay man, and, to a lesser extent, my identity as an Asian-American. 10

Yet this is not a standard "coming out" narrative or racial memoir. I follow the Romantics here in their belief that if a human life is described with enough particularity, the universal will begin to speak through it. What interests me about my story, and the stories of others, is how similar they are in revealing the bones of our common human endeavor, the yearning for human emancipation that stirs within us all.

The New Civil Rights

To describe the new civil rights, I return to the source of my argument. What most excited me about gay civil rights was its universal resonance. Unlike other civil rights groups, gays must articulate invisible selves without the initial support of our immediate communities. That makes the gay project of self-elaboration emblematic of the search for authenticity all of us engage in as human beings. It is work each of us must do for ourselves, and it is the most important work we can do.

In looking for a vocabulary for this quest for authenticity, I found psychoanalysts more helpful than lawyers. The object-relations theorist D. W. Winnicott makes a distinction between a True Self and a False Self that usefully tracks the distinction between the uncovered and covered selves. The True Self is the self that gives an individual the feeling of being real, which is "more than existing; it is finding a way to exist as oneself, and to relate to objects as oneself, and to have a self into which to retreat for relaxation." The True Self is associated with human spontaneity and authenticity: "Only the True Self can be creative and only the True Self can feel real." The False Self, in contrast, gives an individual a sense of being unreal, a sense of futility. It mediates the relationship between the True Self and the world.

What I love about Winnicott is that he does not demonize the False Self. To the contrary, Winnicott believes the False Self protects the True Self: "The False Self has one positive and very important function: to hide the True Self, which it does by compliance with environmental demands." Like a king castling behind a rook in chess, the more valuable but less powerful piece retreats behind the less valuable but more powerful one. Because the relationship between the True Self and the False Self is symbiotic, Winnicott believes both selves will exist even in the healthy individual.

Nonetheless, Winnicott defines health according to the degree of ascendancy the True Self gains over the False one. At the negative extreme, the False Self completely obscures the True Self, perhaps even from the individual herself. In a less extreme case, the False Self permits the True Self "a secret life." The individual approaches health only when the False Self has "as its main concern a search for conditions which will make it possible for the True Self to come into its own." Finally, in the healthy individual, the False Self is reduced to a "polite and mannered social attitude," a tool available to the fully realized True Self.

This paradigm captures my coming-out experience. My gay self, the True Self, was hidden behind an ostensibly straight False Self. Yet it would be wrong to cast the closeted self as purely inimical to the gay one. In my adolescence, this False Self protected the True Self until its survival was assured. Only at this point did the False Self switch from being a help to being a hindrance. And even after I came out, the False Self never disappeared. It was reduced to the minimum necessary to regulate relations between the True Self and the world.

I could slot other civil rights identities into Winnicott's paradigm. The importance of the paradigm, however, lies in its self-conscious universality. Winnicott posits that each of us has a True Self that must be expressed for us to have the feeling of being switched on, of being alive. And if the True Self embodies the importance of authenticity, the False Self embodies our ambivalence about assimilation, which is both necessary to survival and obstructive of life. The goal is not to eliminate assimilation altogether, but to reduce it to the necessary minimum. This is what the reason-forcing conversation seeks to do.

When I describe the uncovered self in Winnicott's terms, many people respond immediately with stories that attest to the concept's universality. Most of these have little to do with conventional civil rights categories. They often pertain to choices about people's careers or personal lives, like the woman who left a career in law to write plays, or the man who left his fiancée at the altar to pursue his first childhood love. I nonetheless hear the same themes threading through these stories as I do through the traditional civil rights cases. These individuals cannot articulate what authenticity is, but know an existence lived outside its imperative would be a substitute for life.

Parents often respond to the concept of the True Self by speaking of their children. Based on extensive clinical research, psychologist Carol Gilligan argues that children have an authentic voice they lose as they mature, with girls retaining it longer than boys. (The breaking of this emotional voice mirrors the breaking of the physical voice, as the voices of boys break earlier and more dramatically than those of girls.) Gilligan's work is replete with instances of parents awed by the directness and realness of their children. These parents suggest that one of the most agonizing dilemmas of parenting is how much they should require their children to cover in the world.

This psychological discourse about authentic selves sounds distant from current civil rights discourse. We must close that gap. The new civil rights must harness this universal impulse toward authenticity. That impulse should press us toward thinking of civil rights less in terms of groups than in terms of our common humanity. 20

Two recent cases show that the Supreme Court is sympathetic to that shift. In the 2003 case of *Lawrence v. Texas* . . . the Supreme Court struck down a Texas statute that criminalized same-sex sodomy. Many assumed the Court would use this case to decide whether to give gays the judicial protections currently accorded to racial minorities and women. But while the Court struck down the statute (and overruled *Bowers v. Hardwick* in the process), it did not do so based on the equality rights of gays. Rather, it held that the statute violated the fundamental right of all persons—straight, gay, or otherwise—to control our intimate sexual relations.

Similarly, in the 2004 case of *Tennessee v. Lane*, the Supreme Court considered the question of whether two paraplegic individuals could sue Tennessee for failing to make its courthouses wheelchair accessible. (One plaintiff was forced to crawl up the courthouse steps to answer criminal charges against him; the other, a certified court reporter, alleged she had lost job opportunities because some county courthouses were inaccessible.) Again, the Court ruled in favor of the minority group without framing its ruling in group-based equality rhetoric. Rather, it held that all persons—disabled or otherwise—have a "right of access to the courts," which had been denied in this case.

In an era when the Supreme Court has closed many civil rights doors, it has left this one wide open. It is much more sympathetic to "liberty" claims about freedoms we all hold than to "equality" claims asserted by a subset of the population. It is easy to see why. Equality claims—such as group-based accommodation claims—inevitably involve the Court in picking favorites among groups. In an increasingly pluralistic society, the Court understandably wishes to steer clear of that enterprise. Liberty claims, on the other hand, emphasize what all Americans (or more precisely, all persons within the jurisdiction of the United States) have in common. The claim that we all have a right to sexual intimacy, or that we all have a right to access the courts, will hold no matter how many new groups proliferate in this country.

The Supreme Court's shift toward a more universal register can also be seen in its nascent acceptance of human rights. I worked on a friend-of-the-court brief in the *Lawrence* case produced by a team centered at Yale Law School. With the former President of Ireland and U.N. High Commissioner Mary Robinson as our client, we argued that decisions by international tribunals and courts in other Western democracies had recognized the fundamentality of the right to adult consensual sexual intimacy. We knew this argument would be resisted by some justices on the Court, who do not take kindly to arguments that decisions outside the United States should guide their jurisprudence. But to our surprise, the majority opinion cited our brief for the proposition that *Bowers* violated "values we share with a wider civilization."

At the end of their lives, both Martin Luther King Jr. and Malcolm X argued for this transition from civil rights to human rights. Both believed that civil rights unduly focused on what distinguished individuals from one another, rather than emphasizing what they had in common. As Stewart Burns, one of the editors of the King papers at Stanford, observes, King "grasped that 'civil rights' carried too much baggage of the dominant tradition of American individualism and not enough counterweight from a tradition of communitarian impulses, collective striving, and common good." Similarly, Malcolm X exhorted Americans to "expand the civil-rights struggle to the level of human rights," so that the "jurisdiction of Uncle Sam" would not prevent us from allying with our "brothers" of other nations. 25

The universal rights of persons will probably be the way the Court will protect difference in the future. I predict that if the Court ever recognizes language rights, it will protect them as a liberty to which we are all entitled, rather than as an equality right attached to a particular national-origin group. And if the Court recognizes rights to grooming, such as the right to wear cornrows or not to wear makeup, I believe it will do so under something more akin to the German Constitution's right to personality rather than as a right attached to groups like racial minorities or women.

One of the great benefits of analyzing civil rights in terms of universal liberty rather than in terms of group-based equality is that it avoids making assumptions about group cultures. I've touched on the problem that the covering concept might assume too quickly that individuals behaving in "mainstream" ways are hiding some true identity, when in fact they might just be "being themselves." A female colleague of mine gave me a powerful version of this critique: "Here is what I dislike about your project. When I do something stereotypically masculine—like fixing my bike—your project makes it more likely people will think I'm putting on a gender performance rather than accepting the most straightforward explanation for what I'm doing. I don't fix my bike because I'm trying to downplay the fact that I'm a woman. I fix it because it's broken."

She gave another example: "When I was in graduate school, there was an African-American man who studied German Romantic poetry. Under your model, I could easily see someone saying he was 'covering' his African-American identity by studying something so esoteric and highbrow. But it was clear to me he was studying Romantic poetry because he was seized by it. And if someone had assumed he was studying it to 'act white,' they would have diminished him as a human being."

The coup de grâce: "Your commitment is to help people 'be themselves'—to resist demands to conform that take away their ability to be the individuals they are. But the covering idea could perpetuate the stereotypes you want to eliminate. One way minorities break stereotypes is by acting against them. If every time they do so, people assume they are 'covering' some essential stereotypical identity, the stereotypes will never go away."

I have literally lost sleep over this criticism.

I have literally lost sleep over this criticism. But in my waking hours, I take it more as a caution than as a wholesale indictment. I agree that we must not assume that individuals behaving in "mainstream" ways are necessarily covering. My ultimate commitment is to autonomy as a means of achieving authenticity, rather than to a fixed conception of what authenticity might be. 30

(Here I follow Winnicott, who observes the True Self is not susceptible to specific definition, as its nature differs for each of us.) In talking about classic civil rights groups, I have focused on the demand to conform to the mainstream because I think that for most groups (except women) these are the demands that most threaten our authenticity. But I am equally opposed to demands that individuals reverse cover, because such demands are also impingements on our autonomy, and therefore on our authenticity.

In practice, I expect the liberty paradigm to protect the authentic self better than the equality paradigm. While it need not do so, the equality paradigm is prone to essentializing the identities it protects. Under an equality paradigm, if a woman who wore a lot of makeup were protected by a court because makeup is an "essential" part of being a woman, this could reinforce the stereotype that women wear makeup. But if the same woman were given the liberty right to elaborate her own gender identity in ways that did not impinge on her job performance, she would be protected from demands to be either more "masculine" or more "feminine." Marsha Wislocki-Goin would be protected for wearing "too much makeup" and Darlene Jespersen would be protected for not wearing it at all. Each woman would then have the full panoply of options from which she could fashion her gender identity. And in protecting that range, the law would not articulate any presupposition about what an "authentic" or "essential" woman would look like. Authenticity would be something these women, and not the state or employer, would find for themselves.

Group-based identity politics is not dead. As I have argued, I still believe in a group-based accommodation model for existing civil rights groups. This is in part because I believe we have made a commitment to those groups to protect them from such covering demands. The statutory language of the Civil Rights Act and the Americans with Disabilities Act already protects racial minorities, religious minorities, women, and individuals with disabilities *as groups* against covering demands. It has been the courts that have erroneously limited the ambit of those protections. Such a group-based equality paradigm is completely consistent with the individual liberty paradigm. In fact, the equality and liberty strands of antidiscrimination law are inextricably intertwined.

Moreover, even if we shift the focus of civil rights law away from equality to liberty, identity politics will still be crucial. If it weren't for the gay rights movement, or the disability rights movement, cases like *Lawrence* or *Lane* would never have made it to the Court. But I'm sympathetic to the Court's desire to frame these cases not as "gay" or "disability" cases, but as cases touching on rights that, like a rising tide, will lift the boat of every person in America. Ironically, it may be the explosion of diversity in this country that will finally make us realize what we have in common. Multiculturalism has forced us to vary and vary the human being in the imagination until we discover what is invariable about her.

While I have great hopes for this new legal paradigm, I also believe law will be a relatively trivial part of the new civil rights. A doctor friend told me that in his first year of medical school, his dean described how doctors were powerless to cure the vast majority of human ills. People would get better, or they would not, but it would not be doctors who would cure them. Part of becoming a doctor, the dean said, was to surrender a layperson's awe for medical authority. I wished then that someone would give an analogous lecture to law students, and to Americans at large. My education in law has been in part an education in its limitations.

For starters, many covering demands are made by actors the law does not—and in my view should not—hold accountable, such as friends, family, neighbors, or people themselves. When I hesitate before engaging in a public display of same-sex affection, I am not thinking of the state or my employer, but of the strangers around me and my own internal censor. And while I am often tempted to sue myself, this is not my healthiest impulse.

Law is also an incomplete solution to coerced assimilation because it has yet to recognize the myriad groups subjected to covering demands outside traditional civil rights classifications like race, sex, orientation, religion, and disability. Whenever I speak about covering, I receive new instances of identities that can be covered. This is Winnicott's point—each one of us has a False Self that hides a True one. The law may someday move to protect some of these identities. But it will never protect them all.

Most important, law is incomplete in the qualitative remedies it provides. I confronted this recently when I became a plaintiff in a lawsuit against the Department of Defense. Under a congressional statute called the Solomon Amendment, the department threatened to cut off $350 million of federal funding from Yale University if the law school did not exempt the military from the law school's policy of protecting gays against discrimination by employers. Our suit argues that the statute is unconstitutional. I believe in this lawsuit, and was heartened that the vast majority of my law school colleagues signed on as plaintiffs. I was also elated when the district court judge, Judge Janet Hall, granted summary judgment in our favor. (As the government has taken an appeal, the case is still pending.) But there is nothing like being a plaintiff to realize that lawsuits occur between people who have no better way of talking to each other.

When I think about the elaboration of my gay identity, I am grateful to see litigation has had little to do with it. The department is the only entity I have ever wanted to sue. Even when I encountered demands for assimilation, my best response was to draw my interlocutor into a conversation. Just as important, framing the project of self-elaboration in purely legal—and therefore adversarial—terms would fail to honor all those who were not adversaries. I have described in these pages many individuals who helped me toward myself. But there were many more. I think here of my law professor Charles Reich, who wrote a memoir about coming out in 1976, when it was an act of real courage to do so, and who let me write the essay that begins this book in his class, though its relationship to the law was then entirely unclear. I think of the chair of my midtenure review committee, who sat me down when I was the only untenured member of the faculty and, unsurprisingly, a mass of nerves, to give me the verdict of the committee. He told me his only advice for the coming years was that I should be more myself, that instead of reasoning within the law as it existed, I should speak my truth and make the law shape itself around me. And I think of my parents, whose response to this manuscript was to say, with calm and conviction, that they were proud of the man I have become.

For these reasons, I am troubled that Americans seem increasingly to turn toward the law to do the work of civil rights precisely when they should be turning away from it. The real solution lies in all of us as citizens, not in the tiny subset of us who are lawyers. People who are not lawyers should have reason-forcing conversations outside the law. They should pull Goffman's term "covering" out of academic obscurity and press it into the popular lexicon, so that it has the same currency as terms like "passing" or "the closet." People confronted with demands to cover should feel emboldened to seek a reason for that demand, even if the law does not reach the actors making the demand, or recognize the group burdened by it. These reason-forcing conversations should happen outside courtrooms—in workplaces and restaurants, schools and playgrounds, chat rooms and living rooms, public squares and bars. They should occur informally and intimately, where tolerance is made and unmade.

What will constitute a good enough reason to justify assimilation will obviously be controversial. But I want to underscore that we have come to some consensus that certain reasons are illegitimate—like white supremacy, patriarchy, homophobia, religious intolerance, and animus toward the disabled. I ask us to be true to the commitments we have made by never accepting such biases as legitimate grounds for covering demands. Beyond that, I have sought to engender a series of conversations, rather than a series of results—what reasons count, and for what purposes, will be for us to decide by facing one another as individuals. My personal inclination is always to privilege the claims of the individual against countervailing interests like "neatness" or "workplace harmony." But we should have that conversation. 40

Such conversations are the best—and perhaps the only—way to give both assimilation and authenticity their proper due. These conversations will help us chart and stay the course between the monocultural America suggested by conservative alarmists and the balkanized America suggested by the radical multiculturalists. They will reveal the true dimension of civil rights. The aspiration of civil rights has always been to permit people to pursue their human flourishing without limitations based on bias. Focusing on law prevents us from seeing the revolutionary breadth of that aspiration, as law has limited civil rights to particular groups. I am not faulting that limitation, as I think prioritization is necessary, and that the law's priorities are correct. But civil rights, which has always extended far beyond the law, may now need to do so more than ever. It is only when we leave the law that civil rights suddenly stops being about particular groups and starts to become a project of human flourishing in which we all have a stake.

We must use the relative freedom of adulthood to integrate the many selves we hold. This includes uncovering the selves we buried long ago because they were inconvenient, impractical, or even hated. Because they must pass the test of survival, most of the selves we hold, like most of our lives, are ordinary. Yet sometimes, what is consequential in us begins to shine.

Questions for Critical Reading

1. What does Yoshino mean by the *"new" civil rights*? Define the term as you reread his essay by locating passages from his text. What makes it new? How does it differ from "old" civil rights? Use Yoshino's text to define *liberty* and *equality paradigms* as part of your response.

2. What is *covering*? Define the concept using Yoshino's text and then offer your own example.

3. How does Yoshino think we can achieve the new civil rights? Identify passages that show his position, and then respond to it. Do you think his vision is possible? Is it something we should strive for? To prepare for your response, read Yoshino's text critically to locate points of connection between his position and yours.

Exploring Context

1. Explore the website for the U.S. Commission on Civil Rights (usccr.gov). Which paradigm does it reflect, *liberty* or *equality*? Use your definition of these terms from Question 1 of Questions for Critical Reading.

2. Yoshino uses recent Supreme Court decisions to make his argument. Visit the website for the Supreme Court at supremecourtus.gov. What recent cases have concerned civil rights? What impact do these cases (or the lack of such cases) have on Yoshino's argument?

3. According to Yoshino, changes in civil rights should come not from legislation but through conversation. Search internet blogs and forums for "civil rights" and related terms. Are people talking about these issues online? What does this say about Yoshino's argument? Connect your exploration to your response to Question 3 of Questions for Critical Reading.

Questions for Connecting

1. Kwame Anthony Appiah also extols the power of conversation in "Making Conversation" and "The Primacy of Practice" (p. 35). Place his ideas in conversation with Yoshino's essay, synthesizing the authors' ideas about the power of conversation. Is Yoshino also calling for cosmopolitanism? How do civil rights function like other social practices?

2. Yoshino discusses some of the social costs of covering but how do the pressures of cultural assimilation contribute to other forms of trauma? Expand Yoshino's ideas about covering using Sarah Stillman's "Hiroshima and the Inheritance of Trauma" (p. 371). What role does covering play in Shoji's trauma, both within her culture and within a larger American context? Your work with covering in Question 2 of Questions for Critical Reading might be a good place to start.

3. Francis Fukuyama argues for the necessity of a concept of human dignity in his essay of the same name (p. 137). What role might human dignity play in civil rights? Is Factor X an essential component of a new civil rights? Synthesize the ideas of Fukuyama and Yoshino into an argument about human rights.

Language Matters

1. Every part of speech and every punctuation mark has certain "rights"; for example, the period has the right to end a sentence and the comma does not. How can we describe the rules of grammar using Yoshino's ideas of liberty and equality paradigms?

2. Defining terms is an important part of academic writing. Locate a passage where Yoshino defines a term. What strategies does he use? Does he offer a dictionary definition? An example? An authority? How should you define terms in your own text?

3. Is there a form of covering that takes place in peer revision? Are people tempted to tone down unfavorable comments? How does Yoshino's discussion of covering offer advice for more effective peer revision?

Assignments for Writing

1. Yoshino discusses the concept of groups and individuals covering in order to conform to the mainstream. Locate your own example of covering and then write an essay that extends or complicates Yoshino's argument through your example. Does your example reinforce or refute Yoshino's ideas about covering? Are any civil rights at stake in your example? What relation is there between covering and civil rights? You will want to use your definition of the term *covering* from Question 2 of Questions for Critical Reading.

2. Yoshino discusses the challenges to civil rights posed by the proliferation of groups engendered by a diverse society; he offers his own vision of how to transform civil rights to account for these groups. Write a paper in which you suggest what changes we should make to civil rights and how we might achieve those changes. Draw on your work in Questions for Critical Reading and Questions for Connecting in making your argument. Consider, too: Should we use a liberty paradigm or an equality paradigm? Would you propose a different paradigm of your own? Is legislation the best way to achieve your vision for civil rights? Is conversation?

3. In response to Question 3 of Exploring Context, you examined current online conversations about civil rights. Yoshino suggests that such conversations are the best means of achieving a new civil rights. Write a paper in which you argue for the role of conversation in social change. Is talking about an issue enough to engender change? Does it matter who is doing the talking? How does change happen in society?

Part Three
ASSIGNMENT SEQUENCES

SEQUENCE 1

How Is Technology Changing Us?

MARIA KONNIKOVA

SHERRY TURKLE

NICK PAUMGARTEN

ROBIN MARANTZ HENIG

CHUCK KLOSTERMAN

PETER SINGER

In this sequence, you will consider the ways in which technology such as social media is changing who we are and how we relate to one another. You'll begin by reading Maria Konnikova to examine the quality of relationships in the age of social media. Then, using Sherry Turkle, you will relate these changes to our growth and development as human beings. Nick Paumgarten will help you examine the psychological impact of these changes and then, using Robin Marantz Henig, you will determine how these changes shape the way we grow and mature as adults. Alternate assignments ask you to expand on the biological, emotional, and ethical dimensions of these changes using Chuck Klosterman and Peter Singer.

Assignment 1. Analyze: KONNIKOVA

How does social media change the nature of relationships such as friendships? Write a paper in which you evaluate the quality of relationships in the digital age, drawing from the work of Maria Konnikova. In making your argument, you may want to use your work on the qualities of friendship from Question 2 of Questions for Critical Reading (p. 260), your reflections on your own experiences from Exploring Context (p. 260), and your work on the impact of virtual friendships from Question 1 of Assignments for Writing (p. 261).

To help you begin your critical thinking on this assignment, consider these questions: Does the Dunbar number remain relevant in the digital age? How does technology enable us to sustain relationships? What is lost when we use technology to do so? How does your own experience confirm or complicate Konnikova's argument?

Assignment 2. Connect: KONNIKOVA AND TURKLE

Sherry Turkle examines the impact technology has on our abilities to talk with and relate to each other. Does Maria Konnikova's argument complicate this analysis? Write a paper in which you determine the relationship between social media and social relationships, using ideas from both Turkle and Konnikova. You might begin by working with your responses to Questions 1 and 2 of Questions for Critical Reading (pp. 387–88) for Turkle as well as Questions 1 and 2 of Assignments for Writing (p. 389).

To help you begin your critical thinking on this assignment, reflect on these questions: How does our use of social media and technology impact our development as human beings? What role does connection play in our ability to act as adults? What about empathy?

Alternate Assignment 2. Connect: Konnikova and Paumgarten

Both Maria Konnikova and Nick Paumgarten are interested in the ways we connect to others as well as to ourselves. Both, too, examine the ways in which technology changes these connections. Using both Konnikova and Paumgarten to support your argument, write a paper in which you assess the impact of technology on our abilities to connect.

To help you begin your critical thinking on this assignment, ask yourself these questions: Does the GoPro help or hinder our ability to connect to others in ways that reflect Konnikova's argument? What is the value of experience, and how are real-world interactions vital to experience? Can technology allow us to connect in different (if not better) ways? What role does memory play in both essays, and how do memories affect our connections?

Assignment 3. Synthesize: Konnikova, Turkle, and Henig

Both Konnikova and Turkle examine the impact of technology on our abilities to connect to others. Henig, meanwhile, explores the emergence of what might be a new stage of life in her discussion of emerging adulthood. To what extent does technology impact our development? Write a paper synthesizing the ideas of these authors in which you determine the relationship between technology and emerging adulthood.

You will probably want to start your work on this question by revisiting your answer from Question 1 of Questions for Connecting (p. 260) that you may have completed after reading Konnikova's essay. Question 1 from the Assignments for Writing (p. 261) following Konnikova's essay might also be useful. Consider also these questions: What general conclusions can you reach about the effects of connection and fragmentation on our development as individuals? How does technology *enable* us to mature?

Assignment 4. Emerge: Klosterman and One Other

Chuck Klosterman uses the figures of Kim Dotcom and Julian Assange to consider the villainy of each man. And while he does identify a cultural narrative promoting the inevitability of the future, Klosterman doesn't seem to address the larger question of whether or not technological progress itself is villainous. Using the ideas of Klosterman and one of the other authors from this sequence, write a paper in which you determine the villainy and virtue of technological progress. You will want to use your work from the Questions for Critical Reading (p. 253) that accompany Klosterman's essay as well as Questions 1 and 2 of Assignments for Writing (p. 254).

Think also about these questions: How does the persistence of the Dunbar number complicate Klosterman's claims about the inevitability of technology? Is villainy a matter of ethics or emotions? How does technology's impact on our brains and emotions confirm or challenge Klosterman?

Alternate Assignment 4. Emerge: Singer and One Other

Although Peter Singer fears an erosion of privacy in the age of digital technology and social media, he also uncovers the ways in which these tools can be used to empower people and hold governments accountable. Using Singer's ideas and one other author from this sequence, write a paper in which you expand Singer's argument to identify the ways in which technology promotes social change.

Consider: How do virtual friendships empower collaborative action? What qualities of emerging adults might make them inclined to use technology for social change? Is the GoPro a kind of sousveillance?

SEQUENCE 2

How Do We Face the Challenge of Race?

Anna Holmes

Ta-Nehisi Coates

Andrew Cohen

Greg Lukianoff and Jonathan Haidt

Kenji Yoshino

Ethan Watters

Wesley Yang

This sequence asks you to confront the entrenched and troubling problems of race and ethnicity: What can we do to resolve the mounting racial tension in this country? The first assignment, Anna Holmes, asks you to look at the disjuncture between our stated commitment to diversity and our failure to fulfill those goals. You will then extend this understanding by looking at Ta-Nehisi Coates's examination of the fraught relationship between race and education; an alternate assignment asks you to work with Andrew Cohen to look similarly at the racial dimensions of law and justice in the context of drug epidemics. You will then use your understanding to reevaluate Greg Lukianoff and Jonathan Haidt's arguments about race, trauma, and education. An alternate assignment uses Kenji Yoshino to consider the future of civil rights in light of all you've discovered about race and ethnicity. Finally, working with either Ethan Watters or Wesley Yang you will consider the final implications of your analysis.

Assignment 1. Analyze: Holmes

According to Anna Holmes, institutions like businesses and the media claim to embrace diversity but fail so completely in achieving it that the word itself is almost without meaning. Write a paper in which you analyze the problem of racial and ethnic diversity. You will want to start with your analysis from Questions for Critical Reading (p. 220) and Questions 1 and 3 of Assignments for Writing (p. 221).

Also consider these questions: How does racial capitalism reflect continuing issues with race? What would it take to be more inclusive? Is equity a realistic goal? How does the lack of diversity reflect continued racism?

Assignment 2. Connect: Holmes and Coates or Cohen

Ta-Nehisi Coates shares his personal experience with the racial dimensions of education. His narrative shows the both the depth and breadth of the problem of race.

Andrew Cohen similarly illustrates that the differing legal responses to the current opioid epidemic and past drug epidemics may have a lot to do with the different racial compositions of those populations.

Write a paper in which you extend Holmes's argument about race in the United States by using the analyses of Coates *or* Cohen. Consider using your responses to Question 1 of Questions for Connecting (p. 95) and Question 2 of Assignments for Writing (p. 96) for Coates or Question 1 of Questions for Connecting (p. 100) and Question 3 of Assignments for Writing (p. 101) for Cohen.

Also ask yourself these questions: Do divisions of race extend much deeper than Holmes suggests? Can Coates's solution to the problem of education be used to address diversity more generally? What are the costs, both personal and cultural, of racial division? How does race shape the lived experience of people of all colors in this country? What is the relationship between race and justice?

Assignment 3. Synthesize: Lukianoff and Haidt, Holmes, and Coates

Greg Lukianoff and Jonathan Haidt seems to suggest that we have gone too far in our response to race, particularly on college campuses. Synthesize these authors to write a paper in which you determine the best approach to dealing with issues of race, ethnicity, and racism in education. Draw from your work in Questions 1 and 2 of Assignments for Writing (p. 277) for Lukianoff and Haidt.

Also think about: How can we balance the concerns of people of color on campus with the larger educational mission? How might critical thinking provide a rubric for locating the best approach?

Alternate Assignment 3. Synthesize: Yoshino, Holmes, and Cohen

Kenji Yoshino offers a new model of civil rights and strategies for achieving them. Synthesize his work with the work of Holmes and Cohen to write a paper in which you propose strategies we can use to address racial injustice and civil rights in the United States. Questions 1 and 3 of Questions for Critical Reading (pp. 460–61), Questions 1 and 3 of Exploring Context (p. 461), and Question 2 of Assignments for Writing (p. 462) for Yoshino may be useful in forming your response.

Consider these questions as well: What are the obstacles to achieving a new model of civil rights? How do we promote equity in law and society?

Assignment 4. Emerge: Watters and One Other

Ethan Watters's argument seems to suggest that the entire controversy about race and ethnicity could be a purely Western phenomenon. Bound as we are by our cultural perspective, is it possible that our categorization of people by race and ethnicity reflects "WEIRD" notions of the self? Write a paper using Watters and one of the other authors from this sequence in which you determine the limitations of racial and ethnic categories. Consider using your work on diversity from Question 1 of Assignments for Writing (p. 434) for Watters.

Consider: Based on Watters's argument, might we consider Western identity itself as an ethnic category? If so, how might the insights about race and ethnicity from the other authors be applied to the concept of WEIRD? Are the categories universal or uniquely Western? How might other cultures encode human variety? Does WEIRD transcend race and ethnicity? To what extent does it reinforce those categories instead?

Alternate Assignment 4. Emerge: Yang and One Other

Wesley Yang looks at the challenges Asian Americans face in the United States, extending this discussion to other racial and ethnic groups. Using Yang and one other author, write a paper about the impact of race on all Americans. You might want to start from your work on Questions 1 and 3 of Questions for Critical Reading (p. 450), Question 2 of Questions for Connecting (p. 451), and Questions 1 and 2 of Assignments for Writing (p. 451) for Yang.

You might start by asking yourself: What does the American Dream mean and does it still have relevance today? Can legal protections ever mitigate the damage caused by stereotypes? How? Should economic rights be considered as well as civil rights? Could such rights dismantle the "Bamboo Ceiling"?

SEQUENCE 3

How Does Gender Shape Us, and How Do We Shape Gender?

JULIA SERANO

ROXANE GAY

MICHAEL CHABON

MALCOLM GLADWELL

DANIEL GILBERT

In this sequence, you will explore the consequences of our current system of gender. You will begin by using Julia Serano to look at the ways in which gender shapes men in relation to sexuality and rape culture. Roxane Gay will then help you articulate the relationship between women and representations of feminism. Using Michael Chabon, you will synthesize these authors to articulate a nuanced understanding of the impact of gender on men and women. The final series of assignments and alternate assignments asks you to consider tools we can use to promote changes in how gender is implemented and received, using Malcolm Gladwell or Daniel Gilbert.

Assignment 1. Analyze: SERANO

According to Julia Serano, when it comes to sex nice guys finish last, a result of a powerful set of cultural assumptions that shape both men and women in relation to rape culture. Write a paper in which you extend Serano's analysis to suggest strategies we can use to mitigate the stereotypes that influence men in our culture. You will want to start with your analysis from Question 3 of Questions for Critical Reading (p. 351) as well as Questions 2 and 3 of Assignments for Writing (p. 352).

Also consider these questions: Who is responsible for rape culture? How do our cultural understandings of gender victimize both men and women? How can we change gender-based stereotypes? What role might the media play? How can our personal behaviors contribute to this effort? Is there a strategy that will allow nice guys to finish first? What would it look like? Or are gendered expectations so entrenched that there is no solution?

Assignment 2. Connect: SERANO AND GAY

While Serano considers the impact of stereotypes on men, Roxane Gay looks instead at her personal relationship to the expectations that come with the term *feminist*. Using both of these authors, write a paper in which you determine how categories related to gender limit our abilities to act personally and politically. Use your work from Questions for Critical Reading (pp. 350–51) as well as Question 3 of Assignments for Writing (p. 352) for Serano.

You might also use these questions to help you think about your response: How does Serano's use of binaries relate to Gay's understanding of a good or bad feminist? What kind of feminist—"good" or "bad" or something else—might work with men to dismantle gendered stereotypes? Does essential feminism empower people to act? Which people? How might individuals take action while avoiding the kinds of labels that come with stereotypes?

Assignment 3. Synthesize: Chabon, Serano, and Gay

Michael Chabon's narrative touches on many of the themes of this sequence, including gender (in particular masculinity and what it means to be a man), the consequences of failing gender norms (in this case through bullying), and the search for understanding and community. Synthesizing all three authors, write a paper in which you propose strategies and practices for building communities within and across the lines of gender. You may find your work from Questions 1 and 3 of Questions for Critical Reading (p. 70) useful as well as your work from Questions 1 and 3 of Assignments for Writing (p. 72) for Chabon.

Consider, too: How do individuals resist the pressures to conform to gender expectations? And at what costs? How do they build community? How does that community sustain them?

Assignment 4. Emerge: Gladwell and One Other

Malcolm Gladwell examines tools used to promote change, contrasting our celebration of technology's potential to generate change with the strong ties used in the civil rights movement. Using Gladwell and one of the other authors in this sequence, write a paper in which you determine what tools we can use to promote gender equity. You may find your responses to Questions for Critical Reading (p. 199) and Assignments for Writing (p. 200) for Gladwell helpful.

Also think about these questions: What kind of ties are most common within a gender? What kind of ties are there across genders? Does technology offer us any means of changing gender?

Alternate Assignment 4. Emerge: Gilbert and One Other

Daniel Gilbert explores our failure to predict happiness but he also looks at the ways in which ideas spread rapidly through a culture. Using his essay and one other author from this sequence, write a paper in which you articulate strategies for finding happiness in the face of gender constrictions.

Consider: What sorts of surrogates exist for gender? Who serves as a surrogate for Gay? For Abe? How does gender operate as a super-replicator? Can alternate understandings of gender be spread this way?

SEQUENCE 4

What Does Ethical Conflict Look Like in a Globalized World?

Sarah Stillman

Torie Rose DeGhett

Tomas van Houtryve

Kwame Anthony Appiah

David Foster Wallace

In this sequence, you will consider the complexities of war and conflict within our deeply connected world. Sarah Stillman will introduce you to the lasting effects of conflict, which can span generations. Then, using Torie Rose DeGhett, you will consider the ethics of conflicts when they occur, particularly in relation to economic systems of media and technology, an understanding you will then develop by incorporating the work of Tomas van Houtryve. Kwame Anthony Appiah will offer you tools we might use to resolve the problems of conflict in a global economy while David Foster Wallace will ask you to consider notions of pain and preference as a means of developing a more nuanced ethical framework.

Assignment 1. Analyze: Stillman

Sarah Stillman examines the possibility that trauma from conflict can act as a form of disease. To what extent should we consider the lasting effects of conflict before taking action in the global arena? Write a paper in which you weigh the consequences of conflict. Draw from your work in Question 3 of Questions for Critical Reading (p. 376) and Question 3 of Assignments for Writing (p. 377).

Also consider these questions: In what cases is conflict worth the cost? What role does shame play in relation to conflict? How might we shape an ethics for determining when to intervene in conflict? Might intervention prevent more trauma?

Assignment 2. Connect: Stillman and DeGhett

The horrific image of war at the center of Torie Rose DeGhett's essay echoes the narratives of the survivors examined by Sarah Stillman. Each offers powerful testimony about the consequences of conflict. Using both of these authors, write a paper in which you examine the role of memory in war. How can we use memories of war to prevent future conflict? What happens when these memories are obstructed? Consider expanding your response to Question 2 of Questions for Connecting (p. 376) for Stillman or draw from your work in Questions 1 and 3 of Assignments for Writing (pp. 120–21) from DeGhett.

Assignment 3. Synthesize: Stillman, DeGhett, and van Houtryve

Torie Rose DeGhett and Tomas van Houtryve each explore the role of the image in modern conflict. These images are not only connected to the technologies that captured them but also embedded in global economic systems, whether the system of publication at play in DeGhett's essay or the system that allows van Houtryve to buy a drone of his own. Connect one of these two essays to Stillman's essay in order to write a paper in which you propose ethical standards for military products in global economic systems. What questions should we ask, and what standards should we use in making decisions about technologies or products when it comes to war? You may wish to use your work from Assignments for Writing (pp. 120–21) for DeGhett or Question 3 of Questions for Critical Reading (p. 119) and Question 1 of Assignments for Writing (p. 398) for van Houtryve.

You might also use these questions to help you think about your response: Do corporations have an ethical obligation to mitigate conflict? Do they have an ethical obligation to display the consequences of conflict? Who makes decisions about conflict, technology, and media in these essays? What ethical considerations, if any, seem to govern their decisions?

Assignment 4. Emerge: Appiah and One Other

Kwame Anthony Appiah states that cosmopolitanism names the problem as much as the solution, suggesting that the challenge facing us is how to get along in a crowded and interdependent world. Using his ideas and those of one other author in this sequence, write a paper in which you propose strategies for ending and avoiding armed conflicts.

You may find these questions helpful: Can practices of economic interdependence enhance peace in the world? What role do both collaboration and conversation have in this process? How might images of war change our values and practices in relation to conflict? Do remote technologies like drones make it easier to wage war? How might the lingering impact of trauma be used to change conversations about conflict?

Alternate Assignment 4. Emerge: Wallace and One Other

David Foster Wallace seems to be concerned not just about lobsters but about ethics. In looking at their capacity for pain he is also asking us about larger issues such as ethical standards. Using his ideas and one other author in this sequence, write a paper about the ethics of conflict.

What factors should be considered in ethical conflict? What about pain, shame, trauma, or displacement? How can we form an ethical framework flexible enough to offer guidance on issues as diverse as what we eat and how we relate to each other globally?

SEQUENCE 5

How Can You Make a Difference in the World?

MALCOLM GLADWELL

RHYS SOUTHAN

KENJI YOSHINO

NAMIT ARORA

HELEN EPSTEIN

ROBINSON MEYER

What tools can you use to change the world around you? In this sequence, you will examine ideas that will help you advocate for social change. Malcolm Gladwell's examination of the power of social ties online and in person will help you think about the ways in which you can use the relationships you have to make a difference in the world. Rhys Southan then offers a very different and very stark approach to change by looking at Effective Altruism. You will then synthesize these approaches with ideas about civil rights from Kenji Yoshino or with ideas about economic justice from Namit Arora. Ultimately, you will test your facility with these tools for social change by either looking at ways to halt the spread of HIV, using the ideas of Helen Epstein, or confronting issues of climate change, using Robinson Meyer.

Assignment 1. Analyze: GLADWELL

Malcolm Gladwell questions whether or not the ties enabled by technology can create social change by contrasting them to the relationships that powered the civil rights movement. In particular, he suggests that the weak ties enabled by social media do not have the ability to promote true social change. Write a paper in which you evaluate Gladwell's ideas about tools for changing the world. In order to do so, you will first need to *identify* these tools; then you will need to *assess* how effective they are; and finally you will need to *predict* their potential usefulness in other contexts of change.

Consider also these questions: How do relationships create change? How can we use that knowledge to shape the changes we want to see? What are the drawbacks of these methods? What is the most powerful tool Gladwell examines, and what makes it so powerful?

Assignment 2. Connect: GLADWELL AND SOUTHAN

Rhys Southan also writes about changing the world, examining in his essay the potential (and potential problems) of Effective Altruism. While Gladwell's analysis focuses largely on the potential of relationships, Southan's analysis of Effective Altruism seems to depend much more on individuals alone. Write a paper in which you determine the power of the individual in producing social change.

You might want to think about these questions to help you get started: Does change start with individuals or in our relationships with the world around us? Do weak and strong ties play a part in Effective Altruism? How do friendships and other relationships complicate the notion of replaceability? Are individuals more important than Effective Altruism suggests? If you want to make a difference in the world, how would you use the tools offered by these authors?

Assignment 3. Synthesize: GLADWELL, SOUTHAN, AND YOSHINO

What is the best way to use law to protect the rights of all individuals? You might locate an answer to that question by synthesizing Kenji Yoshino's discussion of civil rights with the ideas of Gladwell and Southan. Write a paper in which you identify an effective approach to protecting the rights of all individuals through civil rights and other legislation. Your work from Question 2 of Assignments for Writing (p. 462) for Yoshino might be a particularly good place to begin this work.

Also consider: How can the conversations that Yoshino calls for leverage the power of strong and weak ties? What role might technology and social media play? Can Effective Altruism's economic focus be applied to civil rights?

Alternate Assignment 3. Synthesize: GLADWELL, SOUTHAN, AND ARORA

Namit Arora looks at different economic models to raise questions about economic justice and what, exactly, we deserve. Write a paper in which you synthesize the ideas of Gladwell, Southan, and Arora in order to propose mechanisms for promoting social justice.

You might also find these questions helpful: What causes practices to shift? How can we change our understanding of economic justice? How do groups, cultures, and organizations play a role in making change happen? What role can strong and weak ties play in locating equitable economics? Does Effective Altruism offer a means of change?

Assignment 4. Emerge: EPSTEIN AND ONE OTHER

Helen Epstein examines the HIV epidemic in Africa, considering some reasons why certain prevention programs work better than others. Her examination of this disease offers a useful case study for you to continue to explore ideas about how to promote change. Using Epstein and one other author in this sequence, write a paper in which you propose strategies for effectively combating the spread of HIV not only in Africa but globally as well. You may want to start with your response to Question 3 of Questions for Critical Reading (p. 134); your work in Assignments for Writing (p. 135) for Epstein might also inform your response.

Consider, too: What role do strong ties play in preventing the spread of HIV in Africa? How might we harness Effective Altruism? What role can conversation play in disease prevention?

Alternate Assignment 4. Emerge: Meyer and One Other

Robinson Meyer asks whether or not it's acceptable to enjoy warmer winters caused by global changes in climate and, in asking that, he also asks how we can best make decisions about climate change. Using Meyer and one other author in this sequence, write a paper in which you identify a course of action for confronting climate change.

Consider: Can we use strong and weak ties to generate solutions for climate change? What role could Effective Altruism play? Does addressing climate change require legal solutions? What can individuals do to help solve the problem?

SEQUENCE 6

What Should Be the Goal of an Education?

Yo-Yo Ma

Michael Pollan

Ta-Nehisi Coates

Wesley Yang

Daniel Gilbert

Lukianoff and Haidt

Is education only about getting a job or should it have other goals as well? In this sequence of assignments, you will explore the goals of education, a topic that may be particularly relevant to your life today. To start, you will use Yo-Yo Ma to consider the role that different disciplines can play in education and in the world. You will then develop that understanding by looking at Michael Pollan's discussion of integrated farming. Using either Ta-Nehisi Coates's narrative about race and education or Wesley Yang's discussion of Asian Americans you will test your developing ideas against specific, challenging situations. Then, using either Daniel Gilbert or Greg Lukianoff and Jonathan Haidt, you will consider the role that education plays in our future happiness and our ability to be resilient in our critical thinking.

Assignment 1. Analyze: Ma

Yo-Yo Ma argues for the value of the "necessary edges" found at the intersection of different kinds of thinking and learning; in doing so, he also argues for the value of the arts in education. Using Ma's ideas, write a paper in which you evaluate the value of a liberal arts education in a world driven by science and technology. Your work with Questions 1 and 3 of Questions for Critical Reading (p. 282) and Questions 2 and 3 of Assignments for Writing (p. 283) may be useful.

You might also find these questions helpful: What does an education in the liberal arts add to understandings of science and technology? How does education relate to empathy? Is empathy something we learn? What role does education play in collaboration?

Assignment 2. Connect: Ma and Pollan

On the surface, Michael Pollan seems primarily concerned with how farming happens at Polyface Farm. But much like Ma, Pollan has a lot to say about education, both the kind of education needed for this approach to farming and, more generally, the ways in which parts and wholes fit together in a system. Using the ideas of both of these authors, write a paper in which you evaluate the general education or core curriculum at your school. Your responses to Questions for Critical Reading (p. 324) and Question 2 of Questions for Connecting (p. 325) for Pollan might be useful places to start.

Also think about these questions: How are the necessary edges that Ma describes like the integrated systems and holons of Pollan's essay? Does your school's curriculum allow for productive interchange? Does it relate individual courses to a larger goal? How might it prepare the whole person and avoid brain drain?

Assignment 3. Synthesize: Ma, Pollan, and Coates or Yang

Ta-Nehisi Coates and Wesley Yang both examine some of the problems particular populations confront in relation to education, whether African Americans or Asian Americans. Using either Coates or Yang as well as both Ma and Pollan, write a paper in which you determine what responsibility, if any, educational institutions have to student populations.

Also consider: Do educational institutions have a responsibility to keep students safe? To offer them intellectual challenges or a certain kind of environment? How much of education is the responsibility of schools, and how much is the responsibility of students?

Assignment 4. Emerge: Lukianoff and Haidt and One Other

Greg Lukianoff and Jonathan Haidt believe that oversensitivity to issues of race, gender, and sexuality on college campuses hurts learning and critical thinking. Using these authors and one other essay from this sequence, write a paper in which you propose the best compromise between the goals of learning and the goals of diversity, inclusion, and respect. Questions 2 and 3 of Questions for Critical Reading (pp. 275–76), Question 2 of Questions for Connecting (p. 276), and Questions 1 and 2 of Assignments for Writing (p. 277) for Lukianoff and Haidt might be useful as you form your response.

Also consider: How do authors like Coates deal with trauma? Do you think their solutions might offer an alternative to trigger warnings? Do students function as holons in the educational setting? How can we use necessary edges to reach a compromise?

Alternate Assignment 4. Emerge: Gilbert and One Other

Daniel Gilbert illustrates the difficulties we have when we try to make decisions that move us toward our future goals. Given that the choices we make in our education are particularly important to our future happiness, use Gilbert and one other author in this sequence to write a paper in which you determine the methods you should use in making decisions about your education that provide the best chance for your future happiness.

Also consider: Do authors like Ma act as surrogates? Can working within necessary edges help us avoid super-replicators? How do Coates's and Yang's essays act as surrogates? Can we find reliable ways to make decisions about our education?

SEQUENCE 7

How Can We Get Along?

Francis Fukuyama

Sharon Moalem

Leslie Jamison

Adrian Chen

Sherry Turkle

We live in a world that feels increasingly polarized, where people seem to find it challenging just to get along. What can we do to address this problem? In this sequence, you will first work with readings that help you think about the issue and then move into your own research to consider possible solutions. You will begin by considering the nature of human dignity using Francis Fukuyama. Sharon Moalem's work with epigenetics will then help you consider the biological effects of one troubling consequence of not getting along, bullying, or you may work with Leslie Jamison's essay about the mysterious condition known as Morgellons disease. Adrian Chen and Sherry Turkle both focus on conversation and empathy, and you will work with the ideas of one of these authors to think about what role these elements might have in addressing polarization. Having worked across these essays, you will end this sequence by locating your own sources to help you address bullying.

Assignment 1. Analyze: Fukuyama

Francis Fukuyama considers the nature of human dignity and what it means to be human while also considering the ways in which biotechnology threatens both. When we refuse to get along with others different from us do we also deny them basic human dignity? Write a paper in which you propose essential measures we must take to preserve human dignity. Your responses to Questions for Critical Reading (p. 159) might be useful as you compose your response.

You might also think about these questions: What actions (taken or not taken) explicitly or implicitly deny people their human dignity? What are the consequences when human dignity is violated? What role does Factor X play in maintaining human dignity? How can we promote the preservation of dignity? Law? Cultural norms?

Assignment 2. Connect: Fukuyama and Moalem

Both Sharon Moalem and Francis Fukuyama suggest that questions of ethics, morality, and philosophy are closely bound with issues of biology. Traumatic experiences which result from the friction of getting along with different others, such as bullying, thus have extended ramifications not only on our psyche but on our bodies as well. Using the insights of both of these authors, write a paper in which you determine the consequences of bullying. Your response to Question 2 of Assignments for Writing (p. 299) for Moalem may be useful.

Also think about these questions: What are the epigenetic consequences of bullying? How does bullying affect human dignity? How long do the effects of bullying last? Does bullying people diminish their humanity?

Alternate Assignment 2. Connect: Fukuyama and Jamison

Leslie Jamison's essay is about "what kinds of reality are considered prerequisites for compassion" (p. 230). What role do compassion and empathy play in human dignity? Using the ideas of both of these authors, write a paper in which identifying with others can help us to resolve conflict.

Consider these questions: How does empathy resolve polarization? How might we disagree in a way which preserves human dignity? Can we identify with others without confirming their understanding of the world?

Assignment 3. Synthesize: Fukuyama, Moalem, and Chen or Turkle

Conversation and empathy play transformational roles in the essays by both Adrian Chen and Sherry Turkle. They thus offer useful texts for exploring potential of these solutions to the problems of polarization. Using ideas from Fukuyama, Moalem, and either Chen or Turkle, write a paper in which you suggest solutions to the kinds of polarization that take place in the world today.

Also consider: Across all of these essays, what can we do to help things get better? What role does technology play in making a difference? What does it take for us to get along? To work together?

Assignment 4. Emerge: Research Project

So far, you've considered the problem of how we get along using much larger ideas, ranging from the notion of human dignity to epigenetics. These ideas have offered you a broad context for considering this issue, and you've used them to look at specific instances of the consequences of polarization such as bullying. For your research project, locate two academic sources with specific ideas and theories about how to promote cooperation across lines of difference. Then, using these two sources and one of the other authors you've read in this sequence, write a paper in which you determine the most effective approach to solving the problem of polarization by applying ideas from your sources or synthesizing your sources to propose an idea of your own.

SEQUENCE 8

What Is the Role of Art in the World?

RHYS SOUTHAN

TORIE ROSE DEGHETT

TOMAS VAN HOUTRYVE

KAVITA DAS

ALEXANDER PROVAN

OTTO VON BUSCH

Often we think of art as something removed from the world, locked away in museums or displayed in galleries or available only to the very rich. But how does art function in the world around us to reflect and promote change? In this sequence you will explore this question, starting with Rhys Southan's interrogation of art's usefulness in the world. Then, using an author who looks at the power of the image to act in the world—either Torie Rose DeGhett, Tomas van Houtryve, or Kavita Das—you will consider how the question of art intersects with factors ranging from war to nationalism. Then you will think about either the future of art, through Alexander Provan, or the function of craft in social resistance, using Otto von Busch. Finally, you will conduct your own research on an issue related to art that means something to you.

Assignment 1. Analyze: SOUTHAN

Rhys Southan looks at art through the lens of Effective Altruism to determine its usefulness in the world. Write a paper in which you assess the usefulness of artistic production. Question 2 of Questions for Critical Reading (p. 369) might be a useful starting place as you shape your response.

Consider, too: According to Effective Altruism, under what conditions would art be useful? Are there other lenses of social change we might use to look at art? How would art's usefulness change based on the lens we use?

Assignment 2. Connect: SOUTHAN AND DEGHETT, VAN HOUTRYVE, OR DAS

Torie Rose DeGhett, Tomas van Houtryve, and Kavita Das all consider the power of photographs. For DeGhett, that power has to do with censorship and the ethics of armed conflict; van Houtryve also considers the image in relation to armed conflict while looking as well at the commercial enterprises that support those efforts; for Das, photographs stand in relation to ethnic stereotypes and racially inflected notions of national citizenship. Using ideas from Southan and one of these authors, write a paper in which you analyze the potential of the image to create social change.

Also think about these questions: How do these authors represent Effective Altruism? What makes a photograph able to make change happen? Do photographs also prevent change, by reinforcing stereotypes for example? What are the necessary elements for tapping into the power of images to enact change?

Assignment 3. Synthesize: Provan, Southan, and DeGhett, van Houtryve, or Das

Alexander Provan looks at the impact of digital technologies on art while considering both the past and the future of museums. Synthesizing his ideas with Southan and one other author, write a paper in which you speculate on the future of art in relation to social change. You might find your work in Question 2 of Questions for Critical Reading (p. 341), Question 1 of Questions for Connecting (p. 341), and Questions 2 and 3 of Assignment for Writing (p. 342) useful.

You might also find these questions helpful: How do digital copies actually help the power of photographs by allowing the widespread distribution of images? Who owns an image? What might a social justice art museum look like or do? Are originals valuable? Why?

Alternate Assignment 3. Synthesize: von Busch, Southan, and DeGhett, van Houtryve, or Das

Otto von Busch continues the conversation about art and change by looking at craft as a form of resistance. Synthesizing his ideas with Southan and one other author, write a paper in which you delineate the essential elements for using creative acts as a form of resistance for social change. You might find your work in Question 2 of Questions for Critical Reading (p. 403) and Questions 1 and 2 of Assignment for Writing (p. 405) for von Busch useful as your prepare your response.

You might also find these questions helpful: Which of these authors offers the most useful lens for considering these issues? Does social change through creative activity depend on the artist/maker or the viewer/consumer? How does it challenge the relationship between the two?

Assignment 4. Emerge: Research Project

So far, you have explored only very limited areas of the much larger questions surrounding art's power to change the world. For this research project, you will draft a specific question of interest to you and then locate two academic sources with specific ideas and theories that help you answer your research question. Write a paper using these two sources and one of the other authors you've read in this sequence to make an argument that responds to your own research question.

Acknowledgments (continued from page ii)

Kwame Anthony Appiah, "Making Conversation" and "The Primacy of Practice" from *Cosmopolitanism: Ethics in a World of Strangers*, copyright © 2006 by Kwame Anthony Appiah. Used by permission of W.W. Norton & Company, Inc.

Namit Arora, "What Do We Deserve?" originally appearing in *The Humanist*, May/June 2011. Copyright © 2011 by Namit Arora. Used with permission.

Michael Chabon, "My Son, the Prince of Fashion," originally appearing in *GQ Magazine*, Sept. 27, 2016. Copyright © 2016 by Michael Chabon. Reprinted by permission of ICM Partners.

Adrien Chen, "Unfollow," *The New Yorker*, Nov. 23, 2015. Copyright © 2015 Conde Nast. Used with permission.

Ta-Nehisi Coates, excerpt(s) from *Between the World and Me* by Ta-Nehisi Coates, copyright © 2015 by Ta-Nehisi Coates. Used by permission of Spiegel & Grau, an imprint of Random House, a division of Penguin Random House LLC. All rights reserved.

Andrew Cohen, "When Heroin Hits the White Suburbs," *The Marshall Project*, Aug. 12, 2015. Reprinted with permission from the author.

Kavita Das, "(Un)American, (Un)Cool," *Asian American Writers' Workshop Website*, Aug. 4, 2014 by Asian American Writers' Workshop. Used with permission from the author.

Torie Rose DeGhett, "The War Photo No One Would Publish," *The Atlantic*, Aug. 8, 2014, is reprinted by permission of the author.

Helen Epstein, "AIDS, Inc." from *The Invisible Cure: Why We Are Losing the Fight Against AIDS in Africa*. Copyright © 2007 by Helen Epstein. Reprinted by permission of Farrar, Straus and Giroux, LLC.

Francis Fukuyama, "Human Dignity" from *Our Posthuman Future: Consequences of the Biotechnology Revolution*. Copyright © 2002 by Francis Fukuyama. Reprinted by permission of Farrar, Straus and Giroux, LLC.

Roxane Gay, "Bad Feminist," *Virginia Quarterly Review*, Fall 2012, by permission of the publisher.

Daniel Gilbert, Chapter 11, "Reporting Live from Tomorrow" from *Stumbling on Happiness*. Copyright © 2006 by Daniel Gilbert. Used by permission of Alfred A. Knopf, an imprint of the Knopf Doubleday Publishing Group, a division of Penguin Random House LLC. All rights reserved.

Malcolm Gladwell, "Small Change," originally appearing in *The New Yorker*, October 4, 2010. Copyright © 2010 by Malcolm Gladwell. Used with permission.

Robin Marantz Hehig, "What Is It about 20-Somethings?" *New York Times*, August 18, 2010. Copyright © 2010 The New York Times. All rights reserved. Used by permission and protected by the Copyright Laws of the United States. The printing, copying, redistribution, or retransmission of this Content without express written permission is prohibited.

Anna Holmes, "Has 'Diversity' Lost Its Meaning?" *New York Times*, Oct. 27, 2015. Copyright © 2015 The New York Times. All rights reserved. Used by permission and protected by the Copyright Laws of the United States. The printing, copying, redistribution, or retransmission of this Content without express written permission is prohibited

Leslie Jamison, "Devil's Bait" from *The Empathy Exams: Essays*. Copyright © 2014 by Leslie Jamison. Reprinted with the permission of The Permissions Company, Inc., on behalf of Graywolf Press, www.graywolfpress.org.

Chuck Klosterman, "Electric Funeral" from *I Wear the Black Hat*. Copyright © 2013, 2014 by Chuck Klosterman. Reprinted with the permission of Scribner, a division of Simon & Schuster, Inc. All rights reserved.

Maria Konnikova, "The Limits of Friendship," *The New Yorker*, Oct. 7, 2014. Copyright © 2014 Conde Nast. Reprinted with permission.

Greg Lukianoff and Jonathan Haidt, "The Coddling of the American Mind," as first published in *The Atlantic Magazine*, Sept 2015. Copyright © 2015 The Atlantic Media Co. All rights reserved. Distributed by Tribune Content Agency, LLC. Used with permission.

Yo-Yo Ma, "Behind the Cello," *The Huffington Post*, online, Jan. 21, 2014. Reprinted by permission of Yo-Yo Ma.

Robinson Meyer, "Is It Okay to Enjoy the Warm Winters of Climate Change?" *The Atlantic*, February 23, 2017. Copyright © 2017 by The Atlantic Media Co., as first published in *The Atlantic Magazine*. All rights reserved. Distributed by Tribune Content Agency, LLC.

Sharon Moalem, Chapter 3, "Changing our Genes: How Trauma, Bullying, and Royal Jelly Alter Our Genetic Destiny" from *Inheritance: How Our Genes Change Our Lives and Our Lives Change Our Genes*. Copyright © 2014 by Sharon Moalem. Used by permission of Grand Central Publishing.

Nick Paumgarten, "We Are a Camera," *The New Yorker*, Sept. 22, 2014, is reprinted by permission of the author.

Michael Pollan, "The Animals: Practicing Complexity" from *The Omnivore's Dilemma: A Natural History of Four Meals*. Copyright © 2006 by Michael Pollan. Used by permission of Penguin Press, an imprint of Penguin Publishing Group, a division of Penguin Random House LLC. All rights reserved.

Alexander Provan, "Unknown Makers," *Art in America Magazine*, Oct. 1, 2016. Used with permission from the author.

Julia Serano, "Why Nice Guys Finish Last" from *Yes Means Yes!: Visions of Female Sexual Power and A World Without Rape* edited by Jaclyn Friedman and Jessica Valenti. Copyright © 2008 by Jaclyn Friedman and Jessica Valenti. Reprinted by permission of the Seal Press, an imprint of Hachette Book Group, Inc.

Peter Singer, "Visible Man: Ethics in a World without Secrets," *Harper's Magazine*. Copyright © 2011 by Harper's Magazine. All Rights Reserved. Reproduced from the August issue by special permission.

Rhys Southan, "Is Art a Waste of Time?" *Aeon*, online, March 20, 2014. Reprinted by permission of the author.

Sarah Stillman, "Hiroshima and the Inheritance of Trauma," *The New Yorker*, Aug. 12, 2014. Copyright © 2014 Conde Nast. Used by permission.

Sherry Turkle, "The Empathy Diaries" from *Reclaiming Conversation: The Power of Talk in a Digital Age* by Sherry Turkle, copyright © 2015 by Sherry Turkle. Used by permission of Penguin Press, an imprint of Penguin Publishing Group, a division of Penguin Random House LLC. All rights reserved.

Tomas van Houtryve, "From the Eyes of a Drone," *National Geographic*, Aug. 15, 2014 is published by permission of the author and VII Photo Agency LLC.

Otto von Busch, "Crafting Resistance" from *Craftivism* published by Arsenal Pulp Press. Reprinted by permission of the author.

David Foster Wallace, "Consider the Lobster." Copyright © 2005 by David Foster Wallace. Used by permission of Little, Brown and Company.

Ethan Watters, "We Aren't the World," *Pacific Standard Online*, Feb. 25, 2013 is reprinted by permission of the author.

Wesley Yang, "Paper Tigers," originally published in *New York Magazine*, May 16, 2011. Reprinted by permission of the publisher.

Kenji Yoshino, excerpt(s) from *Covering: The Hidden Assault on Our Civil Rights* by Kenji Yoshino, copyright © 2006 by Kenji Yoshino. Used by permission of Random House, an imprint and division of Penguin Random House LLC. All rights reserved.

INDEX OF AUTHORS AND TITLES